MIXED BLOOD

Intermarriage and Ethnic Identity in Twentieth-Century America

PAUL R. SPICKARD

THE UNIVERSITY OF WISCONSIN PRESS

The University of Wisconsin Press
1930 Monroe Street
Madison, Wisconsin 53711

3 Henrietta Street
London WC2E 8LU, England

4 6 8 7 5

Printed in the United States of America

Library of Congress Cataloging-in-Publication Data
Spickard, Paul R., 1950–
Mixed blood: intermarriage and ethnic identity in twentieth
-century America/Paul R. Spickard.
532 pp.   cm.
Bibliography: pp. 474–522.
Includes index.
1. Intermarriage—United States—20th century.
2. Ethnicity—United States—History—20th century.
HQ1031.S75   1989
306.8′46—dc 19   89-31235
ISBN 0-299-12110-0

MIXED BLOOD

To Donald E. Spickard,
whose stories fired a small boy's imagination.

And to the memory of Mary Alice Spickard,
who talked late at night about Galileo and Kepler,
and caused the fire to burn.

Contents

Acknowledgments

This book could not have been produced without countless acts of help, encouragement, and kindness from hundreds of individuals. Lawrence Levine gave guidance, patience, friendship, and faith in me from my entrance into graduate school to the completion of the book. Winthrop Jordan had the good sense to tell me at the outset that this project was impossible, and the good friendship to see me through it nonetheless. Albert Raboteau and Stephen Cornell believed in me and in the project, and offered perceptive criticism as well. All four read the manuscript and made it better.

Richard Alba, Harumi Befu, Stephen Fugita, Christine Hall, Gene Levine, Stanley Lieberson, Darrel Montero, David O'Brien, John Moritsugu, Jonathan Sarna, Sonnet Takahisa, Hiroshi Wagatsuma, and Barbara Waters lent me their manuscripts and their encouragement. Roger Daniels, Orlando Patterson, Alvin Poussaint, Moses Rischin, Ron Toby, and Greg Thompson gave me leads. Jim Morishima added gentle ridicule and unfailing support. Curt Anderson performed perceptive research assistance. Richard McIntosh did my computer work and was good company. Jim Kettner not only read part of the manuscript, but early in my career intervened to keep me in the history business when I might have gone elsewhere; over the years he has had the good grace never to admit his mistake. Rod Addington, Kevin Cragg, Lynn Dumenil, Danielle Fauth, Jack Potter, Caroll Smith-Rosenberg, Bill Tuttle, and Joan Ullman read chapters and saved me from errors.

My friends at the following libraries and archives know who they are and how little I would have been able to do without their help:

American Jewish Archive, Cincinnati; Bancroft Library, Berkeley; Bethel College Library, St. Paul; Doe Library, Berkeley; Federation of Jewish Philanthropies, New York; California State University Library, Fullerton; Hebrew Union College Library, Cincinnati; Hoover Institution Archives, Stanford; Fisk University Library, Nashville; Howard University Library and Archives, Washington; National Archives, Washington; Schlesinger Library, Radcliffe College; University Research Library, UCLA; Widener Library, Harvard; Wilson Library, University of Minnesota; and YIVO Institute Library, New York.

Thanks also to Buffy and Steve Caflisch, Bobby and Suzanne Fong, Wing, Owen, and Ed Fong, Gloria Saito and Dan Chao, Reese Stone and Jennifer Eng, and Victor and Nancy Wong, for feeding and giving shelter to a wandering scholar, and making life on the road pleasant and homelike.

Several score individuals, anonymous in this report but identified in my memory, shared themselves in interviews. Special thanks go to them, and to the many other mixed couples and individuals of mixed parentage who have been my friends over the years, who have taught me much, but whose stories do not appear in this manuscript.

The University of California awarded me a travel fellowship in 1978–80. Bethel College provided a place to finish the project and helped pay for typing.

Portions of this book have been published in other forms. I am grateful to the American Historical Association for permission to use sections from "Mixed Blood," which appeared in the Association's *Proceedings* in 1982; and to the Immigration History Society for allowing me to use a few paragraphs from "Injustice Compounded," which was published in the *Journal of American Ethnic History* in 1986.

I owe a special debt to my former colleagues at Bethel College, who created a uniquely stimulating and supportive environment in which to work. There are others who did not contribute directly to this project but who deserve mention, for they helped form me intellectually. I think particularly of Donald and Mary Alice Spickard, Joseph Frankel, Jean Hundley, Roger Dingman, and Albert Craig. I stand in their debt.

Barbara Hanrahan of the University of Wisconsin Press is an exemplary editor, as anyone who has worked with her knows. I am grateful to her, to Carolyn Moser, to David Reimers, and to an unnamed reader recruited by the Press.

There are many friends and relatives whom I have neglected while writing this book. I pray that they will regard whatever profit or pleasure they may derive from reading it as partial repayment for their steadfast love and friendship. Naomi and Daniel Spickard forgave a frequently absent or preoccupied father. Rowena Fong loved me, listened to my ideas, read the manuscript, helped with the typing, chided me when I needed it, and worked hard to make our life together successful. I am grateful to her and to each of the people mentioned above. Each, in one way or another, contributed to make this a better book. Of course, I alone am responsible for the shortcomings that remain.

Tianjin, China
September 1988

MIXED BLOOD

1. The Problem of Intermarriage

"Don't you feel ashamed," the woman asked, "promoting mixed marriage like this?" The woman's daughter, a farm girl from South Dakota, was a student in a course I was teaching on interethnic romance and marriage. The mother was visiting her daughter on campus and did not like what the younger woman was learning. In the course in question her daughter had had her first contacts with people who were very unlike her. The young woman was White, rural, and middle class. Now she was making friends—female and male—who were different: Black, Asian, Hispanic, urban, and working class. For the first time in her life, race relations were an issue. She responded in the manner her parents had taught her: with openness, honesty, interest, and respect for the feelings of others. One of the things she did when her parents came to campus was to introduce them to some of her new friends. Before long it became clear to the mother that some of those friends—Black and White, male and female—had romantic interests in each other. The mother, who viewed college largely as a market where one selected one's mate, feared that her daughter, too, might become romantically involved with someone who was not White, rural, and middle class.

This mother, whatever her concerns for her daughter, mistook the purpose of my teaching about mixed relationships. I have no particular wish—in teaching about intermarriage or in writing about it—to promote it as a social goal. Nor do I wish to condemn it as a practice of individual choice. I hope to understand it, to describe it, and to explain it.

It is worth explaining. The mixing of peoples is one of the great themes of world history. The history of the world is a story of peoples on the move: invading, conquering, migrating, trading. Rome spread over the Mediterranean world and brought together peoples as varied as Hebrews and Britons. The Mongol colossus took Chinese civilization to the gates of Europe and Persian culture to Cathay. The modern age of trading and empire prompted mixing on an ever-wider scale: Arabs and Bantu in East Africa; Dutch and Javanese in Indonesia; English, Africans, Native Americans, and a horde of other Europeans in North America. In each setting, mixing began in a political or economic context: Normans conquered Saxons, Arabs traded with Indians. Soon they began sharing culture: Saxons and Normans mixed their languages, Indians and Arabs their religions. Ultimately they shared their personal lives as well, mixing socially and, eventually, maritally.[1]

This pattern of mixing is especially prominent in the American past. People came to America from all over the world. They bore every conceivable color, religion, and national heritage. Within a generation or two after arriving here, most socialized and mated with people who were not like them—who did not share their color, their religion, or their national heritage. America was founded, in one sense, upon a vision of intermarriage. Hector St. John de Crevecouer wrote shortly before the American Revolution:

What then is the American, this new man? He is either a European or the descendant of a European, hence that strange mixture of blood, which you will find in no other country. I could point out to you a family whose grandfather was an Englishman, whose wife was Dutch, whose son married a French woman, and whose present four sons have four wives of different nations. *He* is an American, who, leaving behind him all his ancient prejudices and manners, receives new ones from the new mode of life he has embraced, the new government he obeys, and the new rank he holds. He becomes an American by being received into the broad lap of our great *Alma Mater*. Here individuals are melted into a new race of men, whose labours and posterity will one day cause great changes in the world.[2]

Here was the first recorded expression of the melting-pot myth, a powerful part of America's self-image. According to this vision, people of all sorts were to come to America, contribute their part, intermarry, create a new mixed people, and enjoy the unprecedented liberty of life in this place. Although that was the ideal, in practical fact not all sorts were equally welcome. Africans and Native Americans stood outside the promise from the beginning; Mexicans soon joined them. The founders recommended civic rather than ethnic qualifications for citizenship, but they could afford that luxury in a nation whose white population was 80 percent English.

The founding generation was still alive when the first steps at limiting the vision were taken with the Alien and Sedition Acts of 1798. Not many decades later, in the 1840s and '50s, anti-Catholicism came to flower as the nativist response to immigrants streaming in from Europe. Soon, Anglo-Californians drew the first line against immigration, by excluding Chinese. By the turn of the twentieth century, the dominant Anglo-American minority was divided in two over the issue of what to do with non-Anglos. One viewpoint, drawing on the Anglo-Saxon racialism that flourished in the latter nineteenth century, said either "Americanize" non-Anglos—force them to give up distinctive cultural traits—or remove them. The other, harking back to Creve-couer's dream, called for continued social and marital mixing, to make America a vast, homogeneous melting pot. The proponents of Anglo-Saxon domination won in the short run. They achieved the promise of a mainly Anglo-Saxon America through the immigration act of 1924, which sharply limited migration from southern and eastern Europe and eliminated Asian immigration almost entirely. These two strands of thought among Anglo-Saxons—America's most powerful minority group—set much of the context for interethnic relationships and intermarriages throughout the twentieth century.[3] Anglo-Americans did not set the context by themselves, however, for other American minority groups had agendas of their own. We shall see the ideas of Anglos, Blacks, Jews, and Japanese Americans at work over the course of the twentieth century, shaping the settings of interethnic relationships in which intermarriages took place.

Barriers between ethnic groups have fallen over the course of the twentieth century, most particularly in the last few decades. Since 1960 Americans have elected an Irish Catholic president and sanctified a slain Black civil rights leader. First Catholics, then Jews, then Asians, then Blacks have been allowed into formerly all-White Protestant schools, neighborhoods, and clubs. Some fairly intimate mixing —including intermarriage—has taken place. Where in the 1920s the union of a Norwegian American man and a Swedish American woman might have caused a scandal in Minnesota, by the 1980s almost no one would have noticed any ethnic difference between them at all. As we shall see, intermarriage by other groups has increased as well, though at different rates and with different degrees of acceptance.

Ideas about Intermarriage

From the beginning, then, and increasingly of late, intergroup mixing and intermarriage in particular have been important aspects of American society. Intermarriage has also been a topic of considerable study by sociologists, who have constructed a variety of theories about how intermarriage works. Almost all those theories point toward elements of social structure, from demography to class status, to explain intermarriage behavior. Social structure is very important, even when one may dispute the particulars of some of the theories. But social structure is not everything. Culture also counts. People from one group have ideas about people from other groups and ideas about themselves, and those ideas, too, shape behavior. The present study of intermarriage is different from most others in that it examines both social structure and ideas—specifically, mutual images—as bases of action. It is also distinctive in two other respects: it examines and compares the intermarriage experiences of three different ethnic groups, and it traces change over a considerable period of time. Those two comparative dimensions—ethnic context and time—make it possible to evaluate the usefulness of the various theories that have emerged from more narrowly focused studies. The theories are enumerated in the paragraphs that follow. They will be recalled and evaluated in the concluding chapter.[4]

There are several theories, not necessarily mutually exclusive, about what social and economic factors encourage intermarriage. Many students agree that an unbalanced sex ratio leads to outmarriage by those surplus members of a minority group who cannot find mates among their own people. Thus, white males in colonial Jamaica and the Hawaiian kingdom, and Filipino American males in the first half of the twentieth century, were likely to look for wives outside their respective groups because there were not enough ingroup women.[5]

Another theory deals with the absolute size of the minority group in a given location. As Romanzo Adams put it, "The larger the group the higher the percentage of in-marriage, irrespective of any sentiment relative thereto." Thus, in Hawaii, which had 139,631 Japanese Americans in 1930, the intermarriage rate was very low because, Adams said, every Japanese had a large number of potential mates to choose from. A contrasting case would be Eskimos in Vermont. In 1980, the state had only eight Eskimos; each had few, if any, Eskimo marital prospects; and nearly all would be expected to choose non-Eskimo partners. A corollary here is tied not to absolute numbers, but to percentages. Milton Barron regards it "a sociological truism that the percentage of intermarriage increases as the proportion of the group in the community decreases."[6]

A third theory notes that intermarriage has increased steadily over the course of the twentieth century and predicts that it will continue to do so. This observation is based on the perception that American society at large has markedly, if not steadily, become more open to racial and cultural heterogeneity over the course of the twentieth century, most especially in the decades since 1960. This general social change has found expression not just in the rise of intermarriage but also in such broad movements as those for religious ecumenism and minority civil rights. Other social changes of recent decades, such as declining segregation of residence and workplace, plus beginning steps toward interethnic income equality, should abet the general trend toward increasing intermarriage. This theory is tied to a corollary, which says that there is a steady increase of outmarriage in successive generations: very few immigrants intermarry, more of the second generation marry out, still more of the third, and so on. The third generation, made up of the grandchildren of immigrants, shows the sharpest rise, according to the proponents of this corollary.[7] Finally, there is the question of the relation of class to intermarriage. No one is willing to assert that intermarriage is primarily undertaken by members of a single social or economic class. But there are at least two theorists who posit the existence of a college-educated, intellectually—and artistically—inclined stratum of people who hold their ethnicity lightly, mix rather freely with others of similar bent, and are likely to intermarry.[8]

A second batch of theories deals with which groups marry which. The "triple melting pot" hypothesis, associated with Ruby Jo Reeves Kennedy, maintains that there are three major religious groupings in the United States—Protestants, Catholics, and Jews—and that each of these groups constitutes a melting pot in itself. That is, Protestants increasingly are marrying Protestants irrespective of their races or ancestral nationalities, and the same is true of Catholics and Jews. Kennedy goes on to predict indiscriminate marriage within each of these groups in the not too distant future, together with relatively firm barriers between the groups.[9] The second theory in this group tries to rank types of intermarriage as to their frequency. This theory says that boundaries between what we call racial groups are the least easily crossed, religious differences are more easily surmounted, and barriers of national origin are most easily permeated. Thus, marriages between White and Black are very unlikely, between Jew and Christian somewhat more likely, and between German and Swede quite likely indeed. According to this theory, the "social distance," in Emory Bogardus's phrase, is greater between people of different religions than between people of different nationalities, and greater still for people of different races.[10]

A third type of theory tries to predict the gender of intermarrying people according to whether they belong to the majority or the minority group. One of these asserts that intergroup marriage in America follows a system of *hypogamy*. This theory, associated with Robert Merton, posits a hierarchy of status among American ethnic groups and a compensatory system of intermarriages. It says that men of lower caste—such as Blacks, Jews, and Filipinos—marry women of higher caste, such as Gentile Whites. Certain upwardly mobile lower-caste men—those who are conspicuously handsome, talented, rich, or well-educated—trade those assets in a marriage contract for the higher-caste status of women who have status but lack beauty, talent, wealth, or intellect. Some of the same writers assert that *informal* intergroup sex, by contrast, follows the rule of *hypergamy*. That is, males of the dominant group frequently visit their sexual attentions upon females of subordinate groups, but because the males have power, they are not bound to marry those women.[11]

A fourth type of theory is concerned with the ethnic identity choices of mixed couples and mixed children. Most scholars, viewing the families from the perspective of the majority group, assume that such people will live in and regard themselves as members of minority communities. Merton writes of "ostracism and the ascription of lower-caste status" being visited upon the children of interracial marriages. Other scholars speak of intermarriage as a "widely recognized indicator of minority assimilation into the majority." As we shall see, this is as much a matter of the observer's point of view as of the objective status of the people in question.[12]

Many of these theories about intermarriage have considerable merit. Others have less. The present book does not offer a unified theory of all intermarriage behavior, but it does present an analytical scheme for thinking about intermarriage. It contends that a number of structural factors—such as class, generation, and ethnic concentration in the surrounding population—shape intermarriage patterns. But those patterns are also shaped by cultural factors, such as the images that one group has of another and of itself. The present study also suggests that the intermarriage behavior of each ethnic group under study shows a distinctive hierarchy of intermarriage preferences, which endure over several generations, even as the group intermarries more frequently. This book is built around detailed descriptions of the intermarriage experiences of three American minority groups over the course of the twentieth century and one international encounter after World War II, plus some comparisons drawn from studies of other American and foreign ethnic groups. After telling those stories and describing the patterns of intermarriage, the book returns to evaluate the intermarriage theories in the final chapter.

Ideas about Ethnicity

First a word must be said about the relationship between ethnicity and race. There was a time when most Americans who thought about ethnicity would divide the human population conceptually first into races: red, yellow, black, brown, and white on the North American continent. Ethnic groups, according to such thinking, were simply subdivisions of these larger phenotypic categories. Thus, a person whose ancestors came from Bavaria belonged to the German ethnic group and the Caucasian race, while a person from Kyoto was seen as a member of the Japanese ethnic group and the Mongolian race. Most American laws governing race relations in the nineteenth and early twentieth centuries employed such racial categories, and a large number of lay people continue to use them in everyday speech. In the increasingly egalitarian and polyglot atmosphere that has emerged in

the last three decades, however, the number of categories has multi-
plied, and the mechanical distinction between a large category called
"race" and subsidiary divisions called "ethnic" has blurred. The 1980
U.S. Census, for instance, divided people into White, Black, Hispanic,
Japanese, Chinese, Filipino, Korean, Vietnamese, American Indian,
Asian Indian, Hawaiian, Guamanian, Samoan, Eskimo, Aleut, and
Other. In Britain, the distinctions were very different: White, West
Indian, African, Arab, Turkish, Chinese, Indian, Pakstani, Bangla-
deshi, Sri Lankan, and Other.[13] Some of these categories corresponded
to the old "races." Others would formerly have been called "ethnic
groups." The point here is not to argue that race is unimportant; on the
contrary, phenotypic categories are still the great dividers in American
social relations. Rather, it is simply to assert, along with most theorists,
that the issues at work between what have been called races have a
common basis with the issues at work between what have been called
ethnic or nationality groups. The accepted overall term for such issues
is "ethnicity."[14]

This study of intermarriage is intricately bound up with ideas about
ethnicity. Nearly every major theorist of ethnicity believes that intermarriage is an important index of it. Milton Gordon, the premier writer
on American assimilation systems, sees intermarriage as the ultimate
form of assimilation, the step by which a minority group finally loses
its distinct ethnic identity and is obliterated in a mass of homogeneous
Anglo-American culture: "If marital assimilation takes place fully, the
minority group loses its ethnic identity in the larger host or core society." Other sociologists agree, describing intermarriage as "one of the
most telling indicators of the degree of assimilation of one ethnic group
into another," "one of the last rungs on the ladder to final integration
and assimilation," and "the surest means of assimilation and the most
infallible index of its occurrence."[15]

Lay people intuit the same conclusion. When they talk about interethnic issues, sex and marriage are seldom far from the surface of
their thinking. A White male student wrote a letter to the editor of
the West Seattle High School student newspaper in 1969, protesting
the proposed integration of his school. He offered a clear exposition
of then-current conservative arguments against integration: cultural incompatibility, the hardships of busing, and the like. His argument

might have stood well as written, had he not undercut it by adding a final sentence that did not relate to anything he had written before, in which he expressed outrage at the imminent "mongrelization of the race." Clearly, despite his articulate rhetoric, a major concern was for sexual protection from people he regarded as unlike himself.[16]

Ethnicity is more than just important to the study of intermarriage: it is a basic, inescapable fact of our world. Liberal thinkers, from the 1800s through the middle of this century, expected that in America and around the world "modernization" would soon wipe out ethnic differences. The "liberal expectancy," in Milton Gordon's phrase, was that industrialization would bring national systems of education, communication, economics, and politics, which would in turn reduce older distinctions among peoples. In time, according to some, there would emerge one world society. Not just ethnic, but also national divisions would wither. The expectancy of socialist thinkers had different bases but a similar end product: as people in industrial societies came to realize their true interests, ethnic and national divisions would be replaced by class consciousness. After the revolution, even class distinctions would fall before the steamroller of egalitarianism.[17]

These are powerful visions, but they have not come to pass. Everywhere one looks, ethnic division persists. In India, Assamese fights Bengali and Hindu kills Sikh. In Europe, Germans and Swiss draw ever sharper lines between Teutonic natives and Italian and Turkish guest workers. Iranians kill Kurds. Lapps demand autonomy in Scandinavia, as do Basques in Spain. Anglo-Americans beat up Vietnamese immigrant fishermen, demand immigration controls, and call for a constitutional amendment to make English the national language. Even the socialist countries are not immune. China finds itself unable to assimilate non-Han peoples as planned, and Great Russians fear being overrun by fecund hordes of Central Asians. Far from fading away, ethnicity is one of the dominant issues of our age.[18]

Although ethnicity is important, and although it is importantly related to intermarriage (without ethnicity there would be no ethnic intermarriage), the precise nature of that relationship is not yet clear. One of the tasks of this book is to shed some light on the relationship. To do that, one had better develop a clear idea of what ethnicity is and how it works. The sociologists are not much help here. The literature on ethnicity is voluminous, contradictory, and not very precise.[19] Perhaps most observers would recognize what they take to be ethnicity in the following definition by Richard A. Schermerhorn:

An ethnic group is . . . a collectivity within a larger society having real or putative common ancestry, memories of a shared historical past, and a cultural focus on one or more symbolic elements defined as the epitome of their peoplehood. Examples of such symbolic elements are: kinship patterns, physical contiguity (as in localism or sectionalism), religious affiliation, nationality, phenotypical features, or any combination of these. A necessary accompaniment is some consciousness of kind among members of the group.[20]

It is important to emphasize that the item which sets ethnic groups off from other types of groups most sharply is, as Max Weber told us years ago, real or fictive kinship, a sense of common provenance and history.[21]

Studies of ethnicity almost all fall into one of four categories. They are oriented toward ethnic culture, social networks, interests, or identity.[22] Most of the old-time students of ethnicity talk mainly about *culture*. They might describe the political functions ethnic groups played or the economic niches into which they fit, but their main concern is for ethnic behavior. In this view, where people speak a common language, eat the same food, discipline their children in a similar way, and articulate the same values—*there* is ethnicity. Thus, many sociologists talk of measuring degrees of Jewish ethnicity by the degree to which individuals participate in Jewish religious observances or eat Kosher food. This view tends to focus on ethnicity as a minority group phenomenon and on a straight-line process of cultural disintegration, by which, it is alleged, people have been inexorably giving up minority cultural practices and adopting those of Anglo-America. People who view ethnicity as culture see intermarriage primarily in the context of *acculturation*. The questions about intermarriage that concern them surround whether or not intermarriage affects cultural practices: do intermarried Jews, for example, say the seder less frequently than those who have married Jews?[23]

A second group of students contends that ethnicity is really about *social networks*. In this view, where there are Polish neighborhoods, Italian churches, Irish pubs, functioning kinship groups—*there* is ethnicity. Thus, Milton Gordon could in the early 1960s admit substantial acculturation to Anglo-American norms by white immigrants, yet proclaim that ethnicity was alive and well because ethnic institutions remained. In his words, "cultural assimilation" was nearly complete, but "structural assimilation" had not taken place. Two decades later, Richard Alba can look through similar lenses and proclaim "the twilight of ethnicity" in America because, in his view, Italian Americans have given up independent social networks for participation in the larger American social structure. The questions about intermarriage that interest scholars of this persuasion surround its effects on the maintenance of social networks. Do intermarried Poles still go to mass in Polish churches, do they play in predominately Polish softball leagues, and do they still visit their Polish relatives?[24]

Theorists of both these schools tend to see ethnicity as a dying phenomenon in the United States. Their observations of the cultural practices and social connections of European immigrant groups lead them to see a straight-line, one-way process of giving up minority culture and connections in favor of generalized American substitutes. Some scholars who study ethnic groups in other parts of the world or nonwhite American groups recognize that it need not necessarily be so. Groups can *form* social networks and communities of culture as well as eschew them. But few scholars of this sort ever attempt to apply that abstract possibility to the American scene.

The members of a third set of theorists often see ethnicity as a two-way street. For this group, ethnicity is really about *interests*. Where people who perceive a common heritage come together to pursue common economic or political agendas—*there* is ethnicity. Thus, although Nathan Glazer and Daniel Patrick Moynihan talk about culture and social networks, their deepest concern lies in the play of power politics among New York City's ethnic blocs. In similar fashion, Abner Cohen's focus is on the ways dispersed Hausa come together in Yoruba towns to function as independent political entities and control the economic niche of long-distance trade. Some writers, such as William Kornblum and William Julius Wilson, perceive a decline in ethnic-group political and economic functioning, in favor of larger class orientations. Some, such as Karen Blu, detect ethnic groups in the making. Perhaps because they have access to international comparisons, thinkers of the ethnicity-is-interests school frequently depict the formation (or at least the activation) of ethnic groups, not just their weakening and dissolution.[25] Since people operating from this angle of vision seldom look at individual behavior, intermarriage is not one of their major concerns. The treatment of intermarriage in the present book will have relevance for the ideas of the interest-ethnicity school only insofar as intermarriage may, over generations, change the sets of people who form ethnic interest groups and therefore change the boundaries of ethnic groups.

Nearly all of those who see ethnicity as culture, social networks, or interests concentrate mainly on the formation, maintenance, and dissolution of groups. As sociologists and political scientists, they show little concern for the relationship of individuals to their ethnicity.[26] Since intermarriage, like many social phenomena, is bound up not just with forces that act on groups but also with choices made by individuals, it is important that this study consider ethnicity from a viewpoint which also takes individual choice seriously.

A fourth school of thought does this. It says ethnicity is really about *identity*. For people of this persuasion, where a group identifies itself as an ethnic group, where it is so identified by its neighbors, where an individual identifies herself and is so identified—*there* is ethnicity. Herbert Gans calls this "symbolic ethnicity" and regards it as the trivial residue of a now-degenerated real ethnicity. It is, in his view, little more than a label—all that remains after ethnic culture, social networks, and interests have all disappeared. Thus, Gans and fellow heirs to the liberal expectancy might see Irish or Italian Americans today as scarcely more than symbolically ethnic. Having been melted in the crucible of American ethnic relations, they may continue to call themselves Irish and Italian, to cook Italian food and visit Irish pubs on weekends. But, in Gans's view, they know none of the "real" ethnicity of their immigrant grandparents. They are on a straight-line train to ethnic oblivion.[27]

I do not propose to predict the fate of Italian or Irish American ethnicity. But I am not convinced that ethnic identity is as trivial as Gans says. Erik Erikson writes of the power that ethnic identity has for an individual locating himself in the world. Fredrik Barth regards it as the essential issue in group ethnicity—the way of drawing lines between Us and Them. Daniel Bell compares identity to interest as a way of holding groups together: "Ethnicity has become more salient because it can combine an interest with an affective tie. Ethnicity provides a tangible set of common identifications—in language, food, music, names—when other social roles become more abstract and impersonal." Note that, for Bell, it is not the content of cultural practices, but the fact of their existence and the way people use them to tie themselves together in groups, that is important. A. L. Epstein suggests that Jews in New York City, now several generations in the United States and divided by class and other barriers, no longer have much in the way of common interests. Many have ceased Jewish cultural practices. Although some continue to connect with other Jews, the various social networks do not connect with one another, and some Jews connect with none at all. Yet all see themselves—and are seen by others—powerfully as Jews. On some issues, such as the survival of Israel, they act decisively together. Identity is important.[28]

Epstein is trying to create an understanding of ethnic identity that is more than just a label: "I am a Finn." Rather, it is something emotionally powerful—the sense that, on being with some other Finn, "I do not have to explain myself; because we are both Finns, he will know." And, at the level of the group rather than the individual, "All of us are Finns and we all basically understand each other." This idea of ethnicity as a sense of being a group is not simply a group label. It is not the same as a sense of all having gone to General Sherman Elementary School together. It is founded on Weber's notion of imputed common descent and is reinforced by the power of kinship. This angle on ethnicity is especially important for understanding intermarriage attitudes and behavior. People making marriage choices, and other people reacting to those marriage choices, do so largely around the notion of who is within their group. Perceptions of class and culture, and knowledge of social connections, all play parts in these decisions. But ultimately, after an individual's feelings for another individual, marriage choices seem mainly to embody judgments as to whether a particular person is one of us or not. Is she of our group? If not, is she of a group that is close to or compatible with our group? This strikes me as founded on the concept of ethnicity as identity, more than on ethnicity as interest, network, or culture.

One problem with nearly all the studies of ethnicity is that scholars have treated ethnicity as a two-category problem. Either one has ethnicity or one does not. It may be true that one is either a Chinese American or one is not. But a conception that stops there misses a great deal. For within the Chinese American group there are ethnic subgroups—Cantonese, Hakka, Hunanese, Manchu, and so forth—with whom a given Chinese American individual may feel greater or lesser affiliation. Likewise, the tendency among members of ethnic groups to grade people outside their own group in consistent patterns indicates different degrees of perceived similarity and affiliation. As we shall see, these varying senses of closeness, within what most outsiders conceive to be the group and also outside it, have important bearing on intermarriage.[29]

Another problem with most treatments of ethnicity is that they fail to distinguish between *latent* and *active* ethnicity. This is particularly true of the ethnicity-is-interests school.[30] Most American White Protestants do not recognize they have ethnicity. They do, in fact, have ethnicity, but it is latent until thrown into high relief by face-to-face contact—say, by an afternoon in Harlem. In a similar pattern, most middle-class people do not imagine they have a class identity— they are "just people"—until they have to deal closely with the very rich or the very poor. Then their class identity comes out, in their behavior if not in their self-consciousness. When Chinese Americans are together in a group with no non-Chinese around, they do not spend much time thinking about themselves as ethnic. They are just normal people in the company of other normal people. In this case, the norms are Chinese American norms. These Chinese Americans, if viewed surreptitiously by an outsider, would be perceived to behave in ethnic ways—talking in Chinese American slang, eating Chinese food (not of the sort non-Chinese people eat) with chopsticks, telling jokes that make sense only if one assumes a knowledge of Chinese American culture. They *are* ethnic, but their awareness of their ethnicity is latent. The same group of Chinese Americans, at work or school or on the street in the company of non-Chinese Americans, engage in many of the same behaviors (probably not all), but now they have a heightened sense of their ethnicity because it stands in contrast to the people around them. Their ethnicity may in this second instance be said to be active. By Schermerhorn's definition, ethnicity is something we all have. That is, all humans are members of a subgroup of society that has some sense of common ancestry and history, a cultural focus, and all the rest. White Protestant Americans have ethnicity as much as do Jews or Mexican Americans. They may be the largest ethnic group in America, and their ethnicity may be latent much of the time, but they are ethnic nonetheless. The Daughters of the American Revolution is as much an ethnic institution as Temple Beth Israel (both may also be class institutions; that is another matter).[31]

When I started this study, I assumed, along with nearly everyone else who has touched the subject, that intermarriage represents a fixed point at the limit of ethnic identity. Upon intermarriage, ethnicity disappears. There is some truth in that perception. For two groups of people to intermarry substantially they must perceive each other as similar and attractive. But that does not mean they see each other as *the same*. For Poles and Italians to intermarry does not mean they have the same ethnic identity, only that they see each other as compatible. Thus, Gordon and others who see ethnic identity being obliterated by intermarriage have jumped the gun. Does a woman cease to be black or brown or yellow or white if she marries someone of another color? Of course not. Do her children? That depends on the particulars of their social setting. If there is near-complete intermarriage between her group and another, does that mean her group disappears? That, too, depends. Sometimes it does; sometimes it does not (see Chapter 12). So what is most worth looking at is not the bare fact of intermarriage—that signifies little beyond perceptions of compatibility—but at those circumstances surrounding intermarriage which signal loss of group identity and those which do not.

The Scope of This Study

Each of the prevalent ideas about intermarriage or ethnicity has been put together to explain the attitudes and behaviors of a particular group in a particular time and place. Now what is needed is for someone to take a longer and larger view, comparing several groups and observing change over a fairly significant period of time. One ought not try to take the larger view, however, at the sacrifice of the vividness, depth, and relative certitude that come with a detailed look at specific groups. Therefore, rather than attempt to survey all varieties of intermarriages, the following narrative is grounded primarily in the twentieth-century experiences of three American ethnic groups —Japanese, Jews, and Blacks—and one international encounter, between Japanese women and American men after World War II. On occasion, data from before 1900 are used to illuminate the twentieth century. Also, the concluding chapter makes a brief comparison of the intermarriage experiences of these four groups with those of other American and foreign peoples, in order to assess more accurately the worth of the various theories about intermarriage and ethnicity.[32]

Part I comprises three chapters on the intermarriage experiences of Japanese Americans. The first of these—Chapter 2—outlines the history of this ethnic group and recounts the ways Japanese Americans viewed other Americans and the ways they were in turn viewed over the course of the twentieth century. Chapter 3 describes the dimensions of Japanese American outmarriage over time, generation removed from the old country, sex, region, social class, and other variables. It also tells of the changing ways both Japanese Americans and non-Japanese reacted to Japanese American outmarriage. Chapter 4 offers some interpretations of the Japanese American intermarriage experience and comments on such special issues as the relationship between intermarriage and divorce for Japanese Americans and the fate of the children of intermarriage.

Part II tells not a domestic but an international story, about intermarriage between American men and Japanese women in the decades after World War II. Part III returns to the American scene and depicts the intermarriages of American Jews. Like Part I, it is divided into three chapters, the first (Chapter 6) about the background to twentieth-century Jewish intermarriage, the second (Chapter 7) giving the dimensions of intermarriage, and the third (Chapter 8) reflecting on some special issues and questions of interpretation. Part IV, on Black Americans' experiences with intermarriage, is divided into three chapters on the same basis as Parts I and III.

A few words should be said about why these particular groups were chosen. Nearly all the theories about intermarriage were constructed with one of two types in mind, either Blacks married to Whites or Jews married to Gentiles. Even those studies that included other groups took their idea structures from the Black-White and Jewish-Gentile studies. This book begins from a different angle. It starts by looking at marriage between Japanese and non-Japanese Americans, and follows with comparative sections on Jews and Blacks. Japanese Americans have the advantage of comparability with each of the other groups: like Jews, they are an immigrant group, the bulk of whose antecedents came to America between 1880 and 1924; like Blacks they are set off from the majority of Americans by color. One of the arresting things to observe about Japanese Americans is the extraordinary change that has taken place in their status over the time this book covers, at least as measured by intermarriage and related phenomena. Around the turn of the century, most observers would have placed Japanese at the bottom of the American social scale along with Blacks, Mexicans, and Indians—well below the status of recent European immigrants. By the time the study ends in the 1980s, the position of the Japanese (in other Americans' eyes if not their own) was much more like that of the European immigrant group under study, Jews, than like other people of color. Chapter 5, on Japanese women married to American men, affords an international comparison while at the same time retaining some elements of continuity with the Japanese American case.[33]

This book is history, in that it surveys changes in human behavior over time. It is not sociology, although it deals with a subject that has hitherto belonged primarily to sociologists. It is both social and cultural history. The former—for example, the work of the *Annales* school—tends to treat social structures as causal and examines their effects on human behavior. Cultural history, such as Robert Darnton's *The Great Cat Massacre*, treats culture as causal and studies expressive human behavior. My work is about the interplay of culture and structure, and their effects on perception, attitude, and behavior.[34] People's experiences regarding intermarriage, this book contends, are shaped by both ideas and social structure. For example, intermarriage rates *are* shaped by demography. Where there are lots of Jews there is a lower percentage of intermarriage than where there are few Jews. Intermarriage patterns *do* reflect evolving class positions of minority groups. As more Japanese Americans have become middle class, their outmarriage rate has shot up. But intermarriage patterns, particularly gender patterns, are not just functions of social structure. They depend in large part on the images that people of the various ethnic groups have of each other and of themselves.

The book is intended as a benchmark for further intermarriage studies. It looks deeply at the intermarriage experiences of these four groups. Then, relying on data from other, more narrowly focused studies, it also compares them with the experiences of other ethnic groups in the United States and abroad. In making these comparisons, it attempts to say: "This is what we know. This makes sense. That does not. This other topic needs further investigation."

Terms

The use of terms in writing about intermarriage is impressively idiosyncratic and imprecise. I try in the pages that follow to use terms consistently and with as much clarity as I can muster. *Intermarriage* here means any marriage across ethnic or racial lines; hence, "inter-marriers" and "the intermarried" are people who have married others not of their own ethnic group. A marriage between a Jew and a Gentile, for instance, is an "intermarriage." *Outmarriage* is much the same phe-nomenon, but viewed distinctly from the point of view of one group. Thus, when I write about the attitudes of Japanese Americans toward "outmarriage," I mean their attitudes toward other Japanese Americans marrying non-Japanese Americans. *In-marriage* is marriage within the group, for example, between two Blacks. This book sometimes uses "intermarriage" in such a way as to include lasting intergroup unions that have not been made formal by marriage. This seems preferable to repeatedly burdening the reader with "intermarriages and other inter-group liaisons" or some such cumbersome phrase. Those occasions that involve the use of "intermarriage" in this way should be clear from context. "Intermarriage" here never includes casual liaisons such as interracial prostitution. *Amalgamation* and *miscegenation* are two old and still serviceable words for sexual mixing—with or without marriage—across racial lines.

Mixed marriage is a term used sparingly, and only as a synonym for "intermarriage." Some writers on American Jewry have tried to draw a distinction between the two terms, using "mixed marriage" to refer to marriages between Jews and non-Jews where the Gentile does not convert, and "intermarriage" to describe the same combination when the Gentile partner does convert to Judaism. This is a distinction worth making, but it is not one recognized by the general public nor one that inheres in the terms themselves. To draw a distinction between "mixed marriage" and "intermarriage" would add little clarity and much con-fusion, so I do not make the distinction. As the reader will learn, just who is within an ethnic group and who is outside does not always stay the same, so just what constitutes an "intermarriage" varies according to context.

Another problem is what to call the children of intergroup mating. The most common term used throughout the period under study is *mixed blood.* The term arose from the blood theories of race common in the latter nineteenth century. In our selectively more genteel era, "mixed blood" has acquired something of a vulgar ring. Accordingly, it is used very little in the narrative that follows. It remains in the title, however, because it accurately connotes many of the emotions surrounding intergroup mating in the period under study. In most instances in the text, *children of intermarriage, people of mixed ancestry, people of mixed parentage, mixed people,* and similar circumlocutions are employed. *Mulatto* is sometimes used to describe the progeny of Black-White couples, but I do not make such finer distinctions as "quadroon," "octoroon," and so forth. Some people have encouraged me to use *Eurasians* for part-Japanese people, but I have resisted, except where one parent was clearly of European ancestry. I sometimes use *Amerasian* instead, to denote part-Japanese people whose non-Japanese parent might be white, black, brown, or yellow. However, I limit use of this term to the children of Japanese "war brides" after World War II, for that is the only group, save recent part-Indochinese immigrants, to whom "Amerasian" was historically applied. Although some Japanese Americans called mixed people "Hapa" and some Jews called part-Jews "Mischling," I refrain from using these terms because they are not generally used even within the groups in question.

Occasionally the term *mixed people* is applied to persons of mixed ancestry, without any intended connotation that they may be mixed-up people. So, too, sometimes *mixed couples* describes their parents and *mixed families* describes their families.

Finally, a word about ethnic labels is in order. *Jew* and *Japanese American* are universally recognized terms. Though I lean toward using "Chicano" and "Pilipino" for ideological reasons, I recognize that these terms are not universally regarded as the appropriate designations for their respective ethnic groups. Moreover, they were not used much in the bulk of the period under study. In their stead I use *Mexican American* and *Filipino.* I use *Native American* and *Indian* interchangeably, except where otherwise noted.

What to use in referring to the descendants of Africans is more problematical. Most students of nineteenth- and early twentieth-century Black history use the word "Negro," since it was the most polite term in use during the time about which they write. Joel Williamson uses "Negro" to denote anyone of African ancestry, "black" for that subgroup whose ancestry is unmixed, and "mulatto" or "brown" for people of brown color or mixed parentage.[35] I cannot bring myself to adopt his scheme, in part because I deal mainly with a later period when those were not the distinctions being made within Black communities. Instead, I use *Black* or *Afro-American* to refer to anyone, regardless of actual skin color, who has known African ancestry. *Mulatto* refers specifically to the children of mixed couples, not to people of brown or tan color who have two brown parents. At those points where I wish to make distinctions about color, the meaning should be clear from context.

White and *Black* are capitalized because I regard both as proper nouns in contemporary usage. Neither is a descriptive adjective: the skin of most Black people is one shade of brown or another, while the skin of most Whites is pink or beige.

In all of this, I am likely to have offended the sensibilities of some readers, who prefer one or another term for personal, etymological, or political reasons. I can only plead that I mean no offense, and ask the reader to look beyond terminology to the analysis of intermarriage which is the primary subject of this book.

I

JAPANESE AMERICANS

2. Background and Images: Fu Manchu and Charlie Chan

> Near my home is an eighty-acre tract of as fine land as there
> is in California. On that tract lives a Japanese. With that
> Japanese lives a white woman. In that woman's arms is a
> baby. What is that baby? It isn't white. It isn't Japanese. It is
> a germ of the mightiest problem that ever faced this state; a
> problem that will make the black problem of the South look
> white.[1]

These were the words of a White minister named Ralph Newman,
revealing what he thought about an interracial marriage between an
anonymous Japanese American man and an equally anonymous White
American woman near Sacramento in 1913. Part I will investigate
such marriages between Japanese Americans and non-Japanese. It
introduces the reader to Japanese American history and describes the
images Japanese Americans and non-Japanese have held of each other.
It surveys Japanese Americans' attitudes and behavior with respect to
outmarriage over three generations and the first four-fifths of this century. It describes variations in rates and patterns of intermarriage for
immigrant Japanese, their children, and their grandchildren by class
and by region. It recounts the ways some Japanese Americans and
some non-Japanese tried to stop intermarriages. It tells the stories of
individuals who built successful intermarriages and those who failed,
and of people of mixed parentage in various times and circumstances.
It describes the impact on Japanese American intermarriage of outside forces, such as the imprisonment of the Japanese American people
during World War II and the general liberalization of race relations in

the postwar period. It notes changes in the ways Japanese Americans have defined their own ethnic boundaries, and it develops a system of categories for analyzing intermarriage behavior by other ethnic groups.

Issei, Nisei, Sansei

Japanese American history can be divided into five periods: (1) the frontier period, when young Japanese men established a beachhead in the American West; (2) the era of family making, when Japanese women came to America; (3) the youth of the Nisei, or second generation; (4) the trauma of imprisonment during World War II; and (5) the postwar period, when Japanese Americans moved toward joining the American mainstream.

The first official record of Japanese coming to America dates from 1861, when a single individual crossed the ocean. For more than two decades thereafter, only a trickle of students, traders, and perhaps a few immigrants made the journey. The flow picked up in the 1880s, when the Japanese government lifted its ban on emigration and labor contractors began to recruit Japanese to work in Hawaiian cane fields. Some Japanese were coming to the mainland as well. These were the Issei, first-generation Japanese immigrants to America. About 2,000 Japanese emigrated to the United States in the 1880s, 28,000 in the 1890s, and 225,000 in the first two and a half decades of this century.[2] The Japanese called them *dekaseginin*, "men who go out to work," rather than *teiju*, "permanent residents abroad." Like Japanese farmers who worked temporarily in Japanese cities, or Greeks and Italians who came to work on America's East Coast, *dekaseginin* expected to go to America and make money and then return to Japan. Most of the *dekaseginin* came from a few prefectures in southwestern Japan, where labor contractors had established networks of contacts and successful emigrants encouraged others to follow their path. In these prefectures, middle peasants who had fallen victim to crop failures and deflationary government policies sought to regain their lands and fortunes by going abroad to work. Most succeeded: 75 percent went back to Japan with enough money to redeem their mortgages.[3]

That the overwhelming majority of the early workers who went to America were male should surprise no one. They went to work, not to stay and raise families; their families remained in Japan. A few wives went along, in these early years, as well as some women who were sold or tricked into prostitution. But most of the women stayed home, awaiting their men's return. Less than 6 percent of the Japanese who came to America before 1905 were women, compared to 16 percent in 1905–08 and over 50 percent in 1909–14.[4]

The Japanese did not pick a very good time to begin their migration to America. Anti-Chinese agitation, long a favorite West Coast political activity, reached its peak in the 1880s. Congress voted in 1882 to exclude all Chinese laborers, who were deemed a threat to the jobs and living standards of White workers. Throughout the decade anti-Chinese violence erupted all over the western United States, taking scores of lives and rendering hundreds homeless.[5] When many Chinese went back to China and others retreated into ethnic slums, Japanese immigrants came to take their places in Western agriculture and industry. Now the demagogues turned their attention to the Japanese and applied to them all the racist ideas that had been concocted for the Chinese.

The new anti-Japanese feelings stemmed not only from racist imagery and economic competition, but also from international political developments. The Japanese had vaulted from prostration before Western military might in the 1850s to world power by the turn of the century, culminating in their thrashing of China and Russia in wars in 1894–95 and 1904–05. The defeat of a major European power, however weak, by a small Asian nation was a rude shock to those who had calmly assumed that the Caucasian powers would always reign supreme. In 1905 the editors of the *San Francisco Chronicle*, edgy about Japan's growing military presence in Asia, began a crusade against Japanese Californians. They hauled out many of the old charges that had been used against the Chinese. Japanese immigrants, they said, were coming in hordes and would soon "crowd out the white race." They were sneaky, said the *Chronicle*, and they tried to get around immigration and citizenship laws. They stole White people's jobs. "Crime and poverty go hand in hand with [Japanese] labor." And, according to this school of thought, the Japanese were a menace to American women.[6]

A growing group of White racists formed an Asiatic Exclusion League which, together with California labor unions, tried to add the Japanese to the list of barred peoples. They did not achieve exclu-

sion, but they did manage in 1906 to precipitate an international incident by persuading the San Francisco Board of Education to take all
Japanese and Korean students out of the regular public schools and
segregate them with the Chinese. The Japanese government lodged
a furious protest with President Theodore Roosevelt. Roosevelt, who
shared many of the California agitators' racist ideas about Asians but
did not want to risk antagonizing this new world power, put pressure
on the Californians to stop harassing Japanese Americans. In return,
he said he would get the Japanese to stop sending laborers to America.
In 1907 the United States and Japan concluded what has been called
the Gentlemen's Agreement. The American government would kill
all discriminatory legislation against Japanese Californians. In return,
the Japanese government agreed to screen future emigration to keep
laborers at home. Harassment and beatings of individual Japanese did
not stop, but the organized anti-Japanese movement entered a period
of quiescence.[7]

The Gentlemen's Agreement did not change Japanese emigration
policy a great deal. Since 1900 the Japanese government, conscious
of its international image, had discouraged *dekaseginin* laborers from
going to America. Now the ban was simply made more firm, and emigration by laborers continued to drop off. Yet other types of Japanese
immigrants kept coming. About this time, those Japanese men who
had come earlier as temporary sojourners were beginning to rethink
their position. Some had made as much money as they wanted, or else
feared the anti-Japanese agitators, and they returned to Japan. Others
still wanted to go back to Japan in style but were coming to realize that
it would be a long time before they could afford to do that. Members
of a third group were beginning to think that America might be a good
place to stay. The latter two groups of men began to think seriously
about establishing families in America. The Gentlemen's Agreement
said nothing about Japanese women, so these men were free to return
to Japan, marry, and bring their brides back to America with them.
Others wrote to relatives in Japan to find them wives, exchanged letters and pictures with prospective mates, and then sent money for the
women to come to America.[8]

The arrival of the Issei women wrought a dramatic change in the
nature of life for Japanese people in America. Not only did they bring
the comforts of home and family life to lonely Japanese American men,

but their arrival occasioned the creation of Japanese American communities. Before the arrival of Issei women, Japanese American men had lived a transient existence. A man might work one season on the levees of the Sacramento River Delta, the next in the Washington hop fields, and the third in an Alaska salmon cannery. Some stayed longer in one job or another, but few put down roots. Since few Japanese men stayed in one place very long, and since most intended to go back to Japan soon, few ethnic community institutions developed in the early years. Labor contractors' offices, bars, and boarding houses constituted the main gathering points for Issei laborers. Japanese America was transformed in the decade of the 1910s from a collection of lonely males to a family society. In 1900 there were nearly five Japanese men for every Japanese woman in the continental United States. Ten years later the ratio had begun to drop, to 3.5 to 1. By 1920, thanks to the massive influx of Japanese brides and the return of some men to Japan, the ratio was down to 1.6 to 1. Nearly every adult female was married. This still meant that there were many single Issei men, but they were far fewer than a decade earlier.[9]

Throughout the decade of the 1910s, Japanese workers were changing not only their marital condition but also their jobs and community connections. Marriage and stable, long-term employment went hand in hand. Issei men who had decided to stay in America for a while got permanent jobs or started out in business for themselves and secured wives. In this period the occupational pattern for Issei men shifted from laboring to farming and small business. In this period, too, Japanese community organizations—the Japanese Associations, the prefectural societies, the Buddhist and Christian churches—began to flourish. What had formerly been a loose, informal, ever-shifting set of acquaintances among transient Issei men became a series of stable community networks in various towns and rural areas on the Pacific Coast.[10]

But there were men who were left out of these emerging Japanese communities. Some men continued their transient pattern, either because they liked that life or, more often, because they had no economic alternative. They had only fragile connections to other, more sedentary groups of Japanese Americans. Other men had wandered far afield from concentrations of Japanese Americans and had put down tentative roots in such far-off places as Montana, Texas, and New York. There were Japanese Americans in every state in 1920. There were 110,000 of them in Hawaii and 93,000 on the West Coast, but 10,000 lived in the Rocky Mountain states and 3,600 in the Northeast.[11]

Even those Issei who settled down and raised families did not always join Japanese communities geographically. Darrel Montero gathered data on Issei who stayed in America and had children here, and found that in 1915 only three in ten lived in neighborhoods dominated by Japanese Americans. A third of his sample lived in mixed neighborhoods, and 37 percent lived away from other Japanese people entirely.[12]

Although Japanese Americans were settling down, starting families and businesses, and generally becoming stable members of American society, White anti-Japanese agitators were not convinced that they should be allowed to remain. The period of quiescence that followed the Gentlemen's Agreement did not last long. Soon an anti-Japanese chorus led a crescendo of cries for action against the Japanese. Some felt betrayed that the Gentlemen's Agreement had not stopped Japanese immigration entirely, as they had expected, but only deflected it from men to women. The anti-Japanese forces won a round in 1913 when the California Assembly passed the Alien Land Law, denying the right to own real property to "aliens ineligible to citizenship." This meant the Japanese and Chinese, though it was no secret that Japanese Americans were the main target. Soon other western states passed similar laws. The agitators were quiet during World War I, partly because the land law seemed to work (the number of Issei giving up and leaving for Japan increased sharply after 1913 and continued to be high through the 1930s) and partly because Japan was an American ally in the war against Germany. After the war, however, anti-Japanese feeling swelled again. This time it spoke to a national audience. Nativism was in bloom all over America. In 1920 the California Assembly plugged some loopholes in the Alien Land Law. Four years later, as part of a sweeping attempt to make America a nation of northwestern Europeans, Congress passed a law strictly limiting immigration in general and stopping Japanese immigration entirely.[13]

Despite harassment from non-Japanese Americans, many Japanese immigrants stayed in America and raised families. Their children, the Nisei, or second generation, led lives very different from the parents. The abrupt cutoff of immigration in 1924 made for two distinct age-generation groups. The Nisei were also very different from their parents in cultural terms. They exhibited many of the characteristics of Everett Stonequist's Marginal Man: "He belongs neither to America nor to the Orient. Culturally he is an American; racially he is of the Orient. He cannot identify himself completely with either civilization."[14]

As members of the Nisei generation moved out of their parents' homes and into American streets and schools, much of the parents' Japaneseness was left behind. To be sure, Nisei exhibited a number of cultural similarities to immigrant Japanese, particularly in psychological dimensions.[15] But many Nisei came to reject their parents and to question the value of their own Japaneseness. According to Minako Kurokawa Maykovich, "As soon as the Nisei reached school age, the most crucial reference group became the Audience Group of Caucasian peers. The desire for acceptance and recognition by the white group was so great that the Nisei tried to conform as closely as possible to their values and norms." The Nisei aspired to be accepted into middle-class American society, but found themselves shut out because they came in the wrong color. Some acknowledged the part of them that was Japanese, but also wanted the American part of them to gain recognition. Others wanted, if possible, to be accepted as fully American. Ichiro Yamada, the hero of John Okada's novel *No-No Boy*, put the dilemma well. There was a time in his childhood, he said, when, surrounded by his family, he felt only his Japanese identity. But as he grew up, "There came a time when I was only half Japanese because one is not born in America and raised in America and taught in America and one does not speak and swear and drink and smoke and play and fight and see and hear in America among Americans in American streets and houses without becoming American and loving it. But I did not love it enough, for . . . I was . . . still half Japanese. . . . I wish with all my heart . . . that I were American." Ichiro was speaking of an inner conflict between his Japanese and his American identity, but that conflict was caused in no small part by White America's refusal to recognize his dual identity. White Americans looked at Nisei and saw Japanese. They insisted that, because the Nisei bore yellow skins and Japanese names, they must be wholly Japanese. (The imprisonment of all people of Japanese ancestry during World War II is testimony to this fact.) In response, many Nisei protested that they were not Japanese at all, but were 100 percent American.[16]

The Nisei's yearning to be accepted by White Americans caused many of them to be ashamed of the Issei. As Jeanne Wakatsuki put it, "I was ashamed of him [her father] . . . for being so unalterably Japanese. I would not bring home my friends for fear of what he would say or do." Many young Nisei rejected their parents, their Japanese heritage, and even parts of themselves. Daisuke Kitagawa, a Japanese American Christian minister, probably overstated the case, but his comments on the Nisei's rejection of the Issei are not without foundation: "A Nisei, in order to be a respectable member of the Nisei community, had to be rebellious against his parents and the Issei in general. . . . the adolescent Nisei revolted against his parents, not merely because they belonged to a bygone generation, but also, more primarily, because they were Issei, an alien group. Here the rebellion took on a complexion of self-hate. In his parents the Nisei found that element in himself which made it difficult for him to be accepted by American society." One sensitive young man spoke bitterly: "No matter how much I look in the mirror, I cannot change; it is the same old Ichiro—my face is that of an Oriental. I want to be a Caucasian, accepted and comfortable, but when I look at myself honestly, I must face the painful reality that I am a Japanese, a member of a minority group which I reject, and I hate it." Lest one conclude that all Nisei despised themselves unequivocally, however, one should note that many were quite happy about being Japanese.[17]

Many Nisei associated freely with other Americans in their younger years. But in high school, in college, and on the job they found social segregation. In his first years of high school, Hideo Sangano* hung around with a group of Caucasians and was comfortable with White friends of both sexes. But as the group began to pair up into dating couples, he found that none of the girls were interested in him. He began to feel "very self-conscious." It got to the point that he imagined they were always talking about him behind his back, so he stopped seeing them and retreated into the solitude of his own company. In college, and especially in the world of work, Nisei found themselves shut out of social intercourse with non-Japanese Americans. As the bars of discrimination were raised, members of the second generation began to form all-Nisei social groups—holding Nisei dances, fielding Nisei

*Asterisks here and elsewhere denote pseudonyms.

softball teams, bowling in Nisei leagues. One Nisei in 1940 character-ized the majority of his age-mates as "socialites . . . whose main pre-occupations were dates, dances, movies, and sports." These groups in-cluded almost no non-Nisei, and anyone who had non-Japanese friends was suspect. Yet, although the Nisei separated themselves—or found themselves separated—from Whites, Blacks, and other minorities, at the same time they avidly pursued all the outward trappings of White, middle-class American behavior. Chotoko Toyama reported in 1926 that the Los Angeles Nisei worked very hard at appearing as American as possible, "in dress, in manners, in social organization, in customs and in ideas." [18]

No matter how American the Nisei looked, felt, and acted, they could not avoid the traumatic rejection of their American identity that came their way during World War II. Shortly after Pearl Har-bor, the entire Japanese American population of the Pacific Coast was herded into concentration camps. There, in enforced social segrega-tion, they sat out much of the war period. They suffered humiliation, economic loss, and social dislocation. The wartime experiences of Japa-nese Americans have given birth to a vast and rich literature.[19] During the war, the bulk of the Nisei generation, led by the Japanese American Citizens League, worked hard to prove themselves worthy Americans. They pronounced their loyalty to the United States, tried to make the concentration camps into model American communities, joined the Army when they were allowed, and fought with unprecedented valor in Europe and the Pacific. As their generation took the reins in Japa-nese American society after the war, they directed their people toward assimilation and upward mobility.[20]

In the decades after World War II, Japanese Americans made large, rapid steps toward entering the American mainstream. They spread throughout the country. Their largest concentrations were still on the West Coast and in Hawaii, but colonies appeared in the cities of the Midwest and Northeast, and nearly every region had a significant Japanese American presence by 1970. In cities where Japanese Ameri-cans had formerly congregated, the distribution of their population changed. In 1950, Japanese Americans still clustered around the ethnic neighborhoods of prewar years, but by 1960 they were moving rapidly out of those urban ghettoes. By 1970, few Japanese remained in central cities; instead, they were dotted over the suburban landscape.[21]

Postwar Japanese Americans pursued education with renewed vigor. As early as 1940 they were the most highly educated of American racial groups. Their lead widened consistently thereafter. There were holes in the achievement story, of course. Japanese Americans' occupational status, although high, never matched their educational achievement. Income lagged even farther behind. Middle-class Japanese were often relegated to middle management or technical positions or jobs serving primarily their own ethnic constituency, rather than being free to achieve their highest potential. And not all prospered. There were some signs by the 1960s of distinct social classes developing among Japanese Americans, with working and middle-class people traveling separate paths. Despite such limitations, however, the postwar integration of most Japanese Americans into middle-class American society is striking.[22]

This integration was partly the fulfillment of prewar Nisei strivings and postwar efforts to gain entry to mainstream American society. In the 1960s a new generation, the Sansei, came of age. Children of the upward-striving, largely assimilationist Nisei, born mainly after the war, the Sansei inherited many of their parents' goals and attitudes. Some grew up in Japanese American enclaves, others in White suburbs. The Sansei, like their parents, pursued higher education and middle-class careers. A significant minority of them were affected by the liberal ideals of the 1960s. These chose to direct their efforts toward the betterment of society at large and the Japanese American people in particular. But a larger number of Sansei passed through the 1960s and early 1970s relatively untouched by liberal ideas. They emerged as the quintessential people of the late 1970s and 1980s: ambitious, career-oriented, acquisitive, and unconcerned about broad social questions. Among the concomitants of Sansei dispersion and upward mobility in the 1960s and 1970s was a stunning increase in the rate of outmarriage.[23]

How, in sum, shall one characterize Japanese American society at each stage of its development? In the frontier years, Japanese American men who came to work in America did not usually form stable communities. They lived transitory existences and seldom connected with the non-Japanese around them, nor even with their fellow countrymen. The arrival of brides from the homeland did not bring integration into the larger American society, but it did mean that Issei men settled down, took more or less permanent jobs, and formed ethnic communities that both supported and circumscribed their existence. As the Nisei grew toward maturity, they often expressed a common second-generation attraction to American culture and ambivalence—even hostility—toward their immigrant heritage. The developments of these early decades took place against a backdrop of White racism which denied even most Nisei close relationships with non-Japanese Americans. Rejection took very tangible form when the Nisei and their parents suffered incarceration during World War II. After the war, many Nisei made dramatic steps away from what some viewed as the limitations of their ethnic background and toward the American mainstream. Although some among the third generation disputed the wisdom of assimilation, it nonetheless was the dominant trend of the postwar years.

Changing Images of Japanese Americans

From the earliest years of Japanese immigration to America, White people's images of Japanese American men were negative and unflattering, hardly the sort to encourage interracial romance. White people's visions of Japanese women, by contrast, underwent a metamorphosis, from an extremely negative image to one of submissiveness and sensuality that made romance and marriage quite attractive.

In the first quarter of this century, various White Americans debated the character and worth of Japanese immigrants. The dominant view was that they were somehow "unassimilable"—not like Americans and unwilling to become like Americans; that they were unclean and degraded; that they constituted an aggressive economic threat to White farmers and working people; and that they were an aggressive sexual threat—fecund, immoral, and (paradoxically, in view of the first objection) desirous of physical assimilation.[24]

The idea of a sexual threat from Japanese men loomed large in many White men's minds. Japanese immigrants—boys and men—were beginning to try to accommodate to life in America by learning English in the California schools. Since there were no adult classes, teenagers and mature men were put in elementary school classes with native American students whose English skills were similar to their own. Progressive politician Hiram Johnson, a future U.S. senator, complained: "I am responsible to the mothers and fathers of Sacramento County who have their little daughters sitting side by side in the school rooms with matured Japs, with their base minds, their lascivious thoughts, multiplied by their race and strengthened by their mode of life. . . . I have seen Japanese twenty-five years old sitting in the seats next to the pure maids of California. . . . I shudder to think of such a condition."[25]

In 1905, the California Assembly, anxious lest White womanhood be torn from the pedestal by yellow hands, made miscegenation between Asians and Whites illegal.[26] But that prohibition did not assuage White fears completely. A leader of the Native Daughters of the Golden West warned White women in 1923: "It is not unusual these days to find, especially the 'better class' of Japanese, casting furtive glances at our young women. They would like to marry them." Marshall DeMotte, chairman of the California State Board of Control, saw intermarriage as part of a Japanese government plot to conquer America. He perceived an "ambition on the part of the Japanese to win by intermarriage if they are denied their present plan to overcome by occupancy." A *San Francisco Chronicle* editorial summed up the views of many White Californians: "The Japanese boys are taught by their elders to look upon . . . American girls with a view to future sex relations. . . . What answer will the fathers and mothers of America make . . . ? The proposed [physical] assimilation of the two races is unthinkable. It is morally indefensible and biologically impossible. American womanhood is by far too sacred to be subjected to such degeneracy. An American who would not die fighting rather than yield to that infamy does not deserve the name."[27]

This image was filled with ambivalence, combining both loathing and grudging respect. If a White male genuinely feared a Japanese immigrant would take his job or his woman, then he recognized that that immigrant had a certain measure of intelligence, power, ambition, and attractiveness. The movies, mirror of popular taste, accurately reflected that recognition. A Japanese, Sessue Hayakawa, was one of the most compelling stars of the 1910s and '20s. He was suave, dashing, and sophisticated—the complete movie idol.[28]

By the time the bulk of the Nisei became teenagers in the 1930s, the dominant image of Japanese men was even less flattering. Drawing on old fears of the Heathen Chinese and the Yellow Peril, the movies pictured Asian men, both Chinese and Japanese, in three stock roles. One was the malevolent Chinese (later Japanese). In the 1930s, the major figure on the theme was Dr. Fu Manchu, a diabolical genius bent on destroying Western civilization and compromising the virtue of White womanhood. By the 1940s, this evil creature had been transformed into the sickening Kamikaze pilot, grinning devilishly and intoning mystical poetry as he plunged his plane into the side of an American battleship.

A second, more benevolent role for Asian male actors (and for the White actors who played most Asian parts) was what Frank Chin has called "the Chinese who dies," the loyal sidekick of Alan Ladd or John Wayne who died defending China against Japanese invaders.[29] A variation on this theme was the suffering peasant role played by Paul Muni in *The Good Earth* (1938). These were not negative images, but they were not very flattering, either. In such roles, Asian men were seen as noble sufferers, but not as commanding figures who offered any challenge to the dominance of White males.

The preeminent Asian male role, however, was created by Warner Oland in the character of Charlie Chan. Forty-six Chan films reflected and reinforced an image of Asian men that was to dominate White thinking for decades. Detective Chan outsmarted a lot of Whites, but he was not a vigorous, manly figure like the characters played by John Wayne, Tyrone Power, or even Dick Powell. Despite the fact that the Chan character was given a wife and several children, there was never any romantic chemistry between him and any female on screen. He was in fact portrayed by Oland and his successors, Sidney Toler and Roland Winters, as sexless, even effeminate. Whatever positive effect Chan's intelligence might have had on the image of Asian men was mitigated by the fact that everyone knew Chan was not really an Asian, but a White man acting in an Asian role. All the real Asian men in the Chan films were buffoons, like Number One Son Keye Luke, who bumbled through several episodes, getting in his father's way and muttering, "Gee, Pop!" whenever his adolescent impulses were thwarted.

These images of Asian men—the malevolent Fu Manchu, the suffering peasant, the emasculated Charlie Chan—dominated majority Americans' view of Japanese American men from the 1930s through the 1970s. Japanese American men complained with good reason that non-Asians saw them as short, skinny, emotionally unexpressive, often bespectacled, and effeminate—the opposite of dominant American notions of desirable male qualities. Whites did perceive some positive characteristics in Japanese American men, as in other Asian males: intelligence, earnestness, and steadiness, for example. Japanese American men were seen as good technicians and middle management people, but not creative, enterprising individuals with flair, men who could make things happen.[30]

In the 1970s, the negative image of Asian males was modified a bit. The early seventies popularity of Kung-fu stars such as Bruce Lee showed White America an Asian face it had not seen before. Here was a small, compactly built Asian man who did not talk in Charlie Chan's fortune-cookie maxims. He not only outsmarted White men; he also beat them up. He did wonders for the public image—and self-image —of Asian American males. No longer did little Asian boys get beat up on the bus, for bullies learned to fear that a karate expert lurked beneath the seemingly mild exterior. About the same time, several Japanese American men won seats in the U.S. Senate and House of Representatives, from which position they showed Whites that Asians could lead. Also in the 1970s, many American women became less interested in macho, John Wayne types and sought out men who were more androgynous by former standards. In a social climate where a significant number of women were attracted to the Alan Alda image, Japanese American men met with greater romantic interest than ever before.[31]

Throughout most of the twentieth century, Japanese American women enjoyed a much more attractive public image than did their brothers. To be sure, immigrant women were not seen in flattering terms. White people saw Issei women as either prostitutes or faceless drudges through the 1930s. In the late 1930s, for the first time, Japanese women began to be seen as fit partners for White American men.

The change was due partly to the fact that an increasing number of non-Japanese men had by then grown up and gone to school with Nisei women. As long as all the Japanese women came from across the Pacific, their interaction with White American men was severely limited, and intimate social relationships were unlikely to occur. But for the Nisei, growing up side by side with Whites in public school classrooms meant that at least some White boys would have to notice that Japanese girls were female, attractive, and eligible. Out of such situations grew a few prewar interracial marriages, together with an image held by at least some White Americans that Nisei girls were bobby-soxers and gum-chewers just like their non-Japanese sisters.

A more dramatic shift in the image of Japanese American women came out of the Pacific War. Japanese women came to be seen by many American men as exotic, erotic creatures able to please men in special ways. American boys were sent off to remote islands to die hellish deaths. Yet their leapfrog race across exotic Polynesia, land of palm fronds and frangipani blossoms, took on a romantic aura. Soldiers, sailors, flyers, and newsmen came back to tell stories of their South Pacific adventures. James Michener rode to literary stardom on a collection of stories about the Pacific War. One of his great fixations in *Tales of the South Pacific* and later books was on the attractiveness of Asian and Polynesian women. One of the love stories in *South Pacific* was about Joe Cable and Liat, a Tonkinese girl played in the movie version by France Nuyen. Michener described this beauty, who in his mind combined the qualities of Asia and the Pacific, as slight, with "finely modeled" bones and "very black hair," a "rare beauty . . . exquisite . . . altogether delectable." Michener was particularly fascinated, here and in other books, with the bedtime contrast in skin color between Asian women and White men, and with those women's sexual skills.[32]

The image of exotic sensuality grew in the years after World War II, nurtured in part by the presence of several thousand Japanese war brides in America. The stereotype painted Asian women in general and Japanese women in particular as small, quiet, beautiful, submissive, soft, loving, self-sacrificing, uncomplaining, and eager to serve. This view became so pervasive as to prompt caustic rejoinders from Asian women. In a 1973 polemic titled "The Myth of the Erotic Exotic," Elaine Louie protested that she had become "a China object as well as a sex object," the fulfillment of fantasies for White men looking for mystical, "Oriental" experiences. *Playboy* and *Penthouse* did not heed Louie's complaint, for they persisted in playing on the stereotype in several photoessays as late as 1981. Movies and pulp fiction joined in, portraying Asian women as both enthusiastic and exceptionally skilled in the sexual arena. Eurasian women were deemed to be especially sexy.[33]

Increasingly in the 1950s, '60s, and '70s, those White men who were not sex-obsessed came to regard Asian women as normal Americans and fit partners for non-Asian men. The fact that the 1974 Miss Teenage America and the 1980 Rose Bowl Queen could be Sansei says a good deal about the American public's acceptance of Japanese American women (if not men). Asian women began to appear in movies as accepted, unremarked-upon partners to White men. Tina Chen, for instance, played Robert Redford's woman friend in *Three Days of the Condor,* a 1975 release, without significant reference to her ethnic origin. The October 2, 1981, cover of *Christianity Today,* a conservative Protestant magazine aimed at America's heartland, showed a Middle American family at Bible study: mother and father, both graying and solid-looking; two wholesome-appearing sons, one in his late twenties, one in his teens; and a young woman, apparently the daughter-in-law. She was Asian, and there was every indication that she was an accepted member of the family. Asian women had even achieved equal opportunity as candidates for White men's concubines. A 1981 advertisement in the personals column of a Seattle newspaper ran thus: "Good looking, trim, youthful (mid-50s), successful, good natured, married Caucasian executive; seeks arrangement with very attractive and intelligent 25 to 40 year old Caucasian or Oriental mistress, based on friendship, shared interests, and your possible needs to cope with a changing economy."[34]

Although Sansei women were attractive in the minds of many non-Asian men as partners or sex objects, often the women did not view themselves as so desirable. Some actually fit the stereotype; others recognized the elements of the stereotype and played on it, wearing their hair long, talking in quiet voices, and affecting demure postures around men. But many felt inferior to the image of White female beauty that was held up to them by television, magazines, and other cultural paraphernalia. Jan Masaoka expressed her frustration on this subject: "The typical sexy American women are fair with long, slender legs, big eyes and big breasts while Asian women are dark, have short, stocky legs, almond eyes and small breasts. The American ideal is ridiculous and sick for American women, but it's much harder when you're Asian and know you'll never live up to that. When I was a little girl I thought that the epitome of beauty was blonde hair and blue eyes, a pretty common vision for little girls in America, I guess, but when I looked in the mirror, I just knew I was hopeless."[35]

Nor did Japanese American men always see Sansei women as desirable. Ron Tanaka's tongue was planted firmly in his cheek when he wrote "I hate my wife for her flat yellow face," but the attitudes he criticized in himself and in other Sansei males were real enough:

> I hate my wife for her flat yellow face
> and her fat cucumber legs, but mostly
> for her lack of elegance and lack of
> intelligence compared to judith gluck.
> She's like a stupid water buffalo from
> the old country, slowly plodding.

Tanaka reflected an image held by some intellectual and political Sansei men, who criticized Japanese American women as ugly, uneducated, and uninspiring. His specific point of comparison was White women. Other Japanese American men criticized Sansei women for what they regarded as lack of pulchritude compared to White women, less than enthusiastic responses to sexual advances, and mercenary motivations. Some Japanese American men, however, saw beautiful inner qualities in Sansei women that more than compensated for any perceived deficiencies in physique. Tanaka pictured Japanese American women as gentle, kind, and long-suffering. Poet Lawson Inada described them as righteous Asian sisters.[36]

To recapitulate, one may say that Whites' images of Japanese American men made the transit from the sexual threat of the Issei years, to the emasculated Charlie Chan of the century's middle decades, and then to a position of somewhat greater romantic attractiveness. From the late 1930s on, Japanese American women enjoyed (or suffered from) an exotic image that added luster to their beauty and attractiveness in men's eyes, even if they did not always feel quite so beautiful. In the decades after World War II, Japanese American women increasingly came to be accepted by non-Japanese as fit partners for majority group men.

Japanese Americans' Ideas about Non-Japanese and about Intermarriage

Just as White Americans harbored a number of unflattering ideas about the Japanese, so the Issei brought with them mostly negative ideas about foreigners and about intermarriage. And just as Whites' negative views moderated over time, so by the Sansei generation Japanese Americans came to look on outsiders with greater favor.

The Japanese term for foreigner, *gaijin*, carries pejorative connotations that are not found in the English equivalent. *Gaijin* might be translated "outside person"—this in a society in which people depend more than in Europe or America on being inside people. One's whole life in Japan is bound up in a web of personal relationships. While most Japanese are polite and will be friendly to a *gaijin*, they are not likely to admit her or him to the world of inside people, to their web of personal relationships.[37]

Anthropologists George DeVos and William Wetherall speak of an intense and "pervasive Japanese sense of racial . . . purity and superiority," claiming that the Japanese look down on all non-Japanese, as well as on some within their own group. Cullen Hayashida, a Japanese American sociologist, goes further. He contends that the Japanese see themselves as a pure race, indigenous to their islands, and superior to other people. They see others as polluted, as hereditarily stained. They have gone to great lengths, including sponsoring an industry of pseudoscientific bloodline investigators, to maintain distinctions between themselves and outsiders. Ichiro Kawasaki, however, sees the attitudes of superiority often expressed by the Japanese as a mask for "the inferiority complex from which the Japanese invariably suffer toward Westerners and Western civilization . . . the other face being profound reverence in which the Occidentals are held in the mind of the Japanese."[38]

Japanese feelings toward other, non-Western peoples in the modern era have been less ambivalent. For nearly a century Japan has been the most powerful nation in Asia. Although some Japanese have from time to time avowed a pan-Asian sense of peoplehood, the vast majority have felt distinctly superior to the other peoples of Asia since the mid-nineteenth century.

Japanese attitudes toward the racial characteristics of foreigners have particular revelance to the study of intermarriage between Japanese emigrants and other Americans. Hiroshi Wagatsuma has done subtle and intelligent work in this field which deserves to be described at some length.[39] In surveying a variety of historical materials, Wagatsuma found that long before the Japanese had experienced any sustained contact with non-Asian peoples, they already had strong ideas about skin color. Briefly put, the Japanese from very early times liked white skin, which they associated with spiritual refinement and upperclass status, and disliked black skin, which they saw as a sign of primitiveness. The Japanese saw themselves as white and other peoples, such as Okinawans, as black; they did not have terms to describe intermediate shades of skin color. Yanagi Rikyo, a late-eighteenth-century warrior and poet, summed up the position of premodern Japan on feminine attractiveness. A woman ought to have "a small and well-shaped face, white skin, gentle manner, an innocent, charming and attentive character. . . . Disagreeable features for a woman are a large face, the lack of any tufts of hair under the temple, a big, flat nose, thick lips, black skin, a too plump body, excessive tallness, heavy strong limbs, brownish wavy hair and a loud, talkative voice." By such criteria, both Africans and Caucasians would be unpleasing to Japanese.

When Europeans first came to Japan in the sixteenth century, they were viewed as a curiosity, but their appearance did not occasion pejorative moral comment. Not so for the Black sailors and servants who accompanied them. Morishima Churyo described the Negroes he encountered: "The black ones on the Dutch boats are the natives of countries in the South. As their countries are close to the sun, they are sun-scorched and become black. By nature they are stupid. . . . They are uncivilized and vicious in nature." Other Japanese were not entirely sure whether the Black people they saw were humans or monkeys.[40]

Soon, largely for internal political reasons, the Japanese excluded nearly all Europeans from their islands. They ordered that the children of Iberian men and Japanese wives be put to death or deported. Yet they continued to tolerate communities of Chinese and Korean traders in their midst, and a few of those traders married Japanese women, though they did not become full members of Japanese society.[41]

More recently, twentieth-century Japanese have come to use the term *yellow* to describe their own skin for the first time, and have begun to view Caucasian skin as whiter than their own. With respect to color, some might even prefer Caucasian skin, for they associate its whiteness with purity, cleanliness, and spirituality. But they still do not like the hairiness and rougher skin texture of White Americans.

Admiring the skin of Caucasians is not the same thing as wanting to be intimate with them. Even in the 1960s, when Europe and America set much of the cultural tone in Japan and when Western movie stars were Japanese idols, there remained a basic sense of discontinuity in Japanese minds between themselves and Caucasians. One Japanese described his feelings: "When I think of actual Caucasians walking along the street, I feel that they are basically different beings from us. Certainly, they are humans, but I don't feel they are the same creatures as we are. There is, in my mind, a definite discontinuity between us and the Caucasians. Somehow, they belong to a different world. Deep in my mind, it seems, the Caucasians are somehow connected with something animal-like. . . . The first thing that comes up to my mind is a large chunk of boneless ham." Such a deep and persistent sense of difference, of the existence of a yawning chasm separating themselves from Caucasians, which Wagatsuma contends is typical, would be likely to make the average Japanese reluctant to intermarry or otherwise share intimate relations with Whites.[42]

The Issei who came to America in the first part of this century were heirs to Japanese thinking about race and intermarriage. It is likely that they shared the feelings of other Japanese: that they were a pure race; that White skin was attractive and pure, while dark skin was not; that a wide gap separated them from other peoples, with other Asians closest, Europeans perhaps next, and Africans farthest away; and that marriage to non-Japanese was a distinctly unattractive option.

The social situation of the second generation was radically different from that of their parents. Sometimes the ambivalence many Nisei felt toward their Japaneseness, and their desire to emulate White culture and to be connected with White society, extended to a desire for inter-racial romance. Hatsuye and Mineko, heroines of Toshio Mori's World War II-era story "Tomorrow and Today," dreamt, like many of their non-Japanese, early adolescent contemporaries, of romantic affairs with Robert Taylor and Clark Gable. They filled their room with movie magazines and plastered their walls with photographs. One may dismiss such expressions of love and longing as mere romantic fantasies, but it is significant that their romantic dreams centered on Caucasian, not Asian, men. These girls were sufficiently part of American culture to fantasize in the American idiom and long for the embrace of White movie stars. A shy Nisei girl echoed their adulation of a White male of mythic proportions, but like them, she had little hope of satisfying her dreams. She said, "Gee, I'd like to marry a Caucasian. It'd be like my best dreams. But it's so far beyond reach. . . . I just don't think about it." Novelist John Okada's male characters shared the girls' longing for a White partner, or for one who seemed like a White American. In *No-No Boy*, Ichiro and Kenji made it clear they considered it a coup to be seen with a White woman; at the same time they jealously criticized Bull, one of their Nisei contemporaries, for daring to seek a White partner. They betrayed a sense of inferiority about Japanese physiognomy and manners by deriding Bull's "swarthy" complexion, his "short legs and awkward body," and his crude behavior. It was important to Okada that his hero Ichiro have his first sexual experience with a White girl. Similarly, it was important that Emi, the Japanese woman whom Ichiro chose to save him as he sought to become an American in his own eyes, be as much like a White woman as possible: "Emi was several inches taller than Kenji. She was slender, with heavy breasts, had rich, black hair which fell off her shoulders and covered her neck, and her long legs were strong and shapely like a white woman's." Beautiful, cultured, and removed from the Japanese community that was stifling Ichiro, Emi was everything Okada's other Japanese women were not. Those others he depicted as short, flat-chested, bandy-legged, and shallow and mean-spirited to boot. In a last, desperate, and admittedly futile attempt to achieve the stature of an American in his own esteem, Ichiro vowed to "find a girl that's not Japanese that will marry me."[43]

One must use caution, however, in dealing with this type of material. Even if Okada's heroes and these Nisei girls longed for White partners, many other Nisei preferred romance within the Japanese American group. Even those who longed for interracial romance seldom were willing to venture beyond White partners to embrace members of other non-Japanese groups. Okada's Nisei and the Nisei whom Charles Kikuchi interviewed in Chicago in the 1940s were almost universal in their revulsion at the thought of contact with Blacks and Filipinos, and had negative stereotypes of other groups as well. Frances Nishimoto* told Kikuchi, "I just hated the Filipinos because they

stared at me and they always wanted to talk to me. I never saw any
Negroes [while growing up] but even now I don't like to be near one.
I shouldn't feel that way, I know. I'll talk to a Negro but I don't think
I'll ever have a Negro friend. . . . You can't trust a Filipino. . . . I like
the Jews, though . . . I never had any prejudice against them. I guess
that was because I never had any business dealing with them." These
were not just Nishimoto's idiosyncratic prejudices. Sylvia Yanagisako
reported that among prewar Nisei in Seattle, "social interaction with
blacks was unthinkable." Many of Kikuchi's middle-class Nisei were
similarly repelled by Chicanos, although some working-class Nisei
were close to and thought well of people of Mexican ancestry.[44]

Sansei men's and women's images of White women and men were
about what one would expect. Third-generation Japanese Americans,
men and women, tended to see White women as tall, blonde, shapely,
self-confident, cultured, and articulate, like Ron Tanaka's Judith Gluck.
White men's qualities were enumerated by a woman who was very
critical of Sansei men: "1) tall, 2) handsome, 3) manly, 4) self-confident,
5) well-poised, 6) protective, 7) domineering, 8) affectionate, 9) imagi-
native." Other women added blonde and well-biceped. That these
qualities applied to only a tiny fraction of the White population was
recognized by many Sansei. But many still carried these exaggerated
images of Caucasian attractiveness, along with artificial notions of Japanese American inferiority, into romantic encounters with Japanese and
non-Japanese alike.[45]

Japanese immigrants in the early years of this century saw themselves
as a pure race, widely separated and superior to non-Japanese peoples.
They perceived other Asians as somewhat close to themselves, Europeans somewhat more distant, and Africans further away still. Many
Nisei, by contrast, found Whites attractive even as they recoiled from
darker peoples. By the third generation, the attraction to Whites, at
least, was even stronger.

3. Dimensions of Intermarriage: Old Barriers Fall

Generations and Intermarriage

The pattern of outmarriage by Japanese Americans over the course of the twentieth century reflects their declining sense of separation from other American ethnic groups and resembles the intermarriage patterns of several other immigrant peoples. Very few members of the first generation married non-Japanese. Outmarriage was somewhat more common among the Nisei, but still it was the practice of only a small minority. It was not until the third generation, in the context of a high degree of assimilation and general acceptance by other American ethnic groups, that a large number of Japanese Americans chose non-Japanese spouses.

Issei. The rate of outmarriage by Japanese immigrants in California was very low, because it was where the Japanese population was heaviest, because both Japanese and non-Japanese opposed the practice, and because the sex ratio in Japanese communities was not so lopsided as it was among other immigrant peoples. Constantine Panunzio examined Los Angeles county marriage records from 1924 to 1933. He found that fewer than 3 Japanese men in 100 married non-Japanese women. Only 1.7 percent of the Los Angeles Issei women married non-Japanese men. The Japanese outmarriage rate was the lowest for any people of color in the Los Angeles population. None of the ethnic groups approved of intermarriage, and marriages of Blacks and Chinese to Whites were forbidden by law. Yet all the other groups married out more frequently than the Japanese: 11.3 percent of the Negroes married non-Negroes, 23.7 percent of the Chinese married non-Chinese, 56.9 percent of the Native Americans married non-Indians, and 70.1 percent of the Filipinos married non-Filipinos. In other locations on the West Coast, Issei outmarriage was hardly more frequent than in Los Angeles.[1]

Legal and social pressures against intermarriage are the subject of the next two sections of this chapter. Here, it is important to note that the low rate of Issei outmarriage stemmed in part from Japanese American demography. When brides stopped arriving from Japan in 1924, the ratio of Japanese American men to women was about 3 to 2. That is high and certainly must have exerted pressure toward intermarriage. The surplus males would have to either remain celibate, patronize prostitutes, or find mates in other ethnic communities. But the demographic pressure favoring intermarriage was much more intense for other immigrant groups. Among Chinese residents of Los Angeles in 1920, there were 9 men for every 2 women. Among Filipinos, the ratio was more than 20 to 1. Not surprisingly, both these groups had higher rates of outmarriage than the Japanese. Alongside such groups, the Japanese American population looks relatively well balanced.[2]

It is necessary to consider not just how many Issei intermarried, but which Issei, and to whom. Gender is one criterion to note. Both the California marriage records and community wisdom suggest that more Issei men than women married non-Japanese. This makes sense, because a substantial number of Japanese men came here single, while only a few women came without at least promises of marriage to Japanese men. What is more, the sex ratio favored intermarriage by Issei men rather than women. Yet the census takers found a larger percentage of Issei women than men who actually were partners in mixed marriages. How can this have been? It is true that not all marriages between California Japanese and Whites took place within California. Because such marriages were illegal in California and Oregon, couples who could afford it would take a boat or train north to Washington to be married. But there is nothing to indicate that these marriages were predominately between non-Japanese men and Japanese women, nor that they occurred in numbers large enough to make a difference in the overall statistics.[3]

It is more likely that many of the Japanese women in question did not come from Japanese American communities, but instead were wives of American men who had met and married them in Japan or elsewhere outside the West Coast. Such was the case of Mr. and Mrs. A. D. Riddle. He was manager of the Jardine, Matheson Shipping Company, and she was an upper-class, highly educated woman. They married in New York, so they would not have been counted in the California marriage statistics, but they constituted a California mixed marriage in the eyes of the census takers. Since most of these intermarried couples did not settle in Japanese communities, their existence would not have been recorded by the community grapevine. The fact that a slight majority of intermarried Issei were women, in the face of contrary demographic imperatives such as the ratio between the sexes, points to a trend that endured in later generations. At least until the 1970s, the bulk of Japanese American outmarriages were by women, not men.[4]

The Issei women and men who married non-Japanese came from several distinct parts and periods of Japanese American society. Some transient Issei formed temporary liaisons with non-Japanese men and women in the early years before Japanese communities were formed. Throughout the West, from the turn of the century to World War I, Japanese men engaged the services of both Japanese and White prostitutes, and Japanese prostitutes served both Japanese and non-Japanese clients. Some prostitutes formed stable living arrangements with patrons, and some of those arrangements crossed racial lines. Elaine Yoneda reported rooming during World War II at the Manzanar prison camp with a White madam who had lived before the war with an Issei man and had stuck with him when he was imprisoned. Significantly more of the Issei who were born before 1890 married out than those who were born later. This suggests that more intermarriages occurred in the restless, unsettled pioneer years than in the more stable period that followed. When Japanese women became available, Japanese men preferred them to non-Japanese. Moreover, the emerging Japanese American communities enforced marriage within the group.[5]

Some White observers of Japanese-American intermarriages propagated the myth that Caucasian women who married Japanese men did so only because they were old, ugly, and desperate for any mate. One sociologist went to interview an intermarried woman with this image in mind: "I thought she would be a very common unattractive person . . . who had gotten tired of being an old maid and had in despair decided after all that marriage to an Oriental would be better than no marriage at all." No doubt some women did dare to cross the color line largely because they were desperate. American men do not as a rule like fat women, and Evelyn Snow Sera* stood five feet four and weighed 184 pounds. But other women turned down offers from White Americans because they saw special qualities in Japanese men. The sociologist's anticipated "old maid" turned out to be a very attractive woman who saw in her husband a love for God, cleanliness, kindness, and consideration which she had not found in her Caucasian suitors.[6]

Nisei. As with other immigrants, so with Japanese Americans: intermarriage increased with the advent of the second generation. But outmarriage was less common among the Nisei than among other second-generation immigrants, due to the peculiarities of Japanese American history (see Chapters 7 and 12).

Interracial dating was an issue in Japanese communities before World War II. Most Issei expected to dictate their children's social lives. Their own marital partners had been chosen by their families using Old World marriage arrangers. Many Issei were frankly aghast at their children's desires to go to dances and proms, to go out on dates, to go steady, to become engaged, and to marry partners of their own choosing.[7] Most only wanted to do these things with other Nisei, but some chose to date non-Japanese. Some did so out of mere curiosity or a desire to escape the Japanese community gossip system: the family and friends of a White or Mexican date had no access to that system. More Nisei dated non-Japanese out of a sense that they possessed status or social skills that other Nisei lacked. Cindy Matsushita*, who associated with Whites, male and female, at Berkeley, felt the other Nisei were shallow defeatists who retreated into social foolishness and acceptance of White rejection rather than fighting to achieve. She would have no part of them. Hazel Nishi* zeroed in on social graces as the reason she preferred White to Nisei dates:

I enjoyed going out with the Caucasian boys because they were full of fun and not limited in their thinking. They treated me like they would any girl and none of them ever got fresh with me. I thought they were very considerate of me, and they had good manners. . . . I appreciated this more since the Nisei boys did not seem to know the proper manners. It was only little things like helping me into the car, etc., but it indicated their lack of training. And the Nisei boys rarely had anything interesting to talk about except how good they were in sports or all about dancing. There would be long moments of silence and they never acted at ease. . . . They just lacked the poise that most normal people have. I didn't try to act superior or anything like that. I just did not have much in common with them and I preferred my Caucasian friends who acted much more at ease.[8]

That some prewar Nisei dated non-Japanese did not mean they married interracially. In fact, very few Nisei—fewer than 1 in 5— married at all before the outbreak of World War II. Just a tiny fraction of those older West Coast Nisei who married before World War II chose non-Japanese mates: 3.1 percent of the men and 2.3 percent of the women. This is roughly comparable to the percentages of first-generation men and women who had married non-Japanese. These are extremely low numbers for the second generation of an immigrant group. In looking at New York City marriage records for the years 1908–12, Julius Drachsler found that over 30 percent of the children of European immigrants married people from outside their own ethnic group.[9]

It is possible that as the Nisei generation came of age, a larger percentage would have taken non-Japanese spouses had not World War II intervened. Nearly the entire mainland Japanese American population was herded together in concentration camps from very early in the war. The politics and the cultural and human cost of that experience have been amply documented elsewhere.[10] Here it may be useful to note that the concentration camp episode was a time of enforced ethnic closeness for most Nisei. Before the war, most had experienced at least some contacts with non-Japanese people, and some had lived mainly outside their ethnic community. Had the war not happened, some might have surmounted Issei pressures and White discrimination to meet, date, and marry non-Japanese. But that was not to be. Just at the age when most Nisei were beginning to make their choices of life partners, they were thrust into intimate contact with other Japanese. By the time they got out of the camps, shed the psychological burdens of their wartime experiences, and overcame the stigma of being Japanese, the vast majority of the Nisei had already married or become engaged.

The average Nisei was seventeen in 1942. Ninety percent of the Nisei were under thirty, 77 percent under twenty-five. This meant that perhaps only a quarter of the American-born generation were old enough to have married before the war began. As we have seen, not many of those chose non-Japanese mates. Of the group under twenty-five in 1942, 56 percent would reach age twenty-five within a decade. Those people probably chose their mates during that decade, a period when they had contact mainly with other Japanese Americans and during which they were not looked upon favorably by non-Japanese Americans. Under such circumstance, intermarriage by anyone from this large part of the Nisei generation would seem very unlikely. Charles Kikuchi, one of the most acute observers of the Nisei scene, put it this way: "Prior to the war only a tiny percentage of the Nisei intermarried with other racial groups, and the isolation of the evacuation period reduced this percentage even more."[11]

The months in camp were a time of intense social life for most Nisei. There was not much for people to do in the camps. Among the activities with which young Nisei filled their hours was a hectic round of dances and parties. Kisako Yasuda*, a shy Los Angeles girl, first learned to dance, dress fashionably, and talk to boys in camp. Sue Kunitomi and Shizuko Hattori* each had a string of boyfriends at Manzanar. Harry Ando* bragged to Charles Kikuchi that he had enjoyed sex with dozens of girls in the Topaz camp, and forced himself on several more when they were let out together to work in the fruit harvest. Hazel Nishi* was disgusted by people like Ando, but she, too, reported that her social life picked up when she entered Tule Lake. She dated heavily and widely, observing as she did so the blossoming Nisei dance culture and an explosion of sexual activity in the firebreaks and empty barracks after the dances. All this socializing did not include the non-Japanese War Relocation Authority employees who worked in the camps, though many of them were single and about the same age as the Nisei. Some avidly pro-American inmates, Nishi and Rhonda Kaneshiro* among them, would have preferred to socialize with the Caucasian staff members. But anyone who did so was labeled an *inu* (that is, a "dog" or "collaborator"), a "boot-licker," or a "white-man's Jap" by the more extreme pro-Japanese people in camp.

In similar fashion, most of the White staff despised any of their number who consorted with the inmates. The Nisei social scene extended beyond dances and sex to marriage. Robert O'Brien surveyed scores of college-age Nisei in the latter years of the war. In camp, he said, the Nisei "found an elementary solution for the apparent purposelessness of their lives in an epidemic of marriages that swept the centers." He quoted the letter of a young Nisei woman: "It seems that everyone is getting married, and I mean the little kids the age of my younger sister. Several of the boys have asked to marry me, but I am either going to marry a soldier or someone who has been relocated [i.e., released from concentration camp], as I want to get out of here before I go crazy." Altogether, this intense atmosphere, in which the Nisei were thrust together with little to do except socialize with the opposite sex under constant pressure from family and peers, meant that a tremendous number of them got married or at least engaged before leaving camp.[12]

The concentration camps were also temporary homes for at least 1,400 intermarried Japanese Americans, a few of their non-Japanese spouses, and at least 700 people of mixed racial ancestry. From the start, the Army and the War Relocation Authority, which ran the camps, seem to have had doubts about the wisdom of incarcerating such people. The Japanese American population at large was imprisoned chiefly on the ground of suspected disloyalty (political fictions such as "protective custody" need not detain us here). The government very early expressed a desire to take some of the intermarried families out of the prison camps and return them to their homes. This was partly because the government thought intermarriers were more likely than other Japanese Americans to be loyal to America. But more importantly, it was because they did not want Amerasian children who had grown up among Caucasians to be tainted by contact with Japanese people. A meandering policy developed whereby some individuals—those who seemed least likely to present a threat to American security—were allowed to return home, some were permitted to leave the camps but had to stay away from the West Coast, and others remained incarcerated. The criteria for choosing these groups had little to do with individual loyalties and a lot to do with racial and sexual attributes.[13]

The government spoke a lot about "infectious Japanese thought" and tried to keep people of mixed racial ancestry away from it. Government administrators sought to take mixed children who had grown up among Caucasians or other non-Japanese people out of the prison camps and deposit them back in their presumably healthy, prewar, non-Japanese environments. There was a not-so-subtle sexism that went with the racism in this selection system. The government assumed that males would dominate the culture and loyalties of their households. Thus, mixed people who had White fathers and Japanese mothers could return to the West Coast, because their Caucasian fathers presumably had created American environments for their families. By contrast, mixed children who had White mothers and Japanese fathers could leave the camps, but they could not go home. Because their fathers had made them, presumably, more than half Japanese, they did not qualify for a complete return to normal life. Yet, on the off chance that Caucasian mothers had had some salutary effects on their offspring, such children were offered a limited kind of freedom. They could leave camp but could not return to the West Coast war zone. In either case, whether the offending Japanese parent was the mother or the father, the entire family was allowed to leave prison together.[14]

An intermarried couple who did not have children, or one whose children had reached adulthood, had to stay in prison. That is, the Japanese spouse had to stay. Theoretically, the non-Japanese spouse could go whenever he or she pleased, since it was only the Japanese partner who represented a threat to national security. But any non-Japanese who had stuck with his or her partner through the rigors of imprisonment was hardly likely to abandon the family at this point. The only intermarried Japanese Americans without minor children who were permitted to leave camp were women whose non-Japanese husbands were serving in the armed forces. Like Japanese women with Amerasian children, they were allowed to go back to the West Coast, apparently in reward for their husbands' service. The government also allowed adults of mixed parentage to leave the camps if they wanted to, but only if they had "fifty per cent, or less, Japanese blood," and could demonstrate that their prewar environment had been "Caucasian."

Most of the members of mixed families, however, stayed in the concentration camps. For them, the effects of the camp experience were not very different than they were for other Japanese Americans.

Japanese Americans lost hundreds of millions of dollars in property that had to be abandoned or sold at fire-sale prices. They suffered the anger and frustration, the fear and hopelessness, of being sent to jail without cause and without recourse. Once-strong Japanese families lost cohesion as fathers found their authority and their breadwinning capacity usurped by the government. Issei community leaders lost their positions to members of the second generation. Lives were interrupted, careers sidetracked, goals abandoned. Intermarried Japanese Americans suffered all these privations in much the same degree as their homogamous friends and neighbors. In addition, they felt the pain of family separation, as many of the non-Japanese spouses tried to keep going on the outside while mixed children and Japanese adults went to prison. The intermarried and their children also suffered harassment and social isolation at the hands of distrustful, full-blooded Japanese.[15]

As time went on, others besides people of mixed ancestry managed to leave the camps. Many of the young, upwardly mobile Nisei left under a selective government leave program starting in 1943. Forbidden to return to the West Coast, they spread out all over the eastern two-thirds of the United States. Since they were highly acculturated and out of touch with West Coast Japanese communities, one might think them likely candidates for intermarriage, but few actually intermarried. Some, like Gordon Asahi*, advocated interracial mixing and marriage as a positive social program for Nisei uplift: "The important thing was to get more Caucasians to see how Americanized we were and we only had a limited time to do it in. . . . if the Nisei say to themselves that they want to be segregated, then the opportunities will become limited in all phases of their life. . . . I advocated that there was nothing wrong with inter-marriage. . . . Integration [Asahi's goal for the Nisei] is the ultimate freedom to have biological union with members of other racial groups without any social pressure existing against it."[16]

Asahi's vision of Nisei amalgamation was unusual. More common was Isamu Furuta's* conviction that wholesale intermarriage was generations away, but that the Nisei must pursue other forms of social and economic assimilation in the meantime. Some knew and dated non-Japanese, but only a tiny number actually intermarried. Of more than a hundred Chicago Nisei interviewed by Charles Kikuchi in 1944, only one—Rose Hayashi*—ended up with a non-Japanese partner, and she was not formally married.[17]

After the war, more than half the Japanese Americans returned to their former homes, farms, and neighborhoods. But they did not return to their former lives. Japanese Americans came back from exile after 1945 intent on rebuilding their lives. For many of the Issei it was too late. They were too old to start over and rebuild from scratch the farms and businesses that had taken a lifetime of hard work to establish. That task was left to the younger generation. In Japanese American communal life, too, the torch had passed to the Nisei. No longer did the Issei stand at the head of most community institutions. The communities themselves, once cohesive entities which deeply touched the lives of nearly all Japanese Americans, now seemed tangential to many. Immediately after the war there was some reclustering in the old ethnic neighborhoods: Nihonmachi in San Francisco, Little Tokyo in Los Angeles, the Yesler Way area in Seattle. But by 1955 flight from the ghetto had begun, first to surrounding White neighborhoods, then into the suburbs. By 1970 it had reached the point that, except for a tiny number of ethnic pockets such as Gardena, California, one would have been hard pressed to find two mainland Japanese families living next door to each other. The dispersion was not just from ghetto to suburb, but also across the nation. Many Nisei resettlers never went back to the West Coast, preferring instead to seek their fortunes in the Midwest and the East.[18]

Nor was the expansive drive of the postwar Nisei confined to geography. The decade and a half after the war constituted a period of unparalleled social and economic ascent for the Japanese American people. This was not a smooth process. The immediate postwar years, from 1945 through the early 1950s, were a hard time for Japanese Americans; discrimination was still strong, and the Nisei were just finding their feet economically. But the decade of the 1950s witnessed a stunning rise in occupational and educational status, so that by 1960 Japanese Americans had the highest average amount of schooling and highest average occupational status level of any American ethnic group, including White Protestants. To be sure, discrimination continued to hamper the aspirations of many. Income levels never matched occupational status and educational achievement. Even the highest

Nisei achievers seldom made it past middle-management positions. Lots of Issei and some Nisei were left in poverty as class lines hardened within the Japanese American people. And upward mobility was much greater in some areas than others—higher, for instance, in Illinois than in California, on the mainland than in Hawaii. But the overall economic achievement of the Japanese American people in the immediate postwar period was monumental.[19]

There were costs to all this mobility. The Nisei suffered a general lessening of ethnic identity, a declining concern for the maintenance of Japanese culture and institutions in America, and an increasing desire to become indistinguishable from White Americans as they entered the suburban middle class. Daniel Okimoto, a Nisei graduate student, decried these tendencies in a book called *American in Disguise:* "This drive to adapt to White standards of success has recently prompted some postwar Nisei [Okimoto among them] to make the charge that behind our conformity and ambition lies a strong desire to become White." Okimoto linked the assimilationist, accommodationist bent of many Nisei to their increasing materialism, saying, "It is unfortunate that so many Nisei, climbing up the social ladder, have given primacy to material over humanistic values. Gradually, many have assumed some of the less desirable features of their newly acquired status. Preoccupied with materialism as are the majority of Americans, many are deeply committed to the stylish life. Comfortable houses, sleek cars, and fashionable clothes are the accouterments of the middle-class success they have pursued so single-mindedly."[20]

Part of the Nisei's searing ambition to make it in the White middle class was merely the working out in adult life of their prewar, teenage identification with the American part of themselves, rather than with their Japaneseness. But part of it was a result of the war. Many Nisei by the 1950s had determined that they did not ever again want to be told they were not American enough to be treated fairly. They went to work, even during the war, to prove to themselves and to Whites that they were good enough to be unhyphenated Americans. Their segregated unit, the 442nd Regimental Combat Team, took as its motto "Go for Broke!", attacked America's enemies with suicidal zeal, and emerged the most decorated unit in American military history— largely to prove to the rest of America that Japanese Americans were good Americans and should be let out of the concentration camps. After the war, Nisei throughout the country plunged desperately into the race for middle-class status and identification with White Americans. Meanwhile, they developed what Tetsuden Kashima has called "social amnesia." Many Nisei consciously refused to acknowledge any of the uglier parts of their concentration camp ordeal; indeed, not a few Sansei reached adulthood without ever hearing that their parents had been imprisoned.[21]

The younger Nisei, those who finished their education and reached adulthood after the war, met more success in this upward striving than did their older siblings. This is not surprising, since they enjoyed more flexibility. Their education and career choices were before them in the postwar world. Also, as younger siblings, they were less likely to have to make occupational compromises in order to support other family members. Tad Kurushima*, for instance, an older Nisei who had fought in the 442nd, had to quit college and go to work in a cleaning establishment in order to support his parents, brothers, and young wife. Tad's younger brother, Albert*, got to complete his education. Tad worked hard and built up a moderately successful small business while Albert became a wealthy architect. More of the younger Nisei went to college and graduate school than did their elders. More got professional, technical, and managerial jobs. And, significantly, more of them had White friends.[22]

It should surprise no one, then, that an increasing number of these younger Nisei, those who married in the years after World War II, should choose non-Japanese mates. Whereas only 2–3 percent of prewar California Nisei married non-Japanese, by the latter 1950s 10 percent of the Nisei men and 17 percent of the women were intermarrying. But one should also remember that the Nisei generation was petering out by this time. Probably 60 percent of the Nisei who would ever take mates had done so by 1950, and virtually all had married by 1960.[23]

Sansei. The interracial relationships of the Sansei represented the natural outworking of their parents' assimilationist trend. Compared to their parents, members of the third generation knew far more non-Japanese Americans and knew them more intimately. More Sansei lived in non-Japanese neighborhoods and had non-Japanese friends than their elders. More, far more, of the younger generation had romantic relationships with non-Japanese. Most Sansei dated non-Japanese Americans. Gene Levine and Colbert Rhodes surveyed Japanese Americans nationwide in 1967 and found that 55 percent of the Sansei who were engaged or dating steadily had chosen non-Japanese partners. Five years later, that figure had risen to 67 percent. In both surveys, about three-fourths of the non-Japanese partners were Caucasians.[24]

As with the Nisei generation, more Sansei women than men dated non-Japanese. Precise figures are not forthcoming, but impressionistic evidence gathered on four West Coast campuses during the 1970s confirms this conclusion. Perhaps the difference had something to do with the different images non-Japanese Americans held of Sansei women and men. Also, in the power system of American race relations, it was easier for a person from the dominant group to step out to make contact with a minority person than the other way around. In similar fashion, the gender power system dictated that it would be easier for men to make amorous advances than for women. Thus White men would have little difficulty stepping across the racial line to make contact with Japanese American women, but Sansei men and White women would have more trouble surmounting the barriers to reach each other.[25]

As with dating, so with marriage. Year by year, members of the Sansei generation continued not only to date but to marry non-Japanese Americans, and non-Asians, in ever-increasing numbers. In Seattle in 1960, 8 percent of native Japanese American men and 7 percent of the women married non-Japanese. Five years later the percentages jumped to 20 and 29 percent, and in 1975 to 43 and 49 percent, respectively. In Los Angeles, the 1979 figure was 43 percent for both sexes. Nationwide in 1970, 42 percent of Sansei men and 46 percent of Sansei women were married to non-Japanese, a dramatic increase over the Nisei generation, and the numbers continued to climb through the end of the decade.[26]

Which Sansei married non-Japanese Americans? A study by Darrel Montero indicates, not surprisingly, that the intermarried Sansei were those who had fewer ties to their ethnic roots. Fewer of the intermarried than the in-married lived in neighborhoods where other Japanese Americans lived. Fewer spoke Japanese. Fewer had Japanese American relatives nearby. Fewer were members of Japanese organizations. Fewer knew much about their families' histories in Japan. Far fewer were Buddhists. What is striking about Montero's findings is that the intermarriage gender disparity, which had been reflected in high female outmarriage and low male outmarriage in the Nisei generation, was disappearing. Fully as many Sansei men as women in his study married non-Japanese Americans. One should not make too much of this datum by itself, for the method by which Montero's data were collected—through Japanese American associations and telephone book searches—would miss many intermarried Sansei women. But other studies point to a similar trend. Nationwide census data from 1970 show outmarriage by Sansei men approaching—and in some areas surpassing—outmarriage by Sansei women. A 1979 study of Los Angeles County showed equal percentages of Sansei men and women in the outmarrying population. It appears that by the 1970s non-Japanese Americans were coming to see Japanese American men as no less attractive than Japanese American women. John Tinker suggests that Sansei men may have been especially attractive in the 1960s and '70s, precisely because they were often more conservative than Whites. At a time when many White men were questioning the traditional male role of head of household, Japanese American men who were willing to shoulder that responsibility offered welcome stability to more than a few non-Japanese women.[27]

What shall one make of the sudden increase in intermarriage by the Sansei generation? Harry Kitano points to this as one indication of a high degree of structural assimilation by Japanese Americans. Sansei intermarriage may be one fruit of the tremendous impulse toward assimilation exhibited by the Nisei. Nisei stress on education, professional achievement, upward mobility, suburban living, and smooth melting into the surrounding White, middle-class population could not help but encourage intermarriage. But one need not view Sansei intermarriage as unnaturally high. It may simply have been part of the orderly progression of generations among American immigrant groups: a low rate of outmarriage in the immigrant generation, a higher rate in the second, and a very high rate in the third. In Bessie Wessel's 1926 survey of immigrant groups in Rhode Island, 4 percent of the immigrant generation married outside their ethnic group. In the second generation, about 12 percent married out. By the third generation, the intermarriage figure was over 20 percent. Compared to these figures, the Sansei intermarriage rate was high, but not much higher, perhaps, than the general loosening of ethnic tensions in America over the course of half a century would warrant. What is striking about the Japanese American numbers is the fact that Nisei intermarriage was unnaturally *low*. This was because the Nisei came of age during and after World War II, when Japanese Americans were a particularly unpopular group. Intermarriage was not an option for very many of them. By the time anti-Japanese sentiment eased, most Nisei had already taken mates from inside their ethnic group. From one angle of vision, the explosion of Sansei intermarriage in the 1960s and 1970s may be seen simply as restoring the generations to their natural progression.[28]

Japanese American Reactions to Intermarriage

Among the Issei and Nisei, one factor which inhibited interracial marriage was the opposition of many Japanese Americans to such unions. By the advent of the Sansei, that opposition had all but disappeared.

Issei. Issei were not interested in marrying non-Japanese themselves, and they were not shy about harassing others who did not share their prejudice. Joe Tominaga put it bluntly when he turned down offers from his White classmates to get him a date. "Why should American girls think Jap boys want to marry them? I came here to study, not to marry—most Jap boys do so too. We do not want American wives anyway—they are mostly too self—what shall I say?—always talking about self. We do not think them so pretty, either, as they think themselves. Not many of these people have 'family trees' rooted so far in the past as Japanese have. Queer girls, I don't think they know Japanese people dressed in silks when white men still roamed around in skins." Some members of Japanese communities ostracized Japanese Americans who married non-Japanese. Chloe Holt talked in 1924 to a White Los Angeles woman who had married a Japanese man. They had no friends, either Japanese or White, and, according to Holt, "One felt an isolation and loneliness which was not expressed." The husband's family had been polite to the wife, but she sensed they were not pleased with her: "It must have been a great disappointment to his parents when he married."[29]

While most Japanese Americans opposed intermarriage, a few were willing to make exceptions. Chotoku Toyama thought Japanese Americans should fight against intermarriage, but he allowed grudgingly that, "if there is a man and a woman who love each other and well understand their future life," then he would not stand in their way. Others thought that intermarriage by upper-class people who had enough money to cushion their lives might work out all right, but that it was a big mistake for ordinary people. Still others, who saw intermarriage as impractical in the racial climate of the 1910s and 1920s, saw in intermarriage hope for the eventual solution of racial antagonisms and looked forward to a day when intermarriage would be common. S. Minami, a Seattle banker, put it this way, "I doubt the desirability of intermarriage right now, nevertheless I favor ultimate intermarriage; because the rapid advancement and complexity of commercial relations, transportation and communications among the nations and races do not allow civilized races to remain isolated. This is especially true of the Japanese and whites in America. Until we intermarry real friendship and social and economic harmony and cooperation is very hard and we cannot be free from prejudice, which is a great enemy of civilization." Yet such hopes seemed remote to Minami and other Japanese Americans in the 1920s because not only Whites but also most Japanese Americans opposed intermarriage vigorously.[30]

Nisei. Anti-intermarriage feeling was nearly as strong a generation later, when the Nisei came of age. Issei parents did everything in their power to prevent Nisei unions with non-Japanese. In addition to the general antipathy that existed between Japanese and non-Japanese Americans in the years leading up to World War II, there were other reasons for the Issei opposition to Nisei intermarriage. One was a Japanese feeling of racial superiority. There was a social stigma attached to intermarriage, and it was felt by the whole family. Other hesitations touched on moral issues, such as the feeling that Americans did not take marriage seriously enough. Increasingly, Issei objections were phrased in terms of predictions of incompatibility for the couple themselves rather than social stigma attaching to the whole family. One Issei asserted that children of mixed parentage "would have a hard time." Another saw a "conflict in folkways." Another said, "I am well convinced that marriage with members of other races always ends in divorce. . . . Marriage of this kind just would not work. . . . You can't expect to be happy with a Haole [White] woman or a Portuguese woman because our culture, our modes of living, our philosophy are not the same as theirs."[31]

The experience of Sue Kunitomi Embrey reveals the depth of Issei opposition to intermarriage. When she decided to marry a White man, "The biggest resistance came from my mother. She felt that I was really marrying beneath me. The Japanese consider themselves quite superior to everybody else. She couldn't understand why I couldn't marry a nice Japanese boy, and she kept telling me this two years after my husband and I were married. I'd go see her and she'd say, 'Why don't you divorce your husband and marry a nice Japanese boy?'" The mother's animosity was so intense that she threw her daughter out of the house shortly before the wedding, refused to come to the ceremony, and ignored Embrey's repeated attempts at reconciliation. Relations thawed only moderately when grandchildren arrived. Ruth Uyesugi told of an incident which occurred in a Portland Japanese family shortly before World War II: "The beautiful Corinne with the smoldering eyes . . . head-strong and proud" came home one day and announced she intended to marry a Chinese American boy. "Two weeks later Corinne was bound for Japan and nursing school, where she would learn to become an obedient Japanese girl and fall in love with a proper Japanese boy." Corinne was allowed to return to America only after she had been safely married to a Japanese man.[32]

The following account by a young Nisei bride whose White husband had come to Hawaii in 1942 to work in a war industry shows the kind of strain undergone by all parties to an intermarriage:

My mother objected very much. My father was not living. She was concerned for my happiness, but the strongest argument was the shame that would come to the family. She cited cases where the Haole [i.e., White] husband had deserted their Japanese wives. I was determined to marry Bob anyway, although I regretted very much the way my mother was affected when I told her about Bob. Because of her attitude about Japanese girls marrying Haoles, I never took Bob over to see my family while I was going with him. Even the night before the wedding, my older sister tried to talk me out of taking the step. My older brother, taking the role of the head of the family, told me, "You need not expect to come home if you marry him." I took that as cutting me off from family ties, although my mother never told me in so many words that I was to be disowned. My younger brother, who was seventeen then, was the most violent in opposing the marriage. He even struck me. My husband sent my family invitations to our wedding, but no one showed up.

After my marriage in 1944, I had no direct contact with my family for several months. Some girl friends of mine at times gave me news of my family but I didn't feel that they were ready to take me back in the family, so I didn't do anything about it until one day my mother came to our home. My husband couldn't speak Japanese and my mother couldn't speak English, so the first meeting was strained for all three of us. But it broke the ice and since then our relations became gradually better and better and we now visit our family and they visit us. My younger brother is now in the Army on the Mainland and our relations haven't had a chance to improve but I sent him a Christmas present this year after I asked my husband about it. My older brother's attitude has changed for the better, but my sister is still cool to us. Whenever we visit my mother's home and my sister and her husband and their children are there, they would leave right away. My sister speaks to me but is usually cool. We used to be very close to each other before my marriage.[33]

In this instance, as in others, the Nisei opposed intermarriage as much as their parents did. This was particularly true of that segment of the Nisei who were known as Kibei. The Kibei were Nisei who had been taken or sent to Japan by their parents at a relatively early age. They had received most of their education there, had imbibed Japanese culture, and had returned to America, usually in their late teens. On their return to America, some fit right into Nisei society, but more remained aloof, clinging to Japanese ways and forming a subsociety of their own. Many Kibei were bewildered and outraged by what they saw as immorality in dating, dancing, and other Nisei social activities. They were even more incensed by the thought of Japanese American youngsters entering into romantic or sexual relations with White Americans. Kanichi Niisato expressed some of this perspective in a book published in Japan called *Nisei Tragedy,* which purported to chronicle the decline of virtue among Japanese American young people. He based his report mainly on "hearsay," he said, but he did not hesitate to conclude that "the young nisei of to-day are indulging in a riotous life, which will only lead to tragedy. . . . Girls sell their bodies to Americans, in night apartments in town."[34]

The opposition of some other Nisei to intermarriage and interracial romance seems to have stemmed less from disgust at the practice and more from jealousy directed against those acculturated Nisei who consorted with Whites and against the White intruders themselves. Hazel Nishi* complained about the way Nisei gossiped about her when she went out with White boys: "There were some small minded Nisei in town. Whether it was due to jealousy or some other cause, they spread some nasty rumors around by saying that I was 'fast' and hot stuff, none of which was true." Rose Hayashi* found some of her critics were willing to confront her with their indictments of her dating behavior. She was not shy about stating her side of the issue: "The nisei there [at high school] made fun of me because I still went around with hakujin [White] and Kurombo [Black] kids. None of the other nisei did that at all. They just stuck in their own group with their noses up in the air as if they were so good. They made me sick. I used to argue with them about it. They did not agree with me on anything, because they were the quiet type and they were afraid of being with a hakujin." Hayashi and Nishi pointed to envy and fear as two motives for Nisei censure of interracial dating. If their analysis is correct, then things had changed since the first generation. Issei who shrank from social contact with non-Japanese in the 1910s and 1920s did so in the main because they felt different from and superior to those other peoples. But these Nisei girls described their contemporaries as fearful of Whites and envious of those Nisei who dared make contact with Caucasians. If they were correct, then the Nisei they described must have seen Caucasians as clearly superior, desirable, and perhaps unattainable. In one generation, disdain based on feelings of superiority had given way to fear based on feelings of inferiority. In either case, the two groups—Whites and Japanese Americans—remained separate; but their relationship had changed, at least as perceived on the Japanese side.[35]

Nisei men, particularly in Hawaii, gave rising voice to resentment against White men who dated Nisei women. A young Nisei man explained:

One probable reason behind the resentment of Japanese males toward service men becoming so intimate with Japanese females seems to rest upon the fact that this relationship, insofar as sex is concerned, is unquestionably an unchallenged, one-sided privilege. In this case, it is the Haole service men taking liberal sex advantage of the less sophisticated, and in many cases innocent, Japanese women; not Japanese men taking advantages of Haole women. The importance of this fact as having a causal relation to the popular resentment towards service men-Japanese women association is ordinarily overlooked in the medley of more sensational criticisms. . . . The sight of the more aggressive service men, who by crude force and forwardness try to make impressions upon defenseless Oriental girls in public, is an obnoxious one to the average Oriental boy. This unruly, publicly dallying-around attitude is, generally speaking, an attitude that is still "foreign" to local-born Orientals and is therefore frowned upon.

University of Hawaii sociologist Andrew Lind commented, "Thus the local men conceived of themselves as the natural guardians of the Nisei girls who, presumably, were too naive to recognize they were being victimized by the G.I. 'slickers.' The failure of the girls to recognize and appreciate this protective role of the local boys simply added to their exasperation and resentment." They were even less pleased when such outrageous romances turned into marriages.[36]

After World War II, Japanese American opposition to outmarriage continued, but it weakened as more such marriages occurred and as many Nisei entered the middle class. Tolerance grew to the point that, in a 1962–64 survey, fully 43 percent of the Issei approved Nisei marrying Caucasians. Intermarried couples began to be accepted into Japanese community institutions. In 1951–52, the annual report of the Centenary Methodist Church, a Japanese American congregation in Los Angeles, listed 2 mixed couples out of a total membership of about 450. In 1960, 5 intermarried couples were included with about 375 other families in the directory of the Pasadena Union Presbyterian Church. And in 1962, Centenary had 11 mixed families out of a total of about 800. These figures suggest that intermarried Nisei were beginning to be accepted by other Japanese Americans, at least on a limited basis. But one should observe that the church directories recorded a far smaller percentage of intermarried couples than existed in the Japanese American population at large. Although intermarriage was on the rise, especially among the younger, upwardly mobile Nisei, it still was not generally accepted by Japanese Americans.[37]

Sansei. It was not until the third generation that a significant number of Japanese Americans came to approve outmarriage. Even into the 1960s, the Issei retained their opposition. In a 1969–72 study of Sacramento Japanese, John Connor found that fewer than one-fifth of the Issei approved of their grandchildren dating non-Japanese. More than half were adamantly opposed. Issei opposition to Sansei *marriage* across racial lines was even stronger. In Connor's study, over half the Issei men and 70 percent of the Issei women were definitely opposed to Sansei outmarriage, while only 1 in 10 thought it a good idea.[38]

The Nisei, however, were more lenient. Fully 40 percent expressed

some enthusiasm for Sansei outmarriage. About half approved of interracial dating, and only 20 percent completely opposed the practice.
Some saw it as the fulfillment of their dreams for full acceptance into
American society. Other Nisei, however, had an impulse toward interracial tolerance, but could not bring themselves to be totally open
when it came to their own children's friends. One Sansei woman told
Fumiko Hosokawa, "Well, my dad says it's okay to have friends of
another race but it would be nice if you had a Japanese boyfriend.
. . . He would rather have my real good friends be all Japanese and
my casual friends be whatever." Another woman reported, "We could
bring home blacks as long as we were just friends and there was no
romantic thing. I mean, if they were of the same sex it's okay. They
wouldn't have liked it too much if one of us brought home a black boy
friend or something like that, but as friends, it was okay." Nisei prejudice came out in subtle restrictiveness: "It's really funny. When I go
out with a Japanese, hardly any questions would be asked. They aren't
very strict. They ask like, 'Where are you going?' but there wasn't any
curfew for me. . . . But if I went out with a guy of another nationality,
they would ask, 'Where are you going? What time will you be getting
back?' . . . All of a sudden you get asked all these questions. 'If you are
going to be late, be sure to call.'"[39]

Many Nisei parents had particular trouble accepting their children's Black romantic partners. Judy Ohashi* found out just how upset
such parents could become. Raised in a racially mixed neighborhood,
Ohashi fell in love with a Black high school classmate. Her parents,
otherwise gracious people, were adamant in their desire not to meet
the boy or his family. They forbade their daughter to continue seeing
him. On graduation from high school, Ohashi briefly considered elop-
ing with her boyfriend, but could not bear to break from her family.
She gave him up. Fifteen years later she remained single and embit-
tered against her parents, doting on the memory of her former lover.[40]

The Sansei generation split on the desirability of interethnic dating.
The majority liked the idea, but a vocal minority dissented. Most Sansei grew up in predominantly non-Japanese environments. Yet there
were some areas on the West Coast and in Hawaii, especially in inner
cities, where a significant percentage of the population was still Japanese through the 1960s. There, Sansei appeared in large enough numbers that all-Japanese social groups could form. These cliques exerted

pressure on individual Sansei to associate only with other Japanese Americans. They ran a variety of community activities, from church groups to basketball leagues to drum and bugle corps, designed to keep Sansei together. Debbie Hirano* reported that, growing up in inner-city Los Angeles, she dared not date a White or Mexican boy for fear she would be shut out of her school's Japanese clique. Clara Nagai* said she was ostracized from her high school's Asian social clique and shunned by her best friends of many years' standing because she went out with a White boy. Frederick Samuels found that Hawaiian Sansei from working-class families, especially, preferred to associate with Japanese or other Asians rather than with non-Asians.[41]

One group which especially resented interracial dating was made up of pan-Asian activists who appeared on West Coast college campuses about 1970. The Asian power movement was a response to a century of oppression of Asian Americans, from massacres of Chinese miners in Wyoming in the 1880s, to the wartime imprisonment of Japanese Americans, to contemporary stereotypes and limits on occupational advancement. Taking their cue from Black activists, young Asian Americans—Chinese, Japanese, and Filipinos, mostly—banded together to protest these wrongs and try to bring about changes. Since Whites saw them all as "Orientals," an undifferentiable mass, and since their ancestors had all come from more or less the same part of the world, they tried to break down the historic barriers between their separate national identities and form a pan-Asian alliance. Asian activists created Asian American studies programs and held Asian cultural fairs in schools and communities. They protested media stereotyping and job discrimination. They lobbied for health care and special education programs for Asian communities. Some took the radical posture that American society needed a basic restructuring in order to provide freedom and justice for their people.[42]

Asian activists extended their pan-Asian imperatives to the realm of social relationships wherever possible. Results were not uniform, but the attempt was made to discourage social contact with non-Asians, especially Whites, and to encourage relationships with other Asians. Mark Gehrie interviewed a Sansei woman who "had been dating a white boy for two and one-half years but broke up with him because of an 'obligation' she felt 'toward her race.'" Her race was broadly conceived. It included, for the first time, not just Japanese Americans, but other Asians as well. Thus, a Sansei man might date or live with a Chinese woman within the movement and receive encouragement for doing so, instead of the opprobrium he might have felt from Japanese Americans a few years earlier. The intra-Asian ethnic lines still existed, of course. Chinese and Japanese tended to see Filipinos as a little different from themselves. But the pan-Asian ideological commitment was a powerful thing. In this period, Asians attacked, among other things, the negative stereotypes put on Asian men by White Americans. Mayumi Tsutakawa, a University of Washington student leader, became indignant at a hair spray commercial which pictured a cool, graceful, muscular, blonde man playing ping-pong with a jerky, sweaty, skinny Asian opponent. The White man lost the match, but walked off with an adoring Asian woman on his arm. Tsutakawa and other Asian women rejected emphatically the advertisement's implication that Asian women preferred White men to Asians.[43] Margaret Woo decried "Asians who preach Asian political unity and yet reject themselves and their own kind for white mates." She went so far as to pronounce that any trace of White ancestry disqualified one for access to an Asian American identity, saying people "of Euroasian descent can not identify themselves nor understand the full meaning and feeling of being Asian."[44]

Yet such reservations were shared by only a small minority. As one might expect from the large number of Sansei intermarriages, by far the majority approved the practice. Two-thirds said they thought it a good idea, while only 1 in 6 opposed intermarriage unequivocally. Some Sansei saw intermarriage as a way for Japanese Americans to solve their problems by blending into the American mainstream. One woman said, "It seems to me that Sanseis marrying Sanseis will grow up to be exactly like their parents. . . . I have much higher aspirations," so she intended to marry a White male. Laura Fujino* saw intermarriage as a chance for Sansei to lose their separate identity, which she conceived to be a positive development. She thought it odd that Japanese Americans should show interest in Japanese culture or "brand their children for life" by giving them hard-to-pronounce Japanese names. She did not like her own last name and looked forward to taking on a White man's name that was easier to pronounce. Some Sansei still drew the line at Filipinos and Blacks. Some of Judy Ohashi's* friends shunned her once it came out that she was considering marriage to a Black man. But others supported her against her parents and community gossip. Some Asian activists remained ideologically opposed to intermarriage. But others redefined the in-group, so that unions with Chinese and Filipinos were no longer, in their eyes, intermarriages. Even among the activists there were many individuals who married or lived with Whites. It might have caused them some ideological anguish, but it was a choice they frequently made.[45]

In summary, during the era when the Issei were marrying, nearly all Japanese Americans opposed intermarriage with what they saw as inferior peoples, and Japanese communities and individuals acted to prevent it. Japanese American hostility to the practice had not abated when the Nisei were marrying in the 1940s and '50s. Despite the extent of their acculturation, most Nisei opposed intermarriage as strongly as their parents, though often from different motives. By the time the Sansei generation came of age, most Japanese Americans outside a small group of pan-Asian activists found intermarriage basically acceptable. Some of those activists began to define their own ethnicity more broadly, by including Chinese and other Asians within their own group.

Other Americans' Reactions to Intermarriage with Japanese

Japanese Americans were not the only ones who opposed intermarriage. Whites and others also acted to halt or harass intermarriages during the Issei and Nisei generations. During the 1910s and '20s, when the Issei were seeking mates, non-Japanese Americans stood firmly opposed to intermarriage and backed up their sentiments with the force of law. Marriage between Whites and Asians was illegal in California and much of the West. This law was not always enforced meticulously. Constantine Panunzio found that one-quarter of the interracial marriages in early Los Angeles were illegal unions between Japanese and Whites. But the law was sometimes enforced with Draconian severity. In 1914 a Japanese man was convicted of White slavery and his White bride threatened with deportation when it came to light they had taken an ocean cruise in order to get married outside territorial waters and thereby avoid the law. What happened to this tragic pair is not clear. He may have served a prison sentence, and they may both have been deported. She could have been deported, despite being born in America, because of a sexist facet of American law in those days: if an American man married a foreign woman, American law viewed them both as Americans; but if an American woman married a foreign man, the woman lost her U.S. citizenship regardless of her wishes. Furthermore, since this woman had become a Japanese citizen, she could never regain her American citizenship by naturalization. This too, may have served as a powerful impediment to intermarriage. A woman would have to think carefully before giving up American citizenship in favor of Japanese, especially when Japanese law had even less regard than American law for the rights of women.[46]

Non-Japanese people opposed intermarriage not only in theory but also in individual cases. About 1920, when an anonymous White woman married a Japanese man, she and her family were ostracized: "Because of my marriage to a Japanese, my family was 'frozen out' and I have been moving away from whites ever since. I now live in a Japanese district and I wouldn't live near a white person." Whites were not the only ones who opposed intermarriage with the Japanese. Mrs. C. S. Machida of Los Angeles was cut off by her Chinese friends and relatives for marrying a Japanese man in the 1910s. In the 1920s, a Mexican American suffered ostracism from her family for marrying a Japanese man, and neither the Mexican nor the Japanese community would have anything to do with their son. With such a pattern of nearly universal nonacceptance, Japanese men and women had to think very carefully before entering into interethnic unions.[47]

Non-Japanese opinion had moderated but little by the time the Nisei came of age in the 1930s and '40s. To be sure, some White boys sought dates with Nisei girls before the war drove a wedge between the races. And some members of other subordinate groups—Blacks, Mexicans, and Filipinos, mostly—socialized with Japanese young people in California towns. But most non-Japanese would neither date nor marry the Nisei, especially during and after the war. In 1948, Nisei tied Blacks as the least liked students in Seattle's Garfield High School. None of the Chinese, Jewish, Black, or White Gentile students wanted Japanese Americans as leaders or workmates. Only the Chinese could conceive of them as dates or friends, and the Nisei were low on their list. Andrea Sakai had a White boyfriend in Portland, Oregon. But his friends and family pressured him to get rid of her. "His Haole [White] friends considered him wasted on me, to put it mildly. People often stared at us. . . . It seems that he lost a desirable fraternity affiliation during his college days because we dated steadily. . . . Bob's aunt and uncle came to visit him and I was completely snubbed by his aunt. His uncle was very nice, but his aunt would neither acknowledge our introduction, nor would she speak to me at all. She spent the entire evening discussing at length how well-educated, well-bred and socially acceptable her daughter-in-law was. I could hardly miss the point." Andrea and Bob broke up. A psychologist (apparently White) for the War Relocation Authority not only opposed interracial romance, but in his reports labelled all Nisei who had dated Caucasians as "maladjusted" and recommended that they not be released from the Tule Lake concentration camp.[48]

There was an understanding on the part of many servicemen who married Nisei women during the war that they would have to remain in Hawaii's liberal racial climate for the rest of their lives, for they knew their wives would not be accepted on the mainland. That conclusion led more than a few men to curtail their relationships with Nisei women, for they wanted badly to go home when the war was over. But even in the islands intermarried people encountered some opposition. Sailors and soldiers had to have their commanding officers' permission to be married, and that was not always easy to get. One soldier recalled that "the chaplain of our outfit, a fiery Southern Baptist but intelligent and reasonable, tried for seven hours altogether on two different occasions to talk me out of the marriage," before giving up and recommending approval. As this soldier noted, the chaplain was conscientiously trying to prevent irresponsible men from shacking up with local women under the guise of marriage and then abandoning them when their units moved on. The soldier had no quarrel with that objective, for there were some cases of such exploitation of local women by servicemen, but he was not certain that the chaplain would have pursued his goal with such zeal had the bride been White. Another soldier, mustered out at war's end and about to marry his Nisei sweetheart, went looking for a place to live in Waikiki. "The Haole landlady agreed to rent me the place, but when I told her that my wife was going to be a Japanese, she said that she could not rent the place to me after all." Later the couple tried to buy a house in a White neighborhood and were informed discreetly that they were not welcome there. Even friends ostracized some biracial couples. Officer friends tried to discourage one soldier's intermarriage by telling him that "Oriental girls were structurally different, that children by them would be confused and unnatural."[49]

Negative reactions of the sorts described here persisted through the 1950s, but died in the more liberal racial climate of the 1960s. Whites began to see upwardly mobile Japanese Americans as much like themselves. A few World War II veterans objected to their children marrying people whom they identified with their erstwhile enemies. But in an era that saw many Whites begin to accept marriage with Blacks (see below, Chapter 10), a Japanese-White union came to seem hardly worth mentioning. After the 1960s, such opposition as there was to Sansei outmarriage came mainly from the Japanese American side.[50]

Regional Differences in Intermarriage

The account thus far has concentrated on the intermarriage behavior and attitudes of Japanese Americans on the West Coast. In other parts of the country, the patterns were rather different.

Hawaii presents a distinctive pattern of intermarriage behavior. There, because of the nature of Japanese community formation, Issei outmarriage was even less common than in California. The Japanese came earlier to Hawaii than to the mainland, and they came in larger numbers. Already in 1890, over 12,000 Japanese lived in Hawaii. Throughout most of this century the Japanese population of the islands exceeded that of the mainland.[51] A more important difference lay in the structure of communal organization among Hawaiian Japanese. On the mainland in the early years Japanese social organization was fluid, reflecting the transience of the population. Men moved from place to place, sometimes living with other Japanese but often working off on their own in a sea of Whites, Mexicans, Chinese, and others. In Hawaii geographic mobility was much more limited. Most Japanese went to Hawaii in the early years as contract laborers, tied to a particular sugar or pineapple plantation for a term of years. They spent nearly all their time on that plantation, living and working with other Japanese. They had very few contacts with members of other groups, except perhaps with White *lunas,* or overseers. Certainly they did not develop easy and friendly social relationships with other Hawaiian peoples. Whereas on the mainland, communities that could monitor individual behavior, were not established until the arrival of Japanese women after 1905, considerable social controls already existed on the Hawaiian plantations. For a Japanese Hawaiian laborer, mixing with non-Japanese and liberation from the scrutiny of other Japanese came only with the end of his contract and his move off the plantation. Even after contract labor was abolished, Japanese towns in the plantation districts—Kona, for example—remained isolated from the rest of Hawaiian society. It was only when many Japanese Hawaiians moved to Honolulu after their terms were up that they began to mix with non-Japanese.[52]

Even in Honolulu, social intercourse between the races was limited. Many Japanese were insecure about their lack of American cultural skills, and so avoided contact with Whites wherever possible. One Issei put it this way: "I feel very much afraid to speak to a Haole [White] woman who comes to have her hair cut. She is a doctor's wife. I am very self-conscious because I cannot converse with her very well. It is very hard to talk with Haole people with my very meager knowledge of English. All the while I cut hair I wish that she would not ask me any questions."[53]

The result of this isolation was that, despite Hawaii's liberal ideas about racial mixing, intermarriage was even less frequent among Hawaiian Issei than among their mainland counterparts. Romanzo Adams found that from 1912 to 1916 only 1 in 200 Issei men married a non-Japanese woman, and only 1 Japanese woman in 500 married out. Other studies and census data suggest that the intermarriage rate in the 1920s may have gone as high as 2 percent, but still the number of Issei intermarriages was tiny.[54]

Intermarriage was a grand tradition in Hawaii. It began early in the nineteenth century, when some European men became advisors to Hawaiian kings and were given Hawaiian wives of royal lineage to seal their loyalties. Before long, ambitious European and American men were marrying Hawaiian women of property with some frequency. These early high-status unions set the tone for a successful pattern of intergroup marriages. Soon, Chinese laborers began to come to the islands, and many of them, too, married Hawaiian women. Both the Chinese and the Euro-American influxes were almost uniformly male. Some of these men had wives at home, but if any of them were to have wives in Hawaii, they had to marry Hawaiian women. Hawaiian women saw both Caucasian and Chinese men as hard workers, good providers, and the bearers of advanced civilizations; for many Hawaiian women, to marry a White or Chinese man was a mark of status. The Hawaiian men were the odd men out. The first non-Hawaiian families to settle in Hawaii were White missionaries from New England after 1820. Some of them opposed intermarriage, but there was little they could do in the face of established custom, especially since permission to evangelize depended on the good will of the kings' advisors, many of whom were intermarried themselves. Once the practice of intermarriage became entrenched, it was very hard for anyone publicly to mobilize opposition to it. As the nineteenth century turned into the twentieth, the Whites ascended to a position of political and economic hegemony in the islands. But they were never able to dominate culturally. Hawaiian people and Hawaiian culture remained highly revered. Because of the intermarriages that had taken place, part-Hawaiian (that is, White-Hawaiian mixture) and Asiatic-Hawaiian subcultures formed and enjoyed relatively high status. Other groups came: Portuguese, Koreans, Japanese, Filipinos. Each had its separate sphere economically, and stereotypic myths grew up about the supposed characteristics of each, but all bought into the dominant ethos of marital mixing.[55]

All, that is, except the Japanese. In the first generation they intermarried in only a tiny number of cases. This was due partly to the fact that so many Japanese women came over; in 1930 the male to female ratio was only 1.6 to 1, the lowest of any of the new immigrant groups. With many Japanese women available, Japanese men did not have to look outside the group for mates. But there were extra males in all the groups—why did Japanese women not acquire more of them? That state of affairs was partly due to the enforcement powers of the Japanese community. On the mainland, Japanese community life was relatively loose until large numbers of women began to come in the 1910s. In Hawaii, the women began to come earlier, and even before they came, the Japanese worked together in gangs and lived together on plantations and in towns. This communal life meant that the group could enforce its ideas on individuals more effectively. An equally important factor was that most of the Japanese women who came to Hawaii were already married or betrothed to Japanese men at the time of their entry.

And the Japanese community in Hawaii had something bad to say about nearly every other Hawaiian people. Koreans were sneaky and servile. Filipinos were "dumb" and "savages" and addicted to violence. Hawaiians were good-hearted but dirty and lazy. Portuguese were the hated *lunas*. The Hawaiian Issei saw the Whites as clearly superior in power terms, but perhaps not so superior in other ways. It took one Japanese laborer several years to shed his disparaging preconceptions and come to the conclusion that "Haoles are not so dumb as I thought they were." In particular, the Issei did not care for Haole women. "I hate the superior role which the Haole woman assumes in her own home. She thinks that she runs the whole world. . . . Such a thing as this would never occur in a Japanese home. A Japanese woman knows her role in the family. She is very warm and kindhearted. She is obedient and submissive to her husband." Haole men might have been more attractive to Japanese women than Haole women were to Japanese men, but the vast preponderance of the Japanese women had come as wives of Japanese men, so they were not free to choose, and their very submissiveness meant that large-scale intermarriage with non-Japanese men would have to wait a generation.[56]

An additional reason for the miniscule intermarriage rate was simply that the Japanese population in Hawaii was so large that there were a lot of potential Japanese mates available to any individual who went looking for one. The Issei constituted the largest ethnic group in the islands, and they lived mainly in segregated areas, whether on plantations or in towns. They had a strong sense of community identity, which engendered mutual loyalty and supervision, and they very seldom married non-Japanese.[57]

The cosmopolitan character of Hawaiian society began to erode Japanese American exclusiveness in the second generation. World War II played a pivotal role in turning around Japanese Hawaiian intermarriage rates. During the Second World War, Hawaii (especially the island of Oahu) was flooded with soldiers and sailors from the mainland as the islands became the main staging area for the war in the Pacific. This military presence boosted the islands' economy, but it also caused "a general relaxing of moral controls," in the words of University of Hawaii sociologist Andrew Lind. Servicemen, mainly Caucasians, far from home, living in the company of other young males and having access to few White women, found companionship, exotic romance, and sometimes matrimony among women of other races. The overall rate of outmarriage among all races in Hawaii rose during the war from 28 percent in 1940–41 to over 36 percent in 1944–45 (see Fig. 3.1). These new intermarriages were mainly between mainland servicemen and island women. Every nonwhite group of women in the islands registered an increase in its rate of outmarriage during the war years. Overall, outmarriage rates for Hawaii's women jumped 40 percent between 1940 and 1944. The largest increases were by Filipinas and Japanese women, whose intermarriage rates rose 200 and 163 percent, respectively. In this, Nisei women continued a prewar trend: 7 percent of Nisei women married non-Japanese men in 1936–39; 9 percent in 1940–41; 12 percent in 1942–43; and 21 percent in 1944–45. Altogether, close to four hundred Caucasian servicemen married Nisei women between Pearl Harbor and V-J Day. White women were also marrying servicemen from the mainland in large numbers, which meant that their rate of outmarriage actually dropped 38 percent in those years. Nonwhite men had a hard time standing up to the competition from the mainland. Excepting Koreans and Caucasians (most of the latter from the mainland), outmarriage by men dropped in those same years. Outmarriages by Japanese American men held steady at about 4 percent while their sisters were marrying non-Japanese men in unprecedented numbers. In part, this reflected the fact that eleven thousand Japanese American men were off fighting the war. Their places in the arms of Nisei women were taken by soldiers and sailors from the mainland, mainly Whites (see Fig. 3.1).[58]

What types of Nisei women were most likely to marry non-Japanese men during the war years? There was considerable talk in the community that they were loose women, given over to wild behavior and questionable moral conduct. Hester Kong told of the mood in her home village of Palama: "The general community conception of the girls who go out with servicemen is that they are of loose morals. One Japanese lady said, 'If my daughter go out with the soldiers, I give good lickings.'" Some support for this view comes from the observation that illegitimate births to Nisei women more than doubled between 1940 and 1945. But George Yamamoto's interviews with fourteen intermarried couples show only one woman who might have had less rigorous moral standards than the rest of the Japanese community, and several who were extremely moral, religiously motivated women.

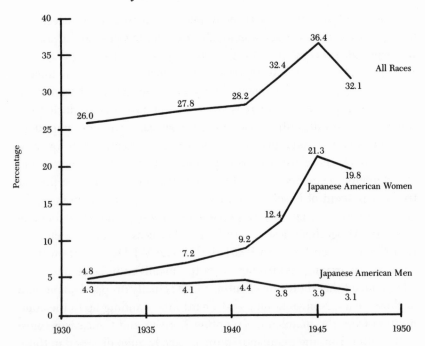

Figure 3.1. Hawaiian Intermarriage Rates (Percentage of All Marriages)
  Source: George K. Yamamoto, "Social Adjustment of Caucasian-Japanese Marriages in Honolulu" (M.A. thesis, University of Hawaii, 1949)

Andrew Lind found a class bias in the selection of Nisei women for intermarriage: "First to be affected were the Nisei girls of the lower classes who were employed as waitresses, bar maids, store clerks, and in other places where they came into constant contact with the public." While Lind's thesis makes some intuitive sense, neither his data nor Yamamoto's sustain such a conclusion.[59]

  More often, Hawaiian Nisei who married servicemen stood out from their sisters by their greater degree of acculturation to Anglo-American norms and their desire to be accepted by non-Japanese than by any difference in class status or moral standards. One intermarried Nisei woman said that "on the whole, I've had friendly contacts with Haoles [Whites] since childhood." Another was deeply involved throughout her youth in a multiracial Christian church. A Nisei girl expressed little surprise at her cousin's marriage to a serviceman: "The family should have anticipated it, at least I did. She was like a Haole. She couldn't speak Japanese. . . . From very early years she loosened the tie that bound her to the family. . . . She liked Haole people and mingled with them. I always felt she looked on the Japanese people with a certain air of condescension." An intermarried Nisei woman described her side of the story: "My upbringing and my feelings about the kind of husband I wanted sort of excluded Japanese boys in the sense that in general, they play the role of husbands and fathers in the traditional Japanese manner and I couldn't stand living with a man like that. I don't mean that my husband had to be a white man. If a good Chinese boy or a Japanese boy met my specifications as to what a husband should be like, why I should have married him. But I never met that kind, they are so scarce." Other Nisei, women and men, pointed to a lesser degree of acculturation on the part of Nisei men as one reason for Japanese American women choosing non-Japanese husbands. Such assimilationist feelings as these were heightened by the war. After bombs stopped dropping on Pearl Harbor, everything American took on a special attraction for the Nisei and everything Japanese faded from prestige. This was the same sort of assimilationist impulse we observed among Nisei on the mainland in the prewar period. According to Yamamoto, "The sudden change in status of the immigrant generation into enemy aliens . . . made the already waning control a difficult matter to maintain." Parental authority declined, and Americanist impulses, including desires for intermarriage, could no longer be contained.[60]

If Nisei women saw intermarriage and dating Haole servicemen as a social step into the American mainstream, the soldiers and sailors stressed instead the attractive physical and personal qualities of Nisei women. A White housewife idly asked a soldier which of the women in Hawaii he found most attractive. "He answered that the Japanese girls were more attractive to him than the mainland girls." Some servicemen were attracted to Nisei women initially because of their exotic, Eastern image, but they stayed with them because of their pleasing personalities and beauty. A soldier went out with a Japanese girl on a blind date; later he recalled, "The novelty of knowing an Oriental girl . . . plus her natural charm, enchanted me, and impelled me to see quite a bit of her." He found her naive, "young and . . . innocent," which pleased him. He solicited the opinions of his fellow soldiers and found that "unanimously the servicemen find themselves physically attracted to the Oriental girls . . . their dark hair, their sometimes not light-colored skin, their physical poise and grace, their slender waists and gratifying curves, but above all their smoother and lovely complexions. . . . The service men agree that most of the Oriental girls they know are shy, humble, quiet and reserved, but capable of being excellent partners for swimming, dancing, cinemaing, and romancing . . . splendid company." One lonely White GI had a hard time attracting White women whom he liked, but found a Nisei woman whose moral qualities he admired: "Down here there wasn't nobody to talk to, no women folks. The girls I went out with were all right at first, pretty 'n' nice, then they weren't any more. I ain't never gone around with that kind. Then I met this [Nisei] girl at an eating place. I went there a lot o' times and she asked me to her house. She was so darn decent. Didn't smoke or drink, never went to dancing places." They were married.[61]

Thus, at the same time that the Second World War blocked Nisei intermarriage on the mainland, it brought a boost to intermarriage by Hawaiian Nisei. In both places, the war upset established Japanese community structures and changed the lives of individuals. On the mainland, Japanese Americans were uprooted from their homes and herded into barbed-wire pens. There the intermarried and mixed people were subjected to harassment from their fellow inmates until the government let many of them leave and rejoin their families. There, too, the Nisei's social life was so intense that many, perhaps most, had chosen their life partners by the time they got out. Even among those relatively acculturated Nisei who left the camps during the war and headed east, intermarriage does not seem to have been much of a factor. In Hawaii, by contrast, the war's upheaval rendered ineffective much Issei criticism of intermarriage and brought thousands of young non-Japanese men to the islands. There they married Nisei women in increasing numbers as the war went on.

The upward trend of intermarriage rates continued into the Sansei generation. But there was no sudden leap, as on the mainland, nor did Hawaiian Sansei ever post quite such high rates as their mainland contemporaries. Twenty percent of the men and 28 percent of the women married non-Japanese during the 1960s. In 1970, 25 percent of the men and 42 percent of the women chose non-Japanese mates. In 1980, nearly 42 percent of Japanese Hawaiians, men and women, married non-Japanese.[62]

It should be noted that there were variations of intermarriage rates not only between regions but within them. Again the presence or absence of a cohesive Japanese American community seems to have been the crucial factor. Where Japanese American population and culture were concentrated, outmarriage was less frequent. Sansei raised in West Coast suburbs, away from other Asians, dated Whites much more frequently than they dated Japanese Americans. Laura Fujino* grew up in San Jose, California, and went to school with Whites and Chicanos. All her dates were Whites. At college in New England she avoided dating Asian men, whom she regarded as "wimpy." Twenty-seven percent of Los Angeles Sansei men and 35 percent of the women married non-Japanese. But in California as a whole, including suburban and rural areas, 41 percent of the men and 47 percent of the women married out.[63]

In other parts of the country Japanese Americans were always fewer and more scattered than on the West Coast or in Hawaii. In the Rocky Mountain states, the East, the Midwest, and the South, the rates of outmarriage by Japanese Americans were high.

The Rocky Mountains and Southwest were pioneer regions long after the West Coast Japanese had entered into a more settled way of life. The considerable number of Issei who inhabited these areas lived far apart from one another. Few Japanese community institutions developed in the Rocky Mountain region until after World War II. The Issei population here was even more overwhelmingly male than that on the West Coast. In 1940, the ratio of Issei males to females in Utah was 1.8 to 1, for instance, compared to 1.5 to 1 in Washington.[64] The isolated existence of Issei miners, farmers, cowboys, and others inhibited interactions with other Japanese and encouraged ultimate intermarriage with non-Japanese. Although hard numbers are hard to come by, it is clear that more than a few Issei men settled down in communities which were ethnically strange to them, married, and ceased to have any significant connection with other Japanese.

Several such intermarried couples matched Issei men and Mexican women in the Phoenix-Tucson area. Frank Yoshioka*, an Issei farmer, married Antonia Esquibel*, an immigrant from Mexico, about 1917 and settled near Hayden, Arizona. They had two daughters and became part of the local Mexican community. Ted Yanagi* married Maria Gonzalez* about the same time, likewise had two daughters, and raised vegetables near Phoenix. Fred Kochiyama* married Celia Montoya* about 1930 and farmed near Phoenix. They also were the parents of a pair of daughters. Joseph Kaneko* and Esmerelda Martinez* were married about 1920, had two sons, and ran a Hayden grocery store. All these families were part of the local Mexican American community. They seem to have known each other, but there is no evidence they had Japanese connections beyond their area. All of the women except Antonia Esquibel were born in the United States. All the children were bilingual in English and Spanish, but none could speak Japanese.[65] High intermarriage rates continued into the second and third generations. Texas Nisei such as Rose and Yasuko Hayashi* and Montanans such as Allen and Masako Ihara* grew up among Whites and Mexicans, and many chose their mates from those groups. The 1980 Denver outmarriage rate of nearly 60 percent was much higher than the 43 percent figure for Los Angeles in 1979. According to sociologist Gordon Hirabayashi, over 80 percent of Alberta Sansei married non-Japanese.[66]

East of the Mississippi lived Issei who were even more lonely and spread out than their brethren in the mountain states. Eleanor Gluck studied the Japanese of New York City in 1940 and reported that "by and large the Japanese in this city do not know each other." There were two thousand Japanese New Yorkers, out of a total population of seven and a half million. Unlike the more numerous Chinese, they were not concentrated in one neighborhood but were spread out over all five boroughs and the surrounding counties. The men's loneliness was exacerbated by a great disparity between the sexes: there were four Issei men for every woman in the East in 1940. Manchester Boddy wrote in 1921 that "in the Eastern part of the United States a majority of the Japanese have married white women." He exaggerated the case, but in fact outmarriage by both men and women was much higher in the eastern states than anywhere to the west. A census taken by the Japanese consulate in New York in 1931 found 211, or 33 percent, of the married Japanese men to have married non-Japanese wives. Census data put the figure at about 29 percent of New York Issei men and 19 percent for men from Illinois. This meant, first, that only a very small fraction of the Issei men who went east married at all, and second, that of those who did marry, between a quarter and a third married non-Japanese women. For the women the percentages of outmarriage were just as high: 31 percent in New York and 24 percent in Illinois. Most Issei in the East were either schoolboys who had come to America to pursue education or else factory and service workers. But there were also a few well-to-do internationalists—businessmen, artists, and intellectuals whose lives and careers crossed national boundaries. Many such men married American women. They included Jokichi Takamine, perhaps the richest and certainly the best known Japanese in turn-of-the-century America. He was a chemist, scion of a distinguished samurai family, and head of the team that first isolated adrenalin. Sent to New Orleans by the Japanese government in 1884, Takamine met and married Catherine Hitch, daughter of a former Confederate officer. Her immediate family seems to have accepted the match, but few others did. The couple met cold formality from many White Americans and most Japanese; they lived in lonely isolation on an estate in rural New York.[67]

Nisei who grew up in the eastern part of the United States married non-Japanese more frequently than their western contemporaries. Of Illinois Nisei born before 1925, 9 percent of the men and 15 percent of the women married non-Japanese. The percentage of outmarriage was higher in Chicago. Of the 187 Nisei living there before World War II, 37 were married, 12 to Caucasians. In New York, the numbers were every bit as high: 16 percent of the men and 35 percent of the women were married to non-Japanese.[68]

Sansei who lived in the Midwest and the East came mainly from middle-class homes, and they seldom associated with other Japanese Americans outside their immediate families. Anthropologist Mark Gehrie noted that in Chicago, "Nisei consider themselves white. . . . There has never been a sense of identity given to the Sansei by the Nisei." Chicago Sansei felt uncomfortable around other Japanese Americans. One woman said, "I know a lot of Oriental people whose parents don't know why . . . they date Caucasian boys or girls and they don't date Orientals. . . . It doesn't dawn on these parents that they have created a world where the majority of the people are Caucasian and they have no relationship at all with the Oriental world . . . so what do you expect? . . . You can't raise a child in that environment and not expect them to respond to the environment."[69]

Japanese American students at Harvard in the 1960s and 1970s came mainly from upper-middle-class eastern suburbs. In 1974 several of them spoke of the dread with which they regarded other Asians. Trying to blend into their White surroundings, they recalled crossing the street or going around the block to avoid being seen near another Asian. They dreaded blind dates, they said, for fear their partner would turn out to be Japanese. Many shared the sentiments of one of their Chinese fellow students, Tim Hsu: "I preferred to play down my ethnic roots. It was a matter of convenience; when the entire school system is one gigantic suburban homogeneous and rather intimidating peer group, it may be wiser not to dwell on such hopefully irrelevant differences. . . . Without the extra closeness that a shared Chinese-American subculture might have provided, there's really no reason to prefer Chinese company to any other, and it just seems better to avoid the whole ethnic business altogether. . . . Seeking out another Chinese for amorous purposes is far too conspicuous for comfort, and smacks distastefully of mate-hunting. . . . It's simpler just to avoid Chinese prospects entirely." In the Midwest and South, more than 40 percent of Sansei men and more than 60 percent of Sansei women married non-Japanese. The percentages were nearly as high in the Northeast.[70]

The differing rates of Japanese American outmarriage in parts of the country outside the West Coast can be traced mainly to structural factors. In Hawaii, because of the large number of Japanese and the power of community institutions, tight surveillance resulted in a lower percentage of intermarriages than on the mainland, even though Hawaii's racial climate was relaxed and intermarriage by other groups a common thing. During World War II, even as mainland Nisei were being forced together in concentration camps just when they came to marriageable age, Hawaiian Nisei women were subjected to the attentions of thousands of mainland servicemen. Intermarriage by Japanese American women shot up during the war years, although Nisei men did not share in the trend. Because of the continued power of Japanese American communal life after the war, intermarriage by Hawaiian Sansei never reached rates comparable to those on the mainland. In the Midwest, South, and East, away from concentrations of Japanese Americans, intermarriage rates were always higher than on the West Coast and in Hawaii.

Intermarriage and Social Class

The class makeup of Issei intermarriages is not clear. Jesse Steiner reported that by far the largest number of interracial marriages were formed by middle- and working-class Japanese American men. Keitoku Watanabe thought just the opposite: "In the east there are more intermarriages among the cooks and chauffeurs and that class of Japanese, but out here [on the West Coast] it is more with doctors and lawyers and that class of people." My own research has uncovered more or less equal numbers of each: some intermarriages by obscure, working-class Issei, and others by prominent, professional people. One gets a vague impression of more mixed marriages occurring at the top and the bottom of the social scale than in the middle. This would accord with W. Lloyd Warner's notion that members of upper and lower classes feel more free to break social norms than do those in the middle. But that is only an impression. There are not enough hard data.[71]

Examples of working-class intermarriages abound. Joe Ininn was a chef who worked in a hotel in El Centro, California, and married an American woman, Catherine, of mixed Black, White, and Native American ancestry. George Miyamoto* was a Japanese immigrant who married Donna Emerson*, the daughter of a Baltimore barkeep. They lived in various places in the eastern half of the United States before settling in San Francisco, where George set up business as building contractor. A twenty-seven-year-old Japanese gardener who worked for a white family in Southern California fell in love with the family's fifteen-year-old White cook. They were married, endured ostracism from her parents and friends, had five children, and eventually opened a nursery.[72]

Intermarriages also involved couples who were members of the social and professional elite. Perhaps the most famous West Coast American-Japanese intermarriage was between Emma Fong and Yoshi Kuno, a professor of Japanese at the University of California. Mrs. Kuno was a strong-willed White woman who had been brought up in the cosmopolitan atmosphere of San Francisco's North Beach district. While a student at Stanford she met Rev. Walter Ngon Fong. After considerable soul-searching on her part they were married in 1897. He was a Stanford student at the time, but soon he would take a prominent place in Bay Area society. He was a lawyer in San Francisco, a minister in Oakland, and a teacher of Chinese at Berkeley. In later years he was prominent in China's first modern revolutionary movement. After Fong's death, Emma married Kuno, a close friend of her late husband. She became a mother figure to generations of international students at Berkeley. She and Kuno achieved some notoriety when she wrote about her experiences in a thirty-one page article that was reprinted nationwide. Emma Kuno freely compared her two marriages, saying that she preferred Fong because he was not so domineering: "While my Chinese husband always accorded me the major part of the 'say,' my Japanese husband is absolutely unbossable." But by all accounts their marriage was a stable and happy one. Her chief complaint—and she was very bitter about this—was that the government had taken away her American citizenship. If Fong or Kuno had complaints, one cannot learn of them from her manuscript.[73]

Another member of this upper-crust, internationalist fraternity was Kiyoshi Karl Kawakami. Kawakami's writings extolled the virtues of interracial marriage, and he put his marriage where his mouth was. He was an internationalist and a socialist, a founder of the Japanese Social Democratic Party. In 1901 at age twenty-five he went to America, ostensibly to continue his education, but also because his party had been outlawed. He changed his name from Miyashita to Kawakami to avoid harassment from Japanese agents. He worked and attended college in Iowa and Washington. By 1907 he had met and married Mildred Clark of Momence, Illinois, "a great, big, corn-fed, beautiful blonde," according to their daughter. They lived for several years in rural Illinois, where they had three children and where Kawakami made a living writing books and articles about America for the Japanese and about Japan for the Americans. The couple did not report any prejudice from either family, nor from the citizens of Illinois at large. Kawakami was dapper, intelligent, engaging, and obviously successful. The family encountered more prejudice after they moved to San Francisco in 1913. They never became part of the local Japanese community; they lived apart and traveled in very different circles from most Japanese Americans. In later years they lived on both coasts and occasionally in Japan.[74]

Jesse Steiner and others have contended that upper-class marriages such as Kuno's and Kawakami's were likely to succeed: education, understanding, and if possible money were necessary to surmount the obstacles in an intermarried couple's path. Dr. F. T. Nakaya, a Los Angeles Issei physician who married a White woman and had a substantial Japanese American practice, put it this way: "I am very much in favor of inter-marriage. My own has been very happy. I have never had any cause to regret it and as far as I know my wife has not. I think that it was very hard for her at first because she did not understand the Japanese people, but she understands them now and enjoys them. In regard to this inter-marriage, though, I do think that it must take place between people of education and understanding. They must understand the prejudice they will have to share and the position of the children, and they must love each other enough to go through these things. If inter-marriage came to take place in about six out of every ten cases, the race problem would be solved." In surveying a large number of Issei intermarriages involving couples from many stations in life, I have not noticed that marital success flowed with more conspicuous regularity to those with wealth and education than to those who possessed fewer material blessings.[75]

One subgroup of Japanese Americans that seems to have intermarried more than others consisted of people with fervent commitments to Christianity. Issei Christians had very positive attitudes toward White Christian workers based on their associations with Christian missionaries in Japan. Some came to America in the first place because of the ideals about freedom and the virtues of Western civilization that had been implanted by Christian teachers. One woman explained her reverence for her White Christian mentors in this way: "It is very natural for me to have a very friendly attitude toward the American people, because my contacts with them were limited to the missionary teachers in Japan. These missionary teachers were to us students as the living Christ. They were more than the teachers; they were our best friends." There are no records of devout Buddhists marrying Americans, and zealous Buddhists were among the most adamant opponents of the practice. Harry Kitano reports that it was common for Issei men to fall in love with the young White women who taught them English and Bible classes at Japanese churches. These women were introducing the Japanese men to a new world of American culture. It should surprise no one that the men may have taken to such women, perhaps the only White Americans who treated them kindly. For their part, some of the women seem to have gone into teaching immigrants in part to fulfill romantic ideals, seeking to minister to downtrodden people. It is not unreasonable to suppose that their romantic feelings should extend to personal relationships with their students. A Seattle minister reported that the woman who married T. Torikai "had gone into missionary work among the Japanese . . . [because] she was young and romantic and flighty and should never have been placed in the field. She met Mr. Torikai and married him but was not ready to settle down and this led to family friction . . . and eventually . . . divorce." Another White woman was more hard-headed about marrying one of her night school students. She knew him for seven years and prayed hard before deciding to turn down other suitors and marry him. "I felt convinced that it was all in God's plan that we should marry. I did not care what my friends would think, for I knew that the true ones would realize that God made one blood of all nations." The couple was on good terms with both families, and they were pillars of the local Japanese church even though the services were in Japanese and the wife understood only a few words.[76]

It is a difficult task to determine the class makeup of Nisei intermarriages. As was the case with the Issei generation, there does not seem to have been any clear occupational grouping. But education, another indicator of social class, seems to have been a factor. Darrel Montero and Ronald Tsukashima surveyed Nisei intermarriages—not just prewar intermarriages on the West Coast, but those among Nisei from other parts of the country and those which occurred after the war as well. Although their sample was broad, their findings are suggestive. Only 6 percent of the Nisei with a high school education or less were married to non-Japanese, compared to 9 percent of those who had attended some college, 12 percent of those who had a bachelor's degree, and 22 percent of those Nisei who had done postgraduate work.[77]

This points to the one group of Nisei who were most likely to break the bonds of ethnic loyalty and marry someone non-Japanese. Intellectuals and artists had few connections with Japanese American communities. They traveled in mixed-ethnic social circles of their own and did not feel the pull toward endogamy with as much force as did their generation-mates. Then, too, they daily came into contact with a class of non-Japanese people who were less likely than others to exhibit prejudice against Japanese Americans. Two examples will suffice. Arthur Ishigo was a San Francisco artist who married Estelle Apffel. Sue Kunitomi was an intellectual, a Unitarian, and a political activist before and after her marriage to artist Gar Embrey. Milton Gordon is probably right when he posits the existence of a multi-ethnic class of "marginally ethnic intellectuals" who, while they recognize the existence of racial and ethnic divisions, tend to act as if those distinctions are unimportant.[78]

There was another group of Nisei who enjoyed even more frequent contact with non-Japanese Americans, although they seldom married. These were zoot-suiters, prostitutes, and others whose aggressive, outlandish behavior—whose very existence, in fact—embarrassed most other Japanese Americans. They were sufficiently embarrassing that no prominent writer of Japanese American history has taken notice of their existence. This lack of emphasis is as it should be, for the deviant population among the Nisei was tiny. But this group was significant, partly because the other Nisei were so embarrassed by it, and partly because it was members of this group who had the most frequent romantic and sexual encounters with non-Japanese.[79]

Sus Kaminaka*, Barry Shimizu*, Harry Ando*, Lester Kimura*, and Blackie Najima* all were young toughs who in 1944 had left the concentration camps for Chicago and who wore the extreme wide-brimmed hats, padded shoulders, pleated pants dropping to tight cuffs, and floor-length chains of the zoot-suiter. Most of their prewar friends were similarly outfitted Chinese, Filipino, Mexican, and Nisei youths from the streets of Los Angeles, San Francisco, and Stockton. Most had jobs in Chicago, although their prime activity was hanging out on street corners. Frances Nishimoto* and Yoriko Machida* complained that gangs of these young men would break up Nisei dances, shouting and picking on a couple by cutting in repeatedly until the girl was reduced to tears and the boy to impotent rage. Worse, in Nishimoto's view, they brought their Mexican friends to some of the dances: "They really looked greasy. I don't know why in the world the Nisei have to associate with Mexicans. . . . Some of the girls showed off by jitterbugging. . . . I didn't like the way some of them jitterbugged with the Mexican fellows because it didn't look decent. . . . I'm glad no respectable hakujin [Caucasian] saw that crowd. . . . I think it hurts our reputation."[80]

The zoots told Charles Kikuchi they enjoyed frequent sex with both Nisei and non-Japanese women. Like other Nisei who had settled in Chicago, they were lonely, but they dealt with their loneliness in ways that were less socially acceptable. Blackie Najima* and his friends would go out at night and have gang sex with street women, with or without those women's permission. Other Nisei youths passed women from hand to hand. One told Kikuchi, "I'm living with a white girl right now, but she is just a tramp. When I get tired of her I will throw her out. She is making the rounds of the Nisei fellows on Clark street and she lives with them for a while so she can have a place to stay." Sus Kaminaka* found it easier to have recreational sex with White women than with Nisei: "I think that most girls are pretty easy to get. I like to fool around with the Caucasian girls better because they don't take you seriously. I have more fun with them because they are a little more experienced." One White teenager hung around him for weeks, trying to get him to marry her, until his Nisei girlfriend appeared from camp to end the affair.[81]

Barry Shimizu* went to bars, dances, and bed with a string of Caucasian women who hung around the Nisei zoots. He "found it pretty easy to have sex with these hakujin girls as they didn't have funny ideas about these things. We began to bring them to our empty rooms and sometimes I would sleep all night with one of these hakujin girls. I thought it was great stuff. . . . Most Caucasian girls are pretty casual about sex affairs and not timid like the Nisei girls and that's why I went for them. They didn't seem to think much about the difference in race and they didn't mind going out in public with me." But the group began to be harassed by outraged neighbors, local police, and the FBI. Moreover, Shimizu began to have second thoughts. "I thought that it would only bring me a bad reputation and it wouldn't do the Nisei any good, if I were seen in public all the time drunk with a hakujin girl. This one girl was pretty young . . . she said she wanted to get married. I never thought of inter-marriage and I didn't think it was possible. Always in my mind, I felt that inter-marriage would not work as there were too many things to consider. I felt that our types of living would be entirely different and that there would be a lot of discrimination against us . . . these things made me realize that inter-marriage was out of the question, so I finally crawled out of the picture after thinking it over seriously." He then began taking out Nisei women, looking for one to marry.[82]

Not just Nisei men, but a few women, too, inhabited this underworld. Charles Kikuchi recalled that, in Chicago, "there were several Nisei prostitutes, but the seamy side of resettler life was carefully hidden from public view" by the other Nisei. Hiromasa Minami* told of a Nisei woman named Pauline who worked for a Nisei pimp servicing the lusts of both White and Japanese men, and several witnesses recalled other women who were also prostitutes with mixed clienteles.[83]

One woman who was generally regarded as a prostitute, but who seems to have been sexually active for play rather than for pay, was Rose Hayashi*. When interviewed by Charles Kikuchi in the fall of 1943, she was a twenty-year-old drifter.[84] Hayashi had held twenty-nine jobs in the previous four years, mostly in pool halls and beer parlors on the West Coast. Born and raised in Texas, she was the daughter of a Japanese American artist. Most of her childhood friends were Anglos and Mexicans, for there were few other Nisei in Texas. Her family moved to Los Angeles when she was thirteen. Three years later, in 1939, she ran away from home. From then until evacuation she lived on her own and carried on affairs of varying intensity with dozens of men, mainly Japanese Americans but also Chinese, Filipinos, and Whites. "I guess I was quite wild," she said. During that time she had "many" proposals of marriage, but turned them all down. "I had always planned to go someplace where nobody knew me at all. . . . There was so much talk going around about me and I got pretty tired of it. They thought I was a prostitute and I was spreading syphillis among the Nisei. That wasn't true at all."

It is arresting to realize that the Japanese community gossip system kept track of Hayashi throughout her escapades up and down the coast, made regular reports to her parents, and put some pressure on her to mend her ways. She told Kikuchi that she was not a prostitute, just a beer hall waitress who would show men a good time if they would show her a good time. "I wasn't doing it for money." Hayashi did not identify with other Japanese Americans, partly because of the pressure they put on her to change and partly because of the general anti-Japanese tone of the time.

When evacuation came, she hid out in a Chinatown nightclub, passing for Chinese, but finally was caught and interned. At Tanforan Assembly Center her reputation made her an outcast, so she hung around with other untouchables: half-Japanese youngsters and Nisei women who had been seeing Filipino men. "There were lots of rumors spread about us. They said we were prostitutes." Transferred to the Topaz concentration camp, Hayashi finally managed to get out of prison by volunteering to work on a Utah turkey farm. There, Nisei men preyed on female workers in the fields, but they dared not go near

Hayashi because of her awesome reputation. She left the farm and began working in a Salt Lake City cafe, where she met a truck driver named Walter Henderson* and fell in love, by her own account, for the first time in her life. She had by this time acquired a bad marriage, a divorce, and a daughter by another man. Hounded by her ex-husband and threatened with reimprisonment by the WRA, Hayashi fled to Chicago. There she and Henderson set up housekeeping, awaiting her final divorce decree and his so they could get married. Ultimately she intended to go back to Los Angeles with Henderson when the coast was reopened to Japanese Americans, pretending she was Korean so that Whites would not hate her and Japanese Americans would not bother her any longer.

Such declassé individuals as Hayashi, Kaminaka, and the others were exceptional, both in their seamy lifestyles and in their frequent choice of non-Japanese partners. Most other Nisei—including most intermarriers—were aspiring members of the respectable middle class. That was true of the Sansei generation as well. Middle-class, college educated, upwardly mobile Sansei were particularly likely to date and marry non-Japanese. Clara Nagai*, an upwardly mobile girl from a poor but well-educated Seattle family, dared to date a White boy in the 1960s when other, less ambitious girls did not. From a very early age she found herself looking toward a wider world, bigger challenges, and broader intellectual and cultural horizons than most of her Sansei peers. Ten years later she was married to a non-Japanese and pursuing a professional career thousands of miles from home, while her high school friends were secretaries and housewives in their old neighborhood in Seattle.[85]

One set of ambitious Sansei who suffered particularly poignant internal conflict over interracial liaisons were certain of the pan-Asian activists. Many were intellectuals who had long looked outside their community for stimulation and friendships. Many had non-Asian partners of some years' standing when they became involved in pan-Asian politics. They were torn between their non-Japanese lovers and their newfound Asian American ideology. Jan Masaoka described her dilemma:

> I guess that one of the most difficult things for me to understand is how to relate to my boyfriend who is white. Sometimes I flash back on all the ideas my parents taught me such as the idea that to marry a white man was to sort

of degrade myself, and it's really hard to know how to deal with these kinds of feelings.

I once read this poem by an Asian woman where she said that after looking into blue eyes for so long she forgot hers were black. I really feel this, and it's hard to understand: I identify so strongly with this man I love and that's inevitably tied up somewhat to the way he looks, which conflicts with me and my background and the way I look.

So I look at him and all the feelings I have get mixed up and make me upset and dizzy: loving him, hating myself for loving a white man, hating him because he's white, hating white people in general, feeling underneath that I'm superior to white people, and even deeper underneath that I'm inferior to white people, especially men, feeling guilty for not having an Asian boyfriend, feeling that I'm taking unfair advantage of my social and sexual mobility racially when Asian men don't have that mobility, and being afraid of what other people think about my going with a white man—it's just really frightening.[86]

Strict class analysis of Japanese American outmarriage patterns, though important, is not possible, given the paucity of historical data on class. Fragmentary testimony suggests that outmarriage was more common among the educated elite than among members of the working or middle classes, and that interracial romance (if not marriage) was fairly common among *lumpen proletarians*.[87]

4. Issues and Interpretations: Japanese, American, or Something in Between?

Intermarriage within the Japanese Group

Now it is time to turn to questions of interpretation and issues of special concern. In the early years, Japanese communities enforced endogamy, not only with regard to divisions of race and nationality, but also with regard to divisions that non-Japanese people did not even know existed. These lines were more clearly articulated in Hawaii because of the more rigid Japanese community structure there, but they were evident on the mainland as well. Not all Issei were willing to talk to outsiders about these divisions, and some members of later generations were not fully aware of their existence. But divisions within what we call the Japanese American people did exist. They affected social behavior generally and marital choice in particular.

The most notorious social cleavage was between ordinary Japanese and *eta*. The eta are an outcast class whose roots go deep into the Japanese past. Their exact origins are not known. Since at least the eighth century, eta have been associated with certain occupations: animal slaughtering, disposal of the dead, tanning of hides, and other jobs that involve contact with dead bodies. Such occupations are thought to be ritually polluting, according to the Japanese fusion of Shinto and Buddhist beliefs. There are both class and racial undertones to

Japanese treatment of the eta. Some Japanese have asserted that the eta are descendants of another race of people who became slaves of the Japanese, but there is no biological or historical evidence to suggest that this is true. Other Japanese think of eta as subhuman and genetically polluted, much as many Whites regard Black Americans. The eta have for centuries been a people apart, living in separate communities and forming a social world distinct from ordinary Japanese. In 1871, the Meiji government, mindful of Japan's international image, legally emancipated the eta. But discrimination has persisted. Today the eta (or *burakumin,* as many prefer to be called) constitute a more or less permanent, impoverished, but increasingly militant underclass. Some individual eta succeed in passing as ordinary Japanese, for they are physically indistinguishable. But they live in constant fear that someone will connect their names or their birthplaces with other burakumin. When a couple got married in prewar Japan, a go-between, or *baishakunin,* would set up the match and check out the background of each party. Usually, a family which had a history of leprosy, tuberculosis, insanity, or eta status would have a very hard time finding mates for its offspring. That kind of checking was easy to do because detailed family records were kept in every village in Japan. Any birth, death, or marriage had to be reported to one's home village register.[1]

When the Issei came to America they maintained the wall between eta and other Japanese. No one would talk about such things openly, but it was common knowledge that certain Japanese communities, such as the one in Florin, California, were made up almost entirely of eta families. It was easier for eta to pass as ordinary Japanese in America than in Japan. The fluid nature of Issei society on the mainland in the early years did not lend itself to exhaustive background checks before social relationships were formed. Moreover, the village registers that contained background data were thousands of miles away in Japan. But before long the Japanese consulates in many cities began to act as conduits of *baishakunin* inquiries. And as mainland Japanese communities formed, they brought together larger numbers of people from various parts of Japan who could offer background information on marriage candidates. All this meant that by the 1920s at the latest, passing as non-eta was very hard to do. Because the anti-eta prejudice of other Japanese was so virulent, almost no marriages were contracted between the two groups. Since the Issei eta group did not contain a vast pool of eligible men and women (about 2 percent of Japanese today are of eta origin), many of them had a hard time finding mates at all. Some ended up marrying close relatives. Romanzo Adams has suggested that most of the Hawaiian Issei who married non-Japanese were either eta or members of another outcast group, the Okinawans.[2]

The Okinawans were not a polluted caste within Japanese society; they were a subject people. They came from the Ryukyu Islands, which stretch south from Japan toward Taiwan. The Ryukyus were independent until the Tokugawa period, and then were only nominally controlled by Satsuma, which in turn was the most independent fief in feudal Japan. Since the Meiji era the Japanese government has tried to integrate the Okinawans into Japanese society, but they have continued to regard themselves, and have been regarded, as a distinct people. Many Okinawans are readily identified by other Japanese on the basis of darker complexions, curly hair, more body hair, rounder eyes, and distinctive family names. Others cannot be distinguished. The Japanese in Japan proper—Naichi, as they are called—have long discriminated against Okinawans and regarded them as savages. Some Naichi Japanese have made up myths about the supposed simian origins of the Okinawan people. Their hairiness and dark coloring have not fit well with Japanese notions of beauty, and there has been little intermarriage between the two groups.[3]

Okinawans constituted only a tiny fraction of the Japanese migration to the American mainland, but in Hawaii they formed a significant minority within a minority—between 10 and 15 percent of the Japanese Hawaiian population. In Peru, the Japanese immigrant community was about evenly split between Okinawans and Naichi Japanese. There, a dual social system developed, with two parallel sets of community institutions and almost no social intercourse between them. Naichi Japanese immigrants in Hawaii referred to Okinawans as *yaban*, or barbaric; as *heta*, or clumsy and stupid; as "loud, rough, and coarse"; as uncultured; as dirty and smelly; as unscrupulous in business, undercutting their Naichi competitors; and as "lower than an Eta." One Issei woman told her daughter about Okinawans: "They are an alien people. Their practices are unclean. . . . They seldom bathe. They are like animals. I forbid you to associate with them." In the intense social climate in Hawaii, almost no Okinawans married Naichi Issei, and on the mainland only a few more crossed the boundary during the first generation. The Okinawans in Hawaii further isolated themselves by sharply drawing the line between themselves and the other outcast group, the eta.[4]

Part of the social chasm between Naichi Japanese and Okinawans must be attributed to their different status as colonizer and colonized. But part of it was simply that they came from different parts of Japan. Japan was hardly a monolith. Though it was only the size of California, it had been divided for centuries into a multitude of separate regional units. Each had evolved its own distinct subculture and loyalties. Those loyalties were strong enough that a marriage between people from different regions might also be called an intermarriage. Even in highly integrated modern Japan, according to Harumi Befu, "Most Japanese at one end of the Japanese island chain feel little kinship with those at the other end." The Issei in America tended to live in towns and neighborhoods dominated by people from one prefecture or another. Their primary social organizations were *kenjinkai*, or prefectural associations. The Issei generally married people from their own or a neighboring village if possible. This ensured they were getting a known quantity and assuaged family fears of losing control of their offspring. When Hazel Nishi's* father went back to Japan to seek a wife, "his parents wanted to arrange a marriage with a girl from the local ken [prefecture] whose family they knew well." Edward Strong's 1930 study of California Issei found a striking correspondence between the percentages of males and females from each prefecture, suggesting a high degree of endogamy by prefecture. In Hawaii during the 1930s Edwin Burrows found "a whole cluster of Japanese rules against marriage to persons of different local origin. The feeling seems to be that if the two families have been neighbors for generations, they know what kind of people they are dealing with, and what to expect at every turn in the new relationship. Hence it is considered preferable to marry into a family that came from the same village; failing that, at least from the same prefecture. The question of marriage to people from another island in Japan, let alone outside of Japan altogether, probably never came up in the old country." Still, Issei in-marriage by prefecture was not uniform. Some, like Nishi's father, overturned social expectations and married people from other prefectures. And most saw the divisions among the various prefectures as less significant than the enormous

gap between ordinary Japanese on the one hand and Okinawans or eta
on the other.[5]

Another split within the Issei community that had an effect on marital choice was the religious division between Buddhists and Christians.
Data on this are scant, but it seems likely that there were few marriages between Christian and Buddhist Issei. About two-thirds of the
Issei were Buddhists; most of the rest were Christians. Almost all the
Christians were themselves converts from Buddhism. Many of them
came to America under the influence of Christian missionaries, specifically because they saw this as a Christian country where they could
practice their new faith free from harassment by their families, neighbors, or the Japanese government. In rural California, Hisao Shimada*
reported intense animosity and "a great rift between the Buddhist and
the Christian" amounting to "two Japanese communities" with separate
institutions and activities. Shimada's view may have been extreme, but
clearly Buddhists and Christians did not get along. In view of the biblical injunction "Be ye not unequally yoked together with unbelievers,"
it seems unlikely that Issei converts would marry non-Christians. Buddhists were traditionally more tolerant of other religions, but the opposition of the two groups in America may have intensified their dislike
for the renegades.[6]

Many Nisei knew that their parents drew lines between ordinary
Japanese and such outgroups as Okinawans and eta. But the Nisei paid
less attention than their parents to such distinctions. One Nisei of eta
parentage was elected president of the Japanese American Citizens
League (the premier Nisei civic club) in the 1940s and apparently was
a popular leader among his generation. But the Issei still wielded a lot
of power in their children's lives, especially when it came to such an
important matter as marriage. They might not forbid their children to
associate with an eta or Okinawan, but they were quite likely to forbid
marriage. Some conservative Issei, especially in Hawaii, disapproved
of their children marrying even ordinary Nisei whose families came
from different parts of Japan. One Hawaiian girl reported: "My middle
brother is planning to get married. My mother put up a big fuss about
that. He is marrying a Japanese, but mother was mad because he didn't
pick one from Hiroshima." There is not much evidence to indicate
that the Nisei themselves cared about Japanese geographical or caste
distinctions. But the parents did, and the young people often bowed
before pressure from the older generation.[7]

The Nisei did recognize another kind of geographical distinction, one made in America. Nisei from different regions in the United States saw each other as culturally alien. Sylvia Yanagisako found that Seattle Nisei regarded California Nisei as "different" and Hawaiian Japanese Americans as "even stranger." Those sentiments, she said, led to a kind of local "community endogamy," whereby prewar Nisei tended to marry only other Nisei from their own regions. Several Nisei gave evidence of this sort of attitude. Doris Ihara*, raised in Montana, found Pasadena Japanese Americans arrogant and shallow when she first moved to California in 1934. "The California Nisei always thought they were superior to everyone else. They always judged by looks, clothing and money." The Seattle Nisei she had met struck her as "much more sincere than the California Nisei as they don't think of dances and the immediate present." She felt shut out by her Pasadena peers. Fusako Tanaka*, a Seattle native, thought of California Nisei as "zoot suiters. . . . We blamed the California Japanese for the evacuation as we thought that the Washington Japanese would not have been evacuated if the California ones had behaved themselves. We felt that the California Japanese acted too much like the Filipinos and not enough like the Caucasians . . . the California Japanese did not mix enough with the Caucasians. We really believed they were quite different from us." These comments point to several ways in which northwestern Nisei differed from Californians. The Californians, because of their greater numbers and higher density, especially in the Los Angeles area, formed their own societies, distinct from non-Japanese Americans, with a much greater degree of completeness than did Nisei from other regions. Northwesterners (and other Nisei from the mountain states and elsewhere on the mainland) interacted more with Whites. Yet, at the same time that the California Nisei maintained their separate ethnic social structures, they seem to have imbibed more liberally the culture of White, teenage America. They were seen, and saw themselves, as better dancers and dressers, and as generally more skilled in the ways of American youth. Northwesterners saw themselves, and were perceived, as both more integrated in a structural sense and less assimilated in a cultural sense.[8]

There also was a barrier between mainland Nisei and their contemporaries from Hawaii. World War II–era Hawaiian Nisei called mainlanders "Kotonks," after the sound their heads were supposed to make as they hit the floor in army fistfights. The mainlanders responded by calling the Hawaiian Japanese Budda–heads and Pineapples. Harry Kitano recalled that "the mainlander was considered standoffish, materialistic, too careful about impressing the majority group, too acculturated, and, in one word, too *haolified*." Andrea Sakai, a Portland native, said she was criticized in Hawaii "because I spoke like a Haole, behaved like a Haole, thought and had interests like a Haole." While mainland Japanese Americans saw islanders as insufficiently Americanized, the Hawaiian Nisei thought the mainlanders lacked ethnic pride. Ida Shigaki* was outraged when she and her California date were refused entrance to a dance hall because they were Japanese. "I was absolutely mortified by this experience but my Nisei escort seemed to take such a thing for granted. I couldn't understand that because back in the islands we would have made a terrible fuss and never stood for such a thing. The difference was that there were more hakujin in California so that the Nisei felt a little inferior. In the islands the Japanese were in the majority so we didn't envy the white people so much." Although Shigaki and other Japanese Hawaiians envied the money and sophistication of mainland Nisei, they despised the cost in ethnic pride that was paid for such cultural and material benefits. It is not clear whether this cultural and attitudinal barrier between Hawaiian and mainland Nisei inhibited intermarriage, although there was at least one case in which the mother of a Nisei boy got terribly upset over her son's marriage to a person whom she regarded as a loose woman from the mainland.[9]

There was another, more radical kind of intermarriage that faced many Nisei: marriage to people who were culturally Japanese. The most common marriage of this sort occurred between Nisei women and Issei men. The Issei generation had many fewer females than males, an insufficiency only partly made up by the immigration of Japanese women in the 1910s. After 1924, by American law, no more Japanese women could come, and Issei men found they had to look elsewhere for partners. The best available candidates seemed to be Nisei women. In Japanese America, as in Japan, husbands usually were several years older than their wives. This factor, together with the dismal economic prospects of most Nisei men, meant that they did not offer the Issei men much competition for the hands of older Nisei women. Jiro Ishimoto* told a poignant story of a desperate quest for wives by several Issei men, himself included. "There were only two Nisei girls in Chicago then [early 1920s]. They were sisters, one eighteen and the other nineteen. I was in love with the nineteen year old and her father wanted to match me with her because I was making good money and had a fine job. But these sisters were very much spoiled. Because they were the only single girls all the Issei . . . went to visit them all the time and gave them presents. They began to think that they were high class and too good for the Japanese boys." When the women chose to marry a pair of wealthier Issei men, Ishimoto was crushed.[10]

Such Issei-Nisei intermarriages were not uncommon. Over half of the Chicago Nisei women who were wedded before World War II chose Issei husbands. The percentages were lower in Los Angeles, and they declined as time went on: in 1937–38, 19 percent of the Nisei men and women who married took immigrant spouses; in 1941–42, only 7 percent did the same. This reflects the fact that, by the 1940s, there were relatively few unmarried Issei left, and there were lots of second-generation mates available for Nisei women to choose from. The War Relocation Authority's census revealed a striking number of Issei-Nisei intermarriages, undertaken not only by Nisei women, but also by Nisei men. The census also recorded a trend away from Issei-Nisei intermarriages in the years before World War II.[11]

Some parents sent away to Japan for wives for their Nisei sons, in the hope that proper Japanese women would accord the young men the kind of submission and support which the parents expected, and which they feared American-born women did not know how to give. A lot of Issei parents also encouraged their daughters to marry Issei men, feeling that they would be more secure economically than with Nisei husbands. The parents also felt more comfortable knowing that their daughters would be treated like Japanese wives, rather than according to the more liberal manners of Americans. Many marriages between Issei men and Nisei women seem to have been quite successful. Some Nisei women, like Margaret Suzuki*, were eager to marry Issei men. At UCLA she met a Japanese student about ten years her senior, whom she found to be more mature than her Nisei friends. "I was fascinated with him because he was so sophisticated and cosmopolitan," she said, and she wanted to marry him. But her father called off the match. He was afraid that a man raised in Japan would mistreat his daughter. An increasing number of Issei and Nisei came to echo the elder Suzuki's fears. Robert Ross surveyed Los Angeles Japanese of both generations

and found that the overwhelming majority opposed Issei-Nisei marriages in 1939. William Smith, a sociologist and lifelong student of
Japanese America, observed that "unhappy unions with foreign-born
mates" were a common topic of conversation in the 1930s. "There have
been cases of divorce and even suicide where American-reared girls
have married immigrants much older than themselves." Hazel Nishi*,
after a trip to Japan, recoiled in horror at the thought of marrying an
Issei man: "A woman just means nothing to the Japanese men. All they
were supposed to do is to bear sons for their conceited husbands. . . .
All they did was belittle women so that I would know my place."[12]

In addition to cultural conflicts between some Nisei women and
their Issei spouses, there were legal consequences to consider as well.
One of the objections Margaret Suzuki's* father raised was that she
would lose her U.S. citizenship if she married an Issei man, and unlike
American women who married men from other countries, she would be
rendered permanently ineligible to reestablish her American citizenship by naturalization. This was a powerful impediment to Issei-Nisei
marriage in the eyes of many Nisei women. Still, many such marriages
did occur. Japanese women who married Nisei men found themselves
in the very different position of acquiring, not losing, American citizenship. Whether they objected to that change of status is not recorded.[13]

One group of Nisei who were particularly likely to consent to
unions with Issei were the Kibei. These Nisei had spent much of their
childhood in Japan and were culturally closer to their parents' generation than to the other Nisei. Generally more conservative and more
submissive to parental control than other Nisei, the Kibei were more
likely to view marriages to Issei as advantageous and less likely to
regret the loss of American citizenship. In a certain sense, one might
even view a marriage between a Kibei and an ordinary Nisei as an
intercultural marriage, so different were their cultural orientations in
many cases. Sue Kunitomi Embrey recalled that, growing up in the
relatively acculturated Nisei community in central Los Angeles, she
and her peers viewed the Kibei with scorn and hostility, and their
antagonism was reciprocated.[14]

To summarize, it appears that the old lines within the Japanese group
—between ordinary Japanese on the one hand and Okinawans and eta
on the other, and between Japanese from different prefectures—had

blurred somewhat by the second generation. The Nisei did not generally make such distinctions, though they did recognize their parents' prejudices and sometimes bowed before them. In place of those prejudices there arose new divisions—American geographical differences and the cultural split between Issei and Nisei—that had an effect on cultural perceptions, on social relations in general, and on marriage choices in particular. But those new divisions do not seem to have been so ironclad as the old caste barriers.

Few Sansei recognized the intragroup distinctions that had channeled their parents' and grandparents' marital choices. They seldom knew or cared if a friend or prospective mate had Okinawan or eta heritage. Regional distinctions, whether Japanese or American, did not matter. There were a number of marriages between younger Nisei and older Sansei, and they caused little comment. What mattered to the Sansei were not distinctions among Japanese Americans, but rather whether to draw lines between Japanese Americans and other outside groups.[15]

A Hierarchy of Choice

It is now possible to construct a picture of the social preferences exhibited by Japanese immigrants with regard to potential mates. What emerges is hierarchy of preference, both within the Japanese group and without. With passing time and succeeding generations, distinctions near the top of the hierarchy began to blur, and Japanese Americans proved willing to accept mates further and further down the ladder.

Within the Japanese group, a person from one's home village or its immediate surroundings was first choice, followed by someone from farther away within one's own prefecture. More than a few Issei seem to have married people from other parts of Japan, though often only after local options had been exhausted. That was about as far as most Issei were willing to go. They recognized the theoretical possibility of marriage to other people and had a hierarchy of choice for such an eventuality, based roughly on skin color, prestige, and perceived cultural compatibility. Next after Japanese would come Caucasians. Perhaps this choice was related to the long-standing Japanese preference for pale skin, but it certainly was due at least partly to the superior wealth and status enjoyed by White people in America. Within the White group, some Issei distinguished between people of northern European and southern European origin. One Issei told Marion Svensrud, "I do not feel any prejudice towards other races. I feel more comfortable with my own race, but I would not object to my children marrying any northern European like an American, Canadian, Dutchman, Russian, or Scandinavian." This same Issei expressed hesitation at the thought of marriage to someone from the Balkans.[16]

Following closely behind the Whites in the Issei hierarchy were the Chinese, whom they saw as culturally much like themselves and therefore compatible. The Chinese had similar ideas about such things as family life and the value of education and hard work. One Nisei woman told Mildred Kosaki: "I don't think my mother like us marry outside the Japanese. But maybe Chinese not too bad." Hatsu Furuya, a Seattle Issei woman, made the hierarchy clear: "I would rather they married Japanese, but if they wish to marry white men it is all right." She added, "If they marry Negroes or Chinese I will not object," but that was a distinctly less preferable choice. In the islands, Hawaiians and part-Hawaiians came after the Chinese. Next, in Hawaii or on the mainland, would come Koreans, who suffered by comparison with the Chinese because they, like the Okinawans, were a colonized people. After the Koreans came various categories of genuinely despised peoples: Okinawans, eta, Filipinos, Mexicans, Puerto Ricans, and finally Blacks. On the mainland, many Japanese lived in ghettoes that lay adjacent to Mexican barrios. Often they employed Mexican, Filipino, or Negro laborers in their businesses. The Issei drew back from any but the most formal economic contact with these darker, subject peoples. They attributed rampant sexual appetites and criminal tendencies to such groups. For the Issei, intermarriage with the people at the bottom of this scale was well-nigh unthinkable.[17]

This hierarchy suggests the Japanese immigrants had a subnational sense of ethnic identity. They regarded themselves first as inhabitants of their respective villages and prefectures, and only secondarily as members of the Japanese nation. As Harumi Befu indicates, the much-touted, all-consuming Japanese nationalism, the emperor worship, was a product of a later period—the 1930s—long after the Issei had left for America. Moreover, that nationalism was not so much an outpouring of feeling from the masses as it was an idea propagated from the top by Japan's military rulers.[18] Even within what the Issei recognized to be the Japanese people, there were groups—the Okinawans and eta—whom they refused to treat as their fellows.

If one may draw a line that was the limit of the Issei's ethnic identity, it was there: it included all other Japanese except the Okinawans and eta, but no one else. But what is arresting is that not everyone outside the group was equally out. Some groups were perceived to be closer to the Japanese group, or more desirable associates, than others. The ranking for those outside groups ran something like this: Caucasians; Chinese; Koreans; the outcast Japanese groups; Filipinos, Mexicans, and Puerto Ricans (in no particular order); and Blacks.[19]

When it came time for the Nisei to marry, the hierarchy remained in force, but the distinctions within the Japanese group had blurred. Some Issei still wanted their children to marry someone from the right kind of family from the proper village in Hiroshima, but few Nisei knew or cared about such distinctions. More recognized the lines their parents drew between majority Japanese and the outcast Okinawans and eta, but that distinction, too, seems to have meant less to the second generation than to their parents. The majority of the Nisei chose Japanese Americans over other possible mates, but a significant minority began to venture beyond the bounds of national origin, especially after 1950. In the minds of some of the younger, more upwardly mobile Nisei, marriage to a White or Chinese American became an acceptable alternative. Beyond that, intermarriage was still forbidden. The few Nisei who married Filipinos, Mexicans, or Blacks found themselves ostracized by other Japanese Americans. By the 1950s, then, the distinctions at the top of the hierarchy had blurred, and some Nisei were willing to venture a bit further down the ladder, but the hierarchy remained in force, with few willing to tread its bottom rungs.[20]

In the Sansei generation, both men and women showed a muted adherence to the hierarchy of outgroup preferences they had inherited. First on the list were other Japanese Americans, though they were not so far ahead as in previous generations. Then, for some Sansei, came Whites. For others, notably ethnic activists, the second spot was held by Asians broadly conceived. All these groups were fundamentally within the margins of acceptability for most Sansei. After Asians and

Whites came people of darker pigment. For many Sansei, as for Debbie Hirano*, marriage to a Black or Chicano was "inconceivable," but to others it was quite possible, if still a distinctly lower preference.[21]

Outmarriage and Divorce

Many observers predicted that Japanese American intermarriages would prove unhappy for both partners. Outside pressures and intra-familial culture conflicts would result in a high percentage of divorce. In the early part of the century, Jesse Steiner thought that "social con-siderations—differences in standards of living, social customs, family system, ideals of home, and even moral standards" would make wrecks of many intermarriages. Those intermarriages that did not succumb to culture conflicts would be battered from outside: "Public opinion will not allow it to remain a merely personal matter." Other commentators, on the contrary, saw a happy future for interracial marriages. H. A. Millis predicted cheerfully that "many intermarriages will take place . . . the couples have lived happily."[22]

For the Issei generation, such optimism as Millis expressed hardly seems justified by the facts that currently are available. According to the 1942 War Relocation Authority census of West Coast Japanese then held in concentration camps, intermarried couples suffered a much higher rate of divorce and separation than did couples within the Japa-nese group. Less than 3 percent of in-married Issei men were divorced or separated from their wives. Over one-quarter of the out-married men were divorced or separated. The figures for women were lower: 1 percent and 13 percent for the in- and out-married, respectively.[23]

One should not, however, leap to the conclusion that all Issei inter-marriages were miserable affairs. If one-quarter of them ended in sepa-ration or divorce, then three out of four must have been relatively stable. In view of the pressures exerted on such marriages, especially the strains brought on by wartime imprisonment, perhaps it would be more appropriate to talk about rates of success than rates of failure. Some endured considerable strain and yet remained intact. George Miyamoto* married Donna Emerson* in Baltimore about 1923. The couple bounced from town to town for several years, had four daugh-ters along the way, and ended up in San Francisco on the eve of World War II. When George and the girls were due to be shipped off to prison camp, Donna insisted that nothing break up the family. The whole family lived in Topaz Relocation Center together. Divorce and separation were more common among intermarried couples than among homogeneous Japanese families, but they were hardly universal.[24]

Data for the Nisei and Sansei generations on the relationship between intermarriage and divorce are even harder to find. According to the WRA's 1942 census, among the small portion of older Nisei who were married before the war, the divorce rate for intermarriages was much higher than for homogamous Nisei unions. Twenty percent of the intermarried Nisei men were either divorced or separated, compared to 1 percent of the in-married couples. Eleven percent of the intermarried women were divorced or separated, compared to 1 percent of the in-married. But the size of the sample was so tiny that it is hard to be sure how much these numbers really mean. Besides, these numbers do not describe the experiences of those who married in the more liberal postwar climate. In any case, compared to other American ethnic groups, even the Nisei outmarriage divorce rate seems very low.[25]

That was precisely the point made by Andrew Lind in a 1964 study of interracial marriage and divorce in Hawaii. There were certain groups in Hawaii, he found, the Japanese among them, who had very low rates of divorce. He attributed this to their being highly "organized" groups—that is, ethnically cohesive and effective at controlling the behavior of group members. When people from a highly organized group married members of a disorganized group, their divorce rate was higher than the organized group's in-married divorce rate, but lower than the in-married divorce rate for the disorganized group. Lind wrote of the "striking . . . degree to which outmarriages of Filipinos and Koreans with persons of Japanese ancestry have proved so much more stable than the in-marriages of either Filipinos or Koreans. Thus, the divorce rate among Japanese-Filipino couples is only about half of what it is among in-married Filipino couples, this despite the strongly anti-Japanese sentiment engendered among Filipinos during World War II. The vastly higher viability of certain types of outmarriages as compared with in-marriages is further illustrated by the divorce rate of 28.5 [divorces per 100 marriages] among the Japanese-Korean couples as compared with 57.3 among in-married Korean couples." Thus, the success or failure of Nisei outmarriages depends on one's angle of vision. Compared with Japanese American in-marriages, the divorce rate for outmarriages was higher. But it was still not very high compared to divorce rates for non-Japanese people. At this writing, the Sansei generation is yet too young to sustain definitive analysis of divorce trends.[26]

Children of Japanese American Intermarriage

One of the major concerns of those who opposed intermarriage was the welfare of the children of those unions. In the early years of this century, the dire predictions of the naysayers had some merit. But as intermarriage increased and race relations improved, the pain and isolation of mixed people declined sharply.

Many of the children of Issei mixed marriages had difficulty establishing ethnic identities that satisfied them, and few identified with the part of them that was Japanese American. Demographically speaking, it seems that Japanese American mixed people were younger than other Nisei. Over 85 percent of the mixed people who were imprisoned by the War Relocation Authority during the Second World War were under twenty years of age in 1942. Only 55 percent of the other Nisei fell into that age range. This means that the parents of mixed people waited longer than other Issei to have children, especially since intermarried Issei were, on the average, older than those who married other Japanese.[27]

The general assumption of both Japanese and Caucasian commentators seems to have been that people of mixed ancestry would have an especially hard time in life because they would not be accepted by either Japanese or Americans. Jesse Steiner described the future of such people in Japan in dark terms in 1917. Citing Japanese anti-foreign prejudice as the cause of much unhappiness, he concluded that "even the majority of the Eurasian children of the better classes cannot be said to enjoy in Japan a favorable opportunity for proper development. Prejudice closes many doors in their faces and makes it hard for them to succeed unless gifted in a more than ordinary way." Even though White Americans had less prejudice about intermarriage, according to Steiner, mixed people would do little better in the United States. Nonetheless, Steiner took pains to dispel any notion that racial hybrids might be genetically inferior to their parents.

Sidney Gulick shared Steiner's concern for the biological prospects of the mixed population. He comforted biologists with the assurance that the offspring of matches between Japanese and Americans, unlike the progeny of horses and donkeys, would indeed be capable of reproducing themselves. Nor would they be "weak and defective," nor give any other evidence of genetic inferiority. Gulick did not think much of the social prospects of mixed people, however. In his view, unless the parents were wealthy and highly educated and could protect their children, the children would suffer social deprivation. Toyokichi Iyenaga and Kenosuke Sato went further than either Steiner or Gulick on the biological front. They pronounced Eurasians genetically superior. Hybridization would invigorate the stock of both Asians and Americans (whereas mating by groups that were "further apart" genetically—Blacks and Asians or Blacks and Whites—would degenerate both groups). Notwithstanding any such genetic advantages, Iyenaga and Sato thought Eurasian mixed people would probably be unhappy because of social discrimination.[28]

Karl Kawakami was the only commentator who was sanguine about the outlook for Amerasian children. An optimist by nature and very pleased with his own half-White children, Kawakami referred to all such people as "strikingly handsome, bright, intelligent and charming," the products of happy homes and the possessors of pleasant prospects. He felt that Caucasian-Japanese children would fare better than Black-White youngsters (whom, he assumed, led miserable lives) for three reasons. First, he said, Japanese and White Americans were more alike culturally than Negroes and Caucasians. Second, yellow was closer to white than black was, so any traces of non-White genes would wash out within two generations at most. Finally, according to Kawakami, American Whites did not hate the Japanese as much as they hated American Blacks.[29]

There seem to have been grounds for both Steiner's and Kawakami's positions. Some people of mixed American and Japanese parentage adjusted very well; others had a miserable time. Success or failure in adjusting to a biracial identity does not seem to have had much to do with whether the person in question resided near or away from other Japanese Americans, nor did it depend on education or social class.

Kathleen Tamagawa, daughter of a Japanese businessman and a midwestern socialite, did not like being half-Japanese and half-American. She opened her autobiography with these words: "The trouble with me is my ancestry. I really should not have been born." In her view, her Japanese father wanted her to be an American girl, her mother wanted her to be Japanese, and neither the Japanese nor the American public was much interested in having her around except as a curiosity. In America as a girl, "I felt myself to be a comicality, a toy. I was often spoken of as a 'Japanese doll', or worse still as the 'cute' little Japanese. . . . I had never been to Japan; I was as innocent of any real knowledge of the Japanese as those white Americans who visited us, but whatever I did, of good or of bad, was sure to be because I was Japanese." Her mother, too, treated both Kathleen and her father as exotic oddities. Sometimes people's curiosity turned to abuse: "There was the dirty-faced boy who sat on the back fence calling, 'Chink! Chink! Chink!' whenever I ventured into his presence in search of a playmate. He was a nice little boy, but my romantic background had fired his imagination. . . . Hurrying back to my mother and weeping real tears brought small comfort for she only said, 'Why didn't you tell him you were not a Chink?' She did not seem to understand my problem, for she never, even to her dying day, admitted that there was, or could, be a problem. . . . What could I have told the young warrior on the back fence? That I was not a 'Chink'—only a 'Jap'?" Living in Japan as a teenager was no better, for Kathleen never made much of a connection with Japanese culture, nor with any Japanese people. She felt as out of place and scorned there as in America. She wondered, "Would I ever be completely anything? . . . If there was anything I longed for above all others . . . it was the ordinary. To be simple—insignificant—and to melt inconspicuously into some environment." So she left her family (both father and mother in their respective ways had made her stand out), married a nondescript White American man, and settled into suburban homemaking. There she found the peaceful, anonymous, White American identity she had sought for so long.[30]

Kathleen Tamagawa never thought of making connections with other Japanese Americans. Her sole point of reference was the White American upper class. But other mixed people grew up among Japanese Americans, and some of them fared little better. Mildred Yoshi-kawa* had a hard time finding friends in Los Angeles in 1925, either among Whites or among Japanese Americans. Her teachers admired her intelligence and leadership abilities, and they thought her well-liked, but her friends described her situation in darker terms: "[Mildred] isn't Japanese, you know. Her mother is American and she doesn't look like a Japanese girl, she looks American. She is rather wild. . . . She comes here to the Union Church and she goes with Japanese boys some. But I don't think the boys like her very much, either. I think she has more Japanese than American friends. She says it is kind of hard on her because she looks like an American and if she goes with Japanese boys people look at her, but if she goes with American boys they soon find out she is Japanese."[31]

Peter, a half-Japanese, half-Mexican boy, had a tougher time of it in Los Angeles in the early 1920s. His Mexican mother died when he was very young, and he never established ties to any Mexican Americans. His father remarried, this time to a Japanese woman who did not like Peter. She beat him, ridiculed him, refused to feed him, and finally threw him out of the house. School authorities found him running unsupervised in the streets at age seven. Peter's father told him that "he wished that I had never been born; and at times I have even wished that myself. I have often wished that I were an American and not a Japanese or Mexican." Peter tried to make friends with Japanese boys rather than Mexicans, "because the Japanese would look down on me if I had too much to do with Mexicans," but he was not able to establish any solid relationships. A Japanese pastor took an interest in Peter, but got little support from his church. "Among the Japanese," he said, "there are very few boys who become delinquent because the entire group feels a sense of responsibility and it would be a disgrace to them to have a delinquent. In the case of Peter, however, it would rather seem that the group does not feel the same sense of responsibility, because he is only half Japanese." The local Japanese community attributed Peter's growing delinquency to his Mexican ancestry. Juvenile court authorities found Peter "an outcast" from both Japanese and Mexican American communities. They tried to find a foster home for Peter, but no one would take him because of his mixed ancestry. He finally was sent to the state reformatory.[32]

Dismal though these few instances seem, there were other mixed people whose lives turned out quite happily. Karl Kawakami's children, Clarke and Yuri, spoke positively of their Eurasianness when interviewed in 1968. Clarke was a Harvard-educated journalist, Yuri the wife of a Denver attorney. They grew up almost exclusively among

White people, with the exception of their father. They looked more White than Japanese. They reported very little discrimination from Whites and very little contact with Japanese Americans. Clarke worked before World War II for a Japanese news agency and married a Japanese movie star. Yuri's husband was White. Both advocated intermarriage—Yuri said it would strengthen the human race—and both spoke proudly of their children's marriages to people of Portuguese and Mexican ancestry. Like the Kawakamis, the offspring of Junzo Hachimonji* identified with their non-Japanese mother. Hachimonji was a career Navy man and naturalized U.S. citizen who married a Black woman and had six children. Only two of the young Hachimonjis had married by the time the United States entered World War II, one to a Negro and the other to a man of mixed Black and Chinese parentage. None of the family had much to do with other Japanese Americans. Doubtless that was partly their own choice, but it also reflected the particular aversion most other Japanese Americans felt to contact with Blacks. Most children of mixed American and Japanese parentage, happy or unhappy, seem to have grown up away from other Japanese.[33]

Observers of Japanese-American intermarriages spoke a good deal of pious nonsense as to the supposed qualities of the offspring. The general consensus, even of those friends of the Japanese who opposed intermarriage, was that Eurasians were beautiful and smart. Sidney Gulick spoke highly of their mental ability and stated further that "there is a tendency to striking beauty in American-Japanese." A Seattle high school teacher named Rowell had taught some Amerasian girls and said they were all "very attractive . . . and splendid students." The *San Francisco Examiner* reported the genius-level IQ scores of Sophronia, John, Dorothy, and Donald Aoki and suggested that "the unusual brilliance of the children is due to the mixture of races." Kawakami found Eurasians equally beautiful and intelligent. Further, Kawakami believed that mixed people invariably took after their Western parent. "In appearance, in temperament, in manner such children are so completely American that one can hardly detect Japanese blood in their veins." A White observer, H. G. Schroeder, thought just the opposite. He saw the Eurasian children he knew as "characteristically Japanese" in features and habits.[34] It may have been that Kawakami dealt only with mixed children—his own—who in fact looked very Caucasian, and that Schroeder had experience only with those who looked Japanese. But it strikes this observer that people have a tendency to note the characteristics which are different from their own and generalize from those qualities as they view Eurasians. Japanese people, used to looking at Asian features, looked at Eurasians and pronounced them White. Whites, used to Caucasian features, looked at the same people and pronounced them Asians. Thus, to White Americans, Kathleen Tamagawa was a "Japanese doll." To Japanese she looked fully American. In fact, her features probably fell somewhere in between, blending both parts of her inheritance.

What emerges, then, from this description of the children of Issei intermarriages? Some seem to have achieved, or been blessed with, means of comfortable adjustment to their biracial status. Others did not do so well. For the most part, but not exclusively, those who adjusted well did not live among nor attempt to identify themselves with Japanese Americans. They sought to identify themselves with the social group of their non-Japanese parent. They did this in some cases because the Japanese would not have them. Some found their non-Japanese group of choice willing to take them in, and they found a comfortable niche. Others, like Kathleen Tamagawa, had a harder time finding a non-Japanese place for their ethnic identities to reside.

The half-Sansei children of Nisei intermarriages fared, on the whole, rather better than did mixed people a generation earlier, although their lives were not without trials. Some of the early mixed Sansei had a difficult adjustment to make because they had poor starts in life. Since intermarriage and mixed babies were frowned upon before World War II, some mixed children found themselves abandoned. There were nineteen such children, most of them infants or toddlers, in the Japanese Children's Home of Los Angeles when the war broke out. Others were placed in foster homes or put up for adoption. Such foster or adoptive parents were almost never Japanese. But most mixed children were raised in somewhat more comfortable circumstances than these, with at least one consistent parent and a reasonably stable pattern of existence.[35]

Although many Japanese Americans were ill-disposed toward the mixed offspring of their friends and relatives, more, probably, were won over by that special charisma that nearly all toddlers possess in abundance. However much an Issei grandparent might oppose his or her child's intermarriage, when the first grandchild arrived some sort of reconciliation was seldom far behind. Non-Japanese people, too, seem to have been relatively open—to Japanese-White mixtures, at least, and sometimes to other combinations as well. In this respect, White-Japanese children fared better than those who were half White and half Black. Ursula Thrush, head of a preschool in San Francisco, dealt with many interracial children and found that "Asian mixtures do not have the defensiveness that black mixtures do." Barbara Ricks, a White-Indian mix herself, had two sons, one by a Japanese-Hawaiian father, the other by a Black man. She found her son of Japanese parentage had an easier time in his early years because "less bigotry is directed toward Asian mixtures."[36]

Though Sansei Eurasians were seldom actively discriminated against, the way they were seen by Whites on the one hand and by Japanese Americans on the other reveals much about the way Americans conceive of racial groupings. In terms of such physical attributes as skin color, eye shape, and hair color and texture, the mixed children Sister Julie Kelley studied in Hawaii in the late 1950s fell, on the average, midway between their Japanese and their White parents. Yet Japanese Americans looked at them and saw Whites. One Hawaiian mixed person complained, "The Japanese in my class were a smug majority who had definite prejudices toward other nationalities in general. I was determined to be liked and accepted [by them, but] I was not Japanese as far as they were concerned, so that I was never quite one of the bunch." One day, before a class debate in which she was scheduled to take part, she overheard "one of the class ringleaders convincing the others in our group to choose another boy and girl because they were Japanese," while she, in the view of that ringleader, was not. Whites would look at the same Eurasians and see Japanese. Gene Levine and Colbert Rhodes, in an otherwise fine sociological study of Japanese Americans, betrayed this tendency when they decided that "mixed marriages would seem to breed mixed marriages" and that the children of Nisei intermarriages "follow in the exogamous footsteps of their parents." What they meant was that these mixed people were dating and marrying Whites. By their reasoning, a Eurasian who married a Japanese American was marrying within his or her own group, but a mixed person choosing a Caucasian spouse was an intermarrier.[37]

With which parental culture, which half of him- or herself, a mixed child identified depended a good deal on the child and on his or her parents. Some children of Nisei intermarriages chose to identify themselves with their Japanese side, calling themselves Japanese and associating mainly with other Japanese Americans. Some chose the non-Japanese side. Most had friends from both groups. But there were almost never enough mixed people in one place for them to fashion a separate subculture of mixed people after the pattern of the *metis* of Canada (see Chapter 12). A stable, intermediate identity does not seem to have been a option for very many. Often one parent would pressure the child to identify strongly with that parent's heritage, insisting, for example, that the child attend Japanese language school. An observer might expect that the ethnic character of one's surroundings would be decisive; that is, that a mixed person raised among Whites would identify with Whites, while one raised among Japanese Americans would see him- or herself as Japanese. Yet a study of Eurasians in Washington State in the 1970s turned up surprising evidence that about half the subjects chose to identify, not with the group among which they were raised, but rather with the group that was in the *minority* during their childhood. This identification with the outgroup of their childhood may have stemmed in part from the tendency of Whites to label Eurasians Japanese, and of Japanese to label them Whites.[38]

Often one's choice of identity depended on how one looked. Sue Kunitomi Embrey's older son looked more like his father; hence, he associated mainly with Whites and saw himself chiefly as White, although during his teenage years he came to accept his Japanese half as well. His younger brother, by contrast, looked more Japanese, was more readily taken for Japanese by others, and saw himself chiefly as Japanese. Jim Morishima tells a story of a woman named Kimiko Johnson*, whom on the basis of her last name and appearance he took to be a Sansei married to a Caucasian. She had a good deal to do with other Japanese Americans and for a time even worked for the Asian American Studies department at the University of Washington. When Morishima asked her about her husband, she replied cryptically that she was not married and had never been married, but would show him his mistake. Soon she reappeared with a Black youth whom she introduced as her brother. The brother spoke in Black dialect and identified himself as Black. The two Johnsons had the same set of parents —a Black father and a Japanese American mother—yet they identified themselves differently, one as Japanese, one as Black, because that is the way they looked. When telling this story, Morishima is quick to point out his belief that an individual of mixed parentage is entitled to identify with whichever group he or she chooses, or with both. His point is simply that the way one looks has a powerful effect on the way one is treated and, ultimately, on the choice of identity one makes.[39]

Some mixed children of Nisei intermarriages were buffeted between their two identities, unsure which to choose, or even whether it was possible to embrace one or the other. Some of these managed in time to find peace and strength in choosing to be *multi-ethnic* individuals. Ai, a woman of Japanese, Black, Native American, and White ancestry, was pressured by Black fellow students at the University of Arizona to join the Black students' union and "be immersed in the black struggle." She did not feel comfortable doing that because the Japanese part of her was important too. She took courses on Asian culture, which she found pacifying. Finally she decided "to be loyal to myself as a multiracial person. . . . People whose concept of themselves is largely dependent on their racial identity and superiority feel threatened by a multiracial person. The insistence that one must align oneself with this or that race is basically racist. And the notion that without a racial identity a person can't have any identity perpetuates racism . . . there is no identity for me 'out there.' I have had to step back into my heart's own cathedral" to gain a sense of self.[40]

Joy Nakamura* underwent a similar odyssey at a large eastern university. She grew up in Brooklyn, in most respects a normal, not-very-observant Jewish girl in a Jewish neighborhood, except that her father was Japanese. She could recall only a few instances of any sort of discrimination from family, friends, or strangers. "Everyone liked my father," she wrote, "and everyone thought my long, straight dark hair was beautiful, and my slightly slanted eyes made my face pretty." Her father seldom talked about his childhood in California, her Japanese American relatives were far away, and although she felt somehow connected to Japan, she never had an opportunity to explore the connection until she went to college. "I met more Asians my first year [in college] than I had ever known. When one Japanese-American called me on the phone to invite me to join a Japanese-American discussion group, I was very excited. I went to the group meetings a few times, but my 'white-half' began to feel uncomfortable when the others began putting down whites," so she stopped going. She took classes on Japanese language and culture and enrolled in a seminar on Asian Americans. "I was desperately trying to find myself as an Asian-American woman, but I was not succeeding." She had clashes with her White boyfriend over racial issues, and she tried to ignore her Jewishness. Pressure from a Black activist friend helped Nakamura clarify her feelings. He said, " 'You must decide if you are yellow, or if you are white. Are you part of the Third World, or are you against it?' I laughed at his question. How could I possibly be one and not the other? I was born half-yellow and half-white. I could not be one and not the other anymore than I could cut myself in half and still exist as a human being." At length she decided, "I do not feel guilty about not recognizing my Asianness; I have already done so. I have just readjusted my guilt feelings about ignoring my Jewish half. . . . My Jewishness is something that can be easily hidden. I do not want to hide that fact. I want to tell the world that I am a Jew. . . . I am not an Asian-American in the same way the others are. . . . My uniqueness separates me from everyone else. This is a scary idea. I am all alone. I cannot even find group solidarity from a gathering of Eurasians; we are all too different." Joy Nakamura's embrace of both her Japanese and her Jewish identities was not achieved without a good deal of inner conflict. Yet it was a lasting achievement. She is today a Jew and a Japanese American, and she remains well-adjusted to both her ethnic identities.[41]

Life has become easier for the children of Japanese American intermarriage. In the early decades of this century, most observers predicted social isolation and ethnic disorientation for people of mixed parentage. They were not disappointed, although some mixed people seem to have adjusted well. In particular, children of mixed marriages seem to have been shunned by other Japanese Americans. Children of Nisei intermarriages did not suffer such isolation, however. The greater degree of acceptance they received allowed many to choose Japanese American identities, others to align themselves with their non-Japanese parent's ethnic group, and some to embrace both parts of their inheritance.

Summary of Part I

What conclusions may one draw about the nature of Japanese American intermarriage? Outmarriage was very low in the first generation, though higher in the frontier period than after communities had formed. There were slightly more intermarried Issei women than men, despite a sex ratio that pushed in the opposite direction. The rate of outmarriage did not increase much among the prewar Nisei. It was much lower than for other second-generation immigrant groups. Despite the yearning of many Nisei to be accepted as Americans they were discriminated against, and this contributed to the low intermarriage rate. The bulk of the Nisei generation made marriage choices during and just after the highly segregated war years. From the 1950s to the 1980s there was a rapid increase in the rate of outmarriage as a concomitant of Japanese American class mobility, geographical dispersion, and a general softening of ethnic barriers in America in those years. Japanese American females far outstripped males in the rate of their outmarriage during the Nisei and Sansei generations, although recently the men have begun to catch up. The predominance of women among the Japanese American intermarriers flies in the face of Robert Merton's hypogamy theory. As we shall see, this idea finds little support among other American minority groups.

Some of this was related to the images other Americans held of Japanese. The image of Issei males as a sexual threat rapidly passed to the emasculated Charlie Chan of the Nisei years; that relatively unattractive image dominated non-Japanese people's thinking about Japanese American men and impeded outmarriage well into the 1960s, although Japanese American men have begun to appear more attractive to non-Japanese women in recent years. By contrast, the exotic image of Japanese American women since about 1940 has enhanced intermarriage possibilities.

During the time when the Issei and Nisei were making their mar-

riage choices, most Japanese and most non-Japanese Americans reso-
lutely opposed intermarriage. Japanese American communities, where
they existed, were especially effective in hindering outmarriage. By
the Sansei era, such controls were largely gone except for the opposition of a few Asian ethnic activists.

There were significant regional differences in intermarriage patterns. Structural factors—tightly knit Japanese communities and a
nearly even male-female ratio—inhibited Japanese outmarriage in Hawaii despite a Hawaiian cultural disposition in favor of intermarriage.
Consequently, outmarriage in Hawaii was always lower than on the
mainland, although it did show a steady increase with the generations, particularly during World War II. By contrast, structural factors
—the lack of Japanese American communities—allowed the intermarriage rate to be much higher in those parts of the country where few
Japanese lived.

Another structural factor—class—is probably important to intermarriage behavior, but existing historical materials do not permit sys-
tematic class analysis. There is some suggestion that people at the
top and bottom of society felt freer to engage in interracial sex and
marriage than those in the middle.

Unbeknown to outsiders, Japanese of the immigrant generation
made distinctions among themselves—between ordinary Japanese,
eta, and Okinawans, and between people from different parts of Japan.
These distinctions helped shape marriage choices. In fact, the Issei
exhibited a hierarchy of preferences both within and outside what we
ordinarily conceive to be the Japanese American group. That hierarchy
remained unchanged over three generations, except that Nisei and
Sansei lost track of distinctions within the Japanese American group
and showed themselves ever more willing to accept people from further down the ladder.

Statistics on intermarriage and divorce are sketchy, but those that
exist suggest a higher divorce rate among intermarriers than among
purely Japanese couples.

The children of Issei intermarriages seem to have had a considerable struggle with their ethnic identities, and very few were allowed
or chose to identify with their Japanese half. In the more relaxed racial
atmosphere of the 1950s and '60s, children of Nisei intermarriages
chose various responses to their ambivalent ethnic identities and sel-

dom suffered the ostracism experienced by the previous generation. By the 1970s and '80s, a significant number began to claim both parts of their biracial identity.

The following chapter describes a particular variety of Japanese American intermarriage. In some senses, it is part of the story of Japanese Americans, but in the main it is an international story.

II

MADAM BUTTERFLY
REVISITED

5. American Men and Japanese Women after World War II

The romantic encounter after World War II between Japanese women and American military men has long fascinated people on both sides of the Pacific. When the war ended in 1945, American soldiers took over Japan as a conquered province. By the time they gave it back in 1952, tens of thousands of American men had become involved with Japanese women. Some enjoyed casual dates, some transient affairs, some temporary living arrangements, some enduring marriages. Harassed at first by Americans and Japanese alike, many couples split rather than endure the pressure. Others stuck it out and lived together in Japan or in America. Thousands of children came from these marriages and fleeting unions. Some never knew their fathers, growing up under their mothers' care alone. Others did not know their mothers either. They were orphans, cast upon the uncertain benevolence of relatives, children's homes, or private families.

The experiences of these latter-day Madam Butterflies, their American mates, and their mixed children have, during the last four decades, provided the material for a host of movies, novels, television shows, magazine articles, and scholarly studies, in both Japanese and English.[1] Some of that outpouring of creative energy has resulted in sensible treatment of its subject. But much nonsense has also issued forth. Some sources tell one part of the story, some another; no one source tells it all. The tasks here are to survey the material on the relationships between Japanese women and American men, to attempt a balanced analysis, and to provide an international comparison for the purely American intermarriages that appear in other chapters.

GIs and Japanese Women

Fear attended the first meetings of Japanese and Americans after the bombing of Hiroshima and Nagasaki. Japanese civilians, prepared by years of propaganda, expected the American invaders to choose rape and pillage as their mode of greeting. The Americans, mindful of the suicidal zeal of some Japanese soldiers in the South Pacific and conditioned to think of the Japanese as vicious and treacherous, expected to see grandmothers defending their homes with sharpened bamboo poles and children creeping into American bedrooms at night with knives in their teeth. Very soon it became clear that neither side was as fearsome as the other thought. The emperor's surrender message convinced nearly every Japanese not to resist, and the Americans turned out to be less barbaric than was previously supposed.

Some Japanese like to remember the early months of the Occupation as a time of gentle reconciliation, with the Americans graciously sharing their abundance with their erstwhile enemies and helping them rebuild their shattered nation. Some of the Americans who were in Japan at the time hold the same opinion. But those were not, in fact, such happy days. The fabric of Japanese society had been rent, as much by wartime shortages as by the bombs that levelled Japanese cities. Economic life was at a standstill. Food was scarce. Hundreds of thousands were homeless. People were dead, wounded, or demoralized, and the living harbored deep resentments toward their conquerors. But to show outward signs of bitterness served no useful purpose; besides, it ran counter to the Japanese ethic that one did not openly confront others with hostility. Since the Americans were clearly in command and must be obeyed, one might as well cooperate. Cooperate the Japanese did, repressing hostile feelings or redirecting them against safe targets: the politicians and military men who had led them so recently. Secure in their role as conquerors, the Americans soon lost their fear of the Japanese people and settled down to reshaping Japanese society. Nonetheless, the war's bitter memories lingered just below the surface of Japanese and American consciousness.[2]

In such a climate of barely suppressed mutual fear and hatred, it is remarkable that some intimate, personal relationships came into being. Japanese men and women worked with their conquerors in rebuilding their country. Some became friends. Others formed recreational relationships. Very soon after the troops landed, early in the fall of 1945, bars, nightclubs, and houses of prostitution appeared around American bases. There, encounters between GIs and Japanese women often became intimate long before they became personal. Just how intimate was clear on June 28, 1946, when Japanese radio announced the first recorded birth of a baby of mixed parentage.[3] Some Japanese women took up with American men as an extension of their wartime professions; more entered prostitution or shady entertainment out of a desperate need for food and shelter. Japan's utter devastation, with people starving in the streets, drove previously respectable women to barter their bodies for food and shelter for themselves or their families.[4]

The attentiveness, grace, and sexual ingenuity of Japanese bar hostesses and prostitutes quickly passed into legend. That legend encouraged other men to try their luck. Like soldiers in other wars of conquest, the Americans in Japan did not hesitate to eschew whatever moral standards they had brought with them and pursue the local women with relish.[5] They showed a degree of enthusiasm that alarmed their superiors. Six months into the Occupation, the Eighth Army's Chief Surgeon, Col. Phillip Cook, reported that 27 percent of his men had venereal diseases of one sort or another. How many brought those diseases with them or got them from other soldiers is unclear, but there can be little doubt that much disease was passed from soldier to soldier via Japanese women. Out of these shadowy encounters on the outskirts of American military posts came an image that has endured: the Japanese woman as sexually enthusiastic courtesan. Gerry McDonough's retelling of a sexual exploit brings the image to life: "Keiko-san slipped into the quilts . . . pressed her extraordinarily smooth-skinned body to [mine] and said, 'Show me how American man make love.'" This image owed something to the exotic, erotic preconceptions held by American men who went overseas, but it had more to do with the meeting of libidinous American men and impoverished Japanese women in the early years of the Occupation. The image has colored relationships between American men and Asian women ever since. The Japanese, based on their experience, came out with a similar picture of American men. One reporter on the scene recalled that "the Japanese, in general, looked upon Americans as sex-obsessed."[6]

Alongside these informal connections there also grew in 1946 and 1947 more enduring relationships between GIs and Japanese women. Some of these ultimately became marriages. More were long-term living arrangements, where the woman would live near a military base and keep house for her GI partner as long as he was in Japan. Some of the women who were involved in such unions sought or were willing to accept the companionship of American men for much the same reasons as those who went into prostitution. They needed to eat, and American soldiers could help them do that. Some were able to extract a measure of financial security not only for themselves but for their families as well. Bok-Lim Kim did social work among the Asian wives of U.S. servicemen and found that many had economic motives for marrying: "The women considered themselves rescued from their insecure socioeconomic position. . . . The United States evoked romantic impressions of physical and economic security. . . . Marriage to American soldiers symbolized eternal security and happiness."[7]

Other Japanese women chose American men in part because there were so few Japanese men available. Hundreds of thousands of young Japanese men died in the war, and many more did not return from China or the Pacific until many months after the end of hostilities. For some Japanese in their middle and late twenties, marriage to an American was preferable to no marriage at all. Some evidence of this situation may be found in the fact that on average, the Japanese women who married American men were older than their sisters who married Japanese.[8]

It may be suggested that there was something distinctive about the background, personality, or aspirations of certain Japanese women which drew them to unions with the conquerors. More than half of the Japanese population lived in rural areas in 1945, yet most of the women who married American men came from the big cities of Tokyo, Yokohama, Osaka, and Fukuoka. Since those areas housed the main concentrations of the Occupation troops, it is not surprising that it was mainly women from those areas who married American men. The fathers of these women included few farmers, but otherwise they ran the gamut of Japanese society from corporate magnate to day laborer, with especially large numbers of small proprietors. Their occupational distribution was thus typical of the urban population of the time. These women averaged ten years of education—just about the norm for Japanese women. Thus, there was not much in their backgrounds to separate the war brides from other Japanese women.[9]

George DeVos and his students at the University of California thought they found a distinctive personality pattern among the Japanese women who married American men and took up residence in northern California. They saw the women they interviewed as passive-aggressive: outwardly subservient to the men around them but inwardly demanding and usurping of family power and authority. DeVos and his colleagues went so far as to describe these women as marginally pathological. But the Berkeley scholars' conclusions were marred by several limitations of technique: (1) They used the Thematic Apperception Test to evaluate their subjects. The TAT is a suggestive interpretive tool, but it is also highly susceptible to tester bias. (2) It is clear from their hypotheses that DeVos and his students assumed their client population to be emotionally unbalanced and then went out looking for pathology. They wrote: "Our guiding hypotheses saw these women as . . . rebellious, . . . overtly passive, . . . subtly controlling, . . . masochistic, . . . passive-aggressive." With such hypotheses, it is hardly remarkable that the Berkeley researchers found pathology. (3) By their own admission, the authors found a number of war brides who did not fit their model, who were "relatively well adjusted." But DeVos and his associates could not find space to describe those women's experiences in their report.[10]

If there is no serious evidence that the Japanese women who chose mates from the Occupation troops differed from their urban sisters in background or personality, there is some indication they differed in aspirations. The Occupation was a time when Japanese culture was changing rapidly.[11] Among the many changes was the emergence of a new kind of woman, one oriented toward the culture of the West and less willing than her elders to assume the docile posture of the traditional Japanese female. Ijichi Junsei wrote at the time that "the emancipation of women [was] much encouraged by the Occupation regime." He described the groping of Japanese women for a "new interpretation and philosophy of love and marriage . . . to achieve free love and free marriage with their newly-gained freedom," and concluded that "the impact of American culture upon Japanese women is undermining the foundations of their manners and morals." Ijichi complained that some Japanese women wanted to know a wider range of experiences than was appropriate to their traditional situation, wanted higher status than had previously been their lot, and wanted to be treated like Western ladies by their men.[12]

There is some evidence that these new Japanese women, still a minority, had trouble finding Japanese men they were willing to marry. Daniel Okimoto, a Japanese American, reported in the 1960s that "some of the most interesting women I have met in Japan have had to forego the usual aspirations of marriage and children; not many men are willing to wed those who shatter established roles in order to develop their minds or pursue professional careers."[13] What would become full-blown rebellion—incipient women's liberation—in Okimoto's day was only the first stirring of unrest two decades earlier. But it was enough to ensure that more than a few ambitious, forward-looking Japanese women would have a problem finding Japanese husbands with whom they could get along.

Some such women found American men to be their answer. One was Matsue Kobayashi*. The beautiful, strong-willed daughter of an old samurai family, she chafed at the restrictions placed on her as a young Japanese woman. She wanted to see the world, to experience all that life had to offer. Frustrated by her family's opposition to her desire to become an actress, she sang with a band for a while until they put a stop to that, too. She got a job in Manchuria, as much to get away from parental scrutiny as anything. There she was pursued by a number of men. But she did not marry any of them because, in the words of her daughter, "She always felt that they weren't going to go anywhere." She saw her opportunity for escape in the person of Phillip Fitzpatrick*, who possessed the status and relative wealth of an American soldier in Japan. Her daughter recalled: "I think a lot of the reason she married my father was the money. . . . Even though he was, I think, a private or something. . . . At least she would get to come to America and the children would have a better start, better chance at education, things like that." She carried her half-white baby proudly in the market as a badge of her association with an American and her liberation from the traditional role of a Japanese wife.[14]

Nobuko "Cherry" Sakuramoto's biographer tells of Cherry's similar pride at being associated with an Australian soldier—not only because of the status he reflected on her but also because of his exotic good looks and his very un-Japanese attentiveness to her comfort: "Cherry felt it strange but exciting to be walking in step with the Goshujin, he so tall, she barely up to his shoulder, a man who walked on the outside of the pavement and helped her over ditches and gutters. She intercepted sidelong glances from other Japanese and she was proud of the way they stared at the barbarian's height and fairness." Ritsuko Parks reported that similar qualities attracted her to her husband: his care for her as a person and his ability to take her away from Japan. She told a reporter for *Ebony* magazine, "I like being married to an American man. In most things my husband puts me first. In Japan the husband is the boss. It is true that many Japanese girls married Americans just to get away from Japan and come to this country, but most of us love our husbands."[15]

The women who chose American men, then, tended to be urban dwellers from a variety of backgrounds, who were united in their interest in pursuing life beyond the restrictions that bound their more traditional sisters. What about the men? What made them different from other Americans, those who did not marry Japanese women? All the American soldiers who went to Japan were far away from home. Most were young and single. There were very few American women in Japan, and most of those were preempted by officers. Yet why did some enlisted men find enduring relationships with Japanese women while others limited themselves to casual affairs at most? Here a distinctive pattern emerges in background and personality. Most of the men seem to have come from blue-collar homes. A surprising number, perhaps as many as half, came from farms and small towns. These concentrations in the lower middle class and in rural environments were not fully representative of the American population at large. In other demographic aspects—age and education, for example—the men who took Japanese mates do not seem to have differed greatly from their fellows.[16]

DeVos and his helpers predicted emotional instability in the husbands of war brides to complement the pathology they postulated for the wives. They "hypothesized that these men would have serious questions about their personal adequacy, . . . lack self-assertion, . . . feel a need to act aggressive, but more from a defensive compensatory standpoint than from a direct impulse expression. . . . For these men the appeal of the Japanese woman would . . . not be in terms of companionship or mutual enjoyment, but almost soley from the standpoint of serving to fulfill strong dependent needs." And that is what these researchers found: they concluded that these intermarrying American men felt generally inadequate, especially regarding their masculinity; that they were unable to cope with a host of normal social relationships, particularly those involving American women, whom they saw as too aggressive; and that they therefore sought out Japanese women, whom they perceived to be docile, submissive, and unthreatening. Furthermore, DeVos and his associates concluded that these were symptoms of fundamental maladjustment on the part of most of their male subjects.[17]

It would be easy to dismiss DeVos and company's findings about these men as merely the predictable results of fixed preconceptions carried through sham investigation, if it were not for corroborating evidence from other sources. Bok-Lim Kim found similar characteristics in the husbands of war brides she studied. These men, she said, did not marry their Asian wives for their beauty, education, personality, or social status. Rather, they chose them to suit the men's peculiar dependency needs: "They perceived these women as a limited threat to their masculinity compared to American women. . . . For the first time they felt accepted by solicitous, unquestioning women who respected them." Almost unanimously, her male patients declared of their Asian brides, "She is the first person who makes me feel important." Admittedly, Kim did not deal with a random sample of Asian-American marriages, but only with those whose members sought help from social service agencies. It seems logical to assume there would be more maladjusted people in such a group than in the general run of the population.[18]

Yet other sources lend some support to her view. Jean Grogan* spoke about her father's less than admirable character traits. Besides a violent temper, she said, he had "a big failure complex," made worse by his inability to rise above sergeant. He was the child of an alcoholic father and a mother who was "a domineering, strong-willed bitch," said his daughter, and he was "like an outcast." He felt inferior about his lack of height and social graces. "He was a shrimp, and I think he got pushed around a lot. . . . He's handicapped socially. He can't mix with people. . . . It's almost embarrassing to watch him interact with people because he's so clumsy. He offends people without realizing it." In Grogan's estimate, her father took a Japanese wife at least partly because he felt that she would treat him like a big man in spite of his flaws.[19]

Still, yearnings for a nurturing, supportive Asian wife need not be taken for signs of emotional ill health. Other men may have chosen Japanese wives with the same qualities in mind, yet without the neurotic motivations perceived by Lim, DeVos, and Grogan. One GI told an *Ebony* reporter what attracted him to his wife: "Man, try to find a girl on Seventh Avenue that is as kind and sweet as these little mooses. They appreciate the least little thing you do for them." Isobel Carter interviewed Australians who married Japanese women and reported, "The small-boned delicacy and fragility of the more attractive Japanese girls was very appealing to the womanless troops. Used to Australian girls who demanded co-partnership, they found the polite submissiveness, the desire to please, of the Japanese *musume* intoxicating." There is male chauvinism here, and forthright appreciation of female attractiveness. But there is little to indicate that emotional instability was the norm.[20]

GIs met Japanese women, then, in circumstances guaranteed to yield romance. Young men far from home, possessing the power and status of conquerors, encountered women who badly needed a square meal. Add to this the fact that many of the women were highly Westernized and sought the nurturant husband more typical in America, while many of the men were looking for women to wait on them, and the prospects for dating and mating were good. The prospects for successful marriage, however, were not so good. Many of the men were looking for the docile Asian women that American stereotypes had led them to expect, while many of the women were looking for men who would allow them to leave that role. It was a situation ripe for conflict.

Dating and Marrying

GIs met the Japanese women who would become their girlfriends and brides in the service industries that sprang up around American bases. Sometimes the women worked as entertainers or bar hostesses. More often, women who entered steady relationships with American men held more prosaic jobs. Mishiko Kawashima met Paul Shaw while ushering at the GI movie house in Gifu. Cherry Sakuramoto made beds and cleaned up after a group of Australian soldiers at Kure. Emiko Hibino* worked for the PX in Tokyo. Other women met the Americans who would become their husbands and lovers through mutual friends.[21]

The young women were not familiar with the courtship behavior of their American suitors. Dating was not a Japanese custom, but they quickly adjusted to being asked to go out for movies, picnics, and boat rides. They enjoyed the consideration that the men showed by opening doors for them and helping them on with their coats.

Neither the Army nor individual Americans in Japan seem to have brought much pressure to bear to stop GIs from dating Japanese women. The Army's anti-fraternization rules simply proscribed public displays of affection or staying past eleven at night in Japanese homes. Even those rules were not rigidly enforced. The general Army ethos tolerated dates between GIs and Japanese women.[22] In fact, according to William Worden, the occupation authorities sometimes encouraged dating, consorting with prostitutes, and even informal living arrangements in order to prevent soldiers from taking what they saw as the more drastic step of entering into formal marriages.[23] A lot of individual soldiers who did not mind their comrades dating Japanese women or visiting Japanese prostitutes expressed anger and disbelief at the thought of a marriage. More just dismissed the possibility as preposterous, much after the fashion of General Webster in James Michener's novel *Sayonara:* "First-class men sometimes fall in love with native girls, of course they do. But they get over it. They forget the girls and they go home. They go back to work."[24]

Insofar as they addressed the interracial romance issue at all, the military (and the U.S. government, generally) bent their energies toward keeping GIs from marrying the Japanese women they loved. When they failed in this, the government tried to keep the Japanese spouses out of the United States. In December 1945 Congress passed Public Law 271, which came to be known as the War Brides Act. It was designed to enable American GIs to bring back the spouses and children they had acquired overseas by waiving the usual immigration quotas, visa requirements, and restrictions on "physical and mental defectives" in their cases. But Congress assumed that American soldiers, sailors, and airmen would be marrying Caucasians. The law was based on studies of GI needs in Europe and excluded spouses of "racially ineligible races"—i.e., Japanese. This distinction was based on the 1924 act that forbade Asian immigration. That act was amended during the war to allow Chinese immigration, because it was not seemly for the United States to continue to deny entry to its Asian allies. But the Japanese were another matter. They must stay out, including the wives and children of U.S. servicemen in Japan. The effect was that Germans and Italians were free to marry American servicemen and come to the United States, but Japanese were not.[25]

By 1947, however, many American GIs had married Japanese women and were clamoring for permission to bring them home. In response, Congress passed an amendment to the War Brides Act that allowed Japanese spouses to enter during 1947 and 1948. That act expired before more than a tiny number of husbands could fight through bureaucratic opposition and bring their families home. After another series of protests by intermarried GIs, Congress approved another period, from August 1950 to February 1952, during which soldiers might take their families to America. But during those months most American troops were tied down in Korea and unable to take their brides home. Moreover, if a soldier died in Korea, his wife had to stay in Japan. If he was wounded, he was likely to be sent straight home from Korea, leaving his wife stranded. Finally, in late 1952, Congress passed the McCarran-Walter Act, which removed overt racial restrictions on immigration and put narrow, racially motivated national quotas in their place. That meant no increase in immigration by most of the world's darker peoples, for their countries were given tiny allotments. The Japanese war brides fared better, however, for they were designated nonquota immigrants and were now legally free to come.[26]

Legal restrictions were only one impediment to intermarriage. The military's unparalleled ability to create bureaucratic obstacles was another. To get permission to marry a Japanese woman, a soldier had to fill out an endless parade of documents. He had to get his commanding officer's permission to marry, which usually meant refusal and a lecture on the virtues of Anglo-Saxon purity. He had to endure a similar, well-intentioned harangue from his chaplain and perhaps harassment from his peers as well. One soldier, intent on marrying a Korean woman, complained: "The minute I told my commanding officer that I was going to marry Yung-ja, he acted strange. He asked me to write my parents about my intended marriage. He also asked me to talk with the base chaplain. The trouble was that my parents had been dead for more than ten years and I am not a church-goer. Even the guys in my barrack started to act concerned. They invited me for drinks and showed pictures of their sisters and cousins." His wife-to-be reported that she also was harassed: "As soon as people around my office [at an American military base] heard about my engagement to John, they looked down on me. I was made to feel dirty and unworthy. Some soldiers asked me to go out with them obviously thinking that I was now an easy mark for propositions. I quit my work rather than put up with such nonsense." Some commanders went beyond racial considerations to discourage a marriage between any American soldier and an Asian woman. An Asian American, Vietnam-era soldier articulately expressed frustrations felt not only in the 1960s but in the 1940s and '50s as well:

First, I went to my section chief, and he said, "Man you don't want to marry one of these 'gooks' over here. They're not civilized, and if you take her back home with you, people won't be able to handle her cause she's not civilized," and so I said, "Well, that's my problem." So then I went to the Gunnery Sergeant, and he lectured me for like all day, and he told me to come back. And I came back, and he lectured me and told me to come back again. Then I got to the First Sergeant and he did the same thing. Finally, I got to the CO and he ran down all the bureaucratic stuff that I'd have to go through before I could even get the consent to get married. You see, you have to go through this waiting period, and they make you wait until after your rotation time, like if you have five months before you're moved out, then they'll give you a waiting period of six months so they can get you out of there.

Man, they'd say stuff like, "She's not an American so she wouldn't be able to handle it in the States; and you wouldn't be able to trust her once you got back to the States." They said, "Okay. You think you want to marry her now, but that's because there are no round-eyed chicks around." They said that to me, you know, I'm Asian too, but they said that to me. They'd always talk about "round-eyed" chicks—you know, Caucasian chicks. They'd say, "And once you get back, you'll see all those blondes and stuff, and you'll look at your wife and she'll be this old farmer chick—this gook—and you'll want to get rid of her. You'll be embarrassed when you get back because she's Vietnamese."[27]

If a couple could get permission from the husband's commanding officer, their application still had to be approved by higher military authorities. The government would check the groom's background to make sure he was single, a U.S. citizen, and able to support a wife. They would ask Japanese officials to run a security check on his fiancee. All the paperwork usually took about six weeks, but it could easily take twice that. By the time the papers came through, many soldiers had been transferred away from their sweethearts, sent to the front, or shipped home. John Connor found that "in some organizations it was policy of the commanding officer to treat applications for marriage as requests for transfer back to the United States." If a soldier had been sent to America, there was no way his Japanese fiancee could join him except via the tiny quota for regular immigrants.[28]

The actual marriages, when they occurred, were simple affairs, consisting merely of registering at an American consulate in front of witnesses. The frustration of fighting through the bureaucratic opposition led many couples to take shorter routes to marriage, either by being married in a Buddhist or Shinto ceremony or simply by living together without formal sanction. In either of these cases, the U.S. government refused to recognize the marriage as legitimate. If the husband was killed or shipped home, his wife and children were left without benefits and unable to enter the United States. More than a few husbands were sent home before they were able formalize their marriages. Many of these men had to make two or three trips back to Japan before they could arrange for their families to come to America. Some gave up and abandoned their families in Japan.[29]

The total effect of the U.S. policy and practice with regard to marriages to Japanese nationals during the Occupation and the years that followed was to prevent intermarriages wherever possible and encourage GIs to opt for informal, unstable relationships—even prostitution —instead of marriage.

The Japanese government and people were no more kindly disposed toward intermarriages. The new Japanese government, installed and directed by the Americans, cooperated with its overlords in this area, as in others. Japanese officials published U.S.-ordered regulations for intermarriages and did much of the legwork in background checks on the prospective brides. Some Japanese families disowned daughters who consorted with American men. Others seemed more concerned for their daughter's welfare than outraged. They were afraid—rightly, in many cases—that the American suitors were not serious in their attentions, but were merely out for some fun at their daughters' expense. One soldier had to take drastic steps to convince his girlfriend's father of his sincere intentions: he invited the old man's friends along on their dates. The father set a strict, early curfew and lifted it only gradually over more than a year's time until finally he came to trust the boy. For many families the thought of an intermarriage brought visions of shame and defilement. In Ariyoshi Sawako's novel *Not Because of Color*, a mother burst out at her daughter's proposed marriage to a Black serviceman: "You, a member of a respectable [samurai] family, wish to marry a man of such blackness! How shall we apologize to our ancestors?" Many families forbade their daughters to be anywhere near American men.[30]

Other Japanese opposed intermarriages and did their best to make mixed couples unhappy. They stared at the couples on the street with undisguised hatred, insulted them, spat on them, and shut them out of social groups. Some Japanese felt that the women had betrayed their country and challenged the rule of Japanese men by consorting with the conquerors. Cherry Sakuramoto perceived that, "humiliated in war, the Japanese [men] were now humiliated by losing their social superiority over their own women, forced to watch them walking out with foreign conquerors." Hiroshi Wagatsuma believed that "when Japanese men feel a vague sense of annoyance or discomfort at the sight or notion of a Japanese woman marrying a white man, especially an American, the feeling may be related to their unconscious understanding that a Japanese woman, by choosing a white man, is challenging their worth as men and their masculinity potency." Many Japanese were convinced that any woman who was seen with a Western man must by definition be a prostitute. A policeman arrested Cherry Sakuramoto when she and Don Parker were walking in Hiroshima. His explanation: "Because she was seen with an Australian soldier she's a tramp and a prostitute!" One woman decided to combat the harlot image by making it a point to carry books when she went out in public, hoping she would be thought an intellectual and not a prostitute. It is not possible to determine how many couples were broken up by all this opposition from the Japanese side, but the number cannot have been small.[31]

There were exceptions, of course. Matsue Kobayahi's* family was pleased with her American marriage and the children it produced. Her eldest daughter, Jean Grogan*, recalled, "My grandmother was very proud of me. She was carrying me on her back and taking me into the markets with her. . . . My grandmother's kind of an eccentric person. She's very independent. . . . And she's never really respected the mores of society." Grogan's experience was not unique. Christine Hall interviewed two Black-Japanese whose relatives and neighbors in Japan treated them with warmth and affection. But, even if not unique, these clearly were exceptional cases.[32]

Despite opposition from both Americans and Japanese, international couples did marry. This was when the hardships set for in many. Few military bases provided housing for dependents of enlisted men, and nearly all those units went to women from the States. But Japanese houses remained off limits to GIs for some months after Congress passed the first bill allowing Japanese-American marriages. Husbands and wives often had to live apart. Many times a baby would come before a couple could start living together, or before they were formally married. Those who lived together off base often had trouble getting medical care. Wives of servicemen were supposed to be able to shop at PXs, but sometimes they were denied admission.[33]

Whatever logistical problems couples faced, they also had to deal with the fact that they came from very different cultures. Almost no GI spoke any Japanese, and few Japanese women spoke English well. One soldier said, "At first I needed an interpreter to talk to her." Lacking an interpreter, many couples could communicate only by gestures. This led to all manner of misunderstandings. Eventually, many women learned enough English to handle daily affairs, but few ever were able to share their innermost feelings with their husbands. Almost none of the husbands ever learned more than pidgin Japanese. Cut off from other Japanese, many of the women felt a loneliness they had never known.[34]

Most wives were eager to learn American ways. Their husbands generally showed less enthusiasm for things Japanese. One frequent area of conflict was food. Husbands insisted that wives learn to cook American food, even though meat, for instance, was very expensive, particularly in American cuts. Even those men who did learn to tolerate Japanese cooking seldom grasped the subtleties of Japanese customs, social relationships, and ways of thinking. In a few cities wives who wanted to learn how to become American housewives took classes in American-style cooking, grooming, childcare, housekeeping, budgeting, and English sponsored by the Red Cross. From 1951 to 1954, two thousand brides took such courses. Realizing that "most of these girls will go to the farming and poorer sections of the United States," after the artificially high standard of living some enjoyed in Japan thanks to PX privileges, the Red Cross tried to introduce the women to the "Sears, Roebuck form of existence rather than the Vogue pattern."[35]

Most couples that stayed together chose to come to America within a year or two after being married. Only a tiny number of Asian war brides came to America during the Occupation. Many more came once the Occupation had ended, Americans were being shipped home, and entry rules had been relaxed. Nineteen fifty-two was the first year that many made it past the tangle of immigration laws; 4,220 came that year. Between 2,000 and 5,000 brides of international marriages came each year thereafter through 1965. By that time a total of more than 40,000 had come. Many of the women in later years were married to American civilians traveling or working in Japan, though a large proportion continued to marry servicemen. Bok-Lim Kim says that between one-fourth and one-third of that total married Japanese Americans; the rest married Whites, Blacks, and other Americans.[36] The source of her estimate, however, is not clear. Certainly many more marriages took place than women came to America. A few marriages involved Japanese men and American women. Many other couples chose to stay together in Japan. Still others split up, the woman remaining in her homeland and the man returning to his. How many such couples existed, it is not possible to tell. U.S. embassy figures do not help, for embassy analysts consistently estimated far fewer marriages than actually took place.

Adjustment to America

When the intermarried couples arrived in America, they spread out all over the landscape. Just how many went where is not clear. But since the husbands came from all parts of the country and most returned to their homes, it is reasonable to assume that the Japanese brides were spread rather thinly over the country initially. This meant that many a rural or southern district saw its first Asian face in the 1950s when a war bride took up residence. The largest numbers of Japanese brides followed their husbands to the Pacific coast, Hawaii, and the South.[37]

At first, these couples met mixed reactions from other Americans.

A lot of American families were initially dismayed at the thought of their sons marrying Japanese women. More than a few shared June Parker's reaction when she learned her brother intended to marry Cherry Sakuramoto. She said, "No Jap tart is coming to this house!" But once they adjusted to the idea, most families offered a somewhat warmer welcome. Esther Pfeiffer insisted that her son and his wife move in with her when they came from Japan. Generally, parents and siblings, because of their close relationship to the men in question, were more willing than more distant relations to accept the marriages. Even among those parents who opposed the marriages, only a very few treated their sons' wives as cruelly as did one woman, who called her daughter-in-law a "Jap" and told people that the couple's child had not been fathered by her son. Even the parents who most vehemently opposed the marriages often came to accept their daughters-in-law once they got to know them. As with other intermarriages, the arrival of grandchildren often brought rapprochement. After four years of estrangement, one war bride took her baby to see its grandmother. By the end of the visit, the grandmother exclaimed, "I think Sachiko is the best mother in Chicago. . . . I wish every mother in the world could see her son as well married as my Frank." Good family relationships were enhanced by the determination of most brides to get along with their husbands' families. On first entering her in-laws' home, Cherry Parker thought, "I must learn everything and learn quickly. . . . I must show Don's father and mother I am a good and thrifty housewife, worthy to have married him . . . not just some no-good Japanese girl who had caught their son."[38]

If most families granted their new members at least grudging acceptance, some other Americans were less welcoming. Witness the following excerpts from letters in the *Cincinnati Enquirer* in 1952:

If we were put here in different colors, it must have been for a purpose. Why don't we stay that way. The boys . . . are getting like the man that had a cabin in the North Woods. No other human was there except an old Indian squaw. . . . One morning he got up and the old squaw looked like Hedy Lamarr . . . so he knew it was time to get back to civilization. Maybe it is time for our boys to come home.

On the whole the American women have much higher ideals, morals, intelligence than Japanese women. Anyone connected with news knows the low morality among most Japanese women. Ask other servicemen that have been there! All these women that snared our GIs are only interested in entering the United States under any means, even to having children before marriage, next a meal ticket; most of all, after a short time over here wait and see how much respect they will show their husbands. I'd like to bet two-thirds will be divorced before three years.

We do not hold our party girls and prostitutes in respect and envy as the Japanese do their "geisha" girls. Apparently our standard of morals is higher than theirs. . . . It is absolutely criminal to allow interracial marriages to fill this country. We are all greatly opposed to extending the time limit for marriages and entry into this country, as enough damage has been done.

We have too many foreigners in this country now.

This group of boys is maladjusted in thoughts, words, and action, that no high-thinking, red-blooded American girl will have. His only choice is to pick a wife from another country that doesn't realize what sort of fellow he really is. . . . I'm rather glad they sent those 8,000 boys to Japan, they are no threat to my American daughters.[39]

Japanese brides reported being stared at on the street and treated rudely. Kishi Morrison was harassed on the streets of Albany, New York. She told a reporter, "There were several ex-GIs who spoke a little Japanese, and they would yell to me as I was walking down the street. The words they used were not very nice. Of course, the people around didn't know what they said, but I did. I was very embarrassed, but could only keep on walking, not saying anything." But not all Americans were rude and crude. Morrison was treated far better by other Albany residents. Most of the thirty-five women interviewed by Leon Walters reported predominantly happy experiences with their neighbors and people on the street. Mieko Malloy was surprised to report that she was not discriminated against in any way she could detect: "I vaguely expected a waiter to say to me in a restaurant, 'We don't serve Japs here.' It never happened." Yet even though most women who were willing to talk to reporters or sociologists did not stress prejudice and discrimination suffered at the hands of white Americans, it is difficult to believe that the hatred expressed in the letters to the *Enquirer* was not made manifest in some fashion.[40]

In America the couples continued the process of adjustment they had begun in Japan. Like all newly married pairs, they had compromises to make as they learned to live with each other. In outward aspects of culture, most brides shed their own mores as best they could and took on American ways. Even though many longed for Japan, they had chosen America and they would try to live as Americans. Sachiko Pfeiffer put it this way: "I content to lose my Japanese blood stream in America. I gonna die in America. Here is my home forever." Japanese women learned to like and to cook American food. They said they seldom cooked Japanese dishes after their arrival in America because ingredients were expensive and because their husbands often did not like Japanese food. The women began to observe American holidays and social rituals such as shaking hands and sending birthday cards. Religion was seldom a problem, for most of the brides and their husbands held only nominal affiliations with their respective faiths. The couples had more trouble with language. Few of the women ever became completely fluent in English, and their husbands were not much help. Many husbands prided themselves on their flexibility because they occasionally ate Japanese food or spoke a word or two of their wives' language. But almost none of the men ever tried to achieve fluency in Japanese (and seldom did they help with domestic chores). Walters found that "the majority of [the husbands] could not carry on even a simple conversation in Japanese." Nor did many understand the subtleties of Japanese emotional behavior. That left them incapable of helping their wives cope with loneliness, fear, and uncertainty about social relationships or the future.[41]

One of the subjects for miscommunication and conflict was money. Some of the brides had once known some wealth in Japan, even if they had become destitute by war's end. Women of Western-oriented education and outlook usually came from the middle and upper classes. Some had had servants. Whether they came from wealthy families or not, after they married most had enjoyed relatively high standards of living in Japan on account of their husbands' overseas pay and PX privileges. When they came to America, however, they found their living less grand. Those men who stayed in the army kept some of their monetary advantages, but they no longer had the high status of conquerors. Those who entered civilian life seldom found high-paying jobs right away. Some went to school. Many ended up living with relatives or in housing projects. The adjustment to a less prosperous lifestyle put strain on some unions. When Masai Endo* found out how little her husband was making in America, she left him, divorced him, took back her own name, and started working to support herself. After nearly two decades in America, Matsue Fitzpatrick* had not yet achieved the security she desired. Her daughter reported, "My mother's working as a maid now. I think that really depresses her." Other brides, however, found life in America more comfortable and secure than the life they had known in Japan. Sachiko Pfeiffer, when asked if she wanted to go back to Japan, replied, "Oh, no! I not answer that question. I not dumb. Japan I be slave. Cold water. Work all day. No rugs on the floor. I stay here!"[42]

Many women suffered loneliness. They were spread all over America, most of them homemakers, isolated from other Japanese, often unable to communicate verbally with their husbands the subtleties of their feelings, and fearful of hostility from other Americans. Life was somewhat less lonely for women who lived near military bases—where there were other Japanese brides—and for those who found jobs outside the home. But still, many women grew homesick and depressed. The arrival of children gave them someone to talk to, but it made them even less likely to venture outside the home and make contact with others. Homesickness led to anxiety about America, to the point that women would become fearful, unable to perform relatively simple tasks such as taking a bus or going shopping. Mieko Malloy described her sense of isolation: "The first night I spent in the United States, in a third-rate hotel, . . . I broke down and cried, lonely and frightened. My husband tried to console me helplessly. But I could not explain for the life of me how I felt. It was as if there was a curtain between us and I couldn't get to him." Most couples had few friends or institutional connections, except for other mixed couples. In their fear and loneliness, many war brides sought out each other's company. That was easy for women whose husbands remained in the military, for most bases had at least a few intermarried couples. Civilians' wives persuaded their husbands to move to places like Chicago, where war brides congregated, or to Los Angeles, where there were many Japanese Americans. Many longed to go back to Japan. But most wanted only to visit the country of their birth. They had made firm commitments to staying in America.[43]

The men's readjustment to life in America often added to their wives' difficulties. Some of the men were "marginal individuals in that they had no great emotional ties to their families or to the prevailing mores of society," according to John Connor. In some of the families that Bok-Lim Kim studied, "out of his own need for support, the husband expected the wife's speedy acculturation and adjustment. His own insecurity, frustration, and anxiety were projected onto the wife, and bitter complaints about her total dependency accompanied the frequent and violent fights." Hiroshi Wagatsuma expressed the opinion that "many of these husbands, once out of the military life and back in their home country, show little sense of responsibility, do not support their family, drink heavily, and are unfaithful and even physically abusive." Evelyn Nakano Glenn reported that many "war brides internalized responsibility for the problems they encountered—marital breakups, low-status jobs, difficulty in dealing with authorities— so their self-esteem suffered." Yet by no means did all the husbands fall apart in that manner. Mieko Malloy reported that her relationship with her husband Pat was strong despite strains, that he had direction and purpose to life, that he treated her well, and that other war brides had the same experience. She said that "many Japanese girls who married Americans tell me that for the first time they were made to feel they were human beings and were loved." Sachiko Pfeiffer told James Michener that because she and Frank had complementary personalities, "we never have one bad fight since we married."[44]

The experiences described above were shared to one degree or another by the majority of the Japanese brides. However, those women who married Black or Japanese American men had other issues to resolve as well. America's ambiguous racial caste system presented some difficulties for the wives of Black men. On a trip through the South, one woman found that she was allowed to stay in White hotels while her husband had to sleep in the car. But there were advantages for Black-Japanese couples, too. Black men had experienced discrimination from Whites and could teach their wives how to deal with it, whereas few White husbands could offer strategies for coping. Most Black Americans seem to have had sympathy for these women of color and welcomed them to their communities. Still, there were signs of resentment from some Black women who did not want anyone trespassing on their male territory. And some Black women and men, like some Whites, nursed lingering hatreds from World War II.

Japanese women who took Japanese American husbands found

themselves in unexpected difficulty. Both sides in such marriages expected them to be felicitous unions. Japanese women often felt they were lowering themselves by marrying into families of emigrants, people they regarded as having gone to America because they "just could not make it in Japan." But they sensed they shared values with Japanese Americans. That sense led them and their families to be optimistic about their prospects with Japanese American men. Daniel Okimoto said of his dating experiences in Japan: "Had I been an ordinary foreigner . . . the parents might have tried to discourage the girl from seeing any more of me. But because I was of Japanese descent, the parents had confided, they could feel assured their daughter would be properly looked after." The fact that most Japanese regarded Nisei, second-generation Japanese Americans, as, if not cultured, at least rich, added to Okimoto's attractiveness. For their part, Japanese American parents, Issei, looked favorably on unions with Japanese women. Tamiko Yamamoto interviewed Japanese Hawaiians who had sons marrying Japanese women: "Many parents were pleased. Some were highly elated and made elaborate preparations for a reception. Their sons were bringing home 'model wives' from Japan—wives who would be 'domestic, obedient, refined, submissive, hard-working— unlike the young Nisei in Hawaii.' "[45]

The Japan of the 1950s was not the Japan the Issei remembered, however. Since they had left, more than four decades earlier, Japan had been transformed by industrial development, military government, changing social structure, and waves of new ideas from the West. The women of the new Japan diverged from Issei expectations as much as did the Nisei. Initial relations between Issei and Japanese daughters-in-law, founded on fond hopes, quickly deteriorated. The families often lived together, and the brides seldom could endure the expectations placed on them. Yukiko Kimura surveyed 124 families and reported: "To the Japanese [American] in-laws an additional member of the family should mean an additional producer of family income. The parents-in-law, keenly conscious of their hard work and sacrifice in raising their sons, remind their daughters-in-law of it constantly. In Hawaii, the words, 'filial piety' are much more used that in Japan. . . . In contrast, none of the Japanese war brides interviewed considered their cardinal duty after marriage to be service to their parents-in-law." Many Japanese American parents were also uncomfortable because they were conscious of the fact that "their daughter-in-law knows about things Japanese and is therefore in a position to criticize them." Disillusionment was often rapid and bitter. Brides complained that their in-laws were old-fashioned, uncultured, and restrictive. The parents saw their daughters-in-law as immature, lazy, extravagant, and "too Westernized." Not a few couples had to move away from the husbands' families in order to save their marriages. The result of all this conflict was unhappy marriages. Yukiko Kimura surveyed 124 couples in four categories: (1) Japanese women and their non-Japanese husbands; (2) European war brides and their Japanese American husbands; (3) European women and non-Japanese husbands; and (4) Japanese women and Japanese American husbands. When she asked them how well they had adjusted to their marriages, she found, to her surprise, that the mixed racial couples expressed more satisfaction than the homogeneous pairs. Marriages between Japanese women and non-Japanese American men were the most happy, followed by unions of European women and Japanese American men, then European women and non-Japanese American men, and finally Japanese women and Japanese American men. The chief reason given for the very low rating for Japanese–Japanese American marriages was conflict with in-laws.[46]

In general, Japanese Americans quickly withdrew their welcome from Japanese wives of American men, whether the husbands were Nisei or non-Japanese Americans. Especially those women married to White and Black men were stigmatized as immoral women. They were denied access to many Japanese American community institutions. Only a tiny percentage, for example, ever felt comfortable enough to attend Japanese American churches. The intermarried women's problems were ignored by most Japanese Americans. Only with the rise of pan-Asian activism in the 1970s did a significant number of Japanese Americans begin to address the special problems faced by the Japanese brides of American men.[47]

In sum, American-Japanese marriages in the immediate postwar years suffered intense opposition from the military and from private citizens in America and Japan. When a couple did succeed in marrying, they faced an arduous adjustment period. They were pressed by economic insecurity, loneliness, an inability to communicate deeply held feelings, cultural differences, family demands, hostility from some

Americans, and a lack of support systems. Did these so-called war bride marriages weather the storm? Were the individuals involved able to make the necessary adjustments?

That depends a great deal on one's point of view. Bok-Lim Kim concluded that most such unions were unhappy and conflict-ridden. George DeVos went farther to describe them as pathological. But Kim's sample was skewed, for it was based on her social welfare practice; she was unlikely to encounter intermarried couples who did not have severe problems. DeVos's conclusions must be suspect because he went looking for pathology, used an instrument highly susceptible to tester bias, and found just what he expected. On the other side were several investigators who saw American-Japanese marriages as relatively successful. Leon Walters consistently discounted any conflict in the thirty-five marriages he studied and found them generally felicitous. John Connor found similar happiness (after a difficult period of adjustment) in the twenty-five marriages he surveyed. Yet the sanguine findings of Walters and Connor may have been partly due to their being predisposed to find bliss in war bride marriages. Christine Hall also found positive adjustment in a study of the children of Black-Japanese couples. But Hall is Black-Japanese and might be suspected, despite her considerable scientific skills, of some desire to see families such as her own portrayed in a positive light.[48]

With evidence on both sides and most of it susceptible to some criticism, it may be left to a person without a discernible axe to grind to settle the debate. Anselm Strauss surveyed American-Japanese marriages for the University of Chicago in the early 1950s and concluded that such unions stood a good chance of success, precisely because of the "severe selective process for those who did marry." Concerted opposition from Americans, Japanese, and the military, said Strauss, had kept all couples apart except those whose members were most dedicated to each other. The couples he studied looked long and hard before marrying. As individuals, they were less likely than others to feel the pressures exerted by family, religious institutions, and the general public, for most had long since cut outside ties. They adjusted well to each other's circles of friends and career aspirations. In short, Strauss found American-Japanese marriages that showed every sign of succeeding.[49] To agree with Strauss's finding of reasonable harmony in war bride marriages is not to ignore DeVos's, and particularly Kim's, contrary findings. Without question, there were couples who experienced tremendous difficulties. The cultural chasm between East and West was hard to bridge, and not a few marriages fell to destruction in the middle. Yet many unmixed marriages failed, too. Severe though the problems of individuals and couples were, there is little evidence to show that the rate of failure was higher for war bride couples than for others.

Children of War Brides in America

In having children, these couples were aware that their offspring might be subject to abuse because of their mixed parentage and that their very mixture might someday lead to confusion about their ethnic identities. Most of the parents chose to raise their children as Americans. They gave them English names, spoke to them mainly or exclusively in English, and chose American child-rearing practices over the more relaxed Japanese methods. Sachiko Pfeiffer expected to remain in America and to have her children grow up as Americans, marry Americans, and raise American grandchildren. Often husbands and extended family members pressed Japanese women to make Americans of their children. Don and Cherry Parker lived in Australia, but their attitudes were typical of American couples, as well. Don forbade Cherry to speak Japanese to their girls or teach them anything about Japan. "If they grow up to speak Japanese they'll speak it to each other at school," he said. "That will make them different. They'll stand out among the other kids as it is. But they're not Japanese, they're Australians, and they're going to speak English." In response to such pressure, Cherry counseled her daughters, "You're not Jap, you're Australian girl . . . I'm Australian girl, too." The brides generally put up with this sort of pressure to deny their ethnic identity, often because they had few resources to combat it. They were alone in a foreign land, whose language they spoke imperfectly, whose folkways they did not fully understand, at the mercy of their husbands and in-laws. If the family wanted them to raise their children as Americans, there was little they could do about it save drag their heels. On the other hand, many of the women may have wanted to adopt American ways and identify with American culture. Leon Walters believed that "a desire to reject Japanese culture was one of the motivations for some of these marriages to Americans."[50]

There were some ways, however, in which Japanese women sought to communicate their heritage to their children. Many of the children spent some time in Japan before coming to America. There, pressures to be American were not so great. Japanese extended families encouraged children to speak Japanese and learn Japanese behavior patterns. Even in America, while few mothers encouraged their children to identify themselves as Japanese, many taught them such traditional Japanese values as filial piety, courtesy, humility, and stoicism. Moreover, some who recognized the harassment their children would suffer taught them not to be ashamed of their Japanese heritage even as they identified themselves as Americans. In this effort the mothers usually acted alone, for most fathers did not anticipate that their children would face identity problems. Several fathers described to Leon Walters their lack of strategies for dealing with prejudice and identity questions: "I don't think they'll run into much trouble." "Just let him shift for himself." "I believe . . . she will be able to meet [prejudice] herself. Trying to teach her would only make her more conscious of prejudice." Some fathers, however, did address issues of prejudice and identity choice. One father felt he had an advantage in this area of child rearing: "My children will also face prejudice because of being Negro. Having met similar problems myself, my children could not have a better teacher." Another father had talked with his wife and worked out a plan for handling these issues: "We are going to teach them that their mother is different from most Americans and that they are different too. We want them to be proud of their ancestry on both sides. They'll be taught that differences aren't to be condemned."[51]

Whether parents made preparations or not, mixed children often experienced harassment and internal questioning as they grew up. Bok-Lim Kim reported that the women she interviewed chose to come to America at least in part because "they felt the children would experience less discrimination here for their racial mixture and would encounter better opportunities for education and employment." As we shall see shortly, they were correct. But life was not without hardships for mixed children in America. Schoolchildren—White, Black, and Japanese—called them derogatory names. Black-Japanese reported being turned down for dates or refused admission to black student union meetings because they were "not Black," and harassed by Black women for dating Black men. Others reported that "the Japanese never accepted me as Japanese," either. Discrimination from Whites was not constant for White-Japanese children, partly because they did not bear Japanese names. With features intermediate between Asian and European, such people might have been the targets of anti-Asian prejudice had they been known as Japanese. But with their fathers' European surnames, most were taken by casual observers to be un-mixed Caucasians with slightly exotic features. Such mistakes hardly lent confirmation to their biracial identities but did spare them some discrimination. Black-Japanese children, by contrast, often suffered not only whatever discrimination came their way as Japanese, but the greater burdens reserved for Blacks as well. John Connor concluded, after studying many interracial families, that "by and large the prejudice was more severe and sustained against the boys than the girls."[52] Connor did not hypothesize as to why that might have been the case. Perhaps it had something to do with the fact that Asian women in general met a warmer reception from Whites than did most Asian men in this period.

Erik Erikson has made the adolescent identity crisis a prominent feature of modern self-consciousness.[53] Part of the identity crisis for each person is deciding to what categories he or she ought to belong. For American youths of mixed race, the identity decision process takes on an especially significant tone, for they must decide to what ethnic group they want to belong. Children of American-Japanese marriages chose American identities, either Black or White, depending on the race of their fathers; they chose Japanese identities; or they chose bicultural identities, emphasizing their claim to both halves of their heritage.

The major study of this subject is "The Ethnic Identity of Racially Mixed People: A Study of Black-Japanese," a UCLA Ph.D. dissertation by Christine Hall.[54] Hall found that most of her subjects went through a process of choosing an ethnic identity between the ages of fourteen and eighteen. Over half of them chose to regard themselves as Black Americans, lived in Black neighborhoods, spoke Black English, and had predominantly Black friends. Some had to work at achieving a Black identity. For instance, those who had spent much of their childhood in Japan could not speak Black English and had to "learn . . . how to be black" as teenagers in America. They found themselves more readily accepted by Blacks than by other Americans, so they chose to identify themselves as Black. In similar fashion, a great many children of White fathers and Japanese mothers grew up among Whites, came to identify themselves as White, and were accepted by other Whites more or less as members of that group.[55]

One of Hall's subjects chose a Japanese identity. She had spent most of her childhood in Japan and could imagine no other identity for herself. Yet her identity was not complete. She spoke Japanese as well as English, ate Japanese foods, observed Japanese holidays, and sang Japanese songs to her children, but she professed to feel more comfortable among Blacks than other Americans, she lived in a Black neighborhood, she dated only Black men, and she married a Black man. Other mixed people who grew up in Japanese American communities blended rather effectively into those communities. A Caucasian-Japanese man grew up in Seattle's Japanese community, went to a Japanese church, played basketball in a Japanese league, and married a Sansei woman. In general, it seems to have been easier for half-White individuals to choose a Japanese identity than for those who were half-Black. Japanese Americans as a group had prejudices against Whites which they leveled against White-Japanese mixed people, but their prejudices against Blacks and Black-Japanese were stronger. A talented, intelligent, and beautiful Black-Japanese woman was much admired by Whites, Blacks, and Japanese in Seattle in the 1960s. She looked more Japanese than Black, but she could not find close friendships among Whites or Japanese Americans, and ended up identifying herself as Black.[56]

Perhaps Hall's most interesting finding is that a substantial number of mixed race people refused to choose either a Black or a Japanese identity. Instead, they held out for a biracial and bicultural identity that emphasized both portions of their inheritance. They saw themselves, not as a marginal people, trapped between Black and Japanese identities, but as bicultural people—fully Black, fully Japanese, and fully "Black-Japanese . . . a new people—a new race!" Hall may be forgiven for waxing enthusiastic about the virtues of the choice these people made, for it is the choice she herself made. But she may be right that their decision—like Joy Nakamura's in Chapter 4—to affirm all parts of their heritage was an especially satisfying way out of the dilemma of mixed racial status. As Velina Houston, the child of a Black father and Japanese mother, described herself: "What I am is 'whole' Japanese and 'whole' American."[57]

Konketsuji: Mixed Children in Japan

No matter how difficult growing up was for mixed children in America, it was infinitely more difficult for their peers in Japan. Mixed children in Japan were often called *ainoko* by other Japanese, but since that term took on a pejorative meaning, most preferred to be called *konketsuji*. The Japanese government has largely ignored the existence of mixed people, and reliable numbers are hard to come by. The best estimates show 20,000 to 25,000 konketsuji in Japan in the latter 1960s; perhaps 2,000 of them had one Black parent, and the rest, White.[58] About half of these children came from stable, two-parent households. The American parents were servicemen or business people who had opted to make their homes in Japan on a long-term basis.[59]

The other half of the children were fatherless. Their fathers had left Japan, perhaps with promises to return or to send for their families. Few had been heard from again. Many of the mothers were middle-class Japanese who expected lifelong commitments from their men but did not get them. Others were prostitutes or bar hostesses who harbored fewer illusions.[60] Though this last category of mother, the woman of ill repute, was a minority, most Japanese fixed on it as typical of the whole. In the eyes of most Japanese, every person of mixed ancestry in Japan was the child of a prostitute, and no amount of corrective information would convince them otherwise. Thus, mixed people in Japan bore the stigma of parental prostitution and illegitimacy. In the years after the war they were also regarded as traitors. They were the living evidence that Japanese women had consorted with the conquerors, and they were therefore despised. Sociologist Hiroshi Wagatsuma bought the argument that "most of these children are illegitimate," but he had a clear grasp of the social implications of their mixed parentage: "Whether or not their mothers actually were street walkers makes little difference in the mind of the Japanese—preferring a foreign victor to a Japanese man was no better than prostitution."[61]

Some of these fatherless children were motherless, as well. Pressured by society, family, and circumstance, many mothers abandoned their babies to the uncertain mercies of relatives, neighbors, and charities. Darrell Berrigan told the story of Yoshiko, who had a child by a by-then-absent American man. "Yoshiko's family considered the entire romance a 'shameful thing.' They sent the baby away to an orphanage and shut the weeping mother in the house to hide her shame." That child was lucky. Berrigan also reported a large increase in the legal abortion rate and hundreds of babies left to starve. "Babies with un-Japanese pigmentation are found dead in refuse heaps. More are found alive in crowded railroad stations, in the park, . . . and in public baths." A Japanese woman who recognized that she had made a poor bet in taking up with an American sometimes tried to salvage a marital future for herself by looking for a Japanese husband. Her mixed child then became an unwanted burden. If she kept the baby, she might not find a mate, or her husband might abuse the child. Since most women did not choose abortion or infanticide, their babies fell to others for care. Grandparents were pressed into service. Neighbors sometimes stepped forward to bring up the unwanted child. That was a courageous act, for the child could bring stigma on them as well as on its natural mother. Their love and generosity did not go unappreciated. Jill Joiner*, a Black-Japanese brought up by her natural mother's former employers, recalled, "Whatever pain I had to endure [from Japanese who ridiculed her] was not as great as the love that they [her foster parents] gave me." In other instances, grandparents or aunts and uncles braved public opinion to care for a child.[62]

More often, konketsuji were left to the care of orphanages. The Japanese government and American military authorities preferred to pretend that such children did not exist, so significant government help was not forthcoming. The largest number of children went to Catholic orphanages, such as Our Lady of Lourdes Home in Yokohama. Many went to the highly publicized Elizabeth Saunders Home, run by Mitsubishi heiress Miki Sawada. The Lourdes and Saunders orphanages tried to raise their children apart from Japanese society, to teach them both Japanese and English, place them in American homes if possible, and help them establish mixed identities without daily harassment from other Japanese. In this they encountered opposition from the Japanese government and several other orphanages, which wanted to mix the children in with pure children in the hope that their distinctive qualities would disappear.[63]

As mixed children grew up in Japan, they were subjected to years of prejudice and discrimination by other Japanese. Those who came from intact, American-oriented families or orphanages that followed the separate development theory espoused by Sawada and the Yokahama sisters seem to have weathered harassment fairly well. Those who had to fend for themselves had a tougher time.

The Japanese for centuries showed extreme prejudice against people they considered outsiders. After World War II they attached anti-foreign ideas to native-born people of mixed ancestry. People of part-Black parentage, especially, were made outcasts. Majority Japanese put Black-Japanese and other konketsuji in a category close to eta, hereditary outcasts, and atom-bomb survivors as ritually polluted people. The sense of pollution, of filth attaching to people who were connected with non-Japanese, can be seen in a notion held by some uneducated Japanese that the womb of a woman who had given birth to a baby by a Black man would be stained permanently. If she gave birth to a second child or a third—these by Japanese men—the babies would nonetheless emerge with tinges of blackness.[64]

Prejudice led to discrimination against konketsuji. Discrimination seems to have been levelled more against Black-Japanese than White-Japanese, and more against men than women, but all felt its effects to some degree. Schoolchildren would call their mixed classmates names such as *gaijin* (foreigner), *kurombo* (nigger), and *hitokui kinshu* (cannibal). One Black-Japanese suffered the embarrassment of having his co-workers run from a public bath when he entered. A White-Japanese was arrested as a spy. Barbers refused to cut the curly hair of Black-Japanese youngsters. Schools refused konketsuji entrance. A PTA father protested the presence of mixed people in his child's class, saying, "Even if legally Japanese, a Negro is a Negro!" Ostracism took its toll on individuals. Jill Joiner*, a Black-Japanese woman, sobbed, "They never let me forget that I am different. I know I'm different. They know it. Why do they have to keep telling me? Why can't they just let me be?" The pressure was so great that more than a few konketsuji youths attempted suicide.[65]

Majority Japanese insisted on treating konketsuji as foreigners, even if they spoke only Japanese and had no connections with any other country. They expected them to be more at home with White and Black Americans than with other Japanese. Much as some nineteenth-century White Americans hoped to end the problem of slavery by exporting

Blacks to Africa, so many Japanese hoped to end the mixed-blood irritation by sending konketsuji abroad. They encouraged Americans to adopt the mixed children. Under the leadership of Miki Sawada, they began a grand experiment, shipping a few dozen off to farm the jungles of Brazil. Adoption by Americans helped only a handful of individuals. The Brazil experiment was beset by economic difficulties and local resistance and seemed unlikely to succeed. Neither addressed the fundamental problem of Japanese racism.[66]

On top of social ostracism came economic discrimination. Konketsuji were relegated to menial jobs at subsistence wages. They were discriminated against in education, hiring, promotion, and pay. There were exceptions, of course. Some half-Whites from business and military families got college educations and middle-class jobs, usually in America or in the Western-oriented sector of Japanese business. A few mixed people—those with particular beauty or talent—achieved success in the entertainment industry and in modeling. In the 1960s and 1970s, in fact, there arose a new, stereotypical image of the konketsuji as gifted entertainer. But for every individual who found such a pathway to success, ten or twenty went nowhere.[67]

Japanese of mixed parentage found themselves in a difficult position with regard to romance and marriage. On one hand, a myth of sexual voracity surrounded konketsuji. Hiroshi Wagatsuma wrote of a "chain of association" in Japanese minds linking mixed people with sex: "In their minds . . . white [and black] men are sexually more passionate and stronger than the Japanese; these mixed-bloods must have inherited that quality from their fathers; their Japanese mothers must have been unusual women if they preferred and could cope with sexually powerful men; these mixed-bloods must have inherited that quality from their mothers; *ergo*, they are sexually precocious, energetic, and enjoyable." Mixed people in Japan were often the targets of insistent sexual interest. Mike Ogita traded on this interest to put together a string of affairs with full-blooded Japanese women, including one in which he was kept by a much older woman. Unmixed Japanese frequented konketsuji bars and night clubs, looking for sexual opportunities with people of mixed ancestry. Mixed women, especially those with one Caucasian parent, found jobs as bar hostesses and models relatively easy to obtain in the 1960s and 1970s, and they often were paid two to three times as much as their full-Japanese colleagues. Pornographic magazines sought after mixed women, especially White-Japanese, almost as avidly as they pursued foreign White and Black women—and much more than they sought pure Japanese women.[68]

This erotic image might get a person a job. It might get her a date, a lover, or a rape. But it did not get a husband or a wife for many konketsuji. Most of the mixed people were culturally Japanese and wanted Japanese mates. Most found, however, that though they might excite ordinary Japanese they did not inspire in them a desire to wed. Some of the more American-oriented konketsuji were interested in American Black or Caucasian partners, and these they might well find. But those who saw themselves as wholly Japanese faced a difficult problem. Few seemed interested in marrying other konketsuji— partly, perhaps, because they were so few that there was not a large selection from which to choose. But for many, their choice of a Japanese ethnic identity demanded that they marry a full Japanese, and there were not many such partners to be had.[69]

Added to the other problems faced by the konketsuji was the question of their citizenship. Under Japanese law, an individual is entitled to Japanese citizenship in only three cases: if the person's father was a Japanese citizen when that person was born; if the father was unknown or stateless and the mother was Japanese; or if both parents were unknown or stateless and the child was born on Japanese soil. This is a much narrower definition than that to which the United States subscribes. Any child born in the United States or born elsewhere to a U.S. citizen is entitled to American citizenship, provided he or she resides in the United States for five consecutive years during his or her young adulthood. These conflicting laws threw many konketsuji into awkward postures. Any mixed person whose father was known was assumed by Japanese authorities to be a U.S. citizen, regardless of his or her wishes. That was all right for people from intact families. But in many cases where the American man had deserted his family and gone back to America, the children were left stateless. Few could afford to come to America to claim their citizenship, and not many could prove their American parentage to the satisfaction of immigration authorities. Fewer wanted to. Many would rather have had Japanese citizenship. At least three out of five konketsuji surveyed by Nathan Strong had no intention of living anywhere but Japan. But Japanese citizenship was not an option for them, even though they had been born and raised in Japan, their mothers were Japanese, they spoke only Japanese, they were culturally pure Japanese, and they knew no other land. To avoid that sort of statelessness, some mothers declared their children illegitimate at birth, even when they knew the fathers' identities. That made the children Japanese citizens, but saddled them for life with the stigma of illegitimacy. Such cases only abetted the majority Japanese tendency to view all konketsuji as illegitimate, and therefore disreputable, people.[70]

For some individuals citizenship coincided with choice of national identity. When konketsuji came from the intact families of American military or business men, they held American citizenship and almost always identified themselves as primarily Americans. They may have spoken Japanese as well as English and have gone to Japanese schools, but their primary orientation was to the land of their fathers' birth. They tended to travel in military or international business circles, insulated from mainstream Japanese life. Those who were interviewed by Nathan Strong exhibited more self-confidence and less ambivalence about their identities than did konketsuji from broken families or institutions who chose Japanese identities.[71]

For other konketsuji, citizenship and identity did not necessarily go together. Irrespective of their citizenship, people who grew up without fathers, cared for by their mothers, other relatives, or institutions, saw themselves as Japanese. They spoke mainly Japanese, seldom much English. Their socialization, ideals, habits, and values were all Japanese. Often they felt pain when other Japanese refused to accord them the position they felt was theirs. Jill Joiner* complained, "I know that I look black, but my heart is Japanese." More than a few other mixed people echoed her thoughts. They saw themselves as Japanese and hoped that other Japanese would see them that way too. Nathan Strong interviewed many konketsuji who identified themselves as Japanese. He divided them into two types: those who were members of distinct konketsuji social networks and those whom he called "isolates." Both were striving to find places for themselves in Japanese society, but the network konketsuji were having a better time of it. Mainly graduates of places like the Elizabeth Saunders Home, where they had established friendships with other konketsuji and been introduced to both parts of their heritage, they frequented konketsuji social circles surrounding a Tokyo university and a Nagoya night club. From those circles they drew strength and companionship to endure the lot assigned to mixed people in Japan. The isolates had more difficulty. They wanted badly to be accepted as pure Japanese and wanted nothing to do with other konketsuji. Strong found many of them trying unsuccessfully to pass as unmixed. They were lonely, fearful, and conflict-ridden.[72]

Life, then, was not easy for mixed people in Japan. Many knew only one parent, some none. They suffered the stigma of assumed prostitution and illegitimacy. They were harassed by other Japanese and made to feel they did not belong in Japan. Some were denied Japanese citizenship. Others were denied jobs or education or marriage partners. They were stereotyped as sexually promiscuous and cast in the role of entertainer. Yet, despite all these difficulties, some konketsuji were able to fashion relatively stable niches for themselves, as half-Japanese members of Japanese society.

Summary of Part II

American men met Japanese women in the years after World War II under circumstances conducive to romance and marriage. Entering Japan as conquerors, they found the Japanese people impoverished. They also found some Japanese women who yearned for more autonomy than would be theirs in a traditional Japanese marriage. The men, for their part, often were drawn by images of tender and submissive Asian women. The young couples dated, mated, and married. Despite intense opposition from the Japanese populace and the American military, thousands of couples married. Many more were cruelly driven apart. In Japan and in America, these couples had a lot of adjusting to do. Many could not verbally communicate their deepest feelings, either in Japanese or in English. Their styles of living, values, choices of food, and ways of thinking were often in conflict. American families sometimes overcame their initial prejudices to help the couples adjust. Other Americans, particularly Japanese Americans, made life hard for the intermarried people. Yet, despite opposition and internal difficulties, the weight of evidence points to a reasonable rate of success in these marriages.

Children of mixed parentage were raised in America as Americans, Black or White, depending on the race of their fathers. Few learned very much about the Japanese parts of themselves. Some were harassed by majority Americans on account of their mixed race. Prejudice and discrimination were greater for mixed people in Japan. Konketsuji suffered the added stigma of being stereotyped as illegitimate children of prostitutes. In both Japan and America, people of mixed race underwent periods of profound self-questioning as to their ethnic identities. Most who had intact American families resolved their doubts in favor of an American identity. A few others were able to establish a meaningful identity as people of mixed race—full members of either Japanese or American society, but at the same time not unmindful of the other part of their heritage. Most who sought a purely Japanese identity were doomed to frustration, for Japan would not have them.

III

JEWISH AMERICANS

6. Background and Images: Shikse and Jewish Mother

Like Japanese Americans, Jews are an immigrant people. Most of their ancestors came to America from Eastern Europe in the same decades in which the Issei were crossing the Pacific—the 1890s, 1900s, and 1910s. The Japanese and the Jews in America shared several common characteristics: a history and culture in which they took great pride, an entrepreneurial spirit, a drive to achieve, and, significantly for this study, an endogamous imperative. Jewish American history, like Japanese American, may be divided conveniently into three epochs: the immigrant, second, and third generations. Their class structures are similar. Immigrants of both groups toiled long hours under difficult conditions to gain a foothold in America. By diligence, study, aptitude, communal self-help, and good luck, the majority in each group earned places in the middle class by the third generation. Those are some of the similarities between Jewish and Japanese Americans. But there are differences aplenty, as will become clear. Part III sets out the patterns which Jewish outmarriage has followed over the years, and makes a start at comparing them to the Japanese experience. But first, a bit of background.

Jewish Intermarriage in the Ancient World

The Jews are a historically minded people. Much of their sense of themselves in the modern world derives from their experiences as a people over the last four thousand years. So, too, their attitudes toward intermarriage derive in part from the intermarriage experiences of Jews in biblical and talmudic times. Most Jews today think of the Bible and Talmud writers as strenuously opposed to intermarriage. While that was largely true, it was not uniformly the case.

Throughout the Hebrew Bible there is a tension between a desire to make marriages only within the Hebrew nation and an acknowledgment that many Jews were in fact marrying non-Israelites. Among the patriarchs, not just inmarriage, but kin-marriage, was the norm. Abraham married Sarah, his half-sister. He made his servant "swear by the Lord, the God of Heaven and the God of earth, that you shall not take a wife for my son from the daughters of Canaan, among whom I live, but you shall go back to my country and to my relatives and take a wife for my son Isaac." So Isaac married Rebekah, a relative. Later he charged his son Jacob to go to the same source. Jacob's wives, Leah and Rachel, were his first cousins.[1]

All this inbreeding was designed to preserve the identity of a tiny family of nomads in a sea of foreign peoples. But at the same time, some of the patriarchs intermarried with the peoples around them. Abraham picked up an Egyptian concubine named Hagar, whose son Ishmael became a focus of contention in family circles. Jacob's brother, Esau, married Judith and Basemith, both Hittite women, much to his parents' grief. At least three of Jacob's sons married foreign women. Judah married a Canaanite woman, as did Simeon. Centuries later, Judah came in for criticism on account of his choice, but there was no such objection raised at the time. And when Joseph, one of the noblest figures in all the Bible, took Asenath, the daughter of an Egyptian priest, for his wife, he suffered no criticism at all.[2]

During the sojourn in Egypt, Israel maintained a distinct tribal identity, all the while mixing with the peoples around it. Moses wrote of Israel as "a nation that lives alone," yet acknowledged that "a mixed multitude also went up with them" when they fled Egypt. Moses himself married Zipporah, a Midianite, and perhaps a Cushite, or Ethiopian, woman as well. Israelites of lesser stature also took spouses from among the Egyptians and other surrounding peoples.[3]

As Abraham's descendants neared the promised land, however, Moses became quite concerned about interethnic mixing. He feared for Israel's military security and its religious integrity. Enumerating seven specific neighboring tribes, Moses told Israel, "You shall not intermarry with them; you shall not give your daughters to their sons nor shall you take their daughters for your sons. For they will turn your sons away from following me to serve other gods." Instead, Israel was to "utterly destroy" the peoples who lived in Canaan.[4] At the same time, Moses recognized and made provision for a certain inevitable amount of intermarriage. He told Israel's soldiers that enemy women they captured might be taken as wives and insisted that, once the fighting was over, "The stranger who resides with you shall be to you as the native among you, and you shall love him as yourself."[5]

Once secure in Canaan, the people of Israel established a regular pattern of social, commercial, and sexual intercourse with those of their neighbors who had not been annihilated. Judges records God's anger that Israel's men were mixing freely with women from six of the seven tribes which Moses had so recently put off limits. Samson petulantly demanded a Philistine bride over his parents' feeble protests. Ruth, one of the greatest models for Jewish and Christian womanhood, was not a Hebrew at all, but a woman of Moab—one of the proscribed peoples—who married an Israelite and threw in her lot with her husband's tribe. David had a number of wives, not all of whom were Israelites, without a hint of disapproval from the Old Testament writers. Solomon, Israel's greatest king, concluded an alliance with Egypt by marrying Pharoah's daughter. His vast harem included scores if not hundreds of foreign wives and concubines, whom later writers credited for a decline of religious devotion during and after his reign.[6]

In subsequent generations, as Israel was split into two nations and then carried off into captivity, substantial mixing took place, to the point that large numbers of Abraham's descendants lost their Hebrew identity through intermarriage and the adoption of surrounding religions. National and religious authorities tried to keep the people together, but were generally successful mainly near the center of Israelite civilization and not on the geographical margins. Also, they were more stringent in opposing outmarriage by Jewish men than by Jewish women: the women would go to their husbands' tribes, but intermarrying Jewish men would bring foreign religious and cultural elements into the nation of Israel. While the people of Israel lay captive in Babylon and later Persia, some tried to preserve their ethnic and religious distinctiveness. Others mixed with their captors and other elements of the empire. One Hebrew woman, Esther, entered the harem of the king of Persia and used her position to save her people from sure destruction. She is remembered as one of the greatest of Jewish heroines; seldom does anyone notice that she intermarried.[7]

Beginning in the sixth century B.C., the Persian monarch allowed a number of Israelites to return to their ancestral homeland. A century later, the rebuilding nation underwent a national and religious revival under the leadership of Ezra and Nehemiah. Part of these leaders' program for national reform involved rigid separation from surrounding peoples. They objected to social intercourse and intermarriage less on the theory that contact with foreigners would sway Jews away from the God of their ancestors and more on the ground that it would destroy Israel's national solidarity. They pushed an ethnic definition of Jewish national and religious identity, complaining that "the holy race has been intermingled." Nehemiah cursed the intermarrying men of Israel, and Ezra demanded that they put away their foreign wives— not just those of the previously proscribed seven tribes, but others as well. What fate met the wives is not recorded. For centuries thereafter, strict Jews looked back to Ezra and Nehemiah as the authors of the definitive word on intermarriage: it is forbidden.[8]

Yet there followed several centuries of domination by Greece and Rome, in which time considerable assimilation took place. Much of the assimilation of this period involved not Jews into Hellenistic culture but rather members of other groups into the Hebrew orbit. Many non-Jews became Jews, and not a few of them married Jews, while a few Jews also slipped into the surrounding milieu. This general trend toward assimilation and intermarriage was punctuated by brief revivals of Jewish nationalism, as with the revolt of the Maccabees against their Seleucid overlords in 168 B.C. At such times, intermarriage and other symbols of accommodation to the surrounding culture were loudly denounced, but the revivals were brief. Converts continued to flow into Judaism, including the tiny Jewish sect called Christianity, and foreign genes continued to flow into the Jewish pool.[9]

In the latter years of the Roman epoch, the writers of the Talmud grappled with many issues, among them the question of intermarriage. As they looked back at the writers of the biblical era, they sided with the prohibitors rather than the permitters of intermarriage, and with Ezra's call for solidarity on nationalist grounds more than Moses's concern for religious purity. As Christianity rose as a separate, and ultimately the supreme, religion in the Roman world, the church legislated against marriage between Christians and Jews. The rabbis responded in kind by keeping up a stiff prohibition against exogamy.[10]

Intermarriage and Jewish-Gentile Relations in Europe

Throughout the Middle Ages, Jews existed in small communities scattered across Europe, the Middle East, and other parts of the Old World. Our concern in this book is with Central and East European, or Ashkenazic, Jews rather than with the Sephardim—those from Iberia, Africa, and the Middle East. The former supplied nearly all of the Jews who came to America. Several authorities suggest that Jewish-Christian marriage was fairly common in the early Middle Ages, despite opposition from leaders on both sides. The Council of Elvira first forbade Christians to marry Jews—or to have any social relations with them at all—about A.D. 303. There followed a steady stream of similar church edicts for more than a millennium. The chief fear seems to have been loss of Christians into Judaism. Not a few Christians, including some priests, converted to Judaism in order to marry Jews. By Jewish law, their children—and any children born of Jewish mothers—would be Jews.[11]

On the other side, many Jews became Christians and married Gentiles. One wealthy eleventh-century Italian Jew named Baruch Pierleoni converted to Christianity and married a Christian woman. Their great-grandson, Petrus Leonis, was chosen pope in 1130. In the early Middle Ages the wealth and relatively high status of some Jews made intermarriage and conversion to Judaism attractive to some Christians. With the coming of the Inquisition, the rise of anti-Jewish propaganda, and the decline of Jewish fortunes, intermarriage became much less frequent. Confronted by the church militant, nearly all the couples who did intermarry chose Christianity, and not Judaism. The church had no use for unconverted Jews, but it welcomed, and approved intermarriages with, any Jews who would renounce the faith of their parents. In this same era, Jewish leaders, such as Rabbi Moses of Coucy, spoke out angrily against conversions and against intermarriage. From the thirteenth century until the beginning of the nineteenth, very few marriages took place between Jews and Christians in Europe. Penalties for intermarriage varied enormously. In most times and places, government authorities refused to acknowledge the legitimacy of such unions. In some instances they prescribed heavy penalties, such as whippings or even death, for offenders.[12]

Western European Jewry underwent a vast change in the nineteenth century. Part of the legacy of the French Revolution was a push toward egalitarianism in most West European societies, including emancipation from centuries-old disabilities for Jews. Jews were allowed to enter occupations, schools, and social stations that had long been closed to them. Disraeli, an English Christian born to Jewish parents, rose to become prime minister of England. Parallel to the emancipation of West European Jewry was a decline in Jewish religiosity and communal life. Many Jews adopted the tongues of their various nations and gave up Yiddish. Many joined the Reform movement, an attempt by assimilationist Jews to modernize Judaism, shed the ritual and superstition they associated with Orthodoxy, and make their religion more estimable in the eyes of their non-Jewish peers. Others practiced other diluted forms of Judaism, became skeptics, dropped Judaism entirely, or became Christians.[13]

Along with the desire to assimilate came a desire on the part of some to intermarry. Increasingly, Christian nations ceased to stand in the way. France, Belgium, Holland, Great Britain, Germany, and the Scandinavian countries all legalized marriage between Christians and Jews by 1875. It has been suggested that the reversal of so many governments' positions on intermarriage occurred because it was now clear that intermarriage in this period meant a net gain to the ranks of Christianity, not a loss as in the early Middle Ages. Yet it may have been simply that marriage was now seen increasingly as a civil matter between two contracting parties, not a religious one involving two households of faith. Governments saw themselves as civil entities, not arms of ecclesiastical powers, and felt less bound to protect the interests of churches than once was the case.[14] Jewish authorities went along with the trend toward toleration of intermarriage. Under pressure from Napoleon, the Paris Sanhedrin declared in 1807 that it would recognize Jewish-Gentile marriages contracted through civil authorities as civilly binding and would not punish Jews who intermarried. In 1844, a rabbinical conference in Braunschweig, Germany, went further, stating that "the intermarriage of Jews and Christians, and, in general, the intermarriage of Jews and adherents of any of the monotheistic religions, is not forbidden, provided that the parents are permitted by the law of the State to bring up the offspring of such marriage in the Jewish faith." Neither body sanctioned rabbis to perform intermarriages, yet some liberal rabbis began to do just that: as early as 1849, Samuel Holdheim, one of the founders of Reform Judaism, married a Jew and Gentile in Leipzig. Soon other rabbis followed suit.[15]

Comprehensive, reliable statistics on intermarriage in Europe are not available until the twentieth century. What numbers there are show an increasing amount of outmarriage by Jews in the countries where Reform and assimilation flourished: in Prussia, for instance, 5 percent outmarried in 1875–84, 11 percent in 1905–8, and 22 percent in 1928. Intermarriage was more common in the cities, where Jews constituted a tiny minority and where pressures to assimilate were greater, than in the countryside. There is some evidence that eighteenth- and early-nineteenth-century Jewish outmarriage was mainly by women. This was, perhaps, partly because of a Jewish law of the womb: children were deemed to follow the religion of their mother, not their father. Thus, there would be no loss to Judaism if a woman married a Gentile, but if a man married out, his offspring would forever be lost. Still, by 1900 far more Jewish men than women intermarried, and the gender imbalance was increasing.[16]

In Eastern Europe, the story was rather different. There, especially in tsarist Russia, oppression of Jews continued unabated into the modern period. Jews did not enter into the social, cultural, or commercial life of their countries. They remained segregated and largely impoverished. They clung to Yiddish rather than adopting their nations' tongues, to Orthodoxy rather than embracing Reform. There was some liberalization and some intermarriage for Jews in relatively cosmopolitan central Russia. But the heartlands of Jewry—places like Galicia, White Russia, Latvia, and the Ukraine—remained largely untouched by the trends that affected their West European co-religionists. As late as the 1920s, Jewish outmarriage rates in such places were very low: 17 percent in central Russia, but only 5 percent in the Ukraine, 3 percent in White Russia, 2 percent in Latvia, and 1 percent in Galicia.[17]

American Jewish Intermarriage:
Sephardim and German Jews

The first Jews to come to North America were Sephardim: Spanish and Portuguese Jews fleeing Old World persecution for the relative safety of British and, especially, Dutch colonies in the New World. Coming as early as 1654, they formed outposts of Judaism in places like Rhode Island and New Amsterdam (later New York). These were Orthodox Jews, but possessors of a culture far removed from the life of East European Jewry. Most Sephardic Jews entered the world of commerce and finance. Several, like Haym Solomon and Aaron Lopez, were prominent financiers of the American Revolution. Others fought in that war. At the time of America's first national census in 1790, Jews numbered only 1,500 out of 3.9 million Americans. By the early years of the nineteenth century, Sephardic immigration had all but stopped, and Sephardim were fast losing their distinct identity, blending either into the Gentile population or into the mass of Ashkenazic newcomers.[18]

Outmarriage was not popular with Sephardic religious organizations, but it was a prominent feature of Sephardic life nonetheless. Genealogist Malcolm H. Stern found 699 Jewish marriages in continental North America between 1776 and 1840; 201 of them, nearly 30 percent, were mixed marriages. Most Sephardic families seem to have been absorbed, usually by Gentiles but sometimes by Ashkenazim, by the third generation. The intermarriage and assimilation came in part because there were more Jewish men than women in many locations, especially outside eastern seaboard cities. If a Jewish man wanted to find a bride, he often had to look for a Gentile woman. In the cities, where most Sephardim settled, intermarriage was spurred by close social and commercial relations between Gentile and Jew, and by the lack of key Jewish institutions in America. Those Gentiles who married Jews might have wished to convert to Judaism, but Orthodox law called for three rabbis to preside over any conversion, and there were no ordained rabbis residing in North America before 1840. Sometimes itinerant rabbis from Europe would perform a conversion, or a congregation would wink at the rules and approve a conversion on its own. But more often, even people with intense pride in their Jewishness found themselves converting to Christianity or at least becoming involved in Christian churches in order to preserve family unity. Genealogical records show Jewish-Gentile intermarriages very early in colonial history. Moses Simonson came to Plymouth with the second boatload of Pilgrims. His daughter married a Gentile named John Soule; that couple's son married Sarah Standish, the granddaughter of John Alden and Miles Standish. Intermarriages seem to have been especially prevalent during the period of intense nationalism and religious tolerance that accompanied the War for Independence. Families as prominent as the Schuylers and Delanceys in New York and the Hurlburts and Wenhams in Massachusetts admitted Jewish men and women to their ranks. Despite theoretical opposition on the part of Sephardic congregations, many prominent Jews intermarried. Members of great commercial families with names like Hart, Franks, Lopez, Salomon, and Levy, and synagogue leaders named Mordecai, Cohen, Da Costa, Seizas, and Judah, all married Gentiles. In many cases Gentile brides or husbands converted to Judaism, but just as often it was the Jew who converted. Even in the former case, children and grandchildren most often were raised as Christians, particularly as Episcopalians. Some of these intermarriages were performed by synagogue officials, though it was more common for intermarrying couples to look for a minister or contract a civil ceremony.[19]

After about 1825, the Sephardim were rapidly overtaken by a wave of Ashkenazic immigrants. In 1840, the American Jewish population stood at about 15,000—a tenfold increase in five decades. In 1850, the population was 50,000; in 1860, 150,000; and in 1880, 250,000. By that time, almost all American Jews were of Germanic origin; even those who came from Hungary, Austria, Bohemia, and Western Poland spoke German and were influenced by German Jewish culture. These were years of emigration for many sorts of Germans besides Jews— Protestant sectarians, Catholics, Lutherans, political dissidents, and Germans who merely sought a chance at raising their standard of living. Many German Jews were caught up in those other movements. Others came for specifically Jewish reasons, fleeing the humiliations and economic restrictions that were the lot of their people in Europe. Unlike the relatively well-to-do Sephardim, whose family connections stretched to merchant houses all over the New World, the German Jewish immigrants were mainly poor people. Many men became peddlers. They hawked their wares not just in the seaboard cities but also

throughout the South and West, and established small Jewish communities wherever they went.[20]

These German Jews brought with them a jumble of theological persuasions, from strict Orthodoxy to radical free thought. One of these
was Reform Judaism. Anxious to be accepted into American (and German) Gentile society, the Reformers tried to "modernize" Judaism,
to deemphasize ritual aspects and Mosaic imperatives that set their
religion apart from others. They discounted the age-old notion that
the Jews were a people somehow different from other peoples and
presented Reform Judaism as just another denomination. Their rationale was that Judaism had always changed its face to accommodate
the tastes and level of knowledge of the time. They also stressed that
Jews had a special "mission" to reach all people, not just to recreate
the historic nation of Israel, and so must be flexible in their appeal.
Orthodox leaders in America and especially in Europe looked upon the
Reformers with horror. They felt that Reform struck at the very heart of
proper Judaism: ritual adherence to Mosaic law. But in America, unlike
Europe, the Reformers had a relatively free hand to change Judaism
as they pleased, for there were no official ecclesiastical structures and
few long-established Orthodox bodies to stand in their way. In 1880,
by far the majority of American Jews were adherents of Reform.[21]

Along with dispersion across the American landscape, assimilationist impulses, and liberal theology came mixing and mating with non-
Jews. In remote areas of the South and West, Jewish men lived alone
and had long since given up the thought of keeping kosher homes or
finding Jewish wives. Most New Orleans Jews who married in the nineteenth century took French Catholic or Black wives. On the frontier,
Jewish men often married Gentile White, Indian, or Mexican women.
Solomon Bibo was not long off the boat from Germany when he left
New York City for New Mexico to open a series of dry goods stores.
He learned to speak several Indian languages in addition to Spanish
and English, married an Indian woman named Juana, and served a
five-year term as chief of the Acoma tribe in the 1880s. He was the first
chief to enforce compulsory education for Acoma children. Wiped out
by a depression in the 1890s, Bibo moved to San Francisco, opened
a chain of grocery stores, and was very active in Jewish religious and
community affairs.[22]

In areas where there were more Jews, intermarriage was uncommon but not unheard of. There were 202 Jewish-Gentile intermarriages in San Francisco in 1883, with 163 involving Jewish men and 39 involving Jewish women. In 1880, Benjamin M. Goldberg married Jennie Sibley near Milwaukee. The wedding might not have occasioned much comment, but it was presided over by I. S. Moses, a radical Reform rabbi. Some conservative Jews condemned the couple, but more excoriated Moses: a couple might intermarry through the services of a minister or justice of the peace, they reasoned, but for a rabbi to sanctify the match amounted to betrayal of his office. Rabbi Isaac M. Wise, the foremost leader of American Reform, viewed Moses's action as a threat to the Reform movement, for it cast the Reformers as proponents of intermarriage in the minds of many Jews. Wise protested angrily that "a Jewish minister has no right . . . to unite in marriage Jew and Gentile" without a prior and thoroughgoing conversion to Judaism on the part of the Gentile. Moses, for his part, claimed the right to act before God as his conscience dictated, and his congregation backed him up. Other rabbis, such as Philadelphia's Samuel Hirsch, claimed a similar right to perform intermarriages, but their congregations did not go along. There does not seem to have been much complaint from Gentiles about this or other intermarriages.[23]

Just three years after the Goldberg-Sibley wedding, Isaac M. Wise's own daughter Helen eloped with James Molony, an indifferent Presbyterian of Irish descent. An outspoken feminist as well as an intermarrier, Helen Wise Molony brought down a hail of criticism on her father's head. Orthodox Jews had long maintained that Reform diluted Judaism to the point where it was Judaism no longer. Helen Wise's intermarriage seemed to prove that Reform led inevitably to loss of Jewish identity. Yet Isaac M. Wise was philosophical about the marriage, and Reform continued to thrive. Helen Wise Molony continued to identify herself as a Jew and to attend synagogue, and she raised her children to be proud of their Jewish heritage.[24]

Rabbis, both Orthodox and Reform, generally condemned intermarriage, whether performed by a rabbi or by someone else. Reform leader David Einhorn loudly protested that "each intermarriage drives a nail in the coffin of Judaism." The rabbis were split on the issue of whether intermarriage was a threat to Jewish religious solidarity or to racial purity, but they all agreed that it must be condemned.[25] Jewish lay people agreed. Delaware Jews sent their children as far away as Pennsylvania, Georgia, and North Carolina in the 1880s and 1890s on Jewish mate-hunting expeditions, rather than let them take Gentile spouses at home. The Milwaukee B'nai B'rith lodge ruled in 1870 that "1. A candidate for membership into this Lodge, if married to a non-Jewess, shall not be admitted. 2. A brother who marries a non-Jewess, or does not circumcize his male child according to the Mosaic faith, shall be expelled." Benjamin Gratz, a prominent businessman, was denied a plot in Philadelphia's Hebrew cemetery in 1882 because he and his children had married Gentiles. He had to go as far afield as Cincinnati before he could find a place of eternal rest. Yet intermarriage continued apace. The responses of the Milwaukee B'nai B'rith and Philadelphia cemetery may have been out of tune with their times. The changing opinions of New York Jews over several decades are instructive. During the era of Sephardic domination, intermarriage was condoned and spouses of intermarriers welcomed to New York synagogues. With the rise of German immigration in the 1830s and '40s, this tolerance disappeared. Intermarried Jews were stripped first of their leadership posts and then of their membership benefits in Shearith Israel synagogue, and zealots called for their complete ouster. By the 1850s, intermarried Jews had been pushed out of most synagogues and had little contact with other Jews. Yet, in the Civil War decade and after, some Reform synagogues began to restore the intermarried to membership and approve conversions for their spouses.[26]

The descendants of the first two waves of Jewish immigrants, then, included a large number of people who intermarried. The colonial-era Sephardim were largely absorbed into the Gentile population by the early nineteenth century. Their successors, German Jews, proved more successful at maintaining a separate Jewish identity. But structural factors such as geographical dispersion and upward class mobility, plus such cultural factors as liberal theology and an assimilationist impulse, pushed them in the direction of increased intermarriage.

The Orthodox Invasion

The 1880s witnessed the beginning of a new era for American Jewry. A vast tide of Jews washed out of Eastern Europe, across Western Europe, and onto the Atlantic shore of the United States. The tide began in 1881, reached its height at the turn of the century, and receded only with the coming of war to Europe in 1914. Altogether, between 1881 and the nearly total cutoff of immigration in 1924, 2.3 million East European Jews came to America. Not only did this vast folk invasion dwarf the existing Jewish community in America; these were a different kind of Jews. They were very orthodox, having lived for centuries in a segregated, intensely Jewish environment. Many had had no contact with the Enlightenment ideas which their German predecessors had imbibed. Those among them who had experienced a broader intellectual world had learned not Goethe but Marx. They were free-thinkers and Zionists and laborites and socialists, not seekers after Protestant refinement. Driven by Russian oppression and by poverty, these and their Orthodox brethren walked across Europe, loaded the steerage of leaky boats, and crammed into America's eastern cities, principally New York. They brought vibrance, life, a cacophony of voices, and a host of social problems to that city's Lower East Side. The contrast was so great between the East Europeans and the by now middle- and upper-class German Jews who had preceded them that most Germans did not at first want to be associated with the new immigrants. The existing Jewish community dutifully, and gingerly, extended a helping hand to coreligionists, but did not welcome them as brothers and sisters. Nor did American Gentiles accord the new immigrants a place of honor in their midst. The East European Jews were stuck, along with other new immigrants from southern and eastern Europe, near the bottom of the heap, and defied to climb up.[27]

The Orthodox invasion was so vast that it soon became possible, especially in the eastern cities, to speak of American Jewry and have in mind only the characteristics of the East Europeans. The Germans remained at the head of many community institutions, and Sephardim continued to come in small numbers, but their lives and concerns no longer were central to the American Jewish experience. It is to this East European group and its dealings with intermarriage that the remainder of Part III is devoted.

Mutual Images

First, however, it is important to understand something about the ways Jews and Gentiles, male and female, saw each other over the first

three-quarters of the twentieth century. Gentile stereotypes of Jewish
women and men, though consistently negative in some respects, in
others showed a progression toward images that tended to encourage
intermarriage. The outraged Gentile mother who stormed in the 1920s
about her daughter's Jewish man friend could have been talking in
the 1960s, though she might have been a bit more polite in the later
decade. She shouted: "Jews are sensual, aggressive, ostentatious, cun-
ning. . . . They are shrewder than Christians and never hesitate to seize
an unfair advantage. . . . Full of sex and sensuality . . . the Jews' god
[is] money."[28] Public opinion surveys from 1938 through 1962 showed a
similar set of negative images of Jews in the minds of Gentiles: greedy,
dishonest, aggressive, clannish, selfish, loud, overbearing, and discriminatory against non-Jews. In the era of the immigrant generation
—before about 1930—Gentiles also saw Jews as lecherous, unclean,
uncultured, impoverished, and given over to bizarre religious practices. Telemanchus Thomas Timayenis attacked Jewish men in an 1888
broadside:

Next to his lust for money, the strongest passion in the Jew is his licen-
tiousness. This, like every other vicious trait of which the Jew is possessed,
takes a peculiarly prominent and objectionable form.

The average Jew is disgustingly bawdy in his talk, and interlards his
conversation with filthy expressions and obscene words. On the verandas at
summer-resorts, in hotel-corridors, in the lobbies of theatres, on steamboats,
on railway-cars, and in public places in general, the Jew indulges in this repulsive peculiarity, to the great annoyance and disgust of respectable Christian
women and decency-loving Gentile men. . . .

Overdressed, with mincing gait and dandified mien, these Jew "mashers"
are daily to be seen strutting up and down the leading streets, ogling, with
amazing effrontery, every woman who passes them by. Young girls of tender
age are especially marked by these Jew "mashers" as their particular prey. . . .

In many of the factories operated by the Jews throughout the country, the
life of an honest girl therein employed is made simply a hell, by reason of the
Jews' predominant lechery. . . .

The Jew . . . is one of the most assiduous patrons of houses of prostitution
throughout the country. Without the Jew clientele, it is safe to say that fully
sixty-six per cent of the houses of ill-fame in the various cities of the United
States . . . would be compelled to go out of existence. . . .

The insatiability of his carnal appetites . . . exceeds the ordinary limits
of lust. Those certain hideous and abhorrent forms of vice, which have their

origin in countries of the East, and which have in recent years sprung into existence in this country, have been taught, . . . fostered, elaborated, and encouraged, by the lecherous Jew![29]

With the exception of lechery, most of the negative traits ascribed to Jews might from another angle be seen as positive. By the time the second generation reached adulthood—the 1930s, '40s, and '50s —Gentiles were increasingly disposed to see the positive side of the coin. Thus, many admired Jews for their business ability, their loyalty to family and religion, their ambition, persistence, and thrift. And in the second generation some new positive traits were added to the image. Jews became associated in the 1930s and after with the avant-garde politically and culturally, and with a high level of intellectual attainment in many fields. Few Americans were unaware in the 1940s that Einstein, Freud, and Marx were Jews.[30]

Many of the characteristics, negative and positive, were applied to both men and women, but they seem to have been associated particularly with Jewish men. The negative image doubtless made immigrant-generation Jewish men unattractive in the eyes of many Gentile women. But beginning with the rise of a substantial, educated middle class in the second generation, the growing positive image made Jewish men look good to an increasing number of Gentile women. Israel Ellman described the phenomenon: "In the course of 'emancipating' themselves many of the bright middle-class non-Jewish girls are attracted by the political liberation characteristic of Jewish students and by their equally characteristic avantgardism in intellectual and aesthetic matters. . . . The average well-educated Gentile girl does not want too much of a Bohemian for a husband but nevertheless would like someone who is 'different.' The Jew fits this category admirably." Add to this exotic, liberating picture the stability implied by the stereotypes ascribing drive, business ability, and a strong sense of family, and Jewish men appeared attractive indeed. Thus, by the 1940s and '50s, when the younger members of the second generation were coming of age, the stereotypes regarding Jewish men were of a type that would attract many Gentile women, much as the submissive, erotic, exotic image of Nisei women attracted many non-Japanese American men.[31]

Gentile minds perceived in Jewish women many of the negative qualities ascribed to Jewish men: loudness, aggressiveness, lust for money and position. These were fairly constant images over the generations and were not likely to make Jewish women attractive to non-Jewish men. But there was a competing image of the Jewish woman as motherly, earthy, exotic, sensual, and uninhibited; to certain sorts of Gentile men these thoughts were enticing. Nowhere is this picture more vividly presented than in Thomas Wolfe's 1937 novel *The Web and the Rock*. Wolfe's protagonist, George Webber, found the older Jewish woman, Esther Jack (modelled after Wolfe's Jewish lover, Aline Bernstein), exotic and inscrutable: "smiling gently, and with that musing and tranquil expression touched with sadness . . . which already had power to wound his suspicion and to awaken in him a jealous curiosity. . . . It was a somber, dark, passionate look . . . giving a masklike grief, an almost Slavic and undecipherable passion to her face. . . . An inner and remote absorption from which the world was excluded." Webber also saw this Jewish woman as domestic, warm, sheltering, motherly, a "matronly figure of middle age." Yet she was voluptuous, sensuous, and uninhibited. He saw all Jewish women—rich and poor—as having these qualities:

Wealthy and cultivated [Jewish women] . . . were very elegant and fashionable, beautifully gowned, dark, tall, some of them exotically lovely. . . . Some of them valued fine intelligence and the ability to create more than they valued money, but most of them had both. . . . The Jews loved what was beautiful and pleasant in life. Rich Jews and poor Jews were full of life and curiosity. . . . They had a glorious time. . . . As for the poor Jews. . . . They swarmed, they fought, they haggled . . . they ate, drank, and fornicated with a will. The poor Jews also enjoyed life. . . . He saw a dark regiment of Jewish women in their lavish beauty, their faces melting into honey, their eyes glowing, their breasts like melons . . . their proud bodies opulently gowned and flashing with somber fires of ancient jewels as they paced with the velvet undulance of an intolerable sensuality the proud and splendid chambers of the night. They were . . . the living cross on which the flesh and marrow of Christian men had been crucified."[32]

Perhaps more Gentile men saw the crabbed, shrill, overbearing Jewish female image than the icon that so fascinated Wolfe, but the earthy, sensual, exotic Jewish woman was also seen by many.

To most immigrants fresh from Eastern Europe, Gentiles might be admired for their wealth or accomplishments, but for their personal qualities they were to be hated or feared. Henry Hellyer recalled what he learned about Christians as a boy in Odessa: "The word Christian was in itself enough to make the hair stand on end with terror on any Jewish head; for, as everybody knew, the Christians were the boys with the brutal faces who ran about bare-footed with whips and cudgels in their hands, attacking every Jewish boy they met." In Yiddish America, many Jews did not have enough contact with Gentiles to form a new opinion. Gentiles were remote and distinctly, irrevocably different from Jews. Even if the animosity faded in America—and it might not if a Jew had suffered anti-Semitic oppression here—the sense of distance did not. It was only with the rise of the second generation that what Julius Shore called "the cult of 'Goy-worship' "—unabashed reverence for all things Gentile—set in. Like the Japanese American second generation, a tremendous number of American-born Jews saw themselves primarily as Americans and sought to assimilate into mainstream society as rapidly as they could.[33]

Gentile women—*shikses* in Yiddish—held a special appeal for certain second- and third-generation Jewish men. Part of the allure was related to class aspirations. Philip Roth's Alexander Portnoy went on and on about button-nosed bevies of Gentile girls, "so gorgeous, so healthy, so blond," and so upper-class, while he was so homely, so uptight, so Jewish, and so hopelessly lower-middle-class. George Benedict converted to Christianity in no small part because of an image of Christian womanhood riveted in his young mind by a grammar school teacher: "She was so sweet and beautiful, with blue eyes and light brown, curly hair" that he felt mortifed to be a Jew in her presence. This vision of Gentile womanhood—beautiful, graceful, cultured, pure, fully and unambiguously American—contrasted sharply with Portnoy's picture of Jewish women: large, loud, bossy, castrating.[34]

Part of the shikse appeal, however, was purely sexual. This was actually a compound of three notions. First there was the idea that Gentile women were particularly good at sex. Jewish men told Louis Berman that "Gentile girls are hotter." A ditty sung on the Lower East side around 1915 went

> In der Toyre steyt geshribn
> Mit a shikse tor me nisht lign—
> Oy—der bester srore oyf der velt!

That means

> In the Torah it is written
> With a shikse you cannot sleep,
> Oh, the best piece in the world![35]

Second was the conviction—quite contrary to Portnoy's vision—that Gentile women were unclean, animalistic, and eager to have sex. In *The Slave,* Isaac Bashevis Singer had Polish peasant women "perpetually pulling up their skirts to show [his main character] . . . their hips and thighs. 'Lay me,' a girl would shamelessly demand." Another Yiddish rhyme treated Gentile women brutally as sex objects:

> In the Torah it is written,
> With a shikse you may sleep,
> But if the girl does not let you have her,
> May she be afflicted with cholera.

The root word for *shikse* means "abomination" or "despicable thing" and was associated with ritual prostitution in Canaanite religion. Maria and David Levinson found Jewish men who regarded Gentile women as "devalued, morally inferior and [therefore] an object of carnal desires."[36] The third notion was that sex with Gentile women was safe, for they were not Jewish. According to Berman, for many Jewish men, "a Jewish girl arouses a young man's incest horror . . . she reminds him of his sister or mother," while a Gentile woman, in the Levinsons' words, represented "a relatively legitimate and anxiety-free sexual object."[37]

Jewish women's ideas about Gentile men have not been so amply discussed. On the one side is a woman who said that "a Gentile husband beats his wife but a Jewish husband never does," expressing a fear of non-Jewish men. On another side there is the pure, lofty, intellectual, cultured, Anglo-Saxon male who lurks in the pages of Anzia Yezierska's novels—not unlike Portnoy's omnipresent preppie shikses, but lacking the constant, explicit sexual references. Then, too, there is the Jewish college student who said that, while Jewish men "make better husbands . . . Gentile men make better lovers."[38]

By the time the second generation reached adulthood, the mutual images of Jews and Gentiles, females and males, had set the stage for interethnic mixing. Gentiles viewed Jewish immigrant men as vulgar, grasping, and generally unattractive. But they saw their sons as bright, ambitious, and avant-garde. Some saw Jewish women as loud and pushy, but others saw them as exotic, sensual, and nurturing. To Jewish men, shikses—Gentile women—were either the personification of beauty and grace or the symbol of animal sexuality. The image that Jewish women had of Gentile men was ambivalent and less distinct.

7. Dimensions of Intermarriage: Separate Identity amid Growing Acceptance

The Generations and Intermarriage

The pattern of Jewish outmarriage over three generations in America was like that of Japanese Americans: little outmarriage in the immigrant group, more in the second generation, and substantially more in the third. First-generation immigrants from Eastern Europe felt conflicting pulls between a desire to assimilate rapidly to American culture and a wish to preserve their distinct Jewish identity. Many immigrants, especially the younger ones, came to America with a strong desire in Irving Howe's words, "to be an American, dress like an American, and even, if only in fantasy, talk like an American." A popular guidebook advised Jewish immigrants: if you want to get on in America, you had better "forget your past, your customs, and your ideals." Yet enthusiasm for things American did not make the average immigrant forget that he or she was a Jew from the Pale. Howe observed that "most wanted to maintain a distinctive Yiddish cultural life while penetrating individually into American society and economy; most wanted to insure their survival as a people while feeling free to break out of the ghetto." The vast majority of the immigrants did not stray very far from the ethnic enclave. Only a tiny fraction extended emancipation to include intermarriage. In New York between 1908 and 1912, less than 1 percent of Jewish immigrants married non-Jews. Outmarriage by Jewish immigrants was somewhat more frequent in the 1920s and '30s: perhaps as much as 2 to 3 percent, but certainly not more than that. Several sources suggest that a few more first-generation women than men married Gentiles, but the numbers for both sexes were so small that no significant trend is apparent. Many of the individuals who did intermarry chose Irish and Italian mates who lived in their neighborhoods and worked with them in New York's clothing trades.[1]

One intermarried man wrote to the "Bintel Brief" section of the *Vorwarts,* the Lower East Side's most prominent newspaper:

February 20, 1906
Dear Editor!

Working for a very long time with a Gentile woman in the shop, I came to know her very intimately, and we began to go out very often and the end was that we fell in love with each other. Naturally, we decided that I should not be a Gentile nor she a Jewess. But in the course of a year I realized, that we were garments of a different cut. Whenever an acquaintance, a friend, comes home, I note a great dissatisfaction on her face. And when she sees me reading a Jewish paper her face changes color. She does not it is true tell me anything, but I see that the woman is wasting away like a candle. I feel that she feels very unhappy with me although I am certain she loves me. On top of that she is to become a mother soon, and her tie to me becomes stronger on account of that. Only a few weeks ago Christ awoke within her; every Sunday she rises at dawn and hurries to church and comes back with eyes swollen from crying. Whenever I go out with her and it happens that we pass a church, tremors seize her.

Give me, dear Mr. Editor some advice as to what I should do. I— become converted to Christianity is out of the question. That she should cease going to church, I see, there is no hope for that. What then remains to be done, in your opinion, that there may not be so much trouble in our home?

Another immigrant, a learned and pious Jew, fell in love with his Gentile night school teacher and gave in to her pleadings to marry her in 1908. She and her parents then supported him during his continued studies. A third immigrant, a freethinking socialist named Chajah Nitz, became pregnant by her Gentile lover in 1906, but refused to marry him because "If I was going to live with a Christian then I wanted it to be a free relationship."[2]

Like Japanese Americans, Jews can be divided fairly easily into

discrete generations. Since East European Jewish immigration began
a little earlier, each Jewish generation is about a decade older than its
Japanese counterpart. Thus, the members of the first generation were
almost all born before 1910, the second generation between 1900 and
1930, and the third generation after 1940. Like the Nisei, and like
the second generation of most immigrant groups, many American-born
Jews considered themselves fully American and chafed against what
they saw as backward separatism on their parents' part. Harry Roskolenko recalled his Lower East Side youth, saying, "As children, we
were American-grained from the start. But to our parents we were
always Jews, never American." He and his friends resisted, proudly
asserting their right to be fully American. Harry Golden wrote of the
second generation's "hurry up to be assimilated. . . . Anything suggesting the old country was naturally considered a bit embarrassing."
An American-born youth bemoaned his parents' humiliating Jewishness to the editor of the "Bintel Brief" in 1933: "Our parents know
English too, but they speak only Yiddish, not just among themselves
but to us too, and even to our American friends who come to visit us.
We beg them not to speak Yiddish in the presence of our friends, since
they can speak English, but they don't want to. . . . A great deal of
quarreling goes on between our parents and ourselves because of it.
. . . Imagine, even . . . in a store on Fifth Avenue, New York, [our
father] insists on speaking Yiddish. . . . Is that nice?"[3]

With such an assimilationist mentality common among members of
the second generation, it is not surprising that intermarriage jumped
sharply. As early as 1908–12 in New York City, second-generation outmarriage was much higher than first: 7 percent of the American-born
men and 5 percent of the women intermarried, compared to less than
1 percent of the first generation of both sexes. Over the whole second generation, probably 10 percent of the men and 7 percent of the
women married Gentiles. As these numbers indicate and other authorities attest, more second-generation men than women intermarried.
There were exceptions to this trend, however. In the upper income
brackets and among Reform Jews, more women than men seem to
have intermarried. And there was a big surge of female outmarriages
in the 1940s—from less than 1 percent in the 1930s to nearly 9 percent
in 1941–45—that was not matched by any parallel increase in outmarriages by Jewish men. Precisely what sorts of people intermarrying

Jews chose as mates is not clear. There is some indication that about 40 percent of the intermarriages were with Roman Catholics, which is substantially more than the percentage of Catholics in the general population and would indicate either more contact or a special affinity for people of Roman Catholic background. Most of the Catholics in question were Italian or Irish.[4]

All sorts of members of the second generation married Gentiles. Some marriages met outstanding success; others, equally spectacular failure. George Sokolsky, son of a Polish immigrant rabbi, went to China, married an educated, upper-class Chinese woman, and enjoyed a happy, stable marriage in that country's international community. Michael Klein, a department store manager, married Katie Neil, a clerk, in New York. The pair had difficulty adjusting to each other and to the discrimination they encountered among Gentiles. But upon moving into a Jewish neighborhood they found most of their problems solved. Some Jews entered intermarriages impulsively and later learned to regret their choices. One Orthodox New York woman married one of the first non-Jews she met, for reasons she could not recall afterward. She admitted in 1937 that although she loved her husband dearly, "I would not marry a Christian again because I feel that it cut me off from my family." A nominally religious Jew married a German American apologist for Hitler. The Gentile wife proclaimed her love for her Jewish husband, but at the same time she demanded that he and other Jews shed as much of their Jewishness as possible. When the wife wrote their story in 1939, their marriage seemed headed for trouble. In many cases, the intermarriers' parents were free-thinkers or others who held their Jewish identity loosely and welcomed the company of Gentiles in their social lives. The children extended their parents' liberal attitudes to intermarriage, sometimes to the dismay of the parents. Some intermarried Jews faced a special crisis with the rise of Hitler to power in Germany and the mass extermination of Jews in Europe. David Blondheim married Eleanor Dulles and seemed happily adjusted to her upper-class, Gentile social world until he was overcome with remorse at having abandoned his people at a time they were being liquidated. He stuck his head in a gas oven. A second-generation Hungarian Jewish woman married a German American Gentile man, only to find out that he had a considerable drinking problem that brought out his latent anti-Semitism. Spurned by both sets of parents, the couple fell to quarreling until he deserted her. In desperation, she wrote the "Bintel Brief" editor asking him to "advise me how to find my husband. I do not want to live with him by compulsion, nor do I ask his support. . . . I merely ask his aid in somehow obtaining a divorce, so that I may return to my people, to my God and to my parents. I cannot stand the loneliness and do not want to be hated, denounced, and spurned by all."[5] It is quite probable that the intermarriages described here were unusually unhappy. Most are taken from journalistic sources, and quiet, stable families do not make titillating reading in advice columns. But two things seem clear from this brief catalogue: (1) intermarrying Jews and their partners came from greatly varying backgrounds, and (2) more than a few of them experienced severe marital difficulty.

Outmarriage rose rapidly in the third generation, just as it did for third-generation Japanese Americans. This was especially true of Jewish men. The male intermarriage rate was only 2.7 percent in 1946–50. It jumped to 6.1 percent in 1951–55, 8.5 percent in 1956–60, 16.6 percent in 1961–65, and a startling 35.8 percent in 1966–72. By 1981, according to one study, 60.1 percent of young Jewish men were married to Gentiles. Outmarriage by Jewish women lagged behind. It stood at only 1.2 percent in 1956–60, though it rose sharply to 6.2 percent in 1961–65 and 9.8 percent in 1966–72. Intermarriage has continued to rise in recent years at an accelerating pace. In the early 1980s, the intermarriage rate for Chicago-area Jews under age thirty was more than three times as high (20%) as for those over forty (6%). In Denver the differential was 6 to 1 (57% to 9%). Many Jewish leaders were very concerned lest American Judaism die because of the high rate of intermarriage coupled with a low Jewish birthrate. Most of the third-generation intermarriers (like most other Jews of their generation) came from relatively comfortable middle- and upper-middle-class homes, where interaction with Gentiles was frequent and Judaism was lightly stressed. Serious consideration of their Jewishness came to many of these individuals only after they had decided to intermarry.[6]

Overall, then, the pattern of Jewish American outmarriage looks much like the Japanese: very little intermarriage in the first generation, more in the second, and considerably more in the third. The major differences are that far more Jewish men married out (for the Japanese it was mainly women who intermarried) and that the third-generation rate for Jews was not as high as for Japanese Americans.

Jews Respond to Intermarriage

In the face of an increasing rate of intermarriage, individual Jews and Jewish organizations had to come to grips with intermarriage and the intermarried Jew. Opposition, which was fairly uniform in the first years of this century, weakened progressively as time went on. Nevertheless, even as late as the 1970s a substantial number of Jews and Jewish leaders still opposed intermarriage.

From the first years of East European immigration to America, official Judaism adopted an Ezra-like posture, consistently discouraging intermarriage and turning its back on intermarried Jews. With few exceptions, this was as true of Reform as of Orthodox rabbis. In the late nineteenth century Rabbi A. E. Dobrin of Cleveland enjoined the girls in his confirmation class "to take an oath that they would never marry a man unless he professes the religion of Judaism." In 1919, rabbis from Syracuse and St. Louis wrote to a Jewish newspaper condemning intermarriage and urging other religious officials not to circumcise sons of intermarried families, nor to admit mixed children to Jewish schools.[7]

The main issue for the rabbis was the survival of the Jewish people. They assumed that anyone who intermarried, and his or her descendants, would be lost to Judaism forever. Fearfully they foretold the end of their people. Max Heller wrote in 1903: "The descendants of the Jew who intermarries are lost to Judaism. . . . The Jew who places social ambition, love of refinement, aesthetic sensitiveness above his loyalty to his brothers has unbound the principle [*sic*] artery of the religious life. A dwindling minority, like ourselves, whose religious principles escape definition, whose church organization lacks all disciplining power, could not retain coherence for any length of time, were it not that the prohibition of intermarriage creates a social inclusiveness which is the most powerful of all preservative agents."[8]

For years the Central Conference of American Rabbis, the Reform association, debated whether to allow its members to officiate at marriages between Jews and Gentiles. The debates were couched in theological terms, but the main issue was ethnic survival. When the

CCAR met in 1909, its members denounced intermarrying rabbis and pledged not to officiate at intermarriages, both because such marriages violated Jewish law and because they threatened Jewish survival. The rabbis split on the issue of whether or not a marriage between a convert and a born Jew was an intermarriage. Heller demanded that Jews, insofar as they could, separate themselves socially and intellectually from non-Jews so that their line might be preserved. Other, more liberal Jewish leaders encouraged social intercourse with Gentiles, but drew the line firmly at intermarriage. Such a liberal rabbi as Henry Berkowitz of Cleveland refused absolutely to perform an intermarriage and tried to talk several mixed couples out of marrying, but he recognized that the marriages they contracted before a justice of the peace were legal, if not, in his eyes, wise. Other rabbis were not so tolerant. They viewed civil intermarriages as no marriages at all and any children of such marriages as illegitimate.[9]

Non-rabbis among the Jewish immigrants also opposed intermarriage, both from gut revulsion and from a desire to maintain ethnic solidarity. Celia Silbert wrote in 1916: "What is the matter with the Jewish girls and boys of the East Side? What is it that makes them break Judea's holiest and most sacred ties and unite with strangers in marriage?" Rebecca Mack, an immigrant from Russia, converted to Christianity and married a Christian. But shortly she felt a longing for her people. "Therefore, I decided to turn back spiritually to where I belong—to the Jewish religion and Jewish customs." She recanted, left her husband, and dedicated herself to keeping other Jews within the fold. Most East Side immigrant men belonged to one or another of the *landsmanshaftn*, mutual aid societies based on one's area of origin in Eastern Europe. Not all of them made an issue of intermarriage, but several did. The constitution of the Plotzker Young Men's Independent Association, organized in 1893, read in part: "A member who leaves the Jewish Faith or marries a non-Jewish woman is automatically expelled from our membership and loses all rights and benefits of our Society."[10]

Some first-generation Jewish intermarriers were shunned by their fellows. Some lost their places in Jewish burial societies and synagogues. The families of some sat *shivah* for them, observing the seven days of ritual mourning. Some had fathers who recited *kaddish*, the Hebrew prayer for the dead. But others, after the marriage had taken place, were reconciled to their people. Michael and Katie Klein found politeness and some sympathy, if not a hearty welcome, when they moved back to a Jewish neighborhood shortly after their marriage, around 1910. Emancipated Jews—laborites, socialists, and freethinkers—were less likely to condemn intermarriers than were religious Jews, for they held their religious identifications less tightly. Secular ideological considerations were often as important to them as their genetic ties to other Jews. Thus Abraham Cahan, socialist activist and editor of the Yiddish-language *Vorwarts*, consistently refused to condemn intermarriage in his responses to letters. In 1908 he answered a query from a young man contemplating intermarriage: "We can only say that some mixed marriages are happy, others unhappy. But then many marriages between Jew and Jew, Christian and Christian, are not successful either. It is true, however, that in some mixed marriages the differences between man and wife create unhappiness. Therefore we cannot take it upon ourselves to advise the young man regarding this marriage. This he must decide for himself." [11] Still, an even-handed attitude such as Cahan's was not common. In the immigrant generation, most Jews, whether observant or not, firmly opposed intermarriage.

In the 1920s, '30s, and '40s, when members of the second generation were taking mates, hostility to intermarriage did not lessen. The rationale for opposition broadened to include other issues besides ethnic survival. A few more individuals were willing to speak up for freedom of choice. Still, immigrant parents generally reacted with horror, revulsion, and shame at the prospect of an intermarriage in the family.

To be sure, there were still rabbis who darkly foretold the extinction of the Jewish people unless intermarriage were stamped out. David De Sola Pool wrote in the 1930s about a "universal conscience of Jewry . . . firmly set against intermarriage," and about the Jew's "instinctive desire for Jewish survival . . . his instinctive protest against Jewish extinction." Reconstructionist leader Mordecai M. Kaplan wrote, "It is certain that if nothing is done to prevent the tendency to intermarriage, Judaism can barely survive another century and even if it survives it will have become hopelessly devitalized." Reform Rabbi Henry Joshua Stern agreed that if intermarriage were not curbed, "the continuation of Jewish group life is in danger." Roland B. Gittelsohn wrote textbooks for Reform youth groups which tried to discourage intermarriage. In them he insisted (without benefit of data) that "only one child out of every ten born of intermarriage remains Jewish; the other nine become Christian," and bemoaned the others, forever "lost to Judaism." On the hostile fringe was Joseph Breuer, who wrote a handbook on Jewish marriage. He threatened divine punishment on any Jewish man who married "the daughter of an alien God." He continued, "The sacred procreative energy of the Jew is to be dedicated to the furtherance of Jewish life, and then he will dare waste that energy and give life to children who, because they are not really his at all, will presently enter into an alien group to tear down someday that Sanctuary to the establishment of which Jewish life must devote itself!" Finally, Breuer hinted that death might be a suitable punishment for the intermarrying Jew. J. L. Zlotnick did not go so far as to suggest the death penalty, but he did think that "the fight against intermarriage is the fight for our very life and existence," and suggested that parents marry off their children while they were still in their early teens so as to insure that they would have proper Jewish mates.[12]

Ordinary Jews were less likely than rabbis to see intermarriage in catastrophic terms, as an issue of survival for a people. They were concerned mainly about their own families. Confronted with an increasing desire on the part of American-born youngsters to socialize with Gentiles and marry them, immigrant parents balked. In the 1920s, the "Bintel Brief" resounded with the anguished cries of parents whose children had intermarried and young people whose parents had cut them off for dating or marrying a *goy*. When a young man told his father he had made a Gentile woman pregnant and therefore had married her, the father replied "that I did not wish to look at him, that I no longer recognized him as my child, and as far as I was concerned it was just as if he were dead." Another father rent his clothing and sat *shivah*. Several mothers threatened suicide. Many of the parents were taken by surprise, altogether unprepared for their offspring to make a Gentile match. Sometimes they thought the children were dating Jews, only to find to their anguish that the prospective partners were Italians or WASPs. One mother wrote the "Bintel Brief" about her son: "Whenever a match is proposed to him, he does not want to listen. So we all thought, that is because of his loyalty to his mother. He does not want to leave her and she sick, because he is very kind and is worshipped by me and by the other children. . . . But to my great surprise I found out, that he has been keeping company with a Gentile for about two years now. I feel, that I am too weak to survive such a great and unexpected blow." One mixed couple could not bring themselves to tell his Jewish parents that they wanted to marry, so they saw each other surreptitiously for more than twenty years. They married, in the end, only because she became pregnant; she was forty-five, he forty-eight. Some pious parents called on dubious theology for comfort in their distress. The sexton of an Orthodox congregation said that "to every Jewish girl when she is born, there is a Jewish mate and God finds a way to bring them together." Though the sexton's son had intermarried, in time "the 'shiksa' will die and God will see to it that his next wife will be a good Jewish girl." People like this sexton used religious categories—Jew and Gentile—to describe their discrimination; however, they seem to have been more concerned with what they regarded as repulsive Gentile character traits, such as alleged wife-beating habits, than with religious beliefs. Long after many of these marriages had been consecrated, Jewish families continued to shut out the miscreants and their Gentile spouses. And for years afterwards, gossip circles rang with tales of their misdeeds.[13]

In the face of rising intermarriage, especially after about 1940, many parents and Reform rabbis took a different tack. They still opposed intermarriage, but in more moderate tones, reasoning with young Jews that intermarriages would be bad marriages for cultural reasons. Harry Stern epitomized this approach when he told Montreal's Temple Emanu-el in 1944: "We modern progressive Jews are not so much motivated by theological reasoning in frowning upon mixed marriage as by sociological and psychological. . . . People of similar backgrounds economically, socially, and religiously have a better chance of having a successful union than those whose backgrounds are dissimilar." Rabbi Barnett Brickner, a radio preacher, wrote: "Our opposition comes from our desire to see people happy—and we know from experience that the chances for marital happiness are infinitely better when the couple are of one faith. . . . A family that prays together stays together." Perhaps the most eloquent statement of the cultural argument against intermarriage was Bernard Malamud's novel *The Assistant*. This haunting, lyrical story of the love affair of Helen Bober and Frank Alpine contained a discouraging message: Interethnic romance is something backed into by miserable, lonely, frustrated people against their better judgment. It does not work, necessitates deceit and self-deception, and ends up hurting everyone involved. Intermarriage, in Malamud's view, is part and parcel of a damaged life.[14]

Despite the increase in outmarriage in the second generation, very few Jews had anything positive to say about mixed marriages. Sometimes a couple would be reconciled to their parents after a baby arrived, but many remained estranged. Even the "Bintel Brief" editors turned against intermarriage, citing cultural incompatibility as their reason. A liberal, midwestern rabbi who acknowledged conducting intermarriages nonetheless opposed such matches: "I officiate at intermarriages. I do so not because I favor them—I do not. My reason for this lies in the desire to hold Jewishly as many of my people as I possibly can." Very few rabbis in the 1920s, '30s, and '40s could be so open-hearted toward intermarriers as Jacob Weinstein, who counseled: "Once [an intermarriage] is consummated—the Jewish parents should receive the non-Jewish son or daughter with open arms, and make him or her a true member of the family. . . . You may, like Naomi, find a daughter-in-law 'who is better to thee than seven sons!' " Very few parents were so blasé as one couple whose third son was about to intermarry; according to a family friend, "His two brothers had already married Gentiles; the parents were used to it. As a matter of fact, they might have been shocked if he married a Jewish girl."[15]

With the advent of the third generation and a tremendous leap in the rate of outmarriage, opposition moderated but did not cease. The 1960s and '70s saw a marked rise in the number of rabbis who performed intermarriages. Those years also witnessed a revival of Jewish religiosity and a widespread concern about intermarriage. Some Jews showed their alarm by denouncing intermarriage and attempting to stamp it out, others by trying to tie the intermarried and their families to Judaism.

The rise of intermarriage in the 1960s brought an outpouring of concern from the rabbinate and officials of Jewish organizations. Jewish leaders wrote volumes and articles, held conferences and strategy sessions to figure out what to do about intermarriage. The Federation of Jewish Philanthropies published books with such titles as *Intermarriage: The Future of the American Jew* and *The Threat of Mixed Marriage*, in which rabbis and social scientists denounced intermarriage and proposed strategies to combat it. The CCAR devoted most of its 1972 convention to debating the intermarriage issue. Yehuda Rosenman of the American Jewish Committee called intermarriage a "perennial danger to Jewish viability and continuity." An Orthodox rabbi warned that "the end of American Jewry is already in sight." Theologian Emil Fackenheim spoke of intermarriage as "the posthumous victory of Adolf Hitler." Reconstructionist leader Ira Eisenstein wrote pamphlets for Jewish children and parents, denouncing intermarriage as an evil for the extended family and the couple, and "a dreadful dilemma into which to place any child."[16]

As in earlier generations, the chief concern of Jewish officials seems to have been for the survival of American Jewry. Marshall Sklare's widely read essay bore that concern in its title: "Intermarriage and Jewish Survival." The leaders' position rested on the assumption that an intermarrier necessarily ceased to be a Jew on his or her wedding day. Ira Eisenstein was especially articulate on this point. "When one marries out of the faith, *causing himself and his offspring to leave the household of Israel,* he is betraying the purpose and meaning of Jewish existence. He is turning his back on an embattled and persecuted people which has stubbornly and courageously maintained itself against extraordinary forces which have throughout history sought to destroy it." Other rabbis took more theological routes to the same survival-oriented position. Thus, Joseph Klein wrote in 1972 that intermarriage ended Jewishness: "Every Jew stands in a covenant relationship with God. He has a commitment to maintain that covenant relationship in all aspects of his personal and family life and to see to it that the covenant relationship is transmitted to his children. . . . A Jew who marries outside the faith is a sinner; he has broken the covenant in that he has made himself incapable of transmitting that covenant to his children."[17]

The remedies that the rabbis proposed ranged from severe to moderate. Like Jewish leaders of yesteryear, New York Rabbi Jacob Goldberg proposed in 1967 that "parents whose children have married a non-Jewish partner sit *shiva* for these children." He said they "must renounce their children. . . . Jewish life cannot be saved without sacrifice." In 1976, Kalman Packouz published *How to Stop an Intermarriage: A Practical Guide for Parents.* He counseled distraught parents to fight a prospective intermarriage with every weapon they could command. They should suggest a trial separation, send their child to Israel, offer him or her money. They should do everything in their power to make their child feel guilty, remind him or her of Jewish persecutions, predict unhappiness, ridicule Gentiles as immoral and unreliable, even threaten suicide. If an intermarriage should take place, parents should shut out the couple entirely and refuse to see them or their children. These were extreme responses. More moderate Jewish leaders, no less opposed to intermarriage but mindful of what they conceived of as a duty to minister to all Jews, even intermarriers, advocated less radical steps. The 1976 Federation of Jewish Philanthropies conference recommended, for example, strengthening Jewish religious education and programs for teenagers and adult singles. They suggested that no intermarrier be given a place of honor or responsibility by any Jewish organization, although he or she should be allowed to participate. Finally, they insisted that "all family agencies supported and sponsored by the Jewish community . . . consider the future of that community in their counseling situations, not only the mental health of the patient." For them, as for other Jewish leaders, Jewish survival loomed uppermost.[18]

In modern times Jewish leaders have replayed the biblical tension, wavering between opposing intermarriage on religious grounds, after Moses, and opposing it, Ezra-like, on the ground of solidarity of the Jewish people. The modern authorities, however, have been less concerned with who enters Judaism and more with who leaves. Ezra's great concern was pollution from without. Modern people talk constantly of Jews "lost to Judaism." Part of this may be gender oriented. In Ezra's time, women entered their husbands' households; it was no great concern to Ezra if they were lost to Israel. His concern was that the women whom Jewish men brought in must not threaten ethnic purity and solidarity. In the modern era, the fear is that Jewish men will leave the tribe to follow the religions of their Gentile wives. This fear is buttressed by the Jewish law, stemming from medieval times, that one must be born of a Jewish mother to be a Jew; children of intermarrying Jewish men would not be available to Judaism. In each age, the concern was over the actions of Jewish men, though the direction of concern was different. In neither case did anyone express much concern over the intermarriage of Jewish women.

As in the youth of the second generation, ordinary Jews seem to have reacted against intermarriage more from gut revulsion than from theological considerations or from a desire to aid Jewish survival. They were worried mostly about their individual families and communities. Parents of third-generation youngsters encouraged their children to mix with Gentiles, and most were pleased when they brought home Gentile friends. But they drew a line sharply at dating, and their sentiments against intermarriage were even stronger. The young people shared their parents' feelings. Jewish students at Columbia University in the 1960s liked to cultivate Gentile friendships. But most would date non-Jews only on a recreational basis. They consciously shied away from serious entanglements.[19]

When parents of the third generation spoke against intermarriage, it was almost always in terms of the inevitability of conflict rather than in terms of a desire to preserve Jewish identity. Their opposition was seldom as uncompromising as a generation earlier. Israel Ellman described the situation clearly: "The big majority of American Jewish parents do not want their children to marry non-Jews, but gone are the days when parents will sit 'shiva' for a child who has married out. When the inevitable has happened, the parent will reconcile himself to the position, especially if there has been a conversion to Judaism. American acculturation and the consequent drop in Jewish consciousness have led to the disappearance of the trauma and rupture which would have been the case several years ago."[20]

In the third generation, as never before, a growing number of Jews —rabbis and lay people—accepted intermarriage as inevitable and worked to keep the intermarried connected to Judaism. Many Reform rabbis began in the 1960s to perform intermarriages. Usually these came at the request of the Jewish partner's parents; the intermarriers seldom cared whether they were married in a Jewish ceremony or not. Most of the intermarrying rabbis took positions much like that of David Max Eichorn: "I do not look with favor on intermarriages per se. . . . [But] if I take the so-called traditional position and refuse to have anything to do with the marriage, what will I accomplish? There is a good possibility that I will drive a Jew away from Judaism. What else will I accomplish? I will also probably destroy whatever possibility there may be for the conversion of the non-Jew to Judaism and the recreation, by this couple, of an acceptable Jewish family life." Eichorn was something of an intermarriage enthusiast. He maintained a nationwide file of rabbis who would perform intermarriages.[21]

One 1970 study suggested that perhaps 40 percent of the marriages performed by Reform rabbis were intermarriages. Many of the rabbis required at least formal conversion to Judaism by the non-Jewish partner prior to the ceremony (Eichorn did not). Other typical stipulations were that the couple promise to rear their children as Jews, give them Jewish religious education, and abstain from any Gentile religious practices. Most intermarrying rabbis, like Eichorn, conducted mixed marriages because they were concerned for Jewish survival and did not want to drive anyone away. Another motivation for some was a desire not to stand in the way of true love. Samuel Glasner questioned "the ethics of sacrificing the possible happiness of these individuals to the preservation of the Jewish group." Still others found denying intermarriage contradictory to Jewish ethical beliefs in the equality of all humankind.[22]

By the 1970s, many synagogues were actively encouraging intermarried Jews and their spouses, whether converted or not, to keep up Jewish ties. Abraham Gordon* longed for his roots after many years away from active Judaism. He joined a local synagogue and brought his children and his Gentile wife. The wife was accepted as a sister by the other women, the boys became *bar mitzvah,* Gordon eventually rose to become chairman of the synagogue, and a family was saved for Judaism. By 1980, San Francisco's Congregation Beth Israel was advertising its classes on Judaism in the daily newspaper and striving to attract a wide audience. The advertisements specifically invited Gentile spouses to attend. By 1985, many Reform and Conservative congregations had adopted similar programs.[23]

An increasing number of Jewish lay people, too, came to accept intermarriage. This was particularly true of members of the third generation. The Columbia study found that students "do not object to intermarriage on moral grounds." Israel Ellman noted in 1971 that while many young Jews had hesitations about intermarriage in principle, "the power of love is seen as overcoming everything."[24] Ira Eisenstein summarized vividly the feelings of many members of the younger generation in the 1950s and 1960s:

We are living now in an age of revolutionary change. The barriers that separated race from race, nation from nation, people from people, are being rapidly broken down. If we are to achieve one world, which is the only kind of world which can survive under present conditions of nuclear armament, the old prejudices will have to go by the board. We will have to learn to live together; and this means, in the final analysis, we should marry one another. To resist intermarriage is to stand in the way of universal progress.

In addition, marriage grows out of the love of a man for a woman, and this kind of love transcends all considerations of religion, group, color; "love conquers all." If a man and a woman truly love one another they must defy all the obstacles that are likely to stand in their way in order that they may unite in domestic bliss.

Moreover, all dire predictions of failure are merely rationalizations on the part of narrow-minded people. The fact is that one can point here and there to very successful marriages between non-Jews and Jews. It all depends on the individual. Anti-Semitism is likely to be found least of all among those who are tolerant enough to allow themselves to become emotionally involved with Jews.

So far as the future of Judaism and the Jewish people is concerned, the issue is totally irrelevant. Those who do not find a rationale for Jewish survival should not be called upon to sacrifice personal happiness in order to assure it, if assure it they will through marriage to a member of the Jewish people. After all, there are many Jews who are uninterested in Judaism, and there is no guarantee that marriage by a Jew to another Jew is going to contribute anything to the survival of Judaism, assuming that this is a desirable end.[25]

Members of the older generation split on the issue of their children marrying non-Jews. While most opposed intergroup dating and marriage, a significant minority expressed only mild objections or none at all. This was particularly true for the parents of boys (apparently parents of girls felt more protective toward their offspring). Parental attitudes were significant: the Columbia study and an early-1970s national survey suggested that parents who did not strongly oppose intermarriage were much more likely to end up with intermarried children than parents who chose adamant opposition.[26] Fred Massarik spoke for a growing number of Jews who were involved in their community of faith yet did not oppose intermarriage when he wrote in 1978:

> If a Jewish man and a Jewish woman who might have married each other, instead both marry non-Jews, we now have two marriages where there would have been one.
>
> Now, if we have two marriages where there would have been one, if only half the children are raised as Jews, there will be as many Jewish children as

there would have been if the two Jews had married each other. So, too, if both raise their children as Jews, then there will be even more Jewish children than there would have been without the two intermarriages.

In short, the fact of intermarriage does not necessarily lead to a decline in the Jewish population. . . .

Precisely because there is a drift towards Jewishness among some intermarried non-Jews, and a drift away from Jewishness among some in-married Jews, the quality of Jewish life may be as rich among some intermarried families as among many of the in-married.[27]

One critical difference between earlier periods and the era of the third generation was that, faced with an intermarriage as a *fait accompli,* Jewish families and communities usually overcame their hesitations and welcomed the couple. That seldom happened in earlier years, but by the 1960s, '70s, and '80s it was quite common. Egon Mayer and Carl Sheingold conducted a national survey of intermarried Jews in the latter 1970s and concluded that "the ties between the couples surveyed and their parents and other relatives were intact. . . . They got along well. . . . In the vast majority of cases their spouses were accepted into the extended family. None of the respondents reported a total break with their families as a result of their marriage." Eugen Schoenfeld found that in the small communities he studied, by the mid-1960s "Jews do not impose the traditional or any other sanctions upon the exogamous." By the 1980s, a majority of St. Louis Jews approved of intermarriage.[28]

As intermarriage increased over three generations, so did tolerance of it. A majority of Jewish leaders and lay people consistently opposed intermarriage, but the size and steadfastness of that majority declined over the course of time. The rabbis were largely preoccupied with maintaining the solidarity of the Jewish people—with race survival, if you will—and with observing theological prohibitions. Faced with the prospect of a drastic decline in adherents to the faith in the third generation, many Jewish leaders began to seek ways to compromise with the intermarriers, to revivify their Jewish commitment, and to win their families to Judaism. Lay people had fewer theological scruples, and few expressed their opposition to intermarriage in terms of Jewish survival or theology. They were concerned, rather, to maintain family and community integrity. They saw Gentiles as foreign, distasteful, untrustworthy, and utterly unlovely, and they wanted no part of them. But as generations passed, as Jews became acculturated to American ways and interacted with Gentiles ever more closely, the sense of foreignness faded away. Jews came to accept intermarriage as an inevitable, and not altogether regrettable, feature of American life. Still, Jewish identity—not always related to religion—lingered and acted to inhibit intermarriage. A highly assimilated, third-generation Jewish intellectual commented on his Jewish identity and its relation to intermarriage: "I'm an atheist. My parents were atheists. Their parents were atheists. But when I get married I want to marry a Jewish woman, and I want our children to be raised as Jews." [29]

Gentiles Respond to Intermarriage with Jews

Gentile attitudes toward intermarriage with Jews underwent a change similar to Jewish attitudes. In the early years of East European immigration, non-Jews were fairly unanimous in despising Jews and rejecting intermarriage. But as generation succeeded generation, Jews and intermarriage became less unpopular with Gentile Americans.

Christian church leaders opposed intermarriage with Jews for centuries before the East European migration to America. Extremists among them viewed Jews as Christ-killers, and even the more moderate regarded Jews with distaste. In the late years of the last century and the early years of this, Gentiles of all classes discriminated against Jews and harassed non-Jews who married them. Katie Néil Klein found young boys and girls pounding on her windows with sticks and shrieking, "Dirty Jews! Dirty Jews!" when she and her husband moved into a Gentile neighborhood about 1910. Although she married a Jew and loved him, this Irish Catholic woman resisted living among other Jews. Furthermore, she said she would not marry him again if she had it to do over, because of the harassment she had received from Gentiles. Still, her family warmed up to Michael after a while. Her brothers, formerly unhappy about the marriage, became Michael's staunch friends and supporters. One Gentile family was so impressed by their daughter's Jewish immigrant friend that they offered to support the couple while he undertook an extensive program of study. Yet these were exceptions. Most Gentiles firmly opposed intermarriage in the early decades of this century.[30]

Gentile opinion had moderated only slightly by the time the second generation came of age. Only a few liberal church leaders were willing to go so far as John Haynes Holmes did in 1931, in exalting true love as the supreme law of marital relations: "Mixed marriages, when they are the fruit of love between the two parties concerned, are not only proper and beautiful but spiritually imperative. . . . Love is the supreme factor in human experience; and, in marital as in all other relations between men and women, must be scrupulously obeyed. . . . Love must be followed even when it leads across the barriers of race and the thresholds of synagogue and church. For life is betrayed when its strongest and noblest incentive is not heeded. . . . If a Jewish maiden loves a Christian man, or a Christian maiden a Jewish man, they must be allowed to marry without opposition from the families concerned, or from the synagogue or church."[31] Much more common were the views of the Simmons family of North Dighton, Massachusetts, who forbade their daughter Thelma to marry Edward Friedland; in despair the couple attempted suicide, and very nearly succeeded. Innumerable mixed couples had to go to new communities and hide the Jewish partner's religion in order to avoid Gentile harassment. Parents who said they had no prejudice against Jews nonetheless insisted that "marriage between Christians and Jews just doesn't work out, and we're determined not to let our daughter risk unhappiness by trying the impossible." Christians surveyed in 1944 overwhelmingly opposed their sons or daughters marrying Jews.[32]

By the 1950s and '60s, Gentile opposition to Jews and to intermarriage had declined considerably, although it had not disappeared. Whereas 57 percent of a national sample queried in 1950 said they "definitely would not marry a Jew," only 37 percent said the same thing twelve years later. Jews were no longer filthy Christ-killers; now they were just a little odd. A Gentile woman in a mixed Protestant-Jewish suburb described her discomfort about Jews in terms of popular cultural symbols: "Christmas is Christmas. There are no wreaths on the doors or trees in our neighborhood. The Jews are so unlike us. Their children don't believe in Santa Claus or the Easter Bunny." Protestant pamphlets no longer decried intermarriage; instead they counseled couples how to manage it successfully. Catholic students were less sanguine than Protestants about the prospects for dating and marriage with Jews, but both groups showed increasing willingness to undertake these previously banned activities. The Gallup Poll recorded a steady rise in Gentile approval of marriage with Jews (at least as an abstract proposition): 59 percent approved in 1968, 67 percent in 1972, 69 percent in 1978, and 77 percent in 1983.[33]

Regional Differences in Intermarriage

Like Japanese Americans, Jews who lived away from ethnic communities intermarried more frequently than those who lived among their own kind. Among immigrants to New York in the 1920s, less than 2 percent married Gentiles. At the same time in California, 9 percent married out. Among third- and fourth-generation Jews in New York City in the early 1980s, the intermarriage rate was 5 percent. In Chicago, it was 9 percent; in Seattle, 16 percent; in Denver, 23 percent. In Indiana, the intermarriage rate in the 1960s was 32 percent. In rural Iowa, it topped 50 percent. All of this meant that the one Jew in twenty who lived in areas where there were very few other Jews was quite likely to pick a non-Jewish mate.[34]

Such areas were more often found in the South and West than elsewhere in America. Abraham Lavender wrote recently that "Southern Jews are facing the potential loss of their youth through assimilation and intermarriage in a pervasive gentile and provincial environment." The Jewish community of El Paso, Texas, was not large enough in its early years to offer wives to all its men; many married Mexican American women and merged into the surrounding Mexican community. Solomon Bibo's rise to the position of chief of the Acoma tribe, by virtue of his marriage to an Indian woman, has already been described. George Sokolsky went even farther from concentrations of Jewish population. He traveled about the globe, finally landing in Shanghai. There, far from the New York Jewish neighborhood of his youth, he met and married a Chinese woman. All these individuals married non-Jews either because few Jews were available or because they felt free to make their own choices unencumbered by the reservations of a Jewish community. By no means did all Jews in areas remote from Jewish communities choose to intermarry. But a striking number did.[35]

The concentration of high rates of intermarriage in certain parts of the United States resembled the pattern in Europe. In Eastern

Europe, where Jews were concentrated, intermarriage was always rare. By contrast, in urban Western Europe, Jews were spread apart and highly assimilated, and intermarriage was common. Regional patterns in Jewish intermarriage are discernible in microcosm in the dating behavior of Columbia University students. Among commuters —those who lived at home in intensely Jewish environments—only 19 percent dated non-Jews. Of students who lived in the regimented dormitories, 31 percent dated Gentiles. Of independent apartment dwellers, invulnerable to parental scrutiny and institutional supervision, 50 percent dated non-Jews.[36]

Some Jews in remote areas tried to stop the trend toward intermarriage. They sent their children to urban colleges that had an abundance of Jewish students, or they imported spouses from out of state rather than submit to intermarriage. But many made their peace with intermarriage, perhaps feeling that small Jewish communities could not afford to lose members, so even intermarriers should be tolerated. Congregation B'nai Israel of Jackson, Tennessee, elected Sam Wahl president about 1950, even though he was married to a Gentile descendant of Henry Clay. In twelve small towns in southern Illinois, nearly half the local Jews were intermarried in 1969. Rather than being ostracized by other Jews, they were usually accepted and took part fully in the affairs of the tiny local Jewish communities.[37]

Class Differences in Intermarriage

Jewish intermarriage followed predictable social class patterns. There was tremendous variation from the first generation to the third, but in all three, people of education, high social status, and independent means married Gentiles more frequently than did other Jews. Only a tiny fraction of the first generation married Gentiles, but of those who did, the majority were professional people. Over three-fourths of the intermarried immigrants in Stanley Bigman's study of Washington, D.C., area Jews were members of the professions, compared with less than a third of other Jews. Only one in ten intermarriers was the manager or proprietor of a business. Very few of the intermarried were clerks, salespeople, or manual workers. Of course, there were intermarriages in the business class—for instance, the one between department store manager Michael Klein and salesclerk Katie

Neil. But the majority of intermarriers were professional people. And only certain professionals were likely to intermarry. Doctors, lawyers, and others whose practices were tied to Jewish communities were less likely to marry Gentiles than those who worked among non-Jews. The latter had more opportunities to meet Gentiles, and they were freer from the scrutiny of other Jews. In the first generation, people with postgraduate education—many of them the very professional people just mentioned—were far more likely to intermarry than people with less schooling. Among immigrant Jewry, one group of people especially prone to intermarry comprised people who put ideals over ethnicity. Leftist intellectuals' ideology made them see classes rather than ethnic groups when they looked at society. Some of them took Gentile spouses. Celia Silbert wrote in 1916 that the people most prone to intermarriage on the Lower East Side were social workers and the "radically inclined."[38]

Outmarriage by all strata increased in the second generation. Intermarriage by professionals tripled, while intermarriage by clerical and sales workers increased many fold. Nearly a quarter of the second-generation clerical workers in the Washington sample married non-Jews. These were the children of immigrant laborers and small business people. Many of them had college educations. They worked alongside Gentiles in Gentile businesses, became their friends, and married them. Such people were as yet a small percentage of the total Jewish population, but they made up a large fraction of the intermarriers. As with the immigrant generation, people who had been to college married out more often than those with less schooling. But those with postgraduate training were now less likely to marry Gentiles than those who stopped with a baccalaureate degree. Perhaps this was related to the fact that many graduate schools had high numbers of Jewish students in those years. If one had not chosen a mate by the time one got to graduate school, one's chances of finding a Jewish partner while there were rather good. As before, leftists seem to have been particularly prone to intermarry. The Communist party and several surrogates were popular with young idealists in the 1930s, Jews and others. The party included more than a few mixed couples in its ranks.[39]

There is a myth, among Jews and others, that the classic intermarrier is the parvenu, the young man on his way up. Possessed of education, pleasing features, or money—and always ambition—he grasps his way to the top. In the classic match, he trades his assets for the higher social status of a WASP bride. Robert Merton and others have called this sort of marital trade-off of male education or wealth for female status "hypogamy" and labeled it the most common form of intermarriage. Harry Golden described how it was supposed to work among Jews and Gentiles: "The Jew must almost always bring something else to the union besides himself. The girl must justify her marriage to a Jew: 'I married a Jew, but he's a composer, a writer, a journalist, a physicist, a college professor,' or 'I married a Jew but he's rich.' A Gentile girl will rarely marry a Jewish shipping clerk or the Jew who pumps gas at a filling station." The neat logic of this formula is very attractive. Quite probably, more than a few marriages were contracted in this calculated fashion. But Maria and Daniel Levinson, the only scholars to match up Jewish men and their Gentile wives and analyze their class backgrounds, could find no such phenomenon. They found "no evidence that any of the Jewish professional men . . . gained in prestige or moved in circles they would not otherwise be accepted in." The Levinsons concluded "that the men did not marry for 'mobility' reasons" and "that Jewish-Gentile marriage is not primarily a 'mobility' phenomenon." Instead, they saw psychological factors, relating to each partner's immersion in or marginality to his or her ethnic group, as primary.[40] If the Levinsons are correct, and if one recalls that for Japanese Americans it was females who did most of the intermarrying, one must seriously question Merton's hypogamy thesis.

In the third generation, professional people again ranked high among the intermarriers. One in five professionals who responded to the Washington survey had taken a Gentile mate. The study of Columbia University students cited earlier repeatedly showed that these Ivy League individuals valued social class over religion as a criterion in date selection. Most of the Levinsons' intermarried subjects were professional people. But there was a new class of people in the third-generation Jewish population, and that class had far more intermarried members than any other. By the third generation, Jews, like many Americans, were moving out of self-employment in business and the professions and into the salaried professions and government service. These people had far more interaction with non-Jews than any previous group and a far higher intermarriage rate: about 35 percent.[41]

College professors are another group frequently pointed out as heavily intermarried. Marshall Sklare in 1964 described the most likely candidates for mixed marriage as "professional groups—mainly in the academy—which are marginal to the community life of American Jewry . . . writers, teachers, scientists, psychoanalysts, and so forth." Jacob Weinstein offered a similar opinion in 1941. Milton Gordon posited this same group of people—artists, intellectuals, writers, professors— as a group that existed in the world of its own created values, with very little reference to ethnicity. It is difficult to verify these observers' impressions with hard data, though there would seem to be some merit to their case. The Columbia study found that the children of Jewish academics were much more likely than the children of other professionals, business people, clerical people, or blue-collar workers to date and marry non-Jews. But the Washington study showed people with advanced degrees—a requirement for nearly all academic jobs— much lower in outmarriage than people with just an undergraduate education.[42]

Denominational Differences in Intermarriage

Contemporary American Jewry can be divided into three major de- nominational traditions: Orthodoxy, Reform, and Conservatism. The Conservative movement arose in Europe and America in the last two decades of the nineteenth century and the first two decades of the twentieth out of dissatisfaction with both Orthodoxy's rigidity and Re- form's radicalism. One would assume that far more Reform Jews than members of the Orthodox or Conservative movements would inter- marry. Leaders of all three denominations opposed intermarriage, but the Reform rabbis were less unanimous, and even those who opposed it were not always unequivocal. Orthodox rabbis, adhering to the let- ter of rabbinic tradition, regularly excluded intermarriers from their congregations and encouraged parents to sit *shivah* for intermarrying children.[43]

Conservatives long held just as fast, although individual rabbis began to waffle under the pressure of growing defections from their congregations as intermarriage swelled in the 1960s. As late as 1963, it was the official position of the Rabbinical Assembly, the Conserva- tive rabbis' union, that people who embark on mixed marriages "shall be excluded from membership." The Assembly went further. "We regard it as the sacred task of responsible Jewish leadership to combat intermarriage," they wrote. "The rabbi shall regard it as part of his duty as a spiritual leader to dissuade any Jew who is contemplating marriage with a non-Jew from this course. He shall further consider it his duty to cooperate with the family that seeks his help in bringing all legitimate pressures and influences to bear upon the young man or woman in order to break up the proposed alliance. He must realize that this is not a matter of concern simply to a particular family, but is the concern of the Jewish people as a whole, and he is their representative." Some Conservative synagogues wavered, allowing intermarrying members to retain their membership even as they excluded other intermarriers from becoming new members. Even so prominent a Conservative leader as Robert Gordis came reluctantly to the point of urging toleration of a certain small amount of mixed marriage as "part of the price that modern Jewry must pay for freedom and equality in an open society."[44]

The leaders of Reform were even more ambivalent. In theory, they agreed with their early leader David Einhorn that "each intermarriage drives a nail in the coffin of Judaism" and must therefore be fought with vigor. In 1909 the Reform rabbis' association, the Central Conference of American Rabbis, passed the following resolution: "Resolved, That it is the sentiment of this Conference that a rabbi ought not to officiate at a marriage between a Jew or Jewess and a person professing a religion other than Judaism, inasmuch as such mixed marriage is prohibited by the Jewish religion and would tend to disintegrate the religion of Israel." Over the next sixty-five years the CCAR met again several times to decide just what that resolution meant, for it was clear that many Reform rabbis continued to officiate at mixed marriages. Others who would not themselves perform intermarriages encouraged couples to go before a civil magistrate; then they let the intermarried Jewish partners take part in their congregations' activities. No less a personage than Isaac M. Wise, the founder of American Reform, found he had to compromise with intermarriage when his daughter Helen ran off with a Presbyterian. Father and daughter were reconciled. The CCAR fought for decades over whether to tolerate intermarriage and how to tolerate it. In 1973, faced with several facts—that between a quarter and a third of its members performed intermarriages, that most synagogues had at least a few intermarried members, and that other intermarried people showed signs of wanting to become involved again in Jewish life—the Conference very nearly capitulated. It still opposed (but did not prohibit) rabbis officiating at mixed marriage, but it counseled synagogues to encourage intermarriers to return, to educate the children of mixed couples, and to try to get non-Jewish spouses to convert. Many rabbis continued to refuse to consecrate intermarriages, but the CCAR tried to keep the intermarried within the fold.[45]

The motives of the three groups of rabbis seem to have been different. The Reform leaders acted out of concern about loss of constituents: they sought ways to bend the rules to keep as many Jews as they could connected to Judaism. For the Conservative, and particularly the Orthodox, the objection to intermarriage was stronger. For them, intermarriage meant consorting with Jewry's enemies and tormentors, and trampling on the sacred laws of Judaism.

The attitudes toward intermarriage of Jewish leaders of various stripes are clear. It is less clear how many Jews from each tradition actually married Gentiles. One would assume that Orthodoxy's strong opposition to intermarriage meant that very few Orthodox believers married out. In fact, there are no numbers to confirm or deny this notion. A 1966 study of Jewish adolescents in New Orleans did find that 70 percent of the Reform youths thought one should marry the person one loves regardless of religion, compared with only 30 percent of the Orthodox and Conservative young people. But no one has counted intermarriers with respect to their denominational allegiance. Certainly, there were people raised in the ranks of Orthodoxy who entered mixed marriages—George Sokolsky was one, and the Levinsons found several more. Reform Rabbi Samuel Silver told of an Orthodox rabbi coming to him and asking him to marry that man's daughter to her Gentile fiance; he could not bring himself to marry the couple, but he wanted "a chance to have Jewish grandchildren." Jacob Marcus suggested that in certain, highly assimilated communities in the Midwest, "there were as many Orthodox as Reform Jews who entered upon mixed marriages." But in all probability, the stronger Orthodox and Conservative sanctions acted to inhibit intermarriage by adherents to those branches of Judaism. Not only were the theological positions of Orthodoxy and Conservatism more firmly against intermarriage, but their subcultures also made intermarriage less likely. Orthodox Jews, by virtue of their religious practices, lived a very different life, far more isolated from Gentiles, than did other Jews. The Conservatives were not so isolated as the Orthodox, but more so than the adherents of Reform. Because of both theological and more general cultural imperatives—especially in places like New York, where half of American Jewry resided and the Orthodox were strong—one would expect to find far more intermarriage by Reform than Orthodox Jews.[46]

8. Issues and Interpretations: According to the Halakhah

The Intermarried Personality

Students of the psychology of Jewish intermarriage generally fell into three camps.[1] The first viewed intermarriage as abnormal and concluded that intermarriers were either rebellious or neurotic. The second group had a neutral or positive attitude toward intermarriage and saw the intermarriers simply as well-acculturated Americans, taking full part in the melting pot. A third group suggested that there may have been some rebellion or neurosis in an intermarriage choice but insisted that, for some individuals, it was the best choice nonetheless. Some of these opinions were based on relatively objective analyses of hard data. Others were built on speculation or pure prejudice.

Most Jewish leaders saw intermarriage as motivated by rebellion or neurotic longings. Such leaders had intense commitments to Judaism and to ethnic solidarity. For anyone to reject or devalue, by intermarriage, the Jewish identity that they held as centrally important must have seemed unreasonable to them. Rabbi Roland Gittelsohn described "the type of personality apt to marry out" as "unorganized or demoralized, . . . detached, . . . rebellious, . . . marginal" in a 1965 marriage manual. Rabbi Henry Kagan asserted a few years later that most intermarriage resulted from "neurotic interaction between parent and child." Samuel Lehrman lent a psychiatrist's imprimatur to this line of reasoning in an article entitled "Psychopathology in

Mixed Marriages." He concluded that most intermarriages resulted
from "1, unresolved oedipus complex and incest-taboo problems (exaggerated phobia of incest); 2, debasement in the sphere of love (special
types of choice of object made by men, misalliance, 'family romance'
in reverse); 3, hostility as a result of disappointment of unconscious
incestuous love impulses, often accompanied by masochism; 4, exaggerated narcissism, including the phallic significance of the marriage
bond; 5, exhibitionism; 6, the conviction that one is an exception;
7, counterphobic and fetishistic attitudes and choices which defend
against castration anxiety."[2]

Bernard Lazerwitz was one of the second group of intermarriage
watchers. He surveyed the intermarriage literature and studied Chicago-area couples, and found very little to suggest maladjustment behind their choices of mates. He saw, rather, "marginal religio-ethnic
members . . . children of parents who had reduced, or marginal religio-
ethnic attachments"—in short, people who had assimilated into American society at large and simply did not care much one way or the
other about being Jewish. Marshall Sklare was another sociologist who
disputed the view of intermarriage as a product of psychopathology.
No proponent of intermarriage, he nonetheless concluded that "assumptions of pathology—social or personal—no longer explain either
the rate or the reasons for exogamy among Jews. . . . It is becoming
impossible to view intermarriage as an indication either of personal
aberration or of social persecution." Erich Rosenthal laid to rest one of
the old assumptions of intermarriage critics: that people entered mixed
marriages at an advanced age, as acts of desperation, fearing that if
they did not intermarry they would never marry at all. He found no
appreciable difference between the ages at marriage of homogamous
Jewish couples and couples with one Gentile partner.[3]

The third group of students recognized that intermarriages might
sometimes proceed out of neurotic motivations, but they did not automatically label such unions bad marriages. Samuel Glasner wrote in
1962 that psychotherapy might be in order for people contemplating
intermarriage because there often were neurotic motives, "but not
all mixed marriages stem from unhealthy motives." Abraham Franzblau observed a decade earlier that "sometimes mixed marriages, even
neurotic ones, solve problems, instead of creating them, when the unconscious needs of a couple meet and match." Other intermarriages,

he said, may be quite healthy, when they are between "emotionally mature people, who are deeply in love, who approach the relationship with mature understanding of the obstacles and responsibilities which such a marriage will place in their path, and who have sufficient character to face what it means not only for themselves but for their children." Louis Birner echoed Franzblau's sentiments: "In situations where the Oedipus complex is resolved with some degree of health, Jews will tend to marry Jews. . . . [However] if an interfaith marriage can reduce the person's sense of guilt and help both parties move in the direction of health it is a successful union."[4]

Maria and Daniel Levinson distinguished between intermarriages that proceeded from neurotic motives and other, healthier intermarriages which had similar motivational patterns but which the Levinsons saw as basically healthy. The former type, which the Levinsons labeled "neurotic exogamy," involved Jewish men who had grown up immersed in Jewish culture, identified strongly with Judaism, and rejected intermarriage on principle. They nonetheless married Gentile women out of incompletely resolved adolescent rebellion, unresolved mother fixations, and inability to relate sexually to Jewish women. For such "reluctant" intermarriers, "the Gentile woman represents, at a conscious level, the female who is the antitheses of mother—someone who is devalued, morally inferior, and an object of carnal sexual wishes. Unconsciously, however, she represents the 'forbidden' mother on whom sexual impulses are fixated." The second group, which the Levinsons called "emancipated" intermarriers, made "contrast choices" of mates. They, too, often came from intensely Jewish cultural environments and went through severe adolescent rebellion, but resolved their rebellion in favor of a lessening identity with Judaism. These men had loosened their grip on Jewishness and become assimilated into the larger society long before they married. They were ideologically disposed to think that ethnic barriers did not matter. Like the neurotics, however, they had problems with domineering, suffocating mothers, and so chose mates who resembled the mothers not at all. The Levinsons' chief reasons for seeing these intermarriages as healthy and the others as neurotic were that this group exhibited fewer signs of anxiety about themselves and that they had left their Jewishness long before taking non-Jewish brides.[5]

J. S. Slotkin and Reuben B. Resnik constructed theoretical models

of several types of Jewish personalities that were prone to intermarriage.[6] Their lists can be reduced to five main types: the neurotic,
the rebellious, the adventurous, the marginal, and the acculturated.
Neurotic intermarriers usually suffered unresolved conflicts with their
opposite sex parents after the fashion described by the Levinsons.
Those conflicts made it impossible for them to form sexual relationships
with Jews of the opposite sex.[7] *Rebellious* intermarriers came from
homes they found cold and lacking in understanding, or had had painful experiences growing up which they identified with Judaism. They
consciously and bitterly chose to reject Judaism and Jewish people.[8]
The *adventurous* could not point to specific conditions that impelled
them toward intermarriage, but they showed enterprising, inquisitive,
risk-taking personalities. They found non-Jewish partners exotic, and
as Lehrman put it, "the exotic is erotic." One intermarried Jewish man
said that "for a young boy there was a certain amount of titillation in becoming involved with" a Gentile woman.[9] *Marginal* intermarriers were
ashamed of their Jewishness and sought ways to eradicate it. Intermarriage was one such way. One intermarrying woman said, "I think that
the reason [for my intermarriage] was my desire to escape from the
stigma of being identified with Jews. I would have a non-Jewish name
and would become part of the non-Jewish group." Armand Schreiber
wrote an article called "The Case for Intermarriage" in which he said
that being Jewish was a "cruel punishment" and a "curse." Another
young Jew said that "he would never marry a Jewish girl because
he had no desire to subject his children to the indignities and discriminations which he suffered as a child."[10] Anzia Yezierska wrote of
intellectual, second-generation Jewish girls who fought their way out
of the Lower East Side ghetto and aspired to places in the American
mainstream alongside non-Jewish American men. In Yezierska's *Bread
Givers*, Sara Smolinsky expounded upon this theme:

> More and more I began to think inside myself, I don't want to sell herring
> for the rest of my days. I want to learn something. I want to do something.
> I want someday to make myself for a person and come among people. But
> how can I do it if I live in this hell house of Father's preaching and Mother's
> complaining? . . .
>
> And then I thought, what kind of a man could I get if I smell from selling
> herring? A son of Zalmon the fish-peddler?
>
> No! No one from Essex or Hester Street for me. . . . I'd want an American-

born man who was his own boss. And would let me be my boss. And no fathers, and no mothers, and no sweatshops, and no herring!

Here and elsewhere, Yezierska held up "Yankees" as symbols of the intellectual and cultural refinement to which her heroines aspired. She showed some affection, but also some loathing, for immigrant Jewish culture.[11] The *acculturated* intermarriers were close to the marginals in their lack of a Jewish identity and in striving for a more generalized American one. But they generally focused more on the positive attributes of Americanism than on the negative qualities of Jewishness, and they seemed generally more at peace: they had made the break with Judaism and had lost the tinge of self-hatred that characterized the marginal group.[12]

The Levinsons, Slotkin, and Resnik, unlike other students, did not fall into a simple debate over whether or not people who intermarried were neurotic. Instead, they posited more complex schemes, in which some intermarriages were seen as healthy, others as neurotic on various grounds, and still others as containing elements of both.

Cleavages within the Group

One area of similarity between Jews and Japanese Americans was the existence of barriers between members of the immigrant generation that were not generally recognized by people outside the broader ethnic group. As with the Issei, these barriers among immigrant Jews proved to be barriers to marriage.

One intragroup cleavage, of minor numerical significance by the twentieth century, but important earlier, was between Ashkenazim and Sephardim. In Europe, these were two very different peoples. Their Judaism was similar, but little else was. The Ashkenazim came from Northern Europe; the Sephardim from Iberia, North Africa, and the Levant. The characteristic language of most East European Ashkenazim was Yiddish. Most Sephardim spoke a Spanish-Hebrew-Arabic mixture called Ladino or one of the Middle Eastern dialects. In America, each group felt superior to the other. The Sephardim came earlier and were well established before the first Ashkenazim came from Germany. As in London, Amsterdam, and other Old World cities where the two lived, Sephardim and Ashkenazim kept strictly apart, attended separate synagogues, and refused to intermarry. When the Ashkenazic Jews of Eastern Europe came to America at the end of the last century, they were shunned by their Sephardic predecessors. As late as 1934, Arthur Ruppin noted that Sephardic-Ashkenazic marriages were still rare. The prejudice came from Ashkenazim as well as Sephardim. An American-born girl of Russian Jewish parents wrote to the "Bintel Brief" in 1939, complaining that her father forbade her marriage to a Jew of Spanish extraction, "on the grounds that he is not an Ashkenazic but a Sephardic Jew. 'Yes, my child,' my father says, 'I know that he is a Jew, but he is still not one of our Jews. By this I mean to say that his past, his upbringing in past generations, is different from ours. The difference can be as great as the difference between an American Yankee and one of our Jews. Your parents are Russian Jews. Your character and habits are altogether different from the character and habits of the Sephardic Jews. I can't see how there can be a complete understanding in everything between the two of you. . . . [He] doesn't even know what *gefilte* fish is.'" Sephardic isolation from other Jews broke down with the advent of World War II. American Jewish soldiers of various traditions lived in unfamiliar communities and mixed and worshipped with other Jews regardless of heritage. In the postwar period, the generally increased geographical mobility characteristic of American society meant that Sephardim and Ashkenazim could no longer keep apart. Distinctly Sephardic congregations declined, the use of Ladino in worship virtually ceased, and intermarriage became the norm. Where nearly 60 percent of Sephardim born in America before 1930 married other Sephardim, less than 15 percent of those born after 1930 did the same.[13]

Denominational splits among the Ashkenazim also affected marriage choices. The classic statement of the Old World Orthodox position on Reform Jews was made by Solomon Poll: "The Orthodox [in Hungary] considered the Reform 'almost as non-Jews,' or religiously speaking 'worse than *goyim*.' Intermarriage between the two groups was not only discouraged and looked down upon, but banned. Some Orthodox families disowned a son or daughter for marrying a Reform Jew, and in extreme cases and circumstances a person who married a Reform Jew was excommunicated because he had 'turned away from the ways of his fathers.'" In America much the same sentiment existed, particularly among immigrant-generation Orthodox Jews. In the early years of the century there were several occasions when Orthodox rabbis proposed to outlaw intermarriages with members of the Reform movement.[14] In 1935 a Reform couple in Easton, New York, vigorously opposed their son's dating an Orthodox girl. As more and more Jews abandoned Orthodoxy for Reform, interdenominational marriages aroused more opposition on the Reform side. In 1967 a Reform girl split with her parents over her desire to marry her Orthodox boyfriend. He lived a strictly observant life, which she wanted to join. Her parents objected strenuously that this was silliness and an infringement on their style of living. Their attempt to break up the impending marriage drove the girl's grandmother to write to the "Bintel Brief" for advice.[15]

The wall between Orthodoxy and Reform was not impenetrable, however. Conservative Jews inhabited a middle position between Orthodox and Reform Jews, communicating with and marrying each. In small Jewish communities, denominational distinctions faded into unimportance compared to the larger difference between Jew and Gentile. The Jewish community in Beloit, Wisconsin, was small enough that viable Orthodox, Conservative, and Reform synagogues were hard to maintain. People from all three persuasions worshipped together, and intra-Jewish intermarriage was common.[16]

Something akin to a denominational split existed between East European immigrants who were Orthodox and those who called themselves Jews but styled themselves "free thinkers." The latter—leftist intellectuals for the most part—were bothered by the notion of marriage to religious Jews, and the Orthodox returned their dislike. One Orthodox family refused in 1906 to allow their daughter to marry an unbelieving Jew unless he agreed to a synagogue wedding. Another sort of religious split—this time between highly assimilated, second- and third-generation Jews and post–World War II Holocaust refugees —was highlighted in Philip Roth's story "Eli, the Fanatic." Roth suggested that many successful, assimilated, suburban Jews may have been more troubled by intermarriage and social mixing with Hasidic Jews—mystical fundamentalists from the *shtetl*—or with immigrants than by similar relationships with Gentiles. In that story, the Jewish community of Woodenton, a bedroom suburb, was embarrassed by the lack of sophistication and country-club manners exhibited by a group of refugees who moved into town. "'Goddam fanatics,' Ted said. . . . 'Pretty soon all the little Yeshiva boys'll be spilling down into town.' 'Next thing they'll be after our daughters.' 'Michele and Debbie wouldn't look at them.' " [17]

Related to the denominational barrier was a distinct ethnic split between German and East European Jews. The German Jews came first and were already well established in the American middle class when their East European brethren began to arrive. Some held positions of cultural eminence, economic power, or political influence. Most of the Germans were Reform, nearly all the East Europeans Orthodox. In Europe, the German Jewish community partook of a higher degree of Gentile culture and education than their East European contemporaries. In America they were also more assimilated. They had German views toward East Europeans: they tended to look on their eastern brothers and sisters as inferior, uncultured, superstitious—altogether rather an embarrassment. For their part, the East Europeans viewed the Germans with a mixture of awe, for their cultural and material accomplishments, and disdain, for their abandonment of Orthodoxy. Irving Engel recalled an Alabama boyhood: "I was always conscious of . . . being the child of Russian Jews among German Jews. At first the . . . line was not as clearly drawn as it became when we were older. I played with the children of German Jewish families. . . . When they became teenagers and began dating, the line began to develop." That line sometimes kept German Jews from marrying Jews of East European parentage. For some East European Jews, marriage into a German family was a step up socially. In the El Paso Jewish community, intra-Jewish distinctions remained even after four generations in America. The Gordons*, a Lithuanian family, spoke in the 1970s in hushed tones about the Cohens*, a German clan. When one of the current generation of Gordons married a Cohen, it was a cause for celebration. The entire Gordon clan was horrified when the marriage ended in divorce; they could not understand how their relative could let loose his grasp on such hard-won status. The Gordons may have been atypical, however. By the 1950s and '60s, barriers between German and East European Jews had begun to dissolve. The rise of Jews of East European parentage to positions of wealth and social status had, in Nathan Glazer's words, "wiped out most of the distinctions between the two." [18]

Not only was there a barrier between German and East European

Jews, but in the immigrant generation there were also a variety of splits between various sorts of East European Jews, and these cleavages affected mate choices. In 1890, the entity "East European Jew" did not exist save in the minds of people outside both Judaism and Eastern Europe. Instead, there were Litvaks and Galitsianers and Ukrainian Jews. They had a sense of commonality with other Jewish immigrants, but in their personal lives they identified themselves as natives of their region and *shtetl*. They joined pan-Jewish synagogues and labor unions, but their strongest ties were with the *landsmanshaftn*, benevolent associations organized by geographical origin. Sometimes interregional acrimony was intense. In 1906, a Galician woman complained to the "Bintel Brief" that a Russian coworker shouted at her that "all Galicians were no good . . . and that he wished all Galician Jews dead."[19] The way this sort of sentiment affected romance and marital choice is illustrated in the following excerpt from the "Bintel Brief" of 1917:

I have been keeping company with a girl. We loved each other and were already discussing our engagement. I am a Russian and she, a Galician. Neither of us worried about this. What is the difference what country we come from? We are all Jews.

My sweetheart took me to her friends and introduced me as her intended husband. They all received me well and we had enjoyable times. They asked me whether I was Russian, Lithuanian, or Galician. I am not ashamed of being Russian and told them what I was.

Then they began to change their attitude toward me. I saw that they did not like it. . . . Several days later, when I called on my sweetheart she said that she did not care to have me because I was Russian. When I protested that she had known that before and had had no objection then, she replied that according to her friends the Lithuanians are passable but the Russians are dangerous people. They all desert their wives and there is not a single upright man among them. That, she said, is what they told her, and she does not want to bring misfortune upon her life.

So I want your answer. Are the Russians the worst of people?[20]

When immigrant Russian Jews married in America, they did not marry East European Jews. They married Russian Jews, and generally Jews from their own part of Russia. Hungarian Jews married Hungarian Jews, Austrians married Austrians, Rumanians married Rumanians. Only the German Jews married large numbers of people from

outside their ancestral region. Non-Jews did not understand these regional distinctions. They scarcely could manage to understand that
there were differences between German and East European Jews.
Since succeeding generations of Jews grew up in an America that
discriminated equally against Jews whatever their ancestral origin,
the American-born began to see themselves as East European Jews,
broadly conceived, and later simply as Jews. Where 85 percent of Russian Jewish immigrants married other Russians, only half their children
did the same. Regional outmarriage by American-born Jews of other
derivations was even more frequent.[21]

The Hierarchy

As was the case with Japanese Americans, Jews exhibited a regular
hierarchy of preferences in choosing their mates. With the passing of
generations, the intra-Jewish distinctions that were important to the
first generation faded away, and second- and third-generation Jews
showed themselves willing to marry further and further down the ladder. A Galician immigrant, for example, would most prefer a mate from
a pious family of appropriate social station who came from the vicinity
of his or her own *shtetl*. Failing that, a candidate from elsewhere in
Galicia would do. Then someone from a neighboring part of Hungary,
Poland, Rumania, or the Ukraine. Finally, a Galitsianer might accept a
match with an Orthodox Jew from somewhere farther afield—Austria,
perhaps, or Germany. Intermarriage with a Reform Jew was out of the
question for most Orthodox immigrants, for they saw members of the
Reform movement as having betrayed their faith. Marriage to a *goy*
was totally outrageous.[22]

As members of the second generation came of age, they began to
lose track of the internal distinctions their parents had made. At the
same time they elaborated on the hierarchy outside the group. In social
relations and marital choices, American-born Jews no longer drew lines
between Litvaks and Warshawskis. They continued to recognize distinctions between Reform and Orthodox, and now Conservative, and
also between Ashkenazim and Sephardim. But those were lines they
frequently crossed. They even began to marry non-Jews in small but
significant numbers, and they began to distinguish among Gentiles.
Highest on their non-Jewish list came White Protestants of liberal denominations, such as Episcopalians and Congregationalists, and those

who rejected religion. Then came White Catholics; then such Protestants as Baptists, who held their religion more tightly and were associated with anti-Semitism; and finally Gentiles who were not White. It was bad, but conceivable, that an American-born Jew might bring home a *goy* to his or her parents. But to bring home a *shvartser*, a Black, was almost beyond comprehension. Color was a tougher barrier than religion. Ten-year-old Harry Roskolenko asked his pious mother, " 'What if your daughter Edna wanted to marry a Negro Jew—what would you do?' She slapped my face and that ended my sociological explorations." [23]

By the third generation, the intragroup cleavages that had seemed so important to the immigrants had long since disappeared. Young Jews in the 1950s and '60s simply did not know or care about differences in their grandparents' birthplaces. Many recognized denominational differences, but those seldom were the deciding factor in a marriage choice. More and more married Gentiles. The intermarriers' choices followed the order of the hierarchy their parents and grandparents had laid out. They chose first other Jews inclusively defined, then liberal, White Protestants, then White Catholics, then conservative, White Protestants, then peoples of moderate color, and finally Blacks. As late as the 1970s, Blacks or Asians—even converts to Judaism— were not accepted as candidates for dating and marriage.[24]

Intermarriage and Conversion

One factor in interreligious marriage not present in interracial marriage is the possibility of conversion. An intermarried Japanese American cannot become White, nor can a White person become Black, however much they may seek to identify with their mates' cultures and social groups. But a Jew can become a Gentile, and a Gentile can become a Jew, although the Jews traditionally were not a proselytizing people and allowed conversion only grudgingly. The possibility of conversion both adds and subtracts tension in cases of religious intermarriage. It adds tension, because relatives and others who care about one partner may fear that he or she will abandon the ancestral faith to take up the mate's religion: Jews fear that the Jewish partner will convert to Christianity. The possibility also subtracts tension, because it offers hope that the Gentile spouse will become a Jew.

Jews have long feared the death of their religion through conversion to Christianity. In nineteenth- and early-twentieth-century Europe, especially in Germany, Jewish leaders bemoaned the drain on Jewish population caused by the apostasy of assimilated Jews. Frequently they linked baptisms with intermarriage. To quiet their fears, Arthur Ruppin wisely observed that, although intermarriage and conversion were both symptoms of assimilation, they seldom occurred in the same social setting: "Intermarriage flourishes where there is no social or religious disrespect for Judaism, and where, therefore, intimate and easy intercourse between Jews and Christians favours marriage between the two. Baptism, on the other hand, is most prevalent where, in spite of legal equality, Jews are socially despised, a condition which they hope to overcome by baptism." Nonetheless, rabbis, sociologists, and lay people continued to think of intermarriage and apostasy as closely related phenomena. The sociologists carefully noted the numbers of intermarriages and conversions, and the rabbis railed against both as harbingers of the death of Judaism. Their concern about baptisms was justified: far more Jews than Christians changed their religion, partly because of anti-Semitic pressures and partly because complex conversion requirements made it hard to become a Jew. But their conviction that intermarriage led to Jewish apostasy may have been misplaced.[25]

During the early years of this century there arose in certain Christian circles a literature of celebration. Hearing pulpit testimonies about transformed lives and reading books like *Christ Finds a Rabbi*, congregations thrilled to tales of Jewish apostasy, of souls saved from the dark night of idolatry. Usually these were brightly burnished stories of triumph. Their protagonists had once lived in sin, but had at last turned to the light, and their whole beings were suffused with the warmth of Jesus. Yet conversion from Judaism was by no means such an easy thing. One might well come to see Jesus as the hoped-for Messiah of the Jews and thus make theological peace with one's turn from Judaism. But it was a harder thing to turn away from the Jewish people. All one's family, one's ancestors, one's sense of self-identity cried out against abandoning Jewishness.[26] H. L. Hellyer, a pious Ukrainian Jew who came to Christ, vividly described his agony at leaving Jewry:

None but a Jew can realize what it means for a new convert to be called by that name [*meshumod*] and to have applied to one all that it implies. Translated literally it means "annihilated." It implies that the Jew called by that name has by his own act annihilated himself from the midst of Israel and from Israel's

God; that his former friends must henceforward be his enemies; that his relatives must hate him as a thing accursed and unclean, and must, in their turn, be hated and despised, on his account, by all Israel; that he can never again be admitted into a synagogue; that he cannot participate in any prayer, nor in any religious ceremony such as circumcision or a wedding. Then I thought of my mother. I could hear her bitter cry of anguish on learning the terrible truth about her son, on whose religious future she had built such grand hopes for herself; I could see her go into mourning for me as for one dead; I could hear her lamenting and wishing rather that I had died a thousand deaths as a Jew than that I had taken the terrible step which made her an outcast for the remainder of her life and condemned her to black darkness for all eternity. Never again would she venture forth in daylight without her neighbors pointing their fingers at her in derision and holy horror and repeating to their neighbors and to the children the shameful fact that her son was a renegade. They might, in their holy indignation and fervent zeal even cast stones at her. My brother and my sister, who were both married, would be in danger of losing their partners in life, for the latter could sue for and obtain divorces from them from any rabbi, on the ground that their brother was a believer in Christ. My little nephews and nieces would no longer find any playmates at school, on account of their uncle; all the other children would consider it an act of worship to abuse them at every opportunity; and should they, in the course of time, find young men and women willing to marry them—which was doubtful—their children would likewise be shunned and abused on account of a Meshumod in the family. In a word I would bring ruin and lifelong misery on my family in the immediate present, and for generations to come. Did I have the right to do so? Then began the struggle between love for Christ and love for my family.[27]

Such an honest, self-critical, multidimensional portrait of a convert's (possibly exaggerated) fears was untypical of the literature celebrating Jewish apostasy. Hellyer's account was typical in one respect, however: although he did convert, it was not as a result of marriage to a Christian. Some converts took Christian spouses after their conversion, but very few did so before. Conversion was a problem, but intermarriage was not its cause.[28]

In cases of intermarriage, conversion of the Christian spouse to Judaism was more common than the other way around. Parents of intermarrying Jews, acting either from religious conviction or from a desire to maintain appearances, frequently pressured their sons- and daughters-in-law to become Jews. Like a pious Jew who wrote to the "Bintel Brief" in 1913, they made conversion a condition for their permission to marry. This father demanded that his daughter's Italian fiance be circumcised, but the young couple refused to go along. Even conversion was not enough to satisfy some parents. Isaac Metzker retold an old Abe Cahan story about "the Italian barber who fell in love with a Jewish girl on Broome Street. He wanted to marry her, but her mother wouldn't bless the match. Finally the mother agreed to the marriage provided the barber converted to Judaism. The mother made the new husband learn Hebrew and he had to pray every morning wearing his *yarmulka*. The Italian barber and his Jewish wife lived with the mother, and the barber did not get his breakfast until he had prayed. But that wasn't all. The wife had a brother named Joe and Joe never prayed before breakfast. So the barber asked his mother-in-law what was the difference between him and the brother. The answer was, 'Joe's a Jew. I know he's a Jew but you've got to prove you're one.' " Other parents were not even that open to accepting converted sons- and daughters-in-law. A "Despondent Mother from the Bronx" wrote the "Bintel Brief" in 1927: "He says he is willing to do anything in the world for [my daughter], even to become a convert to Judaism. But we are not satisfied with that. We are not pious but we are far from accepting a Gentile as a son-in-law." Such uncompromising responses, however, were largely confined to the immigrant generation. Later generations were more kindly disposed toward Gentiles who were willing to convert to Judaism in order to marry their sons and daughters.[29]

Rabbis had rather another standard by which to judge intermarriage-related conversions. In the years when they more or less uniformly opposed intermarriage, they also opposed conversions except for the very small number of people who might be regarded as true proselytes—conscientious converts to the Jewish faith. Conversions simply to satisfy Jewish parents-in-law or to bring religious unity to a home, unaccompanied by heartfelt conviction of the rightness of Judaism, were shunned. In the 1950s and '60s, with the intermarriage rate skyrocketing, some rabbis reassessed their position. Three approaches to the problem of intermarriage and conversion emerged. A large group of Reform and Reconstructionist rabbis, acknowledging that intermarriages were going to take place whether they approved or not, sought to save some of the families for Judaism by performing conversions prior to the marriages. Ira Eisenstein vigorously opposed unconverted intermarriages but thought that "conversion of the non-Jewish party is a valid solution to the dilemma. . . . Of course, this entails a period of study, a formal induction [including circumcision of males, ritual baths, etc.] and a repudiation of all allegiance to religious groups with which one was formerly identified. But once this is done, marriage between a convert and a Jew ceases *completely* to be an intermarriage." Eisenstein and his like-minded colleagues could cite the wisdom of the Midrash for their position, asserting that "those conversions are successful which occur because of the proselyte's desire to secure the benefit of Jewish charity, his love for a Jewess, or his affection for Judaism." A national survey of intermarried Jews showed the effect of this rabbinical position on conversion patterns. Of intermarried Christians who converted to Judaism, only 15 percent did so before meeting their spouse. Forty percent converted with the impending marriage in mind, 28 percent after the marriage had taken place. Thirty-two percent gave their own personal conviction as the reason for the conversion; 38 percent cited pressure from the Jewish spouse and in-laws.[30]

A second group of rabbis, many of them Orthodox, but others holding Conservative or Reform positions, held to the old standard. A group of them published a statement in 1971 which said that conversions "designed in the main to mitigate parental objections and the social stigma attached to intermarriage . . . do not meet the basic condition of genuine conversion to Judaism, namely the sincere commitment to abide by the laws of the Torah and to live by the faith of Israel. The 'convert' remains according to the Halacha (Jewish religious law), a non-Jew as before. These pro-forma conversions constitute a most insidious threat to the integrity of Jewish peoplehood."[31]

Other rabbis agreed that intermarriage-motivated conversions were a sham, but unlike their Orthodox brethren, they performed intermarriages. The leading proponent of this position was "the intermarrying rabbi," David Max Eichorn. He suspected the motives of Gentiles who came for conversion classes simply because they wanted to marry Jewish partners. Rather than grant such quickie conversions, he would marry a couple, then do everything he could to encourage a sincere interest in Judaism on the part of the Gentile partner, pointing ultimately toward a genuine conversion and a truly Jewish household.[32]

Of course, many intermarriages took place without either party ever converting. Christian men who married Jewish women were particularly reluctant to convert. The 1973 National Jewish Population Study showed only 1 in 4 Gentile wives converting to Judaism, and only 1 in 40 Gentile husbands doing the same. Later studies showed even fewer converts. In a male-dominated society such as the United States, it appears that women, not men, were called on to give up their religion in cases of intermarriage. However, the tenfold difference between men and women may also have been a response to Jewish law. Since children were deemed to follow their mother's religion and Judaism generally wanted to preserve as many Jews as possible, it seems likely that more pressure to convert was put on Gentile women than on Gentile men. In general, marital friction seems to have been lower when one or the other partner was a serious convert. Since the converts were usually Christian women adopting Judaism, one would expect to find more tension, overall, in marriages between Gentile men and Jewish women, where few conversions took place.[33]

Accompanying the rise in intermarriage in the 1960s, '70s, and '80s, and the liberalized attitude of some rabbis toward intermarriage and conversion, was a tendency of Jewish groups to accept even unconverted spouses into their fold. In that period more Gentile spouses than ever before were converting to Judaism, perhaps because minority ethnic identity became acceptable—even attractive—to majority people for the first time in American history. But even those who chose to retain their Christian identity often found places in Judaism. Detroit Jewish activist Leonard Simons expressed the growing conviction of many Jews that "marrying someone who is not a Jew does not mean, necessarily, that the Jewish person is lost to the Jewish community." He and others like him felt Jewish organizations should open lines of communication to intermarried couples, strengthen the Jewish partner's faith, and encourage the Gentile partner to participate in Jewish activities wherever possible. Many synagogues advertised classes for non-Jewish partners designed to acquaint them with the fundamentals of Judaism. They hoped some would convert, but were willing to accept those who would go only so far as to support their spouses' Judaism. More and more mixed, unconverted couples became fixtures in Reform and Conservative synagogues. Observers noted that converts were more active and enthusiastic than their born-Jewish mates. Among families where the Gentile partner converted to Judaism, surveys from the 1970s showed a higher degree of Jewish observance—lighting Shabbat candles, holding a Passover Seder, celebrating Rosh Hashana, and the like—than among families where both partners were born Jews. Increasingly, people came to recognize that even spouses who had not formally been converted could be enthusiastic Jews. Nearly half the Gentile partners—male and female—in the National Jewish Population Study identified themselves as Jewish, even though only a quarter of the women and one in forty of the men had formally converted. One Chicago woman summed up the feelings of those Gentiles who had not only married Jews but adopted their Jewishness: "I belong to the sisterhood of a synagogue and all sorts of Jewish organizations. I was never formally converted—it came to me gradually over a period of years. I go to temple now, and it fills my needs—it fills my heart. I have a *seder* passover service at home. . . . I'm a Jew. I've built my life around it. The Jews are my people. I'm a Jew because I want to be—I've read and studied those laws. The other women are Jewish because they can't help themselves; I feel that I'm more Jewish than they are, sometimes."[34]

The general trend was for Gentile spouses increasingly to connect with their partners' Judaism. While conversion and intermarriage were both symptoms of assimilation, intermarriage seldom caused Jews to convert to Christianity. The opposite was not true, however. Due to parental pressure or personal wish, Gentiles who married Jews frequently sought to become Jews themselves. A higher percentage of Gentile women than men sought conversion to Judaism. Most rabbis did not encourage conversions unless the attraction to Judaism was heartfelt, but a rising number, especially of Reform rabbis, were willing to accept converts on any terms. In the 1960s, '70s, and '80s, some Reform and Conservative synagogues began to accept even unconverted spouses into their fellowship.

Intermarriage and Divorce

One of the persistent preoccupations of opponents of intermarriage was the spectre of divorce. Most anti-intermarriage tracts cited a divorce rate two to four times higher than in unmixed marriages. Although the actual numbers were something less than that, it is indis-

putable that intermarriages ended in divorce more frequently than did
other Jewish marriages. In 1919, David De Sola Pool said it was "three
or four times more likely" that an intermarriage would end in divorce.
He called this "clear proof that a mixed marriage is far more likely
to turn out unhappily than a normal marriage." Later generations of
pamphleteers claimed only a 200 to 250 percent disparity.[35]

Proponents of intermarriage, on the other hand, discounted such
assertions. They contended that divorce was only a minor problem and
could be attributed to pressures on couples from family and society and
to insufficient preparation of couples by rabbis. Abraham Shinedling
officiated at scores of intermarriages. In each case he tried carefully to
prepare both the Jewish and the Gentile partner for their life together.
And he claimed that only one out of all those marriages ended in
divorce.[36]

Hard numbers on broken intermarriages are hard to come by.
Those that exist paint a picture less rosy than Shinedling's experience
but less gloomy than the assertions of the pamphlet writers. Maurice
Fishberg's 1905 survey of Prussian records showed an intermarriage
divorce rate of 5.4 percent, compared to 4.1 percent for homogamous
Jewish marriages. In 1933 Harry Linfield wrote about the "high rate of
divorce among Jews married to non-Jews in Hungary," but in fact, the
divorce rate for intermarried Jews in his study was much *lower*, not
higher, than the rate for purely Jewish couples. In Russia in 1926, the
divorce rate for intermarried Jews was 1.3 times that for endogamous
Jews. The only American study to generate divorce statistics, a 1967
study of Jews in Indiana, also found a somewhat higher rate of divorces
among intermarriages than among purely Jewish couples.[37]

What of the Children?

If many observers were bothered about the possibility of divorce
resulting from intermarriage, more were concerned about the fate of
the children. The consensus of Jews was that something bad would
happen to them. Roland Gittelsohn thought that what happened to the
children was the "heart of the problem" of intermarriage. For him,
as for many others, the problem was that the children would not be
Jews. Although Max Heller was less specific about percentages, he
was no less certain that "the descendants of the Jew who intermar-

ries are lost to Judaism." Some people predicted that the offspring of intermarriages would be sterile, generalizing from mules to humans without scientific support. Others expected to see "criminality" and "physical deterioration" in mixed children, again without any evidence to support their theories. Still others expressed their fears in more generalized form. Sidney Goldstein wrote in 1940, "In the case of children in intermarriage the handicaps are too evident to require much discussion."[38]

While some of these fears were either vague or silly, the question of whether mixed children would be Jews or Gentiles was a very real one. Its answer depended upon the time period in which a mixed individual lived, his or her status before Jewish law, and the amount of abuse or support he or she received for his or her mixed status.

Before the Halakhah—Jewish law—children of Jewish mothers and Gentile fathers were Jews; offspring of the inverse combination were Gentiles. This rule of the womb dates from talmudic times, though the reasons for its existence are obscure. Perhaps children followed their mother because often mixed unions were not legal marriages, and the fathers' identities were difficult to determine for legal purposes. In any case, until recent years nearly all rabbis enforced this principle. Since most intermarriages were by Jewish men, this rigid adherence to medieval law had the effect of driving mixed children away from Judaism to the faith of their mothers. Periodically, Jewish leaders would be more flexible and allow a few mixed children of Jewish fathers to enjoy the benefits of Judaism. Reform rabbis took the lead in this development. In 1947, the CCAR agreed that any child should be regarded a Jew who had a Jewish father or mother and both of whose parents declared their intention to raise it as a Jew. Orthodox and Conservative rabbis, however, stuck to the old standard. This meant, for example, that the grandson of David Ben-Gurion, Israel's first prime minister, could not be married by an Orthodox rabbi because he was not a Jew in Orthodox eyes: his mother had not been formally converted at the time of his birth.[39]

Before about 1960, mixed individuals typically endured abuse from both Jews and Gentiles. Rabbi B. Abramowitz of St. Louis in 1919 condemned intermarriage and warned Jews not to circumcise mixed boys, nor to admit mixed children to Jewish schools. They were not Jewish, he said. On the other side, a mixed Jewish-Irish boy was beaten regularly by his New York parochial school classmates because, they insisted, he was Jewish.[40] Such numbers as are available (admittedly most of them from European contexts) suggest that more mixed children in this early period chose Gentile identities than Jewish ones. Two-thirds of the mixed babies born in Hungary in 1932 were baptized as Protestants. Three-fourths of the Prussian mixed babies in 1905 were Protestants. In two small Louisiana towns during the middle decades of this century, nearly all the mixed children were raised as Christians. In Washington, D.C., at the same time, nearly three-fourths of the mixed couples regarded their children as Gentiles. Data from more typical American Jewish communities are not available for that period.[41]

Many mixed individuals were plagued by parents who would not decide what they wanted their children to be. They would let the children decide for themselves whether to be Jews or Gentiles, without giving them any guidance whatsoever. Some families split down the middle, with the mother taking the girls to church and the father taking the boys to temple. Other parents would deny that the children were mixed at all, insisting, according to their ambition, that they were either all Jewish or all Christian.[42] In situations where families were split or identities were left vague, mixed individuals often grew up confused and bitter. A fourteen-year-old boy told his rabbi: "I hate my father and mother. I hate my home. I am a mongrel. Why did I have to be born? The Jews call me a Gentile. And the Gentiles won't accept me because I am a Jew." Ernst Harthern complained: "I don't think my father should have married a Gentile. It would have made matters easier for his children if he hadn't. One is so tortured by divided loyalties."[43]

Increasingly after about 1960, intermarried couples chose to embrace Judaism and communicate it to their children. In 1971 Bernard Lazerwitz noted "the appearance of a substantial minority of intermarried people who have and maintain Jewish religio-ethnic involvement." Two years later the National Jewish Population Study found that an overwhelming majority of mixed children were being raised as Jews.[44] How effective that Jewish upbringing was depended on the type of intermarriage. In 1983 Egon Mayer made a nationwide study of children of upper-class Jewish-Gentile intermarriages. He found a critical difference regarding Jewish identity between those mixed people whose non-Jewish parents had converted to Judaism and those whose Gentile parents had not. In the former case—mainly families involving Gentile women converts and Jewish husbands—the mixed offspring were brought up as Jews, and they saw themselves as Jews and associated with Jewish people as adults. In families where the Gentile spouses did not convert, the mixed children had more tenuous and abstract attachments to Judaism.[45]

To a certain extent the recent trend toward increased Jewish connection represented an awakening to Judaism on the part of intermarried Jews. Partly, it signalled a new willingness by Gentile spouses to pursue Judaism. But in the main, it was a result of changing attitudes on the part of Jews and Jewish institutions. For the first time, they began to welcome the intermarried and seek ways to incorporate them into Judaism. As Eugen Schoenfeld trenchantly observed, "The severance of the exogamous Jew from his community is not a voluntary one; such an action is the result of sanctions imposed upon the deviant by the Jewish community. . . . The exogamous person . . . does not sever his relationship with the Jewish community . . . he continues to declare himself Jewish. . . . In fact, the percentage of exogamous persons who identify themselves as Jewish is greater than the percentage of Jews as a whole." But Jewish communities for many years shut out intermarried people and their offspring, for fear that their presence would encourage others to intermarry.[46] In time, Reform leaders, particularly, but members of the more conservative traditions as well, voiced new sentiments: "Programs have to be created for identifying mixed married families and for reaching out to them. Special attempts must be made to reach the children of mixed marriages with educational and cultural programming. The parents should also be involved as much as possible (and with sensitivity for the non-Jewish partner) in Jewish-content programming."[47]

Such acceptance—even encouragement—from Jewish institutions allowed mixed individuals and their families to embrace Judaism. In the 1970s, people with as little Jewish inheritance as a single grandparent shocked their relatives (and sometimes themselves) by deciding to be Jewish. Sometimes in this new world a person did not have to give up his or her Gentile identity in order to be Jewish. Joy Nakamura* came to see herself as both Jewish and Japanese American—and was allowed to claim that dual heritage—in part because of the more flexible attitude of Judaism in the 1970s and '80s.[48]

In sum, for much of the century the Jewish law of the womb drove most part-Jewish children away from Judaism. However, as intermarriages became more accepted in the 1960s, '70s, and '80s, more and more mixed children chose to identify themselves as Jews.

Summary of Part III

Since biblical times, intermarriage has been a problem for Jews. The patriarchs and their successors tried to prohibit intermarriages, but many such marriages took place anyway. A relatively open society during the early centuries of the Christian ascendancy gave way to persecution of Jews and the intermarried after the thirteenth century. This Christian pressure against intermarriage with Jews was not removed until nineteenth-century West Europeans began to work out the implications of the Enlightenment.

The first Jews to come to America, Sephardim originally from Iberia, were quickly absorbed by the surrounding mass of Gentiles. The German Ashkenazim who followed were better at maintaining their separate Jewish identity, although the dominion of Reform Judaism, the generally assimilationist tenor of their community, and the existence of many single Jewish men in remote parts of the country all tended to encourage intermarriage.

The evolving mutual images of Jew and Gentile increased the chances of intermarriage. Jewish men—who were seen in the immigrant generation as vulgar, grasping, and unattractive—soon changed in the eyes of Gentiles. By the second generation they were regarded as ambitious, avant-garde, and intellectual. Some Gentiles saw Jewish women as loud, aggressive, and domineering, while others saw them as earthy and sensual. The Jewish image of Gentile men is indistinct, but Gentile women were accorded the mythical status of the shikse: beautiful, graceful, and very sexy.

As with Japanese Americans, the rate of intermarriage increased generation by generation. This reflected both increasing structural assimilation and such cultural factors as favorable mutual images and assimilationist impulses, as well as the generally increasing acceptance of ethnic diversity in American society at large. Yet Jewish outmarriage never reached the height experienced by third-generation Japanese Americans, largely because Judaism exerted an ideological pull toward homogamy that had no parallel among Japanese Americans. In both second and third generations, far more Jewish men than women married out. Both Jews and Gentiles opposed intermarriage, but that opposition weakened as time went on. Orthodox and Conservative Jews were more adamant than members of the Reform movement in their opposition to intermarriage. Rabbis attacked intermarriage as a threat to the survival of Judaism, while lay people opposed it on more personal grounds, often predicting marital conflict in mixed families.

As was the case for Japanese Americans, intermarriage was much more common in locations distant from centers of ethnic population. And it was more common among those who worked outside ethnic communities—professionals, clerical people, and government workers—than among those who were surrounded by other Jews. However, in the Jewish experience as in the Japanese, there was little support for Robert Merton's hypogamy theory.

As with Japanese Americans, there were boundaries within the East European Jewish group, at least in the immigrant generation, which outsiders did not recognize, but across which Jews were loath to marry. These boundaries formed the upper rungs of a hierarchy of preference much like the Japanese American ladder. As with Japanese Americans, with the passing of generations, the distinctions at the top of the ladder became blurred, and individuals showed themselves ever more willing to tread the lower rungs.

The psychological factors surrounding Jewish intermarriage were complex. Some psychologists saw intermarriage as *ipso facto* neurotic, and therefore bad. Others viewed it as part and parcel of the progress of assimilation, and therefore good. The most objective observers noted the presence of some factors of motivation that might be called neurotic, but argued that these did not appear in all cases and that, even where they did occur, they did not necessarily make the marriages bad ones.

The relationship between intermarriage and conversion, too, was complex. Intermarriage does not seem to have caused many Jewish conversions to Christianity, although both phenomena were to some extent symptoms of assimilation. On the other hand, the Gentile partner was often forced to convert to Judaism before being allowed to marry a Jew. This requirement seems to have eased in the 1960s and after.

The divorce rate for intermarried Jews was higher than for homogamous Jews, but not a lot higher. The children of intermarriages for many years turned to Christianity, often because Judaism turned them away. After about 1960, however, mixed young people were increasingly welcomed into Judaism. More and more frequently they were choosing to identify themselves as all or part Jewish.

IV

BLACK AMERICANS

9. Background and Images: The Core of the Heart

> In the core of the heart of the American race problem the sex factor is rooted, rooted so deeply that it is not always recognized when it shows on the surface. Other factors are obvious and are the ones we dare to deal with; but regardless of how we deal with these, the race situation will continue to be acute as long as the sex factor persists. . . . It may be innate; I do not know. But I do know it is strong and bitter.
>
> —JAMES WELDON JOHNSON, *Along This Way*

The experiences of Black Americans have been different from those of Japanese and Jewish Americans, and so their patterns of attitude and behavior with respect to intermarriage have been different as well. Their longevity in America, the images Whites assigned to them, the slave status suffered by most of them for much of that time, and the distinctive patterns of discrimination they endured set Blacks apart from the European and Asian immigrants of the late nineteenth century. The twentieth-century position of Black people with regard to intergroup sex and marriage cannot be understood without reference to this distinctive heritage.

Miscegenation before the Civil War

Sexual activity between Whites and Blacks has a long if not honored history in America. Intermarriage, however, is by and large a more recent phenomenon. Throughout the slave period, small numbers of legitimate interracial unions existed alongside widespread concubinage and forced sex, all under an official ideology that denied any mixing at all. The pattern of interracial sexual activity was largely a result of the power relationship that developed between Whites and Blacks from the early days of European domination of the American scene.

No one knows whether the first Africans to inhabit these shores, migrants to Virginia in 1619, were slave or free. But it is clear that a significant portion of the seventeenth-century Negro population enjoyed at least a measure of freedom. Some were indentured servants. Some were independent landowners and employers of servants. Gradually, as the Chesapeake economy expanded over the course of the century, slavery seems to have become the characteristic condition of the majority of the Black population. By the time large numbers of Africans were imported in the eighteenth century, slavery and blackness were closely identified in the minds of most Americans.[1] It remained so until the Civil War, although there always existed, alongside the slaves, individuals and small communities of free people of African descent.

Together with the institution of slavery there developed a distinctive set of images which Whites held of Black people. Many of these ideas predated any significant encounter between Whites and Blacks in America. English people and their American descendants associated blackness with evil, sin, and uncleanness. They associated Africans with the jungle, with primitive culture and social organization, and with savage and violent behavior. Africans, in their view, were somehow closely related to apes and prone to behaving in bestial fashion. Linked to the suggestion of animality was the conviction, deeply rooted in Western culture, that Africans were excessive in their sexuality, passionate, and driven by scarcely controllable lust.[2]

Demography, social structure, and White people's images of Africans combined to produce a relatively high degree of interracial mating in the early colonial decades.[3] America in the seventeenth century was a frontier society, with many more men than women, especially in the southern colonies. It was also a hierarchical society, in which men of relative wealth and status exercised a good deal of control over their social inferiors. It should come as no surprise that more than a few White men took advantage of the women, either slaves or indentured servants, whose lives they controlled. Since many servants and nearly all slaves were Black and most masters were White, many of those couplings were interracial. Because of the patriarchal power exercised by masters in those decades, cases of sexual abuse seldom came to public light. Nonetheless, the frequent appearance of people called mulattoes in records of the time testifies to a good deal of mixing. Romances between Black women and White men of similar status were not always so private. Lorenzo Greene culled court records and found a dozen cases from seventeenth-century New England involving White servants or free men who were named as fathers of illegitimate children by Black slave women. In a society where the line between servant and slave was a good deal less precise than that between bond and free, it stands to reason that some White servant men and Black slave women should choose each other as partners. The fact that both were, at least temporarily, not free people but the property of others meant that most such relationships never received formal legal sanction. In some cases, however, Black women and White men did manage to make formal their attachments. For example, in 1656 Virginian Elizabeth Kay managed to sue for her freedom and wed William Greensted.[4]

It is less well known that there were also marriages and informal liaisons between Black men and White women in colonial America. This happened throughout the colonies. Most often these were fleeting encounters or, at most, informal relationships of some duration. Only a few were sanctified. In Virginia in the 1680s, a White woman named Hester, a servant of James Westcomb, married James Tate, a slave belonging to Patrick Spence. Lemuel Haynes, a prominent Massachusetts preacher, was the son of an interracial marriage and the husband of a White woman. Perhaps the most sensational colonial-era interracial couple was a Black man named Caesar and his Irish-born mistress Peggy Kerry, who were among those executed amid hysteria about an alleged plot by Black slaves, Black servants, and White servants to burn New York City and kill upper-class Whites.[5]

In time, the prohibition on interracial liaisons would become a main pillar of the American racial structure. In the early colonial period that pillar was not yet firmly in place. There are no reliable statistics to prove the point, but Winthrop Jordan believes, credibly, that there was proportionately more interracial mating in the colonial era than at any later time in American history.[6]

That all changed as the color line hardened. Starting early in the eighteenth century, the trickle of Africans imported into the colonies became a stream and then a flood which did not crest until the era of the War for Independence. Although the White and free population was also growing rapidly, the character of American society had irrevocably changed. Throughout much of the seventeenth century, the Black and slave population had been small enough that White colonists could deal with issues regarding race relations on an *ad hoc* basis. With the enlarged presence of African slaves, the Whites could no longer afford that luxury. Starting in the Chesapeake region in the 1660s and continuing through the first decades of the eighteenth century, slave codes were promulgated by legislatures throughout the colonies. They tried to solidify the distinction between slave and free. Simultaneously they placed limits on the free Black populations of most colonies, thus further identifying slavery and blackness.[7]

Among the besetting fears of the White majority (or minority in the case of South Carolina) was servile insurrection: the Whites were, after all, holding their fellow humans in bondage. Many of the laws were designed to keep the slave and free Black population under surveillance with the idea of preventing revolts. White guilt over slavery added to the legitimate fear of insurrection and focused in large part on sex. White men had long regarded Black women as unnaturally passionate, perhaps to excuse their own involvement in sexual exploitation. They also depicted Black men as exceptionally virile, possessors of abnormally large sex organs, promiscuous, and sexually dangerous. At times of slave unrest, fears of sexual attacks by Black men on White women loomed large in White minds. Colonial newspapers had little room for accounts of White men raping Black women, but they reported in lurid detail faraway stories of Black men accused of raping Whites, especially when those Blacks were accused insurrectionists. Several commentators have regarded this fixation on predatory Black male sexuality as a psychological device by which White men assuaged their guilt and anxiety by projecting their own illegitimate desires onto Black men. Meantime, punishments for offenses by Black men often took on a violent and sexual aspect; castration and torture reflected a need by White men to demonstrate their mastery over the Black men they feared.[8]

Opposition to interracial sexual contact found expression in laws and court decisions. This began as early as 1630, when White Virginian Hugh Davis was sentenced "to be soundly whipped, before an assembly of Negroes and others for abusing himself to the dishonor of God and shame of Christians, by defiling his body in lying with a Negro." Davis was guilty not only of miscegenation but also of fornication; in that early period, other interracial unions went unpunished. Courts and legislatures took the next century and more to decide how to handle miscegenation. Gradually, an uneven framework of laws and decisions was erected to inhibit intermarriage by punishing the White or Black spouse, the person who married them, or all three.[9] Typical was a 1741 North Carolina statute:

For Prevention of that abominable Mixture and spurious issue, which hereafter may increase in this Government, by white Men and women intermarrying with Indians, Negroes, Mustees [people of mixed ancestry, usually quadroons or octoroons], or Mulattoes, Be it enacted . . . That if any white Man or Woman, being free shall intermarry with an Indian, Negro, Mustee or Mulatto man or woman, or any Person of Mixed Blood, to the Third Generation, bond or free, he shall, by Judgment of the County Court, forfeit and pay the sum of Fifty Pounds, Proclamation Money, for the use of the Parish.[10]

Such a fine was so large a sum that a free person might well have to sell herself into bondage in order to pay. Penalties in other jurisdictions included whipping, penance, enforced servitude, and banishment. According to Maryland law, a White woman who married a Black slave became the servant of her husband's master for the husband's lifetime, and their children also were to be slaves. Apparently, some masters pushed their White servant women into marriage to slave men, thus gaining the women's service for many years and their children's labor for life. A body of laws and decisions grew up, rendering even free mulattoes second-class citizens. Carter Woodson has argued persuasively that the underlying intent of the antimiscegenation laws and court decisions in the colonial period was not so much to prevent sexual relations between White and Black, as "to debase to a still lower status the offspring of the blacks . . . , to leave women of color without protection against white men," and to prevent the growth of a free Black population.[11]

By the time of the War for Independence, then, a pattern had been established that continued with few modifications throughout the slave era. Mating occurred between Whites and Blacks of both sexes. But it was disapproved of by the White population, and there were severe penalties for making it formal by marriage. Mulattoes often took the status of the slave parent. Even if free, they were second-class citizens at best.[12]

Examples abound of forced sex between White men and slave women in the antebellum period. Indeed, this has long been regarded as virtually the only form of interracial mating to have taken place during the slave period. It was a prominent feature of many of the slave autobiographies that were published by abolitionists in the last decades before the Civil War. May Satterfield recalled that during her Virginia childhood, "In dem times a nigger 'oman couldn't help herself, fo' she had to do what de marster say. Ef he come to de field whar de women workin' an' tell gal to come on, she had to go. He would take one down in de woods an' use her all de time he wanted to, den send her on back to work." Resistance was dangerous. John Brown told of a plantation in Georgia where the master's son made advances on a slave woman, who rejected him. Enraged, "one night he called her out of the gin-house, and then bade me and two or three more, strip her naked; which we did. He then made us throw her down on her face, in front of the door, and hold her whilst he flogged her . . . with the bullwhip, cutting great gashes of flesh out of her person, at every blow, from five to six inches long. The poor unfortunate girl screamed most awfully all the time, and writhed under our strong arms, rendering it necessary for us to use our united strength to hold her down. He flogged her for half an hour, until he nearly killed her, and then left her to crawl away to her cabin." Pauli Murray's grandmother told of her mother, Harriet, being raped repeatedly by Sid Smith, one of the sons of her North Carolina master. Harriet's free Black husband, Reuben Day, attempted to intervene, but was run out of the county by his wife's tormenter, never to be heard from again. Mary Wood said her aunt Fannie was raped and then the man who raped her sold her to the harder slave life in the Deep South, to mollify his jealous wife. Slave women—mulattoes in particular—sometimes were sold openly for the purpose of prostitution. Some apologists for slavery have argued that such sexual abuse of slave women was infrequent and then not the fault of men of the master class, but rather a practice perpetrated by White men of low station. The available testimony, however, indicates that White men of every class, and perhaps especially of the planter class, forced their sexual attentions upon Black women. Even Union soldiers, upon liberating sections of the South, were known to attack Black women.[13]

Yet, if many masters, overseers, and other White men took casual and brutal advantage of slave women, there were also more than a few cases where slave women entered the more stable role of concubine. Sometimes, these were passionate love affairs, tinged on the White side with Gauguin-like dreams of exotic eroticism. Adolf Wolff wrote poetry to his Black Venus, including the following lines:

> You make me dream of distant tropic climes,
> Luxurious vegetation; nights serene
> By burning passion made tempestuous,
> The witching scent of rare exotic languorous
> Of music soft and weird, whose savage rhythm
> Compels each fibre of the frame to dance.
>
> I see you as the princess of an isle
> Whose jungles are replete with beasts of prey
> And whose vast forests are ever alive
> With cries and frolickings of birds and apes,
> Whose villages of bamboo huts are full
> Of dusty-hued and happy naked people.
>
> Your simple-hearted subjects pay you homage,
> Prostrated in the dust, they weirdly chant
> Thy praises, even as in my own way
> I sing your praises sweet, exotic princess.
> Oh, let me enter your enchanted realm
> And make of me your humble slave.[14]

More often, there was an element of coercion involved, and the concubines enjoyed only briefly their elevated status before being sent back to harder forms of slavery. Nancy Weston was a house slave and nurse to the children in Henry Grimké's household. When Henry's wife died, he took Nancy to fulfill the duties of consort and mistress of the household. She gave him three children, and on his deathbed he left instructions that she and their children were to continue to live "as members of the family." But Henry's White son, Montague, took all three boys (his half-brothers) as slaves and sold one, Frank, to another owner. In another instance, a twenty-four-year-old slave named Rachel thought she had a secure position as mistress of the young master. But his mother and sisters made known their disapproval, so Rachel was put on the block and sold by her erstwhile lover.[15]

Some Black women chose the lot of concubine in order to avoid the harder labors of field slaves. Some found their position as master's favorite entitled them to extra food, finer clothing, more spacious living quarters, even a measure of dominion over other slaves. William Wells Brown told of a beautiful quadroon named Cynthia who was offered the choice of being mistress to slave trader James Walker or being sold as a field hand to the most brutal plantation he could find in the Deep South. Choosing the former alternative, she was secure until Walker decided to marry; then he sold her anyway.[16]

Very occasionally, the concubine role meant a lasting, marriagelike relationship. Rumor had it that as prominent a personage as Richard M. Johnson, vice-president under Martin Van Buren, not only had children by a mulatto woman but treated her as his common-law wife. That was only rumor, perhaps, but a number of wills attest to the fact that other White men, particularly single men and elderly widowers, formed enduring relationships with slave women. South Carolina law forbade Elijah Willis to marry his slave mistress, Amy, but his 1854 will directed the executors of his estate to sell his real property, take Amy and her children to Ohio, emancipate them, and buy them land in free territory to farm for themselves. Other slave owners, like Virginian Walter Robertson, did not provide emancipation for their concubines. But Robertson did bequeath all his estate to his slave paramour Ann Rose and leave her to manage his plantation, including other slaves.[17]

In assessing these relationships, especially concubinage, between White men and slave women, one problem is to judge to what extent the women submitted to the advances of powerful White males out of compulsion, and to what extent they acted on the basis of other factors, such as the prestige of association with the master class and the benefits to be obtained in the form of lighter work, better housing, clothing, and food, education for their children, promises of freedom, power over other slaves, love, and affection. Understandably, this has attracted partisan analysis. Recent Black writers and their sympathizers have asserted that nearly all unions were coerced. Apologists for slavery have contended that very little interracial mating happened and that which did take place was largely voluntary. Robert Fogel and Stanley Engerman go through extraordinary statistical gymnastics in attempting to prove that very few White men had sex with slave women. Their evidence will not bear the weight of their main conclusions, but they are certainly right in asserting that slave women and men ardently defended their honor and that the slave family was not hopelessly damaged by forced interracial sex. On balance, it is probably safe to conclude with Eugene Genovese that "much of the plantation miscegenation occurred with single girls under circumstances that varied from seduction to rape and typically fell between the two," and that there were a relatively large number of enduring partnerships between slave women and White men.[18]

Most of the coupling of White men and Black women in antebellum times involved women who were slaves. But in certain southern cities, notably Charleston and New Orleans, free women of color took part in an elaborate cross-racial social structure. The New Orleans situation—known as *placage*—derived in large part from the more relaxed racial system the town had known in its years as a French outpost. Then, slave women had provided their masters with domestic companionship. Throughout the antebellum era, the free offspring of those early interracial unions, plus mulatto women imported from other parts of the South, were bought or hired as concubines by wealthy White planters and merchants. Typically, a free woman of color and her parents would negotiate a contract with a White suitor, whereby he would agree to set her up in an elegant house and keep her luxuriously clothed and fed for as long as their contract lasted, often several years. He would also provide her with enough money to make a living after their relationship expired and to educate any children they might produce. New Orleans society recognized a host of gradations between White and Black: mulatto, quadroon, octoroon, metis, meamelouc, and so on. The most glamourous date on the New Orleans social calendar was the night of the quadroon ball, attended only by White men and light-skinned free women of color. The glamour and wealth of quadroon society in New Orleans could not obscure the fact that a good deal of outright prostitution also took place alongside concubinage there and in other southern cities. The prostitutes in question were often light-skinned, because White men preferred light women, but they were more likely to be slave than free. Charleston operated on this model, although there was concubinage there, too, and a relatively large free mulatto population.[19]

Although most interracial couples involved Black women and White men, there were some cases of the opposite combination. White Southern males were obsessed by the notion that Black men lusted after White women. Yet few would ever have credited the notion that White women reciprocated the sentiment, much less that Black men and White women might actually mate and marry in the Old South. Such was the case, however, to a degree that is just now coming to light. Most interracial liaisons involving Black men and White women were brief encounters, often between lower-class White women and free Black men in southern cities, although some clearly involved women of the planter class. In 1859 Richmond police arrested "two youthful white girls, not of uncomely figures or shape . . . . pandering for lucre's sake to the passions of the negroes." New Orleans police regularly arrested White women for cohabiting with slave men. During the Civil War, a White man named Robinson went off to war and left his wife in the care of a Black slave, who promptly impregnated Robinson's wife. It was from such unions, rather than the emancipated offspring of White men, that the bulk of the free mulatto population probably came. As with the other race-gender combinations, power relationships in Black male-White female couples were uneven. If a White woman had sex with a Black man, she always had the option, like Potiphar's wife, to cry "rape" with the surety of being believed. A smaller number of cases involved durable cohabitation of Black men and White women. These relationships seem to have been as common in rural areas as in the cities. Almost no cases of common-law marriage between upper-class women and Black men are recorded. Overall, the rate of both casual sex and long-term liaisons between Black men and White women seems to have been increasing throughout the South in the two or three decades before the Civil War. Still, the number of such unions was very small, by comparison with either the reverse gender combination or homogeneous mating.[20]

For the most part, Whites were firmly opposed to interracial sex and marriage, though they seem to have been bothered more by marriage than by sex. Casual sex, even extended concubinage, conferred no formal status on the Black partner and posed little threat to the slave system. Marriage, however, reflected an assumption that the two parties were social equals; this the slave regime could not tolerate. Thus, all the southern states except South Carolina outlawed interracial marriage. There was a good deal of public and private anguish over interracial sex, but there was also alongside it a more relaxed attitude that boys will be boys and even—for lower-class Whites—that girls will be girls. Perhaps the most eloquent protest against White men's nocturnal revels in the slave quarters was voiced by Mary B. Chesnut. Significantly, as an upper-class White female tightly limited by her place atop the pedestal, she complained not in public, but to her diary: "God forgive us, but ours is a monstrous system, a wrong and iniquity! Like the patriarchs of old, our men live all in one house with their wives and their concubines; and the mulattoes one sees in every family partly resemble the white children. Any lady is ready to tell you who is the father of all the mulatto children in everybody's household but her own. Those, she seems to think, drop from the clouds." Frequently, a White woman, acting out her own pain and humiliation, would make miserable the life of a slave whom she suspected of submitting to the master's advances. She might load on extra work or punish the slave or her children harshly and without provocation. She might prevail upon her husband to send a house slave into the fields or even to sell her. Caroline Grant, for example, was banished to the fields because her daughter Tissuey looked too White.[21]

Despite the objections of White women and the official ideology that interracial sex was bad, most White men received only mild public censure for crossing the color line. It was reported, for instance, that in some locations, "if a pastor has offspring by a woman not his wife, the church dismisses him if she is a white woman, but if she is colored, it does not hinder his continuing to be their shepherd." By contrast, a White woman with a Black lover stood convicted of a major offense against public opinion. The only exception to this rule seems to have occurred in certain rural enclaves where mixing between lower-class White women and free mulatto men was relatively well accepted.[22]

Slaves, for the most part, resented intergroup mating. Slave husbands and fathers showed themselves angry and frustrated about depredations against their wives and daughters. Some resisted physically, but the power lay against them. They could run away or refuse to work, but most could do little to protect their women. The psychic cost to a

slave husband if his wife went willingly with the master was incalculable. Other slaves frequently marked off a woman who had chosen the
role of concubine and refused to have more than perfunctory dealings
with her.[23] The opinions of free Black people varied. They resented
prostitution, but were rather more tolerant of enduring cross-racial
liaisons, of whichever race-gender combination. The mulatto element
in the free Black population was so large that it was an exceptional
free Black person who, like David Walker, had strong feelings against
miscegenation.[24]

Not all interracial liaisons were between Blacks and Whites. Especially in the colonial period, there were also slaves who were Native
Americans, and Indians who had some Black ancestry. Europeans en-
slaved Indians along with Africans in the seventeenth century, before
they decided the latter constituted a more suitable group for slavery.
Gradually, elements of the two populations merged, so that most
American Blacks came to have a substantial admixture of Native Ameri-
can ancestry. Some other Native Americans lost their freedom along
with their lands as White settlement expanded in the Southeast. Many
Blacks in later years pointed with pride and some veracity to Indian
ancestors. Indians became slaves; Black slaves also became Indians.
Georgia and South Carolina runaways mixed with Creeks to form the
Seminole tribe. Other runaways were held by the Cherokee as slaves.
They made the trip with their Indian masters along the Trail of Tears to
Oklahoma in the 1830s. Many of the descendants of these Black slaves
were emancipated and became members of the tribe. There was anti-
Black prejudice in most tribes; as the nineteenth century progressed,
tribes such as the Creeks raised barriers against intermarriage. But
there was also considerable fusion of the two groups throughout the
slave period.[25]

Another variant on the predominant southern pattern existed in
the North. Most northern states put an end to slavery in the decades
after the War for Independence because slavery did not sit well with
revolutionary ideology about all men being created equal; besides,
no northern state depended on slavery for its economic well-being.
But freedom from slavery for the small Black population in the North
did not mean full citizenship. Shortly after emancipation nearly every
northern state placed careful limits on Black freedom. In some states,
such as Massachusetts, these included a bar against intermarriage.

Even where intermarriage was allowed, it carried painful social consequences. J. Benwell, an English traveller during the 1850s, found in
Buffalo a "well-informed, good-looking" English woman married to a
Black male. "The wife was despised by the wives of white citizens,"
Benwell reported, "and both were shunned. White etiquette would
not let him attend her at their theatre box; they never ventured out
together. If one did go out, it was usually after dark. On one occasion, the man was mobbed and nearly lost his life." One of the major
complaints against abolitionists—White and Black—was that they were
alleged to promote amalgamation and intermarriage. This charge does
not seem to have been true, although William Lloyd Garrison and
others did push for the repeal of the Massachusetts antimiscegenation
law after 1831, as a status issue. Antiabolitionists exposed the nature
of their deepest fears when they attacked Black and White antislavery
people as advocates and practitioners of amalgamation. Sometimes
their attacks took violent form, as in the Philadelphia Passover Riots of
1834. Free Blacks were also subject to attack for alleged sexual mis-
conduct. The spark that lit the Detroit Riot of 1863 was the rape of
Ellen Hover, a Black female, by Thomas Faulkner, a White male. Yet
soon White mobs rampaged through Black neighborhoods, stoning,
burning, and dismembering dozens of Black people. A particular target of these mobs was a small number of White women married to
Black men.[26]

The mulatto population was large and ever-growing in the antebellum years. Statistics are available only for the 1850 and 1860 census
years, and those are subject to varying interpretations.[27] But it is clear
that the increase in the number of people perceived to be mulattoes
—from 405,751 in 1850 to 588,363 in 1860—represented a longer
trend. There was also a much larger percentage of mulattoes in the free
than in the slave population, due both to White masters emancipating
their slave children and to White women giving birth to free children
by Black men. There was a distinct regional difference between the
Upper and the Lower South. The Upper South had the bulk of mulattoes in the population, over 200,000 in 1850. In the Lower South,
there were fewer mulattoes, about 90,000. Moreover, a much smaller
percentage of Lower South mulattoes were free—about one in ten in
1850—compared to over a third of mulattoes in the Upper South. In
the Lower South the free Black population was made up mostly of mu-

lattoes, nearly all of whom lived in New Orleans, Charleston, Mobile, and Savannah, where they formed a middle tier between White and Black, free and slave. By contrast, the free mulatto population of the Upper South was overwhelmingly rural. In a few isolated instances, mulatto families such as the Metoyers of Cane River, Louisiana, came to dominate the countryside and were accorded nearly White status.[28]

Some very prominent people were mulattoes. Benjamin Banneker and Frederick Douglass had White fathers. Alexander Hamilton's mother may have had some slave ancestry. Although proof is highly uncertain, it was widely believed that both Hamilton and Thomas Jefferson sired families by slave concubines.[29]

Sometimes people of mixed ancestry occupied special places on their fathers' plantations, even when the fathers felt constrained not to recognize the children's mothers as their mistresses. People of this sort grew up around the master's house, played with White children, and may have received a little education. Byrl Anderson's experience was unusual but instructive: "My master's name was Powhatan Mitchell. . . . He was a Whig who owned slaves but was against slavery. He took me on his knee when I was about three and a half years ole an' gave me his birthright. He called up an' ole sow that had thirteen pigs all different colors. He said, 'You see them pigs there? They are all different colors but all have the same mother and are all brothers and sisters.' Then he called up his son and said, 'This boy here is your brother an' I am the daddy of both. You are to call me papa henceforth. You are to call this brother of yours [not] master but brother. Never call no white man master.' . . . From that day to this I called the ole master papa and that made me have two papas." Some such slaves, like Pauli Murray's grandmother, identified exclusively with their White fathers. Murray recalled: "Grandmother's uncritical love for her father was intensified by her urgent need for acceptance and for an identity of which she was not ashamed. Her father and his people represented everything desirable in life—power, wealth, privilege and respectability. All her life she would strive to identify herself with the best of her father's world and reject all associations which linked her to slavery." Sometimes a master cared enough for his slave children to emancipate them, either in his lifetime or through his will. Such newly freed mulattoes were seldom allowed to remain in the southern states; some went across the

Ohio River, where small colonies of ex-slaves flourished beginning in the 1840s.[30]

The relatively pampered status of some mulatto children of slave masters was always fragile at best. Henry Ferry reported that on the Virginia plantation where he grew up, a boy named Jim was the master's son by a slave woman. Although Jim's mother Martha had been banished from the big house, Jim was the master's only son and therefore allowed free run of the White family's quarters. That stopped abruptly when a visitor noticed the resemblance between Jim and his father. Thus publicly humiliated, the father's White wife sent Jim back to the slave cabins, never to return. In many instances, creditors, executors, or White family members overturned the wishes of dead masters and denied mulattoes the freedom they had been promised. For example, Samuel Campbell's estate was sold and divided between the White heirs. Among the slaves sold were Campbell's mulatto daughter and her infant son. Judith Logan, one of Campbell's White daughters, protested to her brothers and sisters, "Letty is our own half-sister, and you know it; father never intended they should be sold." They were sold anyway. Sometimes jealous White widows even managed to overturn emancipations that had been accomplished before their husbands died. The reader should not get the impression, however, that all or even very many White men who fathered children by their slave women attempted to treat them as free. There were many men, like Baily Cunningham's grandfather, who cheerfully sold their own children as slaves. Some, in financial difficulty, tried to sell their children to masters they knew to be gentle, but others simply sought the highest bidder.[31]

Other mulattoes, the children of White women or free Blacks, grew up as free people of color—"slaves without masters," as Ira Berlin put it. They constituted something of an elite stratum in southern Black society because of their freedom and their partial White ancestry. But they suffered the severe economic and political limits placed on all free Black people in the antebellum South.

Although antebellum Black people, slave and free, made distinctions of color, not just between White and Black, but between shades of brown as well, the United States never had a three-caste system such as prevailed in Jamaica or other Caribbean lands. In those places, mulattoes were often free and came to form an intermediate social group between Black and White. Except for such towns as Charleston and New Orleans and a few isolated rural pockets, White Americans demanded a two-caste system. All people with any admixture of African ancestry were grouped together, even if the free colored population were lighter than the slave. Still, both Whites and Blacks did make some color distinctions among Blacks. People of lighter complexion, straighter hair, and more angular features tended to think of themselves as superior to unmixed Black people. Because so many free people of color were mulattoes, light people took their color as a badge of elite status. In the rural South, as in New Orleans, free mulattoes typically married other mulattoes and shunned the company of free people of darker pigmentation. In the North, a larger portion of the free colored population was Black, yet there, too, mulattoes assumed superior status. In Philadelphia, for instance, the free mulatto group founded its own church and would not admit Blacks. Yet on the plantation, among slaves, it was not color but relationship to the master which elevated, and that was not an unmixed blessing. Mulattoes were sometimes called on to spy on their fellow slaves. Light slave children, such as William Wells Brown and Dora Curtis's grandmother, may have gained some small benefits from being their masters' children, but those gains were more than offset by the fact that other, darker slaves taunted and shunned them. As for romance, most slaves preferred partners of "a good brown color." Light people stigmatized dark Blacks as drudges and unattractive. But black and brown slaves were vociferous in story and song in their contempt for "yellow" people, whom they regarded as flighty, prideful, and lacking in loyalty. In the decades after slavery, mulattoes came to constitute a genuine elite class among Afro-Americans. But before the Civil War, despite some hierarchical notions about color, dark black and high yellow labored side by side in the fields.[32]

A tiny percentage of mixed people, however, managed to transcend their circumstances, if only by passing as something other than Black. The child of a White person and a mulatto might easily be light enough to be mistaken for unmixed White. Over a series of generations on the colonial Carolina frontier, the clan of Gideon Gibson gradually made the transit from the free Black category to the White. Such open passing was highly unusual, however. More typical was the experience of Thomas Day, son of a free man of color and a Portuguese woman. In the 1820s, young Thomas left his North Carolina home and passed into the White population. His family was thus split, because his decision to live as White made it impossible for him to maintain contact lest he be found out, and his darker brother could not join him on the White side of the line. Not frequently, but on occasion, newspaper advertisements told of the escape hatch used by a few intrepid mulatto slaves. For example:

One Hundred Dollars Reward. —Ran away from the subscriber a bright mulatto slave, named Sam. Light, sandy hair, blue eyes, ruddy complexion; is so white as very easily to pass for a free white man.

—April 22, 1837, Edwin Peck, Mobile[33]

Yet only a tiny number of mulattoes gained freedom as Whites. More, but still a distinct minority, lived as members of a tightly circumscribed free Black caste, North and South. By far the majority worked as slaves. Some of these received special treatment from their White relatives, but others suffered special scorn from both White and Black. As long as slavery lasted, most people of mixed ancestry were simply slaves.

The era of slavery set the pattern for interracial relations in general and interracial mating in particular. American Whites inherited from Europe an image of Black people as lustful and animalistic that helped shape interracial sexual relations from the first. The colonial era probably witnessed the highest incidence of interracial mating in American history. With White servants and Blacks in close proximity and possessing similar class status, sex and marriage were bound to happen. When the Black population increased in the late seventeenth and eighteenth centuries, there arose a band of laws circumscribing Black slave status and punishing interracial sex and marriage. Under slavery, the pairing of White men and Black women frequently took on the brutality of rape, although there was an occasional case of milder concubinage. Some southern cities also supported a *demimonde* inhabited by free women of color. Throughout the era of slavery there were also liaisons between White women and Black men, slave and free. Officially, Whites were horrified by interracial mating, but so long as it involved only White men and Black women and did not include marriage, it was tolerated. Slaves seem to have resented and resisted it, whereas free people of color were more ambivalent. The mulatto population increased steadily through the last decades of the Old South, and mulattoes usually took on the status of their Black parents. Some distinctions and stratifications by color existed, both among slaves and among free people of color, and there was some passing of light mulattoes into the free White population. But by far the majority of mixed people labored as field slaves.

Mutual Images

After the Civil War, a great deal changed for Black Americans. First came a limited kind of freedom, then a massive population shift from the rural South to the urban North and West. The changes affected relations between the races in dramatic ways. White domination continued, but it took on new shapes, with new ideological justifications. All this affected the behavior of Blacks and non-Blacks with respect to intergroup mating and marriage.

Before I describe in detail the patterns of Black outmarriage over the course of the postslavery epoch, it will be useful to sketch the images that twentieth-century Whites and Blacks have held of each other. Although these images have been modified with time and in response to a parade of social forces, nonetheless there have been distinct continuities from the colonial era to our own. These images have had a profound effect on intergroup romantic, sexual, and marital behavior.[34]

White Views of Black Men. As Lawrence Levine notes, Black people, and dark features generally, have long fascinated White Americans. Overt opposition to intermarriage and interracial sex was always a nearly universal sentiment among Whites. But an undercurrent of fascination with Black people and their supposed sexual abilities nonetheless persisted.[35]

The first element in the modern vision of Blacks was a subliminal conviction that Black men were something less than human. They were brutes, possessed of abnormal strength. They were, as Thomas Nelson Page described them, "a race just lifted from African barbarism." The literature of the early years of this century, from Page's novels to Charles Carroll's *The Negro a Beast*, resounded with the conviction that Black people, men in particular, were savage, primitive, elemental creatures, nearer to beasts of the forest than to human beings. Closely related to this was the idea that Black men were violent and rapacious. Over the course of this century, Whites have shown themselves ever ready to believe Black men guilty of violent crimes for which there was little objective evidence, as in the infamous Scottsboro case of 1931.[36]

Another, seemingly contrary image was the Black man as simple, childlike, and dependent creature. In the slavery era, he was Sambo, the gentle, foolish, contented slave. After Reconstruction, Page described this character as "the negro under subjection . . . docile, amiable, tractable." In our time he is television's George Jefferson, the idiotic, nonthreatening Black male, a silly, preening, irrelevant fool. This character is a creature of White people's imagination. A perhaps more benign but closely related vision is the Black male as natural and spontaneous human. In 1948, a White woman enamored of Black men wrote that the Black man was "joyous and bouyant. His voice has a timbre and the lilt unmatched by any other race. His smile is ready and infectious." Other voices added that he was naturally more gentle, "tractable," graceful, sensitive, affectionate, enthusiastic, religious—in short, more like a child—than White men. All these were visions conjured up to soften Whites' fears of darkly predatory Black men.[37]

If Black men were nearer to animals than were other people, they were also, in the eyes of Whites, closer to their own sexuality. Whites conjured for themselves visions of Black men as unnaturally powerful and uninhibited sexual actors. Winthrop Jordan found colonial-era White men worrying that Black men's penises were bigger than their own. In the 1960s, I found White boys casting furtive glances around high school locker rooms, wondering the same thing. Not only did White men fear that Blacks were more generously endowed; they believed Blacks possessed greater sexual skills and enthusiasm, and they thought them less inhibited.[38]

These supposed endowments and enthusiasms became the focus of White men's fears. It has been the abiding conviction of American White men that the prime goal of Black men is to sleep with White women. The anti-Lincoln faction in the election of 1864 accused the antislavery party of trying to bring about the forced "mongrelization" of America. Thomas Nelson Page put it this way in 1907: "Whatever social equality may signify to the white, to the . . . negro . . . it means one thing: the right to stand on the same footing with a white woman as that on which a white man stands with her." More recently, in *The Confessions of Nat Turner,* William Styron strongly implied that desire for Margaret's "bare white full round hips" and "milky white legs and arms," rather than for freedom from slavery, were the central objects of Turner's revolutionary passion. Likewise, psychologist Charles Stember recently devoted an entire volume to attempting to prove that the real ambition of a wide spectrum of Black men was to seduce White women.[39]

The conjunction of a supposedly violent Black nature and an alleged lust for White women was easily translated into a White preoccupation with rape. Again and again in modern history, Black men have been accused of raping White women or wanting to. The thought of the Black man throwing off his chains and raping the master's wife is one of the most powerful scenes in the American imagination. Page's words describe the thinking of many Whites about this hypothetical situation: "The crime of rape . . . is the fatal product of new conditions [since emancipation]. . . . The negro's passion, always his controlling force, is now, since the new teaching, for the white woman. [Lynching is justifiable] for it has its root deep in the basic passions of humanity, the determination to put an end to the ravishing of their women by an inferior race." More recently, several authors have discerned a racist fear of the Black male in the rape scare of the 1970s' White feminist movement. Winthrop Jordan, John Dollard, and others regard the rape fixation as a projection onto Black men of White men's guilt feelings for their own sexual abuse of Black women.[40]

Throughout most of postemancipation history, all this mythology was fastened with special force on the mulatto male. Popular fiction and movies for decades gave a compelling picture of the tragic mulatto, a character torn to the point of derangement between his desire to be White and the certainty that society regarded him as Black. Pseudoscience weighed in with the judgment that mulattoes were "morally and physically the inferior of the pure black" and, of course, of the pure White. Some even went through elaborate "proofs" of declining intelligence and increasing sterility among people of mixed ancestry. Writers such as Page and Thomas Dixon, and filmmakers such as D. W.

Griffiths, chose to focus on the mulatto as depraved creature. Usually the product of the illicit union of a dangerous Black man and a declassé White woman, this mulatto was doubly degraded. Griffiths' mulattoes in *The Birth of a Nation* provide the perfect example. Out of their identity ambivalence, their desire to be White and to have what White men have (status, power, White women), and their moral depravity, mulattoes, of all Black men, lusted most fiercely after the flesh of White women.[41]

How did this image of lustful and potent Black and brown men affect White women? Some were put off. Some were thrilled. Some thought it silly. A large number of White females reported, credibly, that they found Black men unattractive, repugnant, threatening, even loathsome. Christine Berringer* said: "I'm just not attracted to Black men. I can't imagine being interested in one. They're always after White girls and they make me nervous."[42] But another set of White women found themselves titillated by visions of Black sexual mastery. A White prostitute interviewed in Chicago in 1928 was convinced that "colored men are better than white men. I don't enjoy myself anymore when I am with white men." About 1950, another woman asked her therapist: "Is it true that negroes have extra long penises and that they are erect all the time? Wouldn't it be disgusting to have intercourse with a negro?" Later she confided that she "could experience sexual pleasure with her husband only when she phantasied that a 'large black' negro was trying to rape her." In 1968 the White girls of the rock musical *Hair* sang with enthusiasm about the preternatural sexual prowess of Black males.[43] Some White women thought all this talk about the predatory sexuality of the Black male was overdone. Such were the women of the Georgia Women's Inter-Racial Committee, who declared in 1920:

We have a deep sense of appreciation for the chivalry of men who would give their lives for the purity and safety of women. Yet we feel constrained to declare our convictions concerning the methods sometimes employed in this supposed protection. We find in our hearts no extenuation for crime, be it violated womanhood, mob violence or the illegal taking of human life. . . .

Therefore, we believe that no falser appeal can be made to Southern manhood than that mob violence is necessary for the protection of womanhood, or that the brutal practice of lynching and burning of human beings is an expression of chivalry. We believe that these methods are no protection to anything or anybody, but that they jeopardize every right and every security that we possess.

The Georgia women went on to decry White men's unpunished sexual abuse of Black women.[44]

So Whites have seen Black men as primitive, animalistic, violent, childish, and sexually powerful. Over the years, however, overt references to bestial and primitive images have come to be regarded as uncouth. With the Civil Rights and Black Power movements of the postwar period, Black men have sometimes even taken on a positive aspect in White minds. Testimony to this development is the tremendous success after the late 1960s, among Whites as well as Blacks, of the movies and TV shows of such actors as Sidney Poitier and Bill Cosby. These men have uniformly portrayed Black men of honor, articulateness, and noble bearing. Yet the other dominant themes in the imagery surrounding Black males have remained.[45]

White Views of Black Women.   While Black men seemed frightening, yet enticing, to many Whites, Black women suffered an even more severely split image. One theme described them as attractive, easily exploitable sex objects; the other, as bordering on the repulsive.

On the one hand, Black women were seen as possessing a variety of romantically and sexually attractive qualities. Like Black men, they were supposed to be in touch with their elemental selves and to possess exceptional sexual capabilities and enthusiasms. Willie Morris, a White man, told of his youth in the Mississippi Delta region: "I knew all about the sexual act, but not until I was twelve years old did I know that it was performed with white women for pleasure; I had thought that only Negro women engaged in the act of love with white men just for fun, because they were the only ones with the animal desire to submit that way. So that Negro girls and women were a source of constant excitement and sexual feeling for me, and filled my day-dreams with delights and wonders." A Richmond lawyer insisted that "colored women are more passionate, more satisfactory physically," than their White sisters. Numerous southern White men testified that White women were fine for the pedestal, but Black women were essential for the bedroom. Northern men echoed the same conviction (although they may have lacked the Southerners' courage to act on it) when they made

Eartha Kitt the 1950s' prototype Black sex kitten—exotic, forbidden, and tremendously desirable.[46]

Admiration for Black women's beauty and sexual prowess, however, frequently shaded over into the conviction that Black women were by nature sluts and prostitutes. Hundreds of Black women, South and North, from all social strata and time periods, testified to the assumption by White males that Black women were fair game. As Calvin Hernton put it, "To some degree, however microscopic, all white men in America, save a few, carry in their perception of Negro females a dark sexual urge that borders on the vulgar." Mick Jagger went beyond that border when he sang, "Black girls just wanta have sex all night long." This fixation on the Black woman as harlot explains the prurient interest surrounding Vanessa Williams's recent tenure as Miss America. But this is not just a recent phenomenon. In 1902, an anonymous "colored woman, wife and mother" complained in *The Independent* that "a colored woman, however respectable, is lower than the white prostitute" in the eyes of Whites. Lorraine Hansberry said it for all her Black sisters: "In these streets out there, any little white boy from Long Island or Westchester sees me and leans out of his car and yells—'Hey there, *hot chocolate!* Say there, Jezebel! Hey you—"Hundred Dollar Misunderstanding"! YOU! Bet you know where there's a good time tonight.' . . . I can be coming from eight hours on an assembly line or fourteen hours in Mrs. Halsey's kitchen. I can be all filled up that day with three hundred years of rage so that my eyes are flashing and my flesh is trembling—and the white boys in the streets, they look at me and think of sex. They look at me and that's *all* they think. . . . Baby, you could be Jesus in drag—but if you're brown they're sure you're selling!"[47]

A special object for White men's illegitimate fantasies was the mulatto woman. Even more than mulatto males, these women were seen by White society as tragic mulattoes—tempestuous creatures, tormented by their dual natures. From Liza in *Uncle Tom's Cabin* to the mulatto characters brought to the screen by Dorothy Dandridge in the 1950s, women of mixed ancestry had to struggle to survive their twofold heritage. White men associated mulatto women with sin—the sin of their parents' illicit union, magnified in the second generation. That sinful image made them fair game in White eyes.[48] Poet Ella

Wheeler Wilcox analyzed the situation as she spoke up in defense of women of mixed parentage:

> You think me beautiful! I thank you, sir,
> For words like those, in every woman stir
> A sense of pleasure. Be she queen, or slave,
> She would be fair, as all men would be brave.
> But there is something in your voice and mien
> You would not give expression WERE I queen.
>
> Behind the pensive pallor of my skin
> You see bloods mixed by that old
> chemist—Sin.
> You know I stand outside convention's pale
> And take for granted that I am for sale.
>
> .   .   .   .
>
> . . . I would die,
> Rather than sell the virtue you would buy.[49]

If one vision described Black women as alluring to the point of generating constant attempts at sexual exploitation, another pictured them as animalistic and unattractive. Since men are supposed to be the sexual aggressors in our society, the association of Blacks with beasts generally enhanced Black men's sexuality in White eyes. But the same association often acted to decrease the attractiveness of Black women. The Black woman in this mode was "Mammy . . . mother earth, buxom, nurturing, earth brown surrogate mother, whose constant concern is with the oral gratification of her offspring." She was a major figure in many southern novels that glorified the plantation era. In the movies, she was Louise Beaver or Ethel Walters playing the loyal family retainer: strong, articulate, fiercely independent—and sexless.[50]

This view stood in sharp contrast to the image White men—and especially southern White men—created for White women. The White woman was beautiful, charming, pure, and virginal. Perched chastely atop the pedestal, she was the perfect object for White men's adoration, but far too fragile for the heavy hauling of domestic labor or regular sex. By contrast, Aunt Jemima represented the aspect of the Black female image that was so strong, so overpowering in her animalism that she, too, was not fit for romantic encounter. Her strength intimidated White men. Some found her physically unattractive. Psychologist Charles Stember made much of what he believed to be a visceral aversion by White males against intimacy with Black women. But that was not the major issue—after all, there was in fact a tremendous amount of sexual activity involving White men and Black women, in all time periods and in a variety of social contexts, and it was often very matter-of-fact. Rather, it seems the major dynamic here was that insecure White men felt intimidated by the assumed strength, aggressiveness, and sexual voracity of Black women. Tom Bradshaw* put it well: "I've been out with White women and Orientals, and I've had sexual experiences with them that I felt I could handle. And I've met Blacks I thought were exciting, but I couldn't ever bring myself to ask them out. What if they laughed at me? Or worse—what if they were too hot for me to handle?" White male insecurities of this sort, together with the dual image of Black women and the power position of White men in our society, all point toward tight limits on romantic and sexual encounters between Black women and White men, except in situations where White men could offset their fears by overwhelming temporal power, such as rape, prostitution, or quiet concubinage.[51]

In recent years there has been some softening of the hard edges of the Black female image. As Whites have encountered Black women not only in subservient postures but also in the office and boardroom; as such Black women as Yvonne Burke, Barbara Jordan, and Shirley Chisholm have drawn national political attention; and as a few Black women have been allowed to play more fully rounded television and movie roles, there has been some diminution of the mammy/slut image. But for Black women, much more than for Black men, the old sexual stereotypes remain largely intact.

Black Images of White Women. The ways Black people perceived Whites also had an important impact on interracial marital and sexual relationships. White racist literature placed an extraordinary emphasis on what its authors took to be a constant lust by Black men after White women. Black men, so this argument went, were completely taken in by the standards of beauty of the dominant group. White was beautiful. Black men—all of them—wanted White women, the blonder the better. Failing that, they wanted Black women of light skin and Caucasian features—anything to approximate whiteness.[52]

There is, in fact, a strain of this kind of thinking that runs through

Black men's statements about themselves over the course of this century. Undoubtedly, White norms of beauty, including light skin, blue eyes, and silky, blond hair, all influenced Black men's thinking about what was desirable in a woman. White women seemed, for some Black men, icons of beauty, something foreign and feared and above them. Black men's folk songs talked of White women as characteristically wearing furs and diamonds and being far superior to Black women in every respect. White men had forbidden Black men to approach White women. For some, the forbidden became especially desirable. A Chicago prostitute in the 1920s told of the consistent preference among Black customers for a Black co-worker who had blonde hair and looked White, because "many of them were from the South and it was the first time they had ever had a white woman." Blues singer Bill Broonzy was mostly curious. In Mississippi, "lots of times I would wonder why a white man would kill me if he'd seen me with a white woman. What is it she's got that my Negro woman ain't got? . . . So I came North and tried it." Eldridge Cleaver was engaging in hyperbole and racist-baiting, but nonetheless he was onto one aspect of the consciousness of some Black men when he wrote: "I love white women and hate black women. It's just in me, so deep that I don't even try to get it out of me any more. I'd jump over ten nigger bitches just to get to one white woman. Ain't no such thing as an ugly white woman. A white woman is beautiful even if she's baldheaded and only has one tooth. . . . I love her skin, her soft, smooth, white skin. I like to just lick her white skin as if sweet, fresh honey flows from her pores, and just to touch her long, soft, silky hair. . . . Ain't nothing more beautiful than a white woman's hair being blown by the wind. The white woman is more than a woman to me. . . . she's like a goddess, a symbol. My love for her is religious and beyond fulfillment. I worship her."[53]

For some Black men, the White woman represented status, the possibility of achieving an approximation of the freedom enjoyed by White men. Malcolm X recalled that in the 1940s, "in any black ghetto in America, to have a white woman who wasn't a known, common whore was—for the average black man, at least—a status symbol of the first order." For others, achievement of an intimate relationship with a White woman symbolized a way to strike back at White men for centuries of oppression. But with the rise of the Black consciousness movement in the 1960s, whatever status value had been attached to

White women declined as the importance of Black solidarity was more forcefully asserted. Mrs. Melvin McGee perhaps exaggerated in a 1970 letter to *Ebony*, but nonetheless there is truth to her statement: "The era of the 'white woman status symbol' is gone (good riddance)." [54]

Some of the attraction to White women, however, was more interpersonal than status- or power-oriented. It simply reflected a conviction on the part of some Black men that White women were nicer, more pliable, and more enthusiastic about sex than Black women. Danny Davis noted that some Black men believed "the white female often gives the black man certain kinds of recognition that the black woman often times does not give him." Eddie James echoed Davis: "Why does the black man dig the white woman? Because she does him good like a woman should. He digs being treated like a MAN. That's something no black woman will ever do for him." Among the ways that White women were supposed to appreciate and cater to Black men was in enthusiasm about sex. Black male jokes frequently played on the theme of White women being eager for sex with Black men. This view of the White woman as infinitely desirable was usually coupled with a negative evaluation of the Black woman as hard, bossy, and castrating. Cleaver had his character say, "I hate a black bitch. You can't trust them like white women. . . . It would be like trying to pamper a cobra. Anyway, every black woman secretly hates black men. A nigger bitch seems to be full of steel, granite-hard and resisting, not soft and submissive like a white woman." [55]

Yet this portrait of the Black male as lusting after a pure, beautiful, and appreciative White woman is probably overdone. After all, it relies largely on published materials, and it was always easy to find a White publisher for titillating and prejudice-confirming material about Black male fascination with White women. There was a less well publicized countertrend among Black males. In particular, Black militants, from David Walker to Marcus Garvey to Malcolm X, denigrated the fascination of some of their brothers with White women and extolled the virtues of their proud Black sisters. James Weldon Johnson was not radical, but he waxed rhapsodic over the wonders of the Black woman for aesthetic and emotional reasons: "handsome, deep bosomed, fertile. . . . The Negro woman, with her rich coloring, her gayety, her laughter and song, her alluring, undulating movements . . . was a more beautiful creature than her sallow, songless, lipless, hipless, tired-looking, tired-moving white sister." It is likely that most Black men shared his appreciation.[56]

Black Images of White Men. What did Black people think about White men? The first factor to consider here is the overwhelming power of White men as a group throughout most of the century. The abuse of that power through rape and concubinage caused Black women to resent White men and to view them with suspicion. Mary Church Terrell reported in the early years of the century "that it was nearly impossible for a black girl to grow to womanhood unviolated." Consciousness of White men's depradations on Black women led most Black women to reject the notion of affiliation with White men. In 1937 John Dollard reported that "one Negro woman [in a southern town] told me that she had always been proud of the fact that she never cared for any white man. She had always held herself above any such attraction; because white men do such terrible things to Negro men, burning and mutilating them, and cause Negroes so much misery and act in such a superior way." Alberta Robinson*, interviewed in 1984, had internalized the rejection of White men to the point that she did not see them as even remotely potential partners. "I look at this White man and see 'White man.' I look at this Black man and see 'fat legs.'" The Black man was an individual, a conceivable candidate for romance, and was being evaluated as such; the White man was not. Black men supported Black women in rejecting the notion of White men as possible suitors. Sometimes the rejection took the form of ridicule. James Baldwin had Ida, a Black woman in *Another Country*, inveigh against White men in explicit terms: "I used to see the way white men watched me, like dogs. And I thought about what I could do. How I hated them, the way they looked, and the things they'd say, all dressed up in their damn white skin, and their clothes just so, and their weak, little, white pricks jumping in their drawers."[57]

Still, it is not clear that all Black women saw White men only as predators to despise and reject. Some frankly admired the White man's power (and, as Washington power circles have frequently put it, "Power is the ultimate aphrodisiac"). It was reported that around the turn of the century in North Carolina, many Black women, mulattoes especially, were heard to remark that they "would rather be a white man's concubine than a nigger's wife." There was also some suggestion that Black women saw White men as more stable, dependable, gentle, and nurturing than Black men. Several Black male authors agreed with Cleaver that "every black woman at one time or another has experienced, in some dark corner of her being, the illicit desire for a white man; especially those women who claim the contrary." Yet this sentiment, to the extent that it existed at all among Black women, was relegated to a minority position. By and large, Black women throughout the period under study were mindful and resentful of the historic abuse of Black women by White men. What is more, they regarded White men, despite their economic and political might, as less manly, potent, and sexually powerful than their Black brothers.[58]

Black Self-Images. All this had ramifications for the images Black women and men held of themselves. Relative to Whites, Black men had little social, economic, or political power or status from the time of slavery onward. Several observers have argued that, at least until the rise of Black consciousness in the 1960s, many Black men felt degraded by their relative powerlessness. Psychologist Robert Staples wrote, "There is a curious rage festering inside black men because, like it or not, they have not been allowed to fulfill the roles (i.e. breadwinner, protector) society ascribes to [men]." The small, growing Black middle class of the 1970s had a somewhat different experience, but some working-class Black men apparently saw themselves as second-rate goods in the eyes of Black women, whom they perceived to be looking for professional men. Contrasted to the "first prize" professional man —a rarity in Black communities—Ernest Eans saw himself and most Black men as "second, third, and even fourth prize." J. C. Washington told his Black sisters that he "felt real hurt" about being passed over by Black women in favor of middle-class Black men. "Every Black man," he said, "can't be the businessman or superstar that you fancy ladies would like to have." He wished they would look past his limited economic success and appreciate his excellent personal qualities.[59]

For many years, according to this interpretation, one response to the felt devaluation of Black manhood was an attempt by some Black men to appear as White as possible. Some defined Black physical features as less than optimally attractive. One of Jean Toomer's characters described Negroes as "Black, singed, wooly, tobacco-juice . . . ugly as sin." Bill Broonzy recalled having shared this set of emotions: "Negroes . . . don't want to be a Negro and they try not to look like one. They fix their hair, wear their clothes, talk and act like the American white man. . . . I'll spend all the money I have just to dress, ride and look like the white man." Numerous studies cited a preference among Black children for White dolls and light playmates, and Black adolescents and adults altered their lips and noses through plastic surgery and processed their hair in attempts to look White.[60]

Yet adherents to this interpretation may be guilty of hyperbole. There was always a countertrend in Black culture, at least equally strong, which celebrated Blackness, African origins, and Negroid features. This trend came to the fore especially in the Black Power movement of the latter 1960s, when Black became more widely recognized as beautiful. Black men gave up their conks and grew natural hairstyles. In the words of Black psychologists William Grier and Price Cobbs, they gave up "their own unreasoning self-hatred and their pitiful wish to be white."[61] While there has been some retrogression in this area as ethnic chic has declined in the more conservative 1980s, it seems certain that whatever element of White-obsessed self-hatred may have been present at one time is now a thing of the past.

One aspect of the imagery surrounding Black men that tended to enhance rather than denigrate their self-image was the mythology about Black male sexuality. Black men's jokes from many eras were filled with tales of Black men besting Whites in sexual competition, and of White women lusting after Black bodies. One example, a toast heard in Oakland, California, will suffice:

> Now, ladies and gentlemen,
> It has come to the test
> To see what nation
> Can fuck the best
> Get back white folks
> Get back in your class.[62]

Black women sometimes fared less well in those aspects of self-image that had bearing on sex and romance. A Black woman might be bright, interesting, and accomplished, but even so it was sometimes hard for her to feel attractive. Calvin Hernton perhaps exaggerated when he wrote that, "according to the Caucasian standard of beauty and feminity, the American Negro woman hates herself," yet he was not altogether mistaken. Like Black men, most Black women deviated in many respects from the American beauty norms for their sex.

They differed from Americans' preferred image in skin color, lip shape, and especially hair texture. To attract members of the opposite sex in American society, beauty is much more crucial to women's chances than to men's. Very high on many men's lists of desired qualities is long, flowing hair. It was a rare Black woman who could manage this trait without artificial help. Thus, for generations, many Black women, more often than men, tried to alter their features in the direction of Whiteness. M. H. Freeman complained about it as early as 1859: "Flat noses must be pinched up. Kinky hair must be subjected to a straightening process—oiled, and pulled, twisted up, tied down, sleeked over and pressed under, or cut off so short that it can't curl. . . . Thick lips are puckered up. . . . Beautiful black and brown faces by the application of rouge and lily white are made to assume unnatural tints, like the livid hue of painted corpses." For a century and more thereafter, some Black women did their best to approximate White standards of beauty. The female models in *Ebony* ads from the 1940s through the early 1960s were uniformly light and smooth-haired; most had thin lips and pointed noses. They advertised products to make women look whiter. Kotalko ointment would give Black women "lovelier, more lustrous, longer hair" in silky cascades down their backs, as would Silky Strate. Black and White Bleaching Cream proclaimed that "at last you can have shades *lighter,* smoother, softer skin." The competition, Nadinola, promised that "the nicest things happen to girls with light, bright complexions," and that "lighter skin leads the way to brighter evenings" with handsome young men. Many Black women bought these products and diligently applied them to their bodies in an attempt to enhance their beauty.[63]

That attempt speaks volumes for the relatively poor sexual self-image under which some Black women labored. Yet it was not just men's standards of female beauty, but also their treatment of Black women, that lowered still further the self-esteem of some Black women. White men frequently treated Black women as beasts of burden, whores, or, at best, concubines—very seldom as wives, lovers, or partners. Black men sometimes added to the abuse, telling Black women, "The only thing black I want is a Cadillac," "The only thing a black woman can do for me is to lead me to a white woman," or "I don't haul no coal." The result of all this was, for some Black women, a situation much like that described by Grier and Cobbs: "[The Black

woman] finds it difficult to experience herself as a highly valued object to whom any man would be drawn. Rather she sees herself as a
depreciated, unwanted instrument of no inherent value, to be used
by men and society at their pleasure. The bitterness that grows out
of such a self-perception augments her already established self-hatred,
her feelings of being used, and her feelings of worthlessness." Again,
one should not suppose that all or even most Black women suffered
such poor self-images. A later section of this chapter should make clear
that Black preferences in skin color, for example, were highly various.
Yet, while formulations such as that of Grier and Cobbs may have been
extreme, they did point to sets of feelings that were not uncommon.[64]

The Black awakening to self-assertion of the mid-twentieth century
began to bring changes to the poor self-image of some Black women.
With the rise of such slogans as "Black Power" and "Black is beautiful,"
Black people asserted more consistently the beauty in Black women
that some had overlooked. The women in Ebony's ads grew darker and
sported natural hairstyles and African dress. An increasing number of
their brothers began to recognize the truth that many had known all
along; as John Wells put it: "The black woman is the most beautiful,
graceful, tender and precious of God's creations." Black women, from
Kathleen Cleaver to Angela Davis, also began to assert themselves as
powerfully articulate members of the movement for Black liberation.
All these trends pointed toward a healthily enhanced self-image for
Black women after the mid-1960s or early 1970s.[65]

The mutual images of Blacks and Whites remained remarkably constant throughout most of the postslavery epoch, although they have
showed some signs of modification in the last two decades. To Whites,
Black men seemed bestial, primitive, violent, childish, and preter-
naturally sexual. This image proved exciting to many White women.
White people's images of Black women, by contrast, acted to discourage interracial romantic encounters. Black women frequently excited
White men's sexual imaginations, but, in a society where men are
supposed to be the romantic aggressors, the image of Black female
strength and sexuality generally intimidated White men, except in
those situations such as rape and concubinage where temporal power
was overwhelmingly in their hands.

Some Black men doubtless were drawn to White women as forbidden fruit and fantasized about the wonders to be found in their company. Yet there was also always a strong counterstrain in Black male thinking that prized Black womanhood. Black women, for their part, generally found themselves separated from White men by communal memory of slavery-era exploitation. It appears that some Black people's images of themselves were shaped, often negatively, by White evaluations of Blacks. But there was always a strong current of racial pride to counter such denigrating influences, and it became dominant with the moves for Black self-assertion after the 1960s.

10. Dimensions of Intermarriage: The Wall Remains

> "You're not worried about me marrying *your* daughter. You're worried about me marrying your *wife's* daughter. I've been marrying your daughter ever since the days of slavery."
>
> —JAMES BALDWIN to a White segregationist

Black Intermarriage over Time and Generation

The history of Jewish and Japanese Americans is easily divided into discrete generations: the first, or immigrant, generation; their children, the second generation, born in America yet personally connected to their parents' Old World values; and the third generation, several decades removed from direct experience of their ancestors' culture. This trigenerational scheme has been used by both Jews and Japanese Americans to describe their own communities. It has also been employed by a variety of historians and social scientists—for instance, Marcus Lee Hansen and A. L. Epstein—to describe immigrant societies generally. For both Japanese and Jewish Americans, there was very little outmarriage by members of the first generation, somewhat more in the second, and widespread intermarriage in the third.[1]

Some observers have tried to draw a parallel between the generational structure of immigrant groups such as these and Black Americans. This theory suggests that rural Blacks coming to northern cities in the first decades of this century might profitably be viewed as members of a first generation; their children and grandchildren, then, would constitute the second and third generations, respectively. This theory has an attractive neatness to it, holding out the promise of intergroup comparison. Unfortunately, nothing in the intermarriage data or other material examined in this study suggests that the theory is correct when applied to Black Americans. There seem to be hints of a progression in northern Black intermarriage. But the increase in Black outmarriage has been much smaller in scale and slower to come than for other groups. It is by no means clear that Black people have followed a path in fact parallel to that of Jews or Japanese Americans. For purposes of the present analysis, it is more useful to divide recent Afro-American history into four, rather than three, periods, thus: (1) 1865–1920, from the beginning of Reconstruction, through the rise of Jim Crow and substantial Black migration northward, to the end of the First World War; (2) 1920–1945, from World War I to the end of World War II; (3) the postwar period from 1945 to 1960; and (4) the era after 1960, which has seen substantial changes for Black people as a result, largely, of the Civil Rights and Black Power movements. Over these four periods, Black outmarriage has indeed increased, but only very slightly, to a height of just over 1 percent in the 1970s. The predominant fact in all times has been that nearly all Black people, women and men, have married other Blacks.[2] There have, however, been significant shifts in the gender, class, and regional intermarriage mix.

1865–1920. The southern system of interracial sex and marriage did not change much in the first decades after emancipation. White men continued to have both fleeting and long-term relationships with Black women. One difference was that, just after the Civil War, there was a brief upsurge in the number of relationships between Black men and White women. John Blassingame found a number of New Orleans White women who either married or cohabited with Black men during and after the war. Part of the reason they chose to do this, despite significant White opposition, was that White men were in short supply. The war had killed and maimed so many that some White women were forced to violate caste boundaries if they wanted men. Also, during Reconstruction, Black men enjoyed higher status than they had ever before. Blassingame's comments are to the point: "In many cases white females competed openly with Negro women for the sexual attentions of black males. Other white women had assignations with Negro men because the white man, by constant allegations of the black male's extraordinary strength, and exhaustless sexual desire, had created a virtual black Apollo in their minds." The 1880 census found 209 mixed marriages in New Orleans, 29 of them pairing Black men with White women. Numerous informal liaisons went uncounted, not just in New Orleans but in other parts of the South as well.[3]

By far the more common pattern, however, coupled Black women and White men. Before the war, a White master could often compel his slave to submit to his affections. Emancipation from slavery brought only a qualified freedom. Once southern Whites had disposed of Reconstruction governments, many Black people fell back into a debt peonage that did not differ greatly from the slavery they had so recently escaped. In a social situation from the 1880s through World War I that saw power and wealth once again concentrated in the hands of White men, those White men could still easily have their way with Black women. Black writers North and South protested the White men's continued attacks upon the virtue of Black women. Not all interracial liaisons were coerced, however. Men from the most prominent southern White families continued, as before emancipation, to keep Black concubines and mulatto children on the side. Even sympathetic White observers such as Arthur W. Calhoun tended to paint these unions in negative terms, attributing to the men irresponsibility and to the women loose morals. Doubtless that was true in some cases. Mrs. Joseph B. Catus recalled many years later: "I hated that my mother did not marry a colored man and let me live like other folks with a father. . . . I despised my white father and his folks. I might have loved him if he had noticed us and treated us like other folks. . . . His children despised us and I despised them and all their folks, and I despised him. We had to work hard, got no education, and but a little to live on. He had plenty of property but didn't give my mother a thing. . . . I will never forget that old, hateful white father."[4] Yet I am struck by the number of children of such near-marriages who told a different story. Walter Jackson* recalled his turn-of-the-century childhood in North Carolina:

My father was a white man. He had good standing and was recognized by the best white people in the county. He lived with my mother as a husband, only he had a small house on the back of the farm where he kept a bed and his clothes. He called that his home. He gave mother the house out on the road and kept it in good furnishing and repair. He paid the children's school bills. He supervised the farm. . . . He was very attentive to [my mother] and her family. . . . He always consulted her about how was best to spend the money. He would help her choose our company and tell us that even though we were white we were living as colored and must associate with the best colored people.

Jackson's former teacher reported that the father's "relatives took them as his children though not as if they were his lawful children," and added that Jackson's sister

used to tell me that her father used to come to see her mother every day and every night. He would sit around the fire with the whole family and talk just like any other father. If any of their friends would come in he would always go into another room until they had received the company. He did this so that it would not be embarrassing to them and to him. . . . She said that although in public they called him Mr. H., at home they called him daddy, and he was as sweet and loving to them as any father. . . . The girl would show me lots of pretty clothes and would say, "my father gave these to me." If anyone did the least thing she did not like she would remark immediately, "Mr. H. is my father and you must not bother me. You won't walk over me."[5]

It is not possible to know just how common were marriages and other sexual partnerships across racial lines in the decades after the Civil War, for no one counted them. But the census keepers did attempt to count the number of mulattoes in the various states in each census year from 1850 to 1920 except 1880 and 1900. Their methods were often sloppy, their definitions of mulatto varied, and they almost certainly undercounted by a large margin the number of people of mixed ancestry.[6] But their findings are nonetheless startling: they point to a Black population becoming steadily lighter from 1850 to 1910, with a particularly large jump in the number and percentage of mulattoes between 1890 and 1910. This was true in every region. It points to two social trends: (1) continued interracial sexual mixing, and (2) mating by color preference among Afro-Americans, with light people marrying light people and producing an ever-increasing number of noticeably light children (more about this later). It is probable that interracial mixing continued at least through 1920, but census numbers do not reflect the continued trend, for by then the term *mulatto* was falling out of common usage, census takers had become even less dependable at counting mulattoes, and a large number of the lightest Afro-Americans had migrated north and passed as White.[7]

Several authorities point to a gradual hardening of the lines between the racial castes in the decades after slavery. With the national repudiation of Reconstruction in the mid-1870s, southern Whites began to take steps that would lead to a full panoply of laws and customs creating strict segregation by the turn of the century. Joel Williamson sees urban mulattoes as losing their status as a separate caste, intermediate between Whites and Blacks, and being forced into the Black group. His thesis is borne out by the testimony of Uncle Moble Hopson, a former slave from Virginia who talked to a government interviewer in 1936. Before the Civil War, Hopson and his family were regarded by their neighbors as nearly White. But "arter de soljers come back home, it was diff'runt. First dey say dat all whut ain't white is black. An' den dey tell de Injuns yuh kain't marry no more de whites. An' den dey tell usen dat we kain't cum no more tuh church school. An' dey won't let us do no bisness wid de whites, so we is th'own in wid de blacks." This sort of informal pressure on Blacks and mixed people, together with the increasingly complex barrier of Jim Crow laws, undoubtedly acted as a brake on the number of interracial marriages in the South, and probably also discouraged informal liaisons. But the testimony of the children of mixed families from this period, together with the continued mulattoization of the Afro-American population, certifies that interracial mating did continue.[8]

Actual marriage between Whites and Blacks was much more common, in percentage terms, in the North and West than the South. Prior to the great migration that surrounded the First World War, there were very few Black people in the North or West. Some of these were laborers, but many were farmers, artisans, and business people. There are few good numbers on the phenomenon, but it has been suggested that the incidence of intermarriage was as high as 10 percent among Black people who lived in relatively emancipated northern cities such as Boston around the turn of the century. It is known that a number of prominent northern Black leaders, including Frederick Douglass, Archibald H. Grimké, and John S. Durham, married White women. The available survey data suggest that the vast majority of northern interracial marriages in this early period brought together Black men and White women.[9]

Changes began to appear in both the southern and the northern systems of race relations in the two decades after 1900. With Jim Crow in force and an ever-increasing number of lynchings threatening peaceful life in the South, hundreds of thousands of southern Black people opted for the somewhat freer atmosphere and economic opportunities newly available to them in the North. The trend started before 1910 and quickened as war in Europe cut off immigration and northern industries called for new workers. As northern cities accepted larger Black populations, the number of intermarriages rose, but the percentage of northern Blacks marrying non-Blacks declined. Between 1890 and 1920 the number of people classed as mulattoes in the North and West rose only slightly, while the Black population multiplied eight times. Some might take this to indicate that interracial mating was on the decline. But Florette Henri and Eugene Cash rightly point out that a decline in the number of people counted as mulattoes does not mean there were actually fewer mixed people, only that fewer were counted. These scholars insist that the Black migration included an unusually high percentage of light-skinned Blacks and that, in the fluid racial situation attending the migration, many of those who could pass for White did so. They imply, then, that outmarriage by people who were born Negroes increased sharply during the migration, as light mulattoes passed and married Whites.[10]

1920–1945. The system of race relations in postwar northern cities was very different from what Black peasants had known in the South prior to migration. They continued to experience poverty, prejudice, and discrimination. But the urban social system in the North was more fluid than its southern, rural counterpart. Black people hired out their labor as more or less anonymous cogs in an impersonal industrial machine. As in the South, they were oppressed, but it was as anonymous members of an oppressed group, not as persons known and oppressed by White individuals with whom they had lived their whole lives. The anonymity of the North and West brought the opportunity to pass as White for those whose features allowed them—and those who chose —to take that option. Theoretically, removal of some southern restrictions also might have made open interracial sex and marriage easier. But the migration brought a large Black population. As was the case with Jews and Japanese Americans, where numbers of Blacks were great, communities formed; those communities acted as foci of White restriction and also, independently, as brakes on Black outmarriage.

What happened, then, in the decades after the First World War, was that northern, urban Black people began to intermarry with slightly greater frequency than had their predecessors in the South. But their rates of open outmarriage were drastically lower than those of previous generations of northern Blacks. The rate of outmarriage by northern and western Blacks was between 0.5 and 1 percent in the 1920s and 1930s, perhaps double the southern rate. But this represented an extreme drop from a rate perhaps as high as 10 percent or more in northern cities twenty years earlier. These percentages are more or less equivalent to the rates of outmarriage by Japanese and Jewish immigrants during the same era. As before, the heavy majority of intermarriages in the North involved Black men and White women. Over the course of the interwar decades, northern intermarriage continued to drop as Black communities became more tightly organized and Whites developed systems for restricting Black people. For example, Annella Lynn surveyed Washington, D.C., marriage records and found only half as many intermarriages in the mid-1940s as she had found two decades earlier. If anthropological observers are to be believed, miscegenation declined in the South, too, as both Whites and Blacks spoke out against White men's attention to Black women.[11]

Yet there *were* some intermarriages and other interracial liaisons in these years. The mating habits of southern White men died hard. In many southern cities, prostitution was frequently by Black women for the pleasure of White men. Cases of White men taking Black mistresses were not as common as in earlier eras; nonetheless, one can find scores of them in sources from the period, especially in rural areas of the Lower South. For example, in the 1940s Charles S. Johnson wrote about a Black woman who lived with a White man of moderate wealth. She was presented to the world as his cook, but in fact she functioned as his wife while another woman was hired to do the cooking. This couple raised two sons together. The woman inherited the man's property and care of his children when he died. Their relationship was known and acknowledged throughout the community. This was unusual, for in most cases Black mistresses had to be careful not to violate caste etiquette by openly asserting their connections with White men. As before, some White observers attributed interracial quasi-marital behavior only to declassé White men, but that seems not to have been true; White men of every class attached themselves to Black women.[12]

The position of Black men in all this was difficult. Some Black men found their wives, sisters, and lovers involved with White men, and the interracial power relationship in the South was such that they could do little about it. Black men did not usually have equivalent access to White women. There are records of brief romances between Black men and White women in many parts of the South, but few of longer-term relationships, and none of marriages.[13]

In the North, interracial romances, though few, were much more likely to lead to marriage. Most northern states did not have laws against interracial marriage, and the transience and anonymity of city life made it harder for informal antimiscegenation sanctions to be applied. Most northern and western intermarriages seem to have involved middle-class people, such as a Mr. and Mrs. Brown interviewed by St. Clair Drake and Horace Cayton in the 1930s. The Black husband was the college-educated son of a well-to-do Kentucky farm family; his wife, a White office worker. She met him through a co-worker, a Black woman passing for White. After an extended and secretive courtship they married but did not tell Mrs. Brown's relatives or other co-workers, for fear that the family would reject them and that she would lose her job. Over a period of two years, the Browns gradually informed the members of her family and fought their way to acceptance, but when interviewed they had still not told her employer. A less secretive intermarriage took place in 1928 between Josephine and George Schuyler. He was a Black writer from New York; she, a dancer, artist, and daughter of a Texas rancher. She had grown up around, but not among, Black ranch workers in Texas, and had seen her father and brother take Black mistresses. The Schuylers met through the *Messenger* magazine, for which he was a columnist and she an occasional contributor. They had a romantic and highly public courtship in New York nightspots, followed by a marriage of several decades. The Schuylers were extremely prominent in Black intellectual, political, and cultural circles, and seem to have had an easy and successful relationship despite being constantly questioned by curious people.[14]

1945–1960. The years after World War II were a period of transition for American race relations. These years saw Black GIs return from service in that war and Korea, the Supreme Court take a first stand against segregation in *Brown v. Board of Education,* and Black people rise to demand their rights as citizens in the Montgomery bus boycott, the Greensboro lunch counter sit-ins, and scores of other episodes in the early Civil Rights movement. Although intermarriage was not part of anyone's program for Black rights, tiny but significant changes began to take place in the amount and kind of miscegenation.

Nationally, intermarriage rates rose only slightly, from less than 1 percent to just over 1 percent. But in some northern locations, out-marriage began to take off. In Iowa, the outmarriage rate for Black men in 1940–42 was 3 percent. It had doubled by 1950–55 and tripled by 1956–61. In Washington, D.C., the number of Black outmarriages increased tenfold from 1941–45 to 1956–60.[15] Most interracial couples still were made up of White women and Black men, but the preponderance of that combination declined, from nearly four-fifths in Chicago in the 1940s to less than two-thirds a decade later. These numbers describe a modest increase in Black intermarriage that heralded a more substantial rise in later years. Yet the most striking feature here is how tiny are these figures—1 or 2 percent in most places—compared to Jewish and Japanese outmarriage figures of 10 percent and up.[16]

Much of the modest rise in Black outmarriage was due to American servicemen bringing home wives from overseas. Many Black men returned from Europe with a sense of elation, not only at having fought well and defeated the Axis, but also at having been treated as social equals—even as conquering heroes—by European women and men. Black war correspondent Ollie Stewart fairly gloated over the escapades of his mates in France, Italy, and Germany. In a 1946 article for *Negro Digest*, Stewart recalled fine meals, dancing, trying to learn "I'd like to get to know you" in several languages, and romps in the bedroom. He titillated his readers with a country-by-country account of the kissing techniques of European women, and concluded that European women offered a lot that their Black American sisters did not: "Tenderness was the important thing. Tenderness and understanding. A smile, the way her fingers traced silly patterns on your face, the way she catered to your whims."[17] Stewart wrote openly and enthusiastically about romantic adventures with European women at a time when he would not have dared write so brazenly about American Whites.

Some Black GIs were so taken with foreign women that they fought past military objections, married them, and brought them home. It is not recorded how many Black military men married women from Europe and Asia in the years following the war, but the number was substantial. The experience of Japanese war brides was documented at some length in Chapter 5.[18] The lives of European women who followed Black men home were similar in many ways. Buford Simpkins, a college-educated, middle-class Black serviceman from Louisiana, met Hazel Byrne in December 1942. She was a middle-class schoolgirl in Manchester, England, where Simpkins was stationed. After a long, tentative courtship, the couple was married in Chicago in 1947. In between, they enjoyed a relatively peaceful time together in Manchester, until he applied for permission to marry. Then he was immediately transferred out of the area. Byrne was attacked and beaten by a White Southerner for dating a Black man. Her family's friends and neighbors ostracized them, although she found some friends at an interracial club in the area. She was allowed a visa to join her fiancé only after nearly two years' delay and an inquisition at the American embassy in London. Once married, the couple set up housekeeping in Chicago. There was frequent harassment from men—Black and White—who assumed that any White woman accompanying a Black man must be a prostitute and who wanted to share the goods. But Hazel Simpkins got along well with her husband's family, and the marriage seemed likely to succeed. Black-White war bride couples in Los Angeles, Washington, D.C., and Detroit formed clubs in the latter 1940s where they socialized and discussed common problems.[19]

War bride marriages got a lot of play in the Black press in the late 1940s and the 1950s.[20] But most of the mixed marriage space in such new publications as *Ebony* and *Negro Digest* went to celebrities. *Ebony*, in particular, maintained what one Black observer called "an almost lurid interest" in mixed marriages from its inception in the mid-forties down to the 1980s.[21] The intermarriages of singers Lena Horne, Billy Daniels, Anne Brown, Pearl Bailey, and Harry Belafonte; dancers Katherine Dunham and Sammy Davis, Jr.; editor George Schuyler; and novelist Richard Wright all rated major stories in *Ebony* in the period in question. Writers were always careful to note the accomplishments of both partners to such marriages, and seemed positively to glory in the pedigrees of the White spouses. Urban League executive Frank Montero's 1951 bride was "blonde steel heiress Ann Mather of Boston's exclusive Beacon Hill," said *Ebony*, a "31-year old Smith graduate [who] traces family back to Pilgrims."[22]

The most celebrated of the celebrity intermarriages was Walter White's union with Poppy Cannon. When they met in 1929, White was a thirty-five-year-old novelist, the toast of New York literary circles for his recent *Fire in the Flint*. He was small, slim, blond-haired, and blue-eyed. In no place would he have been taken for a Negro. But he had been raised Black in Atlanta and was dedicated to the cause of Black Americans. He spent the better part of his career as executive secretary of the NAACP before retiring to marry Cannon in 1949. Cannon was a businesswoman and journalist. Although she was a Caucasian, her hair, eyes, and skin were several shades darker than White's. The pair were married to partners of their own races throughout most of their on-again, off-again, twenty-year love affair. When White divorced his wife Gladys, a storm of controversy broke out in the Black press. He was accused of having sold out his race for a piece of White flesh, and Cannon, of having seduced one of Black America's most beloved leaders. There was also some criticism from White segregationists, to the effect that White's marriage to a White woman proved that intermarriage, not civil rights, was what Black leaders really wanted. Cannon felt called upon to defend herself and her husband with a book and several articles in *Ebony*. In time the controversy abated, and White went back to work for the NAACP. The marriage lasted until White's death in 1955.[23]

Black magazines paid attention not only to war brides and celebrity intermarriages, but also to celebrating intermarriages by less famous people. They served up articles such as "Mixed Marriage in College" and "Persecution [of a Mixed Couple] in New York," squibs on inter-married dentists and band leaders, and a whole series on how to make mixed marriages succeed.[24] What is remarkable about all this is that intermarriage had increased only very slightly, yet the play it got in the press was extensive. With the advent of glossy Black magazines after World War II, intermarriage was becoming much more public than it had ever been before.[25]

After 1960. The 1960s wrought major changes in American race relations. The Civil Rights movement became a national crusade, with marches and sit-ins, police dogs and water cannons, shown on the nightly news across the country. Blacks in the North and West echoed their southern sisters and brothers in demanding equality. Congress responded with the Civil Rights Act of 1964 and the Voting Rights Act of 1965. Black civil rights became a major issue in nearly every locality. The demands grew more strident with the rise of a new militancy in the Black Power movement in the latter sixties and with violence bred by frustration in ghettoes from Newark to Watts.

Not only did Black people become more visible in American society; they became more attractive to many non-Blacks. Ethnic chic— the cultivation of friendships with minority group members—was one popular form of White liberalism. To say with conviction, "Some of my best friends are Negroes," was a badge of honor at White liberal cocktail parties; even better was to actually invite some dark faces. The 1960s saw Black Americans achieve a formal social equality. White prejudice lingered, to be sure, and animated the anti-busing and anti–affirmative action campaigns of the 1970s and '80s. But beginning in the latter 1960s, for the first time in 350 years of American history, open expression of anti-Black sentiment came to be regarded as uncouth.

Together with an insistent Black political presence and a White liberal interest in socializing with Blacks, the 1960s saw, for the first time, the entry of a small number of Black people into the general middle class. White educational institutions, even in the South, opened their doors a crack, and many began actively to recruit talented Black students. By the early 1970s, White companies were seeking out the services of Black graduates. These opportunities touched only a tiny minority of Black people and left the huge majority as poor and shut out as ever. But the point here is that a small number of Black people began in the 1970s to be integrated into the White middle class. In previous generations, members of the Black elite were mainly professional and business people—lawyers, dentists, newspaper editors— who lived in and served Black communities. Now, the small group of successful Black people was likely to include engineers and corporate personnel directors who lived in recently all-White suburbs.[26]

The event after 1960 that had the most direct relevance for intermarriage was a 1967 Supreme Court decision, *Loving v. Commonwealth of Virginia*. In this action, the court invalidated the laws of several states which had made interracial marriage a crime. The couple, Richard Loving and Mildred Jeter, were residents of Central Point, an insular district in rural Virginia where nearly everyone was about the same color and Black and White had quietly mixed for generations. Richard Loving was a White bricklayer whose father had worked for a wealthy Black farmer. Mildred Jeter was a young Black woman. Neither family nor community objected to the match, so they went off to Washington, D.C., where interracial marriage was legal, to be wed. On returning from their honeymoon, they were rousted out of bed by an irate sheriff, arrested, tried, and sentenced to a year in prison. The angry judge suspended their sentences on the condition they leave Virginia for the next twenty-five years. The Lovings appealed the decision. Trial and appeals took nine years. The Lovings appear to have spent much of that time in and around Central Point, protected by their neighbors from the authorities, the glare of publicity, and the wrath of White segregationists.[27]

The *Loving* decision, the prominence and increased acceptance of Black people in White minds, and the movement of some Black people into the White middle class set a new and unprecedented context for interracial marriage. In that context, the number of outmarriages by Blacks increased sharply. Sister M. Annella counted marriage licenses in Washington, D.C., and found 17 Black outmarriages in 1941–45, 177 in 1956–60, and 493 in 1961–65 (this at a time when the total number of marriages was decreasing). Nationwide, the percentage of Black people who chose to marry non-Blacks between 1960 and 1970 was nearly double that of the previous decade, and it continued to rise through the 1970s. There were 77,000 Black-White married couples in 1970; that figure more than doubled, to 168,000, in 1980. Yet the actual percentages were still tiny: only 1.5 percent of all Black married men had non-Black wives in 1970, and only 0.8 percent of Black married women had non-Black husbands. The percentages were only a bit higher in 1980: 3.6 percent for Black men and 1.2 percent for women. Even though intermarriages constituted over 5 percent of all marriages contracted by Black men in the decade 1970–80 (a fivefold increase over the 1960s), that percentage was still very small by comparison with other ethnic groups.[28] The bulk of interracial marriages continued to be contracted by Black men and White women. The U.S. census reported nearly twice as many intermarried Black men as Black women in 1970, and nearly three times as many in 1977.[29] A 1971 Harris poll pointed to a bifurcation of the White population in its experiences with Black people. Across the country, nearly one White person in five had dated a person of another race (in the West, and among young people age 21–25 everywhere, it was one in three). Yet 55 percent said they did not even *know* anyone who had dated across racial lines. That is, a surprisingly large portion had some interracial social experiences, while a majority was completely isolated.[30]

In the new social situation, Blacks and non-Blacks came together in new circumstances. Once, most interracial contact between people of opposite gender had taken place in hierarchical settings (as White employers and Black workers) or in places such as factories, where social mixing was inhibited by the demands of the workplace. Now, increasingly, Whites met Blacks under conditions of rough social equality.

The most common of these was the college campus. Primary and secondary schools throughout America remained segregated, either by law or by the fact of residential segregation. But Blacks in the 1960s and 1970s entered college in vastly increased numbers. Blonde, lissome Faye Becker dated bronze, handsome Dexter Clarke at the University of Minnesota in 1971, and they were joined by dozens of other interracial couples on campus. Some collegiate dating resulted in interracial marriages. Most of the couples seem to have involved Black men and White women. This may have been partly because White men were less attracted to Black women or were intimidated by them. In any case, it was also at least partly because Black women, responding to the demands of the Black Power movement, stood more strongly against integration than did Black men. Antimiscegenationists, White and Black, reacted with disgust at these campus romances, insisting darkly that "interracial dates without any sexual intimacy are in the minority in the case of Black men."[31]

Another point of interracial meeting was the Civil Rights movement, and the miscegenation issue came up again there. Southern Black young people had been working at achieving racial justice for many years before they were joined by hundreds of Northerners of various colors in the summers of 1964 and 1965. Among the Whites there were more men than women, but it was mainly the women who caused comment. Southern White opponents of Black rights seized on the presence of White women, accusing the civil rights workers of interracial sexual debauchery on a wide scale. There were in fact some interracial romances and sexual activities, involving White men and Black women as well as the other race-gender combination, and some marriages resulted. But several observers pointed to a special set of tensions operating around the coupling of Black men and White women. Some of the young White women—but not most—undoubtedly acted partly out of rebellion or other neurotic motives when they went South. Sometimes they sought to resolve those issues by immersing themselves in intimate relationships with Blacks. White women drew special attention all out of proportion to their numbers in the movement. They were the focus of press reports, and they were sometimes treated specially by Black families with whom they stayed. Black men in the movement exhibited ambivalent feelings toward White women. Some rejected them as troublemakers and players at revolution. Some were attracted to them as the forbidden and therefore revered object of desire. Some Black men approached them sexually, or were approached by the White women. Some Black men used White women sexually as a way of taking out their resentments against White oppression. A White person in the movement could not easily turn down the attentions of a Black person without feeling guilty about, and perhaps being accused of, racism. Altogether, the presence of White women lent an explosive sexual tension to the Civil Rights movement. Blacks, female and male, lashed out at them in ways many White women neither expected nor were equipped to handle. Some, feeling shock, guilt, and confusion, went home in a hurry. But more stayed out their tours of service.[32]

A third new venue for interracial contact began to emerge in the 1970s in formerly all-White residential communities. Sons and daughters of the small Black middle class—what sociologist Harry Edwards calls Buppies (Black Yuppies)—grew up isolated from other Blacks, assimilated the outlook and mores of middle-class Whites, and mixed exclusively with their White peers. While some, just now coming of age, experience discomfort or rejection in the romantic arena, perhaps as many are likely to end up marrying non-Blacks.[33]

Through the 1960s and '70s, the Black and White press continued to find good copy in the interracial marriages of prominent people, from Peggy Rusk, daughter of the secretary of state, to actors Tyne Daly and Georg Stanford Brown. Black magazines continued to report on the trials of intermarriage among the less famous. But as Black-White intermarriage increased in the latter 1970s, the amount of hype declined.[34]

Overall, the trends in interracial sex and marriage are clear. In the decades after slavery, old patterns continued. White men continued to mate with Black women, either in forced, temporary situations or as part of an enduring pattern of concubinage.[35] Actual intermarriages were very infrequent, although there were more in the cities of the

North and West than in the South. There is no pattern of significant increase in outmarriage over three generations as with Japanese Americans and Jews. The percentages did inch upward slightly, but the rate of Black outmarriage as late as the 1970s was more closely comparable to the rate of Japanese or Jewish immigrants than to that of the immigrants' grandchildren. In all time periods, the larger number of actual marriages took place between Black men and White women.

White Reactions to Interracial Marriage

Throughout most of American history, intermarriages and other unions between Blacks and Whites have met with a fairly consistent set of responses: near-hysterical disapproval from the majority of White people and a grudging acquiescence from Black people. But reactions have varied tremendously, depending not just on individual tastes, but also on time, place, social class, the degree of formality of the union, and the race-gender combination of the intermarried couple. Only in the very recent past have White Americans in significant numbers begun to accept interracial marriage.

1865–1920. In the aftermath of slavery, White Americans were at pains to construct a system of understandings by which they might continue to dominate their erstwhile slaves. Other writers have expounded upon this ideology at length.[36] Perhaps it will suffice here to note that this set of ideas argued the necessary superiority and dominance of the White race. From the 1860s through the 1910s, there was a great deal of noise among White Americans, but not much focused debate, over this issue. It started in the election year 1864, when Democratic Copperheads accused Lincoln and abolitionist Republicans of plotting "compulsory inter-marriage" should their party be continued in power. An anonymous pamphlet, widely attributed to New York reporter David Croly, appeared and stirred the soup. Its title coined the term "miscegenation," and it predicted approvingly the inevitable sexual mixing of the races at some future time. Republicans handled the matter gingerly, some offering qualified endorsement and others denying any connection with the pamphlet. Democrats made the Republicans' supposed miscegenation policy a major issue in the campaign. The Republicans won anyway, and the furor abated. In time it appeared that Croly, a Democrat, had fabricated the pamphlet to try to get the radical members of the Republican party to shoot themselves in the foot by taking an unpopular stand on this sensitive issue.[37]

The theme of the 1864 campaign was played out more fully in the decades that followed. The gut-level feeling of most Whites was expressed by E. H. Randle: "All mixed races are inherently violent, incoherent, incapable of national government, revolutionary, and are on the down grade of civilization. . . . Miscegenation is a sin against God and a violation of the laws of nature." In like manner, Charles Carroll attributed all manner of human ills to intermarriage, but gave the paranoia a sharper theological edge in *The Negro a Beast*. Africans, he said, were "not of the human family," not sons of Adam. They were, in fact, the Beast, the Anti-Christ, come to amalgamate with whomever they could seduce and so take over the world. It was they who had miscegenated with Cain and his children, thus rendering them soulless and causing sin to flood the world. Originally, according to Carroll, it had not been God's intention that Christ should die on the cross for human sin; that event had been made necessary by amalgamation.[38]

Carroll was antiscientific as well as anti-integrationist. He believed his treatise had "exploded" the theory of evolution once for all. Yet, although they rejected Carroll's theology, a goodly number of other people who espoused a scientific viewpoint agreed intermarriage was a bad and dangerous practice. The classic statement of pseudoscientific racism was Madison Grant's 1916 volume, *The Passing of the Great Race*. Drawing on the ideas of Joseph LeConte, the Social Darwinists, John H. Van Evre, Frederick Hoffman, and others, Grant wrote a widely published diatribe which helped bring about the legislation cutting off immigration in the 1920s. Briefly put, Grant and his fellows saw Whites and Blacks as two separate species at the top and bottom of a hierarchy of human kinds. Those at the top were superior in talent and temperament to those below, but they were more fragile. The various human species—Black, Yellow, Red, and White—were further divided hierarchically into subspecies (Nordic, Alpine, and Mediterranean, in the European case). Interbreeding of subspecies was bad for the "higher types" (i.e., Nordics). Miscegenation between distinct species, in the words of John Van Evrie, was against "the normal order of creation" and "rapidly tends to [the] extinction" of the higher people.[39]

Beneath such abstract philosophical arguments stood concrete and vicious White reactions against interracial marriage. After the Civil War, White Southerners who had previously turned a winking eye to White men's interracial liaisons began loudly to denounce the practice. The next step was to deny that it happened. The obvious White ancestry of many former slaves ruled out baldfaced denial that masters had ever taken slave women. But White Southerners could announce boldly (and in defiance of the facts) that miscegenation was a sin of the past.[40] They could also speak and act against those few instances of interracial marriage that came into their ken. Frederick Douglass's 1884 marriage to Helen Pitts called down a national round of criticism.[41] White opponents of intermarriage acted with more force against other couples. On July 6, 1905, Joseph Woodman and his White sweetheart decided to leave Arkansas and go to be married in a northern state. They had not gone far when they were apprehended by a sheriff's posse and Woodman jailed. The next morning his body was found dangling from a tree. Between 1885 and 1915 there were at least 2,715 lynchings of Black men and women in America. Only a minority—perhaps one in five—involved charges of rape or miscegenation, but the threat was always present.[42]

Actions against interracial romance and marriage were not confined to the South. William Dixon reported from "the West" in 1867 the story of "a negro seized by a mob for having insulted a white girl; this offence was that of giving the girl a kiss, with an appearance of aiming at a further freedom; and on the girl screaming for assistance, he was collared by a soldier, a native of Ohio, and dragged to Fort Halleck, where he was cuffed and kicked, tarred and feathered, set on fire, skinned alive, and finally stuck, half-dead, in a firkin, and exposed on the open Plains, until his flesh was eaten away by wolves and dogs." Jack Johnson, the Black heavyweight boxing champion, had a string of White wives and mistresses, much to the anger of many Whites. In Illinois in 1912 and 1913 he was charged with abducting one woman, Lucille Cameron, who shortly became his wife. The following year he was indicted and convicted under the Mann Act for allegedly transporting another White woman—Belle Schreiber, a frequent companion—across state lines for immoral purposes.[43]

By the end of Reconstruction, White opponents of intermarriage had come to see the problem solely in terms of Black men and White women. They were much less active in harassing White men with

Black women. Although southern White men continued to take Black women as concubines (admittedly in smaller numbers and perhaps not so openly as before), to this combination the public turned a blind eye. All the rhetoric and action against interracial sex and marriage were focused on Black men.[44]

The tremendous animus against interracial marriage was reflected in antimiscegenation laws in the decades after slavery.[45] The first laws forbidding interracial marriage and cohabitation date from the 1660s in Maryland and Virginia. Antimiscegenation statutes were in place in nearly all the states by the time of independence. They were changed from time to time, and repealed in Pennsylvania and Massachusetts, but in other states the solid front against miscegenation was maintained through the end of the Civil War. With the South's defeat, Congress forced a few states to give up their prohibitions (for example, Mississippi and Louisiana in 1870 and Arkansas in 1874). Other states' laws were left untouched. With the retreat from Reconstruction, the nation split on marriage discrimination, at law if not in attitude. In the South, antimiscegenation acts were restored where they had been removed and strengthened where they had not. In the North, Maine, Michigan, Ohio, and Rhode Island repealed their laws. The period between 1880 and 1920 saw thirteen plains and western states add anti-intermarriage laws to their books. Many of these were new states imbued with frontier racial hatreds; some were afflicted with anti-Asian animus as well. Altogether, thirty of the forty-eight states had antimiscegenation laws in 1920, and all these kept their laws in force until after World War II.[46] (For a summary of these laws, see Appendix A.)

The laws varied tremendously from state to state. In all but four states, interracial marriages were declared not only criminal but null and void. Penalties ranged up to a fine of $1,000 and imprisonment for ten years or more. Not only the offending couple might be fined or put in jail. In many states they might be joined by the clerk who issued the license and the minister who performed the ceremony. Some states forbade only marriages between Blacks and Whites. Others added Native Americans and Asians to the list of those who could not marry Whites. Louisiana even barred Blacks from marrying Indians. Twelve states took pains to define just who was a "Negro." In most cases, one was judged Black if one had "one-eighth Negro blood" or more. This was not a precise accounting of African genetic inheritance. It meant, rather, that one was Black if one had a single great-grandparent who was socially regarded as being of African descent. Other states did not bother with a definition and relied instead on judges' and juries' common sense.[47]

Officially, all these laws applied to interracial marriages involving either combination of race and gender. But practically speaking they were intended mainly to prevent mating of Black men with White women. Just four states—Alabama, Florida, Louisiana, and Nevada— prohibited interracial cohabitation or concubinage, the more common pattern for White men and Black women.[48]

Only a tiny number of White people spoke out against these laws. One who did was former abolitionist Cassius M. Clay, who wrote from Kentucky in 1886:

The law is intended to protect the white, and not the black race. . . . It destroys the self-respect of and degrades the whole black race. . . . I deny the right of society or the state to say whom I shall or will not marry. . . . But, admit that there is an instinctive repugnance between whites and blacks sufficient to warrant a restraining law of intermarriage, then such repugnance is also sufficient without law, and therefore such law is needless in the main issues, while in its degradation of a whole race, it is *per se* criminal. . . . There is reason to believe that those varieties [of Whites] are happiest where intermarriage is confined to the nearest type and closest affinities of rank, education, and sentiment. But as a matter of *right*, . . . let all stand "EQUAL BEFORE THE LAW."

Clay's was certainly a minority voice, and even he spoke, not in favor of intermarriage, but only in defense of the natural right of human beings to equality before the law.[49]

Almost no White people stood with him. State and federal courts consistently upheld antimiscegenation statutes. The U.S. Supreme Court even declared constitutional in 1882 an Alabama law that pre-scribed heavier penalties for interracial than for single-race illicit co-habitation. It did not discriminate, said the justices, because both the Black and the White partner were sentenced to suffer equally; it did not matter that lighter penalties were prescribed for all-White and all-Black couples.[50]

These laws, and judicial support for them, led to some silly and tragic applications. On January 20, 1909, a Richmond judge sentenced Marcus Lindsay and his wife Sophy to eighteen years in the Virginia penitentiary—almost double the statutory maximum for inter-racial marriage. Sophy Lindsay was a Black woman. Her husband be-lieved himself to be a Negro and had always associated with Black people, but the court ruled he had enough White ancestry to be classed a Caucasian. In 1915 an Indiana judge refused the petition of Clifford Yarborough, a wealthy White man from Tennessee, to adopt his seventeen-year-old mulatto daughter. She must remain a bastard, Judge Givens said, because to allow the adoption would amount to sanctioning the marriage of Yarborough and his Black mistress.[51]

There was another flurry of legislative activity during the Progres-sive era. Even states that had never passed antimiscegenation laws tried to enact them. This came largely in response to the highly pub-licized interracial antics of Jack Johnson. Bills were introduced in the legislatures of ten states and in Congress in 1913. One Ohio bill prom-ised not only to jail for five years any Black man who dared marry a White woman, but also to make the penalty retroactive to punish inter-marriers of years past. Politicians continued to push the issue through-out that decade and the next, though only Wyoming and Montana were added to the list of prohibiting states.[52]

1920–1960.   The period from the end of World War I to the Civil Rights movement saw only a modest rise in the number of interracial marriages. Nonetheless, in that period a group of Whites who did not completely condemn the practice began to appear. Sociologists such as Edward B. Reuter, Herbert A. Miller, and Gunnar Myrdal began to argue that race was not so much a biological as a social construct. Phe-nomena such as interracial marriage must be evaluated, they argued, on social rather than biological grounds. And these people were in-clined not to oppose the practice, at least in theory. The rise of inter-nationalism in the era of World War II led more than a few to predict the ultimate demise of racial and national boundaries, in marriage as well as politics. So University of Chicago professor G. A. Borgese in-sisted in 1944 that "only when [the] two bloods mix freely in marriage will [the] color problem be solved."[53]

But an uneven liberalizing trend on race relations in general and a few pie-in-the-sky visions about achieving interracial amity through miscegenation did not change much in the dominant White reactions to interracial marriage. The bulk of White Americans were just as hor-rified at the thought of interracial marriage in 1950 as they had been in

1900 or 1850, although this position had lost some of its academic respectability. The loudest speakers against intermarriage were a clutch of redneck Negrophobes who perceived what they thought to be a conspiracy by Blacks, liberal politicians, Jewish bankers, the Catholic church, and the Soviet Union (they would have said "International Communism" or simply "the Evil Empire") to undermine the strength and vitality of the White American republic by polluting its gene pool. They included people as prominent as Attorney General A. Mitchell Palmer and Senator J. Thomas Heflin of Alabama.[54]

One exceptionally articulate speaker for this viewpoint was Gerald L. K. Smith, disciple of Huey Long and leader of the Christian Nationalist Crusade from the 1930s to the 1950s. Smith could never decide whether he was more angry at Jews, Blacks, the Supreme Court, or Eleanor Roosevelt. But all, he was sure, were part of an ungodly Communist cabal to destroy the United States. In a pamphlet titled *White Man Awaken!* he detailed a plot to force Whites to miscegenate, to make America "a nation of negroid half-breeds." This would happen through allowing breaches in the wall of segregation. If Blacks and Whites shared playgrounds, fire departments, streetcars, and—worst of all—schools, they would inevitably interbreed, and White, Christian America would be doomed. Unlike some of his more genteel compatriots, Smith did not bother with any of the pseudoscientific arguments about the inevitable degeneration of mixed breeds or the *angst* of the mulatto. His was bedrock race-hatred and fear-mongering.[55] Although Smith purported to speak for God on racial matters, other religious leaders disputed his claim. By the 1950s at the latest, many evangelicals, mainline Protestants, Catholics, and Jews all thought God would countenance a position on segregation that was a good deal more liberal than Smith's, and a few were even willing to suggest that intermarriage might be okay. But only the universalist Baha'i faith explicitly encouraged interracial mixing; it constituted a unique bastion of miscegeny.[56]

By the 1950s Smith was something of a fringe character, even though he maintained a following and there were always others far more extreme than he. He was pushed to the margin more because of his lack of couth than because of the content of his program. Smith advocated ideas that had filled most White people's visions of Black Americans for many years—articulate in the South and lying just below the surface in the North—visions of grasping Negroes and radical destabilizers of the social order. Gunnar Myrdal laid these out clearly in 1944, in what he called the "rank order of discrimination." If one were to ask a southern White which aspects of dominance were most necessary to retain, Myrdal said he or she would respond thus:

1. Most important to prevent, in White eyes, was intermarriage, meaning sexual intercourse by a Black man and a White woman.
2. Next most important was to maintain the etiquette of social hierarchy, the behaviors of dominance and submission surrounding handshaking, forms of address, and the like.
3. Then came segregation of public facilities.
4. Then came the denial of the vote.
5. Next came discrimination by police and the courts.
6. And finally economic domination. This was most easily given up, according to Myrdal's understanding of White ideology.[57]

This hierarchy of essential discriminations points to a growing ambivalence in many Whites. People of good will, they did not want Black people necessarily to suffer. They only wanted them to stay away. A southern White officer wrote to Margaret Halsey during World War II expressing his agony over this issue. He described himself as one of the people "who seek democracy in a nation where it is sometimes hard to find," and continued: "Even I am not sure how far I would go to insure that democracy. I want my colored friend to vote; I want him to be free from prejudice in the courts; I want him to go to college; I want him to have the best of living conditions; I want him to be paid what he is worth; I want him to be an active and respected member of any union he desires; I want him to know and enjoy the Four Freedoms. I will work and work hard to see that he—or his sons—gets these things, but—I do not want him to live next door to me; I do not want him to be my house guest; and I do not want him to dance with my daughter." Eleanor Roosevelt was willing to let him dance with her daughter, but even she drew the line at intermarriage. She, and other liberals of the universalist generation who created the United Nations, looked forward to the day when color would not matter in America and intermarriage would happen freely. But, she said, "We haven't reached that time as yet." A mixed couple might be quite happy by themselves, but there would inevitably be too many "reprisals from society and from families, which make for great unhappiness."[58]

During the years Roosevelt was in her prime as a public figure, chinks began to appear in the solid wall of White opposition to interracial marriage. In 1948, the California Supreme Court threw out that state's antimiscegenation law, saying that marriage was more than a contract which the state might regulate at will: it was a "fundamental right of free men." Gradually, over the next decade and more, the number of interracial unions increased, but never did Black-White intermarriage amount to more than a tiny fragment of the total number of California marriages.[59]

Still, California was not the nation, and anti-miscegenation laws stayed on the books in twenty-nine other states. Even where the law was silent, social custom and the determination of individuals kept some interracial marriages from happening and punished those couples who went ahead with their plans. Unlike Eleanor Roosevelt, nearly all southern Whites drew the line well before any sort of social mixing that involved Black men and White women, and they frequently enforced their beliefs with violence. The most infamous episodes came in Alabama in 1931 and Mississippi in 1955. In the Scottsboro, Alabama, case, nine Depression-strapped Black youths got into a fight with a number of Whites on a southbound freight train out of Chattanooga. Getting the worst of the brawl, the Whites jumped off. When the train reached Alabama, the Blacks were arrested for allegedly raping two White women who were also on the train. Alabama Governor B. M. Miller found it necessary to call out the National Guard to prevent a lynching. Eight of the nine Black defendants were convicted by an all-White jury and sentenced to die (the ninth, Roy Wright, was only thirteen), although their sentences were eventually commuted.[60]

Like the Scottsboro incident, the murder of Emmett Till in Sumner, Mississippi, drew national and international notoriety. Till was a fourteen-year-old Chicago boy visiting relatives in the Mississippi Delta. He asked Carolyn Bryant, a young White woman, for a date. She angrily refused. That night, Till was hauled out of bed at gunpoint by Bryant's husband and his half-brother, J. W. Milam. They later admitted pistol-whipping Till, shooting him, and dumping his weighted body in the Tallahatchie River. A jury of twelve White males refused to convict either of the confessed murderers. A howl of protest went up across the country, but more than a few agreed with Richard Lauchli of Collinsville, Illinois: "Roy Bryant and J. W. Milam did what had to be done and their courage in taking the course they did is to be commended. To have followed any other course would have been unrealistic, cowardly and not in the best interests of their family or country."[61]

These were cases that drew national attention, but any relationship between a Black man and a White woman in the South drew harassment throughout this period, and not a few ended as tragically. Black men were beaten, hanged, dismembered, and dragged behind automobiles for having romantic encounters—or for being accused of freshness—with White women. White women were ostracized for their parts in these relationships.[62] A new development of the 1950s, however, was that harassment was extended to White men who dated and married Black women. As late as the 1940s in rural Virginia, Morton Rubin reported Whites' turning a blind eye to the activities of White men and their Black mistresses so long as the couples did not try to marry. Ten years later, White police sergeant Burleigh Lester and his Black sweetheart Sandra Ann Taylor had to endure censure from his family and other Whites, and finally to flee Greenville, Mississippi, on account of their relationship.[63]

Lest Northerners smugly imagine—as they did for many years—that bigotry was a sin peculiar to the South, let the reader be informed that similar harassment, in kind if not degree, was the lot of mixed couples in the North and West. A 1958 Gallup Poll showed that nearly as many northern and western Whites as Southerners disapproved interracial marriages (92 percent as opposed to 99 percent). Many non-southern states did not have laws against intermarriage, but that does not mean they condoned miscegenation. Interracial couples found that clerks would not issue them licenses and ministers refused to marry them. Intermarried people frequently complained of being fired if they told their co-workers of their situation, and of living in constant fear of discovery if they did not. They had difficulty buying homes and renting apartments. One White woman's grandmother even had her committed to a mental institution when she announced her engagement. LeRoy Gardner had to sign a pledge at Bethel College in St. Paul in 1942 promising not to "fraternize" with White women students. When he married a White woman four years later, "People used to wreck their cars staring at us so hard," and his father-in-law threatened to shoot him. White women in interracial relationships usually found they

Table 10.1.   White Americans' Attitudes toward
Interracial Marriage, 1968–1983

Year	Approve	Disapprove
1968	17%	76%
1972	25	65
1978	32	58
1983	43	50

were treated like this: "[White people] promptly infer that my strange preference means that I am either 1) communistic; 2) incapable, for some obscure reason, of getting a white man; or 3) a fallen woman, or at least a woman of lascivious tastes." Interracial couples faced solid, unrelenting opposition from most White parents. When the interracial marriage followed a divorce, several White women found their custody of their children had been revoked by angry White judges. And, of course, many couples had to endure stares, hate mail, and threatening phone calls.[64]

After 1960.   From 1960 to the 1980s the attitudes of White Americans toward interracial marriage softened markedly. At the beginning of the sixties, some Whites wanted to be open-minded in theory, but in practical fact almost all were repelled by the thought of intermarriage with Blacks. By the 1980s, although many still had hesitations about Black people entering their own families, most Whites, North and South, had become used to the abstract idea of Black-White intermarriage and no longer felt threatened by it.

Some of this change was reflected in public opinion polls. In National Opinion Research Center tallies, 60 percent of the White population approved of laws forbidding interracial marriage in 1964; in 1972, only 38 percent approved. Yet opposition to legal discrimination was not the same thing as approval of interracial marriage. Table 10.1 shows the percentages of White Americans who approved and disapproved interracial marriage from 1968 to 1983, according to the Gallup poll. The trend toward greater acceptance of interracial marriage is clear, although as late as 1983 more Whites opposed interracial marriage than approved. Brought down to the realm of one's own family, Whites showed even more reluctance. According to a 1975 Virginia Slims survey, only 14 percent of White women would both accept and approve of their daughters' marrying Black men, 32 percent would accept but not approve, and 44 percent professed neither to accept nor to approve. All this suggests that there was a distinct and rapid change in White opinion over the period roughly 1960 to 1980, away from rejection and toward acceptance of interracial marriage, but that full acceptance had not yet been reached by the end of that period.[65]

The trend toward a measure of White acceptance of marriage with Blacks was reflected in a variety of cultural indicators. In an influential 1963 essay, Norman Podhoretz expressed the growing conviction of White liberals that they had a duty to override their own negative feelings and embrace the idea of intermarriage based on their commitment to human equality: "If I were asked today whether I would like a daughter of mine 'to marry one,' I would have to answer: 'No, I wouldn't *like* it at all. I would rail and rave and rant and tear my hair. And then I hope I would have the courage to curse myself for raving and ranting, and to give her my blessing."[66]

The movies also traced changing attitudes. The 1960s saw two major American films deal with racial intermarriage. In 1964, Bernie Hamilton and Barbara Barrie played a Black and White couple in *One Potato, Two Potato*, a movie with a serious ending that emphasized both the dignity of the couple and the inevitability of White harassment of people in their situation. Four years later, *Guess Who's Coming to Dinner?* emerged as a star vehicle for Sidney Poitier, Katharine Hepburn, and Spencer Tracy. This latter movie had its serious moments, but then breezed to the conclusion that, gosh, intermarriage was okay.[67] The choices of bureaucrats also reflected an increasing acceptance of interracial marriage. For the first time in 1970 the census gave detailed reports on the number and distribution of racially mixed couples, certifying a degree of acceptance, or at least of recognition that intermarriage was a significant social fact.[68]

By the 1980s, many barriers had been broken. Who would have believed, even ten years earlier, that in 1982 radio stations across America would play without comment a top ten hit record, "The Girl is Mine," in which Paul McCartney and Michael Jackson fought over the same woman? Or that, three years later, Black actress, model, and cult figure Grace Jones and her Swedish boyfriend would romp naked across the pages of *Playboy*—and not create a racial stir?[69] The opinion of a lot of Whites on interracial romance and marriage had clearly changed between 1960 and the mid-1980s.

Of course, there were Whites who bucked the trend, especially in the 1960s. Many of these were conservative Southerners actively engaged in resisting the Civil Rights movement. Although religious leaders of every theological persuasion rode at the forefront of the Civil Rights movement and spoke clearly in favor of allowing intermarriage, there were always a few marginal characters. One was South Carolina fundamentalist leader Bob Jones, Jr., who wrote in the 1960s: "The cry today is 'One World, One Race, One Church,' but it will be a corrupt and evil world, a mongrel race, and the church of the Antichrist. Intermarriage of the races is a breakdown of the lines of separation which God has set up and, therefore, is rebellion against God."[70] By the 1970s, however, such open opposition to interracial marriage was considered crude, even in the most conservative circles. Negative opinion usually had to be expressed in more indirect forms, such as psychologist Charles Stember's assertion that the prime motive of Black rights leaders, from W. E. B. Du Bois to H. Rap Brown, was to get into bed with White women. Even these were minority opinions.[71]

Changes in the public mood were reflected in changes in the legal structure. Thirteen states (all but Maryland were in the North or West) repealed their antimiscegenation statutes between the 1948 California decision and 1967. In 1964, the U.S. Supreme Court struck down laws in many southern states which punished interracial cohabitation or adultery more severely than they did the same crimes committed by couples of the same race. And finally, in 1967, the court ended antimiscegenation laws altogether.[72] The courts took longer to decide what to do about custody battles involving interracial couples. For many years it had been the practice in many jurisdictions to revoke a divorced White woman's custody of her children if she remarried interracially. Thus, in 1962 a Detroit judge took three-year-old Donna Potter from her White mother, Sarah Potter, and entrusted her to her White father, Donald, because Sarah had married a Black physician. As late as 1982, in a similar case Georgia judge Faye Martin took four-year-old Nickolas Blackburn away from his White mother, Kathleen Blackburn, and gave custody not to his father but to Nancy Blackburn, the child's White grandmother. Yet the Blackburn case was no longer typical. By the 1970s many judges had ceased to believe that the best interest of the child dictated a monoracial home. Finally, in a 1984 decision, the Supreme Court overrode the Florida judiciary and let

White Linda Palmore keep her White daughter, six-year-old Melanie Sidoti, even though her second husband was Black, and ruled out the use of race as a factor in custody cases.[73]

These gradual changes of public opinion and public policy did not mean that interracial couples lived free of harassment throughout this period. Particularly in the South, at the height of the tensions accompanying the Civil Rights movement, mixed couples were treated badly by Whites. In 1965, White civil rights worker Viola Liuzzo was shot and killed while transporting Black male colleagues near Selma, Alabama. Yet such behavior was not confined to the South. In 1963, Tamara Wright and her Black husband Vincent moved into a middle-class, all-White neighborhood in East Meadow, Long Island. They were promptly greeted by a cross burning on their lawn, a bomb taped to their window, and endless hate mail and threatening phone calls.[74]

Such behavior fell out of fashion over the next decade and a half. In 1967, Peggy Rusk, daughter of then secretary of state Dean Rusk, and Guy Smith found their relationship touted in newsmagazines as "a marriage of enlightenment" and had few problems with either family or the public. A decade later, even southern mixed couples found lessening public pressure. In 1978, Johnny Ford was the young, Black mayor of Tuskegee, Alabama—elected even though his wife, Frances, was White. Married in 1974, the Fords continued to live in their hometown and encountered very little White opposition. Some of Mrs. Ford's relatives criticized the couple and even shunned them, but there was no public pressure. By the early 1980s, Black-White couples still often were stared at and treated with rudeness or stiff formality. But few were subjected to serious harassment from parties outside their own families.[75]

Over the course of more than a century, White opposition to marriage with Blacks remained firm. Laws forbade intermarriage in most states. Custom and the actions of countless individuals made the lives of interracial couples generally miserable. People committed vicious acts against those who dared break the race-sex taboo. Opposition from Whites was even more vehement when the intermarriers were family members. Abuse of couples involving Black men and White women always exceeded maltreatment of the other race-gender combination. Hostile attitudes and behavior began to change, however, not gradually but rather suddenly, in the wake of the Civil Rights struggles of the 1950s and 1960s. Much racist feeling remained. But by the 1970s, giving vent to such feeling had come to be viewed as uncouth. About half the White population still did not approve interracial marriage in the abstract, and more were troubled at the thought of an intermarriage in their own families. But most were willing to let it happen and did not do anything publicly to oppose it.

Black Reactions to Interracial Marriage

From the era of Reconstruction down to the 1980s, Black people had rather a different set of reactions from Whites to the problem of intermarriage. Black people always were, on the whole, more accepting of interracial unions than were Whites. But that did not mean they universally—or even usually—approved.

1865–1920. The early reaction of Black people to intermarriage with Whites was almost overwhelmingly negative. There were very few who would stand with Frederick Douglass in favor of the ultimate amalgamation of White and Black. Said Douglass:

My strongest conviction as to the future of the negro therefore is, that he will not be expatriated nor annihilated, nor will he forever remain a separate and distinct race from the people around him, but that he will be absorbed, assimilated, and it will only appear finally . . . in the features of a blended race. . . . If it comes at all, it will come without shock or noise or violence of any kind, and only in the fullness of time, and it will be so adjusted to surrounding conditions as hardly to be observed. I would not be understood as advocating intermarriage between the two races. I am not a propagandist, but a prophet. I do not say that what I say *should* come to pass, but what I think is likely to come to pass, and what is inevitable.[76]

Yet Douglass's distinction was ignored by most observers, Black and White. He was taken to be not only a champion of Black political rights and a prophet of ultimate assimilation, but also an apostle of intermarriage. Many thought the last title confirmed when Douglass married Helen Pitts, a White woman, in 1884. Some Black leaders, such as T. Thomas Fortune, Blanche K. Bruce, and George Ruffin, were quick to defend Black America's foremost speaker. But more Black people registered shock and anger at what they regarded as a betrayal of their race.[77]

Many Blacks rejected interracial marriage out of an aggressive pride in blackness that grew in the years after Reconstruction. They wanted to build a strong, confident, internally integrated, economically sound, and politically protected Black people. Many were outspoken in their opposition to outmarriage. As Howard University professor Kelly Miller put it, "Self-respect does not lead to amalgamation." Washington realtor Whitefield McKinney told Congress in 1916, "I would almost rather see one of my daughters dead than to see them marry into the white race." Nearly all Black leaders wanted political rights, economic independence, and an end to segregation, but interracial marriage was on almost no one's agenda.[78]

In addition to pride of race, some Black people denigrated intermarriage partly out of fear of reprisals from enraged Whites. Thus, when in 1884 a Toledo court jailed a Black man for marrying a White woman, Ohio Black leaders did not dare protest. Booker T. Washington assured White Southerners, "I have never looked upon amalgamation as offering a solution to the so-called race problem and I know very few Negroes who favor it or even think of it for that matter," and again, "In all things that are purely social we [Black and White] can be as separate as the fingers, yet one as the hand in all things essential to mutual [economic] progress." This was not boot licking. It was partly recognition of real social and cultural differences between Black and White, a recognition—in Du Bois's words—"that a wholesale intermarriage of races during the present generations would be a social calamity by reason of the wide cultural, ethical and traditional differences." It was also realistic politics. These leaders warned Blacks against intermarriage and disavowed any interest in miscegenation, in some fraction because they knew Whites hated the idea, and, if the subject were broached, would take even firmer stands against Black rights in the economic and political areas that really mattered.[79]

Nonetheless, many of these same people—Du Bois most prominent among them—insisted on the abstract right to intermarriage even as they disavowed any interest in actually intermarrying. They called for governments to erase their own antimiscegenation laws on two grounds: respect for Black citizens and protection for Black women. Kelly Miller argued against a proposed intermarriage ban for Washington, D.C., in 1916, saying that the prospective law would be the first-ever federal move to discriminate between native-born Americans by race (for the moment Miller chose to ignore the long-standing segregation of the armed forces). Anti-intermarriage laws, said Charles H. Williams, were not intended to keep the races apart sexually so much as they were "designed as a mark of inferiority" to humiliate Black people. To Du Bois, "To prohibit such intermarriage would be publicly to acknowledge that black blood is a physical taint—a thing that no decent, self-respecting black man can be asked to admit."[80]

An equally strong motive for opposing the anti-intermarriage laws, expressed by countless Black leaders and by Du Bois again and again in the pages of *The Crisis,* was to protect Black women from the advances of White men. With intermarriage illegal, White men could seduce or compel Black women to become their mistresses, and the women had no recourse. If intermarriage were made legal, at least the Black women or their families could go to court and compel the White men to marry them or to support their illegitimate children. As the law stood in the southern states, according to Archibald H. Grimke, it gave White men "for their exclusive possession the women of their own race, and permit[ted] them at the same time to share with the men of the subject race possession of the women of that race," all without any accountability.[81] Du Bois insisted, in a heated criticism of President Harding:

We have not asked amalgamation; we have resisted it. It has been forced on us by brute strength, ignorance, poverty, degradation and fraud. It is the white race, roaming the world, that has left its trail of bastards and outraged women and then raised holy hands to heaven and deplored "race mixture." No, we are not demanding and do not want amalgamation, but the reasons are ours and not yours. It is not because we are unworthy of intermarriage —either physically or mentally or morally. It is not because the mingling of races has not and will not bring mighty offspring in its Dumas and Pushkin and Coleridge-Taylor and Booker Washington. It is because no real men can accept any alliance except on terms of absolute equal regard and because we are abundantly satisfied with our own race and blood. And at the same time we say and as free men must say that whenever two human beings of any nation or race desire each other in marriage, the denial of their legal right to marry is not simply wrong—it is lewd.[82]

Thus, many Black leaders insisted on the right to intermarry as necessary to Black citizens' dignity and self-protection, while at the same time they rejected the act of intermarriage on both practical and ideological grounds.[83]

1920–1960. Most Black people continued to reject intermarriage as social policy for the next four decades, although Black individuals and communities proved a bit more welcoming to interracial couples than did Whites. Significant segments of Black opinion also began to view interracial marriage as a positive social good.

Gunnar Myrdal insisted that Black leaders' priorities exactly inverted the Whites' rank order of fears. Myrdal found in the 1940s that Black leaders wanted for their people first jobs, then equality at law, then political participation, then access to public facilities. An end to such manifestations of petty apartheid as terms of address and marital prohibitions was decidedly less important.[84] Charismatic Black nationalist leader Marcus Garvey took a decidedly stronger tone, not just eschewing the opportunity to intermarry but also actively denouncing the possibility. In a 1924 manifesto, "What We Believe," Garvey wrote: "The Universal Negro Improvement Association advocates the uniting and blending of all Negroes into one strong, healthy race. It is against miscegenation and race suicide. It believes that the Negro race is as good as any other, and therefore should be as proud of itself as others are. . . . It believes in the purity of the Negro race and the purity of the white race. . . . It is against rich blacks marrying poor whites. . . . It is against rich and poor whites taking advantage of Negro women." Hundreds of thousands of Black Americans doubtless agreed with their leader.[85]

Other leaders were no less emphatically pro-Black, yet took a slightly softer stand, emphasizing Black rights rather than compensatory race hatred. Du Bois continued through the 1920s and '30s to repeat his denunciations of White men's depradations on Black women, but also to call for an end to antimiscegenation laws. Sterling Brown chimed in: "Intermarriage is hardly a goal that Negroes are contending for openly or yearning for secretly. It is certainly not a mental preoccupation with them and scarcely a matter of special concern. Nevertheless, they do not want laws on the statute books branding them as outcasts."[86] Scores of other Black leaders and writers agreed— from James Weldon Johnson to Rayford Logan to Langston Hughes.[87]

Yet not every Black American rejected interracial marriage as vehemently as Garvey, nor as gently but firmly as Logan or Hughes. In the 1920s and '30s there arose a generation of young people who did not remember slavery or Reconstruction. Many had come of age in the North, and some were upwardly and outwardly mobile. They continued to value their connection to their Black communities, but they also took on the education and manners of middle-class Whites. It was for this class of Black people that splashy magazines such as *Ebony,* *Jet,* and *Negro Digest* flowered in the aftermath of World War II. The editors of these magazines—*Ebony* in particular—were fascinated by Black people who were accepted by Whites, married Whites, or did the kinds of things White people did. This reflected, perhaps, not so much a longing to be White as simply a desire to be accepted as more or less ordinary, middle-class Americans. Regularly, these magazines printed features on Black artists and entertainers who had married or hobnobbed with Whites. Readers' responses, insofar as one can judge from the letters editors printed, were almost all positive.[88]

Yet most Blacks were not middle class, and very few could realistically aspire to the kind of high life that graced the pages of *Ebony.* More commonly, everyday Black Americans tended to regard interracial relationships as crazy and dangerous, and Black partners in such relationships as disloyal. They protested loudly the marriage of NAACP secretary Walter White and wondered aloud, "Is interracial marriage wrecking the NAACP?" In the 1930s, Harriet Donaldson* told Hortense Powdermaker she thought it "a sin for a colored woman to have relations with a white man," although she did not object to sex with a Black man. May Sutterfield said, "Dey ain't no 'cuse fo' it." Several observers reported Black men in southern towns bitterly resented and ostracized Black women who consorted with White men, to the point where, in one instance, a group of Black men beat up several prostitutes who served White men and drove them out of town. In the '30s and '40s, Calvin Hernton's and Analyn Colter's* families reprimanded them for making opposite-sex White friends. Hernton's grandmother beat him and yelled: "Do you want to git youself lynched! Messing round wit a *white* gurl! A little, trashy, white heifer. Do you want to git me kilt! Get all the colored folks slaughtered." The *Oklahoma Black Dispatch* reminded its readers after the White-Cannon marriage that "thousands of blacks honestly and sincerely . . . feel it is a crime for black people to marry out of their race." Lena Horne's family stopped talking to her when she married White bandleader Lennie Hayton. And shortly after the *Brown* decision against segregated schooling, a Black college president expelled one of his Black students for dating one of the new Whites on campus.[89]

One particular concern of many Black women was their own prospects if Black men married White women. As early as 1929, Palestine
Wells, a columnist for the Baltimore *Afro-American*, lamented: "I have
a sneaking suspicion that national intermarriage will make it harder to
get husbands. A girl has a hard time enough getting a husband, but
methinks 'twill be worse. Think how awful it would be if all the ofay
girls with a secret hankering for brown skin men, could openly compete with us." And so it was. After World War II, some Black women
directed special animus against Black men who brought home war
brides. Pamela Allen of Columbus, Ohio, promised to go get a White
man in retaliation, while "L.B." of Jamaica, New York, just said, "It
makes me sick."[90]

Yet, if most Black people resented intermarriage, that did not mean
they always shunned intermarried people. Black communities in both
the North and the South made places on their margins for interracial
couples. White observers, looking from outside Black communities,
generally concluded that mixed couples lived in Black communities and
became effectively Black. Annella Lynn, for instance, surveyed intermarriage in Washington, D.C., in the 1940s and concluded, "In every
instance of intermarriage with the Negro, the conjugal pair have the
social status of the Negro." So it may have appeared from outside. And,
without doubt, Black people treated mixed couples better than White
people did. But repeated testimony from inside Black communities
placed interracial couples not within those communities but on their
margins. Thus, George and Josephine Schuyler resided in Harlem, but
traveled in White as well as Black circles. Many others lived in mixed
neighborhoods or simply had few friends. Sometimes, lonely mixed
couples banded together in societies such as the Manasseh Clubs in
Chicago and Milwaukee. A group with special isolation problems were
European and Asian women married to Black former GIs after World
War II. Black women and men expressed sympathy for these women,
but still almost none had Black friends or other solid connections to
Black communities. They lived among Blacks because Whites would
not have them, but seldom did they partake fully of Black communal
life.[91]

After 1960.   The split in Black attitudes toward interracial marriage that emerged in the 1940s and '50s became sharper and more
antagonistic as the philosophy of civil rights shaded over into Black

power in the mid-1960s. On the one hand, the editors of *Ebony* and an increasing plurality of Black people expressed a positive attitude toward mixed couples. This did not necessarily mean they advocated intermarriage as social policy, only that they were less disposed than before to reject intermarried people. The long string of *Ebony* inter-marriage articles continued through the 1960s and '70s and into the '80s. But increasingly they were devoted not to a handful of celebrity couples, but to middle-class mixed families and their everyday lives. Opinion polls showed increasing acceptance: the Gallup organization found that 58 percent of Black people nationwide approved interracial marriage in 1972, 66 percent in 1978, and 71 percent in 1983. Larger numbers recognized that, whether they liked it or not, mixed couples would date and marry in rising numbers. Still, only a few expressed a willingness to become interracially involved themselves: a 1982 survey of *Essence* readers found only 37 percent of Black women would "have an intimate relationship" with a White man. Yet this percentage must surely represent a vast increase from even a decade earlier.[92]

On the other hand, with the rise in Black self-assertion in the 1960s, many Black people came to feel that integration into a White world no longer seemed so important. Alongside Martin Luther King's dream of Blacks and Whites joining hands as sisters and brothers there came another vision, not opposed but different in emphasis: a more mili-tant assertion of the value and integrity of the Afro-American people. The Nation of Islam had long preached this message, but now a wider spectrum of people began to listen. Malcolm X was very explicit: "Mr. Muhammad and his followers are violently opposed to intermarriage. . . . Let the white man keep his women, and let us keep ours. . . . Our women are the most beautiful. . . . What would we do married to a white woman? Her people don't want you in the neighborhood around them, and our fast awakening people don't want you to bring her back into our neighborhood any more to live with us." With the rise of the Black Power movement, young Black people heard Malcolm X and Stokely Carmichael call them to pride in their Blackness. They read Frantz Fanon's shattering critique of Black self-hatred and long-ing after Whiteness. Thousands of voices cried out against chasing after the sons and daughters of White people. *Negro Digest*, which formerly published many articles endorsing intermarriage, printed a piece by Charles King in 1964 titled "I Don't Want to Marry Your Daughter," and not long afterward transformed itself into a Black nationalist magazine, *Black World*. Although the Black Panther party did not follow the Muslim lead in banning interracial romance and marriage, there was heavy social pressure on politically oriented young Blacks, men and women, not to date or marry non-Blacks.[93]

This militance with regard to interracial romance was not shared equally by both sexes. It gave rise in the 1970s to a conflict between Black women and Black men that reached the point of considerable public ugliness by the end of the decade. The conflict is complex, has deep roots in the Black past, and is by no means a dead argument today. This is not the place to try to sort it out.[94] Perhaps it will suffice here to outline a few issues. The coincidence of ethnic chic—in this case White interest in the lives and fortunes of Black people—and a loosening of general sexual mores in the latter 1960s made a lot of White women suddenly available to Black men. White men did not show a similar interest in Black women, perhaps in part because of the negative imagery outlined in Chapter 9. Several observers argued that Black males choosing non-Black partners unfairly exacerbated an already difficult mating situation for Black women. Thus, Lisbeth Grant pointed in 1970 to "967,000 more black females than black males" and called on Black men to be true to Black women. To solve a "low sex ratio among Negroes, especially in the nubile years," Jessie Bernard suggested discreet bigamy or "serial polyandry." Robert Staples added that "prison, drugs and homosexuality have done much more [than interracial marriage to further] reduce the number of eligible males available to black women." All three agreed that the relative scarcity of eligible Black men gave these men a powerful position in the mating market, which sometimes led to irresponsibility and abuse against Black women.[95] The marriage dilemma seems to have been especially acute for Black women of high achievement. Black women with college educations and professional jobs far outnumbered Black men of similar status, and were often left with a choice between marrying someone lower in status and education, marrying someone non-Black, or not marrying at all. In a situation where cultural imagery and Black ideology tended to keep Black women from seeking non-Black partners, any outmarriage by Black men was bound to meet bitter resentment on the part of Black women. So, in the 1970s, as intermarriage and less formal interracial liaisons by Black males increased, a great deal of frustration came to be expressed on all sides.[96]

Despite the pressure, intergroup mating did increase during the 1970s. As pressure abated in the more individualistic late 1970s and '80s, mixed couples developed a quiet militance of their own. Forming organizations such as the Interracial Family Alliance and the Biracial Family Network, intermarried Black men and women began to assert their right not to be read out of the race. With the heat of the Black Power era abating, Black families and communities resumed their former welcome to mixed couples. The way for this quieting of angers was paved by a few Black advocates of the view that intermarriage did not necessarily make one less Black. As James Comer and Alvin Poussaint put this thesis: "Blacks are slowly learning that black is beautiful and that they need not feel inferior. Parents should not condemn black men in general because some marry white women. All men and women have the right to date and marry whomever they choose. This right should be respected."[97]

In sum, one can see three strands of thought about intermarriage developing among Black Americans. The first, beginning with Frederick Douglass and brought into the modern era by the editors of *Ebony*, was espoused by people who were proud to be Black, but who also held a universalist vision of the future that made them proud to be included on equal and intimate terms with non-Black people. A second view, initiated by W. E. B. Du Bois and popular among Black intellectuals until the White ban on interracial marriage was lifted, said that Black pride and social circumstances dictated there be no interracial marriage, but that pride also insisted upon the abstract right of Black people as citizens to marry whomever they chose. The third position, an extreme reaction to the first (and whose ancestry included David Walker and Marcus Garvey), more recently was espoused by the proponents of Black Power. For people of this group, Black pride meant that Black people married other Black people, period. The failure of some wholly to endorse this idea led to conflict between Black women and men. In recent years, the trend toward greater Black tolerance of interracial marriage seems clear.

Regional Differences in Intermarriage

The extent to which interracial marriage occurred varied considerably according to where Black people lived. As with Jewish and Japanese Americans, rates of outmarriage were high where there were few members of the ethnic community, low where there were many. In regions and neighborhoods where there were many Black people, a Black person had lots of candidates from whom to choose, and Black and White communities acted to enforce endogamy; hence, outmarriage rates were low. Where there were few Black people, individual Blacks either moved, stayed single, or married a proportionately larger number of non-Blacks.

Thus, when Thomas Monahan studied marriage records in thirty-four states and the District of Columbia between 1967 and 1970, he found high rates of outmarriage in places that had very few Black residents: 30 percent in Maine, 47 percent in Vermont, 28 percent in South Dakota, 27 percent in Hawaii. He calculated much smaller figures—varying quite a lot but circling around 4 percent—in the industrial Northeast and Midwest, and a negligible amount (less than 1 percent) in the Deep South. Even within states, intermarriage rates were lower where there were ethnic concentrations. Thus, in Monahan's study of Pennsylvania, a far higher percentage of outstate Black people married non-Blacks than did residents of Philadelphia. David Heer's study of Black outmarriage between 1960 and 1970 likewise found the highest percentage in rural areas, not just in Pennsylvania but throughout the country. Nonetheless, while it was true that *rates* of intermarriage were higher in rural areas of the North, there were so few northern rural Black people that actual *numbers* of mixed marriages were higher in the cities. Heer found the largest *increase* in the outmarriage rate in the suburbs, which began to receive a significant number of Blacks and mixed couples for the first time in the 1960s.[98]

It was not only the number of Black people that governed intermarriage rates, but also the climate of Black and White opinion. The South has long had the strictest set of race regulations, formal and informal, of any American region. There, White restrictions and phobias, and Black communal self-protection, worked to keep intermarriage rates low. In several polls taken in the 1960s and 1970s, Southerners of both races testified to greater opposition to intermarriage than did Northerners. Despite this opposition to formal intermarriage, however, the South was probably the place of the highest amount of actual sexual mixing until recent years, because of the peculiar power position of White men. Large numbers of Black women served, willingly or under duress, as mistresses to White men. Only in a few isolated rural pockets, and in cities such as New Orleans prior to the Civil War, was there much legitimate intermarriage. Even legal unions in the South more often involved Black women and White men than the opposite combination.[99]

The midwestern states present a mixed picture of intermarriage rates. In some, such as Minnesota, Iowa, and South Dakota, rates were very high. In others the rates were relatively lower. The lowest midwestern rates were found in Indiana, long a fountainhead of Klan activity.[100] Northeastern states and cities with large Black populations, such as New York and New Jersey, had the lowest amounts of out-marriage outside the South, while Massachusetts and northern New England had considerably more. The West, and especially the West Coast, with a newness and lack of entrenched boundaries between Black and White, hosted consistently higher numbers of marriages be-tween Blacks and non-Blacks than any other region. For example, in the 1970s one western Black male in six married a non-Black woman, compared to one in thirteen in the Northeast, one in sixteen in the Midwest, and one in forty in the South. Interracial marriages in the West, Midwest, and Northeast, unlike those in the South, more often coupled Black men with White women than the opposite race-gender combination. Apparently, the mutual imagery that encouraged the Black male–White female combination worked to greater effect away from the South's more repressive racial system.[101]

Class Differences in Interracial Marriage

As with Jews and Japanese Americans, class was a factor in the pat-tern of outmarriage by Blacks. But more than for those other groups, for Black Americans the pattern is fairly clear. Throughout most of this century, the small number of interracial marriages that occurred were contracted mainly by members of the middle class. This is traditionally explained by the most influential idea in the study of intermarriage: Robert Merton and Kingsley Davis's "hypogamy" theory. The idea here is that there is an economy of intermarriage, in which Black men of allegedly lower racial caste but high achievement in education or income "marry up"—that is, they marry White women—by trading their achievement for the women's higher caste status. The women in question are supposed to be members of the White lower class who consent to marrying Black men only because they thus gain men with more education or income than they would be able to command on the White marriage market.[102] Davis and Merton's theory is based on a pair of unacknowledged assumptions. It first assumes that marriage choices work on the basis of exchanges of relatively tangible qualities such as wealth and education. It further assumes the truth of the southern White racist argument, that all or most Black men always wanted to marry White women and lacked only the means. The real problem with the theory, however, is not its dubious assumptions but the fact that it does not work.

It is true that, in every region but the South, more Black men married White women than Black women married White men. And there is a bit of evidence that, at one time, the bulk of the White women who married Black men may have been members of the lower class. Charles Johnson, St. Clair Drake, and Horace Cayton, working in the 1930s and '40s, wrote that the White women in interracial marriages tended to come from the lower classes; and Drake and Cayton added that Black male intermarriers were higher in status than either their White wives or other Black people. Louis Wirth and Herbert Goldhamer, working in the 1930s with data from Boston, found that White women in intermarriages had slightly lower job status than the Black men they married. But these findings can hardly be considered conclusive. Drake, Cayton, and Johnson offer no evidence to support their assertion. Neither the Drake and Cayton nor the Wirth and Goldhamer study deals with a population base larger than a single city. And none of the three studies compares members of intermarriages with Whites and Blacks who did not intermarry.[103]

The 1970 census compared the educational attainments of exogamous and endogamous couples and found that the *best*-educated group of women were White women married to Black men. Second were White women married to White men. Third best educated were Black women married to White men. And last were Black women married to Black men. On the male side, those with the *most* education were Black men married to White women. Then came, in order, White men married to White women, White men married to Black women, and Black men married to Black women. Income data showed a similar pattern, although White men were generally higher on income than on education. As early as 1960, Jessie Bernard found that the general rule in interracial marriages was "educational homogamy," that is, most women married men who had about the same amount of education they did. These data, together with those generated by a number of other partial studies, make it hard to give much credit to the Merton-Davis theory. At least in recent decades, and probably for a considerably longer time than that, it has been the relatively well-off and well-educated members of *both* races who have been intermarrying.[104] How, then, shall one explain the persistence of the hypogamy theory? It would be silly to charge Merton and Davis with unconscious racism. But the hypogamy theory functioned, whatever its authors' intentions, as a way of degrading those White women who intermarried: of saying, in effect, that not self-respecting, but only desperate White women would choose to marry Black men. Clearly this was not true.

To be sure, couples with every combination of race and class background intermarried. Among them were working-class Blacks and lumpen proletarians. For instance, Francine Miller's* mother was a cook and her father an immigrant Italian laborer during her childhood in Washington and Philadelphia in the 1930s. In the years when White men frequently took Black mistresses in the South, many, perhaps most, of those women were lower class, for middle-class Black people shunned such unions. And White men patronized Black prostitutes, just as Black men hired White prostitutes.[105] On the other end of the scale, there seems to have been a disproportionate number of interracial marriages among those segments of the Black group most visible to the public eye: ethnic leaders and entertainers. From James Farmer and Walter White to Pearl Bailey and Harry Belafonte, members of the Black elite often overcame hostile Black and White opinion to wed interracially.[106]

But the elite group of Black entertainers and ethnic leaders was very small, and a genuine Black upper class almost nonexistent. As far as numbers went, the intermarriage issue was largely a middle-class predicament. And for some it was indeed a predicament. Most members of this class throughout modern history have been preoccupied mainly with maintaining positions of economic security and status in society. Any move toward intermarriage would certainly jeopardize that security by bringing White reprisals, and it would also open them to charges of betraying their people. Thus, one feature of the Black middle-class work ethic that developed in the first third of this century was a strong prohibition against interracial marriage. If E. Franklin Frazier is right, there was a good deal of aping of the manners of the White upper class. But members of the Black bourgeoisie drew a sharp line between imitation and interracial mixing. As Kelly Miller put it, "The refined and cultivated class among colored people are as much disinclined to [interracial marriage] as the Whites themselves."[107] For such people it was nearly impossible even to admit that interracial mating took place, especially when it involved White men and Black women in illicit relationships. Thus, when Frazier had his students at Howard—largely members of the mulatto elite—write their life stories in the 1930s, they almost always relegated the interracial coupling in their ancestry to the years before emancipation, even though they and Frazier knew that concubinage and other forms of sexual abuse of Black women continued through their own time and in their own families. Black psychologist Robert Staples and political activist Angela Davis have portrayed White men's advances on slave women not just as lust, but also as a way by which those men symbolized, even ritualized, their power over Black women and men. For middle-class Blacks, even people who were products of such unions, to recognize that such practices continued would have been to validate that ritual power relationship and invalidate the measure of independence they enjoyed as members of the middle class. For Frazier's mulatto students, and for countless Black commentators since, a refusal to acknowledge continued concubinage was one way for them to assert Black autonomy and to shore up their own individual respectability.[108]

Yet it was this middle class, which frowned on intermarriage so strenuously, that felt the strongest pressures toward interracial mixing. John Daniels found the dilemma in Boston's Black community in the 1910s. The Black masses, he said, were a coherent group, sure of their Blackness and intent on earning economic security. The small middle class, according to his analysis, constituted almost a separate community, ambivalent about both White and Black and about where they ought to plug in. Despite the period of identity security that Sidney Kronus feels came with the Black Power movement, in recent years the phenomenon Daniels observed may have returned. A growing number of middle-class Black people have shown renewed signs of ambivalence about the nature and strength of their connection to Black society. The Black working class did not show that kind of ambivalence at any time in history. As Lawrence Levine has demonstrated, Black folk culture talked a lot about color, but very little about intermarriage. But those Black people who were members of the middle class (a tiny number for many years but a growing one recently) had more education, more income, and more contact with non-Blacks. It was among them that most intermarriage took place.[109]

11. Issues and Interpretations: Passing is Passé

The blacker the berry the sweeter the juice.
I wants a real black woman for my special use.
—LEADBELLY

The Psychology of Interracial Mating

The study in Chapter 8 of psychological opinion about marriages between Jews and Gentiles uncovered three characteristic viewpoints: (1) that intermarriage was fundamentally an abnormal, neurotic act born of rebellion or self-hatred; (2) that it was a normal, healthy part of the assimilation of many American peoples into one; (3) that intermarriages may have proceeded in part from rebellious or neurotic motives, but that often they were healthy choices nonetheless. Because of the strong antipathy of White society to marriage with Blacks, very few people expressed the second view—that intermarriage was completely normal and healthy—with regard to marriage between Black and White. But the other two positions were well represented.

Observers who saw intermarrying people as fundamentally neurotic came from both Black and White camps. White sociologists and psychologists who took this view pictured Black men as seeking out White women for one of two reasons. Some saw Black men acting out of an overwhelming desire to possess the virginal forbidden fruit, the White women who represented the society's standard of beauty and therefore could compensate Black men for what these observers saw as their emasculated self-image. Others said Black men acted out of the urge to wreak revenge on White men for discrimination by taking away their women. White women, according to these views, entered inter-marriages out of rebellion against parental and communal standards, out of a desire to feed their own self-hatred by debasing themselves with inferior sexual partners, on account of neurotic fascination with Black men's alleged sexual superiority, because of compulsion to prove themselves liberal on racial matters, or out of desperation at being un-able to attract White men. Those who took this position seldom had much to say about the motives of White men or Black women, but when they did, they usually suggested much the same set of concerns about White men that they had listed for White women, and about Black women that they had noted for Black men. One additional set of motives some saw in White men was simple lust and the desire to dominate and degrade less powerful Black women.[1]

Those Black social scientists who perceived similar pathology in interracial marriages held much the same set of images as the Whites just described. Most who took this view wrote in the context of the Black consciousness movement of the 1960s and 1970s. They expressed pride in their own Blackness and a political commitment to the neces-sity of Black people's preferring their brothers and sisters to outsiders. Such psychiatric authorities as Frantz Fanon, William Grier, and Price Cobbs wrote in detail of the self-hatred and mutually feeding neu-roses they felt underlay most interracial sexual unions. Joyce Ladner summed up this line of reasoning when she wrote of "the tragedy of . . . the pathological hang-ups which almost inevitably emerge within Black male–white female relationships."[2]

A growing number of psychological observers have disputed these contentions, however. They have recognized that some of the moti-vations which others labeled neurotic—closely related to the mutual images described in Chapter 9—have in fact played a part in initial en-counters between many interracial couples. But they have insisted that the presence of such factors do not necessarily make interracial mar-riages abnormal. As Robert Staples, a Black San Francisco psychiatrist, put it, "In interracial marriages, one always looks for ulterior motives. It is said that people marry interracially because of rebellion against their parents, sexual curiosity, and other psychological reasons. But many marriages that are homogeneous take place for the same reasons. . . . People may marry 'their own kind' for the most weird reasons, yet

those reasons do not make each marriage suspect." Several students
have suggested that even in those cases where neurotic motives influenced first encounters, such factors faded as couples got to know one
another and worked their way toward marriage. Certainly, they felt,
such considerations were absent from most interracial couples' interactions by the time they had been married a few years. Alvin Poussaint
suggested recently that changes in the climate of American race relations have reduced whatever neurotic motives might once have been
at work: "It seems that fewer White women are dating Black men
solely to rebel neurotically against society or to inflict hurt on their
families. In turn, more prideful Black men do not require a White
woman to enhance their status or feelings of self-worth. Nor do they
need to compete romantically with White men for the favors of White
women." It may be that once many interracial sexual relations were
largely governed by neurotic and status motivations, but, if Poussaint
is right, that is no longer the case.[3]

Varieties of Black Americans

Among Japanese and Jewish Americans of the immigrant generation, there existed clear lines separating people according to region
of origin and other factors, and those barriers retarded marriage between subgroups. It is likely that similar barriers—separating Ashanti
from Ibo and Hausa from Fon—inhibited communication and social
intercourse among Africans and their descendants during the first few
generations after they came to America in chains. But that happened
a century and more before the time period under consideration here.
By the time with which this study is concerned, the passage of generations and the conscious mixing policies of early slave masters had
combined to blur almost completely the Old World distinctions that
once existed. Therefore, divisions within the Afro-American group did
not in the modern period assume the importance of divisions among
Japanese Americans or Jews of the immigrant generation. Nonetheless,
divisions there were, and they were not without relevance for Black
marriage choices.

Stanley Lieberson has examined possible parallels between northern Black people and immigrants from Europe and Asia. He has
suggested some very limited similarities between the first-generation

immigrants and those Black people who were born in the South and migrated northward as adults. He has found, for instance, differences in education levels between the first and second generations up from the South, much like the differences between first- and second-generation Japanese Americans or East European Jews. There is a good deal of evidence to suggest that, in the early decades of this century, Black natives of Boston, Chicago, and Washington, D.C., viewed southern migrants with a dismay akin to that felt by assimilated German Jews at the first sight of their cousins from Eastern Europe. In the late 1920s, E. Franklin Frazier found Black people of southern origin concentrated in certain Chicago neighborhoods and Chicago-born Blacks more heavily represented in others. The same types of concentrations appeared in job categories, with northern-born people occupying generally higher status slots. The northern-born Blacks he interviewed felt a sense of kinship and responsibility toward their newly arrived southern brethren, but also distaste at the latter's lack of refinement and fear that the southerners would turn Whites against all Black people. One woman asked him, "What are we going to do with all of these Negroes from the South coming in here? They look terrible." John Burke*, from an old, elite, mulatto Washington family, remembered being forbidden to play with the growing number of southern Black children in his neighborhood in the 1920s. Elizabeth Pleck studied the Black community in Boston after the Civil War and decided it was really two communities of roughly equal size: one northern-born and the other immigrant from the South. Only about one person in six married a native of the other region. Moreover, the outmarriage rate to Whites by the northern group was three times as high as the rate for those born in the South.[4]

Another, perhaps more generally perceived division existed between Black people born in America and immigrants from the West Indies. Here the dynamics of division and reluctance to intermarry were clearer. Since the early years of this century, West Indian Blacks have formed separate communities in New York, Boston, Miami, and other American cities. Although their distinctiveness from American-born Black people was not recognized by non-Blacks, that separation was nonetheless almost complete. Blacks of American and West Indian descent suffered many similar forms of discrimination at the hands of Whites. Yet they lived in different neighborhoods, worked at different jobs, and socialized with each other hardly at all. Each group held extremely negative—even abusive—stereotypes of the other. In a survey of New York City Black people taken early in the century, three out of four West Indian men married women from the Caribbean, and nine out of ten Caribbean women married West Indian men. The percentage of endogamy almost certainly increased as more West Indians came in succeeding decades, especially after World War II. Edwin Albert* was typical. Raised by Jamaican parents in a West Indian section of Roxbury, Boston's Black ghetto, Albert returned to Jamaica about 1920 to find a wife from his ancestral neighborhood rather than marry a Roxbury woman. Other people of West Indian ancestry maintained this practice for several generations, either going back to the Caribbean for mates or else marrying West Indians who lived in American cities. Although there was some pressure to identify with American Blacks at the time of the Black consciousness movement, West Indians by and large seem to have resisted that tendency. The large influx of Haitian immigrants in recent years involves an additional barrier of language between Haitians and American Blacks, and there seems to be little social interaction between these two groups. However, as third-generation, English-speaking Black people of West Indian ancestry have grown up in American schools alongside Blacks with southern ancestry in recent years, an increase in social interaction and intermarriage between those two groups appears to have begun.[5]

A third separate group consists of communities of people of mixed Black, White, and Native American ancestry, located mainly in isolated parts of the rural South. Groups such as the Melungeons and Lumbee constituted something of a curiosity in the two-category American racial system. Most existed as separate communities for many generations. Nearly all called themselves Indians and claimed only Native American and White ancestry, yet neighbors and social scientists insisted they had significant Black parentage as well. They were an anomaly, for there was no place for them in the two-caste system. For purposes of segregation, they tended to be regarded as honorary Whites, although sometimes they were segregated with Blacks or kept to themselves. In living memory, they have intermarried with Black people hardly at all.[6]

It is hard to tell whether such people as the Lumbee constituted a special group within the Afro-American people or a different people altogether. But this is perhaps not an issue of critical importance, because their numbers were so small. Similarly, although the line between American Blacks and West Indians was salient, the latter population was also small until recent years. And distinctions between Black people of southern and those of northern origin faded with the rise of a national Black culture. Although these lines among Black Americans existed, they did not much affect the overall pattern of marriage behavior. Not so with another aspect of division: consciousness of color.[7]

Social distinctions based on gradations of color did not affect Japanese or Jewish Americans. But they have been very much a feature of the Black American landscape since the time of slavery. In that early period, although many people of mixed parentage worked as slaves alongside darker Blacks, the small free Black class contained a much larger percentage of light-skinned people. In some places, such as New Orleans and Charleston, these light people formed an elite stratum separate from the Whites above and the dark slaves below. With the fall of slavery, the special middle-tier position of some light-skinned people evaporated, and light people found themselves thrust together with dark Blacks. By virtue of education and a modest degree of financial independence, Black people, many of them light-skinned, who had been free for generations were able to take over positions of leadership in Black communities in the 1870s and '80s. It came to be understood in Washington, Charleston, New Orleans, and several other cities that the Black race was led by the "mulatto elite." Doctors, preachers, business people—all such groups contained more than their share of light people. In some communities, light-toned people maintained their own clubs (such as Nashville's Blue Vein Society), their own churches, and their own neighborhoods, largely separate from both Whites and darker-skinned Blacks. Some Black colleges—Howard and Tougaloo, for example—became bastions of the light upper class. Light-skinned people not only adopted leading positions among Blacks while separating themselves where possible from fraternal contact with other Afro-Americans, but they also often copied the manners of the White upper classes: with colored cotillions, for example, and debutante balls. In the view of E. Franklin Frazier, by the end of World War I Black society had stratified into a small, substantially light-skinned elite, a "brown middle class," and a "black proletariat," at least in most cities.[8]

The conjunction of light skin and upper-class status, together with slightly less White discrimination against light people than dark Blacks, meant that light became the color of status and culture among Black Americans. For much of the modern era, in every social interaction, Black people subtly graded their speech and behavior according to an elaborate color/status hierarchy. This hierarchy was more complex in some situations than others (W.E.B. Du Bois once listed fifty-six different "types" of Black people). But where Whites saw simply Negroes, Black people saw dozens of gradations, from "ash black" to "olive brown" to "high yaller." One's color (and the curl or straightness of one's hair, the breadth or narrowness of one's nose, the thinness or fullness of one's lips) was an important part of one's identity within the Black community. In general, color gradations were more important to women than to men, for men's status depended also on economic achievement, while women in some social connections were defined solely by physical criteria. Bluntly put, the hierarchy said that lighter skin (straighter hair, higher nose, thinner lips) was better, with one important qualification. Light was good, but very light—nearly white, able to pass—was not good. Charles Johnson interviewed hundreds of southern teenagers in the 1930s. He found light brown was their favorite color—for themselves, for friends, for members of the opposite sex —but seldom yellow or white. E. Franklin Frazier also interviewed hundreds of Black young people in those same years in the North and South. Those interviews revealed lots of people wanting to be as light as possible and to associate with light people, but never to be White, and never for the purpose of mating with Whites, or even becoming more acceptable to Whites. Rather, their interest was to achieve status *within* Black communities. As Bonnie Allen put it, "I've never really believed we were trying to look white, because I've met few Blacks who truly wished they were white. We were simply trying to look like that color of Black people who were supposedly getting over."[9]

Afro-Americans developed a set of associations that went with dark skin and African features. Some of the character qualities that were deemed to represent dark people were positive. For instance, Louise, a dark Louisville eighth-grader interviewed by Thelma Colman in 1938, registered her belief that "Honey, black is honest and yellow is low down." But other associations recalled the negative images Whites had of Negroes generally. Dark people were supposed by some to be violent, animalistic, stupid, criminal, and hard to get along with.

Dark people had always to fight the stereotypes expressed by some of Johnson's teenagers: "Black is ugly," "Black people are mean," "Black people are evil," and "Black people don't hold good jobs."[10]

People of lighter skin abused their darker fellows, especially as youngsters. Junior high taunts in the 1950s ranged from "big-lip" and "nappy-head" to "monkey" and "nigger." Very dark children sometimes would be the last chosen for schoolyard games. Ridicule of dark complexions came not just from light people but also from other dark Negroes, and not just from children. A song of the Blue Vein circle, recorded in the 1910s, went in part:

> Stan back, black man,
> You cain't shine;
> You lips is too thick,
> An you hain't my kin'.

Sometimes the best that a light adult could say was, "She's pretty for a black child, smart for a black child."[11]

All this abuse made some dark people wish they were lighter. Johnson and Frazier interviewed dozens of dark Black people who consciously or subconsciously wished to be just a little bit lighter, in order to feel better about themselves and avoid abuse. They did not want to be white, because, Johnson said, "The Negro community is built around the idea of adjusting to being a Negro, and it rejects escape into the white world." But Johnson found that the people he interviewed "consistently rated their own complexions a shade or more lighter than they appeared to be." "Baby," a light girl whom Colman interviewed in 1938, recalled that "in elementary school, there was one very dark little colored girl who used to lick her hand and rub it very hard trying to make her hand as white as mine." Virginia, a high school student interviewed by Colman, said, "I think my color is just fine if I was just a little bit lighter." In order to achieve this, Black people—women especially—invested millions of dollars and incalculable pain and anxiety in hair relaxers and bleaching creams, not trying to be White, just trying not to be dark.[12]

Many Black people did not want to marry someone dark. Mozell Hill asked over four hundred Black teenagers in the early 1940s their preferences in a prospective husband or wife; nearly all stated they wanted someone their own shade or lighter. Dozens of the people

interviewed by Colman and Frazier indicated they would choose light
or tan mates over dark candidates, sometimes even if the dark prospects were more attractive in every other way.[13] Light parents and
dark, hoping for upward mobility for their children, pushed them to
marry light. Eleanor Roberts* told Frazier, "As we became older and
I started to receive company, daddy [a dark man] began to drill me,
that he did not want me to marry a dark man." Belle Winters* recalled
that "there wasn't a brown skin person in my family before I married Robert. When my mother found out that I had married him she
almost died. Honey, it was a shame the way my family treated him,
just because he wasn't light." Bonnie Allen remembered even "dark
parents who were visibly shaken when we brought dark-skinned dates
to parties at their homes."[14] Folksongs sung by Black males frequently
praised light women or made fun of their dark sisters. Newman White
heard this verse in 1928:

> It takes a long, tall yaller gal
> To make a preacher lay his Bible down,
> It takes a long, tall yaller gal
> To make a bulldog break his chain.

Verbal abuse against dark women was more common. Leon Strickland
sang in 1959:

> I don't want no jet black woman
> Oh to fry no meat fo' me,
> Lord, black is evil,
> She like to kill poor me.

And a man passing through Cleveland on a train in 1919 sang, "I don't
want no jet black woman for my regular." Lawrence Levine rightly
points out that only a dark man would have dared say in public such
negative things about dark women. But the positive inclination toward
light women was expressed by men of all hues.[15] Such defamation of
dark people was also much more commonly done by men than by
women. Many observers noted the tendency of successful dark men to
confirm their status by marrying light women. This gender difference
reflected the fact that perceived beauty in American society is more
important in men's mate choices than in women's; in women's eyes,
other qualities such as economic achievement stand higher on the list.[16]

One reason for the interest in a light mate was to produce light children. Often, parents would hope for light babies. They anxiously read articles with titles such as "What Color Will Your Baby Be?" hoping Mendel's laws would work in their favor. If the babies came out dark, they were subject to abuse from parents and lighter siblings. Nadine Allen* told Frazier: "Dad never took us out much. . . . because he was ashamed of my brother and I because we were so very dark. . . . My brother was very dark and unattractive. When my mother scolded him, she would always call him an ugly duckling. Everyone in the family laughed at him. . . . None of my sisters liked to take him out [one even denied knowing him in a store]. . . . On my part, I was glad to be able to ridicule him." While the other children in this family were happy, ambitious, and did well in school, this young boy suffered emotionally: he became careless of his clothing, lost interest in school, and eventually dropped out. Among upper-class, light families in Mississippi in the 1930s, dark babies were regularly sent away to be raised by dark relatives in other towns, rather than embarrass their natural parents.[17]

If light was beautiful, that did not mean that all the folk images of extremely light-skinned people were equally positive. The most debilitating stereotype was the stigma of illegitimacy. Louise again: "Girl, yellah is low down, 'cause mama said yellah comes from messin' around with uh white man an' anytime a niggah goes to layin' aroun' 'em he's low and anything that comes from it is low." In the popular eye, very light people might be rich, but they were likely to be overly thrilled by the wonder of their own beauty. They were apt to be high-strung, flighty, and undependable. They were also seen as sexually loose and dishonest, perhaps because of the association with illegitimacy.[18]

Black adults and children could be just as mean to extremely light people as to the very dark. The youths Johnson interviewed agreed that the "worst color to be," next to black, was yellow. Lena Horne remembered that in Georgia in the 1920s "I was often called little yellow bastard" and other names by darker children. As a small child, Eartha Kitt heard her mother and uncle fighting:

> "You gotta leave here," my uncle said.
> "But I haven't found any place to go."
> "I don't care," my uncle said, "but you can't stay *here!*"

"I'm no trouble to you. . . ."

"I don't want that *yellah gal* in my house. I told you that before!"

So Kitt, her mother, and baby brother had to walk alone across South Carolina until they found a blind woman who would take them in. The abuse was bad enough for the Breneski girls in Chicago in 1950 that their mother taught them to dress, speak, and make themselves look like Whites, so they could pass and leave Black harassment behind.[19]

Some Black people—mainly those of dark hue themselves—spoke of a preference for dark-colored mates. In 1954 Louis Armstrong confided to *Ebony*, "I'm partial to brown and dark-skinned women." He married four. Fifteen-year-old Louise said, "I don't care so much fer real light boys, you know boys with light hair and light eyes, 'cause they jest liable tuh called me black an' I'll be damned if I let any niggah git away with calling me black. As long as they are brown or 'round my color I can stand 'em."[20] Lemon Nash sang in New Orleans in 1959:

> 'Cause some crave for yellow, please give me black an' brown,
> Some say some crave for yellow, please give me black an' brown,
> Your black gal be wit' you, when your yellow gal turn you down.

And Leadbelly and Big Bill Broonzy sang:

> The blacker the berry the sweeter the juice.
> I wants a real black woman for my special use.

Yet, even in the darker range, most people preferred someone their own color or slightly lighter—not darker. And for all the tendency of the dark minority to praise dark skin, almost no one is recorded as hoping to have a dark child.[21]

Although many Black people, especially members of the middle class, were fixated on lightness, while others (perhaps defensively) extolled the virtue of darkness, there were always other trends. The Harlem Renaissance of the 1920s was, from one angle of vision, a cultural celebration of brownness and an attempt to include Afro-Americans of all hues in one brown people, a harmonious middle between militant black and slavish yellow. At the same time, blues singers of all descriptions reflected a strong folk feeling in their frequent statements that brown was to be preferred over both black and yellow. Lawrence Levine even ventures that "brown was held up as the ideal in so many songs that it, rather than lighter shades, may well have been the goal of many of those who used skin lighteners."[22]

In addition to the exponents of brownness, there were always those who stood ready simply to ridicule Black people for what they regarded as an absurd color fixation. Not all the readers of *Ebony* and *Negro Digest* thought the "What Color Will Your Baby Be?" articles were in good taste. George Schuyler wrote a biting, satirical novel called *Black No More* in which a Black scientist discovers a way to turn Black skin to White and immediately upsets both Black and White status systems. Zora Neale Hurston scorned the upper-crust pretensions of light mulattoes. She, too, was mixed, she said, but "I am the only Negro in the United States whose grandfather on the mother's side was *not* an Indian chief. Neither did I descend from George Washington, Thomas Jefferson, or any Governor of a Southern State." In writings and speeches, Malcolm X savagely rebuked Black people for their color mania: "I was among the millions of Negroes who were insane enough to feel that it was some kind of status symbol to be light-complexioned —that one was actually fortunate to be born thus. But, still later, I learned to hate every drop of that white rapist's blood that is in me."[23]

Here were the roots of another kind of consciousness, which re-garded people of African ancestry as one and refused to draw lines of color. With the flowering of the Civil Rights and Black Power move-ments of the 1950s and '60s, the old color/status hierarchy all but died. The Black consciousness movement called on Afro-Americans of all colors to stand together. Ads in Black magazines ceased to feature light, White-looking models and replaced them with people of darker tones. Color became less a factor in the marriage mart. Richard Udry, Karl Bauman, and Charles Chase surveyed Black marriages in Washington, D.C., that occurred in the 1950s and '60s, and found the status and marriage prospects of dark men improved markedly over that period, to the point where they were indistinguishable from the opportunities afforded lighter men. But not all was equal. The study showed that Black men, light and dark, continued to marry wives lighter than they, and continued to leave out very dark women. For all that Black leaders preached the oneness of the race, some vestiges of color consciousness remained. The state of affairs led Alexis De Veaux to conclude, sadly, that "quiet as it's kept . . . in 1982 *color is still a critical issue among our people.* We still discriminate against our own. The darker ones against the lighter ones. The light ones against the dark." [24]

How important were all these distinctions within the Afro-American group? As the twentieth century progressed, some became more important, some less so. The substantial and increasing numbers of West Indians in the 1960s, '70s, and '80s made their distinctiveness from other Black people a live issue. The 1970 Black population of foreign origin (almost all West Indians) was nearly half a million, or slightly more than 2 percent of the total Black population. In 1980, the foreign-*born* Black population alone (not counting American-born people of West Indian ancestry) totalled more than 800,000, or 3 percent of the total Black population. In the industrial Northeast, more than 10 percent of all Black people were natives of the West Indies, and others had West Indian ancestry. [25] Yet the Lumbee and other mixed communities were so tiny as to be inconsequential except for race relations in their immediate localities. With the rise of a relatively homogeneous national Black culture after World War II, the distinction between southern and northern Blacks became no more important than that between southern and northern Whites. And while color differences remained important to some Afro-Americans as late as the 1970s, there was no longer the clear hierarchy of light over dark which once had been common. Altogether, at no time within the purview of this study were intragroup divisions among Black people as important as they were among Jewish or Japanese immigrants. As with those groups, such distinctions declined enormously over the years.

Hierarchies of Choice

Jewish and Japanese Americans showed clear, stable patterns of preference as to whom they would choose to marry. Not only did they select members of their own group first, but their hierarchies of choice as to who else was acceptable showed remarkable stability over the course of the twentieth century. As generations passed and the Old Country became an ancestral memory, both Jews and Japanese grew more willing to consider candidates further down the ladder.

The case of Black Americans is considerably more complex. One can discern hierarchies of preference, based both on whom people talked about as possible partners and on whom they actually married. But Black people's choices were so sharply circumscribed by White power and fears that it is sometimes hard to tell what were Black people's choices and what was imposed upon them. Unlike Japanese Americans and Jews, with Blacks there was no neat progression down the ladder from generation to generation. Hierarchies of actual choices (if not theoretical preferences) can be traced, but categories of people move up or down from period to period, not consistently in a single direction. Finally, the immigration-derived classification scheme of first, second, and third generations simply will not work for Black people. Change did happen in relations between Blacks and other Americans, but it took a longer time than one generation for much movement to make itself visible.

Let me propose, for the purpose of examining Black hierarchies of mate choice, that we consider three periods: the years before emancipation; the era of northward migration and establishment in the industrial economy, roughly 1890–1950; and the period since the height of the Civil Rights movement in the early 1960s.

In the time of slavery, the mate choices of Black people were clearly limited, for most were slaves, and their masters had at least to give assent to any marriage or cohabitation. Slaves did a lot of their own choosing, as Herbert Gutman has shown. But they might also have a choice forced on them, and they were almost always limited to candidates from the immediate neighborhood. Slaves sometimes married free Blacks, but this was not common. There is some fragmentary evidence to suggest that some American-born slaves preferred other native-born, English-speaking people to recent imports from Africa, but that is by no means conclusive. Especially in the seventeenth and eighteenth centuries, a sizeable minority married Indians, although that practice seems to have declined with the removal of most southeastern tribes in the 1830s. From the available evidence and a modest amount of interpolation, one comes up with a hierarchy like the following. A slave would be most likely to choose another American-born slave who lived in the neighborhood and whom the master approved. He or she might also marry a free Black person or a recent arrival from Africa, but that was less likely. It was also conceivable that a Black slave might marry an Indian, although that option became less likely as the nineteenth century proceeded. Marriage to a White partner would be outside the bounds of possibility.[26]

Free Black people had rather a different set of priorities. They had slightly better access to White partners than did slaves. They also showed distinct preferences by color: light people of color fared much better on the marriage market than dark free Blacks. One can construct a hierarchy for free Black people that shows a scheme of color preferences at the top, with light free people preferred over dark. After free people would come slaves. That was as far as most free Black people went. It was conceivable, but unlikely, that a free Black person might marry a Native American or a White. Other varieties of Americans were beyond their ken.[27]

The above hierarchies are admittedly somewhat conjectural. One is on firmer footing when talking about the first half of this century. Here, the elaborate schemes of color and status set forth in the preceding section come into play. People would choose, if they could, a Negro of about their own shade or one a little lighter. Failing that, they would choose someone darker or a very light mulatto. They would also be likely to pick someone born in their own part of the country, South or North. If they failed to achieve their preferences in these areas, they would simply marry an American Black. Black people recognized that it was possible to marry others, such as West Indian Blacks or people of such mixed racial groups as the Lumbee, and a few of them did so. Almost no one married Whites, Native Americans, or others.[28]

As with Japanese and Jewish Americans, so too for American Blacks, in recent years the distinctions within the group which once meant so much no longer had much relevance to mate choice. Divisions among American Blacks by color and region were no longer very important after the era of the Civil Rights movement. Black people whose ancestors came from the English-speaking West Indies were clearly the next choice. It was significantly less likely that an American Black person would marry a French-speaking Haitian immigrant, Caucasian, Mexican American, Indian, or someone else, though all those combinations did begin to occur. If the Black person in question were an ethnic activist, she or he might put other Americans of color before Whites, but other Blacks reacted in just the opposite fashion.[29]

Altogether, one may say that there was some progression down the ladder of preference over the generations. But it was much slower than for Jews or Japanese Americans. Non-Blacks were still, in the 1980s, less acceptable as partners in Black communities than were Gentiles in the eyes of Jews or non-Japanese in the view of Japanese Americans.

Interracial Marriage and Divorce

Those people, Black and White, who opposed interracial marriage and tried to talk their friends and relatives out of entering such unions almost invariably predicted marital breakup in short order. Harassment from relatives and the public, together with the presumed cultural incompatibility of the couple, would tear them apart. Using the traditional tools of the historian—that is, whatever evidence comes readily to hand—one can find many people who stated with conviction that most Black-White marriages ended in divorce or desertion. One can find an equal number who insisted there was no relationship between intermarriage and family instability. Witness the conclusion of St. Clair Drake and Horace Cayton after such a search: "There is, however, no evidence to indicate that the divorce rate is higher among the inter-married than in the population as a whole; indeed there is reason to think that the reverse may be true. The fact that they have violated a taboo together may well act as an additional bond between interacial couples." [30] All this is mere assertion, without benefit of evidence. So, how does one choose between such firmly opposing opinions?

Giving up the fuzzy-thinking eclecticism of traditional historical method, one turns to recent sociologists, who are much better at counting things. One soon finds, however, that much depends on what things they count. David Heer used the U.S. census and counted by racial combination the number of people who had married only once, were first married between 1950 and 1960, and were still married in 1960. Then he compared that to the number of such couples who were still married a decade later. According to his calculations, in the ten-year period between 1960 and 1970, 10.2 percent of the marriages between White men and women had dissolved (through divorce, desertion, or death), compared to 22.2 percent of the marriages between Black men and women, 36.6 percent of those between Black men and White women, and 53.3 percent of those between Black women and White men. Assuming that death rates were equal for each combination, it would seem clear that interracial marriages were less stable than all-White or all-Black marriages, and that the kind of couple in most danger of a breakup was the Black woman married to a White man.[31]

Thomas Monahan, however, looked at a different set of data, used an equally scientific approach, and came up with nearly opposite conclusions. He culled the actual marriage and divorce records for Iowa and Kansas and compared the number of interracial marriages to the number of interracial divorces. He found the divorce rate for all-Black couples was much higher than for all-White couples. But he also found that Black-White couples divorced far less often than pure Black couples; in Iowa they even divorced slightly less often than all-White couples.[32]

Whom shall one believe? Admittedly, there are criticisms to be made of both men's methods. Heer relied on census data. These listed, as married, people who lived together, however temporarily, and recorded, as single, those who lived apart, if only for a short time. Living together and living apart are not the same thing as being married and being divorced. The Heer study also assumed that death affected the numbers for Blacks and Whites equally. This is silly, for the life expectancy of Blacks—and of Black men in particular—was substantially below that of Whites in this period.[33] Yet Monahan's work was also not without flaws. He chose data from Iowa and Kansas, which had only tiny Black populations that were clearly unrepresentative of the majority of Black people in the South or the industrial cities. These criticisms of method, however, do not lead one very far. One can scarcely guess which direction a more representative sample than Monahan's might go. In Heer's case, a proper accounting for death rates would probably move the Black and intermarried couples' divorce rates a fraction closer to the rate for Whites. But the gap between a more representative Monahan and a purified Heer would still be far too large to explain. What is clear, then, is that nothing is clear. We do not know if marriages between Black and White have a higher rate of divorce than homogamous unions, a lower rate, or substantially the same rate. The experiences of outmarried Jews and Japanese Americans would suggest the likelihood of a slightly higher rate, but that is conjecture.

Mulattoes and Passing

Thus, it is not clear whether opponents were correct in their contention that interracial marriages suffered a higher divorce rate than marriages within racial boundaries. It appears, however, that they were not far wrong when they warned that children of those marriages were likely to be unhappy. Mulattoes, taken as a group, were never so lost, bitter, and frustrated as racist mythology described them. Yet for most of this century many mixed people endured abuse from relatives and the larger public on account of their racial mixture, and some suffered significant identity conflicts. Only in the last two decades has the bulk of the mulatto population enjoyed more freedom from such concerns.

Fiction, theater, film, and the scholarly community were nearly unanimous in their depiction of the Tragic Mulatto. In the hands of Whites from Thomas Nelson Page to William Faulkner, the child of an interracial couple invariably grew up tortured psychologically about his or her mixed inheritance. To pioneer sociologist Edward Reuter, "The mixed blood is thus [by definition] an unadjusted person." For some White writers, mulattoes seemed intellectually superior to other Blacks (though inferior to Whites). In the eyes of others they were inferior to both. In the early part of the century, most commentators saw mixed people as physically weaker and more fragile than other Blacks, and therefore as likely to die out. Some saw them as morally degenerate and sexually licentious. Nearly all saw them as psychically divided, torn between the Blackness they were said to despise and the Whiteness toward which, it was said, they aspired and which was denied them. It is worth noting that Black writers shared many of these same ideas. From Charles W. Chesnutt to Nella Larsen, they, too, saw mulattoes as torn between Black and White. But unlike Whites, these Black writers did not see anything characterologically wrong with mulattoes. In the view of these articulate Black people, it was not warring and defective genes but social pressures that tore mulattoes apart.[34]

People of part-Black parentage never found a welcome reception in White society. At best they were always regarded as second-class citizens. During the slavery epoch, a few free mulattoes managed to carve out a social niche between White and Black in certain parts of the South. But with emancipation, Whites exerted ever more pressure on them to join the Black group completely. The rule Whites tried to enforce was that one drop of "Negro blood" made one Black. This dashed the hopes of some late-century mulattoes who would have liked to have been accepted by Whites. People of mixed ancestry encountered all the petty snubs and serious insults that their Black half-brothers and -sisters endured. As children, they were called "Nigger" on playgrounds. As teenagers, they saw their few White friends drift away as the dating urge took over their system of priorities. In adulthood, they found White people staring at them in public, asking them about their racial origins, hesitating to serve them, and politely suggesting they look elsewhere for work. White relatives could be especially brutal. Almost none of the more than three hundred Chicago mulattoes Robert Roberts interviewed in the 1930s, '40s, and '50s had ever enjoyed a close relationship with his or her White grandparents, and most had no such relationship at all (this situation improved slightly in the 1960s).[35]

Black people spread a slightly warmer, though not a unanimous, welcome. Black people's color prejudices worked against very light mulattoes, who were frequently accused of thinking themselves smarter, more beautiful, and generally better than other Blacks. Some stigma of illegitimacy attached to mulattoes, especially those whose fathers were absent and White. Yet Marcus Garvey was alone among major Black leaders in rejecting mulattoes in his speeches and writings (and even he had light-skinned people in his organization). Most Black people seemed willing to accept mulattoes into their communities so long as they committed themselves to other Blacks and did not go chasing after Whites. As one young mulatto put it, "The colored students accept me until I act as if I am interested in becoming friendly with a white girl." Black families were more warmly disposed to mixed children than were Whites. In Roberts' Chicago study, in the 1930s, over half the mulattoes had little or no contact with their Black relatives. But shortly that situation was redressed, and by the 1960s most were reporting "close" or "very close" extended family relationships.[36]

The imagery of American popular culture described mulattoes as anguished and torn between their two ancestral strains. To be sure, there were people who fit this description, but they seem always to have been a fairly small minority. Far more common were those mixed people who identified with Blacks. A certain number were able even to muster stable biracial identities.

Much has been written about the peculiar two-category system of American race relations. With such brief, marginally important exceptions as the small mulatto castes in some antebellum southern cities, the one-drop rule prevailed: any visible admixture of African heritage made one Black. Americans, Black and White (though rather more uniformly Whites), took this for granted. But it need not necessarily have been so. Even South Africa's starkly divided society has had room for an intermediate category, the Coloureds, whose members are largely the products of ancient interracial matings, but also include people added surreptitiously in modern times. Brazilians developed a stratified social system with a series of gradations between Black and White; mixed children (and most were a mix of one sort or another) were assigned positions according to their physical attributes, chiefly color. Among other groups of Americans—we have looked at Japanese Americans and Jews—mixed offspring have not automatically been consigned to the non-WASP group. In fact, since neither Jews nor Japanese would admit mixed people until recent years, such people of necessity became part of the majority group. White Americans also felt differently about Native Americans than about Blacks. After American Indians had been well-nigh exterminated, they ceased to be perceived as a threat to White supremacy. Then, in this century, White individuals could say with some pride that they were "part Indian" (usually some nonthreatening part: a female ancestor several generations removed). But one was not allowed to say she or he was "part Black." The size and very visible oppression of the Black American group, together with the mythology of Black violence and sexual rapaciousness, made Blacks a continuing threat. Once the small proportion of mulattoes who formed an intermediate group had been pushed down into the Black caste, no exit could be allowed.[37]

That was fine as far as most people of half-Black parentage were concerned. Prominent Black leaders from Booker T. Washington to Walter White were pleased to eschew whatever opportunities they might have had to pass as White, in favor of identifying themselves with their Black sisters and brothers. White described his position this way: "I am a Negro. My skin is white, my eyes are blue, my hair is blond. The traits of my race are nowhere visible upon me. . . . [But]

I am not white. There is nothing in my mind and heart which tempts me to think I am." He concluded, "I am one of the two in the color of my skin; I am the other in my spirit and my heart." Countless light-skinned mixed people agreed. Herb Jeffries, popular singer and movie star of the 1940s and '50s, would surely have had a more successful career had he listened to the advisers who tried repeatedly to get him to present himself as a Spaniard of Latin American extraction and thus qualify for parts opposite White leading ladies. Jeffries refused, citing the one-drop rule: "I'd always heard that if you had *any* Negro blood you were a Negro and that was that. . . . Then it can't be such inferior blood, can it? If you had a black paint that was so powerful that two drops of it would color a bucket of white, that'd be the most potent paint in the world, wouldn't it? So if Negro blood is as strong as all that it must be pretty good—maybe I'd better find out where I can get some more of it."[38]

Of course, not all mixed people were as sure of their Black identity as Jeffries or White. Some showed ambivalence and anxiety. Author Jean Toomer went through great swings of mood, sometimes immersing himself in Blackness, finally denying that any African blood flowed in his veins. R. Russo, eighteen-year-old daughter of a Black woman and an Italian man, expressed inner turmoil in a 1951 letter to *Ebony:* "No one can suspect I have Negro blood in me but I don't want to deny it. Yet, if I don't, I can't make a living. You see I find it hard to get along with both races. If I am with whites, they resent me because of my mother. The Negroes also don't accept me as one of them. I tried to go to dances and such but it's even more difficult there. If a Negro asks me to dance and I accept, he immediately thinks I am no good, just 'white trash' out for a thrill. What am I supposed to do? Go around with a sign on me saying I'm half white and half black?" Yet these were varieties of anguish felt only by the lightest of mixed people, and not by all of them. In general, such identity ambivalence was more common where one parent was missing during childhood, or where parents made little or no attempt to help their mixed children make stable identity choices.[39]

Another choice besides a simple Black identity was sometimes available to mixed people: they could choose to see themselves as both Black and White. Occasionally a child of mixed race would be brought up in a situation that allowed him or her this uncommon flexibility. Thus, George and Josephine Schuyler's prominence and relative wealth allowed them in the 1940s to insulate their daughter Philippa from most kinds of discrimination and to encourage her to embrace both parts of her background. Isabelle Rivierez was raised in Europe, where both halves were generally recognized. David Evans simply had an obstinate father who resisted categorization, saying: "People tell me that I must fit in to this system of classification—that I must put David into one racial group or another. . . . I have refused to do it." Francine Miller's* family moved so often from White to Black to mixed neighborhoods that she usually just identified with whichever set of people were around her. Between 1892 and 1932, Chicago's Manasseh Society (named after the biblical Joseph's half-Egyptian son) provided a support system for interracial families and biracial individuals that emphasized embracing both parts of one's identity. These were clearly atypical cases, yet their number grew. Roberts' Chicago interviews revealed that most biracial individuals, from the 1930s through the 1960s, identified themselves as Black and were so regarded by others. A small, growing number gave universalist answers to the identity question, calling themselves "human," "a person," or "just me." But by the 1950s more than a third came to insist on being identified with both White and Black. The patterns of their friendships, neighborhoods, and other cultural indicators showed the same movement, from almost exclusively Black in the 1930s to substantially mixed in the 1950s.[40]

The final option for a biracial person was to identify herself as White. This phenomenon—*passing*—was once far more common than it has been in recent years.[41] It flew in the face of the rules of racial order, but it was nonetheless a popular way out of identity ambivalence. Passing was once studied far out of proportion to the number of people it affected. Perhaps this was because of a lurid fear on the part of some White people that some morning they would wake up and find the person with whom they had slept was not White after all. From the 1920s to the 1940s, no book on Black people or race relations was complete without a section on passing. Novelists treated the subject bountifully.[42] Not all passing was done by people with a White parent. The requirements were light skin, sharp features, and smooth hair; actual White ancestry could be two or more generations distant. Yet a large percentage of those who passed as White doubtless were the offspring of intermarriages. For them, the psychic dilemmas of passing were heightened because of identification with the White parent.

Light people passed as White in a variety of circumstances and for a variety of reasons. For some, passing was unintentional. Several light-skinned northern visitors reported taking their seats in the Black sections of southern buses and ballparks, only to be removed by distraught attendants who refused to believe they were Black and accused them of being "Nigger-lovers." Rayford Logan served as an officer with the U.S. Army in France and Germany during and after World War I. At one point, a colonel's inattention led to Logan's being assigned briefly to a White unit. When his company commander was called away, Logan found himself commanding a White outfit: "For a week white shavetails, non-coms and 'bucks' obeyed my orders with an alacrity that stupefied me. . . . One white orderly was busy shining my shoes. Another was packing my bedding roll. . . . At no time did any one seem to suspect that an unwritten law of the American Army was being merrily trampled underfoot."[43]

Perhaps the most common type of passing was an occasional, brief trip across the color line. Mary Church Terrell admitted, "I have sometimes taken advantage of my ability to get certain necessities and comforts to which I was entitled by outwitting—but never once in my life have I even been tempted to 'cross the color line' [permanently] and deny my racial identity." She and other light people might present themselves as White (or, more often, simply say nothing about racial identity) in order to enjoy an evening in a White restaurant or theater, a more comfortable seat on a train, or just the joy of putting one over on the Whites. Ruby McAllister admitted in 1954: "I really get a kick out of it now. I mingle on both sides." Yet even in this casual sort of passing, there were psychic costs. "L. L." attended a prestigious New England women's college in the 1930s and found that people did not recognize her as Black. She eventually told her classmates, but sometimes went to dances where she was the only Black person. "I found the men interested in me until they learned I wasn't Spanish or South American or something beside Negro. Sometimes I would amuse myself by not stating my racial identity at first, but later in the evening casually drop the word and watch how quickly the young men would fade away." Such experiences left her feeling very alone. Miriam Frederick* told Everett Stonequist how she used to pass in order to get service at a White beauty salon until she silently—for fear of exposure—witnessed the salon's White operators making racial slurs and mistreating a Black nanny who brought in some White children. "She was a neighbor of mine. I hated it, but I had to walk by her without speaking. I've never been back since."[44]

The tension of a double life was more intense for light Black people who held jobs as White but returned to Black friends and neighbors at night. Frank Collier* told his story in 1946: "I pass, myself. Every day from nine to five I'm a white man. I've got a good job downtown; I do the work well, and I've had two raises. But I'd never have been hired if I had said I had Negro blood. When I applied, I gave my race as white and my nationality as Spanish, and neither statement was ever questioned. I keep a little room in a white part of town, to bolster my story if necessary, but I seldom go there. Nearly every night I come home to Harlem because my folks and all my friends are colored." But Collier was tense lest someone find out his deception, for he was certain he would lose his job.[45] Countless light women worked for department stores that refused to hire Blacks, and lived in constant fear that a Black customer would recognize them and inadvertently expose their identity.[46]

After brief experiments and perhaps a stint of living on both sides at once, some brave or driven souls decided to pass across the line completely. This was the most sensational sort of passing, although it probably involved fewer people than the varieties described above. This behavior inspired books such as *I Passed for White* and *The Autobiography of an Ex-Coloured Man* and movies such as *Lost Boundaries* and *Pinky*. Ernest Torregano, a light-colored minstrel show performer, left his Black wife and daughter in New Orleans in 1911. They were soon told that he had died, although his mother and another passing brother knew his whereabouts until the 1940s. Torregano moved to San Francisco, where at first he went as a Black man until deciding to cross the line. He went to law school at night, married a White woman, passed the bar examination, and began a celebrated career as a White bankruptcy lawyer. At his death in 1954 he was one of San Francisco's wealthiest and most prominent citizens, and he had never contacted the family he left behind. For many such passers, the hardest thing was saying goodbye forever to family and friends, or having to leave without saying anything. For others it was the fear of being exposed or the loneliness, knowing no one could be trusted with their secret. Some passers who married White people informed their mates, but usually not until long after the marriages had been firmly established. Others, probably most, never let on. Sometimes two light Black people would marry and cross the line together. For them, the besetting fear was giving birth to a dark baby who would give them away. Ralph and Martha Matthews* had two very light children, but their third, Eve, began to show signs of turning dark. Ralph told John Hewlett, "We love Eve, but we may have to let her go back to relatives in Harlem. It wouldn't be fair to Tom and Annette. It would be too dangerous, too risky. We couldn't take the chance." The loneliness of this type of existence, the sense of betrayal of one's origins—that one had, in James Weldon Johnson's words, "sold my birthright for a mess of pottage"— drove many passers eventually to abandon their pretense and return to their former Black existence. More, however, probably stayed on the White side of the line.[47]

Not much can be known for sure about the dimensions of so clandestine an activity as passing. Nearly all observers agreed that the large majority of those who passed permanently were men, beginning especially with the era of northward migration in the 1900s and 1910s. Men had more freedom of movement than women. They made up a larger proportion of those who left the South—but not of those who arrived in the North, according to census statistics. The conclusion is inescapable that many passed. Attempts to pin down the magnitude of the crossing were based largely on conjecture and varied between 2,500 and 25,000 per year for the first two decades of this century. According to Robert Stuckert's more careful guesses, passing involved about 3,000 people per year in the decades after slavery, 5,000 each year in 1891–1910, and ranged up to a high of 15,000 per year in 1941–50. If numbers must remain in doubt, it is clear that passing was mainly an urban phenomenon, for individuals had to achieve an anonymity they could hardly find in rural areas.[48]

Other Black people viewed all this passing with mixed emotions. Black novelists such as Jessie Fauset, Nella Larsen, and Walter White depicted passers as unhappy, lonely, and tortured by self-doubt until they gave up their pretense and returned to their people. Many other Blacks—especially people with dark skins—agreed. Rosamund, a Louisville high school student interviewed in the 1930s, expressed typical sentiments: "I don't think it is right. Negroes don't have to pass to get good jobs. Some people say they do but those people are just lazy and want something for nothing. I really don't like it. If you're born in one race you should stay in it." But people of lighter complexions could understand the temptation. In most situations, if a Black person encountered someone passing, she would not let on, even if she opposed the practice herself. Dorothy Smith told *Ebony* in 1951 that, in her opinion, "If a person can pass successfully with a clear conscience, it is her business." Others judged that acquiring a good job was an acceptable motive. James Conyers polled over four hundred Black people around 1960 and found most would not pass if they could, but most thought light people were entitled to make their own choices.[49]

There were other passing situations besides adult Black people passing themselves off as White. Sometimes Black children became White without even knowing what was going on. Mary was a Louisville baby whose White mother put up two daughters for adoption. Mary's sister was put in a White orphanage and grew up White, while Mary went from a Black orphanage to a Black family and a Black identity. She wanted so badly to be accepted by other Black people that she used brown cosmetics to darken her skin, dated only dark boys, and deeply resented other Black people with light skin. Lillian Smith, a White woman from Jasper, Florida, told of a brief childhood encounter with Janie, a light mulatto child who had been placed in a Black home. Whites saw this seemingly White girl with her Black adoptive parents, became indignant, and got the authorities to take Janie back and place her with the Smiths. For three weeks, Janie was White, until someone discovered her Black parentage in the records; then she was sent back to be Black again.[50] Occasionally, White people passed as Black. Some, like John Howard Griffin and Grace Halsell, altered their appearance to pass as Black to do research for books on race relations. More commonly, the White party to an interracial marriage might identify himself as a light mulatto so as to avoid public censure. In one southern town, a White man had both a Black wife and a White mistress. In order to avoid being separated from their Black half-sisters, his two daughters by the White mistress passed themselves off as Black.[51] There were also rural pockets in the South —such as Hertford County, North Carolina, and Central Point, Virginia—where people moved back and forth across the color line from generation to generation. Lighter or wealthier relatives tended to be regarded as White, others as Black, but the line between the two was not very formal. People on both sides worked and hung out together, and nearly everyone recognized relatives in the other group.[52]

All these varieties of passing tell a good deal about the operation of the color line and its essential silliness. But it is important to remember that passing for White, however spectacular it might be to recount, was a choice made by only a small number of mixed people. The vast majority, instead, passed for Black.

In recent years, changes have taken place in the identity options of mixed people. The rise of Black consciousness in the 1960s brought greater pressure than ever—from both Whites and Blacks—for people of biracial ancestry to identify with their Black side. Passing was now passé. Light-colored people flocked to affirm their Blackness. The tenor of the times is illustrated in James Carr's account of changing aspirations during his adolescence in the 1960s. Raised in a Black neighborhood, he wanted first to straighten his hair like other Black youths. He told his mother, "Mom, I want a *do!*" even though he knew his hair was already straight. Within a year, styles had changed; now he told her, "Mom, I want a *'fro!*" but found he could not sustain one without an expensive permanent. Black activists generally welcomed Black people of mixed ancestry. After the 1960s, many Black leaders insisted that all people of any degree of Black heritage must identify themselves as Black and give up any identification with their White ancestry. Government agencies generally supported this trend, so that, for instance, orphans of part-Black ancestry were kept in custodial care—sometimes for years—rather than being given in adoption to non-Black couples. Sometimes governments seemed unsure what to do with mixed people. In both the Chicago and St. Paul school systems in the 1980s, some mixed children were classified as Black, others as White, depending on which category was needed in a particular school to meet desegregation guidelines.[53]

Thus, after the latter 1960s, part-Black people found themselves in an ambiguous situation. Some, like Edwin Hiller*, were called on to link arms with their Black brothers and sisters. Hiller felt lost at the thought, because he felt his compatriots did not understand or approve his attachment to his White mother. Most interracial people continued, as before, to choose Black identities. But an increasing number chose, like Christine Hall, to insist on both halves of their inheritance. In doing so, they had the support of new organizations such as the Interracial Family Alliance in Houston and Chicago's Biracial Family Network. (For a list of such organizations see p. 376.) These came into existence in the early 1980s on the explicit premise that both Black and non-Black identities were necessary to the well-being of both interracial marriages and their offspring.[54]

These organizations' viewpoint was endorsed by a growing body of expert opinion. Psychologists and psychiatrists such as Marvin Arnold, Alvin Poussaint, Vladimir Piskacek, Paul Adams, and Prentice Baptiste, Jr., regarded a strong positive self-concept as crucial to emotional health, and a clear racial identity as one part of that self-concept. Increasingly, these and other scholars came to the opinion that for a person of mixed ancestry to neglect one or the other parent's identity was to detract from a clear racial identity. As Arnold put it, "Misidentification lowers self-esteem, and biracial people are just that: biracial." "People who adopt an interracial identity," he continued, "generally form a stronger self-concept" than those who opt for only Black or only White. Piskacek saw numerous interracial families in a clinical setting and found that those mixed people who achieved the strongest personality integration were the ones who had lived in mixed racial neighborhoods, had known love and respect from both sets of grandparents, and had parents who did not have underlying racial animosities. Prentice Baptiste, Jr., wrote in 1983: "These children are born into a society dominated by the social need to categorize its citizens racially as Black or White. Biologically, these children are neither Black or White, but equally a part of both races. But the Jim Crow traditions and laws will attempt to define all of them as Black regardless of their phenotypic appearance. Parents of interracial children must counter this attempt by teaching them that they are and culturally can be members of both races. Positive models of both races must be very apparent to these children during their early years of development."[55]

Summary of Part IV

The slave era set a pattern for interracial sexual and marital relations that persisted well into the twentieth century. White imagery pictured Black people as brutish and oversexed. Interracial marriage existed but was not common, while interracial sex was much more frequent. The latter most often involved White men and Black women, although the opposite combination also existed. The official word among Whites was that interracial mating was terrible, but it was tolerated so long as it did not involve White women or end in marriage. Blacks were not so benignly disposed. People of mixed ancestry did not form a separate group in most places, but instead were lumped in with unmixed Blacks.

White images of Black people carried over into the postslavery epoch. Black men seemed violent, primitive, childlike, and highly sexual. All this made them attractive to some White women. White men saw Black women, on the other hand, as sexually attractive but a bit too strong to handle in marital relations. For their part, some Black men saw White women as extraordinarily attractive sexual or status objects. Black women found themselves much less attracted to White men, perhaps repelled at communal memories of White male advances.

Here is an example where images overwhelmed social structural factors in shaping interracial mating patterns. The power dynamics between Black and White kept interracial marriage low throughout the century after the Civil War. But if power dynamics were the whole story, then there should have been more marriages between Black women and White men than the other way around, for powerful White males did not want Black men marrying their women. Instead, the opposite pattern prevailed, with far more marriages between Black men and White women, precisely because the mutual images of those two sets of people attracted each other, while the mutual images of White men and Black women drove them apart.

Black outmarriage rates showed a stark contrast to those of the immigrant groups previously studied. The second and third generations of those immigrant groups married across ethnic lines quite frequently. Although there was also a slight increase in Black outmarriage over time, it never went much higher than the first generation of the immigrant groups.

Throughout the entire period under study, most Whites opposed the notion of intermarriage with Blacks, especially when it involved members of their own families. They acted through laws, social pressure, and violent behavior to discourage the practice and punish intermarrying people, most particularly Black men married to White women. In the aftermath of the movement for Black rights, however, overt hostility came to be viewed as socially unacceptable even in relatively conservative White circles.

From very early in the era of Black freedom, a small number of Black universalists advocated intermarriage and predicted a raceless future. More Black leaders disavowed any interest in intermarriage at the same time they refused to give up the right to marry whom they pleased. A third group, probably the largest, disapproved of intermarriage entirely. Disagreements over these issues sometimes led to disputes between Black women and men. Yet Black communities consistently showed themselves more willing than White communities to grant mixed couples places on their margins. With the recession of Black nationalist fervor in recent years, Black feeling against interracial marriage also seems to have receded.

As with Jews and Japanese Americans, rates of intermarriage responded to the presence or absence of ethnic community structures. Intermarriage was lowest where Black people were plentiful and ethnic communities strong—in the South and in eastern cities. The rates were much higher in rural areas and on the relatively emancipated West Coast.

The vast majority of intermarriages were by middle-class Blacks and Whites, even though that was the class which frowned on intermarriage most strenuously. As in the Jewish and Japanese American cases, there is no support for the hypogamy theory of Robert Merton and Kingsley Davis. Intermarrying couples were well matched by education and income and could not be accused of trading assets in a marriage contract.

Psychological observers of intermarriages focused on the mutual imagery discussed earlier and tended to see neurotic motives behind many decisions to intermarry. Increasingly of late, however, they have been revising their analyses and perceiving intermarrying couples to be mentally healthy.

Like Jews and Japanese Americans, American Blacks were divided among themselves. But the provenance of the divisions was different for Black people, and the divisions were less salient than for the immigrant groups. The mixing of slavery had long since erased Old World ethnic distinctions. At various times, however, other distinctions were important to Black community life and to intermarriage choices. The distinction between southern-born and northern-born existed from the time of the great migration, but declined in vitality over the course of the century. The same was true for once-important distinctions of color and features. Where light-skinned (but not white-skinned) people once enjoyed higher status than darker people, by the 1960s that hierarchy had lost much of its power to affect social relationships. The one division that continued to grow was between Black people of West Indian origin and those from the North American continent.

As with Japanese and Jewish Americans, there seems to have been a relatively stable hierarchy of marriage preferences which included these intragroup distinctions and also graded people outside the Black group. But the hierarchy was not so simple as for the other groups, nor was there a neat progression down it over the generations.

The available data do not enable one to tell whether Black-White intermarriages have a higher, a lower, or substantially the same divorce rate as homogamous unions.

Where for many years part-Jews and part-Japanese had to find places in White, Gentile America, the opposite was true for most mulattoes. As far as Whites were concerned, anyone with part-Black parentage was all Black. Black people did not see it quite that way until the Black consciousness movement of the 1960s, but Black communities were always more willing than Whites to accept people of mixed ancestry. Most mulattoes were not nearly so torn between White and Black as White mythology would have it, but they did make a variety of identity choices. Some passed for White—more men than women, more in the urban North than in the rural South, more temporarily than permanently. The vast majority of mixed people passed for Black. But an increasing number—perhaps a third or more in recent decades —chose to identify with both halves of their inheritance.

12. Conclusion

> Because a man or woman marries outside his race does not mean that he or she ceases to be a member of it, or ceases to identify with it, or ceases to make contributions to its welfare or progress.
>
> —LOUIS WIRTH and HERBERT GOLDHAMER,
> *Ebony*, December 1949

Some Comparisons

A comparison of the varieties of intermarriage encountered in this book reveals striking similarities between the two immigrant groups, Japanese Americans and Jews. It shows far fewer similarities between the two peoples of color, Japanese Americans and Blacks. This difference suggests that, perhaps, race is not so fundamental a category of social relationships in America as has often been supposed. Beyond this point, however, there are other things to be learned from comparing the intermarriage experiences of the groups treated in this study, as well as those of other American and foreign ethnic groups. Such comparisons provide a basis for evaluating the various theories that have been constructed to explain intermarriage and may shed some light on the nature of ethnicity as well. Intermarriage patterns, this study suggests, can be explained by both structural and cultural factors. Most previous students have concentrated on structural factors, such as the size of the ethnic community or the sex ratio within it, to explain the incidence and varieties of outmarriage. Such factors do explain a good deal, but ideas are also important. Such cultural factors as a group's own perception of its relative social status, the general society's toleration of intergroup relationships, and different ethnic groups' images of

343

each other all seem to have played parts in determining how high the rate of intermarriage would be and who would marry whom.

The overall rate of outmarriage by Jewish and Japanese Americans followed a common sequence: very little outmarriage in the immigrant generation, slightly more in the second generation, and a great deal more in the third. Less than 2 percent of the East European Jewish immigrants married non-Jews. Perhaps 5 to 10 percent of their children and 15 to 30 percent of their grandchildren married Gentiles. Among immigrant Japanese, 2 to 5 percent married non-Japanese; in the second generation, 5 to 15 percent; and in the third, 30 to 45 percent, depending on gender, region, and social class. This pattern reflects the generations' social and cultural situations. Many members of the first generation married in Europe or Japan before coming to America. Others retained strong senses of their Old World identities and were mindful of inherited prohibitions against intermarriage. Second-generation Jews and Japanese Americans, growing up in American streets and schools, were typically enthusiastic about America and highly ambivalent about their minority ethnic heritage. That they should intermarry more frequently than their elders is no surprise.

It is useful to note, for the purpose of further comparison, that outmarriage rates for most other American ethnic groups approximated the pattern for Japanese and Jewish Americans. In 1979, Richard Alba found that Italian immigrants married non-Italians at a rate of 22 percent among men and 17 percent among women. In the second generation, the numbers leaped to 51 and 48 percent; in the third, 67 and 62 percent. According to census data, the outmarriage rate for first-generation Puerto Ricans in metropolitan New York City was 11 percent in 1970, compared to 32 percent for their children. In Albuquerque's Mexican American community, the outmarriage rate was 8 percent between 1924 and 1940, 13 percent between 1940 and 1955, 19 percent in 1964, and 31 percent in 1967. Charles Anderson calculated similar successive leaps in intermarriage over generations and the course of the twentieth century for Scots, Swedes, and Norwegian Americans. Each of the European groups except the Jews started at a high base point, usually about 20 percent in the first generation, and reached well over 50 percent outmarriage by the third.[1]

Lest one conclude, with Alba, that America is marching "into the twilight of ethnicity," it is important to note several qualifications to this trend. The nonwhite groups started at a lower outmarriage rate and never went so high. Chinese Americans, for example, increased their rate from about 10 percent in the 1950s, to 13 percent in the 1960s, and then to 18 percent in the 1970s, according to census records. Black people's rates increased even less, from less than 1 percent before 1940 to something over 2 percent in 1980. These were real increases, but they were nothing like the scale of the marital mixing of White ethnic groups.[2]

Some ethnic groups did not fit the pattern of ever-increasing outmarriage at all. Outmarriage by Filipinos may have reached as high as 90 percent in the latter 1930s, when the male-female ratio was 21 to 1 and further immigration from the Philippines had been cut off. Yet the group did not disappear, for it was joined after World War II by a large number of new immigrants of both sexes. Soon Filipino Americans exhibited outmarriage rates not unlike other Asian groups: 38 percent for women and 19 percent for men in the 1970s. Outmarriage rates for Native American peoples have always been high, hovering around the 50 percent mark at least from 1950 through 1980. Yet there was no increase in outmarriage over that period, nor any particular diminution of Native American ethnicity. Even the Mexican American case must be treated carefully, for a 1971 count saw the Albuquerque rate drop to 24 percent, and other locations had much lower rates throughout the twentieth century.[3]

It is true without doubt that outmarriage by immigrant groups in America tended to increase with each generation removed from the Old Country. But it is also true that there were substantial differences of scale for different immigrant groups. For some—certainly for the White Protestant groups, perhaps for Italians as well—the amount of mixing suggested the possibility that the group might be hard pressed to continue its separate identity. But other immigrant groups and colonized people such as Blacks and Mexicans proceeded more slowly.

It is also clear that changes in the general American social climate had some bearing on intermarriage patterns. In the early years of this century, the dominant ethnic group—White Protestants—did not want to intermarry with anyone (although interracial sex involving White men and Black women was acceptable to many so long as it was not made formal by marriage, and WASPs did not much care if other groups married each other). Harassment was not limited to the part-Jewish, -Japanese, and -Black couples we have witnessed. Filipino men escorting White women were set upon in Chicago streets in the 1920s and '30s, and feared to walk together with their mixed families even after World War II. Petty apartheid caused some major heartaches. As late as 1958, a Minneapolis cemetery refused to allow Ramona Erickson to be buried in the family plot with her husband David because she was a Sioux and he a Swede.[4]

Resistance to intermarriage assumed recognizable patterns. Families were usually the first to object, though often they were the first to become reconciled once intermarriages had been established and grandchildren started to arrive. Ethnic communities usually retained their resentments longer. The White Gentile community was not alone in opposing intermarriage; the wrath of the Jewish and Japanese communities generally exceeded that of the majority group.[5] There was a regional character to opposition: White Protestants of the South were more likely to oppose intermarriages of all sorts than were their ethnic peers in the North. In the early part of the century, West Coast Whites shared White Southerners' animus against intermarriage; in recent decades they have emerged as much more liberal.[6] There were religious variations as well. Jews were by far more favorably disposed than Protestants and Catholics toward the general idea of intermarriage, though not necessarily toward *Jewish* outmarriage. Catholics regularly expressed more liberal opinions than Protestants on all sorts of intermarriages, including those between Catholics and Protestants. Mainline Protestants were generally more liberal than Fundamentalists.[7] Leftists, academics, artists, and intellectuals were almost always more accepting of intermarriage than people from other walks of life.

Majority-group opposition began to crumble after World War II, and that development was reflected in rising intermarriage rates for nearly all groups. The big surge came in the late 1960s and continued through the 1970s, in the wake of the Civil Rights movement and the rise of ethnic chic. By then, almost all the barriers of petty harassment had fallen. Ethnic prejudice had certainly not disappeared, but it had come to be viewed as ill-mannered and anachronistic. Who would have believed, even a decade earlier, that in 1984, when the state of Texas chose as its senator the darling of the hard right, Phil Gramm, it would pass without notice that he was a miscegenator?[8]

What is most striking in all this is the change in the dominant group's understanding of Japanese Americans. At the beginning of the century, Japanese Americans were unquestionably placed along with Blacks at the bottom of the ethnic ladder. All the racist imagery and great and small oppressions heaped on Black Americans were also ladled out for the Japanese. But three-quarters of a century later, with Blacks' position only modestly improved, Japanese Americans had made the transit (in White eyes, not necessarily their own) from Black to White. When I was conducting the research for this book in the late 1970s and early 1980s, and I told people (to keep matters simple) that I was studying interracial marriage, Whites often asked: why, then, was I studying Japanese Americans—were not they just like Whites? This is not to contend that Japanese Americans had in fact lost their ethnic distinctiveness in terms of culture, interest, social structure, or their own view of themselves. Nor is it to suggest that Japanese Americans' change in White eyes was a good thing, nor that it was due to the particular qualities of Japanese American character, nor that it ought to be or could be emulated by other groups. Those are all fundamentally bogus arguments for which there is not space here. It is merely to observe that, whereas in 1900 most Whites despised Japanese Americans and placed them with the lowest of the low, by 1980 they could not see them as very different from themselves, and that fact is remarkable.[9]

Neither for Black Americans nor for Jews nor for Japanese was the intermarriage rate uniform from one region to another. There was very little intermarriage near centers of ethnic concentration: for Blacks, the South and, in later years, northern industrial cities; for Jews, eastern cities; for Japanese, California and Hawaii. The outmarriage rate for Japanese immigrants was low in Hawaii, a bit higher in California, higher still in places like Washington and Oregon, and highest in the South and East. For Jews, intermarriage was rare in eastern cities, but much more common in the South and West. Black people's low rates showed regional variations: lowest in the South, slightly higher in the more liberal and anonymous cities of the industrial North, and a great deal higher on the West Coast.

In each case, it was the presence or absence of an ethnic community that was crucial. A concentrated group of minority people drew sharper discrimination than did a few isolated individuals. Ethnic communities also provided a supply of candidates of the opposite sex that was lacking where Blacks, Jews, or Japanese were sparse. But perhaps most important, where there were clusters of Black people, Japanese Americans, or Jews, along with ethnic institutions such as synagogues and fraternal organizations, the communities actively discouraged intermarriage. They gossiped about intermarriers or those who might attempt to pass, ostracized them, and withheld fraternal privileges. Where such social networks were lacking, individuals were more likely to override any personal internal constraints and marry outside the group.

This pattern of low intermarriage near points of ethnic concentration and a high rate where ethnic fellows were few was followed by every other American ethnic group on record. The interracial marriage rate for Native Americans was tiny (from less than 1 percent to about 10 percent) on reservations in 1970, slightly higher (about 20 percent) in cities such as Albuquerque and Phoenix near Indian concentrations, and much higher (45 to 60 percent) in Chicago, New York, Los Angeles, and Seattle. That same year, Mexican Americans married out at a rate of only 5 percent in the Texas borderlands, 8 to 10 percent in the farm towns of California's San Joaquin Valley, 16 percent in Los Angeles, and more than 35 percent in San Francisco and Detroit. The Puerto Rican rate in Boston was twice as high as in New York City; it was even higher in Los Angeles. Even Alba's Italians married non-Italians much less frequently at their centers of concentration in northeastern cities than they did in other parts of the country.[10]

Class was another factor that had impact on intermarriage rates, but intermarriage did not consistently follow class lines. Once, in a more rigidly hierarchical era, the typical pattern combined wealthy White men and subordinate Black concubines. This was much like the patterns established in other rigidly stratified societies—for example, by Britons and East Indian women and Dutch men and South African women in the early years of those colonies. By the century which is the major focus of this book, however, American stratification had changed. Ethnic relations were still hierarchical, but the near-total subjection of slavery had given way to more subtle subordination mechanisms. In the twentieth century, minority ethnic communities more frequently gave up certain classes of people to intermarriage than others. Generally, it was those people who were most emancipated from their ethnic heritage who chose to intermarry. This meant that those upper-class Jewish, Japanese, and Black Americans whose wealth did not depend on their ethnic fellows intermarried more frequently than those who derived their living from the ethnic community. Generally, people with college educations intermarried more than people without them. Among first-generation Jews, as among Japanese Americans, professional people intermarried the most. The same was not true for Blacks, because nearly all Black professionals—lawyers, dentists, and whatnot—were tied to Black constituencies until at least the 1960s. In later generations, intermarriage by Japanese American and Jewish professionals remained high, and Black professionals' intermarriage rate began to grow. As antipathy eased on both sides of the ethnic line, office workers and business people also began to intermarry. Leftist intellectuals, college professors, artists, entertainers, and people with international elite careers all seem to have been prone to outmarriage. In all three ethnic communities, members of the working class and people with strong ties to ethnic culture and institutions married within the group almost exclusively. The class pattern of intermarriage set up some conflict for elite Blacks and Japanese Americans during the late 1960s and 1970s, when ethnic consciousness was in fullest flower. Since ethnic activists and intermarriers were often drawn from the same high-achievement social sectors—indeed, were all too often the same people—the charge of "talking Black and sleeping White" rang with embarrassment in the ears of many ethnic movement leaders. In general, class homogamy prevailed; that is, both partners to intermarriages usually shared the same social class.[11]

Intermarriage rates were also related to gender, but in complex ways. There were power situations in which dominant-group men mated with (but seldom married) subordinate-group women. There were also settings where factors other than power—such as demography, mobility aspirations, and sexual imagery—conspired to make one gender combination much more likely than another. The power situations were relatively simple ones. In the South under slavery, White men frequently took slave women, either through rape or in more established concubinage. Some Black men also mated with White women, but these were more likely to be marriages and were far less frequent. Similar situations prevailed in the colonial West Indies, in the early years of the British Raj in India, and between Whites and Blacks in South Africa.[12]

Yet this picture of dominant-group males enforcing their will on subordinate females did not represent a host of other situations. Except during the 1940s, far more Jewish men than women married Gentiles. Some observers attributed this to an abiding fascination with the *shikse*, the Gentile woman, on the part of Jewish men. According to this theory, such men saw marriage to a Gentile woman as a symbol of achievement, of acceptance, of assimilation into the American mainstream. Other observers saw the high rate of intermarriage between Jewish men and Gentile women from the Gentile women's perspective—as evidence of the superior qualities of Jewish men. Sensitive, intellectual, and a little exotic, they appealed to Gentile women who were fed up with John Wayne types. Whether or not either theory is correct, neither explains why Jewish women seldom married Gentile men.

A similar situation existed for Blacks. Outside the South (and nearly all intermarriage took place outside the South) far more Black men than women married across racial lines. This may be attributed in some part to popular imagery, which portrayed Black men as supermasculine (if rather menial) and White women as bitch goddesses. Meanwhile, the remembrance of exploitation past kept Black women from seeking White men, even as White men were intimidated by the power and earthiness associated with Black women. Other theories, which posited a class tradeoff between lower-class White women and upwardly mobile Black men, enjoyed attractive conceptual neatness but did not have any factual basis.

There are relevant international comparisons with regard to gender combinations. Most intermarriages in India between caste and outcaste people mirrored the pairings for American Blacks and Jews—that is, subordinate-group males and dominant-group females—although none of the observers of this phenomenon have come up with a convincing rationale for this situation. American servicemen in Japan after World War II were in a similar power position vis-à-vis Japanese women, but in that case the preponderance of American male–Japanese female pairings is surely due to the fact that there were so few American women in the army of occupation. Several varieties of international marriage and intermarriage by American immigrant groups had the same pattern, likewise probably for demographic reasons.[13]

After the first generation, gender patterns in Japanese American outmarriage were more complex. Here, social structure seems a less important factor than imagery. The popular culture of the 1930s and '40s, when the Nisei were coming of age, cast Asian men in unpleasant roles—either as sexless, effeminate Charlie Chans or as snarling, sickening *kamikaze* pilots. Neither image was likely to make Japanese American men seem attractive to non-Japanese women. At the same time, movies and returning GIs' tales of the South Pacific created images of Asian women as submissive, exotic, erotic creatures guaranteed to please men. These images, together with the example set by several thousand Asian war brides who came to America in the 1950s, set the tone for an increasing amount of outmarriage by Japanese American women from World War II through the 1960s. During the same period, intermarriage by Japanese American men stayed low. As the 1960s progressed, and Asian men from actor Bruce Lee to U.S. Senator Daniel Inouye appeared as strong figures on the public scene, the gender imbalance evened out. By 1970, nearly as many Japanese American men as women were marrying non-Japanese.

In the 1950s, '60s, and '70s, outmarriage gender patterns for several other groups followed the Japanese American model: mainly female, with a rising proportion of males. These included Chinese, Filipina, Korean, and Mexican Americans. Some of the Koreans and Filipinas, like some of the Japanese, were brides of U.S. servicemen. But even subtracting such individuals, the female outmarriage dominance was clear. Similar sexual imagery surrounding Asian women may have played a part for Chinese, Koreans, and Filipinas. The reasons for Mexican American women intermarrying more frequently than Mexican American men are less immediately clear.[14]

Ethnic subdivisions played a part in intermarriage choices. In the immigrant generations, Jewish and Japanese Americans were not the monolithic groups they seemed to outsiders. They were, rather, riven by a multitude of ethnic divisions. Japanese immigrants were Japanese, but they were also *Okinawa-jin* or *Naichi-jin, eta* or non-*eta, Hiroshima-jin* or *Wakayama-jin* or *Aichi-jin.* Divisions among various types of Jews—between Orthodox and Reform, between German and Russian, between *Litvak* and *Galitsianer*—were even stronger. As for Black Americans, while Old World ethnic distinctions had long since disappeared, other sorts of intragroup divisions did exist: stratification by color for many years, and a split between native American Blacks and immigrants from the West Indies. All these divisions went largely unrecognized by outsiders, who saw only Jew, Black, and Japanese American, yet they all had some effect on marriage choices.

There are parallels among other American minority groups to these sorts of intragroup divisions. One involves various groups of Chinese Americans. It is common knowledge that most Chinese immigrants came from the vicinity of Canton in southeast China. They spoke a different language than the Chinese of northern or western derivation, and different dialects among themselves as well. The different Chinese regional groups have seldom associated in America, and they hold negative stereotypes of each other. As late as the third generation, intermarriage between Cantonese and Mandarin Chinese was rare enough to cause much clucking of tongues in Chinese communities. Even among the Cantonese immigrants there was a split between Hakka and Punti. The Punti were the Cantonese majority; the Hakka were a people who came to South China relatively late in Chinese history, mainly in the ninth century, and who were subordinate to the Punti at home in South China. The Hakka-Punti division was not transferred to the American mainland, because only a tiny fraction of the mainland Chinese Americans were Hakka. But in Hawaii a substantial minority of Chinese immigrants were Hakka. There, a communal ban on intermarriage between the two groups lasted at least through the second generation, although it seems to have broken down thereafter.[15] Similar divisions existed between various subgroups of the people we call Italian Americans. In the immigrant generation, Lombards and Sicilians saw each other as foreigners and would have been quite as hesitant at the thought of marrying each other as they would have been at the prospect of marrying Frenchmen or Spaniards. Francis Rogers reminds us that Portuguese immigrants divided themselves into Continentals, Azoreans, Madeirans, and Cape Verdeans, even though non-Portuguese divided them very differently: into Portuguese and Blacks. Marriages between Native Americans from different tribes must also be regarded as intermarriages.[16]

Over the years, the notion of just who was within the group and who was outside changed. These divisions within what we conceive to be "the group" affected immigrant social life in general and marriage choices in particular. A given set of people—immigrants from Lublin or Hiroshima, for example—gave evidence of a specific, predictable hierarchy of preferences in choosing mates. An Orthodox Lubliner

Table 12.1. Jewish Intermarriage Hierarchy

	1st generation	2nd generation	3rd generation
Acceptable	Same village Same region East European Orthodox Jew	Orthodox Jew Conservative Jew Reform Jew	Jew
			—— Gentile White ——
Conceivable but unlikely	German Jew Reform Jew	Gentile White	Gentile non-White
Nearly inconceivable	Gentile White Gentile non-White	Gentile non-White	

would choose first a mate from a pious family of the proper social class who came from the area around his or her *shtetl*. Then he or she might take someone from elsewhere in the Lublin district, and then a candidate from some other part of Poland—Warsaw or Grodno, perhaps. Then he or she might accept a mate from Galicia or a nearby part of Russia. Finally, a Lubliner might marry an Orthodox Jew from some place more distant—Prussia or Austria, perhaps. For most of the Orthodox, marriage to a Reform Jew or a Gentile was beyond possibility (see Table 12.1).

An immigrant from Hiroshima would observe a similar hierarchy in choosing a mate. First would come someone from his or her own class and religion (Buddhist or Christian) in his or her own native village. Then someone from a nearby village. Then from Hiroshima at large. Then someone who was simply Japanese, but still probably of similar class and the same religion. That was about as far as most Japanese immigrants were willing to go. There were certain Japanese, even, whom they would not marry—members of hereditary outcast classes such as *eta* or Okinawans. That was particularly true in Hawaii. A marriage between an ordinary Japanese and an Okinawan or *eta* had more psychosocial impact than a Japanese-White marriage would have today. But most immigrants recognized it was at least possible to marry a non-Japanese. They had a hierarchy for these people as well, based roughly on skin color and perceived cultural compatibility. Next after Japanese would come Caucasians, then Chinese Americans. Probably only after exhausting Caucasian and Chinese possibilities would an ordinary Japanese consider marrying an Okinawan or *eta*. Mexicans

Table 12.2. Japanese American Intermarriage Hierarchy

	1st generation	2nd generation	3rd generation
Acceptable	Same village Same prefecture Japanese	Japanese	Japanese Chinese White
Conceivable but unlikely	White Chinese Okinawan Eta	White Chinese	Filipino Black
Nearly inconceivable	Filipino Black	Filipino Black	

and Filipinos might be next, then Koreans, and finally Blacks. It was almost inconceivable to the average Japanese immigrant that he or she might marry someone from the lower rungs of this ladder (see Table 12.2).[17]

Second-generation Jewish Americans did not make all their parents' fine distinctions between different sorts of East European Jews, and they extended the hierarchical concept to relations with people outside Orthodoxy. Whether one's family came from Minsk or Vilna was not an important issue for them. They were willing to socialize with and marry Orthodox Jews whose parents came from any part of Eastern Europe. Although they recognized that Reform, Conservative, and Sephardic Jews were different from them, they were not unwilling to consider marriage with such people. A few were even willing to marry some non-Jews. And the second generation as a whole began to make distinctions among Gentiles. First would come White nonbelievers and liberal Protestants, then White Catholics, then White Protestants from conservative traditions, and finally Gentiles of darker hues.

So, too, second-generation Japanese Americans were willing to mix with and marry people farther down the ladder of preferences their parents had constructed. Nisei tended not to recognize divisions among Japanese Americans: anyone who was a Nisei was an eligible prospect. Below this generalized Japanese category, either Whites or Chinese might come next, depending on one's tastes. That was about as far as most Nisei were willing to go. Marrying someone with darker skin—a Filipino or Mexican or Black person—they recognized as a

Table 12.3.   Black Intermarriage Hierarchy

	Before 1865	1865–1950	After 1960
Acceptable	Same status (slave/free)	Elaborate color/ status hierarchy	American Black
	African	Same region of origin	West Indian
Conceivable but unlikely	Native American	Other Black (West Indian, African)	African White Other
Nearly inconceivable	White Other	White Native American Other	

biological possibility, but few actually contemplated performing what was to them such a radical act.

By the third generation, the intragroup distinctions of village and region the immigrants had made were no longer recognized. Jews were aware of denominational differences, but those seldom were the deciding factor in a marriage choice. Most Jews married Jews, and most Japanese Americans married Japanese Americans. But more and more married out. The intermarriers' choices followed the order of the hierarchies their parents and grandparents had constructed. Jews chose first other Jews broadly defined, then liberal White Protestants, then White Catholics, then conservative White Protestants, then people of moderate color, and finally Blacks. Third-generation Japanese Americans chose first Japanese, then other Asians, then Whites, then people of intermediate skin color such as Mexicans and Filipinos, and lastly Blacks.

The intermarriage hierarchies of Black Americans were less neat than those of Japanese Americans or Jews. In the antebellum era, a slave usually married another American-born slave from the neighborhood, or perhaps a free Black person or slave of African birth. A few, especially in the colonial period and the early years of the republic, married Native Americans. Marriage to Whites and others was nearly inconceivable. A free Black person would most likely choose another free person of color, with a premium on light skin. A slave mate was a clear possibility but a decidedly lower choice. Intermarriage with a

Native American was possible, and so, too—remotely—was marriage
to a White person (see Table 12.3).

In the first half of the twentieth century, another sort of hierarchy
generally obtained. Within the Black population, an individual would
choose a mate partly on the basis of an elaborate set of considerations
surrounding color. If one lived in the North, one would also seek someone from one's own area of origin. Failing to find a compatible candidate who fit these preferences, a person might marry simply another
Afro-American. Marriages to West Indians and to the tiny numbers of
people from mixed communities, such as the Lumbee of North Carolina, happened, but they were extremely infrequent and occurred only
with a sense that one was crossing an ethnic line. Other groups were
graded—White, Mexican, Native American, and so forth—but were
distinctly outside the realm of possibility.

By the 1960s, '70s, and '80s color and regional distinctives among
Afro-Americans had blurred to a tremendous extent. English-speaking
West Indians were a second choice. French-speaking Caribbeans were
a distinct possibility. Marriages to Whites, Mexican Americans, Indians, and others occurred only in the tiniest of numbers.

Other American ethnic groups exhibited similar hierarchies of marital preferences. Even more than Japanese Americans and Jews, Chinese immigrants divided themselves along complex Old Country lines.
In the immigrant generation before World War II, a Chinese from,
for instance, Toisan, would prefer to marry someone from his home
village, or at least from another part of Toisan district. Failing that,
he would choose a mate from one of the other counties (collectively
called *sze yup*) that spoke his native dialect. If such a person were not
available, then someone who did not speak his dialect but who spoke
another variant of Cantonese would do. Beyond that, someone from
Fukien or another part of South China might be acceptable. That was
about as far as a Toisanese immigrant was likely to go. Speakers of Mandarin Chinese or any of the other northern languages were conceivable but unlikely candidates. Whites and other continental Asians were
even less likely. Darker people—Filipinos, Mexican Americans, Blacks
—were out of the question. By the second generation, in the 1960s and
'70s, all the lines separating varieties of Cantonese had blurred. Mandarin Chinese and Japanese were less frequent partners, but they and
Whites were increasingly acceptable. Other types of people, graded

Table 12.4.   Chinese American Intermarriage Hierarchy

	1st generation	2nd generation
Acceptable	Same village/district	Speaker of same Chinese language
	Speaker of same dialect	Speaker of another Chinese language
	Speaker of same Chinese language	Japanese
	Same province/geog. region	
	————————————————— White —————
Conceivable but unlikely	Speaker of another Chinese language	
	White	Korean
	Japanese	Filipino
	Korean	
	————————————————— Mexican —————
Nearly inconceivable	Filipino	Black
	Mexican	
	Black	

by color and perceived cultural similarity, were not likely partners but were within the realm of possibility (see Table 12.4).[18]

White Protestants of various ethnic derivations also exhibited hierarchies of choice in mate preferences. I have done little more than secondary research and a few dozen interviews, but the following seems to be the set of ethnic preferences that might guide a Swedish American in choosing a mate:

> Swede
> Other Scandinavian
> British or German
> Other White Protestant
> White Catholic: German or Irish
> White Catholic: Southern or Eastern European
> Jew
> Asian
> Native American
> Hispanic
> Black

The limit of acceptability in the first generation was very near the top, but it had made considerable progress down the list by the third.[19]

Intermarriages have taken place in ever greater numbers. Have they, on the whole, succeeded or failed as marriages? That is a difficult question to decide and is loaded with value judgments that one is hesitant to make. One imperfect measure of marital ill health is the rate of divorce. More intermarriages than in-marriages ended in divorce— not a lot more, but a significant fraction. Statistics on this issue are not comprehensive, but their trend is clear. In each generation, marriages between Jew and Jew survived at least slightly more frequently than those between Jew and Gentile. Likewise, in each generation there were fewer divorces between Japanese and Japanese than between Japanese and non-Japanese American. Studies of the stability of Black-White intermarriages contradict one another. Marriages between U.S. servicemen and Japanese women probably ended in divorce more frequently than any of the domestic intermarriages, primarily because of the great cultural gap to be bridged. Nonetheless, nothing like a majority of any sort of intermarriage ever ended in divorce. Most intermarriages, like most other marriages until very recent years, survived.

At issue, though, is the provenance of the differential divorce rate where it existed. Was it caused by cultural conflicts between the parties to the marriage or by pressure from outside—from family, other minority group members, or society at large? Clearly there were instances of each, and most marriages which broke up did so from both internal and external pressures. It is worth noting, however, that there was more cultural conflict within Gentile-Jewish intermarriages, and more external pressure on Black-White and Japanese–non-Japanese unions. This resulted from a peculiarity of the American system of racial and ethnic relations. Americans see race as a greater barrier between people than religion, when, in terms of cultural conflict between individuals, just the opposite is true. Jewish-Gentile intermarriage almost always involved bringing together people with two very different cultures, based on volitional adherence (however strong or weak) to two very different religious traditions. By the Nisei generation, Japanese marriages to non-Japanese Americans seldom had to endure such cultural conflict, for Nisei culture and White, middle-class culture were increasingly similar. So, too, Black–non-Black couples were unusually homogeneous as to class, education, values, and other factors.[20]

Nonetheless, people outside the marriage harassed interracial couples more than Jewish-Gentile couples because the physical difference between the races was more visible than that between Jew and Gentile. A Gentile-Jewish couple might have appeared unmixed to the casual observer, but the person in the street could easily spot a racially mixed pair. This is in accord with the general notion in American ethnic relations that racial lines are harder, that they somehow divide people more thoroughly, than national origin or religious lines. It is ironic that the type of intermarriage that generally had a greater amount of actual internal conflict—that between Jew and Gentile—should occasion less overt hostility than the pairing of Black and non-Black or Japanese American and non-Japanese.[21]

Intermarriages, like homogamous marriages, usually suffered some internal conflict. Intermarriages, unlike most other marriages, were besieged from without. Yet one of the major trends of this century was a general lessening of ethnic tensions and of ethnocentric harassment of intermarrying people. That fact, coupled with the growth of a substantial Black middle class and the evolution of Japanese American and Jewish American subcultures into close approximations of the middle-class American mainstream, promised a declining level of pressure on intermarriages from within and without.

Then there is the issue of the fate of the children of intermarriage. Every intermarrying couple has heard the warning: "Do whatever you like with your own lives. That's your business. But what about the children?" Just what evil is expected to befall mixed children is seldom made explicit. But several possible elements come readily to mind: confusion about their ethnic identity, denial of their minority heritage, ostracism by the majority or minority society or both, loneliness, self-hatred, even physical degeneration.

There is no denying that children of mixed couples nearly always faced adjustments in growing up that were in some respects more difficult than those met by children from homogeneous homes. For mixed children growing up in Japan, the adjustments were particularly difficult. Generally speaking, the success or failure of an individual's adjustment to mixed status depended on the amount and kinds of harassment that person had to endure, and upon the support he or she received inside the home. In America during the early decades of this century, White Protestants made life generally miserable for minority people, including people of mixed ancestry. In those same years, both Jews and Japanese Americans viewed intermarriage as betrayal and mixed people as vaguely unclean. Harassed by both majority and minority, mixed individuals often were miserable. Mixed children were taunted by schoolmates. They were often cut loose from their extended families and expected to resolve identity questions for themselves. People like Kathleen Tamagawa did not have much success at this and wished they had not been born. Others, like Clarke and Yuri Kawakami, got more solid family support and adjusted well. The situation was seldom so extreme for part-Black people. Few ever had the option to be considered anything but Black. Although they were occasionally mistrusted and ridiculed by other Blacks, people of part-Black ancestry generally found stable Black identities.

In later years, ethnic tensions eased, and people of mixed status came to be trusted somewhat better by others, both majority and minority Americans. This did not mean full acceptance, but rather a somewhat lower level of abuse. In those circumstances, less painful personal adjustment became the norm. By the 1970s and 1980s, a growing number of individuals, like Joy Nakamura*, found they were allowed to embrace both parts of their bicultural heritage.

Few observers would have thought that possible in an earlier era. Early Jewish leaders assumed that all mixed children would forsake the faith. They fought against intermarriage and ostracized the intermarried. As late as the 1950s, most mixed children were raised as Gentiles, not Jews. But by 1970 many Gentile wives and husbands were converting to Judaism or supporting their partners' faith, and three-quarters of the children were being raised as Jews. This turnaround was due partly to the increasing prestige of minority status in the 1960s and partly to a new willingness on the part of rabbis and other Jews to accept intermarried couples and their children. Then, as never before, intermarried couples could find a home in Judaism even if the Gentile partner did not give up his or her heritage. This meant mixed children could be raised as Jews without having to deny their Gentile identity.

In Japanese America the pattern was similar. Prior to 1960, most mixed children had to make their way outside Japanese American communities, for the minority group would have little to do with them. But in the 1960s intermarriages became so common that Japanese Americans could not cut off their mixed offspring and still expect to maintain basic family and community relationships. As those children grew up in the 1960s and '70s, they were allowed places in Japanese American churches and basketball leagues and beauty pageants.

Early in the century, people of part-Black parentage usually found themselves more or less happily consigned to the Black group. For those who found this unsatisfying, the only option was to pass for White if they could. The 1960s brought intense pressure to deny any connection with the non-Black world and to identify strongly with Black America. Most mixed people took that course. But in the 1970s and after, an increasing number found their heightened ethnic awareness demanded they pay attention to both halves of their inheritance. A growing number found support—whether through interracial organizations or in society at large—for successfully embracing biracial identities.

Something had changed. In the early 1900s, when intermarriage was infrequent and ethnic tensions high, part-Blacks were designated Black; part-Jews and -Japanese were caught, like Kathleen Tamagawa, on the margin, neither fish nor fowl, cut off from both majority and minority Americans. By the 1970s, majority American oppression of Japanese, Jewish, and Black Americans had abated considerably, as had the two former groups' ethnocentrism. With intermarriage a common occurrence, mixed people like Joy Nakamura* found themselves less marginal, able to embrace successfully both halves of their ethnic inheritance.[22]

Intermarriage Theories Reconsidered

We have still to consider the implications of this study for the theories about intermarriage described in Chapter 1. On the basis of the experiences of Black, Jewish, and Japanese Americans and Japanese war brides with intermarriage in this century, it would seem that some of the theories are valid, some are in need of revision, and some may have to be discarded.

The first cluster of theories has to do with social and economic factors tending to encourage intermarriage. One of these theories says that an unbalanced sex ratio leads to a high rate of outmarriage by the surplus members of the more numerous sex. This may be true in some situations—among Chinese men in the Hawaiian kingdom, Filipinos in Depression-era Chicago, or White men in colonial Barbados, for example—but it was the case for only one of the groups studied here: U.S. servicemen who married Japanese women. Japanese American men vastly outnumbered Issei women in the early years, but few of them intermarried. Rather, they waited and sent to Japan for wives, or else remained single. There were intermarriages by Issei, but they were nearly as frequent among the women as the men. What is striking is not how high but how *low* the rate of outmarriage was among the Issei, especially compared to later generations of Japanese Americans. Jewish and Black Americans' sex ratios were about even throughout the century. Contrary to expectations, unbalanced sex ratio does not seem to have been an overwhelming factor encouraging outmarriage.

A second theory in this first group earns more support. It is Romanzo Adams' contention that the size of the minority community is important: where the minority community is large, intermarriage is low; where it is small, intermarriage is high. This seems to have been true for Blacks, Japanese Americans, and Jews. There was always a lower percentage of Japanese American outmarriage in Los Angeles than in Illinois, less Jewish outmarriage in New York City than in Iowa, and less Black outmarriage in Alabama than in rural New England. But the low intermarriage rates where minority group members are numerous may have had as much to do with community supervision as with the wealth of in-group candidates available to any individual.

A corollary, Milton Barron's theory that "the percentage of intermarriage increases as the proportion of the group in the community decreases," seems close to the mark.[23] If community supervision—the gossip system and so forth—is a major inhibitor of intermarriage, then existence of a coherent ethnic community would seem to be a requirement for inhibition to take place. In some southern and midwestern cities, Jews constituted only a small percentage of the population but formed communities concentrated enough geographically and tightly knit enough socially to inhibit intermarriage for a generation or two. One can readily imagine the opposite situation, where Jews might number a larger proportion of the total population but be so spread out geographically and so unconnected socially as to be unable to act to retard intermarriage.

The notion that there has been a steady rise in rates of intermarriage throughout the twentieth century is more or less true, at least for Jews and Japanese Americans. But the rise for these groups was not steady. Rather, it was gentle for the first two generations, then exploded in the third. Part of the vast expansion in intermarriage in the 1960s and after had to do with the general lessening of ethnic tensions in those years. Part may have been attributable to the new attractiveness that went with minority status in the age of affirmative action. And part was certainly because of the coming of age of the third generation, highly assimilated and upwardly mobile. In any case, there was no steady rise in Black outmarriage over the course of the century. Black intermarriage rates were minute until the late 1960s, and then rose only modestly, despite dramatically increased acceptance of interracial unions.

The exact relationship of class to intermarriage is still unclear. There is some evidence, however, that working-class Jews, Blacks and Japanese Americans have intermarried less frequently than people higher up the economic scale, and that college-educated professional people have intermarried the most. Intermarriers from all groups tended to marry people with social standing similar to their own.[24]

The next set of theories, those having to do with which group tends to marry which, would seem in need of substantial revision. Ruby Jo Reeves Kennedy's idea that there are three American melting pots —Protestant, Catholic, and Jewish—within which mixing takes place more and more freely, but between which exist largely impenetrable barriers, has some merit. The strength of this scheme is its prediction of an increasing sense of oneness within each religious group. That has certainly been the case for Jews. Age-old distinctions between various sorts of East Europeans—and even between Sephardim and Ashkenazim—have faded. But Kennedy's idea has a flaw: it is just not true that White Protestants would consistently choose to marry Black Protestants in preference to White Catholics.[25] And her theory does not tell much about the ways people pick mates within their respective pots: do Germans pick Anglo-Americans first or Scandinavians, and why?

The social-distance model of Emory Bogardus and others says race is the hardest line to cross, religion is the next, and national origin the easiest. In terms of the amount of outside harassment visited on intermarried couples, that is true. Mixed racial couples consistently received greater abuse from people outside their circle of acquaintance than interreligious pairs. But Japanese American intermarriage history shows something different from what the social-distance model would lead one to expect. For Japanese Americans, race was a factor in intermarriage choices but not the overriding factor one would expect. Japanese Americans consistently chose White partners over Koreans because of the tensions between Japan and Korea and because of the despised status of Koreans in Japanese society. Most non-Asians were lower on the Japanese American scale of preference than most Asians, but some Asians were lower than some non-Asians. Also, it seems possible that religion may in some cases be a stronger barrier than race. Outmarriage by third-generation Japanese Americans, mainly to Whites, was higher than outmarriage by third-generation Jewish Americans. That may have been partly because the difference between Gentiles and Jews involved differing choices about which culture to adhere to, whereas by the third generation the cultural differences between Japanese Americans and Whites were not so great. Similarly, a survey of twenty-five White, Baptist ministers indicated they approved interracial marriages between believing Christians, but not interreligious marriages. As one expressed his position, "God draws distinctions between Christian and non-Christian, but He does not recognize race."[26]

More useful than either the triple melting pot or the social-distance model for understanding marriage choices may be the notion that each group has a discernible and relatively stable hierarchy of preferences, determined by the group's historical ideas about itself and others, and by its evolving position on the American ethnic scene. These hierarchies have a number of categories, and choices depend on more factors than just religion and race. How far down the hierarchy an individual is willing to go depends on a variety of other social circumstances, such as generation removed from the Old Country in the case of immigrants, the degree to which other groups are perceived as being compatible in culture and status, and external restraints placed by the dominant ethnic group.

Most of the rules about gender patterns in intermarriage will have to be redrawn, for they bear scant relationship to reality. One that may escape the axe is the idea that informal sexual relations tend to follow the rule of *hypergamy:* that is, dominant-group men exploiting subordinate-group women. This seems to have been true in a number of situations where the power gap between groups was great. Thus, in India under the British, in South Africa, and in the American South before World War II, most intergroup mating was informal—concubinage at best—and involved White men exploiting women of color. Yet it is important to remember that White women also mated with Black men in America, especially in those parts of the country that were not so rigidly stratified. There is no evidence this rule applies at all to societies where power is less hierarchically arranged.

The major theory about gender patterns in inter*marriage*, as opposed to inter*mating*, is Robert Merton's generally accepted exchange theory, that lower-caste men marry up. This rule of *hypogamy* seems to confuse as much as it explains. Merton posited an economy of intermarriage, in which lower-caste men of wealth, talent, or beauty traded those attributes for the higher status of upper-caste women who lacked wealth, talent, or beauty. Sometimes intermarriage worked as he predicted: more Jewish men married Gentile women than Jewish women married Gentile men; more Black men married White women than White men married Black women. But educational, income, and occupational figures show that White women married to Black men actually had high achievement in those areas, and no one seems ready to assert that the White women who married Black men were uglier than average. In the cases of the other ethnic groups, the hypogamy idea was off by 180 degrees: far more Japanese, Chinese, Korean, and Mexican American women married White men than Japanese, Chinese, Korean, and Mexican American men married White women.

Merton's approach depends on the assumption that men are naturally more upwardly mobile than women (a dubious contention at best), so only Black men and not Black women would be in position to take advantage of the opportunity to marry up. The problem, of course, is that Black women since World War II have been much more upwardly mobile in education and job status than Black men. One can construct a plausible exchange theory like Merton's to rationalize almost any predominant ethnic-gender combination in intermarriage, but without a good deal of hard evidence, any such interpretation is very difficult to prove.[27]

Merton's theory has a further problem: that of deciding which way is up. Looking at things from a majority-group perspective, he defines any minority person who marries a majority person as someone who is improving her or his status—marrying up. Thus, from Merton's perspective, a Black or Jewish man taking a White Protestant bride is marrying up, and a Japanese American woman taking a White husband is doing the same. Undoubtedly, some Black, Jewish, and Japanese Americans saw ethnic stratification this way. But undeniably, others saw *themselves* as higher status, as superior to Gentile Whites. Which way is up depends very much on one's point of view.

All this suggests that intermarriage is a much more complex matter than Merton imagines, and that such a simple, general rule cannot hold. It seems more profitable to look at the pattern of mutual images —for example, at how Black men and women view White women and men, and vice versa—as well as at social structural factors, before making predictions about which gender will marry outside the group more frequently. That approach has proved more fruitful in dealing with the outmarriage patterns of the three American ethnic groups under consideration here.[28]

As for the ethnic identities of ethnically mixed people, Madison Grant bespoke the conventional wisdom of nearly all theorists in 1916: "The cross between a white man and an Indian is an Indian; the cross between a white man and a Negro is a Negro; the cross between a white man and a Hindu is a Hindu; and the cross between any of the three European races and a Jew is a Jew."[29] It is worth noting that Grant and his fellow theorists were White Christians. It is just not true that children of intermarriage were always consigned to the lower-status group, unless one is prepared to accept uncommon definitions of which groups were lower in status. Some mixed people were assigned to the non-White Protestant group; some were not. Until the 1970s, most part-Blacks had to go as Black, unless they could pass, because Whites would not have them. Most *konketsuji* had no place among Japanese in Japan or America. Until the latter 1960s, most part-Jews and part-Japanese Americans had to go as Gentile Whites, because the minority communities would not have them. As for other groups, children of Punjabi-Mexican families generally followed their mothers. Part-Indians went both ways, as did people from mixed Protestant and Catholic families. Except for these last two instances, there was not much room for individual choice. A mixed individual of a particular ethnic combination almost always had to accept the same status as did others like him. Identity choice rested on the degree of openness of both minority and majority societies to accepting mixed people and on their relative power to enforce their will.

In the 1960s, minority ethnic identity became more acceptable, even fashionable, and both majority and minority groups began to reduce interethnic barriers. At that point, part-Jews and part-Japanese found it both possible and attractive to claim their Jewish or Japanese American identities. As the demands of Black Power receded in the 1970s, mulattoes began to have some access to their non-Black side. In an age of relativism, ethnic identity, like other choices, became partly a matter of individual preference. One could not choose to identify oneself as something for which one's gene pool did not qualify, and the choice one made had enormous social and psychological implications, but if one came from multiple ethnic strains, increasingly one had the option of access to them all. A rising number of people chose bi-ethnic identities and successfully connected themselves to both parts of their heritage. Psychiatric authorities increasingly applauded this as the healthiest choice. Other part-Jews, part-Blacks, and part-Japanese identified with minority communities. Still others (though fewer, and not many mulattoes) saw themselves, and were largely perceived, as Gentile Whites.

What will happen to the ethnic identities of the children of mixed people is anybody's guess. Looking at a national sample, Richard Alba's figures on the cultural practices and ethnic connections of part-Italians suggest that their offspring might leave the ethnic fold. But the experiences of part-Blacks, of part-Mexicans, of many part-Indians, and of part-Chinese in San Francisco's Chinatown point toward continued minority-group identity. In general, in situations where children of intermarriages connected with minority ethnic communities and cultures, their children seem to have done likewise.[30]

What is most striking about the identity situation for mixed people in America is what did *not* happen. Until very recently most types of mixed individuals in the United States, unlike those in many other countries, were assigned to one group or the other. The Cape Coloured in South Africa, *mestizos* in much of Latin America, Anglo-Indians in India, and *métis* on the Canadian frontier all formed intermediate castes between dominant and subordinant groups, each with its own social and economic niche. In Brazil, White and Black were separated by a wide variety of intervening categories. In the United States this never happened, save for small pockets in the Old South. What began to happen in America in the 1970s was not the formation of such a separate group of mixed Jewish-Gentiles or mulattoes or Eurasians. Rather, it was the growth of an opportunity for individuals to resolve their personal identity dilemmas by embracing both halves of their inheritances—not as half-breeds, but as people entitled to identify fully with both.[31]

The fifth type of theory has to do with the fate of ethnic identity for intermarrying people. When a person marries someone from another ethnic group, does that person continue to identify with her own people or does she identify with the group of her partner? Many people assume that any time a member of a minority group marries a White Protestant, that person's minority ethnic identity is automatically wiped out. Thus, Ruby Jo Reeves Kennedy confidently asserted, "Intermarriage is the surest means of assimilation and the most infallible index of its occurrence." More sophisticated analysts such as Milton Gordon would qualify this by asserting that marital assimilation is, rather, the last step *before* identificational assimilation, that is, before the minority group member identifies totally with the majority. But even Gordon sees intermarriage as the death knell of minority ethnic identity: "If marital assimilation . . . takes place fully, the minority group loses its ethnic identity."[32] Gordon is talking about minority groups as whole entities rather than about individuals. He may be right that if (for example) all Japanese Americans marry Whites, there will ultimately cease to be a separate Japanese American ethnic identity. Yet several generations of a 50 percent intermarriage rate have not decreased—but rather, have *increased*—the number of Native Americans. Similarly, Black group identity shows no signs of decline despite incorporating a large number of part-Whites over the generations.[33]

Even to the extent that Gordon's hypothesis may be correct in some cases, it does not help when one is trying to predict the identity dilemma of an *individual* who has intermarried. Many Arizona Japanese immigrant men who married Mexican women seem to have identified in large part if not exclusively with their non-Japanese wives. Their economic and social connections were mainly with Mexican American society, and their children spoke Spanish and English rather than Japanese. Yet the Arizona Japanese intermarriers retained their ethnic identity to the extent that they knew and associated with each other, which would probably not have happened if they had been utterly absorbed in the Mexican population. Thus, it seems likely that they preserved some Japanese ethnic identity, however attenuated. Other situations were less ambiguous. Walter White, Richard Wright, and Frederick Douglass did not lose their Black identities, nor their importance to the cause and culture of Black Americans, when they married White women. Many White brides of Black men were successfully incorporated into Black communities in the 1950s and '6os. Some White women went with their Japanese American husbands to World War II concentration camps, choosing by their actions to identify not with White America but with Japanese America. And some Gentiles joined their Jewish spouses at worship and raised their children as Jews. So it is by no means certain that intermarriage heralds the obliteration of minority ethnic identity. A minority person may intermarry yet retain his or her ethnic identity, and may even persuade the majority partner to come over to the minority side in part.[34]

Intermarriage and Ethnic Identity

This is the place where the study of intermarriage connects with theories about ethnicity: the issue of survival of individual and group ethnic identity. There are four types of theories about ethnicity: those that see it primarily as a matter of interests, those that regard it as based on social networks, those that measure ethnicity by cultural criteria, and those that insist ethnicity is really about identity. Obviously, as Stephen Cornell reminds us, ethnicity is about all four of these things.[35] Intermarriage may or may not be a threat to individual or group ethnicity depending on (*a*) how the individual acts, (*b*) how the ethnic group acts, and (*c*) how the larger society acts, in each of these four areas.

In the first instance, are there pressures or interests acting on mixed couples and people of mixed parentage to identify with the group? Are there pressures to eschew group membership? It has long been assumed that modern society acts to break down primordial distinctions in favor of national or even international identities. But, as Cornell and Michael Hannan demonstrate, ethnic identities may be very contemporary, based on interests peculiar to the modern era. In

Hannan's view, that which is sometimes called modernization acts first to dissolve the effective power of the smallest units of particularity, such as family and kinship, as units of political and economic action. In such a situation, larger units such as ethnic groups become especially effective units of mobilization. There are some instances where a national homogenizing seems to have drawn intermarrying people and their children into a generalized American identity. Most of the White Protestant groups and Alba's Italian Americans may be examples of this. For many years, an official U.S. government policy of assimilation encouraged Native Americans to give up tribal identities and become U.S. citizens, and many—especially intermarriers and mixed people —complied. In other instances, it was the minority ethnic group that pushed away intermarriers and mixed people. Jewish and Japanese Americans in the first and second generations are examples of this. But there were also cases where interests dictated not rejecting but in fact embracing minority ethnic identity. White society pushed mulattoes to be Black throughout history, and the Black Power movement provided a pull factor as well. Once the tribes began to win back land, mineral, and fishing rights in the 1970s, the practical value of Indian identity soared, and the number of mixed people identifying themselves as Native Americans rose accordingly.[36]

The important question regarding the intersection of intermarriage and ethnicity in social networks is whether or not intermarriers and mixed people continue to connect with ethnic communities. Some do; some do not. For many years, Black intermarriers and mulattoes did, and Japanese and Jewish intermarriers and mixed people did not. More recently, the option to connect has been opened to most, if not all. The long-term prospects for continued group identity in the face of heavy intermarriage for such groups as Japanese Americans and Jews will depend on whether such groups can, like Native Americans and Blacks, find ways of encouraging intermarriers and mixed people to commit themselves to minority group identity.[37]

A consistent interest of many observers is to what extent intermarriage has affected cultural practices. Most of the evidence currently available suggests Jewish intermarriers and their half-Gentile children have been less conscientious, on the average, than other Jews in maintaining such religious observances as saying the seder and keeping a kosher home. But in recent years those activities have undergone something of a revival, in mixed as well as purely Jewish homes. For Blacks, there is no long-term evidence yet available that people with substantial White ancestry act in systematically different ways than those who have a larger percentage of Black ancestors. For Japanese Americans, the relevant standard of comparison is other people of the same generation. There is as yet no study which indicates that children of Nisei intermarriage show fewer Japanese American cultural traits than full Sansei, although this is a distinct possibility.[38]

Then there is the question of ethnic identity itself. Have intermarried people and their offspring identified with their minority ethnic heritage or with the majority, or with some other collectivity? Among Black Americans, substantial interracial mixing has clearly not attenuated ethnic identity. For Jews, intermarriage, together with a low birthrate, has brought declining numbers. Recent attempts to connect intermarried and mixed people with Jewish institutions, the continued strength of those institutions, and the experience of having gone through similar periods of membership loss over the centuries and yet survived, all point toward continued strength for Jewish communal identity. For Japanese Americans, the situation is more problematic. Increased acceptance of intermarriage and recent attempts at community mobilization (such as the movement to obtain redress for World War II injustices) have brought many intermarried Japanese Americans and their children back into touch with their ethnic community. Yet Japanese American institutions are not as strong as their Jewish counterparts. If the outmarriage rate were to continue to climb, and the majority of mixed people were not to connect with other Japanese Americans culturally, identificationally, and institutionally, the prospect for the vitality of Japanese American ethnicity would not look good.

A final word must be said about the implications of intermarriage hierarchies for ideas about ethnicity. Most observers have tended to see ethnicity as two boxes: either one has a given ethnicity or one does not. However, the existence of preference hierarchies for mate choices, and changing limits of acceptability over time and generation, suggest a different picture. Ethnic identity seems to include gradations of preference or perceived similarity within it. It also grades those perceived as outside the group. There *is* a perceptible line between Us and Them. But that is not a simple, two-category division. It masks an underlying continuum, a hierarchy of groups with whom one is more or less willing to associate oneself. This hierarchy is held in common by most members of a given minority group. The order of the hierarchy for the groups studied here did not change much over the better part of a century. What did change was the point where the line between Us and Them was drawn.

APPENDICES

NOTES

BIBLIOGRAPHY

INDEX

Appendix A:
Summary of the States' Laws
on Interracial Marriage

(*Loving v. Virginia* 388 U.S. 1 [1967] nullified all laws forbidding interracial marriage.)

States which never had antimiscegenation laws
  Northeast: Connecticut, New Hampshire, New Jersey, New York, Vermont
  Midwest: Kansas, Illinois, Iowa, Minnesota, Wisconsin
  South: District of Columbia
  West: Alaska, Hawaii, Washington

States which repealed their antimiscegenation statutes before 1900
  Northeast: Maine (1883), Massachusetts (1843), Pennsylvania (1780), Rhode Island (1881)
  Midwest: Ohio (1887), Michigan (1883)
  West: New Mexico (1886)

States forbidding intermarriage throughout most of their history
  Northeast: Delaware
  Midwest: Indiana, Nebraska, North Dakota, Oklahoma
  South: Alabama, Arkansas, Florida, Georgia, Kentucky, Louisiana, Maryland, Mississippi, Missouri, North Carolina, South Carolina, Tennessee, Texas, Virginia, West Virginia
  West: Arizona, California, Colorado, Idaho, Montana, Nevada, Oregon, Utah, Wyoming

States forbidding other combinations besides Black and White
  Arizona (White and Mongolian or Indian)
  California (White and Mongolian)

Georgia (White and American Indian, Asiatic Indian, or Mongolian)
Idaho (White and Mongolian)
Louisiana (White and "Persons of Color", i.e., Black and Indian)
Mississippi (White and Mongolian)
Missouri (White and Mongolian)
Montana (White and Chinese or Japanese)
Nebraska (White and Chinese or Japanese)
Nevada (White and Malay or brown, or Mongolian or yellow)
North Carolina (White and Indian; Croatan and Black)
Oregon (White and Chinese, Kanaka, or Indian)
South Dakota (White and "Corean," Malayan, or Mongolian)
Utah (White and Mongolian)
Wyoming (White and Mongolian or Malay).

States declaring interracial marriages void
All those with laws except Alabama, Nevada, Oklahoma, Tennessee

States specifying the degree of Black ancestry that qualifies one for inclusion under the statute (the others simply referred to "Negro" or "Negro and Mulatto")
$\frac{1}{16}$ (one great-great-grandparent):
Louisiana, North Carolina
$\frac{1}{8}$ (one great-grandparent):
Indiana, Florida, Maryland, Mississippi, Missouri, Nebraska, North Dakota, South Carolina, Tennessee
$\frac{1}{4}$ (one grandparent):
Oregon

States by severity of penalty for interracial couples
Severe (maximum imprisonment of more than two years):
Alabama, Florida, Maryland, Missouri, North Carolina, North Dakota, Oklahoma, South Carolina, South Dakota, Tennessee, Texas, Virginia, Wyoming
Medium (more than six months and up to two years):
Arkansas, Colorado, Indiana, Kentucky, Louisiana, Missouri, Nevada, Oregon, West Virginia
Light (up to six months):
Arizona, Delaware, Georgia, Idaho, Montana, Nebraska, Utah
No penalty:
California[1]

Appendix B:
Interracial Family Organizations

A Place for Us
PO Box 357
Gardena, CA 90247

Biracial Family Network
PO Box 489
Chicago, IL 60653

Biracial Family Resource Center
800 Riverside Drive, Suite 5G
New York, NY 10032

Citizens for the Classification
of Biracial Children
3601 NE 73rd Place, #18
Seattle, WA 98115

INTERace
PO Box 7143
Flushing, NY 11354

Interracial Club of Buffalo
PO Box 146, Amherst Branch
Buffalo, NY 14226

Interracial Families, Inc.
700 Second Avenue
Tarentum, PA 15084

Interracial Family Alliance
PO Box 53251
Philadelphia, PA 19105

Interracial Family Alliance—Atlanta
PO Box 20290
Atlanta, GA 30325

Interracial Family Alliance
National Headquarters
PO Box 16248
Houston, TX 77222

I-Pride
PO Box 9641
Berkeley, CA 94709

Multi-Racial Families of Colorado
PO Box 20524
Denver, CO 80220

OURS, Inc.
3307 Highway North
Minneapolis, MN 55422

Parents of Interracial Children
115 South 46th Street
Omaha, NE 68132

Poly-Ethnic Life
PO Box 475
Commerce, TX 75428

Rainbow Circle
c/o First Baptist Church
17th and Sansom Street
Philadelphia, PA 19103

Notes

Abbreviations

AJA   American Jewish Archives, Cincinnati

AJS   *American Journal of Sociology*

AJYB   *American Jewish Year Book*

ASR   *American Sociological Review*

CKI   Interviews conducted by Charles Kikuchi for the JERS in Chicago, 1943–45 (in JERS, cases R and S)

EFF   E. Franklin Frazier Papers, Moorland-Springarn Research Center, Howard University, Washington, D.C.

JARP   Japanese American Research Project Archives, Department of Special Collections, University Research Library, University of California, Los Angeles

JERS   Japanese American Evacuation and Resettlement Study Archives, Bancroft Library, University of California, Berkeley

JMF   *Journal of Marriage and the Family*

JNH   *Journal of Negro History*

SPH   *Social Process in Hawaii*

SRR   Survey of Race Relations Papers, Archives of the Hoover Institution, Stanford University

SSR   *Sociology and Social Research*

WDC   Records of the Western Defense Command, National Archives and Records Center, Washington, D.C., Military Archives Division, Modern Military Branch, Record Group 338, File Number 291.1, "Mixed Marriage File"

Chapter 1. The Problem of Intermarriage

1   Obviously, mixing did not follow this precise pattern in every individual case. It is easy to imagine situations where social mixing or miscegenation might precede significant amounts of cultural sharing. But this pattern fits

most cases. See Romanzo Adams, *Interracial Marriage in Hawaii* (Montclair, N.J., 1969; orig. New York, 1937), v. For a beginning look at intermarriage around the world, try the articles on South Africa, India, Japan, Sri Lanka, Indonesia, Guyana, Australia, Cuba, Trinidad, Puerto Rico, Brazil, the South Atlantic, Hawaii, and the continental United States in Noel P. Gist and Anthony Gary Dworkin, eds., *The Blending of Races* (New York, 1972), and Irving R. Stuart and Lawrence Edwin Abt, eds., *Interracial Marriage* (New York, 1973). See also Susan Benson, *Ambiguous Ethnicity: Interracial Families in London* (Cambridge, 1981); C. R. Boxer, *Race Relations in the Netherlands* (Meppel, 1965); Cedric Dover, *Half-Caste* (London, 1937); George M. Fredrickson, *White Supremacy* (New York, 1981); Noel P. Gist and Roy Dean Wright, *Marginality and Identity: Anglo-Indians* (Leiden, 1973); John Haare, *Maori and Pakeha: A Study of Mixed Marriage in New Zealand* (New York, 1966); Riaz Hassan, "Interethnic Marriage in Singapore," *SSR*, 55 (1971), 305–23; Riaz Hassan and Geoffrey Benjamin, *Ethnic Outmarriage Rates in Singapore* (Singapore, 1972); Esther Holland Jian, *British Girl—Chinese Wife* (Beijing, 1985); Andrew W. Lind, *Interethnic Marriage in New Guinea* (Canberra, 1969); Verena Martinez-Alier, *Marriage, Class, and Colour in Nineteenth-Century Cuba* (London, 1974); Magnus Morner, *Race Mixture in the History of Latin America* (Boston, 1967); Francislee Osseo-Asare, *A New Land to Live In* (Downers Grove, Ill., 1977); Rudolf Sieg, *Mischlingskinder in Westdeutschland* (Baden-Baden, 1955); J. B. Smart, *The Domiciled European and the Anglo-Indian Race of India* (Fort Bombay, 1929); George Dee Williams, *Maya-Spanish Crosses in Yucatan* (Cambridge, 1931). A good summary of theoretical insights is E. L. Cerroni-Long, "Marrying Out: Socio-Cultural and Psychological Implications of Intermarriage," *Journal of Comparative Family Studies*, 16 (1984), 25–46.

2 Hector St. John de Crevecouer, *Letter from an American Farmer*, quoted in Philip Gleason, "American Identity and Americanization," in William Peterson et al., *Concepts of Ethnicity* (Cambridge, 1982), 64.

3 Gleason, "American Identity," 57–143.

4 It is important to note at the outset that interethnic marriage is just one variety of assortative mating. Couples combine individuals who may match or differ in a host of other ways: by age, class, education, geographical origin, physical features (e.g., height), personality characteristics, cognitive abilities, attitudes and opinions, and so forth. In this expanded sense, every marriage is an intermarriage, for surely no couple is made up of perfectly identical people. See David M. Buss, "Human Mate Selection," *American Scientist*, 73 (January–February 1985), 47–51.

5 Winthrop D. Jordan, *White over Black* (Chapel Hill, 1968), 176; Adams, *Interracial Marriage in Hawaii*, 53; Margaret A. Parkman and Jack Sawyer, "Dimensions of Ethnic Intermarriage in Hawaii," *ASR*, 32 (1967), 595; Bruno Lasker, *Filipino Immigration* (New York, 1969; orig. Chicago, 1931), 23, 196, and passim; George Eaton Simpson and J. Milton Yinger, *Racial and Cultural Minorities*, 4th ed. (New York, 1972), 507.

6 Adams, *Interracial Marriage in Hawaii*, 191; U.S. Bureau of the Census, *1960 Census: Nonwhite Population by Race*, Subject Report PC(2)-1C (Washington, D.C., 1963); Bureau of the Census, *1970 Census: Japanese, Chinese, and Filipinos in the United States*, Subject Report PC(2)-1G (Washington, D.C., 1973); Harry H. L. Kitano, *Japanese Americans*, 2nd ed. (Englewood Cliffs, N.J., 1976), 210–11; Bureau of the Census, *1980 Census of Population: General Population Characteristics: United States Summary* (Washington, D.C., 1983), 125; Milton L. Barron, "Intergroup Aspects of Choosing a Mate," in Barron, ed., *The Blending American* (Chicago, 1972), 42. Peter Blau and his colleagues have theorized about and quantified Adams' and Barron's truism at some length: see Peter M. Blau, Terry C. Blum, and Joseph E. Schwartz, "Heterogeneity and Intermarriage," *ASR*, 47 (1982), 45–62; Peter M. Blau, Carolyn Beeker, and Kevin M. Fitzpatrick, "Intersecting Social Affiliations and Intermarriage," *Social Forces*, 62 (1984), 585–617.

7 Barron, "Intergroup Aspects," 43; James A. McRae, "Changes in Religious Communalism Desired by Protestants and Catholics," *Social Forces*, 61 (1983), 709–30; James H. S. Bossard, "Residential Propinquity as a Factor in Marriage Selection," *AJS*, 38 (1932), 219–24; Donald M. Marvin, "Occupational Propinquity as a Factor in Marriage Selection," *Publications of the American Statistical Association*, 16 (1918), 132–50; Scott J. South and Steven F. Messier, "Structural Determinants of Intergroup Association: Interracial Marriage and Crime," *AJS*, 91 (1986), 1409–30.

8 Milton M. Gordon, *Assimilation in American Life* (New York, 1964), 224–32; Barron, "Intergroup Aspects," 43.

9 Ruby Jo Reeves Kennedy, "Single or Triple Melting Pot? Intermarriage Trends in New Haven, 1870–1940," *AJS*, 49 (1944), 331–39; R.J.R. Kennedy, "Single or Triple Melting Pot? Intermarriage in New Haven, 1870–1950," *AJS*, 58 (1952), 56–59. Kennedy's theory has an appealing neatness to it, but it is contradicted by her own data. Her theory would have Protestant Anglo-Americans marrying Protestant Afro-Americans in preference to Catholic Irish Americans, when that clearly was not the case, even in her own study. Will Herberg elaborated on Kennedy's scheme in *Protestant, Catholic, Jew* (Garden City, N.Y., 1955). Samuel A. Meuller supplies a needed, but incomplete, corrective to Kennedy and Herberg in "The New Triple Melting Pot," *Review of Religious Research*, 13 (1971), 18–33.

10 Barron, "Intergroup Aspects," 41; Parkman and Sawyer, "Intermarriage in Hawaii," 593. For discussion of social distance, see several articles and books by Emory S. Bogardus: *Immigration and Race Attitudes* (Boston, 1928); "Changes in Racial Distance," *International Journal of Opinion and Attitude Research*, 1 (1947), 55–62; "Racial Distance Changes in the United States during the Past Thirty Years," *SSR* (1959), 286–90; *Social Distance* (Los Angeles, 1959).

11 Robert K. Merton, "Intermarriage and the Social Structure," *Psychiatry*, 4 (1941), 361–74; Kingsley Davis, "Intermarriage in Caste Societies," *American Anthropologist*, 43 (1941), 376–95; Simpson and Yinger, *Racial and Cultural Minorities*, 500–502. The only scholar to take prominent exception

to this theory is Lewis F. Carter, in "Racial-Caste Hypogamy: A Sociological Myth?" *Phylon* (1968), 347–50. Carter may be right that the data simply do not bear out Merton's theory. An equally disturbing flaw is Merton's assertion that there is an agreed-upon hierarchy that all Americans recognize. It may be, to the contrary, that not all groups can agree about which way is up.

12   Merton, "Intermarriage and the Social Structure"; Simpson and Yinger, *Racial and Cultural Minorities*, 505–6; Michael C. Kearl and Edward Murguia, "Age Differences of Spouses in Mexican American Intermarriage," *Social Science Quarterly*, 66 (1985), 453–60; Stanley Lieberson and Mary C. Waters, *From Many Strands: Ethnic and Racial Groups in Contemporary America* (New York, 1988), ch. 6.

13   Michael Banton, *Racial and Ethnic Competition* (Cambridge, 1983), 32–59; Thomas F. Gossett, *Race: The History of an Idea in America* (New York, 1963).

14   Fredrik Barth, ed., *Ethnic Groups and Boundaries* (Boston, 1969); Arnold Dashevsky, ed., *Ethnic Identity in Society* (Chicago, 1976); George DeVos and Lola Romanucci-Ross, eds., *Ethnic Identity* (Chicago, 1982); Nathan Glazer and Daniel P. Moynihan, eds., *Ethnicity* (Cambridge, Mass., 1975); R. A. Schermerhorn, *Comparative Ethnic Relations* (Chicago, 1970); David Y. H. Wu, ed., *Ethnicity and Interpersonal Interaction* (Singapore, 1982).

15   Gordon, *Assimilation*, 80; Gene N. Levine and Colbert Rhodes, *The Japanese American Community* (New York, 1977); Israel Ellman, "Jewish Intermarriage in the United States," in Benjamin Schlesinger, ed., *The Jewish Family* (Toronto, 1971), 25–61; Kennedy, "Single or Triple Melting Pot?" (1944). See also Richard D. Alba, "Interethnic Marriage in the 1980 Census" (Paper presented at the American Sociological Association annual meeting, 1985), courtesy of the author; Lieberson and Waters, *From Many Strands*, ch. 6; Andrew W. Lind, *An Island Community: Ecological Succession in Hawaii* (Chicago, 1938), 304.

16   Field notes, Seattle, 1969. Other examples abound. A 1986 issue of *Christianity Today*, a middle-American evangelical magazine, ran an editorial exhorting people to be nice about race relations. Three of the five letters in response, whether they favored or opposed the editors' stance, offered some version of the following analysis: "To address the core problem is to face the issue of racial intermarriage." *Christianity Today*, October 17, 1986, 6; October 31, 1986, 8.

17   Milton M. Gordon, "Toward a General Theory of Racial and Ethnic Group Relations," in Glazer and Moynihan, *Ethnicity*, 84–110; Glazer and Moynihan, "Introduction," ibid., 1–26; Cerroni-Long, "Marrying Out."

18   I do not mean necessarily to sing the praises of unbridled ethnic assertion, after the fashion of Michael Novak in *The Rise of the Unmeltable Ethnics* (New York, 1972). Nor do I take the position of Orlando Patterson, seeing in ethnicity "chauvinism" and a likely descent into fascism (*Ethnic Chauvinism* [New York, 1977]). Patterson is probably right, at least about the possibilities—witness the fascist tendencies of Boer ethnicity in South Africa (cf. T. Dunbar Moodie, *The Rise of Afrikanerdom* [Berkeley, 1975]). But his

alternative—complete individualism, with no entity of identification intervening between the atomistic individual and the whole of humankind—is
equally frightening. My point here is only that ethnicity, contrary to many
people's expectations, shows no signs of going away, and therefore needs to
be better understood.

19   A beginning survey of the subject might include the following: Michael
Banton, *Race Relations* (New York, 1967); Banton, *Racial and Ethnic Com-
petition;* Fredrik Barth, ed., *Ethnic Groups and Boundaries* (Boston, 1969);
H. M. Blalock, Jr., *Toward a Theory of Minority-Group Relations* (New
York, 1967); Robert Blauner, *Racial Oppression in America* (New York,
1972); Bogardus, *Social Distance;* Abner Cohen, ed., *Urban Ethnicity* (Lon-
don, 1974); Oliver C. Cox, *Caste, Class, and Race* (New York, 1959); Arnold
Dashevsky, ed., *Ethnic Identity in Society* (Chicago, 1976); DeVos and
Romanucci-Ross, *Ethnic Identity;* A. L. Epstein, *Ethos and Identity* (Lon-
don, 1978); E. K. Francis, *Interethnic Relations* (New York, 1976); John H.
Franklin, ed., *Color and Race* (Boston, 1968); E. Franklin Frazier, *Race and
Culture Contacts in the Modern World* (New York, 1957); George M. Fred-
rickson, *White Supremacy* (New York, 1981); Nathan Glazer and Daniel P.
Moynihan, *Beyond the Melting Pot* (Cambridge, 1963); Glazer and Moyni-
han, *Ethnicity;* Gordon, *Assimilation in American Life;* Herberg, *Protestant,
Catholic, Jew;* H. Hoetink, *Slavery and Race Relations in the Americas*
(New York, 1973); Charles F. Keyes, ed., *Ethnic Change* (Seattle, 1981);
William H. McNeil, *Polyethnicity and National Unity in World History*
(Toronto, 1986); William Newman, *American Pluralism* (New York, 1973);
Robert E. Park, *Race and Culture* (Glencoe, Ill., 1949); Patterson, *Ethnic
Chauvinism;* William Petersen et al., *Concepts of Ethnicity* (Cambridge,
Mass., 1982); Anya Peterson Royce, *Ethnic Identity* (Bloomington, Ind.,
1982); Schermerhorn, *Comparative Ethnic Relations;* Tamotsu Shibutani and
Kian M. Kwan, *Ethnic Stratification* (New York, 1965); Werner Sollors,
Beyond Ethnicity (New York, 1986); Stephen Steinberg, *The Ethnic Myth*
(Boston, 1981); Ronald T. Takaki, *Iron Cages* (New York, 1979).

The reader should note that the above scholars, like the present author,
are concerned primarily with issues of culture and social structure. There is
another, sociobiological view of ethnicity which has emerged in certain quarters recently, connected to nineteenth-century primordialist views of human
nature. The sociobiological view of ethnicity is outside the purview of the
present discussion, not only because it is not generally respected by scholars
of race and ethnicity, but also because it has little to say about intermarriage.
The interested reader may turn to Pierre L. van den Berghe, "Race and Ethnicity: A Sociobiological Perspective," *Ethnic and Racial Studies*, 1 (1978),
401–11; van den Berghe, *The Ethnic Phenomenon* (New York, 1981); and
Harold Isaacs, "Basic Group Identity," in Glazer and Moynihan, *Ethnicity*,
29–52.

20   Schermerhorn, *Comparative Ethnic Relations*, 12.

21   Max Weber, "Ethnic Groups," in Weber, *Economy and Society* (Berkeley,
1979), 385–98.

22 One of the few exceptions is a soon-to-be-published article by Stephen Cornell, whose ideas on the dynamics of ethnicity helped shape the four-category analysis I have just enunciated. I stand in his debt, although I am not sure he would want to claim responsibility for the use to which I have put his ideas here. His work should be read not just for his categories, but also for their usefulness in describing and predicting patterns of ethnic change. See Cornell, "Communities of Culture, Communities of Interest: On the Variable Nature of Ethnic Groups" (Paper presented to the Center for the Study of Industrial Societies, University of Chicago, February 1984), courtesy of the author.

23 See, for example, Steinberg, *Ethnic Myth;* William Petersen, *Japanese Americans* (New York, 1971); Egon Mayer and Carl Sheingold, *Intermarriage and the Jewish Future* (New York, 1979).

24 Gordon, *Assimilation;* Richard D. Alba, *Italian Americans: Into the Twilight of Ethnicity* (Englewood Cliffs, N.J., 1985); Richard D. Alba, "The Twilight of Ethnicity among Americans of European Ancestry: The Case of Italians," *Ethnic and Racial Studies*, 8 (1985), 134–58; William L. Yancey et al., "Emergent Ethnicity," *ASR*, 41 (1976), 391–403.

25 Patricia C. Albers and William R. James, "On the Dialectics of Ethnicity," *Journal of Ethnic Studies*, 14 (1986), 1–28; John A. Armstrong, *Nations before Nationalism* (Chapel Hill, 1982); Karen Blu, *The Lumbee Problem* (Cambridge, 1980); Paul R. Brass, ed., *Ethnic Groups and the State* (London, 1984); Abner Cohen, "The Lesson of Ethnicity," in Cohen, *Urban Ethnicity*, ix–xxiv; Abner Cohen, *Custom and Politics in Urban Africa* (Berkeley, 1969); Jyotirindra Das Gupta, "Ethnicity, Language Demands, and National Development in India," in Glazer and Moynihan, *Ethnicity*, 466–88; June Teufel Dreyer, *China's Forty Millions: Minority Nationalities and National Integration* (Cambridge, 1976); Cynthia Enloe, *Ethnic Conflict and Political Development* (Boston, 1973); Glazer and Moynihan, *Beyond the Melting Pot: The Negroes, Puerto Ricans, Italians, and Irish of New York City;* Glazer and Moynihan, "Introduction," to *Ethnicity*, 1–26; William Kornblum, *Blue Collar Community* (Chicago, 1974); Lucian W. Pye, "China: Ethnic Minorities and National Security," in Glazer and Moynihan, *Ethnicity*, 489–512; Joseph Rothschild, *Ethnopolitics* (New York, 1981); Mark Schneider, *Ethnicity and Politics* (Chapel Hill, 1979); Jimy M. Sanders and Victor Nee, "Limits of Ethnic Solidarity in the Enclave Economy," *ASR*, 52 (1987), 745–73; John F. Stack, ed., *Ethnic Identities in a Transnational World* (Westport, Conn., 1981); William Julius Wilson, *The Declining Significance of Race*, 2nd ed. (Chicago, 1980). Wilson should be tempered by Melvin E. Thomas and Michael Hughes, "The Continuing Significance of Race," *ASR*, 51 (1986), 830–41.

26 An exception here is Orlando Patterson, who sees ethnicity as a calculated individual decision that changes in direct response to costs and benefits—in short, to interests—without limits or interventions from culture, social networks, or other factors. See Patterson, "Context and Choice in Ethnic Allegiance," in Glazer and Moynihan, *Ethnicity*, 305–49.

27 Herbert J. Gans, "Symbolic Ethnicity," *Ethnic and Racial Studies*, 2 (1979), 1–20. Cf. Charles Hirschman, "America's Melting Pot Reconsidered," *Annual Review of Sociology* (1983), 397–423.

28 Erik H. Erikson, "The Concept of Identity in Race Relations," in Talcott Parsons and Kenneth B. Clark, eds., *The Negro American* (Boston, 1966), 227–53; Fredrik Barth, "Introduction," in Barth, *Ethnic Groups and Boundaries*, 9–38; Daniel Bell, "Ethnicity and Social Change," in Glazer and Moynihan, *Ethnicity*, 141–74; Epstein, *Ethos and Identity*, 91–118; Stanley Lieberson, "Unhyphenated Whites in the United States," in Richard D. Alba, ed., *Ethnicity and Race in the U.S.A.* (London, 1985), 159–180; Richard D. Alba, "Ethnic Identity among American Whites" (Paper presented to the annual meeting of the American Sociological Association, Chicago, 1987), courtesy of the author.

29 Jonathan Sarna, "From Immigrants to Ethnics: Toward a New Theory of 'Ethnicization,'" *Ethnicity*, 5 (1978), 370–78; Paola Sesia, "White Ethnicity in America: The Italian Experience," *Berkeley History Review*, 2 (1982), 18–32; Donald L. Horowitz, "Ethnic Identity," in Glazer and Moynihan, *Ethnicity*, 111–40.

30 Cf. Cohen, "Lesson of Ethnicity"; Patterson, "Context and Choice."

31 William J. McGuire et al., "Salience of Ethnicity in the Spontaneous Self-Concept as a Function of One's Ethnic Distinctiveness in the Social Environment," *Journal of Personality and Social Psychology*, 36 (1978), 511–20; Alba, "Ethnic Identity among American Whites." Charles H. Anderson argues for a composite White Protestant ethnic identity in *White Protestant Americans* (Englewood Cliffs, N.J., 1970).

32 A few social scientists have recently written analyses of intermarriage that treat multiple groups. Unfortunately, the most useful of these are not systematically comparative. They are primarily theoretical and use data on various groups only in an illustrative manner. See, for example, Cerroni-Long, "Marrying Out"; Monica McGoldrick and Nydia Garcia Preto, "Ethnic Intermarriage: Implications for Therapy," *Family Process*, 23 (1984), 347–64.

33 This book is about heterosexual, rather than homosexual, relationships. Although the latter seem an increasingly prominent feature of modern life, and although ethnic issues may be relevant to homosexual relationship dynamics, nonetheless, to introduce the homosexual issue would make this book too complicated to write.

34 Robert Darnton, *The Great Cat Massacre and Other Episodes in French Cultural History* (New York, 1984), esp. 3–7, 257–63.

35 Joel Williamson, *New People* (New York, 1980).

Chapter 2. Fu Manchu and Charlie Chan

1 Roger Daniels, *Concentration Camps USA* (New York, 1971), 15.

2 William Petersen, *Japanese Americans* (New York, 1971), 9–11; Harry H. L. Kitano, *Japanese Americans*, 2nd ed. (Englewood Cliffs, N.J., 1976), 11–15; Bill Hosokawa, *Nisei* (New York, 1969), 31–35; Roger Daniels, *The Politics of*

Prejudice (New York, 1968; orig. Berkeley, 1962), 1–3; Robert A. Wilson and Bill Hosokawa, *East to America* (New York, 1980), 17–27; Yamato Ichihashi, *Japanese Immigration* (San Francisco, 1915), 4–5; Dorothy Thomas et al., *The Salvage* (Berkeley, 1952), 573.

3 Yasuo Sakata, interviewed by the author, Los Angeles, December 21, 1979; Petersen, *Japanese Americans*, 9–35; Tadashi Fukutake, *Japanese Rural Society*, trans. R. P. Dore (Ithaca, N.Y., 1972; orig. New York 1967), 5–6 and passim, Edward K. Strong, *Japanese in California: Based on a Ten Per Cent Survey* . . . , Stanford University Publications in Education and Psychology, vol. 1, no. 2 (1933), 236; Kazuo Ito, *Issei* (Seattle, 1973).

4 Ichihashi, *Japanese Immigration*, 4–5, 13; Yuji Ichioka, "Ameyuki-san: Japanese Prostitutes in Nineteenth-Century America," *Amerasia Journal*, 4 (1977), 1–21; Donald T. Hata, "'Undesirables': Unsavory Elements among the Japanese in America prior to 1893 and Their Influence on the First Anti-Japanese Movement in California" (Ph.D. diss., University of Southern California, 1970); D.C.S. Sissons, "Karayuki-san: Japanese Prostitutes in Australia, 1887–1916," *Historical Studies* (Melbourne), 17 (1977), 323–41, 474–88; Michael Berger, "A Once-Taboo Story for Japanese TV," *San Francisco Examiner and Chronicle*, February 25, 1979; Joan Hori, "Japanese Prostitution in Hawaii during the Immigration Period," in Nobuya Tsuchida, ed., *Asian and Pacific American Experiences: Women's Perspectives* (Minneapolis, 1982), 56–65.

5 Elmer C. Sandmeyer, *The Anti-Chinese Movement in California* (Urbana, Ill., 1973; orig. 1939); Mary Roberts Coolidge, *Chinese Immigration* (Taipei, 1968; orig. 1909); Alexander H. Meneely, "The Anti-Chinese Movement in the Northwest" (M.A. thesis, University of Washington, 1922); Chester P. Dorland, "The Chinese Massacre at Los Angeles in 1871," *Historical Society of California Annual Publications*, 3, no. 2, 22–26; A. A. Sargent, "The Wyoming Anti-Chinese Riot," *Overland Monthly*, 2nd ser., 6 (November 1885), 507–12; Jules A. Karlin, "The Anti-Chinese Outbreaks in Seattle, 1885–1886," *Pacific Northwest Quarterly*, 39 (April 1948), 103–30.

6 Daniels, *Politics of Prejudice*, 24–26.

7 Ibid., 16–45.

8 Ito, *Issei*, 188–201.

9 Kitano, *Japanese Americans*, 213.

10 Ito, *Issei*, 247–586, 743–875.

11 U.S. Bureau of the Census, *1960 Census: Nonwhite Population by Race*; Subject Report PC(2)-1C (Washington, D.C., 1963); Bureau of the Census, *1970 Census: Japanese, Chinese, and Filipinos in the United States*, Subject Report PC(2)-1G (Washington, D.C., 1973); Kitano, *Japanese Americans*, 210–11.

12 Darrel M. Montero, "The Japanese American Community: Generational Changes in Ethnic Affiliation" (Ph.D. diss., UCLA, 1975), 41.

13 Daniels, *Politics of Prejudice*, 46–105; Dorothy S. Thomas, "Some Social Aspects of Japanese-American Demography," *Proceedings of the American Philosophical Society*, 94 (October 1950), 460. Cf. John Higham, *Strangers in the Land* (New York, 1975).

14 Everett V. Stonequist, *The Marginal Man* (New York, 1965; orig. 1937), 105. The Marginal Man concept was first enunciated by Robert E. Park in 1928 ("Human Migration and the Marginal Man," *AJS*, 33 [May 1928], 881–93) and was elaborated shortly thereafter by his student Stonequist. Then followed a lively debate as to the meaning of the concept, its validity, and its usefulness. That debate is ably summarized in H. F. Dickie-Carr, *The Marginal Situation* (London, 1966), 7–26.

15 Kitano, *Japanese Americans*, 26–27, 139–42; Monica Sone, *Nisei Daughter* (Boston, 1953), 1–28; William Petersen, *Japanese Americans* (New York, 1971), 59–62, 202–4; Stanford M. Lyman, "Generation and Character: The Case of the Japanese Americans," in S. M. Lyman, *The Asian in the West* (Reno, 1970), 81–97; Minako K. Maykovich, *Japanese American Identity Dilemma* (Tokyo, 1972), 31–34.

16 Maykovich, *Identity Dilemma*, 55; John Okada, *No-No Boy* (Rutland, Vt., 1957), 34–35. Cf. Gary M. Matsumoto et al., "Ethnic Identity: Honolulu and Seattle Japanese-Americans," in Stanley Sue and Nathaniel M. Wagner, eds., *Asian-Americans: Psychological Perspectives* (Ben Lomond, Calif., 1973), 65–74; James Hirabayashi, "Nisei: The Quiet American?—A Re-Evaluation," *Amerasia Journal*, 3 (1975), 114–29.

It should be noted that the "audience group," as Maykovich put it, was not always White, nor was it always middle-class. Working-class Nisei youths in Los Angeles, Stockton, and rural areas of California, for example, sometimes associated and identified with Mexican Americans rather than with Whites or other Japanese Americans. Far too much literature on American ethnic groups assumes that there are only two groups in America: whatever group is being studied and the dominant WASP majority. It is one of the contentions of this book that most Americans have lived not in bi-ethnic, but in multi-ethnic environments. That was particularly true in such cosmopolitan places as California, Hawaii, and any of the large eastern cities. One cannot fully understand the interracial contacts of Japanese Americans by looking only at Japanese and Whites, any more than one can understand the contact system of Whites by looking only at Whites and Blacks. There were other sorts of people involved in each case. Having said all that, it is still true that the primary reference groups for the majority of the Nisei were the Issei on one side and the White middle class on the other. It was usually —though certainly not always—between these two groups that they were torn.

17 Jeanne Wakatsuki Houston and James D. Houston, *Farewell to Manzanar* (Boston, 1973), 144; Daisuke Kitagawa, *Issei and Nisei* (New York, 1967), 29; L. B. Olinger and V. S. Sommers, "The Divided Path: Psycho-Cultural Neurosis in a Nisei Man," in Georgene Seward, ed., *Clinal Studies in Culture Conflict* (New York, 1958), 359–408.

Such feelings were not isolated. Virginia Hertzler's postwar study of a multi-ethnic high school in Seattle found lingering tensions in the years after World War II. Blacks, Jews, Chinese Americans, and White Gentiles held the Nisei in extremely low esteem as potential leaders, work partners, dates, and friends. The Nisei she surveyed shared those low opinions of

themselves. In selecting leaders, they chose all others but Jews before they
looked to members of their own group. They preferred Whites and Chinese
as work partners and dates, but were in fact thrown back on their own
people when seeking friends. Virginia B. Hertzler, "A Sociometric Study of
Japanese Students in a High School Population" (M.A. thesis, University of
Washington, 1949).

M. E. Smith studied Hawaiian Nisei teenagers in the 1930s and found
that their feelings of inferiority differed by sex. The boys' sense of inferiority was broader and deeper than the girls'. The boys felt bad about being
short, physically weak, and awkward; they felt they lacked essential knowledge about American speech and etiquette, and about such social graces as
dancing; they were nervous about their tendency to blush, their choice of
clothing, and their academic performance; and they were embarrassed by
their poverty and their parents' ignorance of American customs. The Japanese girls felt awkward and ignorant in social situations, and they feared they
would blush and betray themselves, although they did not share the boys'
physical and economic feelings of inferiority. No other ethnic group, Smith
concluded, felt as bad about themselves as did the Nisei. M. E. Smith,
"A Study of the Causes of Feelings of Inferiority," *Journal of Psychology*,
5 (1938), 315–32. Robert H. Ross and Clarke Kawakami spoke of the Nisei
they knew as suffering from "a kind of inferiority complex" relative to White
Americans; see Robert H. Ross, "Social Distance as It Exists between the
First- and Second-Generation Japanese in the City of Los Angeles and Vicin-
ity" (M.A. thesis, University of Southern California, 1939), 113, and Clarke
Kawakami and Yuri Morris, interviewed by Joe Grant Masaoka and Lillian
Takeshita, May 22, 1968 (Bancroft Library, Berkeley, Phonotape 1050B:10).
Also see C. W. Kiefer, *Changing Cultures, Changing Lives* (San Francisco,
1974), 115; William C. Smith, *The Second-Generation Oriental in America*
(Honolulu, 1927), 9; George A. Lundberg and Lenore Dickson, "Selective
Association among Ethnic Groups in a High School Population," *ASR*, 17
(1952), 23–35; Gordon K. Hirabayashi, "A Sociometric Study of the University of Washington Students of Japanese Ancestry" (M.A. thesis, University
of Washington, 1949).

18 "The Relocation Program at Tule Lake" (JERS R20.84), 338–48; "Nisei
Attitude Survey" (JERS Carton 3); Doris Ihara* Interview (CKI-39); Rose
Hayashi* Interview (CKI-24); Kitagawa, *Issei and Nisei*, 25; James Sakoda,
"Recreation: Dancing" (JERS R20.87A); Chotoku Toyama, "The Japanese
Community in Los Angeles" (M.A. thesis, Columbia University, 1926). It is
worth noting that such striving to be accepted as full Americans was common
to the second generation of most immigrant groups, not just the Nisei. The
Nisei subculture is a subject ripe for study, though it is beyond the scope
of the present volume. Bill Hosokawa describes elements of that subculture,
although he does not analyze it, in *Nisei: The Quiet Americans* (New York,
1969) and *JACL: In Quest of Justice* (New York, 1982).

19 See, for example, Michi Weglyn, *Years of Infamy* (New York, 1976); Dorothy S. Thomas and Richard Nishimoto, *The Spoilage* (Berkeley, 1969; orig.

1946); Jacobus ten Broek et al., *Prejudice, War, and the Constitution* (Berkeley, 1968; orig. 1954); Daniels, *Concentration Camps USA;* Thomas et al., *The Salvage;* Audrie Girdner and Anne Loftis, *The Great Betrayal* (New York, 1969); Leonard Bloom and Ruth Reimer, *Removal and Return* (Berkeley, 1949); Alexander H. Leighton, *The Governing of Men* (Princeton, 1968; orig. 1945); Morton Grodzins, *Americans Betrayed* (Chicago, 1949); Leonard Broom and John I. Kitsuse, *The Managed Casualty* (Berkeley, 1956); Edward H. Spicer et al., *Impounded People* (Tucson, 1969); Allan R. Bosworth, *America's Concentration Camps* (New York, 1967); Mine Okubo, *Citizen 13660* (New York, 1966; orig. 1946); John Modell, ed., *The Kikuchi Diary* (Urbana, Ill., 1973); Jeanne Wakatsuki Houston and James D. Houston, *Farewell to Manzanar* (Boston, 1973); John Tateishi, *And Justice for All* (New York, 1984); Peter Irons, *Justice at War* (New York, 1984).

20 For one manifestation of this trend, see Paul R. Spickard, "The Nisei Assume Power: The Japanese American Citizens League, 1941–1942," *Pacific Historical Review,* 52 (1983), 147–74.

21 Bureau of the Census, *Nonwhite Population (1960);* Bureau of the Census, *Japanese, Chinese, and Filipinos (1970);* Kitano, *Japanese Americans,* 210–11; Art Chin, *Up Hill: The Settlement and Diffusion of the Chinese in Seattle, Washington* (Seattle, 1970); Field notes, Seattle, 1965–78, Los Angeles, 1973 and 1979, and San Francisco, 1974–81.

22 Calvin F. Schmid and Charles E. Nobbe, "Socioeconomic Differentials among Nonwhite Races," *ASR,* 30 (1965), 909–22; Kitano, *Japanese Americans,* 89–104, 214; Petersen, *Japanese Americans,* 113–22; Yukio Okano, "Correlates of Ethnic Identity in Japanese Americans" (M.A. thesis, University of Denver, 1970), 60–64; Darrel M. Montero, "The Japanese American Community: Generational Changes in Ethnic Affiliation" (Ph.D. diss., UCLA, 1975), 41.

23 Darrel Montero and Gene N. Levine, "Third-Generation Japanese Americans" (unpublished paper, 1974), courtesy of the authors; Eric Woodrum, "An Assessment of Japanese American Assimilation, Pluralism, ad Subordination," *AJS,* 87 (1981), 157–69. Neither dispersion nor mobility nor intermarriage necessarily meant that individual Sansei gave up their Japanese American ethnic identity. Hilla Israely studied Los Angeles Sansei and found that most had distinct compartments for American and Japanese identifications: "Certain attitudes and actions of the Sansei are governed solely by their Japanese subidentity while other spheres of life are controlled exclusively by the American one. . . . Both subidentities enjoy an almost equally important position within the identity structure of the Sansei with a slight edge in favor of the American one." Hilla K. Israely, "An Exploration into Ethnic Identity: The Case of Third-Generation Japanese Americans" (Ph.D. diss., UCLA, 1976), 369–70. Cf. Maykovich, *Japanese American Identity Dilemma,* 65–151.

24 For the dominant, anti-Japanese view, see James D. Phelan, "Why California Objects to the Japanese Invasion," *Annals of the American Academy of Political and Social Science,* 93 (1921), 16–17; John S. Chambers, "The

Japanese Invasion," ibid., 23–29; V. S. McClatchy, "Japanese in the Melting Pot: Can They Assimilate and Make Good Citizens?" ibid., 28–34; Marshall DeMotte, "California, White or Yellow?" ibid., 18–23; Margaret Holliday, "Social Relations between the Japanese and the Californians" (M.A. thesis, Columbia University, 1921), 8; "Are Japanese People?" *Literary Digest,* 81 (April 26, 1924), 22–23. For a pair of mildly hysterical extensions of the Asian hordes theory, see Lothrop Stoddard, *The Rising Tide of Color* (New York, 1920), and Madison Grant, *The Passing of the Great Race* (New York, 1922). For alternative, and largely unheard, voices in the debate, see Jesse F. Steiner, *The Japanese Invasion* (Chicago, 1917), 150–51; Sidney E. Gulick, *The American Japanese Problem* (New York, 1914); H. A. Millis, *The Japanese Problem in the United States* (New York, 1915); Elliot G. Mears, *Resident Orientals on the American Pacific Coast* (New York, 1927); Sidney Gulick, *Mixing the Races in Hawaii* (Honolulu, 1937); E. Manchester Boddy, *Japanese in America* (Los Angeles, 1921); Robert Newton Lynch, "The Development of the Anti-Japanese Movement" *Annals,* 93 (1921), 47–52. Japanese immigrants spoke in their own defense, and also went unheard. See Toyokichi Iyenaga and Kenosuke Sato, *Japan and the California Problem* (New York, 1924); Kiichi Kanzaki, *California and the Japanese* (San Francisco, 1921); Junzo Sasamori, "Social Life of Japanese in America" (unpublished MS, Bancroft Library, University of California, Berkeley, 1927); K. K. Kawakami, *Japan in World Politics* (New York, 1917); idem, *Asia at the Door* (New York, 1914); Juichi Soyeda and T. Kamiya, *A Survey of the Japanese Question in California* (San Francisco, 1913); Tasuku Harada, *The Social Status of the Japanese in Hawaii* (Honolulu, 1927).

25 Daniels, *Concentration Camps USA,* 15.

26 California *Statutes,* Civil Code, 1909, sec. 60; Megumi Dick Osumi, "Asians and California's Anti-Miscegenation Laws," in Tsuchida, *Asian and Pacific American Experiences,* 1–37. Marriages between Blacks and Whites were already prohibited.

27 *Grizzly Bear* (July 1923), 27, quoted in Roger Daniels, *Politics of Prejudice* (Berkeley, 1968), 85; DeMotte, "White or Yellow?"; Dennis Ogawa, *From Japs to Japanese* (Berkeley, 1971), 15, 18.

28 The movie material in this paragraph and those that follow derives mainly from my own late-night watching of old movies over the last two and a half decades. The analysis presented here also draws from Frank Chin, "Confessions of a Number One Son," *Ramparts,* 11 (March 1973), 41–48; Eugene Franklin Wong, "On Visual Media Racism: Asians in the American Motion Pictures" (Ph.D. diss., University of Denver, 1977); Richard A. Oehling, "The Yellow Menace: Asian Images in American Film," in Randall M. Miller, ed., *The Kaleidoscopic Lens* (Englewood Cliffs, N.J., 1980), 182–206; Christine Choy, "Images of Asian-Americans in Films and Television," in R. M. Miller, ed., *Ethnic Images in American Film and Television* (Philadelphia, 1978), 145–55; Herbert Morikawa, "Psychological Implications of Asian Stereotypes in the Media," ibid., 161–65; Irvin Paik, "That Oriental Feeling" in Amy Tachiki et al., *Roots: An Asian American Reader* (Los Angeles, 1971), 30–36; Ogawa, *From Japs to Japanese.*

29 Chin, "Number One Son."

30 In the decades after World War II, jobs that demanded dynamic people seldom went to Asian men. Senior members of a large San Francisco law firm told one of their junior lawyers, an Asian male, that he would never make partner. They acknowledged that he wrote the best law of any of their young prospects, that he worked hard, and that his technical skills were excellent, but they felt he lacked certain undefinable qualities that made one a top-notch trial lawyer. His subsequent career proved how wrong they were, leaving the lingering suspicion that they saw him as a category—Asian male —which they could not associate with dynamism and charisma. In similar fashion, one searched in vain in the 1970s for Asian male faces on the nightly news of West Coast cities with large Asian populations. Asian women there were aplenty, but the men apparently were not seen as dynamic enough to come across well in that medium. Even Asian roles in television series seldom went to Asian men. France Nuyen, Nancy Kwan, Aimee Eccles, and Miyoshi Umeki had enough dynamism to play movie or TV parts for Asian women. But no Asian male could be found with the star quality to play the lead role in the *Kung Fu* series. Under pressure from Asian groups, the producers changed the wandering martial artist's background from full to half Chinese so that David Carradine would not look so out of place, but they would not consider an Asian actor for the leading role. Norman Mar, "Yellow TV Caricatures Become Real," *University of Washington Daily*, Spring 1971; idem, "This Silver Bullet Will Tell You Who I Am" (student paper, University of Washington, 1971); Felicia Lowe et al., "The Portrayal of Chinese in the Media" (paper presented to the National Conference on Chinese American Studies, San Francisco, October 10, 1980); Irvin Paik, "Kung Fu Fan Klub," in Emma Gee, ed., *Counterpoint* (Los Angeles, 1976), 289–94; Jan Masaoka, "I Forgot My Eyes Were Black" in *Asian Women* (Berkeley, 1971), 57–59; Margaret Woo, "Woman + Man = Political Unity," in *Asian Women*, 115–16; field notes, Seattle, Boston, and San Francisco, 1967–85.

31 See the sources cited in note 30, and Jane B. Kaihatsu, "Asian Americans and Outmarriage," *Pacific Citizen* (December 20–27, 1985), A-8.

32 James Michener, *Tales of the South Pacific* (New York, 1967; orig. 1946), 173ff. In the minds of many White Americans—the men, at least—there is a continuity between Asian and Polynesian women that serves to heighten the Asians' sexual attractiveness. White European and American men see Pacific Island women as extremely sexy. Many a harried executive has dreamed of escaping to Tahiti, not only for surf and sun and a relaxed way of living, but also for the legendary attractions of Polynesian women, much as Paul Gauguin fled a shrewish wife in Copenhagen to paint and live with a succession of bare-breasted Tahitian women. It is thought by some that Pacific Island women are possessed by a special enthusiasm for sexual activity. James Michener has one of his heroes, Teroro, overwhelmed by the adolescent sexuality of a girl named Tehani, in the blockbuster *Hawaii*. Generations later, another Bora-Bora girl, also named Tehani, takes up with Hoxworth Hale because she likes White babies. A Hawaiian girl, Iliki, uses the English she learned in missionary school to make her way in the world from man to

man, saying "please" each time she is mounted. In the 1938 movie, *Bird of Paradise*, Joel McCrae found unwedded bliss on a tropical isle in the arms of a topless and enthusiastic Polynesian princess played by Dolores Del Rio. Unfortunately, their happiness was interrupted by an insistent volcano, to which Del Rio had to be sacrificed.

The image of sexual enthusiasm carries over from Polynesian women to their Asian sisters because Whites do not always distinguish between the two. Both sorts of women, in their stereotypical incarnations, have long, flowing black hair and warm, dusky skin. In the minds of Whites, Asian women often take on roles that properly belong to women from the Pacific Islands. In his first book, Michener placed his Asian woman, Liat, on a South Pacific isle. In an infamous television commercial from the 1970s, an Asian woman appeared at Honolulu airport dressed in Hawaiian costume. She bestowed a lei and a kiss on a visiting businessman, only to recoil in horror at her discovery that he had "wing awound the collar." Not only was this advertisement silly and demeaning to all involved, but it also placed an Asian woman in the role of a Hawaiian, and no one seemed to notice that she was out of place, because people did not distinguish between the two groups. When Asian women pose for pornographic magazines, they are often sent to Hawaiian beaches to disrobe. Apparently, Hawaii is thought to be a more natural location for them to exhibit their bodies than an apartment in Philadelphia or the streets of Los Angeles. They don (and then remove) sarongs, leis, and other Polynesian paraphernalia to emphasize their identification with the Pacific Islands. Similarly, more than one TV shampoo commercial has placed a dark-haired woman—Asian or Polynesian, it does not matter— beside a Hawaiian waterfall dressed in a sarong with her long hair cascading down her bare back. The suggestion of luxuriant sexuality is unmistakable.

This connection, in the minds of White men, between Japanese and Polynesian women was not new when James Michener was serving in the South Pacific. A half century earlier Lafcadio Hearn saw his marriage to a Japanese woman as the same sort of act as the marriage of his hero Pierre Loti to a Tahitian. What was different after World War II was the increasing number of American men who were struck with the vision of Japanese women being as exotic and sexually attractive as they believed Polynesian women to be. See Robert Wallace, *The World of Van Gogh* (New York, 1969), 116–35; James Michener, *Hawaii* (New York, 1959) 54–81, 362–72, 912–20; centerfold photo essays in *Playboy*, April 1976, and *Penthouse*, January 1981; and Elizabeth Stevenson, *Lafcadio Hearn* (New York, 1961).

33 *Diamond Head* (Columbia Pictures, 1963); "White Male Qualities" in Amy Tachiki et al., *Roots* (Los Angeles, 1971), 44–45; Debbie Hirano*, interviewed by the author, Berkeley, Calif., February 15, 1980; Ogawa, *From Japs to Japanese*; Elaine Louie, "The Myth of the Erotic Exotic," *Bridge*, 2 (April, 1973), 19–20; "If You Knew Suzee," *Penthouse*, January 1981, 87– 105; "The Girls of the Orient," *Playboy*, December 1968, 172; Ian Fleming, *You Only Live Twice* (New York, 1964); James Clavell, *Shogun* (New York, 1975); Tabor Evans, *Longarm and the Hatchet Men* (New York, 1979);

Gillian Stone, *Land of Golden Mountains* (New York, 1980). The pornographic movie industry was particularly expressive of the Asian-woman-assexual-enthusiast view. The mid-1970s saw a boom in pornographic movies starring Asian women, with such titles as *China Girls, Oriental Blue, Diversions of an Oriental* ("hard core with a new slant on things"), *Oriental Kitten* ("Mishi loves America—it's so big and beautiful. Mishi loves John Holmes —for the same reason!"), and *Erotic Fantasies of a Eurasian Nymph* ("She's a new breed of woman. Part Oriental, part European. She'll jolt you right out of your seat!")—all advertisements from the pornographic movie section, *San Francisco Chronicle*, November 20 and 24, 1975.

34 Lori Matsukawa, "Miss Teenage America 1974," in *Asian American Women* (Stanford, 1976), 37–38; *Three Days of the Condor* (Paramount, 1975); classified advertisement in *Seattle Weekly*, October 7–13, 1981, 39.

35 Masaoka, "I Forgot My Eyes Were Black"; Larry Hama, "I Am Yellow . . . Curious?" *Bridge*, 2 (April 1973), 21–22; Field notes, Seattle, 1970–71.

36 Ron Tanaka, "I hate my wife for her flat yellow face," in Tachiki, *Roots*, 46–47; Hama, "I Am Yellow"; Lawson Inada, "Asian Brother, Asian Sister," in Tachiki, *Roots*, 121–27.

37 Harumi Befu, *Japan: An Anthropological Introduction* (San Francisco, 1971), 125–26. As Chie Nakane demonstrated, Japan is a society of vertical cliques. Foreigners do not belong to any clique, and so do not belong to Japanese society. Chie Nakane, *Japanese Society* (Berkeley, 1970).

38 George A. DeVos and William O. Wetherall, *Japan's Minorities* (London, 1974), 18; Cullen Tadao Hayashida, "Identity, Race, and the Blood Ideology of Japan" (Ph.D. diss., University of Washington, 1976); Ichiro Kawasaki, *Japan Unmasked* (Rutland, Vt., 1969), 75.

39 Hiroshi Wagatsuma, "The Social Perception of Skin Color in Japan," in John Hope Franklin, ed., *Color and Race* (Boston, 1968), 129–65; Wagatsuma, "Some Problems of Interracial Marriage for the Japanese," in Irving R. Stuart and Lawrence E. Abt, eds., *Interracial Marriage* (New York, 1967), 247–64. Information for the rest of this section, except where otherwise noted, comes from Wagatsuma's work.

40 It is quite possible that these unflattering ideas about Africans were not independent creations of the minds of Japanese, but rather were picked up from Europeans, whose prejudices about Black people were not dissimilar. Winthrop Jordan has described the racial thinking of seventeenth-century English people, who associated blackness with evil, danger, ugliness, repulsion, and sin, and who saw Africans as apelike savages, vaguely subhuman, and given over to bestial lusts. Jordan, *White over Black* (Chapel Hill, 1968), 3–43 and passim.

41 This order did not specify any punishment for Japanese women who had consorted with Iberian men. It is not clear whether they were covered by a separate edict or were intended to share the punishments awarded their children here. It is not likely that they were to be allowed to stay in Japan. By this edict not only children of mixed percentage, but even foster parents of such children, were to be deported on pain of death. Charles R. Boxer,

The Christian Century in Japan (Berkeley, 1951), 439–40; G. B. Sansom, *The Western World and Japan* (New York, 1973; orig. 1949), 267–80; Ronald Toby to the author, July 26, 1980; C. R. Boxer "The Rise and Fall of Nicholas Iguan," *T'ien Hsia Monthly*, 11 (1941), 401–39; Torao Haraguchi et al., *The Status System and Social Organization of Satsuma* (Toyko, 1975), 88–89.

42   Wagatsuma, "Social Perception of Skin Color," 143.

43   Toshio Mori, *Yokohama, California* (Caldwell, Idaho, 1949); Setsuko Matsunaga, "The Adjustment of Evacuees in St. Louis" (M.A. thesis, Washington University, 1944), 91–97 (JERS T1.880); Okada, *No-No Boy*, 102–6, 114, 215. Cf. the obsession with whiteness and White womanhood that Endo Shusaku shows in his novel *Up to Aden;* translation of a passage of that novel appears in Wagatsuma, "Social Perception of Skin Color in Japan," 146–47.

44   Frances Nishimoto* Interview (CKI-22); Hiromasa Minami* Interview (CKI-21); Kisako Yasuda* Interview (CKI-51); Shizuko Hattori* Interview (CKI-26); Sylvia J. Yanagisako, "Social and Cultural Change in Japanese-American Kinship" (Ph.D. diss., University of Washington, 1975), 154; Lester Kimura* Interview (CKI-47); Rose Hayashi* Interview; Yasuko Hayashi* Interview (CKI-9); Barry Shimizu* Interview (CKI-46).

45   Tanaka, "I Hate My Wife"; Hama, "I Am Yellow"; "White Male Qualities."

Chapter 3. Old Barriers Fall

1   Constantine Panunzio, "Intermarriage in Los Angeles, 1924–33," *AJS*, 47 (March 1942), 690–701; U.S. Bureau of the Census, *Japanese, Chinese, and Filipinos*, Subject Report PC(2)-1G (Washington, D.C., 1973), 17–23. Cf. Paul R. Spickard, "Mixed Marriage: Two American Minority Groups and the Limits of Ethnic Identity, 1900–1970" (Ph.D. diss., University of California, Berkeley, 1983), 493–96.

2   Panunzio, "Intermarriage in Los Angeles"; Benicio T. Catapusan, "Filipino Intermarriage Problems in the United States," *SSR*, 22 (1938), 265–72.

3   E.S.S., "Interview with Mrs. H———" (SRR major document 235); Jesse F. Steiner, *The Japanese Invasion* (Chicago, 1917), 170; Emma Fong Kuno, "My Oriental Husbands" (SRR major document 53); "Progeny of Jap-White Union Amaze," *San Francisco Examiner*, November 11, 1922 (SRR major document 222); Western Defense Command, "Summary of Mixed Marriage Families" (WDC); U.S. War Relocation Authority (WRA), Tabulation of All Census Forms 26 (JERS Shelf F). Cf. Spickard, "Mixed Marriage," 507.

4   "Japanese Matron Prefers America," *San Francisco Chronicle*, March 3, 1922 (SRR minor document 251); WRA Census Form 26, no. 210767, 956854 (JERS Shelf F); "The Relocation Program at Tule Lake" (JERS R20.84).

5   Chotoku Toyama reported that domestic relations in Los Angeles's Little Tokyo were unstable as late as the 1920s: "Sexual relations between Japanese men and American women are numerous. A Japanese man was killed because of sexual relations with a white married woman on October 10th, 1925. Deserted husbands are much in evidence. We see almost every day advertisements in search of a wife who has deserted her husband." Maude

Madden reported in 1923 on a Japanese woman who had left her husband and son to live with a White man and run a boarding house. Madden attributed desertions and interracial marriages by Japanese women to the picture bride system, which brought many Japanese women to America to marry men they had never seen, with high expectations that were sure to be dashed on the hard realities of life in America. Takiji Morimoto, "The Oriental Pioneer" (SRR major document 336); Kazuo Ito, *Issei* (Seattle, 1973), 765–72; Yuji Ichioka, "Ameyuki-san: Japanese Prostitutes in Nineteenth-Century America," *Amerasia Journal*, 4 (1977), 10–11; Elaine Black Yoneda, interviewed by Betty Mitson, San Francisco, March 3, 1974 (California State University, Fullerton, Oral History Tape OH1377a); Tabulation of all WRA Census Forms 26 (JERS Shelf F). Chotoku Toyama, "The Japanese Community in Los Angeles" (M.A. thesis, Columbia University, 1926), 45; Maude Madden, *When the East Is in the West* (New York, 1923), 129–34. Cf. Spickard, "Mixed Marriage," 506.

6   E.S.S., "Interview with Mrs. H————"; WRA Census Form 26, nos. 506936–37 (JERS Shelf F); K. Lentz, "Intermarriage: A Case Study" (SRR major document 173).

7   Robert Ross and E. S. Bogardus, "Four Types of Nisei Marriage Patterns," *SSR*, 25 (1940), 63–66; William C. Smith, "Changing Personality Traits of Second-Generation Orientals in America," *AJS*, 33 (1928), 922–29; Mildred Doi Kosaki, "The Culture Conflicts and Guidance Needs of Nisei Adolescents" (M.A. thesis, University of Hawaii, 1949), 61–68; George K. Yamamoto, "Social Adjustment of Caucasian-Japanese Marriages in Hawaii" (M.A. thesis, University of Hawaii, 1949), 69; Motoku Shinosaki* Interview (CKI-49); Tamiko T. Yamamoto, "Trends in Marriage Practices among the Nisei in Hawaii," University of Hawaii, Adams Social Research Laboratory Report 21 (1950), 9; F. E. LaViolette, *Americans of Japanese Ancestry* (Toronto, 1946), 109–39; W. C. Smith, *Second-Generation Oriental*, 5–12; Jitsuichi Masuoka, "Japanese Patriarch in Hawaii," *Social Forces*, 17 (1938), 240–48.

8   "Relocation Program at Tule Lake" (JERS R20.84), 315–20, 349–54; Hazel Nishi* Interview (CKI-3); All enlhara* Interview (CKI-34); Ida Shigaki Interview (CKI-56); William C. Smith, "Interview with Susie Yamamoto," August 9, 1924 (SRR major document 77); Charlotte G. Babcock and William Caudill, "Personal and Cultural Factors in Treating a Nisei Man," In Georgene Seward, ed., *Clinical Studies in Culture Conflict* (New York, 1951).

The sense of fear, inferiority, longing, and self-consciousness many Nisei felt toward Whites came through in the words of a Hawaiian Nisei boy from about 1930. He knew an older White woman quite well through their mutual involvement in a religious group. "Once she invited me to a school dance, and told me that I could dance with her. I was determined to dance with her that evening, so after the first dance, I pulled together my nerve and went up to her for a dance. When I went up to her she was speaking with a lady next to her. She did not see me approaching her. This was what came to my mind. 'Would she not feel quite out of place to dance with a Japanese student in a public place like this? Would she not feel cheap to dance with

a Japanese while there are many Haoles watching us?' I turned away and
returned to my seat. I danced with other Japanese girls, but I stayed away
from her even though I knew all the time that she would not refuse me if I
should ask for a dance." Jitsuichi Masuoka, "Race Attitudes of the Japanese
Population in Hawaii" (M.A. thesis, University of Hawaii, 1931), 118.

9   Tabulation of all WRA Census Forms 26 (JERS Shelf F); Julius Drachsler,
    Intermarriage in New York City (New York, 1921), 35. Cf. Spickard, "Mixed
    Marriage," 505–10. Drachsler surveyed 79,704 Manhattan and Bronx mar-
    riage licenses for the years 1908–12 and recorded the intermarriage rates for
    55 ethnic and racial groups.

10 See, for example, Peter Irons, *Justice at War* (New York, 1983); Michi We-
    glyn, *Years of Infamy* (New York, 1976); Dorothy S. Thomas and Richard
    Nishimoto, *The Spoilage* (Berkeley, 1969; orig. 1946); Jacobus ten Broek et
    al., *Prejudice, War and the Constitution* (Berkeley, 1968; orig. 1954); Roger
    Daniels, *Concentration Camps, USA* (New York, 1971); Dorothy S. Thomas
    et al., *The Salvage* (Berkeley, 1952); Audrie Girdner and Anne Loftis, *The
    Great Betrayal* (New York, 1969); Leonard Bloom and Ruth Reimer, *Re-
    moval and Return* (Berkeley, 1949); Alexander H. Leighton, *The Governing
    of Men* (Princeton, 1968; orig. 1945); Morton Grodzins, *Americans Betrayed*
    (Chicago, 1949); Leonard Broom and John I. Kitsuse, *The Managed Casualty*
    (Berkeley, 1956); Edward H. Spicer et al., *Impounded People* (Tucson, 1969);
    Allan R. Bosworth, *America's Concentration Camps* (New York, 1967); Mine
    Okubo, *Citizen 13660* (New York, 1966; orig. 1946); John Modell, ed., *The
    Kikuchi Diary* (Urbana, Ill., 1973); Jeanne Wakatsuki Houston and James D.
    Houston, *Farewell to Manzanar* (Boston, 1973); Richard Drinnon, *Keeper of
    Concentration Camps* (Berkeley, 1987); Thomas James, *Exile Within* (Cam-
    bridge, 1987).

11 Charles Kikuchi, "The Social Adjustment Process of the Japanese American
    Resettlers to Chicago during the Wartime Years" (M.S.W. thesis, Columbia
    University, 1947), 105.

12 Kisako Yasuda* Interview (CKI-51); "Relocation Program at Tule Lake"
    (JERS R20.84), 315–32; Sue Kunitomi Embrey, interviewed by A. A. Han-
    sen, D. A. Hacker, and D. J. Bertagnoli, October 24, 1973 (California State
    University, Fullerton, Oral History Office, Tape OH1366); Shizuko Hattori*
    Interview (CKI-26); Harry Ando* Interview (CKI-31); Hazel Nishi* Inter-
    view (CKI-3); Rhonda Kaneshiro* Interview; "Miscellany" (JERS R20.03);
    Robert O'Brien, *The College Nisei* (New York, 1978; orig. Palo Alto, 1949),
    50.

13 The World War II experiences of intermarried Japanese Americans and their
    mixed racial offspring constitute a story of their own, told by this author in
    "Injustice Compounded: Amerasians and Non-Japanese in America's World
    War II Concentration Camps," *Journal of American Ethnic History*, 5 (Spring
    1986), 5–22, from which the following discussion is drawn.

14 It is interesting to note that the Army saw this environment business, not in
    terms of conflicting *national* loyalties and cultures (that is, American versus
    Japanese), but rather in terms of *racial* loyalties and cultures. Whenever the

leaders of the Western Defense Command spoke of the kind of environment they wanted for these children, they labeled it "Caucasian"—not "American" or "Western," or even "wholesome." Though such an appellation would confound an anthropologist, presumably it meant something to the government planners.

15 Not all of the non-Japanese inmates were relatives of Japanese Americans. In a few bizarre and tragic cases, people of other ethnic groups got caught up in the evacuation and were unable to find a way out. Peter Ogata* was one such person. In 1942, the Army took 145 Japanese Alaskans from their homes and put them in the prison camp at Puyallup, Washington. About 50 of those were the children of Japanese fishermen or cannery workers and Indian or Eskimo women, among them Ogata's two half-brothers. Peter Ogata was born at Taku Harbor in 1915. His Indian mother had become pregnant by an Indian man. To salvage her respectability she married Hajime Ogata* while Peter was still in her womb. She and Hajime had two boys of their own before Hajime deserted the family. The boys were brought up by missionaries among other Indians. They had never been to a city, much less around Japanese Americans, before the government took them to camp. Peter, tall, powerfully built, and dark-skinned, was a full-blooded Tlingit Indian, as were his wife and infant son. But the government took them anyway because they had a Japanese last name—at the same time that they left free full-blooded Japanese Alaskans who had taken Indian names. Peter complained that "when we got to camp all the Japanese people gawked at us." The Ogata family were treated as curiosities by their fellow inmates and were very lonely in camp. But things got worse when they managed to get a leave clearance to settle in Chicago. Unemployed and unused to city life, they grew depressed and bitter, longing for their woodland home. When Peter was interviewed by Charles Kikuchi in 1944, he was bitter against the bungling government bureaucracy for forcing his family into such a degraded state, against the Japanese Americans who had mistreated him in camp, and against his stepfather—both for deserting the family and for giving him the name that had caused him so much trouble. He vowed, "Someday I'm going to slit his neck open if I ever find him, by golly."

16 Gordon Asahi* Interview (CKI-58).

17 Isamu Furuta* Interview (CKI-62); Rose Hayashi* Interview (CKI-24).

18 Gene N. Levine and Colbert C. Rhodes, *The Japanese American Community* (New York, 1981), 46; U.S. Bureau of the Census, *1960 Census: Nonwhite Population by Race*, Subject Report PC(2)-1C (Washington, D.C., 1963); Bureau of the Census, *1970 Census: Japanese, Chinese, and Filipinos in the United States*, Subject Report PC(2)-1G (Washington, D.C., 1973); Harry H. L. Kitano, *Japanese Americans*, 2nd ed. (Englewood Cliffs, N.J., 1976), 210–11; Tomoko Makabe, "Nisei Ethnic Identity," *Rikka*, 3 (1976), 18–22.

19 Tetsuden Kashima, "Japanese American Internees Return, 1945 to 1955," *Phylon*, 41 (1980), 107–15; William Petersen, *Japanese Americans* (New York, 1971), 113–26; Kitano, *Japanese Americans*, 89–104.

20 Daniel I. Okimoto, *American in Disguise* (Tokyo, 1971), 150–51, 154–55.

21 Kashima, "Japanese American Internees Return"; cf. Bob Suzuki, "Education and Socialization of Asian Americans: A Revisionist Analysis of the 'Model-Minority' Thesis," *Amerasia Journal*, 4 (1977), 23–52.

22 Darrel M. Montero, "The Japanese American Community: Generational Changes in Ethnic Affiliation" (Ph.D. diss., University of California, Los Angeles, 1975), 55 and passim; Tad Kurushima*, interviewed by the author, Seattle, August 1972.

23 Larry D. Barnett, "Interracial Marriage in California," *Marriage and Family Living* (1963), 424–25; Akemi Kikumura and Harry H. L. Kitano, "Interracial Marriage: A Picture of the Japanese Americans," *Journal of Social Issues*, 29 (1973), 67–81; Bureau of Census, *Japanese, Chinese, and Filipinos* (1970), 17–23. For the last point, cf. the Nisei age distribution in Levine and Rhodes, *Japanese American Community*, 59. James Bossard might have attributed the intermarriage increase simply to the Nisei dispersion to the suburbs. In an essay entitled, "Residential Propinquity as a Factor in Marriage Selection," in *AJS*, 35 (1932), 219–24, he observed that "romantic love aside, the 'one and only' typically lives within driving distance." While he is undoubtedly correct about the importance of residence, the other factors cited above also contributed to the upsurge in intermarriages by the younger Nisei and the Sansei.

A Note on the Reporting of Intermarriage. There are two common ways of reporting rates of intermarriage. One way, used by Kikumura and Kitano in "Interracial Marriage" is to count the number of marriages that involve two Japanese American individuals and compare that to the number of marriages that involve one Japanese American partner. Thus, they would report the following group of marriages as 50 percent intermarried:

> Jane Watanabe/Harry Hondo Fred Akiyoshi/Aphrodite Tamura
> Alfred Schwartz/Sylvia Aoki George Nagai/Theresa Appleby

That is, Kikumura and Kitano see four marriages, two homogamous and two heterogamous.

The present study counts intermarriages in a different manner. In the example given, I see six Japanese American individuals, two of whom have intermarried. I would record an intermarriage rate of 33.3 percent. My reasoning is that most observers, when looking at a group of Japanese Americans, want to know how many individuals will marry outside the group. That is, they want to know what is the probability that a given person will intermarry.

Any other method of counting intermarriages is artificial and misleading. If one follows the Kikumura-Kitano method for this hypothetical sample, one will report that half the Japanese marriages are intermarriages. Then hearts will flutter and tongues will wag in Japanese American communities, for people will think that half of the Japanese Americans are married to non-Japanese. But that is not the case. In the hypothetical population reported here, only one-third of the Japanese Americans are married to non-Japanese.

24 Levine and Rhodes, *Japanese American Community*, 109–43.

25 See James W. Loewen, *The Mississippi Chinese* (Cambridge, Mass., 1971), 152; Melford S. Weiss, "Selective Acculturation and the Dating Process: The Pattern of Chinese-Caucasian Inter-racial Dating," in Stanley Sue and Nathaniel Wagner, eds., *Asian-Americans: Psychological Perspectives* (Ben Lomond, Calif., 1973), 86–94. Linked with this power dynamic was a pattern that emerged in many West Coast communities where substantial numbers of Japanese Americans lived. Certain single, non-Japanese Americans—White males, usually—made it a practice to hang around with groups of Japanese Americans and date Sansei women exclusively. The motives of such persons are unclear, but the pattern of their behavior is familiar to anyone who spent time among Sansei during the 1960s and 1970s. A White Berkeley student admitted to Fumiko Sagasawara* that he was taking Asian studies courses mainly because he hoped to meet Asian women. Debbie Hirano* and Grace Morizawa were critical of White men they had known because they felt these men were asking them out simply because they were Japanese. These men had erotic, exotic stereotypes of Sansei women to which they expected these two women to conform, and the women resented it. Field notes, Seattle, 1965–71, Berkeley, 1974–81; Debbie Hirano*, interviewed by the author; Grace Morizawa, "Tomas, Where Are You?" in *Asian American Women*.

26 Kikumura and Kitano, "Interracial Marriage"; Donna Lockwood Leonetti and Laura Newell-Morris, "Exogamy and Change in the Biosocial Structure of a Modern Urban Population," *American Anthropologist*, 84 (1982), 19–36; Bureau of the Census, *Japanese, Chinese, and Filipinos* (1970), 17–23; Bureau of the Census, *1980 Census of Population: Marital Characteristics*, Subject Report PC80-2-4C (Washington, D.C., 1985), 175–81; Harry H. L. Kitano, "Asian-American Interracial Marriage," *JMF*, 46 (1984), 179–90. Cf. Spickard, "Mixed Marriage," 491–96.

27 Montero, "Japanese American Community," 72–77; John N. Tinker, "Intermarriage and Ethnic Boundaries: The Japanese American Case," *Journal of Social Issues*, 29 (1973), 49–66; Kikumura and Kitano, "Interracial Marriage;" Bureau of the Census, *Japanese, Chinese, and Filipinos* (1970), 17–23; Kitano, "Asian-American Interracial Marriage." Cf. Spickard, "Mixed Marriage," 493–96.

28 Kitano, *Japanese Americans*, 189; Bessie Bloom Wessel, *An Ethnic Survey of Woonsocket, Rhode Island* (New York, 1970; orig. Chicago, 1931), 128. To arrive at these percentages I have had to convert Wessel's computations to the system used in this study (see note 23 above).

29 Chotoku Toyama, "The Life History as a Social Document," May 27, 1924 (SRR major document 312); Chloe Holt, "Account of a Visit with a White Woman Married to a Japanese," Los Angeles, August 14, 1924 (SRR major document 104). Also Maude Madden, *When the East Is in the West* (San Francisco, 1971; orig. New York, 1923), 39. In general, students and other Issei who had been in America only a short time opposed intermarriage more vigorously than those who had been here longer.

30 Toyama, "Life History"; "A Japanese Physician's Wife," interview of Mrs.

Suie Murakami, Mrs. Tashiro, interpreter, Seattle, June 4, 1924 (SRR major document 46); S. Minami, letter, June 11, 1924, Seattle (SRR minor document 152).

31 Setsuko Matsunaga, "The Adjustment of Evacuees in St. Louis" (M.A. thesis, Washington University, 1944; JERS T1.880), 91–97; "Relocation Program at Tule Lake" (JERS R20.84), 358–62; Kunio Nagoshi and and Charles Nishimura, "Some Observations Regarding Haole-Japanese Marriages in Hawaii," *SPH*, 18 (1954), 57–65; Frederick Samuels, "Colour Sensitivity among Honolulu's Haoles and Japanese," *Race*, 11 (1969), 203–12; George K. Yamamoto, "Social Adjustment of Caucasian-Japanese Marriages in Hawaii" (M.A. thesis, University of Hawaii, 1949), 34–35, 48, 53, 56; Jitsuichi Masuoka, "Race Attitudes of the Japanese Population in Hawaii" (M.A. thesis, University of Hawaii, 1931), 178.

32 Sue Kunitomi Embrey, interviewed by A. A. Hansen, D. A. Hacker, and D. J. Bertagnoli, October 24, 1973 (California State University, Fullerton, Oral History Tape OH 1366); Ruth F. Uyesugi, *Don't Cry, Chiisai, Don't Cry* (Paoli, Ind., 1977), 10–11.

33 Yamamoto, "Social Adjustment," 33.

34 Marvin K. Opler, "Cultural Dilemma of a Kibei Youth" in Seward, *Clinical Studies in Culture Conflict*, 297–316; Kanichi Niisato, *Nisei Tragedy* (Tokyo, 1936), 38 and passim.

35 Hazel Nishi* Interview; Rose Hayashi* Interview, 15. The Hayashi-Nishi thesis would seem borne out by the statements of some of their contemporaries. Tamie Ihara* became a minor celebrity among her Nisei girlfriends for dating a White boy: "I almost swooned the first time he kissed me. The other Nisei girls thought kissing was so daring and I became a sort of heroine among them for a while, because I was daring enough to go out with a Caucasian." One must remember that daters were considerably more staid in the latter 1930s than they are today, and that the Nisei were particularly conservative in such matters, if one is to appreciate the bravado involved in Ihara's actions. She also dated a Black boy named Robert, but she did not record being envied for having made that connection. Tamie Ihara* Interview (CKI-4).

36 Yamamoto, "Social Adjustment," 85; Andrew W. Lind, *Hawaii's Japanese* (Princeton, 1946), 226–28.

37 By this time, Issei approval of Nisei intermarriage did not cost too much: nearly all the Nisei were already married. Levine and Rhodes, *Japanese American Community*, 36; Pasadena Union Presbyterian Church, *Directory* (Pasadena, 1960; JARP Box 361); West Los Angeles Community Methodist Church, *Membership Directory* (Los Angeles, 1963; JARP Box 361); Centenary Methodist Church, *Directory* (Los Angeles, 1962, 1965; JARP Box 361).

38 John W. Connor, *Tradition and Change in Three Generations of Japanese Americans* (Chicago, 1977), 57, 59.

39 Fumiko Hosokawa, *The Sansei: Social Interaction and Ethnic Identification*

among the Third-Generation Japanese (Saratoga, Calif., 1978), 104–7; Connor, *Tradition and Change*, 57, 59.

40 Judy Ohashi*, interviewed by the author, San Francisco, May 22, 1980.

41 Levine and Rhodes, *Japanese American Community*, 114–15, 125–26; Debbie Hirano* Interview; Field notes, Seattle, 1965–71; Frederick Samuels, *The Japanese and the Haoles of Honolulu* (New Haven, Conn., 1970), 63–66.

42 For early expressions of this movement's ideology, see Amy Tachiki et al., eds., *Roots: An Asian American Reader* (Los Angeles, 1971); *Asian Women* (Berkeley, 1971); Frank Chin et al., *Aiiieeeee! An Anthology of Asian American Writers* (Washington, D.C., 1975).

43 Mark J. Gehrie, "Sansei: An Ethnography of Experience" (Ph.D. diss., Northwestern University, 1973), 145–47; Field notes, Seattle, 1970–72; Melford S. Weiss, "Modern Perspectives and Traditional Ceremony: A Chinese-American Beauty Pageant," in Sue and Wagner, *Asian-Americans*, 75–78; Christie W. Kiefer, *Changing Cultures, Changing Lives* (San Francisco, 1974); Togo W. Tanaka, interviewed by Betty Mitson and David Hacker, May 19, 1973 (California State University, Fullerton, Oral History Tape OH1271a); Levine and Rhodes, *Japanese American Community*, 125–26; Jane B. Kaihatsu, "Asian Americans and Outmarriage," *Pacific Citizen*, December 20–27, 1985, A-8.

44 Margaret Woo, "Woman + Man = Political Unity," in *Asian Women*, 115–16. Certain sorts of interethnic romance, then, were approved by Asian leftists—specifically, relationships between members of the various Asian American nationalities. Another sort of relationship, interracial this time, was also kosher in certain circumstances. Yellow Power advocates looked to Black leftists as the American revolutionaries *par excellence*. In certain circles, to have a Black partner was perceived as especially revolutionary. In 1971, a Sansei woman who was active in the Asian American movement in Seattle felt free to criticize her Chinese compatriot for dating a White man, while she herself was living with a Black man—for he had higher status in this political situation than her colleague's White boyfriend. Field notes, Seattle, 1970–71; Debbie Hirano* interview.

45 Connor, *Tradition and Change*, 59; "White Male Qualities," in Tachiki, *Roots*, 44–45; Laura Fujino*, interviewed by the author, Los Angeles, December 17, 1979; Judy Ohashi* Interview; "Autobiography of a Sansei Female" in Tachiki, *Roots*, 112–13.

46 Panunzio, "Intermarriage in Los Angeles"; *Commercial Tribune*, February 14, 1914, 8 (AJA, Deutsch Catalog); Ruth McKee, *Wartime Exile* (Washington, D.C., 1946), 30–43; Mrs. Emma Fong Kuno, "My Oriental Husbands" (SRR major document 53). The policy that women assumed the citizenship of their husbands had one positive aspect: it allowed many illiterate (and, thus, ineligible) European women to become American citizens when their husbands were naturalized.

47 William C. Smith, *Americans in Process* (Ann Arbor, Mich., 1936), 22; Mrs. C. S. Machida, interviewed by William C. Smith, Los Angeles, August

13, 1924 (SRR major document 73); idem, interviewed by Chloe Holt, Los Angeles, July 2, 1924 (SRR major document 251-A).

48   Masako Ihara Tashiro* Interview (CKI-25); Harry Ando* Interview (CKI-31; Bill Katayama* Interview (CKI-13), 55, 71; Allen Ihara* Interview; Rose Hayashi* Interview; George A. Lundberg and Lenore Dickson, "Selective Association among Ethnic Groups in a High School Population," *ASR*, 17 (1952), 23–35; Virginia B. Hertzler, "A Sociometric Study of Japanese Students in a Polyethnic High School" (M.A. thesis, University of Washington, 1949); Tetsuden Kashima, "Japanese American Internees Return, 1945 to 1955," *Phylon*, 41 (1980), 107–15; Jessie Reichel, "A Sociometric Study of Jewish Students in a Polyethnic High School" (M.A. thesis, University of Washington, 1949), 41; Andrea Sakai, "Reflections: An Autobiographical Sketch," *SPH*, 22 (1958), 36–44; "Relocation Program at Tule Lake" (JERS R20.84), 315–57.

49   Lind, *Hawaii's Japanese*, 94–97; Yamamoto, "Social Adjustment," 53–57, 85–86, 88, 93; Napoleon W. Lovely, *Conversations on Success in Marriage* (Boston, 1948), 11ff.

50   Field notes, Seattle, 1965–72, San Francisco, 1974–81; Barbara Kantorowicz, "The Ultimate Assimilation," *Newsweek*, November 24, 1986, 80.

51   Bureau of the Census, *Nonwhite Population* (1960); Bureau of the Census, *Japanese, Chinese, and Filipinos* (1970); Kitano, *Japanese Americans*, 210–11.

52   Lawrence H. Fuchs, *Hawaii Pono: A Social History* (New York, 1961), 106–37; Samuels, *Japanese and Haoles*, 38; Margie Barrows, "Plantation Hegemony in Hawaii, 1890–1920" (Paper presented at the annual meeting of the Association for Asian/Pacific American Studies, Seattle, November 7, 1980).

53   Masuoka, "Race Attitudes," 82–83. Even moderately well-educated Issei felt shy toward non-Japanese, especially Whites. A Japanese language school principal admitted, "I go away whenever I see a white man approaching me, because I don't speak good English. Sometimes I ignore a white man so that he will go away." As indicated by the hairdresser's statement above, class also played a part in keeping the races apart. On the mainland, there was a small, college-educated Issei elite, some of whom mixed with upper-class Whites socially. There was no such elite class of Japanese Americans in Hawaii in the first generation. Ibid.

54   Bureau of the Census, *Japanese, Chinese, and Filipinos* (1970), 17–23; Clarence E. Glick, "Interracial Marriage and Admixture in Hawaii," *Social Biology*, 17 (1970), 278–91; Romanzo C. Adams, *The Japanese in Hawaii* (New York, 1924), 19; Kikumura and Kitano, "Interracial Marriage"; George K. Yamamoto, "Interracial Marriage in Hawaii," in Irving R. Stuart and Lawrence E. Abt, eds., *Interracial Marriage* (New York, 1967); Bernhard L. Hormann, "Hawaii's Mixing People," in Noel P. Gist and Anthony Gary Dworkin, eds., *The Blending of Races* (New York, 1972), 213–33. Cf. Spickard, "Mixed Marriage," 493–97.

55   Romanzo C. Adams, *Interracial Marriage in Hawaii* (Montclair, N.J., 1969); Ernest J. Reese, "Race Mingling in Hawaii," *AJS*, 20 (1914), 104–16; Sidney

E. Gulick, *Mixing the Races in Hawaii* (Honolulu, 1937); S. D. Porteus et al., "Race and Social Differences in Performance Tests," *Genetic Psychology Monographs*, 8 (1930).

56 Masuoka, "Race Attitudes," 77, 82, 130–34, and passim.

57 Nonetheless, there were a few intermarriages undertaken by Hawaiian Issei. Most of the Issei men who intermarried chose Hawaiian or part-Hawaiian wives. The few Issei women who intermarried took mainly Haole husbands. Koreans and Filipinos were particularly unpopular with both sexes; the other groups fell in between. Glick, "Interracial Marriage and Admixture in Hawaii"; Adams, *Japanese in Hawaii*, 19; Kikumura and Kitano, "Interracial Marriage"; Yamamoto, "Interracial Marriage in Hawaii"; Hormann, "Hawaii's Mixing People"; Adams, *Interracial Marriage in Hawaii*, 169. Cf. Spickard, "Mixed Marriage," 497.

58 Lind, *Hawaii's Japanese*, 97, 191; Otome Inamine et al., "The Effect of War on Inter-Racial Marriage in Hawaii," *SPH*, 9–10 (1945), 103–9; Hester Kong, "Through the Peepsight of a Grocery Store," ibid., 11–16; Yamamoto, "Social Adjustment"; Tabulation of WRA Census Form 26 (JERS Shelf F); Andrew Lind, "Attitudes toward Interracial Marriage in Kona, Hawaii," *SPH*, 4 (1938), 19–23; Shigeo Ozaki, "Student Attitudes on Interracial Marriages," *SPH*, 6 (1940), 23–28; Leatrice Wong and Marion Wong, "Attitudes toward Intermarriage," *SPH*, 1 (1935), 14–17. Cf. Spickard, "Mixed Marriage," 505, 516–17.

59 Kong, "Peepsight"; Yamamoto, "Social Adjustment"; Lind, *Hawaii's Japanese*, 191. Japanese opposition to intermarriage on racial grounds was intensified by the generally low status of military people in Hawaii. Nisei women who married Haoles who were not servicemen took pains to emphasize their husbands' civilian status. In protesting her parents' opposition to her marriage, one Nisei woman said, "It wasn't like I was marrying a serviceman." But as the war progressed and Hawaiians of all groups grew more used to the sight of military people and felt more at ease in dealing with them, opposition to intermarriage weakened. Chiyoko Ono* reported in 1943: "We used to look down on the Nisei girls who went around with any soldiers. We thought that they were cheap and vulgar, but all that has changed now." As time went on and Nisei women seemed to be making stable family units out of their intermarriages, more and more families dropped their opposition. Yamamoto, "Social Adjustment," 35, 38–40, 48, 55; Chiyoko Ono* Interview (CKI-12); Lind, *Hawaii's Japanese*, 191; Inamine, "Effect of War."

60 Yamamoto, "Social Adjustment," 17, 48, 69–70, 87–88; Inamine, "Effect of War."

61 Lind, *Hawaii's People*, 91–97; Yamamoto, "Social Adjustment," 57.

62 Glick, "Interracial Marriage and Admixture"; Adams, *Japanese in Hawaii*, 19; Kikumura and Kitano, "Interracial Marriage"; Yamamoto, "Interracial Marriage"; Hormann, "Hawaii's Mixing People"; Kitano, "Asian-American Interracial Marriages." Cf. Spickard, "Mixed Marriage," 497.

63 Laura Fujino* Interview; Harry Kitano, interviewed by the author, Los Angeles, December 21, 1979; David J. O'Brien and Stephen S. Fugita,

"Generational Differences in Japanese Americans' Perceptions and Feelings about Social Relationships between Themselves and Caucasian Americans" (Unpublished MS), courtesy of the authors; Kikumura and Kitano, "Interracial Marriage"; Bureau of the Census, *Japanese, Chinese, and Filipinos* (1970), 17–23. Cf. Spickard, "Mixed Marriage," 491–96.

64 U.S. Bureau of the Census, *1940 Census: Characteristics of the Nonwhite Population by Race* (Washington, D.C., 1943), 98–109.

65 WRA Census Form 26, nos. 206860–63, 206904–11, 209330–35; New World Sun Daily, *Memorial Book of Japanese Families in the USA* (San Francisco, 1939), 462. A fascinating parallel to the experiences of these inland Issei with Mexican wives is described in Bruce LaBrack and Karen Leonard, "Conflict and Compatibility in Punjabi-Mexican Immigrant Families in Rural California, 1915–1965," *JMF*, 46 (1984), 527–37.

66 Yasuko Hayashi* Interview; Rose Hayashi* Interview; Allen Ihara* Interview; Masako Ihara Tashiro* Interview; Russell Endo and Dale Hiraoka, "Japanese American Intermarriage," *Free Inquiry in Creative Sociology*, 11 (1983), 159–62; Gordon K. Hirabayashi, private communication with the author, Seattle, November 7, 1980. Hirabayashi's figures on Nisei and Sansei outmarriage in a southern Alberta metropolitan area:

1950–55	2 percent
1955–60	8 percent
1960–65	31 percent
1965–70	54 percent
1970–75	82 percent

67 Eleanor W. Gluck, "An Ecological Study of the Japanese in New York City" (M.A. thesis, Columbia University, 1940), 28–29; Bureau of the Census, *Characteristics of the Nonwhite Population by Race* (1940), 98–109; idem, *1940 Census: Population, vol. 2, Characteristics of the Population, pt. 5, New York–Oregon*, 157; Manchester Boddy, *Japanese in America* (Los Angeles, 1921), 133; Michiji Ishikawa, "A Study of Intermarried Japanese Families in U.S.A." *Cultural Nippon*, 3 (Tokyo, 1935), 457–87; "Biography 5" (JERS Carton 4); Agnes de Mille, *Where the Wings Grow* (Garden City, N.Y., 1968); K. K. Kawakami, *Jokichi Takamine* (New York, 1928); *Prominent Americans Interested in Japan and Prominent Japanese in America* (1903); Bureau of the Census, *Japanese, Chinese, and Filipinos* (1970), 17–23. Cf. Spickard, "Mixed Marriage," 493–96.

68 MS on Nisei in Chicago (JERS T1.832); Bureau of the Census, *Japanese, Chinese, and Filipinos* (1970), 17–23. Cf. Spickard, "Mixed Marriage," 493–96.

69 Gehrie, "Sansei," 70–81, 144.

70 Field notes, Boston, 1974; Tim Hsu, draft article for *Harvard Yearbook* (1974); Tinker, "Intermarriage and Ethnic Boundaries"; Bureau of the Census, *Marital Characteristics* (1980), 175–81. Cf. Spickard, "Mixed Marriage," 523.

71 Steiner, *Japanese Invasion*, 167; "Biography of a Seattle High School Boy"

(SRR major document 151); W. Lloyd Warner et al., *Yankee City* (New Haven, 1963), 247. The War Relocation Authority's census records show Issei who intermarried and those who married Japanese in various sectors (not classes) of the economy. There is not a great deal of difference between the two groups in any sector except the unemployed. That fewer of the intermarried Issei were unemployed may be attributed to the fact that the intermarried were, as a group, a little older, and therefore more settled economically, than those who married other Japanese. Tabulation of WRA Census Form 26 (JERS Shelf F); cf. Spickard, "Mixed Marriage," 509.

72 A. W. Swanson, interviewed by William C. Smith, El Centro, Calif., n.d. (SRR minor document 333); WRA Census Form 26, nos. 602725–30 (JERS Shelf F); E. K., "Japanese-American Intermarriage" (SRR minor document 420). Of fifty-three intermarried East Coast Issei interviewed by Michiji Ishikawa in 1933, twenty-one were domestic workers, eight were clerks or salesmen, sixteen owned small stores of their own, three were students, three had attained professional positions, and two were unemployed. Ishikawa, "Intermarried Japanese Families."

73 Kuno, "My Oriental Husbands."

74 Clarke Kawakami and Yuri Morris Interview; K. K. Kawakami, *Asia at the Door* (New York, 1914); idem, *Japan in World Politics* (New York, 1914).

75 Catherine Holt, "Interview with Dr. F. T. Nakaya, Japanese Physician," Los Angeles, September 21, 28, 1924 (SRR major document 247).

76 Jitsuichi Masuoka, "Race Attitudes of the Japanese People in Hawaii" (M.A. thesis, University of Hawaii, 1931); Toyama, "Life History"; Harry Kitano Interview; T. Torikai Interview, Seattle, July 8, 1924 (SRR major document 156); E. S. S., "Interview with Mrs. H———." It should be noted that there were proportionately many times more Christians among Japanese American immigrants than there were among those Japanese who remained in Japan. Cf. Thomas, *Salvage,* 607–9.

77 Tabulation of WRA Census Form 26 (JERS Shelf F); Darrel Montero and Ronald Tsukashima, "Assimilation and Educational Achievement: The Case of the Second-Generation Japanese American," *Sociological Quarterly,* 18 (1977), 498; WRA Census Form 26, nos. 702933–34. Cf. Spickard, "Mixed Marriage," 510.

78 Ishigo Papers (JARP Box 80); Estelle Ishigo, "Lone Heart Mountain" (JARP Box 79); Sue Embrey Interview. Cf. Milton Gordon, *Assimilation in American Life* (New York, 1964), 224–32.

79 Cf. Bill Hosokawa, *Nisei: The Quiet Americans* (New York, 1969); Robert Wilson and Bill Hosokawa, *East to America* (New York, 1980); Petersen, *Japanese Americans,* 134–43; Kitano, *Japanese Americans,* 143–59.

80 Sus Kaminaka* Interview (CKI-45); Barry Shimizu* Interview (CKI-46); Harry Ando* Interview; Lester Kimura* Interview; Tadashi "Blackie" Najima* Interview (CKI-32); Frances Nishimoto* Interview (CKI-22); Suski, "Inter-Marriage."

81 Tadashi "Blackie" Najima* Interview; Kikuchi, "Social Adjustment," 112; Sus Kaminaka* Interview.

82 Barry Shimizu* Interview.

83 Kikuchi, "Social Adjustment," 112; Hiromasa Minami* Interview (CKI-21). Cf. deYoung, "Japanese Evacuees in Denver" (JERS T1.874); Tamotsu Shibutani, "The First Year of the Resettlement of the Nisei in the Chicago Area," March 1, 1944 (JERS T1.842), 152.

84 The following discussion is derived from Rose Hayashi* Interview and Harry Ando* Interview.

85 Field notes, Seattle, 1965–80. There is considerable evidence that working-class Sansei, in Hawaii at least, shunned intermarriage more vigorously than Sansei further up the economic ladder. Cf. Frederick Samuels, "Color Sensitivity among Honolulu's Haoles and Japanese," *Race*, 11 (1965), 463–73.

86 Jan Masaoka, "I Forgot My Eyes Were Black," in *Asian Women*, 57–59.

87 The most recent attempt to analyze Japanese American intermarriage patterns by something like class—i.e., by occupation—has yielded only inconclusive results. See Kitano, "Asian-American Interracial Marriage."

Chapter 4. Japanese, American, or Something in Between

1 George DeVos and Hiroshi Wagatsuma, *Japan's Invisible Race*, rev. ed. (Berkeley, 1972); George A. DeVos and William O. Weatherall, *Japan's Minorities* (London, 1974); Cullen Tadao Hayashida, "Identity, Race, and the Blood Ideology of Japan" (Ph.D. diss., University of Washington, 1974). *Eta* is an offensive term for most Japanese so labelled, and so has rightly fallen out of use in Japan. It is used here not out of a desire to offend, but because it is the term that has been used in Japanese American communities.

2 Kazuo Ito, *Issei* (Seattle, 1973); Harry H. L. Kitano, interviewed by the author, Los Angeles, December 21, 1979; John F. Embree, *Acculturation among the Japanese of Kona, Hawaii* (Menasha, Wis., 1941), 74–75; Bernhard L. Hormann, "A Note on Hawaii's Minorities within Minorities," *SPH*, 18 (1954), 47–56; Sanjiro Kawaguchi, interviewed by Joe Grant Masaoka, San Francisco, February 1967 (JARP box 519); Romanzo C. Adams, *Interracial Marriage in Hawaii* (Montclair, N.J., 1969), 170. Fuller data on Japanese American eta, such as their proportion in the population, are not available.

3 Henry Toyama and Kiyoshi Ikeda, "The Okinawan-Naichi Relationship," *SPH*, 14 (1950), 51–65; DeVos and Weatherall, *Japan's Minorities*, 5.

4 Toyama and Ikeda, "Okinawan-Naichi"; Adams, *Interracial Marriage in Hawaii*, 170; James L. Tigner, "Ryukyuans in Peru, 1906–52," *Americas*, 35 (July 1978), 20–44; George K. Yamamoto, "Some Patterns in Mate Selection among Naichi and Okinawans on Oahu," *SPH*, 21 (1957), 42–49; Embree, *Acculturation among the Japanese*, 35; Hormann, "Minorities within Minorities."

5 Harumi Befu, "The Group Model of Japanese Society: A Critique" (Paper presented at the Center for Japanese and Korean Studies, University of California, Berkeley, November 19, 1980), 11; John Modell, *The Economics and Politics of Racial Accommodation* (Urbana, Ill., 1977), 90; Toyama and Ikeda, "Okinawan-Naichi"; Hazel Nishi* Interview (CKI-3); Edward K. Strong, *Japanese in California* (Stanford, Calif., 1933), 236–37; Edwin C. Bur-

rows, *Hawaiian Americans* (New Haven, 1937), 92–93; "Biography 3" (JERS Carton 4); Embree, *Acculturation among the Japanese*, 75; Lawrence H. Fuchs, *Hawaii Pono* (New York, 1961), 110.

6   Dorothy S. Thomas et al., *The Salvage* (Berkeley, 1952), 607–9; "Biography 27" (JERS Carton 4); B. Billigmier, "Miscellany" (JERS R20.03); 2 Corinthians 6:14.

7   Saburo Kido, interviewed by Joe Grant Masaoka and Robert A. Wilson, Los Angeles, January 4, 1967 (Bancroft Phonotape 1050:2); Harry Kitano Interview; Mildred Doi Kosaki, "The Culture Conflicts and Guidance Needs of Nisei Adolescents" (M.A. thesis, University of Hawaii, 1949), 61–68; Edwin C. Burrows, *Chinese and Japanese in Hawaii during the Sino-Japanese Conflict* (Honolulu, 1939), 66–67 (quotation); Robert H. Ross and Emory S. Bogardus, "Four Types of Nisei Marriage Patterns," *SSR*, 25 (1940), 63–66.

8   Sylvia J. Yanagisako, "Social and Cultural Change in Japanese American Kinship" (Ph.D. diss., University of Washington, 1975), 154; Doris Ihara* Interview (CKI-39); Fusako Tanaka* Interview (CKI-40); S. F. Miyamoto, manuscript analysis of Tule Lake Prison camp (JERS R20.42); Masako Ihara Tashiro* Interview (CKI-25); Yasuko Hayashi* Interview (CKI-9); Donna Lockwood Leonetti and Laura Newell-Morris, "Exogamy and Change in the Biosocial Structure of a Modern Urban Population," *American Anthropologist*, 84 (1982), 19–36. For distinctions between structural and cultural assimilation, see Milton M. Gordon, *Assimilation in American Life* (New York, 1964), 60–83.

9   Harry H. L. Kitano, *Japanese Americans*, 2nd ed. (Englewood Cliffs, N.J., 1976), 164–65; Andrea Sakai, "Reflections," *SPH*, 22 (1958), 36–44; Ida Shigaki* Interview (CKI-56); Chiyoko Ono* Interview (CKI-12); Saburo Kido, 1967 interview; Kosaki, "Culture Conflicts," 61–68.

10 Michiji Ishikawa, "A Study of Intermarried Japanese Families in USA," *Cultural Nippon*, 3 (1938), 457–87; Nisei in Chicago MS (JERS T1.832); Kyohei Sakamoto* Interview (CKI-10); Jiro Ishimoto* Interview (CKI-5).

11 Nisei in Chicago MS; Leonard Bloom et al., *Marriages of Japanese-Americans in Los Angeles: A Statistical Study* (Berkeley, 1945); Thomas, *Salvage*, 581.

12 Embree, *Japanese of Kona*, 75; Juni Oyama* Interview (CKI-2); "Relocation Program at Tule Lake" (JERS R20.84), 315–20; Ida Shigaki* Interview (CKI-56); Margaret Suzuki* Interview (CKI-8); Robert H. Ross, "Social Distance as It Exists between the First and Second Generation Japanese in the City of Los Angeles and Vicinity" (M.A. thesis, University of Southern California, 1939), 117; W. C. Smith, *Americans in Process* (Ann Arbor, 1936), 236–37; Hazel Nishi* Interview.

13 Margaret Suzuki* Interview; Saburo Kido Interview; Yamato Ichihashi, *Japanese in the United States* (New York, 1969; orig. 1921), 324–25. The Cable Act of 1931 partly solved this problem by making it possible for a woman to retain her American nationality at the time of her marriage to a foreign national if she chose to do so.

14 Kazuo Nishimoto* Interview (CKI-7); Marvin K. Opler, "Cultural Dilemma of a Kibei Youth," in Georgene Seward, ed., *Clinical Studies in Culture Conflict* (New York, 1951), 297–316; Yasuko Hayashi* Interview; Embrey Interview.

15 Field notes, Seattle, 1965–80; San Francisco, 1974–81.

16 Marion Svensrud, "Some Factors Concerning the Assimilation of a Selected Japanese Community" (M.A. thesis, University of Southern California, 1931), 203–6.

17 Jitsuichi Masuoka in Hawaii and Gene Levine and Colbert Rhodes on the mainland found essentially the same hierarchy expounded here. Masuoka, "Race Attitudes of the Japanese Population in Hawaii" (M.A. thesis, University of Hawaii, 1931), 61–62; Masuoka, "Race Preference in Hawaii," *AJS*, 41 (1936), 635–41; Levine and Rhodes, *The Japanese Community* (New York, 1981), 36; Mrs. M. Furuya Interview, Seattle, July 3, 1924 (SRR major document 196); Kosaki, "The Culture Conflicts and Guidance Needs of Nisei Adolescents," 61–68; Chotoku Toyama, "The Japanese Community in Los Angeles" (M.A. thesis, Columbia University, 1926), 49; Toyama and Ikeda, "Okinawan-Naichi."

18 Befu, "Group Model."

19 The ranking for marriage mates that I have found corresponds closely to rankings found by Levine, Rhodes, Masuoka, and Frederick Samuels, using other measures of social distance. Cf. Levine and Rhodes, *Japanese Community*, 36; Masuoka, "Race Attitudes," 61–62; idem, "Race Preference"; Frederick Samuels, *The Japanese and the Haoles of Honolulu* (New Haven, 1970), 63–66.

20 Levine and Rhodes, *Japanese Community*, 36; Masuoka, "Race Attitudes," 92–93; Kitano Interview; Masuoka, "Race Preference"; Toyama and Ikeda, "Okinawan-Naichi"; Burrows, *Chinese and Japanese in Hawaii*, 66–67; Fuchs, *Hawaii Pono*, 110; Embree, *Japanese of Kona*, 86; Andrew W. Lind, "Attitudes toward Interracial Marriage in Kona, Hawaii," *SPH*, 4 (1938), 79–83; Shigeo Ozaki, "Student Attitudes on Interracial Marriage," *SPH*, 6 (1940), 23–28; Leatrice Wong and Marian Wong, "Attitudes toward Intermarriage," *SPH*, 1 (1935), 14–17; Leonetti and Newell-Morris, "Exogamy and Change." Cf. Paul R. Spickard, "Mixed Marriage: Two American Minority Groups and the Limits of Ethnic Identity" (Ph.D. diss., University of California, Berkeley, 1983), 516–17.

21 Fumiko Hosokawa, *The Sansei: Social Interaction and Ethnic Identification among the Third Generation* (Saratoga, Calif., 1978), 104–7; Field notes, Seattle, 1968–72; "Japanese Americans in California" (Bancroft Phonotape 717A); Darrel Montero and Ronald Tsukashima, "Assimilation and Educational Achievement: The Case of Second-Generation Japanese Americans," *Sociological Quarterly*, 18 (1977), 490–503; Togo Tanaka, interviewed by Betty Mitson and David Hacker, May 19, 1973 (California State University, Fullerton, Oral History Tape OH1271A); Sanjiro Kawaguchi, interviewed by Joe Grant Masaoka, San Francisco, February 1967 (JARP Box 519); Robert C. Schmitt, "Demographic Correlates of Interracial Marriage in Hawaii," *Demography*, 2 (1965), 463–73; U.S. Bureau of the Census, *1980*

Census: Marital Characteristics, Subject Report (PC80-2-4C (Washington, D.C., 1985), 175–81; Debbie Hirano* Interview.

22 Jesse F. Steiner, *The Japanese Invasion* (Chicago, 1917), 162, 172; H. A. Millis, *The Japanese Problem in the United States* (New York, 1915), 275. Cf. Toyokichi Iyenaga and Kenosuke Sato, *Japan and the California Problem* (New York, 1924), 160; Sidney E. Gulick, *The American Japanese Problem* (New York, 1914), 157; Manchester Boddy, *Japanese in America* (Los Angeles, 1921), 134; K. K. Kawakami, *Asia at the Door* (New York, 1914), 70–74.

23 Tabulation of WRA Census Forms 26 (JERS Shelf F); cf. Spickard, "Mixed Marriage," 505. The greater number of in-married Issei men than women who were divorced or separated may be attributed partly to a greater number of broken marriages among couples comprising Issei men and Nisei women, which would not be classified as intermarriages for the purposes of the WRA census. But still the numbers are vexing. Altogether, in-married Issei and Nisei men suffered 273 divorces and 248 separations, while the women had only 127 divorces and 132 separations. These numbers should match, but they do not. Were the other estranged wives all in Japan? It is hard to tell. Another problem crops up when one looks at the number of people who listed themselves as widowed. Forty-two percent of the out-married Issei men and 56 percent of the out-married Issei women said their mates had died. The corresponding numbers for the in-married were only 9 percent and 13 percent. I do not have an explanation for the difference.

24 WRA Census Form 26, nos. 602725–30.

25 Tabulation of WRA Census Forms 26 (JERS Shelf F); cf. Spickard, "Mixed Marriage," 505.

26 Andrew W. Lind, "Interracial Marriage as Affecting Divorce in Hawaii," *SSR,* 49 (1964), 17–25.

27 Tabulation of WRA Census Forms 26 (JERS Shelf F); cf. Spickard, "Mixed Marriage," 506–7.

28 Steiner, *Japanese Invasion,* 163–65, 173; Gulick, *American Japanese Problem,* 152–60; Iyenaga and Sato, *California Problem,* 157–61.

29 K. K. Kawakami, *Japan in World Politics* (New York, 1917), 110–13; idem, *Asia at the Door,* 70–74.

30 Kathleen Tamagawa, *Holy Prayers in a Horse's Ear* (New York, 1932).

31 Catherine Holt, "Interviews regarding Mildred Yoshikawa*, Mixed Japanese-American high school girl . . . . Los Angeles, California" (SRR minor document 446); Kyo Inouye, interviewed by Catherine Holt, Los Angeles, January 16, 1925 (SRR major document 236).

32 William C. Smith, "Life History of Peter" (SRR major document 251-A); William C. Smith, "Adjutant M. Kobayashi on the Second Generation" (SRR major document 236).

33 Clarke Kawakami and Yuri Morris, interviewed by Joe Grant Masaoka and Lillian Takeshita, May 22, 1968 (Bancroft Phonotape 1050B:10); Lt. Col. Claude B. Washburne, memo to Commanding General, Western Defense Command, December 12, 1943 (WDC).

34 Gulick, *American Japanese Problem,* 152–60; "The Okajima Girls" (SRR

major document 144); "Progeny of Jap-White Union Amaze," *San Francisco Examiner*, November 11, 1922 (SRR major document 222); Kawakami, *Asia at the Door*, 70–74; H. G. Schroeder, "Case Brief on Anglo-Japanese Marriage" (SRR major document 62).

35   Helen Elizabeth Whitney, "Care of Homeless Children of Japanese Ancestry during Evacuation and Relocation" (M.S.W. thesis, University of California, Berkeley, 1948), 65–68; *Pacific Citizen*, June 4, 1942, 8.

36   Ruth Farlow Uyesugi, *Don't Cry, Chiisai, Don't Cry* (Paoli, Ind., 1977), 143–45; Bea Pixa, "Stereotypes Have No Place in This Home," *San Francisco Examiner*, July 16, 1976, 15, 17; idem, "Interracial Marriages—What about Kids?" ibid., July 13, 1976, 18 (quotations); idem, "Chinese-Caucasian Children Left to Find Own Identities," ibid., July 19, 1976, 19.

37   Julie P. Kelley, "A Study of Eyefold Inheritance in Inter-Racial Marriages" (M.S. thesis, University of Hawaii, 1960); Bernhard L. Hormann, "Hawaii's Mixing People," in Noel P. Gist and Anthony Gary Dworkin, eds., *The Blending of Races* (New York, 1972), 213–33; Levine and Rhodes, *Japanese American Community*, 142.

38   Yamamoto, "Social Adjustment," 67–69, 76, 84: Richard Slobodin, "The Metis of Northern Canada," in Gist and Dworkin, *Blending of Races*, 143–65; John Moritsugu, Lyn Foerster, and James Morishima, "Eurasians" (Paper presented to the Western Psychological Association, San Francisco, 1978).

39   Embrey interview; James Morishima, "Interracial Issues among Asian-Americans" (Panel discussion presented to the Association for Asian/Pacific American Studies, Seattle, November 1, 1980).

40   Ai, "On Being ½ Japanese, ⅛ Choctaw, ¼ Black, and ¹⁄₁₆ Irish," *Ms.*, May 1978, 58.

41   Joy Nakamura*, letter to the author, May 22, 1974. Dee Dee and Kathy Akiyama, sisters, achieved similar integration of their biracial identities. They chose to identify with both their father's Japaneseness and their mother's Caucasian identity. Dee Dee said, "We are exactly in the middle," and Kathy added, "I come as a package. I'm denying one part or the other part [if I try to choose]." Dee Dee Akiyama and Kathy Akiyama, "Half-Breed: The Unaddressed Perspective" (Paper presented to the Association for Asian/Pacific American Studies, Seattle, November 7, 1980). A similar biracial identity was the choice of Christine C. I. Hall and many of the Black-Japanese people about whom she wrote in "The Ethnic Identity of Racially Mixed People: A Study of Black-Japanese" (Ph.D. diss., UCLA, 1980). It was the choice advocated by George Kitahara Kich, on the basis of his own experience and his psychological study of Caucasian-Japanese ("Eurasians: Ethnic Racial Identity Development of Biracial Japanese/White Adults" [Ph.D. diss., Wright Institute, 1982]), and the choice of numerous other part-Japanese (see, e.g., Lane Ryo Hirabayashi, "On Being Hapa," and Mira Chieko Shimabukuro, "Proud of Being Hapa," both in *Pacific Citizen*, December 20–27, 1985).

Chapter 5. American Men and Japanese Women

1 A selection of the magazine articles and scholarly studies is found in the notes below. For other productions, see, for example, the novels *The Hidden Flower*, by Pearl S. Buck (New York, 1952), and *Sayonara*, by James Michener (New York, 1953); the movies *Sayonara* (1957), *Japanese War Bride* (1952), and *Tea House of the August Moon* (1957); and the 1979 Japanese television documentaries on the mixed children at the Elizabeth Saunders Home (NTV).

2 Junesay Iddittie, *When Two Cultures Meet: Sketches of Postwar Japan* (Tokyo, 1960), 25–26; Hargis Westerfield, "Failures in GI Orientation," *Free World*, 2 (1946), 62–63; Ernest R. Hilgard, "The Enigma of Japanese Friendliness," *Public Opinion Quarterly*, 10 (1946), 343–48; Walt Sheldon, *The Honorable Conquerors* (New York 1965), 176–77.

3 Sheldon, *Honorable Conquerors*, 42–45, 107, 112–19; Elizabeth Anne Hemphill, *The Least of These* (New York, 1980), 80.

4 Yuriyo Watanabe*, interviewed by the author, July 1972; Bok-Lim C. Kim, "Casework with Japanese and Korean Wives of Americans," *Social Casework*, 53 (1972), 273–79. America's armies in Asia continued in succeeding decades to prey on Asian women. Cf. Tom Weber, "The 'Hired Wives' in Thailand—Abandoned, Poor and Much Older," *San Francisco Chronicle*, April 20, 1976, 17; James A. Michener, "Pursuit of Happiness by a GI and a Japanese," *Life*, February 21, 1955, 124–41; J. W. Smith and W. L. Worden, "They're Bringing Home Japanese Wives," *Saturday Evening Post*, January 19, 1952, 26–27; Era Bell Thompson, "Rest and Recreation," *Ebony*, August 1968, 76–78; G. Parise, "Strange Sad Story: Sex and Saigon," *Atlas*, September 1967, 26–31; Jill Joiner*, interviewed by the author, St. Paul, Minn., September 25, 1981; "For Love or Money: Vietnamese-American Marriage," *Newsweek*, September 7, 1970, 50–51; Sheldon, *Honorable Conquerors*, 115–18; Richard Buttny, "Legitimation Techniques for Intermarriage: Accounts of Motives for Intermarriage from US Servicemen and Philippine Women," *Communication Quarterly*, 35 (1987), 125–43.

5 See "For Love or Money"; Evelyn Yoshimura, "G.I.'s and Asian Women," in Amy Tachiki et al., *Roots: An Asian American Reader* (Los Angeles, 1971); Parise, "Strange Sad Story."

6 Sheldon, *Honorable Conquerors*, 42–45, 115–17.

7 Michener, "Pursuit of Happiness"; Smith and Worden, "Japanese Wives"; "For Love or Money"; Kim, "Japanese and Korean Wives."

8 Bok-Lim C. Kim, "Asian Wives of U.S. Servicemen: Women in Shadows," *Amerasia Journal*, 4 (1977), 91–115; John W. Connor, *A Study of the Marital Stability of Japanese War Brides* (San Francisco, 1976), 64, 77; Leon K. Walters, "A Study of the Social and Marital Adjustment of Thirty-five American-Japanese Couples" (M.A. thesis, Ohio State University, 1953), 33; George A. DeVos, *Personality Patterns and Problems of Adjustment in American-Japanese Intercultural Marriages* (Taipei, 1973), 247.

9 Walters, "American-Japanese Couples," 35–48; Connor, *Marital Stability*, 57.

10   DeVos, *Personality Patterns*, 9, 256, and passim.

11   See Kazuko Tsurumi, *Social Change and the Individual: Japan Before and After World War II* (Princeton, 1970); Kazuo Kawai, *Japan's American Interlude* (Chicago, 1960).

12   Iddittie, *Two Cultures*, 135–38.

13   Daniel I. Okimoto, *American in Disguise* (Tokyo, 1971), 191.

14   Jean Grogan*, interviewed by the author, Boston, March 4, 1974.

15   Isobel Ray Carter, *Alien Blossom: A Japanese-Australian Love Story* (Melbourne, 1965), 31; "The Truth about Japanese War Brides," *Ebony*, March 1952, 17–25.

16   Walters, "American-Japanese Couples," 39–45; Connor, *Marital Stability*, 57, 77; DeVos, *Personality Patterns*, 245.

17   DeVos, *Personality Patterns*, 6–7, 241–56, and passim.

18   Kim, "Japanese and Korean Wives." See also Bascom W. Ratliff et al., "Intercultural Marriage: The Korean-American Experience," *Social Casework*, 59 (1978), 221–26.

19   Jean Grogan* Interview.

20   "Truth about Japanese War Brides"; Carter, *Alien Blossom*, 56.

21   "Truth about Japanese War Brides"; Carter, *Alien Blossom*, 7; Tom Sasaki, "Social Organization: Towards Larger Community," August 24, 1946 (JERS carton 4, no. 49); Jean Grogan* Interview; Kim, "Asian Wives," 94.

22   Carter, *Alien Blossom*, 58. Cf. the much stricter controls placed on the Australian troops. On landing in Japan, the troops were told by their commander, Lt. Gen. John Northcott, to avoid "fraternization" entirely, to "be formal and correct," and to keep their distance from any Japanese civilian. The order was not enforced uniformly, but it seems to have kept the Australians away from the Japanese women more successfully than the looser American restriction. Gordon Parker, an Australian, was reprimanded by his commanding officer for swimming at Kure with Cherry Sakuramoto. The couple was broken up on a Hiroshima street by military police, who threw Cherry in jail, called her a prostitute, and roughly forced a venereal disease examination on her. The stricter rules against dating in the Australian zone seem to have stemmed more from the fears of the Australian public at large than from official Allied policy (see Carter, *Alien Blossom*, 34, 44, 53, 58, 69, 80).

23   William L. Worden, "Where Are Those Japanese War Brides?" *Saturday Evening Post*, November 20, 1954, 38–39, 133–34. This policy of encouraging fornication between American troops and local women (including sponsoring prostitution) while putting every possible roadblock in the way of stable unions has been the consistent policy of the U.S. Army throughout its activities in Asia. See Weber, "Hired Wives."

24   Michener, *Sayonara*, 211. Cf. Ben Wickersham, "A Letter from the Far East," *Look*, February 12, 1952, 94–95; "Truth about Japanese War Brides."

25   "War Brides," *United States Immigration and Naturalization Service Monthly Review*, 6 (June 1949), 168; Walters, "American-Japanese Couples," 29–30; U.S. Immigration and Naturalization Service, *Annual Report* (1946),

13–14; "Mission Sent to Europe to Aid 50,000 War Brides," *USINS Monthly Review,* 3 (November 1945), 229–30; "Service Issues Ruling on War Bride 'Visitors,' " *USINS Monthly Review,* 3 (March 1946), 285.

26 "War Brides"; Japan, Ministry of Foreign Affairs, Division of Special Records, *Documents Concerning the Allied Occupation and Control of Japan, vol. 6, On Aliens* (Tokyo, March 1951); Smith and Worden, "Bringing Home Japanese Wives"; U.S. Department of the Army, Special Regulations No. 600-24-6, 17 June 1953, "Personnel. Marriages to Non-Nationals within the Far East Command," American University, Foreign Area Studies Division, *U.S. Area Handbook for Japan* (Washington, 1964), 78–79.

27 Kim, "Asian Wives," 96–97; Yoshimura, "G.I.'s and Asian Women." Cf. "For Love or Money"; A. Lin Neumann, " 'Hospitality Girls' in the Philippines," *Southeast Asia Chronicle,* 66 (January/February 1979), 18–23.

28 Smith and Worden, "Bringing Home Japanese Wives"; George K. Yamamoto, "Social Adjustment of Caucasian-Japanese Marriages in Honolulu" (M.A. thesis, University of Hawaii, 1949), 85–86; John W. Connor, "American-Japanese Marriages—How Stable Are They?" *Pacific Historian,* 13 (Winter 1969), 25–36; Walters, "American-Japanese Couples," 8.

29 Walters, "American-Japanese Couples," 27–30; Smith and Worden, "Bringing Home Japanese Wives"; Jean Grogan* Interview.

30 Japan, Ministry of Foreign Affairs, *Documents Concerning the Allied Occupation;* Walters, "American-Japanese Couples," 23–24; Worden, "Where Are Those Japanese War Brides?"; Hiroshi Wagatsuma, "The Social Perception of Skin Color in Japan," in John Hope Franklin, ed., *Color and Race* (Boston, 1968), 151.

31 Walters, "American-Japanese Couples," 61, 64, 65, 68; Michener, "Pursuit of Happiness"; Carter, *Alien Blossom,* 31, 53, 54, 67, 72, 105; Wagatsuma, "Social Perception of Skin Color," 164.

32 Jean Grogan* Interview; Christine C. I. Hall, "The Ethnic Identity of Racially Mixed People: A Study of Black-Japanese" (Ph.D. diss., University of California, Los Angeles, 1980), 90–93, 98–99.

33 Carter, *Alien Blossom,* 57, 71, 87; Walters, "American-Japanese Couples," 27, 54; Jean Grogan* Interview.

34 Walters, "American-Japanese Couples," 24; Michener, "Pursuit of Happiness"; "For Love or Money."

35 Walters, "American-Japanese Couples," 51, 59–61; Smith and Worden, "Bringing Home Japanese Wives"; "Truth about Japanese War Brides"; Ray Falk, "GI Brides Go to School in Japan," *New York Times Magazine,* November 7, 1954, 54–56; Mrs. William C. Kerr, "On the Frontier of International Understanding," *Japan Christian Quarterly,* 17 (Summer 1951), 48–49.

36 Walters, "American-Japanese Couples," 53; Kim, "Asian Wives."

37 Kim, "Asian Wives."

38 Carter, *Alien Blossom,* 62, 133–34 (Parker quotations); Tamiko T. Yamamoto, "Adjustments of War Brides in Hawaii" (Romanzo Adams Social Research Library report 17, University of Hawaii, August 1950); Connor, "American-

Japanese Marriages"; G. J. Schnepp and Agnes Masako Yiu, "Cultural and Marital Adjustment of Japanese War Brides," *AJS*, 61 (1955), 48–50; Connor, *Marital Stability*, 58; Michener, "Pursuit of Happiness" (Sachiko quotation); Worden, "Where Are Those Japanese War Brides?"; Walters, "American-Japanese Couples," 126–41.

39 Walters, "American-Japanese Couples," 80–87, 135, 158. See also Worden, "Where Are Those Japanese War Brides?"; Michener, "Pursuit of Happiness"; J. P. McEvoy, "America through the Eyes of a Japanese War-Bride," *Reader's Digest*, April 1955, 95–99.

40 Worden, "Where Are Those Japanese War Brides?" (Morrison quotation); Walters, "American-Japanese Couples," 74–76, 90–107; McEvoy, "America through the Eyes of a Japanese War Bride" (Malloy quotation); Michener, "Pursuit of Happiness"; Schnepp and Yui, "Cultural and Marital Adjustment"; Kim, "Asian Wives."

41 Walters, "American-Japanese Couples," 71–73, 90; Worden, "Where Are Those Japanese War Brides?"; Jean Grogan* Interview; Michener, "Pursuit of Happiness" (Pfeiffer quotation); Evelyn Nakano Glenn, *Issei, Nisei, War Bride: Three Generations of Japanese American Women in Domestic Service* (Philadelphia, 1986), 236.

42 Walters, "American-Japanese Couples," 77, 141, 155; Carter, *Alien Blossom*, 136, 149; McEvoy, "America through the Eyes of a Japanese War-Bride"; Schnepp and Yui, "Cultural and Marital Adjustment"; Kim, "Japanese and Korean Wives"; "This War's War Bride"; Yamamoto, "Adjustments of War Brides," 6; Jean Grogan* Interview (Fitzpatrick quotation); Michener, "Pursuit of Happiness" (Pfeiffer quotation).

43 Jean Grogan* Interview; Eiko Murai, "The Enhancement of the Alien's Adjustment through Interpersonal Relationships within the Ethnic Group toward the Socialization into the Host Society: Japanese Women's Case" (Ph.D. diss., University of Michigan, 1972), 109; Frank D. Richardson, "Ministries to Asian Wives of Servicemen," *Military Chaplain's Review* (Winter 1976), 1–14; McEvoy, "America through the Eyes of a Japanese War-Bride" (Malloy quotation); Glenn, *Issei, Nisei, War Bride*, 232–41; Velina Hasu Houston, "On Being Mixed Japanese in Modern Times," *Pacific Citizen*, December 20–27, 1985.

44 Walters, "American-Japanese Couples," 81; Worden, "Where Are Those Japanese War Brides?"; Connor, "American-Japanese Marriages"; Kim, "Japanese and Korean Wives"; Michener, "Pursuit of Happiness"; Hiroshi Wagatsuma, "Some Problems of Interracial Marriage for the Japanese," in Irving R. Stuart and Lawrence E. Abt, eds., *Interracial Marriage* (New York, 1967), 258–59; Glenn, *Issei, Nisei, War Bride*, 240; McEvoy, "America through the Eyes of a Japanese War-Bride" (Malloy); Michener, "Pursuit of Happiness" (Pfeiffer).

45 Daniel I. Okimoto, *American in Disguise* (Tokyo, 1971), 183, 193; Yukiko Kimura, "War Brides in Hawaii and Their In-Laws," *AJS*, 63 (1957), 70–76; Yamamoto, "Adjustments of War Brides."

46 Kimura, "War Brides in Hawaii"; Randall Risdon, "A Study of Interracial Marriages Based on Data for Los Angeles County," *SSR*, 39 (1954), 92–95.

47 Murai, "Enhancement of the Alien's Adjustment," 112–13; Richardson, "Ministries to Asian Wives"; Walters, "American-Japanese Couples," 146; Worden, "Where Are Those Japanese War Brides?"

48 Kim, "Asian Wives"; Kim, "Japanese and Korean Wives"; DeVos, *Personality Patterns;* Walters, "American-Japanese Couples"; Connor, *Marital Stability;* Connor, "American-Japanese Marriages"; Hall, "Racially Mixed People."

49 Anselm Strauss, "Strain and Harmony in American-Japanese War Bride Marriages," *Marriage and Family,* 16 (1954), 99, 106.

50 Carter, *Alien Blossom,* 147–49; Michener, "Pursuit of Happiness"; Walters, "American-Japanese Couples," 108–25.

51 Hall, "Racially Mixed People," 62–63, 91; Walters, "American-Japanese Couples," 108–25; Houston, "Being Mixed Japanese." See also Michael C. Thornton, "A Social History of a Multiethnic Identity: The Case of Black Japanese Americans" (Ph.D. diss., University of Michigan, 1983).

52 Kim, "Japanese and Korean Wives"; Hall, "Racially Mixed People," 65–67, 87, 92–102, 120; Walters, "American-Japanese Couples," 125; Carter, *Alien Blossom,* 149; Connor, *Marital Stability,* iv.

53 Erik Erikson, *Identity: Youth and Crisis* (New York, 1968).

54 Christine C. I. Hall, "The Ethnic Identity of Racially Mixed People: A Study of Black-Japanese" (Ph.D. diss., UCLA, 1980). See also Thornton, "Social History of a Multiethnic Identity."

55 Hall, "Racially Mixed People," 30, 56–58, 68–69, 99–107; field notes, Seattle, 1964–69.

56 Hall, "Racially Mixed People," 38, 90–94; field notes, Seattle, 1965–68.

57 Hall, "Racially Mixed People," 26, 51, 81, 86, 98, 103, 115; Houston, "Being Mixed Japanese."

58 Wagatsuma, "Problems of Interracial Marriage"; Era Bell Thompson, "Japan's Rejected," *Ebony,* September 1967, 42–54; Nathan Oba Strong, "Patterns of Social Interaction and Psychological Adjustment among Japan's Konketsuji Population" (Ph.D. diss., University of California, Berkeley, 1978), 2, 14, 21; Iddittie, *When Two Cultures Meet.*

59 Strong, "Patterns of Social Interaction," 2, 21. In the 1960s and 1970s, an increasing number of the American parents were women married to Japanese businessmen returning to Japan from assignments abroad. See Sonnet Carol Takahisa, "Intercultural Interpersonal Encounters: A Study of Assimilation Patterns of Western-Born Women Married to Japanese Men" (A.B. thesis, Harvard University, 1976).

60 Strong, "Patterns of Social Interaction," 24, 54, 107; Darrell Berrigan, "Japan's Occupation Babies," *Saturday Evening Post,* June 19, 1948, 24–25, 117–18; Thompson, "Japan's Rejected"; Jill Joiner*, interviewed by the author, St. Paul, Minn., September 25, 1981.

61 Wagatsuma, "Problems of Interracial Marriage"; Wagatsuma, "Social Perception of Skin Color."

62 Berrigan, "Occupation Babies"; Thompson, "Japan's Rejected"; Jill Joiner* Interview; Strong, "Patterns of Social Interaction," 52, 97.

63 Berrigan, "Occupation Babies"; Hemphill, *Least of These;* Peter Kalischer,

"Madam Butterfly's Children," *Collier's*, September 20, 1952, 15–18; Charles W. Iglehart, "The Problem of G.I. Children in Japan," *Japan Christian Quarterly* (1952), 300–305.

64 Wagatsuma, "Social Perception of Skin Color"; Strong, "Patterns of Social Interaction," 3, 4, 10–13, 54, 227, 255; Susan B. Scully, "Speaking Out: Yurie Horiguchi," *Mainichi Daily News*, July 27, 1977.

65 Thompson, "Japan's Rejected"; Strong, "Patterns of Social Interaction," 2, 71, 135–38, 148, 190–94; Jill Joiner* Interview.

66 Thompson, "Japan's Rejected"; Strong, "Patterns of Social Interaction," 49; Hemphill, *Least of These*, 132–43.

67 Thompson, "Japan's Rejected"; Wagatsuma, "Problems of Interracial Marriage"; Strong, "Patterns of Social Interaction," 58–62, 92–97, 101–3, 109, 127, 132, 192.

68 Wagatsuma, "Problems of Interracial Marriage"; Strong, "Patterns of Social Interaction," 71, 96, 115–29, 132, 228; Thompson, "Japan's Rejected."

69 Strong, "Patterns of Social Interaction," 152–56; Wagatsuma, "Problems of Interracial Marriage"; Thompson, "Japan's Rejected."

70 Strong, "Patterns of Social Interaction," 158–88; Gilbert Bowles, comp., *Japanese Law of Nationality* (Tokyo, 1915); "Court Rejects Japan Nationality for Children of U.S. Fathers," *Japan Times Weekly*, April 4, 1981; William Weatherall, article on intermarriages and citizenship, *Japan Times*, June 24, 1978, 3; U.S. Congress, *Immigration and Nationality Act*, 82nd Cong., 2nd sess., June 27, 1952 (reproduced in Strong, "Patterns of Social Interaction," 259); Japan, Civil Code, *Nationality Law*, Law No. 147, May 4, 1950 (reproduced in Strong, 262–63). Very belatedly the U.S. government is beginning to take some measure of responsibility for children of Americans in Asia, but not for konketsuji. In 1982 Congress passed an act designed to ease immigration restrictions for some of the 150,000 American children scattered along the Pacific rim, but omitted Japan from the list of countries to which the rule applied. James LeMoyne, "Coming 'Home'—At Last," *Newsweek*, October 4, 1982, 78; "Reagan Signs Bill to Aid Amerasians," *Minneapolis Star and Tribune*, October 23, 1982, 4C.

71 Strong, "Patterns of Social Interaction," 19, 22, 25, 59, 79, 84, 88.

72 Jill Joiner* Interview; Wagatsuma, "Problems of Interracial Marriage"; Strong, "Patterns of Social Interaction," 20, 25, 27, 47, 48, 51, 55–58, 62, 68–75, 86–87, 94, 97–100, 143–45, 152, 265, 219.

Chapter 6. Shikse and Jewish Mother

1 Gen. 20:12; 24:3–4; 28:1–2. All biblical quotations are taken from the *New American Standard Bible* (Carol Stream, Ill., 1971).

2 Gen. 16; 26:34–35; 38:2; 46:10; Mal. 2:11; Gen. 41:45.

3 Num. 23:9; Exod. 12:38; 2:21; Num. 12:1–15; Lev. 24:10; John Bright, *A History of Israel*, 2nd ed. (Philadelphia, 1972), 105–39.

4 Deut. 7:2–4. Cf. Exod. 34:12–16; Num. 25:1–8; Deut. 13; 20:16ff.; 23:3ff.; Josh. 23:12–13.

5 Deut. 21:10–14; Lev. 19:34.

6 Judg. 3:5–8; 14:1–20; Ruth 1:4 and passim; 2 Sam. 3:2ff.; 1 Kings 3:1; 11:1–13; 7:14; 16:31; Song of Sol.

7 Louis M. Epstein, *Marriage Laws in the Bible and the Talmud* (Cambridge, 1942), 145–62.

8 Ezra 8:1–10:44; Neh. 13:23–29; Epstein, *Marriage Laws*, 162–67; Ephraim Feldman, "Intermarriage Historically Considered," *Central Conference of American Rabbis Journal*, 16 (1909), 271–307; Arthur Ruppin, *The Jews of To-Day* (London, 1913), 157; Moses Mielziner, *The Jewish Law of Marriage and Divorce* (Cincinnati, 1901), 45–54.

9 Maurice Fishberg, *The Jews: A Study of Race and Environment* (New York, 1911), 183–88; Book of Jubilees 30:7; Epstein, *Marriage Laws*, 167–77.

10 Epstein, *Marriage Laws*, 166–77; Louis I. Newman, "Intermarriage between Jews and Christians during the Middle Ages," *Jewish Institute Quarterly*, 2 (January and March 1926), 2–8, 22–28.

11 This law, apparently of medieval origin, reversed the ancient practice of children following the religion of the father. In biblical times, Gentile women typically married into Judaism and their children were deemed Jews. In later centuries, when Christian governments made intermarriage illegal, most mixed children were illegitimate and had no religious status if they did not follow the religion of their mothers. This law of the womb has caused difficulty in modern times, when intermarriage has again become legal, yet children of Jewish fathers and Gentile mothers have not been deemed Jews by Jewish authorities. See "The Issue of Patrilineal Descent—A Symposium," *Judaism*, 34 (1985), 3–135.

12 Newman, "Intermarriage during the Middle Ages"; Fishberg, *Jews*, 188–94; Roland B. Gittelsohn, *Modern Jewish Problems* (Cincinnati, 1943), 86–96; Ruppin, *Jews of To-Day*, 157; Feldman, "Intermarriage Historically," 23–25; Arthur Ruppin, *The Jews in the Modern World* (London, 1934), 316. For a haunting account of one intermarriage in medieval Poland, see Isaac Bashevis Singer, *The Slave* (New York, 1962). In other parts of the globe, intermarriages between Jews and local peoples took place rather often; see, for example, John J. Schulter, "Washington's Moroccan Jews," in Abraham D. Lavender, ed., *A Coat of Many Colors: Jewish Subcommunities in the United States* (Westport, Conn., 1977), 289–95.

13 Ruppin, *Jews in the Modern World*, 31–41, 271–98; Ruppin, *Jews of To-Day*, 137–56; Fishberg, *Jews*, 195–209; Feldman, "Intermariage Historically," 26–27; Nathan Glazer, *American Judaism*, 2nd ed. (Chicago, 1972).

14 Ruppin, *Jews in the Modern World*, 317; Gittelsohn, *Modern Jewish Problems*, 96.

15 Mielziner, *Jewish Law of Marriage*, 45–54; Marshall Sklare, "Intermarriage and Jewish Survival," *Commentary*, 49 (March 1970), 55; Feldman, "Intermarriage Historically," 28–32.

16 Deborah Hertz, "Mobility and Assimilation in the Berlin Salons, 1780–1832" (Research proposal, based on University of Minnesota Ph.D. diss., for work to be done at the AJA, 1979); John E. Mayer, "Jewish-Gentile Intermar-

riage Patterns," *SSR*, 45 (1960), 188–95; Ruppin, *Jews in the Modern World*, 319–20; Jacob Lestschinsky, "Mixed Marriage," in *The Universal Jewish Encyclopedia* (1942), 7:594–97; *Digest of Events of Jewish Interest* (1932–36); Milton L. Barron, "The Incidence of Jewish Intermarriage in Europe and America," *ASR*, 11 (1946), 7; Louis Rosenberg, *Canada's Jews* (Montreal, 1939), 100–111; Uriah Z. Engleman, "Intermarriage among Jews in Switzerland, 1888–1920," *AJS*, 34 (1928), 516–523; idem, "Intermarriage among Jews in Germany," *SSR*, 20 (1935), 34–39; idem, "Intermarriage among Jews in Germany, USSR, and Switzerland," *Jewish Social Sciences*, 2 (1940), 157–78; Nathan Goldberg, "Intermarriage from a Sociological Perspective," in Federation of Jewish Philanthropies, Commission on Synagogue Relations, *Intermarriage: The Future of the American Jew* (New York, 1964), 31. Cf. Paul R. Spickard, "Mixed Marriage: Two American Minority Groups and the Limits of Ethnic Identity, 1900–1970" (Ph.D. diss., University of California, Berkeley, 1983), 531–35.

17 See note 15. Also, Ruppin, *Jews in the Modern World*, 317; Fishberg, *Jews*, 195; Lucy S. Dawidowicz, ed., *The Golden Tradition: Jewish Life and Thought in Eastern Europe* (Boston, 1967).

18 The story of American Jewry in its early years is ably told in Jacob Rader Marcus, *Early American Jewry*, 3 vols. (Philadelphia, 1951–53); Hyman B. Grinstein, *The Rise of the Jewish Community of New York, 1654–1860* (Philadelphia, 1957); and David and Tamar de Sola Pool, *An Old Faith in the New World* (New York, 1955). For shorter summaries, see Glazer, *American Judaism*, 12–21, and Stanley Feldstein, *The Land That I Show You* (Garden City, N.Y., 1979), 1–117. Population figures are from Malcolm H. Stern, "Jewish Marriage and Intermarriage in the Federal Period (1776–1840)" (Unpublished MS, AJA), and from the 1790 U.S. census.

19 Malcolm H. Stern to Jacob R. Marcus, New York, February 1, 1966 (AJA); Malcolm H. Stern, "Two Studies in the Assimilation of Early American Jewry" (D.H.L. thesis, Hebrew Union College, 1957), 12–24 and passim; David J. Goldberg, "An Historical Community Study of Wilmington Jewry, 1738–1925" (Student paper, University of North Carolina, Chapel Hill, 1976; in AJA), 12–16; Grinstein, *Jewish Community of New York*, 372–87; Ipswich, Mass., Vital Records (AJA); Harold I. Sharfman, *Jews on the Frontier* (Chicago, 1977), 73–77; certificate of marriage between I. A. Isaacs and Isabella Hastie, December 6, 1817, New York City (AJA); Ellen Jay Lewis, "A Study in Assimilation as Reflected in the Correspondence of the Mordecai Family from the Earliest Days to 1840" (Student paper, Hebrew Union College, 1977; AJA); Mrs. S. J. Cohen, *Henry Luria; or, The Little Jewish Convert* (New York, 1860), 54 and passim.

20 Glazer, *American Judaism*, 22–42; Feldstein, *Land That I Show You*, 118–309; Sharfman, *Jews on the Frontier*, 73–77, 163–70, 184–88, 280–81.

21 Glazer, *American Judaism*, 22–59; Feldstein, *Land That I Show You*, 118–309; M. Doroshkin, *Yiddish in America: Social and Cultural Foundations* (Rutherford, N.J., 1969), 58.

22 Sharfman, *Jews on the Frontier*, xvii, 184, 280–81; Bibo Family Papers (AJA).

23 Rudolf Glanz, *The Jewish Woman in America* (New York, 1976), 2:98; Isaac M. Wise, "A Clandestine Marriage," *American Israelite*, March 19, 1880, 4; responsive articles, *American Israelite*, June 8 and 18, 1880; "Damocles" column in *Israelite*, April 17, 1874, 5–6. All articles in Deutsch Catalogue, AJA.

24 Iphigene Molony Bettman, biographical questionnaire, May 9, 1964 (AJA); Iphigene Molony Bettman, interviewed by Stanley F. Chyet et al., Cincinnati, May 13, 1964 (AJA Tape 215, Cincinnati). Cf. Isaac M. Wise, *Reminiscences* (New York, 1935), which does not mention the Wise-Molony marriage.

25 Isaac M. Wise, "Intermarriages," *American Israelite*, December 21, 1883; S. H. Sonneschein, "Should a Rabbi Perform the Ceremonies at the Intermarriage between Jew and Gentile?" *American Israelite*, May 7 and 14, 1880, 5; M. Mielziner, "Upon the Intermarriage Question," *American Israelite*, May 28, 1880.

26 Sklare, "Jewish Survival"; Goldberg, "Wilmington Jewry," 31; Adolph Moses to William Kreigshaber, Chicago, May 14, 1870 (AJA); Sharfman, *Jews on the Frontier*, 167–68; Grinstein, *Jewish Community of New York*, 372–87.

27 The world of the East European *shtetl* is lucidly evoked in Dawidowicz, *Golden Tradition*, and in the novels of Sholom Aleichem and Isaac Bashevis Singer. The life of Jews on the Lower East Side is vividly described in Moses Rischin, *The Promised City* (Cambridge, 1962), and Irving Howe, *World of Our Fathers* (New York, 1976). Figures on Jewish immigration can be found in Leonard Dinnerstein and David M. Reimers, *Ethnic Americans*, 2nd ed. (New York, 1982), 163–65. No European immigrant group has ever been placed quite so low on the scale as have Black and Native Americans.

28 "I Married a Jew," *Atlantic Monthly*, 163 (January 1939), 38–46.

29 Telemanchus Thomas Timayenis, *The American Jew: An Exposé* (New York, 1888), 81–87, quoted in Stanley I. Kutler, ed., *Looking for America*, 2nd ed. (New York, 1979), 2:260–63.

30 Charles Herbert Stember et al., *Jews in the Mind of America* (New York, 1966), 48–75; Louis A. Berman, *Jews and Intermarriage* (New York, 1968), 390–467; "Experiences of a Jew's Wife," *American Magazine*, 78 (1914), 49–52, 83–86; Henry Berkowitz, "Should Jews and Non-Jews Intermarry?" *Kansas City Journal*, November 2, 1889.

31 Israel Ellman, "Jewish Intermarriage in the United States" in Benjamin Schlesinger, *The Jewish Family* (Toronto, 1971), 52; Berman, *Jews and Intermarriage*, 393. This blend of exoticism and stability is what drew Hope Plowman to Noah Ackerman in the 1958 movie, *The Young Lions* (Twentieth Century Fox), and Charlotte Brown to Jacob Diamond in *Home before Dark* (Warner Brothers, 1968); cf. Lester D. Friedman, *Hollywood's Image of the Jew* (New York, 1982), 156–60.

32 Thomas Wolfe, *The Web and the Rock* (New York, 1937), 369, 513, 434, 476, and passim. Cf. Berman, *Jews and Intermarriage*, 439–446, for a penetrating description of the Esther Jack character in Wolfe's novel. Much of this portion of my analysis is drawn from Berman's work. Corroborating evidence was found by J. S. Slotkin in Chicago in 1942; see "Jewish-Gentile

Intermarriage in Chicago," *ASR*, 7 (1942), 34–39. For amplification of the negative side to the image of Jewish women, see Friedman, *Hollywood's Image*, 204–5, 249–50, and passim.

33 H. L. Hellyer, *From the Rabbis to Christ* (Philadelphia, 1911), 10–11; Julius Shore, *Intermarriage—An Analysis* (Vancouver, 1935), 10; Harry Roskolenko, *The Time That Was Then* (New York, 1971), 18, 34, and passim. The second generation's infatuation with things Gentile gave rise to a large number of assimilationist films in the largely Jewish movie industry, from *Becky Gets a Husband* (Lubin, 1912) to *The Jazz Singer* (Warner Bros., 1927) to *Minnie and Moskowitz* (Universal, 1971); cf. Friedman, *Hollywood's Image*, 26–27, 48–52, 243–56.

34 Philip Roth, *Portnoy's Complaint* (New York, 1969), 86–90, 160–65, 264–72, and passim; George Benedict, *Christ Finds a Rabbi* (Philadelphia, 1932), 19–21; Leslie A. Fiedler, *The Jew in the American Novel* (Ann Arbor, 1976; orig. New York, 1959), 17; Maria H. Levinson and Daniel J. Levinson, "Jews Who Intermarry: Sociopsychological Bases of Ethnic Identity and Change," *YIVO Annual of Jewish Social Science*, 12 (1958–59), 127.

35 Berman, *Jews and Intermarriage*, 489; Roskolenko, *Time That Was Then*, 144–45.

36 Singer, *The Slave*, 9; Milton L. Barron, "The Incidence of Jewish Intermarriage in Europe and America," *ASR*, 11 (1946), 6–13; Sanford Seltzer, *Jews and Non-Jews: Falling in Love* (New York, 1976), 12–16; Isaac Bashevis Singer, *A Crown of Feathers* (New York, 1973), 192; Levinsons, "Jews Who Intermarry," 118.

37 Berman, *Jews and Intermarriage*, 485–515; Levinsons, "Jews Who Intermarry," 118–19; Jacob Rader Marcus, "A Survey of Intermarriage in Small Mid-Western Cities" (AJA).

38 Marion F. Langer, "A Story of the Jewish Community of Easton" (Master of Social Service thesis, Graduate School for Jewish Social Work, New York, 1935), 303; Anzia Yezierska, *All I Could Never Be* (New York, 1934); Anzia Yezierska, *Bread Givers* (New York, 1975; orig. 1925); anonymous interview by the author, Cincinnati, October 12, 1979.

Chapter 7. Separate Identity amid Growing Acceptance

1 Irving Howe, *World of Our Fathers* (New York, 1976), 127–28; Moses Rischin, *The Promised City* (Cambridge, 1962), 75, 110–11; Celia Silbert, "Intermarriage on the East Side," *American Jewish Chronicle*, 1 (1916), 456–57; Arthur Ruppin, *The Jews in the Modern World* (London, 1934), 321; Julius Drachsler, *Intermarriage in New York City* (New York, 1921), 134–40, 185–90; Erich Rosenthal, "Studies of Jewish Intermarriage in the United States," *AJYB*, 64 (1963), 19; Fred Massarik and Alvin Chenkin, "United States National Jewish Population Study," *AJYB*, 74 (1973), 295. German and Hungarian Jews intermarried somewhat more frequently than Jews from other parts of Eastern and Central Europe. Cf. Paul R. Spickard, "Mixed Marriage: Two American Minority Groups and the Limits of Ethnic Identity" (Ph.D. diss., University of California, Berkeley, 1983), 539–41.

2 "Bintel Brief," February 20, 1906, quoted in George M. D. Wolfe, "Study of Immigrant Attitudes Based on an Analysis of Four Hundred Letters Printed in the 'Bintel Brief' of the 'Jewish Daily Forward'" (Diploma thesis, New York Training School for Jewish Social Work, 1929), 75–78; "Bintel Brief," 1908, quoted in Isaac Metzker, *A Bintel Brief* (New York, 1971), 76–78.

3 Sidney Goldstein and Calvin Goldscheider, *Jewish Americans* (Englewood Cliffs, N.J., 1968), 7–9, 43; Harry Roskolenko, *The Time That Was Then: The Lower East Side, 1900–1914* (New York, 1971), 18; Metzker, *Bintel Brief*, 18–19 (Golden quotation), 156–57.

4 Milton L. Barron, "The Incidence of Jewish Intermarriage in Europe and America," *ASR*, 11 (1946), 6–13; Jacob Rader Marcus, "Study of 'Mixed Marriages' in Mid-Western Towns and Cities," 1944 (AJA); S. Felix Mendelsohn, "Intermarriage: A Sociological Problem" (sermon delivered December 29, 1939, Chicago), printed as *Intermarriage* (Chicago, 1939); Julius Shore, *Intermarriage* (Vancouver, 1935), 6; U.S. Bureau of the Census, *Current Population Reports: Religion Reported by the Civilian Population of the United States, March 1957*, Series P-20, no. 79 (Washington, D.C., 1958); "Bintel Brief," January 6, 1947, in Wolfe, "Immigrant Attitudes," 328–29; "Bintel Brief," November 22, 1921, in William I. Thomas, *The Unadjusted Girl* (Boston, 1923), 52; Dachsler, *Intermarriage in New York City*, 134–40, 185–90; Rosenthal, "Studies of Jewish Intermarriage," 19; Massarik and Chenkin, "National Jewish Population Study," 295. Cf. Spickard, "Mixed Marriage," 539–41.

5 George E. Sokolsky, "My Mixed Marriage," *Atlantic Monthly*, August 1933, 137–46; "Experiences of a Jew's Wife," *American Magazine*, 78 (1914), 49–52ff.; Sadie Josephson, "Adjustment Histories of Six Jewish Women" (M.S.S. thesis, Graduate School of Jewish Social Work, New York, 1937), 223–64; "I Married a Jew," *Atlantic Monthly*, January 1939, 38–46; Metzker, *Bintel Brief*, 152–53, 165–66; Leonard Mosely, *Dulles* (New York, 1978), 121–22; Thomas, *Unadjusted Girl*, 51–52; "George E. Sokolsky," *Current Biography* (1941), 805–7.

6 Massarik and Chenkin, "National Jewish Population Study," 295; Peter Friedman et al., *A Population Study of the Jewish Community of Metropolitan Chicago* (Chicago, 1985), 36; Bruce A. Phillips and Eleanore P. Judd, *The Denver Jewish Population Study* (Denver, 1981), 47–48; M. H. Levinson and D. J. Levinson, "Jews Who Intermarry: Socio-psychological Bases of Ethnic Identity and Change," *Yivo Annual of Jewish Social Science*, 12 (1958), 122; Delllight Thompson to Rabbi Stanley F. Chyet, May 4, 1959, Bowling Green, Ohio (AJA); Samuel Glasner, "Counseling Parents on Problem of Intermarriage" (AJA); Joann S. Lublin, "The Crisis in Jewish Identity," *Wall Street Journal*, May 1979. See D. Caplowitz and H. Levy, *Interreligious Dating among College Students* (New York, 1965), and Morton Weinfeld, "A Report on Jewish Intermarriage Rates in Canada and the United States," 1975 (AJA), for similar trends in Jewish dating behavior and in Canadian intermarriage rates, respectively.

7 *Jewish Independent*, Cleveland, May 24, 18?? (Deutsch Catalogue, AJA); letters in *Tageblatt*, April 2 and 10, 1919 (Deutsch Catalogue, AJA).

8 Max Heller, "Judaism and Intermarriage," *American Israelite*, December 10, 1903, 4.

9 Michael Cook, "The Debates of the C.C.A.R. on the Problem of Mixed Marriage: 1907–1968" (AJA); Henry Berkowitz, "Should Jews and Non-Jews Intermarry?" *Kansas City Journal*, November 2, 1889.

10 Silbert, "Intermarriage on the East Side"; Rebecca E. Mack, *You Are a Jew and a Jew You Are!* (New York, 1933); *Constitution, Plotzker Young Men's Independent Association* (New York, 1893), 26. Also *Constitution of the Bombier Benevolent Society, Incorporated* (New York, 1916), 16–17; *Constitution of the Independent First Kudryncer Congregation Sick and Aid Society* (New York, 1900), 26–27; *Kremenitzer-Wolyner Benevolent Association* (New York, 1915); *Constitution of the Kolomear Friends Association* (New York, 1904); *Konstitushon fun di Yunited Disner Benevolent Asosieyshon* (New York, 1923); *Konstitutsion der Progresive Samborer Yong Mens Benevolent Associeyshon* (New York, 1913); *Konstitutsion Ershte Zborower Kranken und Vereyn* (New York, 1896), 14; *Constitution and By-Laws of the First Zborower Sick Benevolent Association*, rev. ed. (New York, 1940), 5–8; Michael R. Weisser, *A Brotherhood of Memory: Jewish Landsmanshaftn in the New World* (New York, 1985), 237. All of these *landsmanshaftn* constitutions are in the archives of YIVO Institute, New York City.

11 Mannheim S. Shapiro, "Intermarriage and the Jewish Community," in Gilbert S. Rosenthal, *The Jewish Family in a Changing World* (New York, 1970), 266; Eugen Schoenfeld, "Intermarriage and the Small Town," *Journal of Marriage and the Family*, 31 (February 1969), 61–64; "Experiences of a Jew's Wife"; "Bintel Brief," 1908, quoted in Metzker, *Bintel Brief*, 76–78 (Cahan quote); "Bintel Brief," 1906, quoted ibid., 37–38; "Bintel Brief," 1909, quoted ibid., 91–92. The Yiddish title *Vorwarts* is frequently translated as the *Jewish Daily Forward*.

12 David De Sola Pool, *Intermarriage* (pamphlet dated 1919, but surely written in the 1930s: it contains material from the late 1920s and mentions Nazism); Bernard Cohen, *Sociocultural Changes in American Jewish Life as Reflected in Selected Jewish Literature* (Rutherford, N.J., 1972), 125 (Kaplan and Stern quotations); Roland B. Gittelsohn, *Modern Jewish Problems* (Cincinnati, 1943), 82–101; Joseph Breuer, *The Jewish Marriage* (New York, 1956), 25–28; Shore, *Intermarriage*, 1–3 (Zlotnick quotation).

All the clamor about an end to the Jewish people seems a bit less hyperbolic if one considers that in this same period six million Jews were dying in Europe, chiefly at the hands of Germans. Many American Jews were aware that pre-1932 German Jewry was perhaps the most assimilated—and intermarried—Jewish community on earth. Perhaps this tragedy was one of the things Sholem Asch had in mind when, in *East River*, he put the following thoughts in the mind of the character Moshe Wolfe, an immigrant whose son had intermarried: "My grandchild is a Christian! I have lost my place in Israel. The ancient chain has been broken. My grandchildren will begin a new line of Christian generations, who will not know my God. They will be the enemies of my people. They will be pogromists against the Jews!" Surely that memory lingered in the mind of Golda Meir when she, an unbelieving Jew, insisted on endogamy because Jewish survival required it. Sholem Asch, *East River* (New York, 1946), 216; Golda Meir, "The Threat of Mixed Marriages," *American Mercury*, 107 (Winter 1971), 51–53.

13 "Bintel Brief," October 14, 1920, quoted in Marvin Bressler, "Jewish Behavior Patterns as Exemplified in W. I. Thomas' Unfinished Study of the 'Bintel Brief'" (Ph.D. diss., University of Pennsylvania, 1952), 219–21; "Bintel Brief," March 12, 1914, quoted ibid., 212–14; "Bintel Brief," November 11, 1913, quoted ibid., 215–17; Marion F. Langer, "Story of the Jewish Community of Easton" (M.S.S. thesis, Graduate School for Jewish Social Work, New York, 1935), 297–303; "Bintel Brief," February 8, 1927, quoted in Wolfe, "Immigrant Attitudes," 429–30; "Bintel Brief," March 22, 1927, quoted ibid., 548–49; "Bintel Brief," January 6, 1927, ibid., 328–29; "Bintel Brief," 1935, quoted in Metzker, *Bintel Brief*, 162–63. See also "Bintel Brief," March 23, 1927, quoted in Wolfe, "Immigrant Attitudes," 550–51; Irving M. Engel, transcript of oral memoir, New York, 1969–1970 (AJA); "Bintel Brief," March 10, 1920, quoted in Thomas, *Unadjusted Girl*, 52; "Bintel Brief," July 7, 1939, quoted in Bressler, "Behavior Patterns," 218–19; Roskolenko, *Time That Was Then*, 13, 37.

14 Harry Joshua Stern, *The Problem of Intermarriage* (Montreal, 1944); Abraham B. Shoulson, ed., *Marriage and Family Life: A Jewish View* (New York, 1959), 219–24; Bernard Malamud, *The Assistant* (New York, 1957).

15 J. S. Slotkin, "Adjustment in Jewish-Gentile Intermarriages," *Social Forces*, 21 (1942), 226–30; "Bintel Brief," 1928, quoted in Metzker, *Bintel Brief*, 149–50; "Bintel Brief," 1953, quoted ibid., 182–83; Claris Edwin Silcox and Galen M. Fisher, *Catholics, Jews, and Protestants* (New York, 1934), 244; Jacob Weinstein, *The Jew and Mixed Marriage* (Cincinnati, 1941); Reuben B. Resnik, "Some Sociological Aspects of Intermarriage of Jew and Non-Jew," *Social Forces*, 12 (1933), 94–102.

16 Werner J. Cahnman, "New Intermarriage Studies," *Reconstructionist*, March 17, 1967, 7–13; Federation of Jewish Philanthropies, Commission on Synagogue Relations, *Intermarriage: The Future of the American Jew* (New York, 1964); Sheldon Zimmerman and Barbara Trainin, eds., *The Threat of Mixed Marriage* (New York, 1976); "A Sampler of Reform Rabbis' Attitudes toward Mixed Marriage," 1972 (AJA); Egon Mayer and Carl Sheingold, *Intermarriage and the Jewish Future: A National Study in Summary* (New York, 1979), 1; Sanford Seltzer, *Jews and Non-Jews: Falling in Love* (New York, 1976), 4; Ira Eisenstein, *Intermarriage* (New York, 1964).

17 Marshall Sklare, "Intermarriage and Jewish Survival," *Commentary*, 49 (1970), 51–58; Eisenstein, *Intermarriage*, 14–15 (italics added); "Reform Rabbis' Attitudes," 25.

18 Abraham I. Shinedling, "On the Problem of Intermarriage," Albuquerque, 1967, (AJA), 53–56; Kalman Packouz, *How to Stop an Intermarriage: A Practical Guide for Parents* (Jerusalem, 1976); Zimmerman and Trainin, *Threat of Mixed Marriage*. I am grateful to Rabbi Paul Kushner of the Federation of Jewish Philanthropies for showing me the Packouz book and several other sources of information.

19 Mayer and Sheingold, *Jewish Future*, 12; American Jewish Committee,

"Jewish Teenagers in Wilkes-Barre" (New York, 1965), cited by Israel Ellman, "Jewish Intermarriage in the United States," in Benjamin Schlesinger, *The Jewish Family* (Toronto, 1971), 25–61; American Jewish Committee, "Survey of Dade County, Greater Miami" (New York, 1961), cited in Ellman, "Jewish Intermarriage"; Levinsons, "Jews Who Intermarry"; Caplowitz and Levy, *Interreligious Dating*, 14, 19–22, 37, 48–49 (the study of Columbia University students).

20 Ellman, "Jewish Intermarriage,"34–37. Also Sklare, "Jewish Survival"; Seltzer, *Jews and Non-Jews*, 12–16.

21 "Reform Rabbis' Attitudes," 5, 13, 21, and passim; David Max Eichorn, "Autobiography of David Max Eichorn" (AJA); Eichorn correspondence (AJA); David Max Eichorn, *Jewish Intermarriages: Fact and Fiction* (Satellite Beach, Fla., 1974).

22 Shinedling, "Problem of Intermarriage," 9; Arnold Schwartz, "Intermarriage in the United States," *AJYB*, 71 (1970), 118–20; Sklare, "Jewish Survival"; Glasner, "Counseling Parents on Problems of Intermarriage" (AJA); Cook, "The Debates of the C.C.A.R." (AJA).

23 Abraham Gordon, interviewed by the author, San Francisco, 1978; "Laboratory in Jewish Living," advertisement in *San Francisco Chronicle*, October 28, 1980, 5; Samuel M. Silver, *Mixed Marriage between Jew and Christian* (New York, 1977), 9, 55, 73–87; Joseph Berger, "Interfaith Marriages: Children's Views," *New York Times*, December 2, 1985, 19. Paul Cowan and Rachel Cowan, *Mixed Blessings* (New York, 1987), constitutes a gentle endorsement of intermarriage and book of advice for intermarriers, from an intermarried couple.

24 Caplowitz and Levy, *Interreligious Dating*, 13; Ellman, "Jewish Intermarriage," 30.

25 Eisenstein, *Intermarriage*, 4–6.

26 Caplowitz and Levy, *Interreligious Dating*, 48–49; Fred Massarik and Alvin Chenkin, "United States National Jewish Population Study," *AJYB*, 74 (1973), 303. An extraordinary degree of acceptance—and perhaps a portent for the future—are indicated by the following, found on a men's room wall at San Francisco State University, May 21, 1981: "1971: Mom asks me to marry a nice Jewish girl. 1981: Mom's glad I married a girl."

27 Fred Massarik, "Rethinking the Intermarriage Crisis," *Moment*, 3 (June 1978), 29–33. Massarik's opinion was widely but not universally shared. David Singer responded tartly, "If widespread intermarriage does not point to the inevitable demographic decline of American Jewry, it certainly poses the threat of a critical weakening of the quality of Jewish life." Singer, "Living with Intermarriage," *Commentary*, 68 (July 1979), 48–53. Some Jews still felt even more strongly—and personally—opposed to intermarriage than did Singer. See, for example, Ken Levitt's account of being kidnapped and "deprogrammed" in 1978 at his parents' arrangement on account of his conversion to Christianity and marriage to a Gentile woman: *Kidnapped for My Faith* (Van Nuys, Calif., 1978).

28 Mayer and Sheingold, *Jewish Future*, 14; Eugen Schoenfeld, "Intermarriage

and the Small Town: The Jewish Case," *JMF*, 31 (1969), 61–64; Gary A. Tobin, *1982 Demographic and Attitudinal Study of the St. Louis Jewish Population* (St. Louis, 1982), 117–18.

29 Ronald Cohen, interviewed by the author, Berkeley, Fall 1978.

30 "Experiences of Jew's Wife"; "Bintel Brief," 1908, quoted in Metzker, *Bintel Brief,* 76–78; Maurice Fishberg, *The Jews: A Study of Race and Environment* (New York, 1911), 209–10.

31 John Haynes Holmes, *Mixed Marriages: Are They Advisable?* (New York, 1931), 6, 17.

32 Gittelsohn, *Modern Jewish Problems*, 83, 85; J. S. Slotkin, "Adjustment in Jewish-Gentile Intermarriages," *Social Forces*, 21 (1942), 226–30; "I Married a Jew"; Charles H. Stember et al., *Jews in the Mind of America* (New York, 1966), 104.

33 Stember, *Jews in the Mind of America*, 106; Benjamin B. Ringer, *The Edge of Friendliness: A Study of Jewish-Gentile Relations* (New York, 1967), 62 (quotation); Caplovitz and Levy, *Interreligious Dating*, 8–10, 20–22, 37; Mayer and Sheingold, *Jewish Future*, 13; *Gallup Report*, no. 213 (June 1983), 10.

34 Rosenthal, "Studies of Jewish Intermarriage," 16, 19, 37, 40; Massarik and Chenkin, "National Jewish Population Study," 295; Gary A. Tobin and Julie A. Lipsman, "A Compendium of Jewish Demographic Studies," in Steven M. Cohen et al., eds., *Perspectives in Jewish Population Research* (Boulder, Colo., 1984), 137–66; Erich Rosenthal, "Jewish Intermarriage in Indiana," in Milton L. Barron, ed., *The Blending American* (Chicago, 1972), 224; Stanley K. Bigman, *The Jewish Population of Greater Washington in 1956* (Washington, D.C., 1957); Fred Massarik, *Report on the Jewish Population of Los Angeles, 1959* (Los Angeles, 1959); Fred Massarik, *The Jewish Population of San Francisco, Marin County, and the Peninsula, 1959* (San Francisco, 1959); Sidney Goldstein, *The Greater Providence Jewish Community* (Providence, 1964); Bureau of Jewish Social Research, "Jewish Population of Los Angeles, California" (AJA); Bureau of the Census, *Religion Reported by the Civilian Population*, 7. Cf. Spickard, "Mixed Marriage," 540–42.

35 Abraham D. Lavender, ed., *A Coat of Many Colors: Jewish Subcommunities in the United States* (Westport, Conn., 1977), 4, 28, 91; Anonymous interview by the author, Berkeley, May 19, 1981; Bibo Family Papers (AJA); Sokolsky, "My Mixed Marriage," 137–46; "Bintel Brief," 1909, quoted in Metzker, *Bintel Brief,* 87–88; "Bintel Brief," 1913, quoted ibid., 168–70; I. Harold Sharfman, *Jews on the Frontier* (Chicago, 1977), 280–81 and passim; Dorothy Dellar Kohanski to Jacob R. Marcus, Passaic, N.J., January 6, 1976 (AJA); Irving M. Engel memoir (AJA); "Bintel Brief," July 7, 1939, quoted in Bressler, "Behavior Patterns," 218–19.

36 Deborah Hertz, "Mobility and Assimilation in the Berlin Salons, 1780–1832" (AJA); John E. Mayer, "Jewish-Gentile Intermarriage Patterns," *SSR*, 45 (1960), 188–95; Ruppin, *Jews in the Modern World*, 319–20; Jacob Lestschinsky, "Mixed Marriage," in *The Universal Jewish Encyclopedia* (1942), 7:594–97; *Digest of Events of Jewish Interest* (1932–36); Barron, "Incidence of

Jewish Intermarriage"; Louis Rosenberg, *Canada's Jews* (Montreal, 1939), 100–111; Uriah Z. Engleman, "Intermarriage among Jews in Switzerland, 1888–1920," *AJS*, 34 (1928), 516–23; idem, "Intermarriage among Jews in Germany, *SSR*, 20 (1935), 34–39; idem, "Intermarriage among Jews in Germany, U.S.S.R., and Switzerland," *Jewish Social Studies*, 2 (1940), 157–78; Nathan Goldberg, "Intermarriage from a Sociological Perspective," in Federation of Jewish Philanthropies, *Intermarriage: The Future of the American Jew* (New York, 1964); Fishberg, *Jews*, 209; Arthur Ruppin, *The Jews of To-Day* (London, 1913), 161; Caplowitz and Levy, *Interreligious Dating*, 36. Cf. Spickard, "Mixed Marriage," 531–35.

37   Metzker, *Bintel Brief*, 146; Lavender, *Coat of Many Colors*, 44; Erich Rosenthal, "Jewish Intermarriage in Indiana" in Milton L. Barron, ed., *The Blending American* (Chicago, 1972), 222–42; Daniel E. Kerman to Jacob R. Marcus, Buffalo, N.Y., April 26, 1967 (AJA); Schoenfeld, "Intermarriage and the Small Town."

38   Stanley K. Bigman, *The Jewish Population of Greater Washington in 1956* (Washington, D.C., 1957); Rosenthal, "Studies of Jewish Intermarriage," 22, 25; "Experiences of a Jew's Wife"; Silbert, "Intermarriage on the East Side."

39   Rosenthal, "Studies of Jewish Intermarriage," 22, 25; Bressler, "Behavior Patterns," 212; Malamud, *The Assistant*, 158–60; Howe, *World of Our Fathers*, 267.

40   Robert K. Merton, "Intermarriage and the Social Structure," *Psychiatry*, 4 (1941), 361–74; Kingsley Davis, "Intermarriage in Caste Societies," *American Anthropologist*, 43 (1941), 376–95; Lewis F. Carter, "Racial-Caste Hypogamy: A Sociological Myth?" *Phylon* (1968), 347–50; Metzker, *Bintel Brief*, 38–39 (Golden quotation); Levinsons, "Jews Who Intermarry," 108–9.

41   Rosenthal, "Studies of Jewish Intermarriage," 25; Caplowitz and Levy, *Interreligious Dating*, 12, 32, and passim; Levinsons, "Jews Who Intermarry," 123–26; Ellman, "Jewish Intermarriage," 44, 50–51; Sklare, "Jewish Survival." The Levinsons also suggest that Jewish professionals who intermarried found more support for their marriages among their peers and therefore were better adjusted than their "less professional" subjects.

42   Marshall Sklare, "Intermarriage and the Jewish Future," *Commentary*, 37 (April 1964), 46–52; Jacob Weinstein, *The Jew and Mixed Marriage* (Cincinnati, 1941); Milton M. Gordon, *Assimilation in American Life* (New York, 1964), 224–32; Caplowitz and Levy, *Interreligious Dating*, 41, 53; Rosenthal, "Studies of Jewish Intermarriage," 22.

43   Marion F. Langer, "Story of the Jewish Community of Easton" (Master of Social Service thesis, Graduate School for Jewish Social Work, 1935), 300; Samuel Silver, *Mixed Marriage between Jew and Christian* (New York, 1977), 66; David Kirshenbaum, *Mixed Marriage and the Jewish Future* (New York, 1958); Fishberg, *Jews*, 221. There are other, smaller groups, such as Reconstructionists, Hasidim, and Messianic Jews, who are not analyzed separately here. Likewise, there are a large number of unaffiliated Jews. Unfortunately, I have unearthed no source of information that would allow me systematically to compare the unaffiliated to members of the three major

traditions. One might surmise that the unaffiliated would have a higher rate of intermarriage than those with synagogue connections, but that is an as yet untested hypothesis.

44 Max J. Routtenberg, "The Jew Who Has Intermarried," 1963 (AJA); Wilfred Shuchet, "The Intermarried Jew and Synagogue Membership," 1963 (AJA); Berger, "Interfaith Marriages"; Schwartz, "Intermarriage in the United States," 101.

45 Sklare, "Jewish Survival"; Central Conference of American Rabbis, "Resolutions, 1890–1962" (Microfilm 892–894, AJA); "Reform and Intermarriage," *Liberal Judaism*, March 1947, 14–17; Cook, "Debates of the C.C.A.R."; Iphigene Molony Bettman biographical questionnaire, May 9, 1964 (AJA); Iphigene Molony Bettman, interviewed by Stanley Chyet et al., Cincinnati, May 13, 1964 (AJA); "Not Wise-ly But Too Well" (Isaac M. Wise Papers, AJA); Isaac M. Wise, "A Clandestine Marriage," *American Israelite* (1880), 4; Isaac M. Wise, "Intermarriages," *American Israelite* (1883), 25; Seltzer, *Jews and Non-Jews*; Shinedling, "Problem of Intermarriage"; Letter from sixteen CCAR rabbis to their fellow members, April 15, 1973 (AJA); Pool, "Intermarriage"; Moses Cyrus Weiler, letter to Rabbi Herman E. Schaalman, New York, May 30, 1973 (AJA); James G. Heller, *Isaac M. Wise* (New York, 1965); Weinstein, *The Jew and Mixed Marriage*; "Reform Rabbis' Attitudes," 1972 (AJA); "Report of the Committee on Patrilineal Descent," *Reform Judaism* (Spring–Summer 1983), 16. The position of Reconstructionist Jewish leaders was similar to that of the leaders of Reform; see Federation of Jewish Philanthropies, *Intermarriage*; Eisenstein, *Intermarriage*.

46 Jewish Welfare Federation of New Orleans, "A Study of Jewish Adolescents of New Orleans," cited in Ellman, "Jewish Intermarriage"; Sokolsky, "My Mixed Marriage"; Levinsons, "Jews Who Intermarry," 110; Silver, *Mixed Marriage*, 66; Jacob R. Marcus, "'Mixed Marriages' in Mid-Western Towns and Cities" (AJA); Gilbert S. Rosenthal, *The Many Faces of Judaism* (New York, 1978), 26–115.

Chapter 8. According to the Halakhah

1 Past tense is used in this section, not because no one studies the psychological dynamics of intermarriage any more, but because the studies examined here all deal with an earlier era. I treat them in part as historical artifacts themselves.

2 Roland B. Gittelsohn, *Consecrated Unto Me: A Jewish View of Love and Marriage* (New York, 1965); Henry E. Kagan, "Reflections on Intermarriage," in Gilbert S. Rosenthal, *The Jewish Family in a Changing World* (New York, 1970), 285; Samuel R. Lehrman, "Psychopathology in Mixed Marriages," *Psychoanalytic Quarterly*, 36 (1967), 67–82. Also see Louis I. Newman, "Intermarriage between Jews and Christians during the Middle Ages," *Jewish Institute Quarterly*, 2 (January 1976), 2–8, and (March 1976), 22–28; Peter Elman, ed., *Jewish Marriage* (London, 1967), 112. The fullest discussion of the psychology of Jewish intermarriage is Louis A. Berman,

Jews and Intermarriage: A Study in Personality and Culture (New York, 1968). His analysis undergirds much of the present discussion, although his conclusions are somewhat different from mine.

3 Bernard Lazerwitz, "Intermarriage and Conversion," *Jewish Journal of Sociology*, 12 (1971), 41–63; Marshall Sklare, "Intermarriage and the Jewish Future," *Commentary*, 37 (1964), 46–52; Erich Rosenthal, "Studies of Jewish Intermarriage in the United States," *AJYB*, 64 (1963), 47.

4 Samuel Glasner, "Counseling Parents on Problems of Intermarriage," 1962 (AJA); Abraham N. Franzblau, "The Dynamics of Mixed Marriage," *CCAR Journal* (1954), 21–25; Louis Birner, "The Interfaith Marriage and Its Effect on the Individual," in Rosenthal, *Jewish Family*, 275–76.

5 M. H. Levinson and D. J. Levinson, "Jews Who Intermarry: Socio-psychological Bases of Ethnic Identity and Change," *YIVO Annual of Jewish Social Science*, 12 (1958), 103–30.

6 J. S. Slotkin, "Adjustment in Jewish-Gentile Intermarriages," *Social Forces*, 21 (1942), 226–30; Reuben B. Resnik, "Some Sociological Aspects of Intermarriage of Jews and Non-Jews," *Social Forces*, 12 (1933), 94–102.

7 Jerold S. Heiss, "Premarital Characteristics of the Religiously Intermarried in an Urban Area," in "Sampler of Reform Rabbis' Attitudes" (AJA); Lehrman, "Psychopathology in Mixed Marriages"; Werner Cahnman, "New Intermarriage Studies," *Reconstructionist*, 33 (1967), 7–13; Israel Ellman, "Jewish Intermarriage in the United States," in Benjamin Schlesinger, ed., *The Jewish Family* (Toronto, 1971), 53.

8 Heiss, "Premarital Characteristics"; Sanford Seltzer, *Jews and Non-Jews: Falling in Love* (New York, 1976), 20; D. Caplowitz and H. Levy, *Interreligious Dating among College Students* (New York, 1965), 42, 44, 54.

9 Lehrman, "Psychopathology in Mixed Marriages"; John E. Mayer, "Jewish-Gentile Intermarriage Patterns," *SSR*, 45 (1960), 188–95.

10 Slotkin, "Jewish-Gentile Intermarriage"; Armand Schreiber, "The Case for Intermarriage," *Harper's Weekly*, January 8, 1916, 33–34; George E. Sokolsky, *We Jews* (Garden City, N.Y., 1935), 109.

11 Anzia Yezierska, *Bread Givers* (New York, 1975), 55; also Anzia Yezierska, *All I Could Never Be* (New York, 1932). Cf. Helen Bober in Bernard Malamud's *The Assistant* (New York, 1957).

12 Slotkin, "Jewish-Gentile Intermarriage"; Egon Mayer and Carl Sheingold, *Intermarriage and the Jewish Future* (New York, 1979), 9; Sklare, "Jewish Future"; Heiss, "Premarital Characteristics."

13 Nathan Glazer, *American Judaism* (Chicago, 1972), 15; Arthur Ruppin, *The Jews in the Modern World* (London, 1934), 317; "Bintel Brief," January 13, 1939, quoted in Marvin Bressler, "Jewish Behavior Patterns as Exemplified in W. I. Thomas' Unfinished Study of the 'Bintel Brief'" (Ph.D. diss., University of Pennsylvania, 1952), 221–24; Marc D. Angel, "The Sephardim in the United States," *AJYB*, 74 (1973), 77–138; Victor D. Sanua, "Contemporary Studies of Sephardi Jews in the United States," in Abraham D. Lavender, ed., *A Coat of Many Colors* (Westport, Conn., 1977), 281–88. The discrimination by Israeli Askenazim against Sephardim is a very different

phenomenon, though it springs from some of the same roots as American cleavages; cf. Bob Levin, "Second-Class Israelis," *Newsweek*, July 13, 1981, 34.

14 Solomon Poll, *The Hasidic Community of Williamsburg* (New York, 1962), 15; Adolph Abbey, letter to the *Hebrew Standard*, July 27 and May 13, 1904 (Deutsch Catalogue, AJA); Report on Orthodox rabbinical conference, New York, May 16, 1916 (Deutsch Catalogue, AJA).

15 Marion F. Langer, "Story of the Jewish Community of Easton" (Master of Social Service thesis, Graduate School for Jewish Social Work, 1935), 299; "Bintel Brief," 1967, quoted in Isaac Metzker, ed., *Bintel Brief* (Garden City, N.Y., 1971), 206–7.

16 David Dorman Gould, autobiographical questionnaire (AJA); Milton L. Barron, "Incidence of Jewish Intermarriage in Europe and America," *ASR*, 11 (1946), 6–13.

17 "Bintel Brief," 1906, quoted in Metzker, *Bintel Brief*, 47–49; ibid., 50; "Bintel Brief," February 20, 1906, quoted in George M. D. Wolfe, "A Study of Immigrant Attitudes Based on an Analysis of Four Hundred Letters Printed in the 'Bintel Brief' of the 'Jewish Daily Forward'" (Diploma in Social Work thesis, Training School of Jewish Social Work, 1919), 75–78; Philip Roth, "Eli, the Fanatic," in *Goodbye, Columbus* (Boston, 1959), 186.

18 Moses Rischin, *The Promised City* (Cambridge, 1962), 95–111; Kurt Lewin, "Self-Hatred among Jews," in Arnold Rose, ed., *Race Prejudice and Discrimination* (New York, 1953), 322; M. Doroshkin, *Yiddish in America* (Rutherford, N.J., 1969), 48; Irving M. Engel memoir (AJA); Anonymous interview by the author, Berkeley, May 19, 1981; Sybil H. Pollett, *Marriage, Intermarriage and the Jews* (New York, 1966), 48; Glazer, *American Judaism*, 106.

19 Anonymous interview by the author, New York, September 18, 1979; Isaac Bashevis Singer, "Grandfather and Grandson," in *Crown of Feathers* (New York, 1973), 299–319; Egon Mayer, *Love and Tradition: Marriage between Jews and Christians* (New York, 1985), 50; "Bintel Brief," 1906, quoted in Metzker, *Bintel Brief*, 52–53.

20 "Bintel Brief," March 5, 1917, quoted in Bressler, "Behavior Patterns," 224.

21 Julius Drachsler, *Intermarriage in New York City* (New York, 1921), 134–40, 185–90; Mayer, *Love and Tradition*, 50. Cf. Spickard, "Mixed Marriage," 546–50. Jonathan Sarna has described the ways Old World distinctions were blurred and new, overarching categories created, in "From Immigrants to Ethnics: Toward a New Theory of 'Ethnicization,'" *Ethnicity*, 5 (1978), 370–78. I am grateful to him for several insights on this matter.

22 Drachsler, *Intermarriage in New York City*, 134–40, 185–90; cf. Spickard, "Mixed Marriage," 546–50.

23 Harry Roskolenko, *The Time That Was Then: The Lower East Side, 1900–1914* (New York, 1971), 13. Also Angel, "Sephardim"; Clarence Edwin Silcox and Galen M. Fisher, *Catholics, Jews and Protestants* (New York, 1934), 267; Langer, "Jewish Community," 299; Norman Podhoretz, "My Negro Problem —and Ours," *Commentary*, 35 (February 1963), 93–101; Drachsler, *Inter-*

marriage in New York City, 134–40, 185–90; Spickard, "Mixed Marriage," 546–50.

24 Glazer, *American Judaism*, 106; Levinsons, "Jews Who Intermarry," 124; William Mitchell, *Mishpokhe* (New York, 1978), 160–61; Robert T. Coleman, "Black and Jewish—And Unaccepted," in Lavender, *Coat of Many Colors*, 229–32; Caplowitz and Levy, *Interreligious Dating*, 8; Dorothy Dellar Kohanski to Jacob R. Marcus, Passaic, N.J., January 6, 1976 (AJA).

25 Arthur Ruppin, *The Jews of To-Day* (London, 1913), 189; *Digest of Jewish Events* for the following dates and pages: January 20, 1933, 7–8; May 5, 1933, 60; May 16, 1934, 66; August 16, 1934, 105–6; September 13, 1935, 65–68. Also Newman, "Intermarriage during the Middle Ages"; Louis Rosenberg, *Canada's Jews* (Montreal, 1939), 112–17; Singer, "Crown of Feathers," in *Crown of Feathers*, 11–36; Isaac Bashevis Singer, *The Slave* (New York, 1962), 47, 156.

26 George Benedict, *Christ Finds a Rabbi* (Philadelphia, 1932); "Apostasy among the Jews," *Review of Reviews*, 36 (September 1907), 356–57; Rebecca E. Mack, *You Are a Jew and a Jew You Are!* (New York, 1933); Ira O. Glick, "The Hebrew Christians," in Lavender, *Coat of Many Colors*, 415–31.

27 H. L. Hellyer, *From the Rabbis to Christ* (Philadelphia, 1911), 80–82.

28 This picture of conversion for theological rather than matrimonial reasons was a change from the early years of the republic. Many of the early converts to Christianity were upwardly mobile, highly assimilated Jews who had already married Gentiles and chose Christianity to create religious unity at home. Other early intermarriages, however, resulted in Christian converts to Judaism. See David J. Goldberg, "An Historical Community Study of Wilmington Jewry, 1738–1925," 12–16 (AJA), and Mrs. S. J. Cohen, *Henry Luria; or, The Little Jewish Convert* (New York, 1860), 54 and passim.

29 "Bintel Brief," November 8, 1913, quoted in Bressler, "Behavior Patterns," 214–17; Metzker, *Bintel Brief*, 14; "Bintel Brief," February 8, 1927, quoted in Wolfe, "Immigrant Attitudes," 429–30. See also "Bintel Brief," January 6, 1927, quoted ibid., 328–29.

30 Ira Eisenstein, *Intermarriage* (New York, 1964), 19–21; Newman, "Intermarriage during the Middle Ages," 3 (citing Yalkut 1:213); Mayer and Sheingold, *Jewish Future*, 21; "A Sampler of Reform Rabbis' Attitudes toward Mixed Marriage" (AJA).

31 "Reform Rabbis' Attitudes" (AJA). See also Moses C. Weiler to Rabbi H. E. Schaalman, New York, May 30, 1973; Abraham B. Shoulson, ed., *Marriage and Family Life* (New York, 1959), 219–24.

32 David Max Eichorn, *Jewish Intermarriages* (Satellite Beach, Fla., 1974), 19, 45, and passim; "Reform Rabbis' Attitudes"; C. E. Silcox and G. M. Fisher, *Catholics, Jews and Protestants* (New York, 1934), 244; Marshall Sklare, "Intermarriage and Jewish Survival," *Commentary*, 49 (1970), 51–58.

33 Fred Massarik and Alvin Chenkin, "United States National Jewish Population Study," *AJYB*, 74 (1973), 296–97; Egon Mayer and Carl Sheingold, *Intermarriage and the Jewish Future* (New York, 1979), 6; Bernard Lazer-

witz, "Intermarriage and Conversion," *Jewish Journal of Sociology*, 12 (1971), 41–63; Ellman, "Jewish Intermarriage," 48; Seltzer, *Jews and Non-Jews*, 18–19; Bruce A. Phillips and Eleanore P. Judd, *The Denver Population Study* (Denver, 1982), 48.

34   It must be noted that these practices of liberal synagogues met stiff opposition from more traditional Jews. Werner Cahnman, "New Intermarriage Studies," *Reconstructionist*, 33 (1967), 7–13; Lazerwitz, "Intermarriage and Conversion"; Leonard M. Simons, taped interview, March 24, 1975 (AJA); "Laboratory in Jewish Living," advertisement in the *San Francisco Chronicle*, October 28, 1980; Samuel M. Silver, *Mixed Marriage between Jew and Christian* (New York, 1977), 73–87; Seltzer, *Jews and Non-Jews*, 21–22; Arthur Gilbert to Jacob R. Marcus, Philadelphia, November 26, 1968 (AJA); Bernard Cohen, *Sociocultural Changes in American Jewish Life as Reflected in Selected Jewish Literature* (Rutherford, N.J., 1972), 138; Joseph Berger, "Interfaith Marriages: Children's Views," *New York Times*, December 2, 1985, 19; David Singer, "Living with Intermarriage," *Commentary*, 68 (July 1979), 48–53; Bernard Lazerwitz, "Jewish-Christian Marriages and Conversions," *Jewish Social Studies*, 44 (1981), 31–46; Mayer, *Love and Tradition*, 55–56, 159; Massarik and Chenkin, "National Jewish Population Study," 297; J. S. Slotkin, "Adjustment in Jewish-Gentile Intermarriages," *Social Forces*, 21 (1942), 226–30 (Chicago woman).

35   David De Sola Pool, "Intermarriage," *Hebrew Standard*, February 7, 1919; Julius Shore, *Intermarriage* (Vancouver, 1935); Eisenstein, *Intermarriage*; Arnold Schwartz, "Intermarriage in the United States," *AJYB*, 71 (1970), 101–22.

36   Abraham I. Shinedling, "On the Problem of Intermarriage," Albuquerque, 1967 (AJA), 22.

37   Maurice Fishberg, *The Jews* (New York, 1911), 217; Harry Linfield, "The High Rate of Divorce among Jews Married to Non-Jews in Hungary," *Digest of Jewish Events*, June 9, 1933, 79; Uriah Z. Engelman, "Intermarriage among Jews in Germany, U.S.S.R., and Switzerland," *Jewish Social Studies*, 2 (1940), 157–58; H. T. Christensen and K. E. Barber, "Interfaith versus Intrafaith Marriage in Indiana," *Journal of Marriage and the Family* (1967), 461–69. Two more recent studies also inferred a higher incidence of divorce among intermarried couples, but could not present figures: Lazerwitz, "Jewish-Christian Marriages"; Allen S. Maller, "Jewish-Gentile Divorce in California," *Jewish Social Studies*, 37 (1975), 279–90.

38   Roland B. Gittelsohn, *Modern Jewish Problems* (Cincinnati, 1943), 91; Max Heller, "Judaism and Intermarriage," *American Israelite*, 50 (1903), 4; Ignaz Zollschan, *Jewish Questions* (New York, 1914), 38; Fishberg, *Jews*, 213; Sidney E. Goldstein, *Meaning of Marriage and Foundations of the Family* (New York, 1940), 70–75.

39   David Saperstein and Marc Saperstein, *Who Is a Jew?* (New York, 1972), 4; Golda Meir, "The Threat of Mixed Marriages," *American Mercury*, 107 (1971), 51–53; Seltzer, *Jews and Non-Jews*, 8; Shore, *Intermarriage*; Hy-

man B. Grinstein, *The Rise of the Jewish Community of New York* (Philadelphia, 1945), 318–20; *Archives Israelites* (1865), 276 (Deutsch Catalogue, AJA); *L'Educatore Israelita* (1863), 288 (Deutsch Catalogue, AJA).

40 *Tageblatt*, April 2 and 10, 1919, 5 (Deutsch Catalogue, AJA); "Experiences of a Jew's Wife," *American Magazine*, 78 (1914), 49–52ff.

41 *Digest of Jewish Events*, January 20, 1933, 7; Ruppin, *Jews of To-Day*, 175; Fishberg, *Jews*, 215; Erich Rosenthal, "Studies of Jewish Intermarriage in the United States," *AJYB*, 64 (1963), 13, 31; *Cincinnati Enquirer*, June 3, 1912 (Deutsch Catalogue, AJA); George E. Sokolsky, *We Jews* (Garden City, N.Y., 1935), xi–xii.

42 Eisenstein, *Intermarriage*, 8–10; "I Married a Jew," *Atlantic Monthly*, 163 (1939), 38–46; Kurt Lewin, "Self-Hatred among Jews," in Arnold Rose, ed., *Race, Prejudice, and Discrimination* (New York, 1953); Gittelsohn, *Modern Jewish Problems*, 92–93; "Bintel Brief," February 20, 1906, quoted in Wolfe, "Immigrant Attitudes," 75–78.

43 Abraham B. Shoulson, ed., *Marriage and Family Life* (New York, 1959), 219–24; Gittelsohn, *Modern Jewish Problems*, 98; cf. "Reform and Intermarriage."

44 Lazerwitz, "Intermarriage and Conversion"; Fred Massarik and Alvin Chenkin, "United States National Jewish Population Study," *AJYB*, 74 (1973), 298. Cf. Mayer and Sheingold, *Jewish Future*, 16–20; Gary A. Tobin and Julie A. Lipsman, "A Compendium of Jewish Demographic Studies," in Steven M. Cohan et al., eds., *Perspectives in Jewish Population Research* (Boulder, Colo., 1984), 165–66.

45 Egon Mayer, *Children of Intermarriage* (New York, 1983); Mayer, *Love and Tradition*, 153–76. The mixed children under study were all sixteen or older in 1981, so their parents presumably were married before 1965.

46 Eugen Schoenfeld, "Intermarriage and the Small Town: The Jewish Case," *JMF*, 31 (1969), 61–64; Eugen Schoenfeld, "Problems and Potentials," in Lavender, *Coat of Many Colors*, 73–75.

47 From "Recommendations" offered by a joint conference of Reform, Conservative, Reconstructionist, and Orthodox rabbis and lay workers, in Sheldon Zimmerman and Barbara Trainin, eds., *The Threat of Mixed Marriage* (New York, 1976), 150. Cf. "Reform Rabbis' Attitudes," 21, 26, 31; David Saperstein and Mark Saperstein, *Who Is a Jew?* (New York, 1972), 5–10.

48 Anonymous interview by the author, Berkeley, May 19, 1981; Joy Nakamura* to the author, May 22, 1974 (see Chapter 4).

Chapter 9. The Core of the Heart

1 Winthrop D. Jordan, *White over Black* (Chapel Hill, 1968), 44–98; cf. Edmund Morgan, *American Slavery, American Freedom* (New York, 1975), 295–337.

2 Jordan, *White over Black*, 3–43 and passim.

3 The summary analysis that follows comes from a multitude of sources, some of which can be found in the notes below. The interested reader might

fruitfully begin with Jordan, *White over Black*, 136–78; Jordan, "American Chiaroscuro: The Status and Definition of Mulattoes in the British Colonies," *William and Mary Quarterly*, 3rd ser., 19 (1962), 183–200; Carter G. Woodson, "The Beginnings of Miscegenation of Whites and Blacks," *Journal of Negro History*, 3 (1918), 335–53; and Joel Williamson, *New People: Miscegenation and Mulattoes in the United States* (New York, 1980), 5–59.

4   Lorenzo J. Greene, *The Negro in Colonial New England* (New York, 1968; orig. 1942), 203–7; John H. Franklin, *The Free Negro in North Carolina, 1790–1860* (New York, 1971; orig. Chapel Hill, 1943), 36; Morgan, *American Slavery*, 334–36; Peter Wood, *Black Majority* (New York, 1974), 98, 234. It is worth noting that the social situation in Britain's West Indian colonies was rather different. There, settled concubinage (but seldom intermarriage) between White masters and Black slave women was an open and common practice, due to the tiny number of White women available and the transient nature of most British settlers. On the continent, by contrast, there were proportionately more Whites, more of them were women, and social life soon took on a more settled character—hence, open cohabitation of White masters and Black slaves was rare.

5   Morgan, *American Slavery*, 334; Greene, *Negro in New England*, 201–2; Franklin, *Free Negro in North Carolina*, 36; Wood, *Black Majority*, 99; Joel A. Rogers, *Sex and Race: Negro-Caucasian Mixing in All Ages and All Lands*, 3 vols. (New York, 1940–44), 2:166, 232–34.

6   Jordan, *White over Black*, 137.

7   Ibid., 101–35.

8   Ibid., 150–63; Wood, *Black Majority*, 236–37.

9   Williamson, *New People*, 7–11.

10   Franklin, *Free Negro in North Carolina*, 35–37.

11   Greene, *Negro in New England*, 207–10; Louis Ruchames, "Race, Marriage, and Abolition in Massachusetts," *Journal of Negro History*, 40 (1955), 250–73; Morgan, *American Slavery*, 335–36; Arthur W. Calhoun, *A Social History of the American Family*, 2 vols. (Cleveland, 1917–19), 1:65–66, 81, 149, 210–11; Rogers, *Sex and Race*, 2:155, 163, 169, 183, 228; Leon Litwack, *North of Slavery* (Chicago, 1961), 16; Carter G. Woodson, *Free Negro Heads of Families in the United States in 1830* (Washington, D.C., 1925), vi–xv.

12   The major work on miscegenation in the antebellum South is a 1937 University of Chicago doctoral dissertation, belatedly published in book form, by James Hugo Johnston, *Race Relations in Virginia and Miscegenation in the South, 1776–1860* (Amherst, Mass., 1970); see esp. pp. 163–339. Other sources for my analysis are recorded in the notes below.

13   Charles L. Perdue et al., eds., *Weevils in the Wheat: Interviews with Virginia Ex-Slaves* (Charlottesville, 1976), 205–332 (Satterfield quotation, 245); John Brown, *Slave Life in Georgia* (London, 1855), 132–33, cited in E. Franklin Frazier, *The Negro Family in the United States* (Chicago, 1939), 55; Pauli Murray, *Proud Shoes* (New York, 1957), 39–44; Dorothy Sterling, ed., *We Are Your Sisters: Black Women in the Nineteenth Century* (New

York, 1984), 18–27; Calhoun, *History of the American Family*, 1:291–95; Rogers, *Sex and Race*, 2:185–98; Herbert G. Gutman, *The Black Family in Slavery and Freedom* (New York, 1976), 389–93.

14 Rogers, *Sex and Race*, 2:218–19.

15 Archibald H. Grimké to Angelina Grimké Weld, February 20, 1868 (Grimké Family Papers, Howard University Archives, Washington, D.C.); J. W. C. Pennington, *The Fugitive Blacksmith* (London, 1850), vi–viii, in Frazier, *Negro Family*, 59–60. Cf. Perdue, *Weevils in the Wheat*, 81; Sterling, *We Are Your Sisters*, 28.

16 Ronald T. Takaki, *Violence in the Black Imagination* (New York, 1972), 217–18; Perdue, *Weevils in the Wheat*, 117; Murray, *Proud Shoes*, 46–47.

17 J. S. Buckingham, *The Slave States of America* (London, 1842), 2:244–45; Frazier, *Negro Family*, 60–61, 65–67; Hill Family Documents (EFF box 92, no. 2); Family Histories—John Burke (EFF box 85, no. 9); Sterling, *We Are Your Sisters*, 29–30. Cf. Kenneth Stampp, *The Peculiar Institution* (New York, 1956), 355–56; Ira Berlin, *Slaves without Masters* (New York, 1974), 267–68; Gutman, *Black Family*, 389–93.

18 Robert W. Fogel and Stanley L. Engerman, *Time on the Cross* (Boston, 1974), 1:130–35; Eugene Genovese, *Roll, Jordan, Roll* (New York, 1974), 415 and passim.

19 John W. Blassingame, *Black New Orleans, 1860–1880* (Chicago, 1973), 17–21; Alice D. Nelson, "People of Color in Louisiana," *Journal of Negro History*, 1 (1916), 359–74, and 2 (1917), 51–78; James T. Haley, comp., *Afro-American Encyclopedia* (Nashville, 1895), 341; Sterling, *We Are Your Sisters*, 27; E. Franklin Frazier, *The Free Negro Family* (Nashville, 1932), 29–33; Calhoun, *History of the American Family*, 1:296–99; Frazier, *Negro Family*, 63–64; Berlin, *Slaves without Masters*, 267ff; Rogers, *Sex and Race*, 2:181–85, 194–96.

20 *Richmond Enquirer*, August 17, 1859, in Berlin, *Slaves without Masters*, 266; Blassingame, *Black New Orleans*, 19; Perdue, *Weevils in the Wheat*, 174–75, 224–25; Family Histories—Alabama (EFF box 5); Stampp, *Peculiar Institution*, 352; Gary B. Mills, "Miscegenation and the Free Negro in Antebellum 'Anglo' Alabama," *Journal of American History*, 68 (1981), 16–34; Franklin, *Free Negro in North Carolina*, 37–38; Rogers, *Sex and Race*, 2:235–47.

21 Mary B. Chesnut, *Diary from Dixie* (Boston, 1949), 21–22; Family Histories —Eloise F. Anderson (EFF box 85, no. 3); Frazier, *Negro Family*, 50–69; Ronald Takaki, *Violence in the Black Imagination* (New York, 1972), 216.

22 Calhoun, *History of the American Family*, 2:300–305; Murray, *Proud Shoes*, 45–47; Stampp, *Peculiar Institution*, 353; Family Histories—Julia Spain Cheevers (EFF box 86, no. 1); Mills, "Miscegenation and the Free Negro."

23 Genovese, *Roll, Jordan, Roll*, 421; Stampp, *Peculiar Institution*, 359; Family Histories—Raymond A. Brownbow (EFF box 85, no. 23); Murray, *Proud Shoes*, 42–43.

24 Mills, "Miscegenation and the Free Negro"; David Walker, *Appeal . . . to the Coloured Citizens of the World* (Boston, 1829), 10–11; Mildred Haskins,

"The Choice of a Mate" (student paper, Fisk University, March 1932, EFF box 82, no. 11).

25 Family Histories—Alabama (EFF box 5); Daniel F. Littlefield, *Africans and Seminoles* (Westport, Conn., 1977), 42, 53, 63, and passim; Tim Gannon, "Black Freedmen and the Cherokee Nation," *Journal of American Studies*, 11 (1977), 357–64; James Johnston, "Documentary Evidence of the Relations of Negroes and Indians," *Journal of Negro History*, 14 (1929), 21–43; Daniel F. Littlefield, *Africans and Creeks* (Westport, Conn., 1979), 84–86, 143–45; Kenneth W. Porter, *The Negro on the American Frontier* (New York, 1971), 8–95; Theresa Taylor, "Black-Seminole Relations" (student paper, University of California, Berkeley, 1981); Murray, *Proud Shoes*, 38; Conway W. Sams, *The Conquest of Virginia* (New York, 1916), 395–96; Arthur H. Estabrook and Ivan H. McDougle, *Mongrel Virginians: The Win Tribe* (Baltimore, 1926); Rogers, *Sex and Race*, 2:177–79.

26 Leon Litwack, *North of Slavery* (Chicago, 1961), 97 and passim; Ruchames, "Race, Marriage, and Abolition"; Calhoun, *History of the American Family*, 2:30; James O. Horton and Lois E. Horton, *Black Bostonians* (New York, 1979), 70; Leonard Richards, *Gentlemen of Property and Standing* (New York, 1970), 114–15, 120–23; *Anti-Negro Riots in the North: 1863* (New York, 1969), 2ff.; Adrian Cook, *The Armies of the Streets* (Lexington, Ky., 1974), 203, 312–13.

27 The Bureau of the Census made counts of mulattoes as well as Blacks for 1850, 1860, 1870, 1890, 1910, and 1920. But the term *mulatto* was interpreted variously. In 1850 and 1860, census takers received no instructions on how to decide if a person were a mulatto. One assumes the enumerators relied on eyeball estimates of color and features, together with whatever background information they might pick up. In 1870, 1910, and 1920, bureau employees were told to regard "full-blooded Negroes" as "black," and "all Negroes having some proportion of white blood" as "mulattoes." In 1890 these vague instructions were briefly replaced by a more precise set of criteria. That year, "blacks" were "persons having from three to five eighths Negro blood"; "quadroons" and "octoroons" had even less African ancestry. The problem, of course, is that the census takers seldom had sufficient family background data on which to base such fine gradations. As the 1890 census report admitted, "These figures are of little value." Yet this was more true for 1890 than the other years. There is *some* value in the general trends reported by these various census documents for the seventy-year period 1850–1920. At the very least, the census reports' finding that the Afro-American population got steadily lighter over this period—and differentially so in different regions —seems indisputable. Cf. U.S. Bureau of the Census, *Negro Population, 1790–1915* (New York, 1968; orig. Washington, D.C., 1918), 207–8; idem, *Fourteenth Census of the United States, 1920*, vol. 2, *Population, 1920, General Report and Analytical Tables* (Washington, D.C., 1920), 16–17.

28 Bureau of the Census, *Negro Population, 1790–1915*, 220–21; Bureau of the Census, *Fourteenth Census . . . Analytical Tables*, 35; U.S. Department of the Interior, *Population of the United States in 1860* (Washington, 1864), xiii;

Williamson, *New People*, 14–42; Gary B. Mills, *The Forgotten People: Cane River's Creoles of Color* (Baton Rouge, La., 1977); Sister Frances Jerome Woods *Marginality and Identity: A Colored Creole Family* (Baton Rouge, La., 1972); Genovese, *Roll, Jordan, Roll*, 414.

29 Maurice R. Davie, *Negroes in American Society* (New York, 1949), 391; Daniel Murray, "Color Problem in the United States," *Colored American Magazine*, 7 (1904), 719–24; Rogers, *Sex and Race*, 2:197–98, 221–22. For accounts of Jefferson's alleged alliance with his quadroon slave, see Barbara Chase-Riboud, *Sally Hemings* (New York, 1979), and Fawn M. Brodie, *Thomas Jefferson* (New York, 1974), 293–318 and passim.

30 Perdue, *Weevils in the Wheat*, 9 (Anderson quotation); Murray, *Proud Shoes*, 48–54; Family Histories—Eloise F. Anderson (EFF 85, no. 3); Stampp, *Peculiar Institution*, 358. Family Histories—Marcelyn R. Cobbs (EFF box 86, no. 4); Ophelia Settle Egypt et al., *Unwritten History of Slavery* (Nashville, 1945), 198–200.

31 Perdue, *Weevils in the Wheat*, 81 (Cunningham incident), 91 (Ferry); Frazier, *Negro Family*, 58–63 (Campbell); Calhoun, *History of the American Family*, 2:301; Sterling, *We Are Your Sisters*, 28; Genovese, *Roll, Jordan, Roll*, 418–19.

32 Genovese, *Roll, Jordan, Roll*, 429–31; Family Histories—Marcelyn R. Cobbs (EFF box 86, no. 4); Jordan, *White over Black*, 167–78; Blassingame, *Black New Orleans*, 21–22; Mills, "Miscegenation and the Free Negro," 21–23; Litwack, *North of Slavery*, 179, 182–83; Hannibal G. Duncan, "The Changing Race Relationship in the Border and Northern States" (Ph.D. diss., University of Pennsylvania, 1922), 98–99; Family Histories of Higher Classes—Mrs. Rose Hutchins (EFF box 93, no. 9); Murray, *Proud Shoes*, 52–53; Takaki, *Violence in the Black Imagination*, 217; Family Histories—Dora R. Curtis (EFF box 86, no. 10); Newman I. White, *American Negro Folk Songs* (Hatboro, Mass., 1965; orig. Cambridge, Mass., 1928), 152–56; Levine, *Black Culture*, 193; Littlefield, *Africans and Creeks*, 84–86.

33 Family Histories—Day Family (EFF box 86, no. 17); Jordan, *White over Black*, 171–74; Unarranged Family Histories (EFF box 93, no. 1); William I. Bowditch, *White Slavery in the United States* (New York, 1855).

34 Calvin Hernton has produced the most thorough exposition of power and sexual imagery between Black and White in *Sex and Racism* (New York, 1965). His work is fundamental to this section; other sources are listed in the notes that follow.

35 Lawrence W. Levine, *Black Culture and Black Consciousness* (New York, 1977), 290–91; George M. Frederickson, *The Black Image in the White Mind* (New York, 1971), 117–24, 294, 321–22, and passim.

36 Thomas Nelson Page, "The Great American Question; The Special Plea of a Southerner," *McClure's*, 28 (1907), 565–72; Charles Carroll, *The Negro a Beast* (St. Louis, 1900); Sterling A. Brown, "Negro Character as Seen by White Authors," in J. A. Emanuel and Theodore Gross, eds., *Dark Symphony: Negro Literature in America* (New York, 1968), 155–57; Sam Dennison, *Scandalize My Name: Black Imagery in American Popular Music*

(New York, 1982), 117; Earnest S. Cox, *White America* (Richmond, 1923); Haywood Patterson and Earl Conrad, *Scottsboro Boy* (Toronto, 1969; orig. 1950).

37 Brown, "Negro Character," 141–48, 151–55; Page, "Great American Question"; Dennison, *Scandalize My Name*, 122–23; Jack Slater, "The Real People behind the Jeffersons," *Ebony*, 35 (September 1980), 83–93; William H. Dixon, "Colour," in Dixon, *New America* (London, 1867), 2:325.

38 Jordan, *White over Black*, 158–59 (Jordan cites evidence that Black men's penises are, on the average, in fact larger than those of White men); I. L. Reiss, "Premarital Sexual Permissiveness among Negroes and Whites," *ASR*, 29 (1964), 688–98; Levine, *Black Culture*, 333–34; Gary I. Schulman, "Race, Sex, and Violence: A Laboratory Test of the Sexual Threat of the Black Male Hypothesis," *AJS*, 79 (1974), 1260–77.

39 Julius M. Bloch, *Miscegenation, Melaleukation, and Mr. Lincoln's Dog* (New York, 1958); L. Seaman, *What Miscegenation Is! And What We are to Expect Now that Mr. Lincoln is Re-Elected* (New York, 1864); Sidney Kaplan, "The Miscegenation Issue in the Election of 1864," *Journal of Negro History*, 34 (1949), 274–343; Lawrence J. Friedman, *The White Savage: Racial Fantasies in the Postbellum South* Englewood Cliffs, N.J., 1970), 66–68; Page, "Great American Question," 565; John Henrik Clarke, ed., *William Styron's Nat Turner* (Boston, 1968), 6, 40–41, 85, 89; Charles Herbert Stember, *Sexual Racism* (New York, 1976).

40 Patterson and Conrad, *Scottsboro Boy*; James Weldon Johnson, "The Washington Riots," *Crisis*, September 1919; Thomas Nelson Page, *The Negro*, quoted in Brown, "Negro Character," 156–57; Nathan Hare, "Revolution without a Revolution: The Psychosociology of Sex and Race," *Black Scholar*, 9 (April 1978), 2–7; John Dollard, *Caste and Class in a Southern Town*, 3rd ed. (Garden City, N.Y., 1957), 162–63; Jordan, *White over Black*, 154. There is a parallel between this imagery and the protective attitudes of upper-caste Hindu men toward upper-caste Hindu women vis-à-vis lower-caste men in India; see André Beteille, "Race, Caste, and Ethnic Identity," *International Social Science Journal*, 23 (1971), 519–35.

41 Thomas Nelson Page, *In Ole Virginia* (New York, 1887); Frederick L. Hoffman, *Race Traits and Tendencies of the American Negro*, Publications of the American Economic Association, 11 (August 1896), 182; Robert F. Foerster, *The Racial Problems Involved in Immigration from Latin America and the West Indies to the United States* (Washington, 1925), 57 (for a refutation of these racist, pseudoscientific tracts, see Juan Comas, *Racial Myths* [Paris, 1951], 12–19); Hugh M. Gloster, *Negro Voices in American Fiction* (Chapel Hill, 1948), 12ff.; Donald Bogle, *Toms, Coons, Mulattoes, Mammies, and Bucks: An Interpretive History of Blacks in American Films* (New York, 1973), 9–18, 147–49.

42 Christine Berringer*, interviewed by the author, Atlanta, August 1984; Dennison, *Scandalize My Name*, 128.

43 Incidents and Characters in the Chicago Community (EFF box 82, no. 1); Robert Seidenberg, "The Sexual Basis of Social Prejudice," *Psychoanalytic*

Review, 38 (1952), 90–95; Gerome Ragni and James Rado, "Black Boys/ White Boys," on *Hair* (RCA Records LSO-1150). Cf. A White Woman, "I Want to Marry a Negro," *Negro Digest*, August 1948, 9–14; "Tate's Night of Passion—Or Sleep? Model Says He Wasn't Alone," *San Francisco Chronicle*, November 2, 1979; George S. Schuyler, *Racial Intermarriage in the United States* (Girard, Kans., 1929), 11; Malcolm X, *Autobiography* (New York, 1965), 67–68.

44 Monroe N. Work, ed., *Negro Year-Book* (1919–21), 8–9.

45 Edward Mapp, *Blacks in American Films* (Metuchen, N.J., 1972), 154–62; Bogle, *Toms, Coons*, 175–83, 215–20. The remaining themes can all be found alive and well in the movies of Jim Brown; cf. Bogle, 220–23.

46 Willie Morris, *North toward Home*, 79 (Richmond lawyer), in Genovese, *Roll, Jordan, Roll*, 427–28; Charles S. Johnson, *Patterns of Negro Segregation* (New York, 1943), 220–21; Eartha Kitt, "The Most Exciting Men in My Life," *Ebony*, 8 (January 1953), 26–36; "Eartha Kitt's Search for Love," *Ebony*, November 1956, 83–88; Joseph Golden, "Facilitating Factors in Negro-White Intermarriage," *Phylon*, 20 (1959), 273–84; Dennison, *Scandalize My Name*, 117.

47 Hernton, *Sex and Racism*, 95; Rolling Stones, "Some Girls," on *Some Girls* (Atlantic Records COC 39108); "Miss N.Y. Becomes First Black Miss America," *Minneapolis Star and Tribune*, September 18, 1983; Cathleen McGuigan, "Miss America: A Title Lost," *Newsweek*, July 30, 1984; Melinda Beck, "For Want of a Bathing Suit," *Newsweek*, August 6, 1984; "A Colored Woman, However Respectable, Is Lower Than the White Prostitute," *The Independent*, 54 (1902), 2221–24, quoted in Gerda Lerner, ed., *Black Women in White America* (New York, 1972), 166–67; Lorraine Hansberry, *To Be Young, Gifted, and Black* (New York, 1969), 98. Cf. Anne Moody, *Coming of Age in Mississippi* (New York, 1968), 184 and passim; Lena Horne, "I Just Want to Be Myself," in Mel Watkins and Jay David, eds., *To Be a Black Woman* (New York, 1970), 103–12; Robert Staples, *The Black Woman in America* (Chicago, 1973), 65–66; Incidents and Characters in the Chicago Community (EFF box 82, no. 1); Reiss, "Premarital Sexual Permissiveness."

48 Brown, "Negro Character," 157–62; Bogle, *Toms, Coons*, 60–62, 125–32, 150–54, 166–75; George Washington Cable, *Madame Delphine* (New York, 1881), 42 and passim.

49 Ella Wheeler Wilcox, "An Octoroon," *New York Evening Journal*, no. 7, 800 (n.d.). The full text of Wilcox's poem is as follows:

> You think me beautiful! I thank you, sir,
> For words like those, in every woman stir
> A sense of pleasure. Be she queen, or slave,
> She would be fair, as all men would be brave.
> But there is something in your voice and mien
> You would not give expression WERE I queen.
>
> Behind the pensive pallor of my skin
> You see bloods mixed by that old chemist—Sin.

You know I stand outside convention's pale
And take for granted that I am for sale.

You are a white man with a pedigree.
A proud white woman and child I see
Full often at your side; God has been kind.
Yet there is some base stratum in your mind,
Which was left out of me; for I would die,
Rather than sell the virtue you would buy.
Fierce midday suns and lawless ebon nights
Mingled to make this beauty which delights.
And lurid in my veins you think must run
United ardors of the night and sun.

I am the Twilight just between the two,
The hour when reckless Day sits down to rue
His wasted moments; when Night, sweet and young,
After the children's lullabys are sung,
Stands near with tender counsel. In my heart
High aspirations germinate and start;
I would be noble in each thought and aim!
Nay, do not sneer—perchance from some great dame
Descends to me, through my degenerate sires,
An unsoiled woman's instincts and desires.
Perchance on Afric's coast was bought and sold
A jet black princess with heart of gold,
Who knew no sin save what the white man taught;
Till death a princess, though to serve her lot.
I know not how my love of virtue came,
But, sir, for you I have but one thought—shame.
Your heart is blacker than the blood in me;
And mine—I feel the nobler pedigree.

50 Pearl Bowser, "The Image of Black Women in the Media" (Vertical File
—Black Women, Schlesinger Library, Harvard University); Bogle, *Toms,
Coons*, 9, 58, 62–67, 150–54, 161–66.
51 Anne F. Scott, *The Southern Lady* (Chicago, 1970); Stember, *Sexual Racism*,
121–43; Tom Bradshaw*, interviewed by the author, San Francisco, April
1980. Cf. Fogel and Engerman, *Time on the Cross*, 135; Berke Breathed,
"Bloom County" (sequence on Binkley and Blondie), *Minneapolis Star and
Tribune*, November 1982; Staples, *Black Woman*, 68.
52 Examples of this sort of argument abound. For one recent example, see
Stember, *Sexual Racism*, 90–120. Stember makes lust for White women the
raison d'être of the Black Power movement.
53 White, *American Negro Folk Songs*, 317; Incidents and Characters in Chicago Community (EFF Box 82, Number 1); Bill Broonzy, *Big Bill Blues*
(London, 1955), 56–64; Eldridge Cleaver, *Soul on Ice* (New York, 1968),
159.

54 Malcolm X, *Autobiography*, 66–68; Daryl C. Dance, *Shuckin' and Jivin':
    Folklore from Contemporary Black Americans* (Bloomington, Ind., 1978),
    103; William H. Grier and Price M. Cobbs, *Black Rage* (New York, 1968),
    77; Mrs. Melvin E. McGee to the editor, *Ebony*, October 1970.

55 Kermit Mehlinger, "That Black Man–White Woman Thing," *Ebony*, August
    1970, 130–33 (Davis quote); Eddie James to the editor, *Ebony*, October
    1970; Levine, *Black Culture*, 333–34; Dance, *Shuckin' and Jivin'*, 106–9;
    Cleaver, *Soul on Ice*, 158–59.

56 Walker, *Appeal*; Amy Jacques Garvey, *Philosophy and Opinions of Marcus
    Garvey*, 2 vols. (New York, 1968–69; orig. 1923–25); Johnson, *Along This
    Way*, 121; Family Histories of Higher Classes—Analyn Colter* (EFF box
    93, no. 9).

57 Gerda Lerner, comp., *Black Women in White America* (New York, 1972),
    205–11 (Terrell quotation); John Dollard, *Caste and Class in a Southern
    Town* (New Haven, 1937; rpt. Madison, Wis., 1989), 141–43; Friedman,
    White Savage, 140–42; Alberta Robinson*, interviewed by the author, Wash-
    ington, D.C., August 1984; James Baldwin, *Another Country* (New York,
    1960), 352. See also Family Histories—Harrietta Davenport (EFF Box 86,
    no. 12); John Burma, "Humor as a Technique in Race Conflict," *ASR*, 11
    (1946), 712.

58 Hertford County Documents (EFF box 92, no. 7B); Hernton, *Sex and
    Racism*, 151; Cleaver, *Soul on Ice*, 169–70.

59 Robert Staples, "The Myth of Black Macho," *Black Scholar*, 10 (March–April
    1979), 24–33; Takaki, *Violence in the Black Imagination*, 222; Ernest Eans,
    Jr., to the editor, *Ebony*, November 1980; J. C. Washington to the editor,
    ibid.

60 Jean Toomer, *Cane* (New York, 1969; orig. 1923), 22; Broonzy, *Big Bill
    Blues*, 62; Bruce L. Maliver, *Anti-Negro Bias among Negro College Stu-
    dents* (Ann Arbor, 1964), 12 and passim; "Plastic Surgery: Many Negroes
    Narrow Noses, Thin Lips through Operations," *Ebony*, May 1949, 19–23;
    Malcolm X, *Autobiography*, 54–55. Lawrence Levine takes issue with the
    assertion that processing one's hair represented an attempt to appear White.
    He notes that a man like Malcolm X, even though he later attributed his
    conk to slavishness toward Whites, did nothing else at the time to please
    Whites. Levine argues that Black men who processed their hair were simply
    acting in accord with urban Black male values. Although Levine is right that
    the desire for straight hair had become a widely shared Black value, it seems
    certain that it came originally from a wish to replace an African physical trait
    with one of European origin. Cf. Levine, *Black Culture*, 290–91.

61 Grier and Cobbs, *Black Rage*, 67.

62 Levine, *Black Culture*, 333–34. Cf. Grier and Cobbs, *Black Rage*, 74;
    Dance, *Shuckin' and Jivin'*, 106–7.

63 Hernton, *Sex and Racism*, 131; David M. Buss, "Human Mate Selection,"
    American Scientist, 73 (January–February 1985), 48–51; M. H. Freeman,
    "The Educational Wants of the Free Colored People," *Anglo-African Maga-
    zine*, 1 (1859), 116–19, quoted in Litwack, *North of Slavery*, 183. Observa-

tions on advertisements come from *Ebony* for the following dates: November and December 1947; April 1948; January, June, November, and December 1949; February and March 1950; September 1951; May and September 1953; February 1954; November 1956; December 1960; March, April, and June 1961; July and August 1965. Cf. Toni Morrison, *The Bluest Eye* (New York, 1970).

64 A Negro Nurse, "More Slavery at the South," *The Independent,* 72 (1912), 197–200; Horne, "I Just Want to Be Myself"; Mehlinger, "Black Man–White Woman"; Dance, *Shuckin' and Jivin',* 101; E. Simms Campbell, "Are Black Women Beautiful?" *Negro Digest,* June 1951, 16–20; Jack Johnson, *Jack Johnson—in the Ring—and Out* (Chicago, 1927), 70–89; Grier and Cobbs, *Black Rage,* 74–75.

65 *Ebony* advertisements, August, September, and October 1970; December 1975; August 1982; January and May 1983; John Wells to the editor, *Ebony,* October 1970; Helen Hayes King and Theresa Ogunbiyi, "Should Negro Women Straighten Their Hair?" *Negro Digest,* August 1963, 65–71; Imamu Amiri Baraka, "Black Woman," *Black World,* July 1970, 7–11.

Chapter 10. The Wall Remains

1 For enunciations of the three-generation view of immigrant cultural history, see Marcus Lee Hansen, *The Immigrant in American History* (Cambridge, 1946); Marcus Lee Hansen, "The Problem of the Third-Generation Immigrant," *Augustana Historical Society Publications* (1938), reprinted in Oscar Handlin, ed., *Children of the Uprooted* (New York, 1966), 255–71; A. L. Epstein, *Ethos and Identity* (London, 1978), 139–56. The chapter epigraph is from James Oliver Killens, *Black Man's Burden* (New York, 1965), 127.

2 Jessie Bernard, *Marriage and the Family among Negroes* (Englewood Cliffs, N.J., 1966), 64–65; Stanley Lieberson, "Generational Differences among Blacks in the North," *AJS,* 79 (1973), 550–65; Thomas P. Monahan, "An Overview of Statistics on Interracial Marriage in the United States," *JMF,* 38 (1976), 228; U.S. Bureau of the Census, *1960 Census: Marital Status,* Subject Report PC(2)-4E (Washington, D.C., 1966), 160–65, 171–72; U.S. Bureau of the Census, *1970 Census: Marital Status,* Subject Report PC(2)-4C (Washington, D.C., 1972), 262–67; James D. Bruce and Hyman Rodman, "Black-White Marriages in the United States," in Irving R. Stuart and Lawrence E. Abt, eds., *Interracial Marriage* (New York, 1973), 151.

3 John W. Blassingame, *Black New Orleans, 1860–1880* (Chicago, 1973), 203; Joel Williamson, *New People: Miscegenation and Mulattoes in the United States* (New York, 1980), 89, 93; Arthur W. Calhoun, *A Social History of the American Family,* 2 vols. (Cleveland, 1917–19), 2:30–31.

4 Daniel Murray, "Race Integrity—How to Preserve It in the South," *Colored American Magazine,* 11 (1906), 369–77; Calhoun, *History of the Family in America,* 2:27–38; Chicago Documents of Families Coming to the Urban League (EFF box 81, no. 18); Family Histories—Wilma Jean Burton (EFF box 85, no. 24); Unarranged Family Histories (EFF box 93, no. 1); Family

Histories of Higher Classes—Walter Jackson* (EFF box 93, no. 9); Ray Stannard Baker, *Following the Color Line* (New York, 1964; orig. 1908), 165, 170–71; Hertford County (N.C.) Documents (EFF box 92, no. 7B) (Catus quotation).

5 Hertford County Documents (EFF box 92, no. 7B).

6 U.S. Bureau of the Census, *Negro Population, 1790–1915* (New York, 1968; orig. Washington, D.C., 1918), 218–21; U.S. Bureau of the Census, *Fourteenth Census, 1920*, vol. 2, *Population, 1920: General Report and Analytical Tables* (Washington, D.C., 1920), 35; Julius Lester, ed., *The Seventh Son: The Thought and Writing of W. E. B. Du Bois* (New York, 1971), 1:320–21.

7 Joel Williamson regards this lightening of Black America as evidence of mulattoes being pushed by White society out of a separate mulatto category, where they had been intimate with Whites, and into the Black caste, where they came to occupy an elite position newly distant from Whites. His argument has much to recommend it. But Williamson does not explain why there was no nationally recognized mulatto category before 1850, nor why separate mulatto social strata were limited to a few isolated locations such as New Orleans and Charleston, while thousands of other mulattoes—slaves— worked in the fields alongside their darker compatriots. His argument that there was once a three-category American racial system, which during this period devolved into two, while attractive, is not proved. See Williamson, *New People*, 61–109; William Kephart, "Is the American Negro Becoming Lighter?" *ASR*, 13 (1948), 437–43.

8 Williamson, *New People*, 78; Charles L. Perdue et al., eds., *Weevils in the Wheat: Interviews with Virginia Ex-Slaves* (Charlottesville, 1976), 146.

9 Robert E. T. Roberts, "Trends in Marriages between Negroes and Whites in Chicago," in R. E. Holloman and S. A. Arutinov, eds., *Perspectives on Ethnicity* (The Hague, 1978), 173–210; F. L. Hoffman, "Race Traits and Tendencies of the American Negro," *Publications of the American Economic Association*, 11 (1896), 198–200; A. H. Stone, *Studies in the American Race Problem* (New York, 1908), 60–65; G. T. Stephenson, *Race Distinctions in American Law* (New York, 1910), 98; R. S. Baker, *Following the Color Line* (New York, 1964; orig. 1908), 172; Julius Drachsler, *Intermarriage in New York City* (New York, 1921), 49–50, 100; L. Wirth and H. Goldhamer, "The Hybrid and the Problem of Miscegenation," in Otto Klineberg, ed., *Characteristics of the American Negro* (New York, 1944), 277–82; J. V. DePorte, "Marriages in the State of New York with Special Reference to Nativity," *Human Biology*, 3 (1931), 394; J. Golden, "Characteristics of the Negro-White Intermarried in Philadelphia," *ASR*, 18 (1953), 177–83; Annella Lynn, "Interracial Marriages in Washington, D.C.," *Journal of Negro Education*, 36 (1967), 429; idem, *Interracial Marriages in Washington, D.C.* (Washington, D.C., 1953); John Burma, "Interethnic Marriage in Los Angeles, 1948–1959," *Social Forces*, 42 (1963), 156–65; D. M. Heer, "Negro-White Marriage in the United States," *JMF*, 28 (1966), 264–65; D. M. Heer, "Intermarriage and Racial Amalgamation in the United States," *Eugenics Quar-*

terly, 14 (1967), 112–20; T. H. Pavela, "An Exploratory Study of Negro-White Intermarriage in Indiana," *JMF*, 26 (1964), 209–11; Nathan I. Huggins, *Slave and Citizen* (Boston, 1980), 157–58; Philip S. Foner, *The Life and Writings of Frederick Douglass* (New York, 1975), 4:115–17; August Meier, *Negro Thought in America, 1880–1915* (Ann Arbor, 1973), 242–43, 313.

10　See note 9. Florette Henri, *Black Migration* (Garden City, N.Y., 1975), 71–72; Eugene Cash, "A Study of Negro-White Marriages in the Philadelphia Area" (Ph.D. diss., Temple University, 1956), 8; Robert S. Stuckert, "The African Ancestry of the White Population," *Ohio Journal of Science*, 58 (1958), 155–60. For contrary opinions, see Kephart, "American Negro Becoming Lighter"; Williamson, *New People*, 119–20.

11　See note 9. Lynn, *Interracial Marriages in Washington, D.C.*, 63; John Dollard, *Caste and Class in a Southern Town*, 3rd ed. (Garden City, N.Y., 1957; rpt. Madison, Wis., 1989), 141, 151; Williamson, *New People*, 111–39 and passim; Maurice R. Davie, *Negroes in American Society* (New York, 1949), 396; Hortense Powdermaker, *After Freedom* (New York, 1967; orig. 1939), 195–96; Bureau of the Census, *Marital Status* (1960), 160–65, 171–72; idem, *Marital Status* (1970), 262–67, 283–88.

12　Charles S. Johnson, *Patterns of Negro Segregation* (New York, 1943), 148. Cf. Allison Davis and John Dollard, *Children of Bondage: The Personality Development of Negro Youth in the Urban South* (Washington, D.C., 1940), 20; Powdermaker, *After Freedom*, 185–96; Dollard, *Caste and Class*, 142–43; Allison Davis et al., *Deep South* (Chicago, 1965; orig. 1941), 31–37; Joel A. Rogers, *Sex and Race*, 3 vols. (New York, 1940–44), 2:306–9, 315, 317; Josephine Schuyler, "Seventeen Years of Mixed Marriage," *Negro Digest*, 4 (July 1946), 61–65. For a riveting fictional account, see Jean Toomer, *Cane* (New York, 1969; orig. 1923), 5–7.

13　Powdermaker, *After Freedom*, 186–89; Johnson, *Patterns of Negro Segregation*, 146–47; Davis, *Deep South*, 27–31; Rogers, *Sex and Race*, 2:298, 308, 312–15, 322. In the 1960s Calvin Hernton interviewed a Black man who had had an affair with a White woman during the Depression. The 18-year-old youth was hoboing from New York to Miami, and stopped to ask for work and a meal at a motel just inside the Florida line. The woman of the establishment said she needed help, since her husband was an invalid, and hired the young man for a week.

"Before three days had passed, you know what that woman did—one night she came up to my room above the garage and told me that she loved me, and wanted to know if I felt the same way about her. Man, I begin to shake my head and say, 'Nom, No mam, I sho ain't feeling nothing like that.' She didn't do anything else then, she just turn around and walked out. Right then I say to myself, 'Man, when the week's up, you better get the hell out of here fast.'

"But I didn't get a chance. The very next day, while I was fiddling around with something in the yard, she called me from up in her room. She said: 'Come up here this minute, I want you to do something rightaway.' Well, I stopped whatever I was doing and went up there. When I got up the stairs that led right into her room— BAM!—my eyes liked to have popped out: there she was lying on the bed with not a rag on her white body. Well, man, you know what I did? I ran back down those stairs like a ball of fire out of hell. But by the time I got to the bottom, she was at the top, and she said: 'If you run, I'll yell and scream and say you attacked me. So you best come back up.'

"I was trapped.

"From then on she started coming out to my room over the garage almost every night. And you know what, I got carried away; I got to like it—I mean with her calling me 'Daddy,' and me only eighteen—I fell in love; I got proud as hell. A young black boy with a white woman carrying on over him like that. And she wasn't no white trash, either. I found out her family was connected with one of the largest manufacturing companies in the nation at that time."

When the seriousness of his situation dawned on him,

"I made several attempts to leave, but she warned me over and over that if I did, she would tear her clothes and say I raped her and that was why I left.

"Trapped again, man.

"The only way I got out of that nightmare was to write my brother in Miami and ask him to send me a telegram saying my father had died and I must come home immediately."

(Calvin Hernton, *Sex and Racism* [New York, 1965], 12–15.)

14   St. Clair Drake and Horace Cayton, *Black Metropolis*, rev. ed. (New York, 1962), 1:149–53; Schuyler, "Seventeen Years of Mixed Marriage"; Mr. and Mrs. George S. Schuyler, "Does Interracial Marriage Succeed?" *Negro Digest*, June 1945, 15–17; G. S. Schuyler, *Black and Conservative* (New Rochelle, N.Y., 1966). Cf. Francine Miller*, "History of an Interracial Marriage" (EFF box 36, no. 9); Rogers, *Sex and Race*, 2:316–23.

15   Thomas P. Monahan, "Are Interracial Marriages Really Less Stable?" *Social Forces*, 48 (1970), 464; Lynn, "Interracial Marriages in Washington, D.C.," 428–33; Bureau of the Census, *Marital Status*, (1960), 171–72.

16   Akemi Kikumura and Harry H. L. Kitano, "Interracial Marriage: A Picture of the Japanese Americans," *Journal of Social Issues*, 29 (1973), 67–81; Constantine Panunzio, "Intermarriage in Los Angeles," *AJS*, 47 (1942), 690–701; Erich Rosenthal, "Studies of Jewish Intermarriage in the United States," *AJYB*, 64 (1963), 16, 37, 40; idem, "Jewish Intermarriage in Indiana," in Milton L. Barron, ed., *The Blending American* (Chicago, 1972), 224; Stanley K. Bigman, *The Jewish Population of Greater Washington in 1956* (Washington, D.C., 1957); Fred Massarik, *Report on the Jewish Population of Los Angeles, 1959* (Los Angeles, 1959); idem, *Jewish Population of San Francisco, Marin County, and the Peninsula, 1959* (San Francisco, 1959); Sidney Goldstein, *Greater Providence Jewish Community* (Providence, 1964); Roberts, "Marriages between Negroes and Whites in Chicago."

17   Ollie Stewart, "What Negro GI's Learned from Women in Europe," *Negro Digest*, September 1947, 24–27.

18   For the Japanese war brides, see in addition to Chapter 5, "War Babies of Japan," *Ebony*, September 1951; "The Truth about Japanese War Brides,"

Ebony, March 1952, 17–25; "Germany and Negro Soldiers" (letters), *Ebony*, April 1952; "The Loneliest Brides in America," *Ebony*, January 1953, 17–24; "Sailor to Movie Star," *Ebony*, August 1953, 46–51; "Letters of a Dying Mother to Her Baby," *Ebony*, July 1954, 16–25.

19 Hazel Byrne Simpkins, "A Negro's British War Bride," in Clotye M. Larsson, ed., *Marriage across the Color Line* (Chicago, 1965), 97–106. Cf. Ollie Stewart, "How War Brides Fare in America," *Negro Digest*, April 1948, 25–30; "German Mail Order Bride," *Ebony*, June 1953, 62–64; "Church Wedding for Mixed Couple," *Ebony*, December 1951, 50–52. These were not the first mixed marriage clubs. The Manasseh Society was founded in Milwaukee in 1890 and soon formed a chapter in Chicago, where it had several hundred members and became an elite organization in the city's Black community after the turn of the century. The Penguin Club was a similar New York group in the 1930s. See "Mixed Marriage Clubs," in Larsson, *Marriage across the Color Line*, 58–61; Lynn, *Interracial Marriages*, 520.

20 See notes 18 and 19, above.

21 Interview with anonymous Black social scientist, by author, Boston, 1984.

22 "Is Mixed Marriage a New Society Fad?" *Ebony*, September 1951, 98–103; "When Celebrities Intermarry," in Larsson, *Marriage across the Color Line*, 89–96; "Famous Negroes Married to Whites," *Ebony*, December 1949, 20–30; Lena Horne, "I Just Want to Be Myself," in Mel Watkins and Jay David, eds., *To Be a Black Woman* (New York, 1970), 103–12; "The Private Life of Lena Horne," *Ebony*, September 1953, 65–70; "Marriage to Lennie Hayton Is Open Secret for Three Years," *Ebony*, October 1950, 36; Pearl Bailey, "This Time It's Love," *Ebony*, May 1953, 122–28; William Gardner Smith, "Black Boy in France," *Ebony*, July 1953, 32–42; Anne Brown, "I Gave Up My Country for Love," *Ebony*, November 1953, 28–38; Harry Belafonte, "Why I Married Julie," *Ebony*, July 1957, 90–95. Other articles trumpeted "Hollywood's Most Tragic Marriage," between blonde follies beauty Helen Lee Worthington and Black physician Eugene C. Nelson (*Ebony*, February 1952, 26–36); "White Queen in Darkest Africa," the story of Ruth Williams, a British woman, and her husband, Seretse Khama, chief-designate of the Bamangwato of Bechuanaland (*Negro Digest*, December 1949, 60–69); and a host of other sensational mixed marriages.

23 Poppy Cannon, *A Gentle Knight* (New York, 1952); idem, "Mr. and Mrs. Walter White," in Larsson, *Marriage across the Color Line*, 140–61; idem, "How We Made Our Mixed Marriage Work," *Ebony*, June 1952, 24–40; idem, "How We Erased Two Color Lines," *Ebony*, July 1952, 47–59; idem, "Love That Never Died," *Ebony*, January 1957, 17–20.

24 "Mixed Marriage in College," in Larsson, *Marriage across the Color Line*, 120–39; "Successful U.S. Dentist in England," *Ebony*, May 1951, 4; "Americans in Ethiopia," *Ebony*, May 1951, 79–80; Mr. and Mrs. William Grant Still, "Does Interracial Marriage Succeed?" *Negro Digest*, April 1945, 50–52; Schuyler, "Does Interracial Marriage Succeed?"; Ruth Burke, "Protecting a Mixed Marriage," in Larsson, *Marriage across the Color Line*, 40–43; Thyra Edwards Gitlin and Murray Gitlin, "Does Interracial Marriage Succeed?"

Negro Digest, July 1945, 63–64; Nathaniel O. Calloway, "Mixed Marriage Can Succeed," *Negro Digest,* March 1949, 24–27.

25 The White press paid some attention to mixed marriages as well, although most of that did not come until the 1960s. Cf. "My Daughter Married a Negro," *Harper's,* July 1951, 36–40.

26 William Julius Wilson, *The Declining Significance of Race,* 2nd ed. (Chicago, 1980); Reynolds Farley, *Blacks and Whites: Narrowing the Gap?* (Cambridge, Mass., 1984).

27 Simeon Booker, "Couple That Rocked the Courts," *Ebony,* September 1967, 78–84. The *Loving* decision was greeted by generally positive comment around the country. It is probably significant that the American Civil Liberties Union chose as its test case the marriage of a Black woman and a White man. The opposite combination, a Black man and a White woman, might have elicited the same legal opinion, but would not have been likely to receive such general acclaim. It should also be noted that the *Loving* decision applied not just to Black-White marriages, but also to several other combinations, including Japanese-White.

28 Bureau of the Census, *Marital Status* (1970), 262–67; idem, *1980 Census: Marital Status,* Subject Report PC80-2-4C (Washington, D.C., 1985), 175–181; Joyce A. Ladner, *Tomorrow's Tomorrow: The Black Woman* (New York, 1971), 281–82; Lynn, "Interracial Marriages in Washington"; U.S. Bureau of the Census, *Perspectives on American Husbands and Wives,* Current Population Reports, Series P-23, no. 77 (Washington, D.C., 1978), 5–6, 9–10; Stanley Lieberson and Mary C. Waters, "Ethnic Mixtures in the United States," *SSR,* 70 (1985), 43–52; idem, *From Many Strands: Ethnic and Racial Groups in Contemporary America* (New York, 1988), chs. 6–7; Barbara Foley Wilson, "Marriage's Melting Pot," *American Demographics,* 6 (July 1984), 34–37ff; Richard D. Alba and Reid M. Golden, "Patterns of Ethnic Marriage in the United States," *Social Forces,* 65 (1986), 202–23. Some observers pegged the rise in intermarriage to the period immediately after the passing of the Civil Rights Act of 1964 or the *Loving* decision in 1967, but the numbers do not bear out either of these contentions. Rather, the increase in intermarriage rates was a longer-term trend.

29 Bureau of the Census, *Perspectives on American Husbands and Wives,* 5–6, 9–10. Other studies generally agreed, although Robert Roberts's Chicago survey suggested a sharp decline in the sex differential in the 1960s. See Robert E. T. Roberts, "Trends in Marriages between Negroes and Whites in Chicago," in Regina E. Holloman and S. A. Artuniunov, eds., *Perspectives on Ethnicity* (The Hague, 1978), 173–210; also U.S. Bureau of the Census, *1970 Census: Negro Population,* Subject Report PC(2)-1B (Washington, D.C., 1973), 172–80.

30 Joan Downs, "Black/White Dating," in Doris Y. Wilkinson, ed., *Black Male/White Female* (Morristown, N.J., 1975), 159–70.

31 Ibid.; Robert Staples, *Black Woman in America* (Chicago, 1973), 67.

32 Alvin F. Poussaint, "The Stresses of the White Female Worker in the Civil Rights Movement in the South," *American Journal of Psychiatry,* 123 (Octo-

ber 1966), 401–7; Sara Evans, *Personal Politics: The Roots of Women's Liberation in the Civil Rights Movement and the New Left* (New York, 1979), 78–82; Mary Aickin Rothschild, *A Case of Black and White: Northern Volunteers and the Southern Freedom Summers, 1964–1965* (Westport, Conn., 1982), 145–47.

33 Dennis A. Williams, "Roots III: Souls on Ice," *Newsweek*, June 10, 1985, 82–84; field notes, St. Paul, 1981–84. The phenomenon of the Black person isolated in a sea of Whites is not totally new. But the degree of acceptance and assimilation experienced by suburban Blacks today greatly exceeds that of earlier generations. Cf. "Young Woman in a 'White World'," *Ebony*, August 1966, 69–74.

34 Simeon Booker, "Challenge for the Guy Smiths," *Ebony*, December 1967, 146–50; "What Tyne Daly Gains from Her Mixed Marriage," *Globe*, September 4, 1984. Cf. Sammy Davis, Jr., "Is My Mixed Marriage Mixing Up My Kids?" *Ebony*, October 1966, 124–32; "Marriage of Eartha Kitt," *Ebony*, September 1960, 37–42.

35 From the 1850s on, a train of apologists for the evolving southern system kept insisting that White men's sexual abuse of Black women was a thing of the past—regrettable, but now happily terminated. Many doubtless believed what they said, but at best they were whistling in the dark. At least as late as the 1950s, the old practices continued. Witness the testimony of John Howard Griffin, a White man who posed as Black and hitched a ride with a White southern man: "He told me how all the white men in the region crave colored girls. He said he hired them, a lot of them both for housework and in his business. 'And I guarantee you, I've had it in every one of them before they get on the payroll.' . . . 'Surely some refuse,' I suggested cautiously. 'Not if they want to eat—or feed their kids,' he snorted. 'If they don't put out, they don't get the job. . . . We figure we're doing you people a favor to get some white blood in your kids.'" This White man may just have been bragging or trying to intimidate Griffin, but Griffin talked to dozens of Southerners, White and Black, who agreed this was a widespread practice. John Howard Griffin, *Black Like Me* (New York, 1960), 100 and passim. Cf. Oskar Heim, "Why I Want a Negro Wife," *Negro Digest*, July 1951, 64–68; Anne Moody, *Coming of Age in Mississippi* (New York, 1968), 30–32, 130–35, and passim.

36 George M. Fredrickson, *The Black Image in the White Mind* (New York, 1971), 165–227; John S. Haller, Jr., *Outcasts from Evolution: Scientific Attitudes of Racial Inferiority, 1859–1900* (Urbana, Ill., 1971); Williamson, *New People*, 61–109.

37 Sidney Kaplan, "The Miscegenation Issue in the Election of 1864," *JNH*, 34 (1949), 274–343; David G. Croly, *Miscegenation* (New York, 1864); L. Seaman, *What Miscegenation Is! and What We Are to Expect Now that Mr. Lincoln is Re-Elected* (New York, 1864); John H. Van Evrie, *Subgenation* (New York, 1864); Forrest G. Wood, *Black Scare: The Racist Response to Emancipation and Reconstruction* (Berkeley, 1968).

38 E. H. Randle, *Characteristics of the Southern Negro* (New York, 1910), 118; Charles Carroll, *The Negro a Beast* (St. Louis, 1900). Carroll drew on

an earlier work, Buckner H. Payne, *The Negro: What Is His Ethnological Status?* (Cincinnati, 1867). Hardly anyone seems to have paid much attention to two careful, step-by-step, scriptural refutations of Carroll's arguments: W. S. Armistead, *The Negro Is a Man* (Tifton, Ga., 1903), and William Gallio Schell, *Is the Negro a Beast?* (Moundsville, W. Va., 1901).

39   Madison Grant, *The Passing of the Great Race* (New York, 1916), 13–20 and passim. The others did not agree in every detail, but they all agreed on the evil of intermarriage. Armistead, *The Negro Is a Man*, 6–31; Hoffman, *Race Traits and Tendencies*, 177–99; Junius Aryan [Wilbert Newton], *The Aryans and Mongrelized America: The Remedy* (Philadelphia, 1912); Alfred P. Schultz, *Race or Mongrel* (Boston, 1908); Oscar Grow, *The Antagonism of Races* (Waterloo, Iowa, 1912), 36–65. Even President Eliot of Harvard agreed; see "Against Mixture of Racial Stocks," *Colored American Magazine*, 15 (1900), 133–34. Only a few, unheard White voices argued the contrary; cf. Richmond Mayo-Smith, "Theories of Mixture of Races and Nationalities," *Yale Review*, 3 (1894), 166–86.

40   Williamson, *New People*, 92–94; Randle, *Characteristics of the Southern Negro*.

41   Nathan I. Huggins, *Slave and Citizen* (Boston, 1980), 157–58; Philip S. Foner, *The Life and Writings of Frederick Douglass* (New York, 1975), 4:554.

42   "A Lynching in Arkansas," *Colored American Magazine*, 9 (1905), 409; "Colored Men and Women Lynched without Trial," *Crisis*, 9 (1915), 145; Booker T. Washington, *The Future of the American Negro* (Boston, 1899), 185–86.

43   William H. Dixon, "Colour," in *New America* (London, 1867), 336; Al-Tony Gilmore, "Jack Johnson and White Women," *Journal of Negro History*, 58 (1973), 18–38; "Jack Johnson," *Crisis* (1913), 121; Al-Tony Gilmore, *Bad Nigger!* (Port Washington, N.Y., 1975), 95–132.

44   Lawrence J. Friedman, *The White Savage: Racial Fantasies in the Postbellum South* (Englewood Cliffs, N.J., 1970), 105–7; Charles H. McCord, *The American Negro as a Dependent, Defective, and Delinquent* (Nashville, 1914), 49–50.

45   The standard work on intermarriage and the law is Robert J. Sickel, *Race, Marriage, and the Law* (Albuquerque, 1972). Sickel's interpretation undergirds much of the analysis of this section. Other sources used extensively include Derick A. Bell, Jr., *Race and Racism in American Law* (Boston, 1973), 259–94; Jack Greenberg, *Race Relations and American Law* (New York, 1959), 343–99; Winston P. Nagan, "Conflict of Laws: Group Discrimination and the Freedom to Marry," *Howard Law Journal*, 21 (1978), 1–46; Edward Byron Reuter, *Race Mixture* (New York, 1969; orig. 1931), 75–103; Albert E. Jencks, "The Legal Status of Negro-White Amalgamation in the United States," *AJS*, 21 (1916), 666–78.

46   A. Leon Higginbotham, *In the Matter of Color* (New York, 1978), 36–47, 158–59, 251, 273; Williamson, *New People*, 97–98; Johnson, *Patterns of Segregation*, 163–69; Gilbert Thomas Stephenson, *Race Distinction in American*

Law (New York, 1909), 78–80; Louis Wirth and Herbert Goldhamer, "The Hybrid and the Problem of Miscegenation," in Otto Klineberg, ed., *Characteristics of the American Negro* (New York, 1944), 359–60. Some states also levied penalties on those officiating at intermarriages or granting licenses to intermarrying couples.

47 Stephenson, *Race Distinction in American Law*, 86–88. See definitions of a Negro in note 27 to Chapter 9, above. It is little wonder attorney William Zabel concluded that "the statutory definitions of Negro are sometimes contradictory, often nonexistent, and usually a combination of legal fiction and genetic nonsense nearly impossible to apply as a practical matter. None of the statutory definitions seems sufficiently precise to meet the constitutional requirement of due process which nullifies a criminal statute that is so vague that men of common intelligence must guess at its meaning and differ about its application." William D. Zabel, "Interracial Marriage and the Law," in Wilkinson, *Black Male/White Female*, 114–23.

48 Stephenson, *Race Distinction in American Law*, 88–89; J. Shirley Shadrach, "Furnace Blasts: The Growth of the Social Evil among All Classes and Races in America," *Colored American Magazine*, 6 (1903), 259–63; U.S. Congress, House of Representatives, *Intermarriage of Whites and Negroes in the District of Columbia* (Washington, D.C., 1916); Johnson, *Patterns of Negro Segregation*, 169.

49 Cassius M. Clay, "Race and the Solid South," *North American Review*, 142 (February 1886), 134–38.

50 Pace v. Alabama, 106 U.S. 583, cited in Allan C. Brownsfeld, "Miscegenation and the Law," *New South*, 19 (July–August 1964), 10–15.

51 Associated Press, January 21, 1909; "Intermarriage," *Crisis*, 11 (1915), 306. The judge agreed to the absurdity of the Lindsay decision, and said he would petition the governor for a pardon, *on the condition that they cease to live as husband and wife.*

52 Gilmore, "Jack Johnson and White Women"; "Chicago," *Crisis*, 6 (1913), 38–39; David A. Gerber, *Black Ohio and the Color Line, 1860–1915* (Urbana, Ill., 1976), 268–70; "Proposed Negro Legislation," *Crisis*, 22 (1921), 65–66; Lynn, *Interracial Marriages in Washington, D.C.*, 61; "Anti-Intermarriage Bill in Michigan," *Crisis*, 22 (1921), 66; "Inter-Marriage," *Crisis*, 29 (1925), 251; "The NAACP Battlefront," *Crisis*, 35 (1928), 49–50; "Race Intermarriage," ibid., 118.

53 Reuter, *Race Mixture;* Herbert Adolphus Miller, "Racial Inter-Marriage," *Crisis* (1931), 337; Gunnar Myrdal, *An American Dilemma* (New York, 1962; orig. 1944); Juan Comas, *Racial Myths* (Paris, 1951); G. A. Borgese, "A Bedroom Approach to Racism," *Negro Digest*, December 1944, 31–35. Cf. Margaret Halsey, *Color Blind* (New York, 1946), 89–130.

54 "Sex Equality," *Crisis*, 19 (1919), 106; J. Thomas Heflin to Sam H. Reading, National News Service, Washington, D.C., October 15, 1929, reprinted in I. A. Newby, ed., *The Development of Segregationist Thought* (Homewood, Ill., 1968), 123–27. See also "The Anglo-Saxon at Bay," *Crisis*, 30 (1925), 10–11; A. H. Shannon, *The Racial Integrity of the American Negro* (Nash-

ville, 1925); Earnest Sevier Cox, *The South's Part in Mongrelizing the Nation* (Richmond, 1926); Jerome Dowd, *The Negro in American Life* (New York, 1926), 410–57; Marilyn R. Allen, *Alien Minorities and Mongrelization* (Boston, 1949); Austin E. Burges, *What Price Integration?* (Dallas, 1956), 53–73; Lambert Schuyler, *Close the Bedroom Door!* (Winslow, Wash., 1957).

55 Gerald L. K. Smith, *White Man Awaken!* (Los Angeles, [1950s]). See also the following pamphlets by Smith, all published in the 1950s in Los Angeles: *The Plot to Undermine the Republic*, 24–27, 34–37; *Handbook for the Courageous*, 90–94; *The Great Issues*, 25–30; *Congressman John E. Rankin*, 7, 21–37; *Matters of Life and Death*, 38–42; *Arkansas: Hungary of America; Supreme Court Tyranny;* and *The New York Jungle*.

56 Protestant Everett Tilson undertook a biblical defense of intermarriage in *Segregation and the Bible* (Nashville, 1958), 32–34. See also Joseph F. Doherty, *Moral Problems of Interracial Marriage* (Washington, D.C., 1949); "Baha'i Faith," *Ebony*, October 1952, 39–46.

57 Myrdal contended that *"the Negro's own rank order is just about parallel, but inverse, to that of the white man. The Negro resists least the discrimination on the ranks placed highest in the white man's evaluation and resents most any discrimination on the lowest level. This is in accord with the Negro's immediate interests. Negroes are in desperate need of jobs and bread, even more so than of justice in the courts, and of the vote. These latter needs are, in their turn, more urgent even than better schools and playgrounds, or, rather, they are primary means of reaching equality in the use of community facilities. Such facilities are, in turn, more important than civil courtesies. The marriage matter, finally, is of rather distant and doubtful interest." An American Dilemma*, 60–61.

58 Halsey, *Color Blind*, 124–25; Eleanor Roosevelt, "Should a Negro Boy Ask a White Girl to Dance?" *Negro Digest*, December 1947, 41–42. Harry Truman, less liberal than Eleanor Roosevelt but nonetheless the first president to take active steps toward integration, still dismissed as preposterous and counter to the teachings of the Bible the thought that his daughter might marry a Black man: Zabel, "Interracial Marriage and the Law." See also T. B. Matson, *Segregation and Desegregation: A Christian Approach* (New York, 1959), 73–80; "Mixed Marriages and Catholics," *Negro Digest*, March 1945, 85–86; Francis James Gilligan, *The Morality of the Color Line* (Washington, D.C., 1928), 82–107.

59 Alfred Steinberg, "What Is the Law on Mixed Marriages?" *Negro Digest*, May 1949, 47–49; John H. Burma, "Interethnic Marriage in Los Angeles, 1948–1959," *Social Forces*, 42 (1963), 163.

60 Haywood Patterson and Earl Conrad, *Scottsboro Boy* (Toronto, 1969; orig. 1950).

61 William Bradford Huie, "The Shocking Story of Approved Killing in Mississippi," *Look*, January 24, 1956, 46–48; Richard Lauchli to the editor, *Look*, March 6, 1956, 12; "Mississippi: The Place, the Acquittal," *Newsweek*, October 3, 1955, 24–29. For a vivid dramatization of the Till tragedy, see James Baldwin, *Blues for Mr. Charlie* (New York, 1964).

62 Chicago Documents of Families Coming to the Urban League (EFF box 81, no. 18); Morton Rubin, *Plantation County* (Chapel Hill, 1951), 98; Ron Borges, "Lightin' 'em Up Down in the Valley," *Boston Globe*, November 24, 1984, 29; Powdermaker, *After Freedom*, 194–95; Richard Wright, *Black Boy* (New York, 1966; orig. 1937), 189–91; Davis, *Deep South*, 29–34, 44–49.

63 Rubin, *Plantation County*, 202. It may be that White Virginians were less bothered by intermarriage than Whites in Mississippi. Yet Allison Davis and Burleigh and Mary Gardner found much the same situation in Mississippi in the 1930s as Rubin found in Virginia a decade later. Davis, *Deep South*, 35–37, 286–88; Alex Poinsett, "A Mississippi Story," in Larsson, *Marriage across the Color Line*, 114–19.

64 Sara Harris, *Father Divine: Holy Husband* (Garden City, N.Y., 1953), 97–115; Eugene Cash, "A Study of Negro-White Marriages in the Philadelphia Area" (Ed.D. diss., Temple University, 1956), 24–25; Joseph Golden, "Social Control of Negro-White Intermarriage," *Social Forces*, 36 (1958), 267–69; George S. Schuyler, *Racial Intermarriage in the United States* (Girard, Kans., 1929), 20–24; Joseph Golden, "Patterns of Negro-White Intermarriage," *ASR*, 19 (1954), 144–47; Ed Lacey, "The Village Is So Quaint," *Opportunity*, 20 (1942), 203–4; "Where Mixed Couples Live," in Larsson, *Marriage across the Color Line*, 44–47; A White Woman, "I Want to Marry a Negro," *Negro Digest*, August 1948, 9–14; "Should a White Girl Marry a Negro?" *Negro Digest*, December 1948, 13–18; "My Daughter Married a Negro," *Harper's*, July 1951, 36–40; "Children in Interracial Homes," in Larsson, *Marriage across the Color Line*, 67–74; Francine Miller*, "History of an Interracial Marriage" (EFF box 36, no. 9); "Interracial College Marriages," *Ebony*, July 1954, 89–94; Michelle Ross, "Is Mixed Marriage Jinxed?" *Ebony*, August 1953, 34–38; Elaine Neil, "Persecution in New York," in Larsson, *Marriage across the Color Line*, 120–39; Drake and Cayton, *Black Metropolis*, 1:129–51; Noel Myricks and Donna L. Ferullo, "Race and Child Custody Disputes," *Family Relations*, 35 (1986), 325–28; Nora Leven, "Love in Black and White," *Mpls./St. Paul*, August 1987, 72–74ff. (Gardner quotation).

65 Hazel Erskine, "The Polls: Interracial Socializing," *Public Opinion Quarterly*, 37 (1973), 291–93; G. H. Gallup, *The Gallup Poll: Public Opinion, 1972–1977* (Wilmington, 1978), 1:72–74; idem, *The Gallup Poll: Public Opinion, 1978* (Wilmington, 1978), 218–19; idem, *The Gallup Poll: Public Opinion, 1983* (Wilmington, 1984), 96–98; Bontemps, "National Poll." On all these points, the more liberal position tended to be taken by people from the North and West, those with high education and high income, people from big cities, the young, Democrats, and Catholics. More conservative postures tended to be taken by people from the South, those with less education and lower incomes, those from rural areas, older people, Republicans, and Protestants.

66 Norman Podhoretz, "My Negro Problem—and Ours," *Commentary*, February 1963, 93–101.

67 Bogle, *Toms, Coons*, 200–202, 217–18; Edward Mapp, *Blacks in American*

Films (Metuchen, N.J., 1972), 96–98, 156–62; "Guess Who's Coming to Dinner," *Ebony*, January 1968, 56–62.

68 Bureau of the Census, *Marital Status*, Subject Report PC(2)-4C, 262–98.

69 Jim Miller, "The Peter Pan of Pop," *Newsweek*, January 10, 1983, 52–54; *Playboy*, August 1985, cited in Cathleen McGuigan, "The Most Amazing Grace," *Newsweek*, July 1, 1985, 63. It is perhaps not irrelevant to note that, even in 1985, *Playboy*, this arbiter of middlebrow, White, male lust, was not yet ready to present a White *woman* and a Black *man* in the throes of carnal passion.

70 William J. Krutza and Philip P. DiCicco, *Facing the Issues 3* (Grand Rapids, 1970), 30. Although evangelical-bashing has become a favorite armchair sport in the 1980s, and Bob Jones gives ample reason for such a practice, it is worth noting that denunciations of Jones's position came from all across the theological spectrum. Evangelical scholar John Warwick Montgomery wrote: "Racial integration is thoroughly Christian, for God created all men and Christ died for all men. The consequence is that 'there is neither Jew nor Greek: ye are all one in Christ Jesus' (Gal. 3:28). . . . 'But, Dr. Montgomery, would you want *your* daughter to marry one of them?' In a word, Yes! Better that my daughter should marry a believing Negro than a bigoted White who has forgotten the love of Christ and 'passed by on the other side.'" Krutza and DiCicco, *Facing the Issues*, 30. Other Evangelicals, mainline Protestants, Catholics, and Jews expressed similar beliefs in the oneness of humankind and the appropriateness of interracial marriages within their theological communities. Cf. Andrew Schulze, *Fire from the Throne: Race Relations in the Church* (St. Louis, 1968), 130–43; C. E. Askew, "Yes, I Would Want My Daughter to Marry a Negro," *Negro Digest*, July 1964, 4–8; Joseph T. Leonard, *Theology and Race Relations* (Milwaukee, 1963), 154–65; Werner J. Cahnman, "The Interracial Jewish Children," *Reconstructionist*, June 9, 1967, 7–12; H. J. Massaquoi, "Would You Want Your Daughter to Marry One?" *Ebony*, August 1965, 82–84.

71 Charles H. Stember, *Sexual Racism* (New York, 1976), 90–120. Cf. Robert E. Kuttner, "Race Mixing: Suicide or Salvation?" *American Mercury*, Winter 1971, 45–48; Carleton Putnam, *Race and Reason* (Washington, D.C., 1961). There is some evidence that a fairly wide spectrum of Whites held subliminal prejudices against interracial marriage. Gary Schulman tested White males for willingness, in an experimental situation, to inflict pain on others. White males from all classes and political persuasions showed a greater willingness to inflict pain on Black men they understood to be involved sexually with White women than on either White men or Blacks who did not have that involvement. Schulman, "Race, Sex, and Violence: A Laboratory Test of the Sexual Threat of the Black Male Hypothesis," *AJS*, 79 (1974), 1260–77.

72 See note 45; also Sickels, *Race, Marriage, and the Law*, 64; A. C. Brownfeld, "Will the Supreme Court Uphold Mixed Marriages?" *Negro Digest*, March 1965, 72–77; Simeon Booker, "Couple That Rocked Courts," *Ebony*, September 1967, 78–84; "The Crime of Being Married," *Life*, March 18, 1966, 85–91.

73 Herbert Feinstein, "Lena Horne Speaks Freely on Race, Marriage, Stage," *Ebony*, May 1963, 61–67; "Court Takes Woman's White Child after She Has Black Baby," *Minneapolis Tribune*, January 12, 1982; Aric Press, "Blackburn v. Blackburn," *Newsweek*, May 17, 1982, 105; "Dad, Son Start New Life after Custody Fight," *Minneapolis Star and Tribune*, November 8, 1983; "High Court to Hear Interracial Custody Case," *Minneapolis Star and Tribune*, October 18, 1983; "Judge Bars Woman from Reclaiming Child after Supreme Court Decision," *Minneapolis Star and Tribune*, April 28, 1984.

74 Feinstein, "Lena Horne Speaks Freely"; "Trials of an Interracial Couple," *Ebony*, October 1965, 66–68. There were at least two kinds of exceptions to the generally more liberal air. One was exemplified by the lunatic behavior attributed to Joseph Paul Franklin, a White hate-monger charged in 1980 with the deaths of several Black men who had been seen with White women. This was an infrequent phenomenon, not often repeated by others. The other was quirky, individual, petty harassment, such as that visited upon dozens of Minnesota mixed couples and interracial adoptive parents by an anonymous leaver of packets of clippings and typed messages against intermarriage in the early 1980s. "Tracing a Pattern of Racial Murder," *Newsweek*, November 10, 1980, 45; "Avowed Racist Is Found Guilty of Killing Two Blacks," *Minneapolis Tribune*, September 20, 1981; field notes, St. Paul, May 1984.

75 "An Honest and Open Look at Interracial Mating" (student paper, Bethel College, January 1982); field notes, Boston, January 1985; "Races: A Marriage of Enlightenment," *Time*, September 29, 1967, 28–31; Simeon Booker, "Challenge for the Guy Smiths," *Ebony*, December 1967, 146–50; Bill Berry, "Interracial Marriages in the South," *Ebony*, June 1978, 64–72; Shawn D. Lewis, "Black Women/White Men: The 'Other' Mixed Marriage," *Ebony*, January 1978, 37–42; Linda Grimes*, interviewed by the author, Boston, March 4, 1985.

76 Frederick Douglass, *The Life and Times of Frederick Douglass* (London, 1962; orig. 1892), 438–39. Richard T. Greener, C. B. Purvis, Charles W. Chesnutt, and William Wells Brown (along with Henry Highland Garnet in an earlier era) were other prominent Black people who favored amalgamation.

77 Howard Brotz, ed., *Negro Social and Political Thought* (New York, 1966), 7–8; Huggins, *Slave and Citizen*, 157–58; Foner, *Life and Writings of Frederick Douglass*, 4:115–17; Francis J. Grimke, "The Second Marriage of Frederick Douglass," *JNH*, 19 (1934), 324–29; Meier, *Negro Thought*, 54–58, 243; Earl Ofari, *"Let Your Motto Be Resistance": The Life and Thought of Henry Highland Garnet* (Boston 1972), 180.

78 Kelly Miller, *As to the Leopard's Spots* (Washington, 1905), 17; House of Representatives, *Intermarriage of Whites and Negroes*, 27–28; Meier, *Negro Thought*, 54–58, 76, 167, 194–95, 204–6; Brotz, *Negro Social and Political Thought*, 10–11, 180–90; Friedman, *The White Savage*, 140–42.

79 David A. Gerber, *Black Ohio and the Color Line, 1860–1915* (Urbana, Ill., 1976), 207; Booker T. Washington, quoted in Jencks, "Legal Status of Negro-White Amalgamation"; Washington, *Address . . . at the Opening of the*

Atlanta Cotton States and International Exposition (1895); W. E. B. Du Bois, "The Social Equality of Whites and Blacks," *Crisis*, 21 (1920), 16–18; Meyer Weinberg, ed., *W. E. B. Du Bois: A Reader* (New York, 1970), 40. The fear involved for some Black people in the rejection of interracial sex and marriage is evident in the following joke recounted by Lawrence Levine: "Two black soldiers sitting on the dock at Brest at the end of the First World War spoke of what they would do when they were shipped home. One said that he would take a lesson from the French, who had no race feelings and drew no color line. On arriving in their home town he would buy a white suit, white tie, white straw hat, and white shoes. 'An' I goin' put'em on an' den I'm goin' invite some w'ite gal to jine me an' wid her on my arm I'm gwine walk slow down de street bound fur de ice-cream parlor. Whut does you aim to do w'en you gets back?' His companion replied, 'I 'spects to act diffe'nt frum you, an' yet, in a way, similar. I'm goin' git me a black suit, black frum haid to foot, and black shoes, an' I'm gwine walk slow down de street, jes' behin' you—bound fur de cemetery!'" Levine, *Black Culture*, 341.

80 House of Representatives, *Intermarriage of Whites and Negroes*, 22; Chas. H. Williams, "The Negro Problem," *Colored American Magazine*, 6 (1903), 460–63; "Intermarriage," *Crisis*, 5 (1913), 180–81.

81 House of Representatives, *Intermarriage of Whites and Negroes*, 3–30; Shadrach, "Furnace Blasts," 259–63; "Emancipation," *Crisis* 5 (1913), 128–29; "Intermarriage," ibid., 180–81; "The Next Step," *Crisis*, 6 (1913), 79; "The Congressmen," *Crisis*, 9 (1914); Booker T. Washington, quoted in Jenks, "Legal Status of Negro-White Amalgamation"; Archibald H. Grimke, "The Sex Question and Race Segregation" (Archibald H. Grimke Papers, box 21, no. 44, Moorland-Springarn Research Center, Howard University).

82 W. E. B. Du Bois, "President Harding and Social Equality," *Crisis*, 23 (1921), 53–56.

83 T. Thomas Fortune was almost alone in expressing his feeling that this was a bad tactic. He complained in 1909 that "a man of Prof. Du Bois' prominence must know that he cannot help the Negro people by insisting upon the abstract right of intermarriage." Better, said Fortune, that Black people should give up such symbolic crusades and get on with the business of achieving prosperity and political participation. Fortune, "Intermarriage and Natural Selection," *Colored American Magazine*, 16 (1909), 379–381.

84 Myrdal, *American Dilemma*, 61. See note 57, above.

85 John Henrik Clarke, ed., *Marcus Garvey and the Vision of Africa* (New York, 1974), 378. Cf. Amy Jacques Garvey, *Philosophy and Opinions of Marcus Garvey*, 1:17–18; Wilson J. Moses, *Black Messiahs and Uncle Toms: Social and Literary Manipulations of a Religious Myth* (University Park, Pa., 1982), 125–31; E. David Cronon, *Black Moses* (Madison, Wis., 1955), 194–95; Brotz, *Negro Social and Political Thought*, 556.

86 Sterling Brown, "Count Us In," in Bucklin Moon, ed., *Primer for White Folks* (Garden City, N.Y., 1945), 364–95. For Du Bois' continued statements, see, e.g., "Correspondence," *Crisis*, 25 (1923), 201–2; response to

letter, *Crisis*, 35 (1928), 24; "Social Equality," *Crisis*, 35 (1928), 61–62; Julius Lester, ed., *Seventh Son: The Thought and Writing of W. E. B. Du Bois* (New York, 1971), 2:5–10.

87 James Weldon Johnson, *Along This Way*, 411–12; Rayford W. Logan, ed., *What the Negro Wants* (Chapel Hill, N.C., 1944), 14, 65–66, 71ff., 217–43, 260, 306; Hugh M. Gloster, *Negro Voices in American Fiction* (Chapel Hill, 1948), 141ff.; Rebecca Chalmers Barton, *Witnesses for Freedom: Negro Americans in Autobiography* (New York, 1948), 75–77, 141, 154, 234–35.

88 Each of these magazines printed large numbers of articles on Black people who worked or played or married with Whites or acted like Whites or looked like Whites. Some examples of major intermarriage articles from *Ebony* are the following: "Famous Negroes Married to Whites," December 1949, 20–30; "Is Mixed Marriage a New Society Fad?" September 1951, 98–103; Poppy Cannon, "How We Made Our Mixed Marriage Work," June 1952, 24–40; Clotye Murdock, "My Daughter Married a White Man," January 1954, 86–88; "Do Negro Stars Prefer White Husbands?" May 1954, 41–46; Harry Belafonte, "Why I Married Julie," July 1957, 90–95; "Marriage of Eartha Kitt," September 1960, 37–42.

89 Franklin Fosdick, "Is Interracial Marriage Wrecking the NAACP?" *Negro Digest*, July 1950, 52–55 (also *Oklahoma Black Dispatch* quotation); Powdermaker, *After Freedom*, 186; Perdue, *Weevils in the Wheat*, 245; Davis, *Deep South*, 33–38; Dollard, *Caste and Class*, 142–54; Hernton, *Sex and Racism*, 57–58; Family Histories of Higher Classes (EFF box 93, no. 9); "Famous Negroes Married to Whites"; Horne, "I Just Want to Be Myself"; Cash, "Negro-White Marriages in Philadelphia." The resentments of Black men against Black women's relationships with White men come through clearly in Lawrence Levine's retelling of the joke "about a Negro sharecropper whose wife gives birth to a light-skinned child. Convinced that the white landowner must be responsible, the sharecropper becomes hostile to him. When the landowner asks him what's wrong, he says, 'Well, you know all my thirteen children are of the same color, and the fourteenth child came up half white.' The white man quickly assures him he has nothing to worry about; such is the way of nature. Pointing to his sheep he comments, 'They all are supposed to be white, but every now and then one comes up black. But I don't worry about it.' The sharecropper thinks this over and replies, 'If you stay out of my house, I'll stay out of your pasture.'" Levine, *Black Culture*, 342.

90 Schuyler, *Racial Intermarriage*, 25–26; "Are White Women Stealing Our Men?" *Negro Digest*, April 1951, 52–55; Pamela Allen to the editor, *Ebony*, November 1951; "Foreign Wives," letter to the editor, *Ebony*, June 1953.

91 Lynn, *Interracial Marriages in Washington, D.C.*, 70–71; Josephine Schuyler, "Seventeen Years of Mixed Marriage," *Negro Digest*, July 1946, 61–65; Drake and Cayton, *Black Metropolis*, 1:141–46; Francine Miller*, "History of an Interracial Marriage" (EFF box 36, no. 9); Chicago Documents of Families Coming to the Urban League (EFF box 81, no. 20); Hertford County Documents (EFF box 92, no. 7B); Family Histories of Higher Classes (EFF box 93, no. 9); Davis, *Deep South*, 30, 37; Golden, "Patterns of Negro-

White Intermarriage"; "The Loneliest Brides in America," *Ebony,* January 1953, 17–24.

92   May Britt, "Why I Married Sammy Davis, Jr.," *Ebony,* January 1961, 96–102; Sammy Davis, Jr., "Is My Mixed Marriage Mixing Up My Kids?" *Ebony,* October 1966, 124–32; Booker, "Couple That Rocked Courts"; Booker, "Challenge for the Guy Smiths"; Alex Bontemps, "National Poll Reveals Startling New Attitudes on Interracial Marriage," *Ebony,* September 1975, 144–51ff.; Lewis, "Black Women/White Men"; Berry, "Interracial Marriages in the South"; Alvin Poussaint, "The Black Male–White Female," *Ebony,* August 1983, 124–28; Gallup, *Public Opinion, 1972–1977,* 1:72–74; Gallup, *Public Opinion, 1978,* 218–19; Gallup, *Public Opinion, 1983,* 96; Downs, "Black/White Dating"; Audrey Edwards, "How You're Feeling," *Essence,* December 1982, 73–76.

93   "Minister Malcolm X Enunciates the Muslim Program," *Muhammad Speaks,* September 1960, 2, 20–22, reprinted in John H. Bracey et al., eds., *Black Nationalism in America* (Indianapolis, 1970), 118–19; C. Eric Lincoln, *The Black Muslims in America* (Boston, 1961), 89; Frantz Fanon, *Black Skin, White Masks* (New York, 1967); C. H. King, Jr., "I Don't Want to Marry Your Daughter," *Negro Digest,* April 1964, 3–7; Moses, *Black Messiahs and Uncle Toms,* 259; Staples, *Black Woman,* 68–69; Ladner, *Tomorrow's Tomorrow,* 89–90. The frustration of a few White men at this turn in interracial politics is exemplified by Bill Medley's 1968 top-forty tune, "Brown-Eyed Woman," in which a White man pledges his love to a Black woman, only to be rebuffed on account of his color.

94   The interested reader can begin to pursue this topic in such sources as the following: Robert Staples, "The Myth of Black Macho," *Black Scholar,* 10 (March/April 1979), 24–33; "The Black Sexism Debate," *Black Scholar* (special issue), 10 (May/June 1979); Michelle Wallace, *Black Macho and the Myth of the Superwoman* (New York, 1980); Louise Meriwether, "Black Man, Do You Love Me?" *Essence,* May 1970, 14–15ff.; Rosemary Santini, "Black Man, White Woman," *Essence,* July 1970, 12–13ff.; Orde Coombs, "Black Men and White Women," *Essence,* May 1983, 80–82ff.; Patrice Miles and Audrey Edwards, "Black Women and White Men," *Essence,* October 1983, 94–96ff.; Diane Weathers, "A New Black Struggle," *Newsweek,* August 27, 1979, 58–60; Hernton, *Sex and Racism,* 123–68.

95   Lisbeth Grant, quoted in Kermit Mehlinger, "That Black Man–White Woman Thing," *Ebony,* August 1970, 130–33; Jessie Bernard, *Marriage and the Family among Negroes* (Englewood Cliffs, N.J., 1966), 83; Staples, "Myth of Black Macho," 29. These observers' contention that there was an unnaturally low number of Black men compared to Black women seems to be true. In 1970 there were 1,083,657—or 10 percent—more Black women than Black men in America. The male-female ratio for White Americans exceeded that of Blacks in every age group and part of the country. This was especially true in urban areas and for people of child-bearing age. For example, the male-female ratio among northern, urban Whites was .93, whereas for northern, urban Blacks it was .77, a difference of 20 percent.

U.S. Bureau of the Census, *1970 Census of Population. General Population Characteristics. U.S. Summary* (Washington, D.C., 1973), 1:286–88. Some authorities have traced this disparity to the effects of poverty and oppression on Blacks, and theorized that poverty in America does especial violence to men as opposed to women. Others—Staples, for example—have suggested that the disparity is more apparent than real, asserting that Black males are simply the likeliest to be underenumerated in census counts.

96   Miles and Edwards, "Black Women and White Men"; Coombs, "Black Men and White Women"; field notes, Cambridge, Mass., February 12 and March 21, 1985; Melinda Robinson*, interviewed by the author, Cambridge, Mass., March 21, 1985.

97   Field notes, Chicago, June 1985; Joseph R. Washington, *Marriage in Black and White* (Boston, 1970); Howard O. Jones, *White Questions to a Black Christian* (Grand Rapids, 1975), 67–72; James P. Comer and Alvin Poussaint, *Black Childcare* (New York, 1975), 373.

98   Thomas P. Monahan, "Interracial Marriage: Data for Philadelphia and Pennsylvania," *Demography*, 7 (1970), 287–99; idem, "Interracial Marriage in the United States: Some Data from Upstate New York," *International Journal of Sociology of the Family*, 9 (1971), 94–105; idem, "Interracial Marriage and Divorce," *Journal of Comparative Family Studies*, 2 (1971), 107–20; idem, "An Overview of Statistics on Interracial Marriage in the United States," *JMF*, 38 (1976), 223–31; David M. Heer, "Prevalence of Black-White Marriage in the United States," *JMF*, 36 (1974), 246–58; idem, "Negro-White Marriage in the United States," *JMF*, 28 (1966), 262–73; Golden, "Facilitating Factors in Negro-White Intermarriage"; idem, "Characteristics of the Negro-White Intermarried"; Todd H. Pavela, "An Exploratory Study of Negro-White Intermarriage in Indiana," *Marriage and Family Living*, 26 (1964), 209–11; U.S. Bureau of the Census, *Negro Population, 1790–1915* (New York, 1968; orig. Washington, D.C., 1918), 207–31; Bureau of the Census, *Marital Status* (1960), 160–65, 171–72; Bureau of the Census, *Negro Population* (1970), 172–80; Bureau of the Census, *Marital Status* (1970), 262–68, 283–92.

99   Dollard, *Caste and Class*, 137 and passim; Charles S. Johnson, *Growing Up in the Black Belt* (New York 1941), 256ff.; Gary B. Mills, "Miscegenation and the Free Negro in Antebellum 'Anglo' Alabama," *Journal of American History*, 68 (1981), 16–34; "Negroes in the Kentucky Mountains," *Crisis*, 22 (1921), 69–71; Drake and Cayton, *Black Metropolis*, 1:143; Erskine, "The Polls: Interracial Socializing"; Jessie Bernard, "Note on Educational Homogamy in Negro-White Marriages, 1960," *Journal of Marriage and the Family*, 28 (1966), 274–76. There is some testimony to an increasing receptivity to intermarriage in parts of the South in recent years; see Ray Jenkins, "The Tuskegee Mayor and His Wife," *New York Times* (1973, in Vertical File: "Marriage," Schlesinger Library, Harvard University); Bill Berry, "Interracial Marriages in the South," *Ebony*, June 1978, 64–72.

100 Lewis, "Black Women/White Men"; "Interracial College Marriages," *Ebony*, July 1954, 89–94. White Iowans were welcoming enough to Black people to

select a Black woman, Cheryl Browne, as their candidate for Miss America in 1970. Judy Klemesrud, "Miss Iowa, the Black Girl from Queens," *New York Times*, June 30, 1970.

101 Thomas P. Monahan, "An Overview of Statistics on Interracial Marriage in the United States, with Data on Its Extent from 1963–1970," *Journal of Marriage and the Family*, 38 (1976), 228; Bureau of the Census, *Marital Status* (1960), 160–65, 171–72; idem, *Marital Status* (1970), 262–67, 283–88; idem, *Marital Status* (1980), 175–81; Bernard, "Educational Homogamy." Of course, many intermarried couples found no part of the United States adequately hospitable. Some found interracial marriage better received in Europe and Africa. Those who went to Asia, usually Asian war brides and their Black American husbands, did not have such salutary experiences. See "Americans in Ethiopia," *Ebony*, May 1951, 79–80; "Marriage That Could Not Work," *Ebony*, July 1967, 119–22; "Darlings of Royalty," *Ebony*, June 1953, 36–40; William Gardner Smith, "Black Boy in France," *Ebony*, July 1953, 32–42; Anne Brown, "I Gave Up My Country for Love," *Ebony*, November 1953, 28–38; "Blues Writer in Sweden," *Ebony*, April 1954, 123–25; Mario Senesi, "Identity Crisis Italian Style," *Ebony*, July 1970, 40–46; Britt, "Why I Married Sammy Davis"; "Sailor to Movie Star," *Ebony*, August 1953, 46–51; "Letters of a Dying Mother to Her Baby," *Ebony*, July 1954, 16–25.

102 Kingsley Davis, "Intermarriage in Caste Societies," *American Anthropologist*, 43 (1941), 338–47; Robert Merton, "Intermarriage and the Social Structure," *Psychiatry*, 4 (1941), 361–74.

103 Johnson, *Patterns of Negro Segregation*, 150; Drake and Cayton, *Black Metropolis*, 1:140; Wirth and Goldhamer, "The Hybrid," 289–96.

104 Bureau of the Census, *Marital Status* (1980), 283–92; Bernard, "Educational Homogamy"; Cash, "Negro-White Marriages in Philadelphia," 34; Heer, "Prevalence of Black-White Marriage," 252–56; John Burma et al., "Comparison of the Occupational Status of Intramarrying and Intermarrying Couples," *SSR*, 54 (1970), 508–19. The reader will note that the hypogamy theory was further undermined by the finding in Chapter 3 that for most of this century it was not mainly Japanese American men who married White women, but, far more often, Japanese American women who married White men.

105 Francine Miller*, "History of an Interracial Marriage" (EFF box 36, no. 9); Incidents and Characters in the Chicago Community (EFF box 82, no. 3); Dollard, *Caste and Class*, 138, 158; Drake and Cayton, *Black Metropolis*, 1:131; "Detroit's Most-Discussed Mixed Marriage," *Ebony*, April 1953, 97–103.

106 The list of prominent Black artists, political leaders, entertainers, and athletes who married non-Blacks after World War II is extremely long, and includes such people as Maya Angelou, Pearl Bailey, Harry Belafonte, Edward Brooke, Rod Carew, James Farmer, Lena Horne, Eartha Kitt, Sidney Poitier, Diana Ross, Bill Russell, Walter White, and Richard Wright. Many of them testified to the ease of interracial relationships in the circles in which they traveled. See *Ebony*, 1945–1980, passim.

107 Dollard, *Caste and Class*, 149–58; Powdermaker, *After Freedom*, 182–83; Drake and Cayton, *Black Metropolis*, 1:131–38. E. Franklin Frazier, *Black Bourgeoisie* (New York, 1957); Miller, *As to the Leopard's Spots*, 17.

108 Staples, *Black Woman*, 13. For Frazier, see EFF, for example, boxes 36, 81–82, 85–93, 109, 112–13, 115–16, 131.

109 John Daniels, *In Freedom's Birthplace* (Boston, 1914), 182–83; Sidney Kronus, *The Black Middle Class* (Columbus, 1971), 14 and passim; Dennis A. Williams, "Roots III: Souls on Ice," *Newsweek*, June 10, 1985, 82–84; Levine, *Black Culture*.

Chapter 11. Passing Is Passé

1 Charles H. Stember, *Sexual Racism* (New York, 1976); John Dollard, *Caste and Class in a Southern Town*, 3rd ed. (Garden City, N.Y., 1957), 153–56 and passim; Abram Kardiner and Lionel Ovesey, *The Mark of Oppression* (Cleveland, 1951), 291–93; Ray E. Baber, "A Study of 325 Mixed Marriages," *ASR*, 2 (1937), 705–16; Hugo G. Biegel, "Problems and Motives in Interracial Relationships," *Journal of Sex Research*, 2 (1966), 185–205, reprinted in Doris Y. Wilkinson, ed., *Black Male/White Female* (Morristown, N.J., 1975), 67–87. There would almost have to be a pathological tinge to the views of Biegel and Kardiner and Ovesey, since theirs were reports on clinical populations.

2 Frantz Fanon, *Black Skin, White Masks* (New York, 1967); William H. Grier and Price M. Cobbs, *Black Rage* (New York, 1968), 65–85; Joyce A. Ladner, *Tomorrow's Tomorrow: The Black Woman* (New York, 1971), 281–82. Also Rose Hedgeman, "Interracial Marriage" (Paper presented at "Crossing the Color Line," Biracial Family Conference, Chicago, June 29, 1985), and Ernest Spaights and Harold E. Dixon, "Socio-Psychological Dynamics in Pathological Black-White Romantic Alliances," *Journal of Instructional Psychology*, 11 (1987), 132–38.

3 Robert Staples, *The Black Woman in America* (Chicago, 1973), 122; Alvin F. Poussaint, "Black Male–White Female," *Ebony*, August 1983, 124ff.; Kermit Mehlinger, "That Black Man–White Woman Thing," *Ebony*, August 1970, 130–33; Calvin Hernton, *Sex and Racism* (New York, 1965); Ari Kiev, "The Psychiatric Implications of Interracial Marriage," in Irving R. Stuart and Lawrence Edwin Abt, Jr., *Interracial Marriage* (New York, 1973), 161–76; Joseph R. Washington, *Marriage in Black and White* (Boston, 1970), 1–32, 324–36; Robert Staples, *The World of Black Singles* (Westport, Conn., 1984), 137–63.

4 Stanley Lieberson, "Generational Differences among Blacks in the North," *AJS*, 79 (1973), 550–65; E. Franklin Frazier, *The Negro Family in Chicago* (Chicago, 1932), 82, 102–7; Family Histories—John Burke* (EFF box 85, no. 9); Elizabeth Hafkin Pleck, *Black Migration and Poverty: Boston, 1865–1900* (New York, 1979), 75, 114–16, and passim. For a differing opinion from Lieberson's tentative and limited conclusions, see Karl E. Taeuber and Alma F. Taeuber, "The Negro as an Immigrant Group," *AJS*, 69 (1964), 374–82.

5   Julius Drachsler, *Intermarriage in New York City* (New York, 1921), 103,
    107–8, 133–34, 156, 158, 160, 184; Family Histories—Doris Albert* and
    Otis Bacon* (EFF box 85, nos. 6 and 11); Family History—Gloria Cheever
    (EFF box 86, no. 2); Family Histories of Higher Classes (EFF box 93, no. 9);
    John Jasper Spurling, "Social Relationships between American Negroes and
    West Indian Negroes in a Long Island Community" (Ph.D. diss., New
    York University, 1962), 1–2, 49–61; Ira DeA. Reid, *The Negro Immigrant*
    (New York, 1969; orig. 1939), 143–45; Margaret Wallace*, interviewed by
    the author, Vallejo, Calif., March 25, 1980; Oscar Glantz, "Native Sons
    and Immigrants," *Ethnicity*, 5 (1978), 189–202; L. P. Jackson, "Culture or
    Color? The Moyetos of San Juan and New York," *Crisis*, 75 (1968), 189–93;
    Constance R. Sutton and Susan R. Makiesky, "Migration and West Indian
    Racial and Ethnic Consciousness," in Helen I. Safa and Brian M. DuToit,
    eds., *Migration and Development* (The Hague, 1975), 113–44; Vera Green,
    "Racial versus Ethnic Factors in Afro-American and Afro-Caribbean Mi-
    gration," ibid., 83–96; Wilda George*, interviewed by the author, Boston,
    April 1973; Roy Simon Bryce-LaPorte, "Black Immigrants," *Journal of Black
    Studies*, 3 (September 1972), 29–56; Lennox Raphael, "West Indians and
    Afro-Americans," *Freedomways*, 4 (1964), 438–45; Richard Blackett, "Some
    of the Problems Confronting West Indians in the Black American Struggle,"
    Black Lines, 1 (Summer 1971), 47–52; Orde Coombs, "West Indians in New
    York," *New York*, 3 (July 12, 1970), 28–32.
6   Mooreland Family Documents (EFF box 92, no. 3); Family Histories—North
    Carolina (EFF box 92, no. 7); Brewton Berry, *Almost White* (London, 1963);
    Karen I. Blu, *The Lumbee Problem* (New York, 1980); A. H. Estabrook
    and I. H. McDougle, *Mongrel Virginians* (Baltimore, 1926); Guy Benton
    Johnson, "Personality in a White-Indian Negro Community," *ASR*, 4 (1939),
    516–23; E. Franklin Frazier, *The Negro Family in the United States* (Chicago,
    1939), 164–89; Mark Harris, "America's Oldest Interracial Community,"
    Negro Digest, July 1948, 21–24; "South Carolina's Raceless People," *Ebony*,
    January 1957, 53–56; "Mystery People of Baltimore," *Ebony*, September
    1957, 70–73; Charles T. Powers, "The Jackson Whites," *Los Angeles Times*,
    September 29, 1978; Virginia R. Dominguez, *White by Definition* (New
    Brunswick, N.J., 1986); Darrell A. Posey, "Origin, Development, and Main-
    tenance of a Louisiana Mixed-Blood Community," *Ethnohistory*, 26 (1979),
    177–92; Frank W. Porter, "Strategies for Survival: The Nanticoke Indians in
    a Hostile World," *Ethnohistory*, 26 (1979), 325–45.
7   It should be noted that color consciousness involved a good deal more than
    just skin tone. Social gradations depended in addition on the texture of hair
    and the shape of nose and lips. Yet color of skin was the most obvious and
    universally recognized marker.
8   E. Franklin Frazier, *Black Bourgeoisie* (New York, 1957), 29–42, 153–73,
    and passim; Joel Williamson, *New People* (New York, 1980), 75–87; E. Frank-
    lin Frazier, *Negro Family in Chicago* (Chicago, 1932), 100–04; Sidney Kro-
    nus, *The Black Middle Class* (Columbus, Ohio, 1971), 3–16; Frazier, *Negro
    Family*, 198–99, 300–08; Gunnar Myrdal, *An American Dilemma* (New York,
    1962; orig. 1944), 695–700; Anne Moody, *Coming of Age in Mississippi* (New

York, 1968), 239ff.; Allison Davis et al., *Deep South* (Chicago, 1965; orig. 1941), 213–16; R. C. Barton, *Witnesses for Freedom* (New York, 1948), 29–34; L. L., "Role of Color in the Development of Personality" (EFF box 108, no. 10).

9 Julius Lester, ed., *The Seventh Son: The Thought and Writing of W. E. B. Du Bois* (New York, 1971), 1:322–25; Hortense Powdermaker, *After Freedom* (New York, 1967), 175–80; Charles S. Johnson, *Growing Up in the Black Belt* (New York, 1941), 260–63; Frazier interviews (e.g., EFF box 82, no. 11; box 92, no. 78); Mozell C. Hill, "Social Status and Physical Appearance among Negro Adolescents," *Social Forces*, 22 (1944), 443–48; Bonnie Allen, "It Ain't Easy Being Pinky," *Essence*, July 1982, 67ff. Both Black people and social scientists who studied color distinctions thought them important. For example, W. Lloyd Warner and his colleagues wrote an entire book on Black personality types, dividing their analysis according to color and class (*Color and Human Nature: Negro Personality Development in a Northern City* [New York, 1969; orig. 1941]).

10 Louisville Girls Interviewed by Mrs. Thelma L. Colman (EFF box 109, no. 8); Johnson, *Growing Up in the Black Belt*, 258–59.

11 J. Richard Udry et al., "Skin Color, Status, and Mate Selection," *AJS*, 76 (1971), 722–33; Family Histories—Nadine Allen* (EFF, box 85, no. 2); Louisville Girls Interviewed by Mrs. Thelma L. Colman (EFF box 109, no. 8); "Conflict in My Family" (EFF box 93, no. 9); Thomas W. Talley, *Negro Folk-Rhymes* (New York, 1922), 10–11; Alexis De Veaux, "Loving the Dark in Me," *Essence*, July 1982, 67ff.

12 Johnson, *Growing Up in the Black Belt*, 265–77, 301–4; Louisville Girls Interviewed by Mrs. Thelma L. Colman (EFF box 109, no. 8). For evidence of the popularity of lighteners, one has only to pick up any copy of *Ebony* from its inception in 1945 to about 1966 and look at the advertisements.

13 Mozell C. Hill, "Social Status and Physical Appearance among Negro Adolescents," *Social Forces*, 22 (1944), 443–48; Life History of Lawrence Higgins*, Life Histories of Higher Classes (EFF box 93, no. 9); Student Documents on "Choice of Mate": Constance Matthews, Julia A. Ewing, Jane Priestly, Lillian Banks, Bontia E. Trimble, Charlotte L. Mahood, M. A. Ashley, Maude Izetta Duncan, Earline Cooper, Howard Bennett, Smithie Sutton, Willie C. Holt, 1932–33 (EFF box 82, no. 11); Family Histories—Martha Hart Green (EFF box 86, no. 33).

14 "Conflict in My Family" (EFF box 93, no. 9) (Roberts quotation); Family Histories—Belle Winters* (EFF box 92, no. 11); Allen, "It Ain't Easy Being Pinky," 67ff.; Family Histories—Muriel Avery (EFF box 85, no. 7); Family Histories—Nadine Allen* (EFF box 85, no. 2).

15 Newman I. White, ed., *The Frank C. Brown Collection of North Carolina Folklore*, 7 vols. (Durham, 1952–62), 3:526; Harry Oster, *Living Country Blues* (Detroit, 1969), 290; Newman I. White, *American Negro Folk Songs* (Hatboro, Pa., 1965; orig. Cambridge, 1928), 327; Levine, *Black Culture*, 288. Cf. Talley, *Negro Folk-Rhymes*, 56; George Washington Cable, *Madame Delphine* (New York, 1881), 104.

16 G. A. Steward, "The Black Girl Passes," *Social Forces*, 6 (1927–28), 99–

103; Gwendolyn Brooks, "If You're Light and Have Long Hair," in Mary Helen Washington, ed., *Black-Eyed Susans* (Garden City, N.Y., 1975), 37–42; Jessie Bernard, *Marriage and the Family among Negroes* (Englewood Cliffs, N.J., 1966), 84–85; Louisville Girls Interviewed by Mrs. Thelma L. Colman (EFF box 109, no. 8); Williamson, *New People*, 118; David M. Buss, "Human Mate Selection," *American Scientist*, 73 (January–February 1985), 48–51.

17 "What Color Will Your Baby Be?" *Ebony*, May 1951, 54–57; Julian Lewis, "What Color Will Your Baby Be?" *Negro Digest*, November 1946, 4–7; "The 'Black Baby' Bugaboo," in St. Clair Drake and Horace Cayton, *Black Metropolis*, rev. ed. (New York, 1962), 1:171–73; Family Histories—Nadine Allen* (EFF box 85, no. 2); Johnson, *Growing Up in the Black Belt*, 267ff.; "Conflict in My Family" (EFF box 93, no. 9).

18 Louisville Girls Interviewed by Mrs. Thelma L. Colman (EFF box 109, no. 8); E. Franklin Frazier, *Negro Youth at the Crossroads* (Washington, D.C., 1940), 51; Mary Virginia Bales, "Some Negro Folk-Songs of Texas," *Publications of Texas Folklore Society*, 7 (1928), 100; "Conflict in My Family" (EFF box 93, no. 9); Johnson, *Growing Up in the Black Belt*, 262, 270.

19 Johnson, *Growing Up in the Black Belt*, 263, 271; Lena Horne, *Lena* (London, 1966), 31; Eartha Kitt, *Alone with Me* (Chicago, 1976), 7–17; Mrs. Jack Breneski, Chicago, to the editor, *Ebony*, April 1950.

20 Louis Armstrong, "Why I Like Dark Women," *Ebony*, August 1954, 61–68; Louisville Girls Interviewed by Mrs. Thelma L. Colman (EFF box 109, no. 8).

21 Levine, *Black Culture*, 288 (Leadbelly); Harry Oster, *Living Country Blues*, 293 (Nash lyrics); Student Documents on "Choice of Mate": Nina M. Harris, Wilona Nicholson (EFF box 82, no. 11); Talley, *Negro Folk-Rhymes*, 63.

22 Williamson, *New People*, 111, 128–30; E. C. Perrow, "Songs and Rhymes from the South," *Journal of American Folklore*, 28 (1915), 136; Paul Oliver, *Blues Tradition* (New York, 1970), 48; White, *American Negro Folk Songs*, 324; Levine, *Black Culture*, 286–87. Levine may be right for some, but the very white faces and long, straight hair of most *Ebony* models from the '40s and '50s suggest he exaggerates.

23 Irene Finch, Los Angeles, Leroy P. Vital, Chicago, and Alberta D. Washington, Cleveland, letters to the editor, *Ebony*, August 1951; George S. Schuyler, *Black No More* (New York, 1931); Barton, *Witnesses for Freedom*, 103 (Hurston quotation); Malcolm X, *Autobiography* (New York, 1965), 2.

24 The dramatic change in *Ebony* ads came between 1965 and 1970. Udry et al., "Skin Color, Status, and Mate Selection"; Kronus, *Black Middle Class*, 38–45; De Veaux, "Loving the Dark in Me."

25 U.S. Bureau of the Census, *1970 Census of Population: National Origin and Language*, Subject Report PC(2)-1A (Washington, D.C., 1973), 1–5; idem, *1960 Census: Nonwhite Population by Race*, Subject Report PC(2)-1C (Washington, D.C., 1963), 1–2; idem, *1980 Census of Population: General Social and Economic Characteristics, United States Summary*, PC 80-1-C1 (Washington, D.C., 1983), 15.

26 Herbert G. Gutman, *The Black Family in Slavery and Freedom* (New York, 1976); Eugene Genovese, *Roll, Jordan, Roll* (New York, 1974), 463–82.

27 Gary B. Mills, "Miscegenation and the Free Negro in Antebellum 'Anglo' Alabama," *Journal of American History*, 68 (1981), 16–34.

28 U.S. Bureau of the Census, *1960 Census: Marital Status*, Subject Report PC(2)-4E (Washington, D.C., 1966), 171–72; Johnson, *Growing Up in the Black Belt*, 260–61; Lynn, "Interracial Marriages in Washington, D.C.," 429; "The Fortune Survey," *Fortune*, 26 (November 1942), 10; Julius Drachsler, *Intermarriage in New York City* (New York, 1921), 103, 107–8, 133–34, 156, 158, 160, 184.

29 U.S. Bureau of the Census, *1970 Census: Marital Status*, Subject Report PC(2)-4C (Washington, D.C., 1972), 262–67; Melinda Robinson*, interviewed by the author, Cambridge, Mass., March 21, 1985; Staples, *World of Black Singles*, 158–61; Thomas P. Monahan, "Are Interracial Marriages Really Less Stable?" *Social Forces*, 48 (1970), 464.

30 Drake and Cayton, *Black Metropolis*, 1:153–54.

31 David M. Heer, "Prevalence of Black-White Marriage in the United States," *JMF*, 36 (1974), 250.

32 Monahan, "Are Interracial Marriages Really Less Stable?" 461–73; Thomas P. Monahan, "Interracial Marriage and Divorce in Kansas," *Journal of Comparative Family Studies*, 2 (1971), 107–20.

33 Thomas P. Monahan, "Critique of Heer Article," *JMF*, 36 (1974), 669–72.

34 E. B. Reuter, *Race Mixture* (New York, 1969; orig. 1931), 129–216; Judith R. Berzon, *Neither Black nor White: The Mulatto Character in American Fiction* (New York, 1978); Lee Jenkins, *Faulkner and Black-White Relations* (New York, 1981), 14, 25–27, 34–36, 48, 229; Hugh M. Gloster, *Negro Voices in American Fiction* (Chapel Hill, 1948), 12–17; Sterling A. Brown, "Negro Characters as Seen by White Authors," in J. A. Emanuel and Theodore Gross, eds., *Dark Symphony* (New York, 1968), 157–63; John S. Haller, Jr., *Outcasts from Evolution: Scientific Attitudes of Racial Inferiority* (Urbana, Ill., 1971), 58; Eileen Landay, *Black Film Stars* (New York, 1973), 26–27; Penelope Bullock, "The Mulatto in American Fiction," *Phylon*, 6 (1945), 78–82; Nella Larsen, *Passing* (New York, 1969; orig. 1929); "Pinky," *Ebony*, September 1949, 23–25; John G. Mencke, "Mulattoes and Race Mixture: American Attitudes and Images, 1865–1918" (Ph.D. diss., University of North Carolina, 1976), 233–45; Oscar Grow, *The Antagonism of Races* (Waterloo, Iowa, 1912), 37–38; Charles H. McCord, *The American Negro as a Dependent, Defective, and Delinquent* (Nashville, 1914), 49–50; Nathan Huggins, "Marginality in American Life: Passing is Passé" (Colloquium paper, Department of History, University of California, Berkeley, November 7, 1979); Langston Hughes, "Mulatto: A Tragedy of the Deep South," in Mel Watkins and Jay Daniel, eds., *To Be a Black Woman* (New York, 1970), 23–28.

35 "White, but Black," *Century*, 109 (February 1925), 492–99; Isabelle Rivierez and Louis E. Lomax, "Between Two Races," *Negro Digest*, February 1962, 3–8; Drake and Cayton, *Black Metropolis*, 1:155–56; Louisville Girls

Interviewed by Mrs. Thelma L. Colman (EFF box 109, no. 8); Anna M. Wirth, "Skin-Deep," *Crisis*, 39 (1932), 126–27; Robert E. T. Roberts, "Self-Identification and Social Status of Biracial Children in Chicago in Comparative Perspective" (Paper presented to the International Congress of Anthropological and Ethnological Sciences, Vancouver, August 20, 1983), 18–20.

36 Johnson, *Growing Up in the Black Belt*, 272–73; John Henrik Clarke, ed., *Marcus Garvey and the Vision of Africa* (New York, 1974), 110, 115, 227; Drake and Cayton, *Black Metropolis*, 1:158; Mary Guess, Buffalo, to the editor, *Ebony*, May 1950; Roberts, "Self-Identification and Social Status."

37 George M. Fredrickson, *White Supremacy* (New York, 1981); Carl Degler, *Neither Black nor White* (New York, 1971; rpt. Madison, Wis., 1986); John Louis Hill, *Negro: National Asset or Liability? The Battle of the Bloods* (New York, 1930), 6–9.

38 E. T. Clayton, "Famous Negro Sons of White Fathers," *Ebony*, October 1950, 96–100; Walter F. White, *A Man Called White* (New York, 1948), 3, 366; Richard L. Williams, "He Wouldn't Cross the Line," *Life*, September 3, 1951, 81–94; "He's Too Light to be Negro and Too Known to be White," *Ebony*, March 1950, 22–26 (Jeffries quotation); Barton, *Witnesses for Freedom*, 9, 29–34, 74. See also Archibald J. Carey, "Riding the Color Line," *Negro Digest*, August 1951, 7–11; "White, but Black," 492–99. Walter White was the son of two very light Black parents.

39 Darwin T. Turner, Introduction to Jean Toomer, *Cane* (New York, 1975), ix–xxv; "Problem of Mixed Parents," letter to the editor, *Ebony*, July 1951. Cf. Alan J. Glasser, "A Negro Child Reared As White," in Georgene Seward, ed., *Clinical Studies in Culture Conflict* (New York, 1951), 41–61; Channing H. Orbach and Carl H. Saxe, "Role Confusion in a Negro-Indian Woman," in Seward, *Clinical Studies in Culture Conflict*, 125–50.

40 Mr. and Mrs. George S. Schuyler, "Does Interracial Marriage Succeed?" *Negro Digest*, June 1950, 15–17; Josephine Schuyler, "Seventeen Years of Mixed Marriage," *Negro Digest*, July 1946, 61–65; Isabelle Rivierez and Louis E. Lomax, "Between Two Races," *Negro Digest*, February 1962, 3–8; David W. Evans, "My Son is a Blonde Negro," *Negro Digest*, March 1949, 43–45; Robert E. T. Roberts, "Children of Interracial Marriage" (paper presented to the Biracial Family Conference, Chicago, June 28, 1985); Roberts, "Self-Identification and Social Status," 19–23. For a further look at mixed children in Europe, see "British Families Adopt Brown Babies," *Ebony*, March 1949, 19–22; "Shirley Temple of Germany," *Ebony*, January 1953, 67–70; Erich Lissner, "We Adopted a Brown Baby," *Ebony*, May 1953, 36–45; "Brown Babies Go to Work," *Ebony*, November 1960, 97–108; "Italian 'War Baby' Seeks Father's Fortune," *Ebony*, October 1962, 64–70; Mario Senesi, "Identity Crisis Italian Style," *Ebony*, July 1970, 40–46.

41 Passing was a phenomenon not limited to the U.S. racial system. It was hardly necessary in Brazil, which had a multitude of color-status categories. In South Africa, however, even up until recent decades, quite a substantial number of Africans and mixed-race individuals passed over into the White

category, sometimes with the explicit knowledge of other Whites. This was possible, according to Hans Hesse, because in the early years of Black-White contact, "unlike in the U. S. . . . genealogy did not play a role in establishing one's 'racial' identity, association with a particular group did." If one were born a slave, no matter what one's parentage, one was an African. If born free or freed by marriage to a free White person, then one became White, regardless of one's ancestry. In addition, more than a few light Coloureds passed for White in the same manner as light American Blacks passed. So dies the myth of Afrikaner racial purity. H. H. Hesse to the author, Bellville, South Africa, March 25, 1985 (cf. his *Groep sonder Grense* [Bellville, 1985]); Fredrickson, *White Supremacy*, 94–135; Pierre van den Berghe, "Miscegenation in South Africa," in van den Berghe, *Race and Ethnicity* (New York, 1970), 224–43; H. F. Dickie-Clarke, "The Coloured Minority in Durban," in Noel P. Gist and Anthony Gary Dworkin, eds., *The Blending of Races* (New York, 1972), 25–38. Anglo-Indians seem sometimes to have passed for White as well; see Noel P. Gist, "The Anglo-Indians," in Gist and Dworkin, *Blending of Races*, 39–59.

42 See, e.g., Drake and Cayton, *Black Metropolis*, 1:159–73; Myrdal, *American Dilemma*, 683–88; Everett V. Stonequist, *The Marginal Man* (New York, 1965; orig. 1937), 184–200; Louis Wirth and Herbert Goldhamer, "The Hybrid and the Problem of Miscegenation," in Otto Klineberg, ed., *Characteristics of the American Negro* (New York, 1944), 301–19; Larsen, *Passing*; Nella Larsen, *Quicksand* (New York, 1928); James Weldon Johnson, *The Autobiography of an Ex-Coloured Man* (New York, 1960; orig. 1912); Walter White, *Flight* (New York, 1926); Jessie Fauset, *Plum Bun* (New York, 1929). The analysis that follows owes much to James E. Conyers, "Selected Aspects of the Phenomenon of Negro Passing" (Ph.D. diss., Washington State University, 1962); cf. Conyers and T. H. Kennedy, "Negro Passing: To Pass or Not to Pass," *Phylon*, 24 (1963), 215–23.

43 Herbert Asbury, "Who Is a Negro?" *Negro Digest*, October 1946, 3–11; Sterling A. Brown et al., *The Negro Caravan* (New York, 1969; orig. 1941); 1047 (Logan incident); L. L., "Role of Color in the Development of Personality" (EFF box 108, no. 10).

44 Barton, *Witnesses for Freedom*, 75–77; Ruby MacAllister to the editor, *Ebony*, May 1954; L. L., "Role of Color in Development of Personality" (EFF box 108, no. 10); Stonequist, *Marginal Man*, 186–88; Nanette Kutner, "Women Who Pass for White," *Negro Digest*, August 1949, 43–46; Leo Swain, "How a Negro Minister Passed in Dixie," *Negro Digest*, February 1948, 4–6; Herbert Asbury, "Who Is a Negro?" *Negro Digest*, October 1946, 3–11; "Why I Never Want to Pass," *Ebony*, June 1959, 49–54.

45 "White by Day . . . Negro by Night," *Ebony*, April 1952, 31–36.

46 Asbury, "Who Is a Negro?"; "I Lived Two Lives for Thirty Years," *Ebony*, December 1958, 156–62; Conyers, "Aspects of Passing," 36–37.

47 Reba Lee*, *I Passed for White* (New York, 1955); Johnson, *Ex-Coloured Man*, 211; Clotye Murdock, "What Happened to the 'Lost Boundaries' Family," *Ebony*, August 1952, 52–66; Gladys Stevens, "My Father Passed for

White," *Ebony*, April 1957, 41–46 (Torregano story); John Hewlett, "Four Who Are Passing," *Negro Digest*, April 1949, 8–13 (the Matthews family); Nanette Kutner, "Women Who Pass for White," *Negro Digest*, August 1949, 43–46; Incidents and Characters in Chicago Community (EFF box 82, no. 1); Family Histories of Higher Classes (EFF box 93, no. 9); Louisville Girls Interviewed by Mrs. Thelma L. Colman (EFF box 109, no. 8); Asbury, "Who Is a Negro?"

48   U.S. Bureau of the Census, *Negro Population, 1790–1915* (New York, 1968; orig. Washington, D.C., 1918), 211–14; idem, *Negroes in the United States, 1920–1932* (Washington, D.C., 1935), 78; Eugene Cash, "A Study of Negro-White Marriages in the Philadelphia Area" (Ph.D. diss., Temple University, 1956), 8; Asbury, "Who Is a Negro?"; Reuter, *Race Mixture*, 70; "The Vanishing Mulatto," *Opportunity*, 3 (1925), 291; Conyers, "Aspects of Passing," 23–26; Williamson, *New People*, 119–20; Robert Stuckert, "African Ancestry of the White Population," *Ohio Journal of Science*, 58 (1958), 155–60.

49   Gloster, *Negro Voices in American Fiction*, 131–46; Louisville Girls Interviewed by Mrs. Thelma L. Colman (EFF box 109, no. 8) (Rosamund quote); John Green, Philadelphia, to the editor, *Ebony*, November 1952; Dorothy Smith, Chicago, to the editor, *Ebony*, May 1951; Conyers, "Aspects of Passing." Many Blacks and some Whites insisted they could recognize passers by the dark semicircles at the bases of their fingernails or by blue gums. There is little evidence to support this conviction, however.

50   Louisville Girls Interviewed by Mrs. Thelma L. Colman (EFF box 109, no. 8); Lillian Smith, *Killers of the Dream* (New York, 1945), 34–39.

51   Griffin, *Black Like Me*; Grace Halsell, *Soul Sister* (New York, 1969); Schuyler, "Seventeen Years of Mixed Marriage"; Asbury, "Who Is a Negro?"; Frazier, *Negro Family*, 196–97.

52   Frazier, *Negro Family*, 171, 203–4; Simeon Booker, "Couple That Rocked Courts," *Ebony*, September 1967, 78–84; Family Histories—Harietta Davenport (EFF box 86, no. 12); Hertford County Documents (EFF box 92, no. 7); Family Histories of Higher Classes (EFF box 93, no. 9); Ohio Documents (EFF box 92, no. 8); Perdue, *Weevils in the Wheat*, 108.

53   Huggins, "Marginality in American Life"; James Carr, comment on Sandy Campbell and Prentice Baptiste, "Biracial Individuals: Self-Identity, Self-Esteem" (Paper presented to the Biracial Family Conference, Chicago, June 29, 1985); Kathryn Anderson, "Transracial/Interracial Adoptions" (Session of the Biracial Family Conference, Chicago, June 29, 1985); Lynn Dunson, "Controversy over Mixed Families," *Washington Star*, August 28, 1977; idem, "Whites Who Adopt Black Children Meet Resistance from Many Sides," ibid., August 29, 1977; Joyce Ladner, "Providing a Healthy Environment for Interracial Children," *Interracial Books for Children Bulletin*, 15, no. 6 (1984), 7–8; Philip Spivey, "Growing Up in Interracial Families," ibid., 11–16; Lynn Norment, "A Probing Look at Children of Interracial Families," *Ebony*, September 1985, 159–62; field notes, St. Paul, 1981–87.

54   Field notes, Boston, 1972; Christine C. I. Hall, "The Ethnic Identity of Racial Mixed People: A Study of Black-Japanese" (Ph.D. diss., University

of California, Los Angeles, 1980); Shawn D. Lewis, "Black Women/White Men: The 'Other' Mixed Marriage," *Ebony*, January 1978, 37–42; notes on general discussion, Biracial Family Conference, Chicago, June 28–29, 1985; Melinda Robinson*, interviewed by the author, Cambridge, Mass., March 21, 1985; Curtia James, "A Black–Native American Harvest," *Essence*, November 1983, 87–88; Ai, "On Being ½ Japanese, ⅛ Choctaw, ¼ Black, and ¹⁄₁₆ Irish," *Ms.*, May 1978, 58; "Children of the Rainbow," *Newsweek*, November 19, 1984, 120–22; Glenn Collins, "Children of Interracial Marriage," *New York Times*, June 20, 1984; Charles T. Waggoner, "Mixed Marriage Clubs," *Communique* (newsletter of the Interracial Family Alliance), June 1984; "Please Check One—White—Black—Other Mixed," *Communique*, September 1984; Prentice Baptiste, Jr., "The Contemporary Interracial Club," *Communique*, April 1985.

55 Marvin Arnold, comments at Biracial Family Conference, Chicago, June 29, 1985; Vladimir Piskacek and Marlene Golub, "Children of Interracial Marriages," in Stuart and Abt, *Interracial Marriage*, 51–61; H. Prentice Baptiste, Jr., "Rearing the Interracial Child," *Communique*, December 1983; Kathlyn Gay, *The Rainbow Effect: Interracial Families* (New York, 1987); Alvin Poussaint, interviewed by the author, Boston, November 28, 1984; Paul L. Adams, "Counseling with Interracial Couples and Their Children in the South," in Stuart and Abt, *Interracial Marriage*, 63–79; Francis Wardle, "Are You Sensitive to Interracial Children's Special Identity Needs?" *Young Children*, 42 (January 1987), 53–59; Nora Leven, "Love in Black and White," *Mpls./St. Paul*, August 1987, 198; Deborah Sebring, "Considerations in Counseling Interracial Children," *Journal of Non-White Concerns in Personnel Guidance*, 13 (January 1985), 3–9; Alvin F. Poussaint, "Study of Interracial Children Presents Positive Picture," *Interracial Books for Children Bulletin*, 15, no. 6 (1984), 9–10; Kate Schackford, "Interracial Children," ibid., 4–6; Thomas J. Buttery, "Helping Biracial Children Adjust," *Education Digest*, 52 (May 1987), 38–41.

Chapter 12. Conclusion

1 Richard D. Alba, *Italian Americans: Into the Twilight of Ethnicity* (Englewood Cliffs, N.J., 1985), 146–47; U.S. Bureau of the Census, *1970 Census: Puerto Ricans in the United States*, Subject Report PC(2)-1E (Washington, D.C., 1973), 104–8; Edward Murguia and W. Parker Frisbie, "Trends in Mexican American Intermarriage," *Social Science Quarterly*, 58 (1979), 374–89; Charles H. Anderson, *White Protestant Americans* (Englewood Cliffs, N.J., 1970), 26, 39, 53–54, 67. See also Celestino Fernandez and Louis M. Holscher, "Chicano-Anglo Intermarriage in Arizona, 1960–1980," *Hispanic Journal of Behavioral Sciences*, 5 (1983), 291–304; Richard D. Alba, "Cohorts and the Dynamics of Ethnic Change," in Matilda White Riley et al., eds., *Social Structure and Human Lives* (Newbury Park, forthcoming), vol. 1 (advance copy courtesy of the author); Ralph B. Casares et al., "Mexican American Intermarriage in a Nonmetropolitan Context," *Social Science*

Quarterly, 65 (1984), 626–34; Richard D. Alba and Reid M. Golden, "Patterns of Ethnic Marriage in the United States," *Social Forces*, 65 (1986), 202–23; Stanley Lieberson and Mary C. Waters, *From Many Strands: Ethnic and Racial Groups in Contemporary America* (New York, 1988), ch. 6 (advance copy courtesy of the authors).

2   U.S. Bureau of the Census, *1960 Census: Marital Status*, Subject Report PC(2)-4E (Washington, D.C., 1966), 160–65, 171–72; idem, *1980 Census: Marital Characteristics*, Subject Report PC80-2-4C (Washington, D.C., 1985); Richard D. Alba, "Interethnic Marriage in the 1980 Census" (Paper presented at the annual meeting of the American Sociological Association, 1985), courtesy of the author. One conceivable explanation for the low Black outmarriage rates compared to high rates for immigrant groups has more to do with internal family dynamics than with discrimination. Marcus Lee Hansen wrote an influential essay on the return of third-generation immigrants to interest in the ethnicity of their grandparents. A. L. Epstein has recently expanded Hansen's understanding in a way that has importance for intermarriage rates. Epstein writes of the critical importance of grandparents in passing group culture on to their children's children. Children often rebel against the explicit values and customs their parents try to teach them; it is the less threatening grandparents, according to Epstein, who succeed in teaching the worth of traditional ways. This might help explain a crucial difference between the group cohesiveness of Black Americans—whose family structures contained three generations throughout nearly all their history—and the relative lack of cohesion among grandparentless second-generation immigrants. It might be argued that continued low Black outmarriage rates were the product, not just of White discrimination, but also of greater internal Black community cohesion. Black people learned ethnic symbols and rules for behavior—including endogamy—at the knees of their grandparents in ways that were not possible for Nisei or second-generation Jews. For Jews and Japanese Americans, to rebel against one's parents was often to rebel against Jewishness or Japaneseness. For Blacks, there might be personal rebellion, but it could not so easily take the form of marrying outside one's ethnic roots. Cf. Marcus Lee Hansen, "The Problem of the Third-Generation Immigrant," *Augustana Historical Society Publications* (1938), reprinted in Oscar Handlin, ed., *Children of the Uprooted* (New York, 1966), 255–71; A. L. Epstein, *Ethos and Identity* (London, 1978), 139–56.

3   Barbara M. Posadas, "Crossed Boundaries in Interracial Chicago: Philipino American Families since 1925," *Amerasia Journal*, 8, no. 2 (1981), 31–52; Bureau of the Census, *Marital Characteristics* (1980); Murguia and Frisbie, "Mexican American Intermarriage."

4   Posadas, "Crossed Boundaries"; Tamara Hanneman, "Woman's Victory Will Be Realized When She Is Buried Beside Her Husband," *Minneapolis Star Tribune*, February 28, 1984.

5   This was true for Chinese Americans as well. Chinese immigrant families were fully as distraught as Jews or Japanese Americans at the prospect of a son or daughter marrying outside their group. Chinese communities used

similar gossip systems to keep young people in line. See Melford S. Weiss, "Selective Acculturation and the Dating Process: The Pattern of Chinese-Caucasian Interracial Dating," in Stanley Sue and Nathaniel Wagner, eds., *Asian-Americans: Psychological Perspectives* (Ben Lomond, Calif., 1973), 86–94; and James W. Loewen, *The Mississippi Chinese* (Cambridge, 1971), 134–38, 142–46. In 1978, Betty Hwang, aged seventeen, and her thirteen-year-old sister Jane were hit by their father after a long series of family battles in their New York City apartment. The father objected to the girls' Puerto Rican boyfriends and threatened to send them back to Taiwan. The girls went up to the roof, waved goodbye to neighbors, and dived off. "Girls Scolded over Dates Leap to Death," *San Francisco Examiner*, November 11, 1978.

6 This regional variation is akin to that Carl Degler found in Brazil, where the climate of opinion about intermarriage (as about other racial matters) was far more open in Bahia and other states of the northeast than it was to the south of Sao Paulo. Degler, *Neither Black Nor White: Slavery and Race Relations in Brazil and the United States* (New York, 1971; rpt. Madison, Wis., 1986), 98ff.

7 The tiny Baha'i sect was certainly the most liberal of all, as it officially recognized no barriers and taught its members to seek to cross whatever boundaries they encountered. G. H. Gallup, *The Gallup Poll: Public Opinion, 1972–1977* (Wilmington, Del., 1978), 1:72–74; Gallup, *The Gallup Poll: Public Opinion, 1978* (Wilmington, Del., 1978), 262–63; Gallup, *The Gallup Poll: Public Opinion, 1978* (Wilmington, Del., 1978), 262–63; Gallup, *The Gallup Poll: Public Opinion, 1983* (Wilmington, Del., 1984), 96–101; Anderson, *White Protestant Americans*, 131; Morgan Strong, "We Must Return to Religious Basics" (interview with fundamentalist educator Bob Jones), *USA Today*, August 22, 1983; "Bob Jones University's Position on Interracial Marriage," Bob Jones University brochure (Greenville, S.C., n. d. [early 1980s]). Other religious traditions close to American Fundamentalism, such as the Dutch Reformed Church of South Africa, adopted similarly strong-minded stances against intermarriage of any sort: see George M. Fredrickson, *White Supremacy* (New York, 1981), 94–135, and Pierre L. van den Berghe, "Miscegenation in South Africa," in van den Berghe, *Race and Ethnicity* (New York, 1970), 224–43.

8 "Apparent Victor," *Boston Globe*, November 7, 1984; Wendy Gramm appeared from publicity photos to be an Asian American.

9 John N. Tinker, "Intermarriage and Assimilation in a Plural Society: Japanese-Americans in the United States," *Marriage and Family Review*, 5 (1982), 61–74. Cf. Loewen, *Mississippi Chinese*, for a similar, though less complete, transit.

10 U.S. Bureau of the Census, *1970 Census: American Indians*, Subject Report PC(2)-1F (Washington, D.C., 1973), 145–53; idem; *1970 Census: Persons of Spanish Origin*, Subject Report PC(2)-1C (Washington, D.C., 1973), 160–64; Edward Murguia, "Intermarriage of Mexican Americans," in Gary A. Cretser and Joseph J. Leon, eds., *Intermarriage in the United States* (New

York, 1982), 91–100; U.S. Bureau of the Census, *1970 Census: Puerto Ricans in the United States,* Subject Report PC(2)-1E (Washington, D.C., 1973), 104–8; Alba, *Italian Americans,* 148. In the United States similar patterns were reported for Cubans (Bureau of the Census, *Persons of Spanish Origin* [1970], 160–64); Chinese (Harry H. L. Kitano and Wai-tsang Yeung, "Chinese Interracial Marriage," in Cretser and Leon, *Intermarriage,* 35–48); Koreans (Kitano and Lynn Kyung Chai, "Korean Interracial Marriage," in Cretser and Leon, *Intermarriage,* 75–89; Kitano et al., "Asian-American Interracial Marriage," *JMF,* 46 [1984], 179–90); and Germans (Anderson, *White Protestant Americans,* 84). Somewhat analogous situations appeared for Boers and Khoikhoi in South Africa (Fredrickson, *White Supremacy,* 94–135); for racial intermarriage in Brazil (Degler, *Neither Black Nor White,* 98ff.); and for various minority nationalities in the Soviet Union (Wesley A. Fisher, "Ethnic Consciousness and Intermarriage: Correlates of Endogamy among the Major Soviet Nationalities," *Soviet Studies,* 29 [1977], 395–408).

11 Sara Evans, *Personal Politics* (New York, 1979); Ann Baker Cottrell, "Today's Asian-Western Couples Are Not Anglo-Indians," *Phylon,* 40 (1979), 351–61; Leigh R. Kambhu, *Thailand Is Our Home: A Study of Some Wives of Thais* (Cambridge, 1963), 7–17; Murguia and Cazares, "Intermarriage of Mexican Americans"; Chester L. Hunt and Richard W. Coller, "Intermarriage and Cultural Change: A Study of Philippine-American Marriages," *Social Forces,* 35 (1957), 223–30; Lieberson and Waters, *From Many Strands,* chs. 6 and 7. Lieberson and Waters point out that although frequently it was the more highly educated members of a given ethnic group who married out, the same was not true for the groups as whole entities—i.e., the best educated ethnic groups were not the most frequent intermarriers.

12 Richard S. Dunn, *Sugar and Slaves* (New York, 1972), 252–56; Noel P. Gist, "The Anglo-Indians of India," in Gist and Anthony Gary Dworkin, eds., *The Blending of Races* (New York, 1972), 39–59; van den Berghe, "Miscegenation in South Africa."

13 Bok-Lim C. Kim, "Casework with Japanese and Korean Wives of Americans," *Social Casework,* 53 (1972), 273–97; idem, "Asian Wives of US Servicemen: Women in Shadows," *Amerasia Journal,* 4 (1977), 91–115; John W. Connor, *A Study of the Marital Stability of Japanese War Brides* (San Francisco, 1976); Leon K. Walters, "A Study of the Social and Marital Adjustment of Thirty-five American-Japanese Couples" (M.A. thesis, Ohio State University, 1953); George A. DeVos et al., *Personality Patterns and Problems of Adjustment in American-Japanese Intercultural Marriages* (Taipei, 1973); Tamiko T. Yamamoto, *Adjustments of War Brides in Hawaii,* Romanzo Adams Social Research Library Report 17, University of Hawaii (Honolulu, August 1950); G. J. Schnepp and Agnes Masako Yui, "Cultural and Marital Adjustment of Japanese War Brides," *AJS,* 61 (1955), 48–50; Anslem Strauss, "Strain and Harmony in American-Japanese War Bride Marriages," *Marriage and Family,* 16 (1954); Man Singh Das, "Touchable-Untouchable Intercaste Marriage," in Das and Panos D. Bardis, eds., *The Family in Asia* (London, 1978), 88–98; Cottrell, "Today's Asian-Western Couples"; Kambhu,

Thailand Is Our Home; Virginia Yans-McLaughlin, *Family and Community: Italian Immigrants in Buffalo, 1880–1930* (Urbana, Ill., 1982; orig. Ithaca, N.Y., 1977), 257; Posadas, "Crossed Boundaries in Interracial Chicago." In Japan today the outmarriage gender pattern may be changing. There is some evidence that more Japanese men than women are marrying foreigners (this sex differential holds both for marriages to Americans and for those to other Asian peoples); see Nicholas D. Kristof, "Tokyo Tacos: The Japanese Look to the West," *New York Times,* September 22, 1987.

14　Loewen, *Mississippi Chinese,* 150–53; Weiss, "Selective Acculturation and the Dating Process"; Kitano and Yeung, "Chinese Interracial Marriage"; Bureau of the Census, *Marital Characteristics* (1980); Kitano and Chai, "Korean Interracial Marriage"; Murguia and Frisbee, "Trends in Mexican American Intermarriage"; Murguia and Cazares, "Intermarriage of Mexican Americans"; Nelly Salgado de Snyder and Amado M. Padilla, "Cultural and Ethnic Maintenance of Interethnically Married Mexican Americans," *Human Organization,* 41 (1982), 359–62; Alba, "Interethnic Marriage in the 1980 Census." Native Americans showed a consistently similar pattern of greater outmarriage by women than men, but the gender difference was much smaller than for the other groups (Bureau of the Census, *Marital Characteristics* [1980]).

15　William Carlson Smith, *Americans in Process* (Ann Arbor, 1936), 344; Cecil Lee, interview, May 26–June 1, 1924 (SRR major document 34); B. L. Sung, *Mountain of Gold* (New York, 1967), 10–20 and passim; anonymous interview by the author, San Francisco, June 1980; Bobby Fong, "A Taxonomy of Group Identity with Examples from Chinese America" (unpublished paper, Berea, Ken., 1982).

16　Paola Sesia, "White Ethnicity in America: The Italian Experience," *Berkeley History Review,* 2 (1982), 19–32; Jonathan D. Sarna, "From Immigrants to Ethnics: Toward a New Theory of 'Ethnicization,'" *Ethnicity,* 5 (1978), 370–78; Yans-McLaughlin, *Family and Community,* 148, 256; Francis M. Rogers, *Americans of Portuguese Descent* (Beverly Hills, 1974); Howard M. Bahr et al., *American Ethnicity* (Lexington, Mass., 1979), 536–37. Other groups, such as Rumanians and Slovaks, seem to have intermarried across regional lines and formed nationality groups quite readily. Josef J. Barton, *Peasants and Strangers: Italians, Rumanians, and Slovaks in an American City, 1890–1950* (Cambridge, Mass., 1975), 58–59. The salience of ethnic divisions among White Americans fluctuated a great deal, depending on era, section of the country, class, generation removed from the Old Country— essentially the same set of variables I have examined in looking at Black, Jewish, and Japanese American outmarriage.

　　Other groups exhibited other sorts of divisions: Mexican Americans between immigrants and members of later generations (Murguia and Cazares, "Intermarriage of Mexican Americans"); Koreans between people derived from distinctive periods and types of immigration (Kitano and Chai, "Korean Interracial Marriage"); and reservation Indians between "mixed bloods" and "full bloods," who were dissimilar less in the character of their ancestry than in the degree of their acculturation (Murray L. Wax, *Indian Americans* [Englewood Cliffs, N.J., 1971], 70–80, 167–71, and passim). Donald Horowitz describes the continuing salience of subethnic identities among Ibo in Nigeria, Bengali in pre-Bangladesh East Bengal, and Tonga in southern Zambia; see "Ethnic Identity," in Nathan Glazer and Daniel P. Moynihan, eds., *Ethnicity* (Cambridge, Mass., 1975), 132–35.

17 The Japanese American hierarchy for non-Japanese was much like the general American status hierarchy, graded roughly from light skin to dark. This was not, however, for American reasons, at least not in the first generation. More likely it stemmed from age-old color prejudices in Japan. See Hiroshi Wagatsuma, "The Social Perception of Skin Color in Japan," in John Hope Franklin, ed., *Color and Race* (Boston, 1968), 129–65.

18 Most of the information here was collected in the Chinese communities of Seattle, Boston, and San Francisco between 1965 and 1985. See also Bureau of the Census, *Marital Characteristics* (1980); Kitano and Yeung, "Chinese Interracial Marriage."

19 Anderson, *White Protestant Americans*, 39, 53, 68, 86, and passim; Hazel Erskine, "The Polls: Interracial Socializing," *Public Opinion Quarterly*, 37 (1973), 283–94; Alex Bontemps, "National Poll Reveals Startling New Attitudes on Interracial Marriage," *Ebony*, September 1975, 144–51; Field notes, St. Paul, 1981–85; Alfred C. Kinsey et al., *Sexual Behavior in the Human Male* (Philadelphia, 1948), 75–76. Several sources point to similar hierarchies exhibited by various Catholic groups. See Harold J. Abramson, *Ethnic Diversity in Catholic America* (New York, 1973), 58–65; Alba, *Italian Americans*, 89–90, 149; Posadas, "Crossed Boundaries in Interracial Chicago"; Douglas T. Gurak and Joseph P. Fitzpatrick, "Intermarriage among Hispanic Ethnic Groups in New York City," *AJS*, 87 (1982), 921–34. For a similar situation in an overseas setting, see Judith A. Nagata, "What Is a Malay? Situational Selection of Ethnic Identity in a Plural Society," *American Ethnologist*, 1 (1974), 331–50. Several recent studies point toward fusion—something approaching random mate selection—among northwest European Protestants: Richard D. Alba, "Ethnic Identity among American Whites" (Paper presented at the annual meeting of the American Sociological Association, Chicago, 1987), courtesy of the author; idem, "Cohorts and the Dynamics of Ethnic Change"; idem, "Interethnic Marriage in the 1980 Census"; Stanley Lieberson, "Unhyphenated Whites in the United States," in Richard D. Alba, ed., *Ethnicity and Race in the U.S.A.* (London, 1985), 159–80; Lieberson and Waters, *From Many Strands*.

20 One measure of the difference is the reaction of different types of couples to the arrival of the first child. In intermarriages of Gentile and Jew, the birth of a baby often increased marital conflict, for the couple had to choose what religion they would teach the child (J. S. Slotkin, "Adjustment in Jewish-Gentile Intermarriages," *Social Forces*, 21 [1942], 226–30). By contrast, the arrival of children frequently solidified Black–non-Black and Japanese–non-Japanese marriages, for it often was the catalyst that brought the couple back into the extended family circle. There are some data to suggest that mar-

riages between Catholics and Protestants ended in divorce more frequently than homogamous Catholic or Protestant unions; see Glenn M. Vernon, "Interfaith Marriages," *Religious Education*, 55 (1960), 261–64; Loren E. Chancellor and Thomas P. Monahan, "Religious Preferences and Interreligious Mixtures in Marriages and Divorces in Iowa," *AJS*, 6 (1955), 233–39; Judson T. Landis, "Marriages of Mixed and Non-Mixed Religious Faith," *ASR*, 44 (1949), 401–7.

21 One type of intermarriage described in this book typically suffered both internal and external difficulty. That was the war bride marriage. Culture and personality differences between Japan and America lent internal pressure, while visible racial differences and rejection by Japanese Americans provided outside pressure. Information on conflict or stability in other sorts of intermarriages is fragmentary at best, although one recent study suggests the rise of interreligious marriages had little effect on marital satisfaction or stability in the 1970s: Norval D. Glenn, "Interreligious Marriage in the United States," *JMF*, 44 (1985), 555–65.

22 People of other mixtures found themselves in similar circumstances. In the 1960s, White offspring of mixed Protestant and Catholic marriages chose to marry Catholics about two-thirds of the time and Protestants the rest. Part-Italians remained connected to both Italian and non-Italian family and community and married Italians and part-Italians more often than one would expect—over 20 percent of the time. Where the children of South Asian–Western couples once were consigned to a separate Anglo-Indian status, by the 1970s they were moving freely in both Indian and Euro-American circles. See Anderson, *White Protestant Americans*, 131–33; Alba, *Italian Americans*, 146–47; Cottrell, "Today's Asian-Western Couples"; Alba, "Ethnic Identity among Whites"; idem, "Interethnic Marriage in the 1980 Census"; Gillian Stevens, "Nativity, Intermarriage, and Mother-Tongue Shift," *ASR*, 50 (1985), 74–83; Larry R. Petersen, "Interfaith Marriage and Religious Commitment among Catholics," *JMF*, 48 (1986), 725–35; Nelly Salgado de Snyder and Amado M. Padilla, "Interethnic Marriage of Mexican Americans after Nearly Two Decades," UCLA Spanish Speaking Mental Health Research Center Occasional Paper no. 15 (1981); Lieberson and Waters, *From Many Strands*, chs. 6–7.

23 Milton L. Barron, "Intergroup Aspects of Choosing a Mate," in Barron, ed., *The Blending American* (Chicago, 1972), 42.

24 Steven M. Cohen argues against a link between class and intermarriage in *Interethnic Marriage and Friendship* (New York, 1980), 166.

25 Cohen punctures the triple melting pot hypothesis (*Interethnic Marriage and Friendship*, 65 and passim).

26 Survey taken by the author, Minnesota, January 1982.

27 For two other attempts at economic exchange theories—neither particularly believable—for two very different gender-ethnic combinations, see Murguia and Cazares, "Intermarriage of Mexican Americans," 96, and Loewen, *Mississippi Chinese*, 150–53.

28 The idea of exchange may have some relevance in the matter of images. It

may be that there is sometimes an emotional economy at work, one that responds to prevailing images about members of the opposite sex of various groups. It may be that a given White man has a need to dominate physically which is satisfied, for instance, by alliance with a smaller (and, according to stereotype, submissive) Japanese American woman. And a given Japanese American woman may have a complementary need to be dominated. While such considerations certainly did not determine all intermarriage choices, they, and the mutual images to which they are related, may have played a part in some.

29   Madison Grant, *The Passing of the Great Race* (New York, 1916), 15–16.

30   Alba, *Italian Americans*, 146–47; Vera Burns* (three-fourths Chinese, one-fourth White), interviewed by the author, Berkeley, May 1979; Peter Denoyer* (half Chinese, half White), interviewed by the author, San Francisco, November 1980; Salgado de Snyder and Padilla, "Interethnic Marriages of Mexican Americans."

31   The reasons that Americans stick to the two-category system, while people of other nations have built more elaborate ethnic stratification systems, are complex. See Fredrickson, *White Supremacy*, 94–135; John Western, *Outcast Cape Town* (Minneapolis, 1981); van den Berghe, "Miscegenation in South Africa"; H. F. Dickie-Clark, "The Coloured Minority of Durban," in Gist and Dworkin, *Blending of Races*, 25–38; Magnus Morner, *Race Mixture in the History of Latin America* (Boston, 1967); Gist, "Anglo Indians of India"; Richard Slobodin, "The Métis of Northern Canada," in Gist and Dworkin, *Blending of Races*, 143–66; Antoine S. Lussier and D. Bruce Sealey, *The Other Nation: The Métis*, 2 vols. (Winnipeg, 1978); Jacqueline Peterson and Jennifer S. H. Brown, eds., *The New Peoples: Being and Becoming Métis* (Lincoln, Neb., 1985); Degler, *Neither Black Nor White*. Some would argue that a similar, intermediate mixed group emerged on various U.S. Indian reservations; see Wax, *Indian Americans*, 50–51, 69–70, 76–77.

32   Ruby Jo Reeves Kennedy, "Single or Triple Melting Pot?" *AJS*, 49 (1944), 331–39; Milton Gordon, *Assimilation in American Life* (New York, 1964), 80.

33   Frederik Barth found that among Pathans in Afghanistan and Pakistan, "boundaries may persist despite . . . 'osmosis' of personnel through them." Barth, ed., *Ethnic Groups and Boundaries* (Boston, 1969), 21. Two recent studies have found little attenuation of minority identity on the part of Mexican Americans married to Anglos: Salgado de Snyder and Padilla, "Culture and Ethnic Maintenance," and idem, "Interethnic Marriages of Mexican Americans."

34   In fact, since some ethnic activists tend to come from the same college-educated stratum as intermarriers, one may find that a larger percentage of Black and Japanese American ethnic activists are intermarried or attached romantically to people outside their group than is true for the group at large. That would probably be less true for Jews because of the volitional nature of religious commitment, but even in that community Eugen Schoenfeld found that in some settings Jewish identity was *stronger* among intermarriers than

among those who married Jews. Schoenfeld, "Intermarriage and the Small Town: The Jewish Case," *JMF*, 31 (1969), 61–64.

35 Stephen Cornell, "Communities of Culture, Communities of Interest: On the Variable Nature of Ethnic Groups" (Paper presented to the Center for the Study of Industrial Societies, University of Chicago, February 1984), courtesy of the author.

36 Michael T. Hannan, "The Dynamics of Ethnic Boundaries in Modern States," in Hannan and John W. Meyer, *National Development and the World System* (Chicago, 1979), 253–75; Stephen Cornell, "The Transformations of Tribe," in Cornell, *The Rise of the Powerless: American Indian Political Resurgence* (New York, 1988), advance copy courtesy of the author. Abner Cohen reports that Hausa migrants in Yoruba towns discouraged intermarriages by telling tales of the "mystical dangers which can afflict a Hausa man who marries a Yoruba woman," because they viewed endogamy as necessary to preserve the Hausa's economic niche. Cohen, *Custom and Politics in Urban Africa* (Berkeley, 1969), 53. There never was structural pressure to create an intermediate ethnic group in the United States, unlike India and South Africa, where the colonial overlords had political uses for a mixed group. See Gist, "Anglo-Indians of India"; Dickie-Clark, "Coloured Minority of Durban."

37 Murray Wax notes that Native Americans long defined Indian ethnicity as "basically a matter of participation and kinship," whereas the U.S. government kept trying to impose "Anglo-Saxon notions of heirship." In the long run, the Indians seem to have won. Wax, *Indian Americans*, 72–73.

38 Gillian Stevens ("Nativity, Intermarriage, and Mother-Tongue Shift") and Salgado de Snyder and Padilla ("Interethnic Marriages of Mexican Americans") have found some evidence of greater attenuation of ancestral language skills among children of mixed marriages than among children from homogamous families.

Appendix A. Summary of States' Laws on Interracial Marriage

1 This summary of state laws is derived from the following sources: A. Leon Higginbotham, *In the Matter of Color* (New York, 1978), 36–47, 158–59, 251–73; Gilbert Thomas Stephenson, *Race Distinctions in American Law* (New York, 1909), 78–80; Chester G. Vernier, *American Family Laws*, 6 vols. (Stanford, 1931), 1:206–8; *The Negro Yearbook* (Tuskegee, Ala., 1921–22), 180–81; U.S. Bureau of the Census, *Marriage and Divorce, 1867–1906*, 2 vols. (Washington, D.C., 1909), 1:200–63.

Bibliography

The bibliography that follows is divided into five sections. The first of these contains sources for the introductory and concluding chapters (1 and 12). It is followed by lists for each of the four parts of the book. Here, as in the text, asterisks denote pseudonyms.

The following abbreviations are used throughout:

AJS   *American Journal of Sociology*
AJYB   *American Jewish Year Book*
ASR   *American Sociological Review*
JMF   *Journal of Marriage and the Family*
JNH   *Journal of Negro History*
SPH   *Social Process in Hawaii*
SSR   *Sociology and Social Research*

Chapters 1 and 12

Abramson, Harold J. *Ethnic Diversity in Catholic America.* New York, 1973.

Adams, Romanzo. *Interracial Marriage in Hawaii.* Montclair, N.J., 1969; orig. New York, 1937.

Alba, Richard D. "Cohorts and the Dynamics of Ethnic Change." In Matilda White Riley et al., eds., *Social Structures and Human Lives,* vol. 1. Newbury Park, forthcoming.

Alba, Richard D. "Ethnic Identity among American Whites." Paper presented at the annual meeting of the American Sociological Association, Chicago, 1987.

Alba, Richard D. "Interethnic Marriage in the 1980 Census." Paper presented at the annual meeting of the American Sociological Association, 1985.

Alba, Richard D. *Italian Americans: Into the Twilight of Ethnicity.* Englewood Cliffs, N.J., 1985.

Alba, Richard D. "The Twilight of Ethnicity among Americans of European Ancestry: The Case of Italians." *Ethnic and Racial Studies,* 8 (1985), 134–58.

Alba, Richard D., ed. *Ethnicity and Race in the U.S.A.* London, 1985.

Alba, Richard D., and Reid M. Golden. "Patterns of Ethnic Marriage in the United States." *Social Forces*, 65 (1986), 202–23.

Albers, Patricia C., and William R. James. "On the Dialectics of Ethnicity." *Journal of Ethnic Studies*, 14 (1986), 1–28.

Anderson, Charles H. *White Protestant Americans.* Englewood Cliffs, N.J., 1970.

Armstrong, John A. *Nations before Nationalism.* Chapel Hill, N.C., 1982.

Bahr, Howard M., et al. *American Ethnicity.* Lexington, Mass., 1979.

Banton, Michael. *Race Relations.* New York, 1967.

Banton, Michael. *Racial and Ethnic Competition.* Cambridge, 1983.

Barron, Milton L. "Intergroup Aspects of Choosing a Mate." In Barron, ed., *The Blending American.* Chicago, 1972.

Barth, Fredrik, ed. *Ethnic Groups and Boundaries.* Boston, 1969.

Barton, Josef J. *Peasants and Strangers: Italians, Rumanians, and Slovaks in an American City, 1890–1950.* Cambridge, Mass., 1975.

Bell, Daniel. "Ethnicity and Social Change." In Glazer and Moynihan, *Ethnicity*, 141–74.

Benson, Susan. *Ambiguous Ethnicity: Interracial Families in London.* Cambridge, 1981.

Blalock, H. M. *Toward a Theory of Minority-Group Relations.* New York, 1967.

Blau, Peter M., Carolyn Beeker, and Kevin M. Fitzpatrick. "Intersecting Social Affiliations and Intermarriage." *Social Forces*, 62 (1984), 585–617.

Blau, Peter M., Terry C. Blum, and Joseph E. Schwartz, "Heterogeneity and Intermarriage." *ASR*, 47 (1982), 45–62.

Blauner, Robert. *Racial Oppression in America.* New York, 1972.

Blu, Karen. *The Lumbee Problem.* Cambridge, 1980.

"Bob Jones University's Position on Interracial Marriage." Brochure published by Bob Jones University, Greenville, S.C., early 1980s.

Bogardus, Emory S. "Changes in Racial Distance." *International Journal of Opinion and Attitude Research*, 1 (1947), 55–62.

Bogardus, Emory S. *Immigration and Race Attitudes.* Boston, 1928.

Bogardus, Emory S. "Racial Distance Changes in the United States during the Past Thirty Years." *SSR* (1959), 286–90.

Bogardus, Emory S. *Social Distance.* Los Angeles, 1959.

Bontemps, Alex. "National Poll Reveals Startling New Attitudes on Interracial Marriage." *Ebony*, 30 (September 1975), 144–51.

Bossard, James H. S. "Residential Propinquity as a Factor in Marriage Selection." *AJS*, 38 (1932), 219–24.

Boxer, C. R. *Race Relations in the Netherlands.* Meppel, 1965.

Brass, Paul R., ed. *Ethnic Groups and the State.* London, 1984.

Buss, David M. "Human Mate Selection." *American Scientist*, 73 (January–February 1985), 47–51.

Carter, Lewis F. "Racial-Caste Hypogamy: A Sociological Myth?" *Phylon* (1968), 347–50.

Cazares, Ralph B., et al. "Mexican American Intermarriage in a Nonmetropolitan Context." *Social Science Quarterly*, 65 (1984), 626–34.

Cerroni-Long, E. L. "Marrying Out: Socio-Cultural and Psychological Implications of Intermarriage." *Journal of Comparative Family Studies*, 16 (1984), 25–46.

Chancellor, Loren E., and Thomas P. Monahan. "Religious Preferences and Inter-religious Mixtures in Marriages and Divorces in Iowa." *AJS*, 6 (1955), 233–39.

Christianity Today, October 17 and 31, 1986.

Cohen, Abner. *Custom and Politics in Urban Africa.* Berkeley, 1969.

Cohen, Abner, ed. *Urban Ethnicity.* London, 1974.

Cohen, Steven M. *Interethnic Marriage and Friendship.* New York, 1980.

Connor, John W. *A Study of the Marital Stability of Japanese War Brides.* San Francisco, 1976.

Cornell, Stephen. "Communities of Culture, Communities of Interest: On the Variable Nature of Ethnic Groups." Paper presented to the Center for the Study of Industrial Societies, University of Chicago, February 1984.

Cornell, Stephen. *The Return of the Native: American Indian Political Resurgence.* New York, 1988.

Cottrell, Ann Baker. "Today's Asian-Western Couples Are Not Anglo-Indians." *Phylon* (1979), 351–61.

Cox, Oliver C. *Caste, Class, and Race.* New York, 1959.

Cretser, Gary A., and Joseph J. Leon, eds. *Intermarriage in the United States.* New York, 1982.

Darnton, Robert. *The Great Cat Massacre and Other Episodes in French Cultural History.* New York, 1984.

Das, Man Singh. "Touchable-Untouchable Intercaste Marriage." In Das and Panos D. Bardis, eds., *The Family in Asia*, 88–98. London, 1978.

Das Gupta, Jyotirindra. "Ethnicity, Language Demands, and National Development in India." In Glazer and Moynihan, *Ethnicity*, 466–88.

Dashevsky, Arnold, ed. *Ethnic Identity in Society.* Chicago, 1976.

Davis, Kingsley. "Intermarriage in Caste Society." *American Anthropologist*, 43 (1941), 376–95.

Degler, Carl. *Neither Black nor White: Slavery and Race Relations in Brazil and the United States.* New York, 1971; rpt. Madison, Wis., 1986.

DeVos, George, and Lola Romanucci-Ross., eds. *Ethnic Identity.* Chicago, 1982.

DeVos, George, et al. *Personality Patterns and Problems of Adjustment of in American-Japanese Intercultural Marriages.* Taipei, 1973.

Dover, Cedric. *Half Caste.* London, 1937.

Dreyer, June Teufel. *China's Forty Millions: Minority Nationalities and National Integration.* Cambridge, 1976.

Dunn, Richard S. *Sugar and Slaves.* New York, 1972.

Ellman, Israel. "Jewish Intermarriage in the United States." In Benjamin Schlesinger, ed., *The Jewish Family*, 25–61. Toronto, 1971.

Enloe, Cynthia. *Ethnic Conflict and Political Development.* Boston, 1973.

Epstein, A. L. *Ethos and Identity.* London, 1978.

Erikson, Erik H. "The Concept of Identity in Race Relations." In Talcott Parsons and Kenneth B. Clark, eds., *The Negro American*, 227–53. Boston, 1966.

Erskine, Hazel. "The Polls: Interracial Socializing." *Public Opinion Quarterly*, 37 (1973), 283–94.

Evans, Sara. *Personal Politics.* New York, 1979.

"Famous Negroes Married to Whites." *Ebony*, December 1949, 20–30.

Fernandez, Celestino, and Louis M. Holscher. "Chicano-Anglo Intermarriage in Arizona, 1960–1980." *Hispanic Journal of Behavioral Sciences*, 5 (1983), 291–304.

Fisher, Wesley A. "Ethnic Consciousness and Intermarriage: Correlates of Endogamy among the Major Soviet Nationalities." *Soviet Studies*, 29 (1977), 395–408.

Fong, Bobby. "A Taxonomy of Group Identity with Examples from Chinese America." Unpublished paper, Berea, Ky., 1982.

Francis, E. K. *Interethnic Relations*. New York, 1976.

Franklin, John H., ed. *Color and Race*. Boston, 1968.

Frazier, E. Franklin. *Race and Culture Contacts in the Modern World*. New York, 1957.

Fredrickson, George M. *White Supremacy*. New York, 1981.

Gallup, G. H. *The Gallup Poll: Public Opinion, 1972–1977*. Wilmington, Del., 1978.

Gallup, G. H. *The Gallup Poll: Public Opinion, 1978*. Wilmington, Del., 1978.

Gallup, G. H. *The Gallup Poll: Public Opinion, 1983*. Wilmington, Del., 1984.

Gans, Herbert J. "Symbolic Ethnicity." *Ethnic and Racial Studies*, 2 (1979), 1–20.

"Girls Scolded over Dates Leap to Death." *San Francisco Examiner*, November 11, 1978.

Gist, Noel P., and Anthony Gary Dworkin, eds. *The Blending of Races*. New York, 1972.

Gist, Noel P., and Roy Dean Wright. *Marginality and Identity: Anglo-Indians*. Leiden, 1973.

Glazer, Nathan, and Daniel P. Moynihan, *Beyond the Melting Pot: The Negroes, Puerto Ricans, Italians, and Irish of New York City*. Cambridge, Mass., 1963.

Glazer, Nathan, and Daniel P. Moynihan, eds. *Ethnicity*. Cambridge, Mass., 1975.

Glazer, Nathan, and Daniel P. Moynihan. Introduction to Glazer and Moynihan, *Ethnicity*, 1–26.

Glenn, Norval D. "Interreligious Marriage in the United States." *JMF*, 44 (1982), 555–65.

Gordon, Milton M. *Assimilation in American Life*. New York, 1964.

Gordon, Milton M. "Toward a General Theory of Racial and Ethnic Relations." In Glazer and Moynihan, *Ethnicity*, 84–110.

Gossett, Thomas F. *Race: The History of an Idea in America*. New York, 1963.

Grant, Madison. *The Passing of the Great Race*. New York, 1916.

Gurak, Douglas T., and Joseph P. Fitzpatrick. "Intermarriage among Hispanic Ethnic Groups in New York City." *AJS*, 87 (1982), 921–34.

Haare, John. *Maori and Pakeha: A Study of Mixed Marriage in New Zealand*. New York, 1966.

Hannan, Michael T. "The Dynamics of Ethnic Boundaries in Modern States." In Hannan and John W. Meyer, *National Development and the World System*, 253–75. Chicago, 1979.

Hanneman, Tamara. "Woman's Victory Will Be Realized Friday When She Is Buried beside Her Husband." *Minneapolis Star Tribune*, February 28, 1984.

Hansen, Marcus Lee. "The Problem of the Third-Generation Immigrant." *Augustana Historical Society Publications* (1938). Reprinted in Oscar Handlin, ed., *Children of the Uprooted*, 255–71. New York, 1966.

Hassan, Riaz. "Interethnic Marriage in Singapore." *SSR*, 55 (1971), 303–23.

Hassan, Riaz, and Geoffrey Benjamin. *Ethnic Outmarriage Rates in Singapore.* Singapore, 1972.

Herberg, Will. *Protestant, Catholic, Jew.* Garden City, N.Y., 1955.

Hirschman, Charles. "America's Melting Pot Reconsidered." *Annual Review of Sociology* (1983), 397–423.

Hoetink, H. *Slavery and Race Relations in the Americas.* New York, 1973.

Horowitz, Donald L. "Ethnic Identity." In Glazer and Moynihan, *Ethnicity*, 111–40.

Hunt, Chester L., and Richard W. Coller. "Intermarriage and Cultural Change: A Study of Philippine-American Marriages." *Social Forces*, 35 (1957), 223–30.

Isaacs, Harold. "Basic Group Identity." In Glazer and Moynihan, *Ethnicity*, 29–52.

Jian, Esther Holland. *British Girl—Chinese Wife.* Beijing, 1985.

Jordan, Winthrop. *White over Black.* Chapel Hill, N.C., 1968.

Kambhu, Leigh R. *Thailand Is Our Home: A Study of Some Wives of Thais.* Cambridge, 1963.

Kearl, Michael C., and Edward Murguia. "Age Differences of Spouses in Mexican American Intermarriage." *Social Science Quarterly*, 66 (1985), 453–60.

Kennedy, Ruby Jo Reeves. "Single or Triple Melting Pot? Intermarriage Trends in New Haven, 1870–1940." *AJS*, 49 (1944), 331–39.

Kennedy, Ruby Jo Reeves. "Single or Triple Melting Pot? Intermarriage in New Haven, 1870–1950." *AJS*, 58 (1952), 56–59.

Keyes, Charles F., ed. *Ethnic Change.* Seattle, 1981.

Kim, Bok-Lim C. "Asian Wives of US Servicemen." *Amerasia Journal*, 4 (1977), 91–115.

Kim, Bok-Lim C. "Casework with Japanese and Korean Wives of Americans." *Social Casework*, 53 (1972), 273–97.

Kinsey, Alfred C., et al. *Sexual Behavior in the Human Male.* Philadelphia, 1948.

Kitano, Harry H. L. *Japanese Americans.* 2nd ed. Englewood Cliffs, N.J., 1976.

Kitano, Harry H. L., and Lynn Kyung Chai. "Korean Interracial Marriage." In Cretser and Leon, *Intermarriage*, 75–89.

Kitano, Harry H. L., and Wai-tsang Yeung. "Chinese Interracial Marriage." Ibid., 35–48.

Kitano, Harry H. L., et al. "Asian-American Interracial Marriage." *JMF*, 46 (1984), 179–90.

Kornblum, William. *Blue-Collar Community.* Chicago, 1974.

Kristoff, Nicholas D. "Tokyo Tacos: The Japanese Look West." *New York Times*, September 22, 1987.

Landis, Judson T. "Marriages of Mixed and Non-Mixed Religious Faith." *ASR*, 44 (1949), 401–7.

Lasker, Bruno. *Filipino Immigration.* New York, 1969; orig. Chicago, 1931.

Levine, Gene N., and Colbert Rhodes. *The Japanese American Community.* New York, 1977.

Lieberson, Stanley. "Unhyphenated Whites in the United States." In Richard D. Alba, ed., *Ethnicity and Race in the U.S.A.*, 159–80. London, 1985.

Lieberson, Stanley, and Mary C. Walters. *From Many Strands: Ethnic and Racial Groups in Contemporary America.* New York, 1988.

Lind, Andrew W. *Interethnic Marriage in New Guinea.* Canberra, 1969.

Lind, Andrew W. *An Island Community: Ecological Succession in Hawaii.* Chicago, 1938.

Loewen, James W. *The Mississippi Chinese.* Cambridge, 1971.

Lussier, Antoine S., and D. Bruce Sealey. *The Other Nation: The Métis.* 2 vols. Winnipeg, 1978.

McGoldrick, Monica, and Nydia Garcia Preto. "Ethnic Intermarriage: Implications for Therapy." *Family Process*, 23 (1984), 347–64.

McGuire, William J., et al. "Salience of Ethnicity in the Spontaneous Self-Concept as a Function of One's Ethnic Distinctiveness in the Social Environment." *Journal of Personality and Social Psychology*, 36 (1978), 511–20.

McNeill, William H. *Polyethnicity and National Unity in World History.* Toronto, 1986.

McRae, James A. "Changes in Religious Communalism Desired by Protestants and Catholics." *Social Forces*, 61 (1983), 709–30.

Martinez-Alier, Verena. *Marriage, Class, and Colour in Nineteenth-Century Cuba.* London, 1974.

Marvin, Donald M. "Occupational Propinquity as a Factor in Marriage Selection." *Publications of the American Statistical Association*, 16 (1918), 132–50.

Mayer, Egon, and Carl Sheingold. *Intermarriage and the Jewish Future.* New York, 1979.

Merton, Robert K. "Intermarriage and the Social Structure." *Psychiatry*, 4 (1941), 361–74.

Moodie, T. Dunbar. *The Rise of Afrikanerdom.* Berkeley, 1975.

Morner, Magnus. *Race Mixture in the History of Latin America.* Boston, 1967.

Mueller, Samuel A. "The New Triple Melting Pot." *Review of Religious Research*, 13 (1971), 18–33.

Murguia, Edward, and W. Parker Frisbie. "Trends in Mexican American Intermarriage." *Social Science Quarterly*, 58 (1979), 374–89.

Nagata, Judith. "What Is a Malay? Situational Selection of Ethnic Identity in a Plural Society." *American Ethnologist*, 1 (1974), 331–50.

Newman, William. *American Pluralism.* New York, 1973.

Novak, Michael. *The Rise of the Unmeltable Ethnics.* New York, 1972.

Osseo-Asare, Francislee. *A New Land to Live In.* Downers Grove, Ill., 1977.

Park, Robert E. *Race and Culture.* Glencoe, Ill., 1949.

Parkman, Margaret A., and Jack Sawyer. "Dimensions of Ethnic Intermarriage in Hawaii." *ASR*, 32 (1967).

Patterson, Orlando. "Context and Choice in Ethnic Allegiance." In Glazer and Moynihan, *Ethnicity*, 305–49.

Patterson, Orlando. *Ethnic Chauvinism.* New York, 1977.

Petersen, Larry R. "Interfaith Marriage and Religious Commitment among Catholics." *JMF*, 48 (1986), 725–35.

Petersen, William. *Japanese Americans.* New York, 1971.

Petersen, William, et al. *Concepts of Ethnicity.* Cambridge, 1982.

Peterson, Jacqueline, and Jennifer S. H. Brown, eds. *The New Peoples: Being and Becoming Métis.* Lincoln, Neb., 1985.

Posadas, Barbara. "Crossed Boundaries in Interracial Chicago: Pilipino American Families since 1925." *Amerasia Journal,* 8, no. 2 (1981), 31–52.

Pye, Lucien. "China: Ethnic Minorities and National Security." In Glazer and Moynihan, *Ethnicity,* 489–512.

Rogers, Francis M. *Americans of Portuguese Descent.* Beverly Hills, 1974.

Rothschild, Joseph. *Ethnopolitics.* New York, 1981.

Royce, Anna Peterson. *Ethnic Identity.* Bloomington, Ind., 1982.

Salgado de Snyder, Nelly, and Amado M. Padilla. "Cultural and Ethnic Maintenance of Interethnically Married Mexican Americans." *Human Organization,* 41 (1982), 359–62.

Salgado de Snyder, Nelly, and Amado M. Padilla. "Interethnic Marriage of Mexican Americans after Nearly Two Decades." UCLA Spanish-Speaking Mental Health Research Center Occasional Paper no. 15, 1981.

Sanders, Jimy M., and Victor Nee. "Limits of Ethnic Solidarity in the Enclave Economy." *ASR,* 52 (1987), 745–73.

Sarna, Jonathan. "From Immigrants to Ethnics: Toward a New Theory of 'Ethnicization.'" *Ethnicity,* 5 (1978), 370–78.

Schermerhorn, R. A. *Comparative Ethnic Relations.* Chicago, 1970.

Schneider, Mark. *Ethnicity and Politics.* Chapel Hill, N.C., 1979.

Schnepp, G. J., and Agnes Masako Yui. "Cultural and Marital Adjustment of Japanese War Brides." *AJS,* 61 (1955), 48–50.

Schoenfeld, Eugen. "Intermarriage and the Small Town: The Jewish Case." *JMF,* 31 (1969), 61–64.

Sesia, Paola. "White Ethnicity in America: The Italian Experience." *Berkeley History Review,* 2 (1982), 18–32.

Shibutani, Tamotsu, and Kian M. Kwan. *Ethnic Stratification.* New York, 1965.

Sieg, Rubolf. *Mischlingskinder in Westdeutschland.* Baden-Baden, 1955.

Simpson, George E., and J. Milton Yinger. *Racial and Cultural Minorities.* 4th ed. New York, 1972.

Slotkin, J. S. "Adjustment in Jewish-Gentile Intermarriages." *Social Forces,* 21 (1942), 226–30.

Smart, J. B. *The Domiciled European and the Anglo-Indian Race of India.* Fort Bombay, 1929.

Smith, William Carlson. *Americans in Process.* Ann Arbor, 1936.

Sollors, Werner. *Beyond Ethnicity.* New York, 1986.

South, Scott J., and Steven F. Messner. "Structural Determinants of Intergroup Association: Interracial Marriage and Crime." *AJS,* 91 (1986), 1409–30.

Stack, John F., ed. *Ethnic Identities in a Transnational World.* Westport, Conn., 1981.

Steinberg, Stephen. *The Ethnic Myth.* Boston, 1981.

Stevens, Gillian. "Nativity, Intermarriage, and Mother-Tongue Shift." *ASR,* 50 (1985), 74–83.

Strauss, Anselm. "Strain and Harmony in American-Japanese War Bride Marriages." *Marriage and Family*, 16 (1954).

Strong, Morgan. "We Must Return to Religious Basics." *USA Today*, August 22, 1983.

Stuart, Irving R., and Lawrence Edwin Abt, eds. *Interracial Marriage*. New York, 1973.

Sung, B. L. *Mountain of Gold*. New York, 1967.

Takaki, Ronald T. *Iron Cages*. New York, 1979.

Thomas, Melvin E., and Michael Hughes. "The Continuing Significance of Race." *ASR*, 51 (1986), 830–41.

Tinker, John N. "Intermarriage and Assimilation in a Plural Society: Japanese-Americans in the United States." *Marriage and Family Review*, 5 (1982), 61–74.

U.S. Bureau of the Census. *1960 Census: Marital Status*. Subject Report PC(2)-4E. Washington, D.C., 1966.

U.S. Bureau of the Census. *1970 Census: American Indians*. Subject Report PC(2)-1F. Washington, D.C., 1973.

U.S. Bureau of the Census. *1970 Census: Japanese, Chinese, and Filipinos in the United States*. Subject Report PC(2)-1G. Washington, D.C., 1973.

U.S. Bureau of the Census. *1970 Census: Persons of Spanish Origin*. Subject Report PC(2)-1C. Washington, D.C., 1973.

U.S. Bureau of the Census. *1970 Census: Puerto Ricans in the United States*. Subject Report PC(2)-1E. Washington, D.C., 1973.

U.S. Bureau of the Census. *1980 Census of Population. General Population Characteristics. United States Summary*. Washington, D.C., 1983.

U.S. Bureau of the Census. *1980 Census of Population: Marital Characteristics*. Subject Report PC80-2-4C. Washington, D.C., 1985.

van den Berghe, Pierre. *The Ethnic Phenomenon*. New York, 1981.

van den Berghe, Pierre. "Miscegenation in South Africa." In van den Berghe, *Race and Ethnicity*, 224–43. New York, 1970.

van den Berghe, Pierre. "Race and Ethnicity: A Sociobiological Perspective." *Ethnic and Racial Studies*, 1 (1978), 401–11.

Vernon, Glenn M. "Interfaith Marriages." *Religious Education*, 55 (1960), 261–64.

Walters, Leon K. "A Study of the Social and Marital Adjustment of Thirty-five American-Japanese Couples." M.A. thesis, Ohio State University, 1953.

Wax, Murray L. *Indian Americans*. Englewood Cliffs, N.J., 1971.

Weber, Max. *Economy and Society*. Berkeley, 1979.

Weiss, Melford S. "Selective Acculturation and the Dating Process: The Pattern of Chinese-Caucasian Interracial Dating." In Stanley Sue and Nathaniel Wagner, eds., *Asian-Americans: Psychological Perspectives* 86–94. Ben Lomond, Calif., 1973.

Western, John. *Outcast Cape Town*. Minneapolis, 1981.

Williams, George Dee. *Maya-Spanish Crosses in Yucatan*. Cambridge, 1931.

Williamson, Joel. *New People*. New York, 1980.

Wilson, William Julius. *The Declining Significance of Race*. 2nd ed. Chicago, 1980.

Wu, David Y. H., ed. *Ethnicity and Interpersonal Interaction*. Singapore, 1982.

Yamamoto, Tamiko T. *Adjustments of War Brides in Hawaii*. Romanzo Adams Social Research Library Report 17, University of Hawaii. Honolulu, 1950.

Yancey, William L., et al. "Emergent Ethnicity." *ASR*, 41 (1976), 391–403.

Yans-McLaughlin, Virginia. *Family and Community: Italian Immigrants in Buffalo, 1880–1930*. Urbana, Ill., 1982; orig. Ithaca, N.Y., 1977.

Part I. Japanese Americans

Archival Documents

Japanese American Research Project (JARP), Department of Special Collections, University Research Library, University of California, Los Angeles.

Centenary Methodist Church. *Directory*. 1962, 1965. Box 361.

Ishigo, Estelle. "Lone Heart Mountain." Box 79.

Ishigo Papers. Box 80.

Kawaguchi, Sanjiro, interviewed by Joe Grant Masaoka, San Francisco, February 1967. Box 519.

Pasadena Union Presbyterian Church. *Directory*. 1960. Box 361.

West Los Angeles Community Methodist Church. *Membership Directory*. 1963. Box 361.

Japanese American Evacuation and Resettlement Study (JERS), Bancroft Library, University of California, Berkeley.

Billigmeier. "Miscellany." R20.03.

"Biography 3." Carton 4.

"Biography 5." Carton 4.

"Biography 27." Carton 4.

deYoung, John. "A Preliminary Survey of the Adjustment of Japanese Evacuees in Denver." November 10, 1943. T1.874.

Johnson, Audrey, et al. "Study of the Relocated Japanese-Americans in Minneapolis." T1.877.

Kikuchi, Charles, "The Social Adjustment Process of the Japanese American Resettlers to Chicago during the Wartime Years." M.S.W. thesis, Columbia University, 1947. T1.836.

Manuscript on the Nisei in Chicago. T1.832.

Matsunaga, Setsuko. "The Adjustment of Evacuees in St. Louis." M.A. thesis, Washington University, 1944. T1.880.

Miyamoto, S. Frank. Manuscript analysis of Tule Lake prison camp. R20.42.

"Nisei Attitude Survey." Carton 3.

"Nisei Autobiography." June 19, 1944. T1.95.

Nisei in Chicago MS. T1.832.

"The Relocation Program at Tule Lake." R20.84.

Sakoda, James. "Recreation: Dancing." R20.87A.

Shibutani, Tamotsu. "The First Year of the Resettlement of Nisei in the Chicago Area." March 1, 1944. T1.842.

"Suski Biography." T1.96.

Suski, Louise. Report on Japanese American resettlement in Milwaukee. T1.868.

Tanaka, Togo. "Report on Madison, Wisconsin, Evacuee Resettlement." April 22, 1943. T1.854.

U.S. War Relocation Authority (WRA). Tabulation of All Census Forms 26. (The forms are on Shelf F. Information from the forms has also been recorded on IBM cards and computer tape.)

Survey of Race Relations Papers (SRR), Archives of the Hoover Institution, Stanford University.

"Biography of a Seattle High School Boy." Major document 151.

E. K. "Japanese-American Intermarriage." Minor document 420.

E. S. S. "Interview with Mrs. H———." Major document 235.

Furuya, Mrs. M., interview, Seattle, July 3, 1924. Major document 196.

Holt, Catherine. "Interview with Dr. F. T. Nakaya, Japanese Physician." Los Angeles, September 21, 28, 1924. Major document 156.

Holt, Catherine. "Interviews regarding Mildred Yoshikawa*, Mixed Japanese-American high school girl . . . Los Angeles, California." Minor document 446.

Holt, Chloe. "Account of a Visit with a White Woman Married to a Japanese." Los Angeles, August 14, 1924. Major document 104.

Inouye, Kyo, interviewed by Catherine Holt, Los Angeles, January 16, 1925. Major document 236.

"Japanese Matron Prefers America." *San Francisco Chronicle.* Minor document 251.

"A Japanese Physician's Wife." Interview of Mrs. Suie Murakami, Mrs. Tanishiro, interpreter, Seattle, June 4, 1924. Major document 46.

Kuno, Emma Fong. "My Oriental Husbands." Major document 53.

Lentz, K. "Intermarriage. A Case Study." Major document 173.

Machida, Mrs. C. S., interviewed by Chloe Holt, Los Angeles, July 2, 1924. Major document 251-A.

Machida, Mrs. C. S., interviewed by William C. Smith, Los Angeles, August 13, 1924. Major document 73.

Minami, S., letter, June 11, 1924, Seattle. Minor document 152.

Morimoto, Takiji. "The Oriental Pioneer." Major document 336.

"Progeny of Jap-White Union Amaze." *San Francisco Examiner,* November 11, 1922. Major document 222.

Schroeder, H. G. "Case Brief on Anglo-Japanese Marriage." Major document 62.

Smith, William C. "Adjutant M. Kobayashi on the Second Generation." Major document 236.

Smith, William C. "Interview with Susie Yamamoto." August 9, 1924. Major document 77.

Smith, William C. "Life History of Peter." Major document 251-A.

Swanson, A. W., interviewed by William C. Smith, El Centro, Calif., n.d. Minor document 333.

Torikai, T., interview, Seattle, July 8, 1924. Major document 156.

Toyama, Chotoku. "The Life History as a Social Document." May 27, 1924. Major document 312.

Western Defense Command Records (WDC), U.S. National Archives and Records Center, Washington, D.C., Military Archives Division, Modern Military Branch, Record Group 338, File Number 291.1, "Mixed Marriage File."

Interviews Cited (asterisks denote pseudonyms)

Embrey, Sue Kunitomi, interviewed by Arthur A. Hansen, David A. Hacker, and D. J. Bertagnoli, October 24, 1973. California State University, Fullerton, Oral History Office, Tape OH1366.

Fujino, Laura*, interviewed by the author, Los Angeles, December 17, 1979.

Grogan, Jean*, interviewed by the author, Boston, March 4, 1974.

Hirano, Debbie*, interviewed by the author, Berkeley, February 15, 1980.

"Japanese Americans in California." Bancroft Library, Berkeley, Phonotape 717A.

Kawakami, Clarke, and Yuri Morris, interviewed by Joe Grant Masaoka and Lillian Takeshita, May 22, 1968. Bancroft Library, Berkeley, Phonotape 1050B:10.

Kido, Saburo, interviewed by Joe Grant Masaoka and Robert A. Wilson, Los Angeles, January 4, 1967. Bancroft Library, Berkeley, Phonotape 1050:2.

Kitano, Harry, interviewed by the author, Los Angeles, December 21, 1979.

Kurushima, Tad*, interviewed by the author, Seattle, August 1972.

Ohashi, Judy*, interviewed by the author, San Francisco, May 22, 1980.

Sakata, Yasuo, interviewed by the author, Los Angeles, December 21, 1979.

Tanaka, Togo, interviewed by Betty Mitson and David Hacker, May 19, 1973. California State University, Fullerton, Oral History Office, Tape OH1271a.

Yoneda, Elaine Black, interviewed by Betty Mitson, San Francisco, March 3, 1974. California State University, Fullerton, Oral History Office, Tape OH1377a.

Charles Kikuchi's interviews (CKI) conducted in Chicago in 1943–1945, in JERS, Cases R and S:

Ando, Harry*, CKI-31.
Asahi, Gordon*, CKI-58.
Furuta, Isamu*, CKI-62.
Hattori, Shizuko*, CKI-26.
Hayashi, Rose*, CKI-24.
Hayashi, Yasuko*, CKI-9.
Ihara, Allen*, CKI-34.
Ihara, Doris*, CKI-39.
Ihara, Tamie*, CKI-4.
Ishimoto, Jiro*, CKI-5.
Kaminaka, Sus*, CKI-45.
Katayama, Bill*, CKI-13.
Kimura, Lester*, CKI-47.
Minami, Hiromasa*, CKI-21.
Najima, Tadashi "Blackie"*, CKI-32.
Nishi, Hazel*, CKI-3.
Nishimoto, Frances*, CKI-22.

Nishimoto, Kazuo*, CKI-7.
Ono, Chiyoko*, CKI-12.
Oyama, Juni*, CKI-2.
Sakamoto, Kyohei*, CKI-10.
Shigaki, Ida*, CKI-56.
Shimizu, Barry*, CKI-46.
Shinosaki, Motoku*, CKI-49.
Suzuki, Margaret*, CKI-8.
Tanaka, Fusako*, CKI-40.
Tashiro, Masako Ihara*, CKI-25.
Yasuda, Kisako*, CKI-51.

Other Sources

Adams, Romanzo C. *Interracial Marriage in Hawaii*. Montclair, N.J., 1969.
Adams, Romanzo C. *The Japanese in Hawaii*. New York, 1924.
Ai. "On Being ½ Japanese, ⅛ Choctaw, ¼ Black, and ¹⁄₁₆ Irish," *Ms.*, May 1978, 58.
"Are Japanese People?" *Literary Digest*, April 26, 1924, 22–23.
Asian American Women. Stanford, 1976.
Asian Women. Berkeley, 1971.
"Autobiography of a Sansei Female." In Tachiki, *Roots*, 112–13.
Babcock, Charlotte G., and William Caudill. "Personal and Cultural Factors in Treating a Nisei Man." In Seward, *Clinical Studies in Cultural Conflict*, 409–48.
Barnett, L. D. "Interracial Marriage in California." *Marriage and Family Living*, 25 (1963), 424–27.
Barrows, Margie. "Plantation Hegemony in Hawaii, 1890–1920." Paper presented at the meeting of the Association for Asian/Pacific American Studies, Seattle, November 7, 1980.
Befu, Harumi. "The Group Model of Japanese Society: A Critique." Paper presented at the Center for Japanese and Korean Studies, University of California, Berkeley, November 19, 1980.
Befu, Harumi. *Japan: An Anthropological Introduction*. San Francisco, 1971.
Berger, Michael. "A Once-Taboo Story for Japanese TV." *San Francisco Examiner and Chronicle*, February 25, 1979.
Bloom, Leonard, et al. *Marriages of Japanese-Americans in Los Angeles: A Statistical Study*. Berkeley, 1945.
Boddy, Manchester. *Japanese in America*. Los Angeles, 1921.
Bosworth, Allan R. *America's Concentration Camps*. New York, 1967.
Broom, Leonard, and John I. Kitsuse. *The Managed Casualty*. Berkeley, 1956.
Burrows, Edwin C. *Chinese and Japanese in Hawaii during the Sino-Japanese Conflict*. Honolulu, 1939.
Burrows, Edwin C. *Hawaiian Americans: An Account of the Mixing of Japanese, Chinese, Polynesian, and American Cultures*. New Haven, 1937.
Catapusan, Benicio T. "Filipino Intermarriage Problems in the United States." *SSR*, 22 (1938), 265–72.

Chambers, John S. "The Japanese Invasion." *Annals of the American Academy of Political and Social Science*, 93 (1921), 23–29.

Cheng, C. K., and Douglas S. Yamamura. "Interracial Marriage and Divorce in Hawaii." *Social Forces*, 36 (1957), 77–84.

Chin, Art. *Up Hill: The Settlement and Diffusion of the Chinese in Seattle, Washington*. Seattle, 1970.

Chin, Frank. "Confessions of a Number One Son," *Ramparts*, 11 (March 1973), 41–48.

Chin, Frank, et al. *Aiiieeeee! An Anthology of Asian American Writers*. Washington, D.C., 1975.

Choy, Christine. "Images of Asian-Americans in Films and Television." In Miller, *Ethnic Images*, 145–55.

Connor, John W. *Acculturation and Retention of an Ethnic Identity in Three Generations of Japanese Americans*. San Francisco, 1977.

Connor, John W. *Tradition and Change in Three Generations of Japanese Americans*. Chicago, 1977.

Coolidge, Mary Roberts. *Chinese Immigration*. Taipei, 1968; orig. 1909.

Daniels, Roger. *Concentration Camps USA*. New York, 1971.

Daniels, Roger. *The Politics of Prejudice*. New York, 1968; orig. Berkeley, 1962.

deMille, Agnes. *Where the Wings Grow*. Garden City, N.Y., 1978.

DeMotte, Marshall. "California, White or Yellow?" *Annals of the American Academy of Political and Social Science*, 93 (1921), 18–23.

DeVos, George, and Hiroshi Wagatsuma. *Japan's Invisible Race*. Berkeley, 1972.

DeVos, George A., and William O. Wetherall. *Japan's Minorities*. London, 1974.

Dickie-Carr, H. F. *The Marginal Situation*. London, 1966.

Dorland, Chester P. "The Chinese Massacre at Los Angeles in 1871." *Historical Society of California Annual Publications*, 3, no. 2, 22–26.

Drachsler, Julius. *Intermarriage in New York City*. New York, 1921.

Drinnon, Richard. *Keeper of Concentration Camps*. Berkeley, 1987.

Dulles, Foster Rhea. *Eastward Ho!* London, 1931.

Embree, John F. *Acculturation among the Japanese of Kona, Hawaii*. Menosha, Wis., 1941.

Endo, Russell, and Dale Hiraoka. "Japanese American Intermarriage." *Free Inquiry in Creative Sociology*, 11 (1983), 159–62.

Eskelund, Karl. *My Chinese Wife*. London, 1946.

Fuchs, Lawrence H. *Hawaii Pono: A Social History*. New York, 1961.

Fukutake, Tadashi. *Japanese Rural Society*. Trans. R. P. Dore. Ithaca, N.Y., 1972; orig. New York, 1967.

Gee, Emma, ed. *Counterpoint*. Los Angeles, 1976.

Gehrie, Mark J. "Sansei: Ethnography of Experience." Ph.D. dissertation, Northwestern University, 1973.

Girdner, Audrie, and Anne Loftis. *The Great Betrayal*. New York, 1969.

Glick, Clarence E. "Interracial Marriage and Admixture in Hawaii." *Social Biology*, 17 (1970), 278–81.

Gluck, Eleanor W. "An Ecological Study of the Japanese in New York City." M.A. thesis, Columbia University, 1940.

Gordon, Milton. *Assimilation in American Life*. New York, 1964.

Graalfs, Marilyn. "A Sociometric Study of Chinese Students in a Polyethnic High School." M.A. thesis, University of Washington, 1949.

Grant, Madison. *The Passing of the Great Race*. New York, 1922.

Grodzins, Morton. *Americans Betrayed*. Chicago, 1949.

Gulick, Sidney E. *The American Japanese Problem*. New York, 1914.

Gulick, Sidney E. *Mixing the Races in Hawaii*. Honolulu, 1937.

Hall, Christine C. I. "The Ethnic Identity of Racially Mixed People: A Study of Black-Japanese." Ph.D. dissertation, UCLA, 1980.

Hama, Larry. "I Am Yellow . . . Curious?" *Bridge*, 2 (April 1973), 21–22.

Harada, Tasuku. *The Social Status of the Japanese in Hawaii*. Honolulu, 1927.

Hata, Donald T. "'Undesirables': Unsavory Elements among the Japanese in America prior to 1893 and Their Influence on the First Anti-Japanese Movement in California." Ph.D. dissertation, University of Southern California, 1970.

Hawaii Department of Health. *Annual Reports*. Honolulu, 1959–78.

Hayashida, Cullen Tadao. "Identity, Race, and the Blood Ideology of Japan." Ph.D. dissertation, University of Washington, 1974.

Hertzler, Virginia B. "A Sociometric Study of Japanese Students in a Polyethnic High School." M.A. thesis, University of Washington, 1949.

Higham, John. *Strangers in the Land*. New York, 1975.

Hirabayashi, Gordon K. "A Sociometric Study of the University of Washington Students of Japanese Ancestry." M.A. thesis, University of Washington, 1949.

Hirabayashi, James. "Nisei: The Quiet American?—A Re-Evaluation." *Amerasia Journal*, 3 (1975), 114–29.

Holliday, Margaret. "Social Relations between the Japanese and the Californians." M.A. thesis, Columbia University, 1921.

Hori, Joan. "Japanese Prostitution in Hawaii during the Immigration Period." In Nobuya Tsuchida, ed., *Asian and Pacific American Experiences: Women's Perspectives*, 56–65. Minneapolis, 1982.

Hormann, Bernhard L. "Hawaii's Mixing People." In Noel P. Gist and Anthony Gary Dworkin, eds., *The Blending of Races*, 213–33. New Yori, 1972.

Hormann, Bernhard L. "A Note on Hawaii's Minorities within Minorities." *SPH*, 18 (1954), 47–56.

Hormann, Bernhard L. "Racial Complexion of Hawaii's Future Population." *Social Forces*, 27 (1948), 68–72.

Hosokawa, Bill. *JACL: In Quest of Justice*. New York, 1982.

Hosokawa, Bill. *Nisei: The Quiet Americans*. New York, 1969.

Hosokawa, Fumiko. *The Sansei: Social Interaction and Ethnic Identification among the Third-Generation Japanese*. Saratoga, Calif., 1978.

Houston, Jeanne Wakatsuki, and James D. Houston. *Farewell to Manzanar*. Boston, 1973.

Ichihashi, Yamato. *Japanese Immigration*. San Francisco, 1915.

Ichihashi, Yamato. *Japanese in the United States*. New York, 1969; orig. 1921.

Ichioka, Yuji. "Ameyuki-san: Japanese Prostitutes in Nineteenth-Century America." *Amerasia Journal*, 4 (1977), 1–21.

Inada, Lawson. "Asian Brother, Asian Sister." In Tachiki, *Roots*, 121–27.

Inamine, Otome. "The Effect of War on Inter-Racial Marriage in Hawaii." *SPH*, 9–10 (1945), 103–9.

"Interracial Issues among Asian Americans." Panel presented to the Association for Asian/Pacific American Studies, Seattle, November 7, 1980.

Irons, Peter. *Justice at War*. New York, 1984.

Ishikawa, Michiji. "A Study of Intermarried Japanese Families in USA." *Cultural Nippon*, 3 (1938), 457–87.

Israely, Hilla K. "An Exploration into Ethnic Identity: The Case of Third-Generation Japanese Americans." Ph.D. dissertation, UCLA, 1976.

Ito, Kazuo. *Issei*. Seattle, 1973.

Iyenaga, Toyokichi, and Kenosuke Sato. *Japan and the California Problem*. New York, 1924.

James, Thomas. *Exile Within*. Cambridge, 1987.

Kaihatsu, Jane B. "Asian Americans and Outmarriage." *Pacific Citizen*, December 20–27, 1985, A-8.

Kantorowicz, Barbara. "The Ultimate Assimilation." *Newsweek*, November 24, 1986, 80.

Kanzaki, Kiichi. *California and the Japanese*. San Francisco, 1921.

Karlin, Jules A. "The Anti-Chinese Outbreaks in Seattle, 1885–1886." *Pacific Northwest Quarterly*, 39 (1948), 103–30.

Kashima, Tetsuden. "Japanese American Internees Return, 1945 to 1955." *Phylon*, 41 (1980), 107–15.

Kawakami, K. K. *Asia at the Door*. New York, 1914.

Kawakami, K. K. *Japan in World Politics*. New York, 1917.

Kawakami, K. K. *Jokichi Takamine*. New York, 1928.

Kawasaki, Ichiro. *Japan Unmasked*. Rutland, Vt., 1969.

Kelley, Jullie P. "A Study of Eyefold Inheritance in Inter-Racial Marriages." M.S. thesis, University of Hawaii, 1960.

Kich, George Kitahara. "Eurasians: Ethnic/Racial Identity Development of Biracial Japanese/White Adults." Ph.D. dissertation, Wright Institute, 1982.

Kiefer, Christie W. *Changing Cultures, Changing Lives*. San Francisco, 1974.

Kikumura, Akemi, and Harry H. L. Kitano. "Interracial Marriage: A Picture of the Japanese Americans." *Journal of Social Issues*, 29 (1973), 67–82.

Kitagawa, Daisuke. *Issei and Nisei*. New York, 1967.

Kitano, Harry H. L. *Japanese Americans*. 2nd ed. Englewood Cliffs, N.J., 1976.

Kitano, Harry H. L., and Akemi Kikumura. "The Japanese American Family." In Charles Mindel and Robert Habenstein, eds., *Ethnic Families in America*, 41–60. New York, 1976.

Kitano, Harry H. L., et al. "Asian-American Interracial Marriage." *JMF*, 46 (1984), 179–90.

Kong, Hester. "Through the Peepsight of a Grocery Store." *SPH*, 9–10 (1945), 11–16.

Kosaki, Mildred Doi. "The Culture Conflicts and Guidance Needs of Nisei Adolescents." M.A. thesis, University of Hawaii, 1949.

La Brack, Bruce, and Karen Leonard. "Conflict and Compatibility in Punjabi-

Mexican Immigrant Families in Rural California, 1915–1965." *JMF*, 46 (1984), 527–37.

LaViolette, Forrest E. *Americans of Japanese Ancestry.* Toronto, 1946.

Leighton, Alexander H. *The Governing of Men.* Princeton, 1968; orig. 1945.

Leonetti, Donna L., and Laura Newell-Morris. "Exogamy and Change in the Biosocial Structure of a Modern Urban Population." *American Anthropologist*, 84 (1982), 19–36.

Levine, Gene N., and Colbert Rhodes. *The Japanese American Community.* New York, 1981.

Lind, Andrew W. "Attitudes toward Interracial Marriage in Kona, Hawaii." *SPH*, 4 (1938), 79–83.

Lind, Andrew W. *Hawaii's Japanese.* Princeton, 1946.

Lind, Andrew W. "Interracial Marriage and Divorce in Hawaii." *Social Forces*, 49 (1964), 17–26.

Lind, Andrew W. "Interracial Marriage as Affecting Divorce in Hawaii." *SSR*, 49 (1964), 17–26.

Loewen, James W. *The Mississippi Chinese.* Cambridge, 1971.

Louie, Elaine. "The Myth of the Erotic Exotic." *Bridge*, 2 (April 1973), 19–20.

Lovely, Napoleon W. *Conversations on Success in Marriage.* Boston, 1948.

Low, Ron. "A Brief Biographical Sketch of a Newly-Found Asian Male." In Tachiki, *Roots*, 105–8.

Lowe, Felicia, et al. "The Portrayal of Chinese in the Media." Paper presented to the National Conference on Chinese American Studies, San Francisco, October 10, 1980.

Lundberg, George A., and Lenore Dickson. "Selective Association among Ethnic Groups in a High School Population." *ASR*, 17 (1952), 23–35.

Lyman, Stanford M. "Generation and Character: The Case of the Japanese Americans." In Lyman, *The Asian in the West*, 81–97. Reno, 1970.

Lynch, Robert Newton. "The Development of the Anti-Japanese Movement." *Annals of the American Academy of Political and Social Science*, 93 (1921), 47–52.

McClatchy, V. S. "Japanese in the Melting Pot: Can They Assimilate and Make Good Citizens?" *Annals of the American Academy of Political and Social Science*, 93 (1921), 28–34.

McKee, Ruth. *Wartime Exile.* Washington, 1946.

Madden, Maude. *When the East Is in the West.* New York, 1923.

Makabe, Tomoko. "Nisei Ethnic Identity." *Rikka*, 3 (1976), 18–22.

Mar, Norman. "This Silver Bullet Will Tell You Who I Am." Student paper, University of Washington, 1971.

Mar, Norman. "Yellow TV Caricatures Become Real." *University of Washington Daily*, Spring 1971.

Masaoka, Jan. "I Forgot My Eyes Were Black." In *Asian Women*, 57–59.

Masuoka, Jitsuichi. "Japanese Patriarch in Hawaii." *Social Forces*, 17 (1938), 240–48.

Masuoka, Jitsuichi. "Race Attitudes of the Japanese Population in Hawaii." M.A. thesis, University of Hawaii, 1931.

Masuoka, Jitsuichi. "Race Preference in Hawaii." *AJS*, 41 (1936), 635–41.

Matsukawa, Lori. "Miss Teenage America 1974." In *Asian American Women*, 37–38.

Matsumoto, Gary M., et al. "Ethnic Identity: Honolulu and Seattle Japanese-Americans." In Sue and Wagner, *Asian-Americans*, 65–74.

Matsunaga, Setsuko. "The Adjustment of Evacuees in St. Louis." M.A. thesis, Washington University, 1944.

Maykovich, Minako. *Japanese American Identity Dilemma*. Tokyo, 1972.

Mears, Elliot G. *Resident Orientals on the American Pacific Coast*. New York, 1927.

Meneely, Alexander. "The Anti-Chinese Movement in the Northwest." M.A. thesis, University of Washington, 1922.

Miller, Randall M. *Ethnic Images in American Film and Television*. Philadelphia, 1978.

Miller, Randall M. *The Kaleidoscopic Lens*. Englewood Cliffs, N.J., 1980.

Millis, H. A. *The Japanese Problem in the United States*. New York, 1915.

Miyamoto, Joanne. "What Are You?" In *Asian Women*, 50–51.

Modell, John. *The Economics and Politics of Racial Accommodation*. Urbana, Ill., 1977.

Modell, John, ed. *The Kikuchi Diary*. Urbana, Ill., 1973.

Monahan, Thomas P. "Interracial Marriage and Divorce in the State of Hawaii." *Eugenics Quarterly*, 13, 40–47.

Montero, Darrel M. "The Japanese American Community: Generational Changes in Ethnic Affiliation." Ph.D. dissertation, UCLA, 1975.

Montero, Darrel M., and Gene N. Levine. "Third-Generation Japanese Americans." Unpublished paper, 1974, courtesy of the authors.

Montero, Darrel, and Ronald Tsukashima. "Assimilation and Educational Achievement: The Case of the Second-Generation Japanese Americans." *Sociological Quarterly*, 18 (1977), 490–503.

Mori, Toshio. *Yokohama, California*. Caldwell, Idaho, 1949.

Morikawa, Herbert. "Psychological Implications of Asian Stereotypes in the Media." In Miller, *Ethnic Images*, 161–65.

Morimoto, Mary. "To Be Young, Gifted, and an Asian American Woman." In *Asian American Women*, 39–42.

Moritsugu, John; Lynn Forester; and James Morishima. "Eurasians: A Pilot Study." Paper presented to Western Psychological Association, San Francisco, 1978.

Morizawa, Grace. "Tomas, Where Are You?" In *Asian American Women*, 34.

Nagoshi, Kunio, and Charles Nishimura. "Some Observations Regarding Haole-Japanese Marriages in Hawaii." *SPH*, 18 (1954), 57–65.

Nakane, Chie. *Japanese Society*. Berkeley, 1970.

New World Sun Daily. *Memorial Book of Japanese Families in the USA*. San Francisco, 1939.

Niisato, Kanichi. *Nisei Tragedy*. Tokyo, 1936.

O'Brien, David J., and Stephen S. Fugita. "Generational Differences in Japanese Americans' Perceptions and Feelings about Social Relationships between Themselves and Caucasian Americans." Unpublished manuscript, courtesy of the authors.

O'Brien, Robert. *The College Nisei*. New York, 1978; orig. Palo Alto, Calif., 1949.

Oehling, Richard A. "The Yellow Menace: Asian Images in American Film." In Miller, *Kaleidoscopic Lens*, 182–206.

Ogawa, Dennis. *From Japs to Japanese*. Berkeley, 1971.

Okada, John. *No-No Boy*. Rutland, Vt., 1957.

Okano, Yukio. "Correlates of Ethnic Identity in Japanese Americans." M.A. thesis, University of Denver, 1970.

Okubo, Mine. *Citizen 13660*. New York, 1966; orig. 1946.

Olinger, L. B., and V. S. Sommers. "The Divided Path: 'Psycho-cultural' Neurosis in a Nisei Man." In Seward, *Clinical Studies in Culture Conflict*, 359–408.

Opler, Marvin K. "Cultural Dilemma of a Kibei Youth." Ibid., 297–316.

Osumi, Megumi Dick. "Asians and California's Anti-Miscegenation Laws." In Tsuchida, *Asian and Pacific Americans*, 1–37.

Ozaki, Shigeo. "Student Attitudes on Interracial Marriage." *SPH*, 6 (1940), 23–28.

Paik, Irvin. "Kung Fu Fan Klub." In Gee, *Counterpoint*, 289–94.

Paik, Irvin. "That Oriental Feeling." In Tachiki, *Roots*, 30–36.

Panunzio, Constantine. "Intermarriage in Los Angeles, 1924–1933." *AJS*, 47 (1942), 690–701.

Park, Robert E. "Human Migration and the Marginal Man." *AJS*, 33 (1928), 881–93.

Parkman, Margaret A., and Jack Sawyer. "Dimensions of Ethnic Intermarriage in Hawaii." *ASR*, 32, (1967), 593–607.

Petersen, William. *Japanese Americans*. New York, 1971.

Phelan, James D. "Why California Objects to the Japanese Invasion." *Annals of the American Academy of Political and Social Science*, 93 (1921), 16–17.

Porteus, S. D., et al. "Race and Social Differences in Performance Tests." *Genetic Psychology Monographs* (1930).

Reichel, Jessie. "A Sociometric Study of Jewish Students in a Polyethnic High School." M.A. thesis, University of Washington, 1949.

Ross, Robert H. "Social Distance as It Exists between the First- and Second-Generation Japanese in the City of Los Angeles and Vicinity." M.A. thesis, University of Southern California, 1939.

Ross, Robert H., and Emory S. Bogardus. "Four Types of Nisei Marriage Patterns." *SSR*, 25 (1940), 63–66.

Ross, Robert H., and Emory S. Bogardus. "The Second-Generation Race Relations Cycle." *SSR*, 24 (1940), 357–63.

Sakai, Andrea. "Reflections: An Autobiographical Sketch." *SPH*, 22 (1958), 36–44.

Samuels, Frederick. "Colour Sensitivity among Honolulu's Haoles and Japanese." *Race*, 11 (1969), 203–12.

Samuels, Frederick. *The Japanese and the Haoles of Honolulu*. New Haven, 1970.

Sandmeyer, Elmer C. *The Anti-Chinese Movement in California*. Urbana, Ill., 1973; orig. 1939.

Sargent, A. A. "The Wyoming Anti-Chinese Riot." *Overland Monthly*, 2nd ser., 6 (November 1885), 507–12.

Sasamori, Junzo. "Social Life of Japanese in America." Unpublished manuscript, 1927.

Schmid, Calvin F., and Charles E. Nobbe. "Socioeconomic Differentials among Nonwhite Races." *ASR*, 30 (1965), 909–22.

Schmitt, Robert C. "Demographic Correlates of Interracial Marriage in Hawaii." *Demography*, 2 (1965), 463–73.

Schmitt, Robert C. "Interracial Marriage and Occupational Status in Hawaii." *ASR*, 28 (1963), 809–10.

Schmitt, Robert C. "Recent Trends in Hawaiian Interracial Marriage Rates by Occupation." *JMF*, 33 (1971), 373–74.

Schmitt, Robert C. "Social and Economic Characteristics of Interracial Households in Honolulu." *Social Problems*, 10 (1963), 264–68.

Seward, Georgene, ed. *Clinical Studies in Culture Conflict*. New York, 1951.

Sissons, D. C. S. "Karayuki-san: Japanese Prostitutes in Australia, 1887–1916." *Historical Studies* (Melbourne), 17 (1977), 323–41.

Smith, M. E. "A Study of the Causes of Feelings of Inferiority." *Journal of Psychology*, 5 (1938), 315–32.

Smith, William C. *Americans in Process*. Ann Arbor, 1936.

Smith, William C. "Changing Personality Traits of Second-Generation Orientals in America." *AJS*, 33 (1928), 922–29.

Smith, William C. *The Second-Generation Oriental in America*. Honolulu, 1927.

Sone, Monica. *Nisei Daughter*. Boston, 1953.

Soyeda, Juichi, and T. Kamiya. *A Survey of the Japanese Question in California*. San Francisco, 1913.

Spicer, Edward H., et al. *Impounded People*. Tucson, 1969.

Spickard, Paul R. "Injustice Compounded: Amerasians and Non-Japanese in America's World War II Concentration Camps." *Journal of American Ethnic History*, 5 (1986), 5–22.

Spickard, Paul R. "Mixed Marriage: Two American Minority Groups and the Limits of Ethnic Identity." Ph.D. dissertation, University of California, Berkeley, 1983.

Spickard, Paul R. "The Nisei Assume Power: The Japanese American Citizens League, 1941–1942." *Pacific Historical Review*, 52 (1983), 147–74.

Steiner, Jesse F. *The Japanese Invasion*. Chicago, 1917.

Stoddard, Lothrop. *The Rising Tide of Color*. New York, 1920.

Stonequist, Everett V. *The Marginal Man*. New York, 1965; orig. 1937.

Strong, Edward K. *Japanese in California: Based on a Ten Per Cent Survey.* . . . Stanford University Publications in Education and Psychology, vol. 1, no. 2. 1933.

Strong, Edward K., *Second-Generation Japanese Problem*. Stanford, 1934.

Sue, Stanley, and Nathaniel Wagner, eds. *Asian-Americans: Psychological Perspectives*. Ben Lomond, Calif., 1973.

Suzuki, Bob. "Education and Socialization of Asian Americans: A Revisionist Analysis of the 'Model-Minority' Thesis." *Amerasia Journal*, 4 (1977), 23–52.

Svensrud, Marion. "Some Factors Concerning the Assimilation of a Selected Japanese Community." M.A. thesis, University of Southern California, 1931.

Tachiki, Amy, et al. *Roots: An Asian American Reader*. Los Angeles, 1971.

Taeuber, Irene B. "Hawaii." *Population Index*, 28 (1962), 97–125.

Tamagawa, Kathleen. *Holy Prayers in a Horse's Ear*. New York, 1932.

Tanaka, Ron. "I hate my wife for her flat yellow face." In Tachiki, *Roots*, 46–47.

Tanaka, Tomi. "From a lotus blossom cunt." Ibid., 109.

Tateishi, John. *And Justice for All*. New York, 1984.

ten Broek, Jacobus, et al. *Prejudice, War, and the Constitution*. Berkeley, 1968; orig. 1954.

Thomas, Dorothy S. "Some Social Aspects of Japanese-American Demography." *Proceedings of the American Philosophical Society*, 94 (1950).

Thomas, Dorothy S., and Richard Nishimoto. *The Spoilage*. Berkeley, 1969; orig. 1946.

Thomas, Dorothy S., et al. *The Salvage*. Berkeley, 1952.

Tigner, James L. "Ryukyuans in Peru, 1905–52." *Americas*, 35 (July, 1978), 20–44.

Tinker, John N. "Intermarriage and Ethnic Boundaries: The Japanese American Case." *Journal of Social Issues*, 29 (1973), 49–66.

Toyama, Chotoku. "The Japanese Community in Los Angeles." M.A. thesis, Columbia University, 1926.

Toyama, Henry, and Kiyoshi Ikeda. "The Okinawan-Naichi Relationship." *SPH*, 14 (1950), 51–65.

Tsuchida, Nobuya, ed. *Asian and Pacific Americans: Women's Perspectives*. Minneapolis, 1982.

U.S. Bureau of the Census. *1940 Census. Population. Characteristics of the Nonwhite Population by Race*. Washington, D.C., 1943.

U.S. Bureau of the Census. *1960 Census: Nonwhite Population by Race*. Subject Report PC(2)-1C. Washington, D.C., 1963.

U.S. Bureau of the Census. *1970 Census: Japanese, Chinese, and Filipinos in the United States*. Subject Report PC(2)-1G. Washington, D.C., 1973.

U.S. Bureau of the Census. *1980 Census: Marital Characteristics*. Subject Report PC80-2-4C. Washington, D.C., 1985.

U.S. Department of the Army. Western Defense Command and Fourth Army. *Final Report: Japanese Evacuation from the West Coast, 1942*. Washington, D.C., 1943.

U.S. War Relocation Authority. *War Relocation Authority: A Story of Human Conservation*. Washington, D.C., 1946.

Uyesugi, Ruth Farlow. *Don't Cry, Chiisai, Don't Cry*. Paoli, Ind., 1977.

Wagatsuma, Hiroshi. "The Social Perception of Skin Color in Japan." In John H. Franklin, ed., *Color and Race*, 129–65. Boston, 1968.

Wagatsuma, Hiroshi. "Some Problems of Interracial Marriage for the Japanese." In Irving R. Stuart and Lawrence E. Abt, eds., *Interracial Marriage*, 247–64. New York, 1967.

Weglyn, Michi. *Years of Infamy*. New York, 1976.

Weiss, Melford S. "Modern Perspectives and Traditional Ceremony: A Chinese-American Beauty Pageant." In Sue and Wagner, *Asian-Americans*, 75–78.

Weiss, Melford S. "Selective Acculturation and the Dating Process: The Pattern of Chinese-Caucasian Inter-racial Dating." Ibid., 86–94.

Wessell, Bessie Bloom. *An Ethnic Survey of Woonsocket, Rhode Island*. New York, 1970; orig. Chicago, 1931.

"White Male Qualities." In Tachiki, *Roots*, 44–45.

Wilson, Robert A., and Bill Hosokawa. *East to America*. New York, 1980.

Wong, Eugene Franklin. "On Visual Media Racism: Asians in the American Motion Pictures." Ph.D. dissertation, University of Denver, 1977.

Wong, Leatrice, and Marian Wong. "Attitudes toward Intermarriage." *SPH*, 1 (1935), 14–17.

Woo, Margaret. "Woman + Man = Political Unity." In *Asian Women*, 115–16.

Woodrum, Eric. "An Assessment of Japanese American Assimilation, Pluralism, and Subordination." *AJS*, 87 (1981), 157–69.

Yamamoto, George K. "Interracial Marriage in Hawaii." In Irving R. Stuart and Lawrence E. Abt, eds., *Interracial Marriage*. New York, 1967.

Yamamoto, George K. "Social Adjustment of Caucasian-Japanese Marriages in Hawaii." M.A. thesis, University of Hawaii, 1949.

Yamamoto, George K. "Some Patterns of Mate Selection among Naichi and Okinawans on Oahu." *SPH*, 21 (1957), 42–49.

Yamamoto, Tamiko T. "Trends in Marriage Practices among the Nisei in Hawaii." University of Hawaii, Adams Social Research Laboratory Report 21, 1950.

Yamamura, Douglas S. "Interracial Marriage and Divorce in Hawaii." *Social Forces*, 36 (1957), 77–84.

Yamamura, Douglas S., and Janet H. Higa. "Dating Preferences of University of Hawaii Students." *SPH*, 20 (1956), 4–15.

Yamamura, Douglas S., and Raymond E. Sakamoto. "Inter-Ethnic Friendship and Dating Patterns." *SPH*, 19 (1955), 35–44.

Yanagisako, Sylvia J. "Social and Cultural Change in Japanese American Kinship." Ph.D. dissertation, University of Washington, 1975.

Part II. Madam Butterfly Revisited

Berrigan, Darrell. "Japan's Occupation Babies." *Saturday Evening Post*, June 19, 1948, 24–25ff.

Bowles, Gilbert, comp. *Japanese Law of Nationality*. Tokyo 1915.

Buck, Pearl S. *The Hidden Flower*. New York, 1952.

Buttny, Richard. "Legitimation Techniques for Intermarriage: Accounts of Motives for Intermarriage." *Communication Quarterly*, 35 (1987), 125–43.

Carter, Isobel Ray. *Alien Blossom: A Japanese-Australian Love Story*. Melbourne, 1965.

Connor, John W. "American-Japanese Marriages—How Stable Are They?" *Pacific Historian*, 13 (Winter 1969), 25–36.

Connor, John W. *A Study of the Marital Stability of Japanese War Brides*. San Francisco, 1976.

"Court Rejects Japan Nationality for Children of U.S. Fathers." *Japan Times Weekly*, April 4, 1981.

DeVos, George A., et al. *Personality Patterns and Problems of Adjustment in American-Japanese Intercultural Marriages*. Taipei, 1973.

Erikson, Erik. *Identity: Youth and Crisis*. New York, 1968.

Falk, Ray. "GI Brides Go to School in Japan." *New York Times Magazine*, November 7, 1954, 54–56.

"For Love or Money: Vietnamese-American Marriage." *Newsweek*, September 7, 1970.

Glenn, Evelyn Nakano. *Issei, Nisei, War Bride: Three Generations of Japanese American Women in Domestic Service.* Philadelphia, 1986.

Grogan, Jean*, interviewed by the author, Boston, March 4, 1974.

Hall, Christine C. I. "The Ethnic Identity of Racially Mixed People: A Study of Black-Japanese." Ph.D. dissertation, UCLA, 1980.

Hemphill, Elizabeth Anne. *The Least of These.* New York, 1980.

Hilgard, Ernest R. "The Enigma of Japanese Friendliness." *Public Opinion Quarterly,* 10 (1946), 343–48.

Houston, Velina Hasu. "On Being Mixed Japanese in Modern Times." *Pacific Citizen,* December 20–27, 1985.

Iddittie, Junesay. *When Two Cultures Meet.* Tokyo, 1960.

Iglehart, Charles W. "The Problem of G.I. Children in Japan." *Japan Christian Quarterly* (1952), 300–305.

Joiner, Jill*, interviewed by the author, St. Paul, September 25, 1981.

Japan. Ministry of Foreign Affairs. Division of Special Records. *Documents Concerning the Allied Occupation and Control of Japan.* Vol. 6. *On Aliens.* Tokyo, 1951.

Kalischer, Peter. "Madam Butterfly's Children." *Collier's,* September 20, 1952, 15–18.

Kawai, Kazuo. *Japan's American Interlude.* Chicago, 1960.

Kerr, Mrs. William C. "On the Frontier of International Understanding." *Japan Christian Quarterly,* 17 (Summer 1951), 48–49.

Kich, George Kitahara. "Eurasians: Ethnic/Racial Identity Development of Biracial Japanese/White Adults." Ph.D. dissertation, Wright Institute, 1982.

Kim, Bok-Lim C. "Asian Wives of U.S. Servicemen: Women in Shadows." *Amerasia Journal,* 4 (1977), 91–115.

Kim, Bok-Lim C. "Casework with Japanese and Korean Wives of Americans." *Social Casework,* 53 (1972), 273–79.

Kimura, Yukiko. "War Brides in Hawaii and Their In-Laws." *AJS,* 63 (1957), 70–76.

LeMoyne, James. "Coming 'Home'—At Last." *Newsweek,* October 4, 1982, 78.

McEvoy, J. P. "America through the Eyes of a Japanese War-Bride." *Reader's Digest,* 66 (April 1955), 95–99.

Michener, James A. "Pursuit of Happiness by a GI and a Japanese." *Life,* February 21, 1955, 124–41.

Michener, James A. *Sayonara.* New York, 1953.

"Mission Sent to Europe to Aid 50,000 War Brides." *U.S. Immigration and Naturalization Service Monthly Review,* 3 (November 1945), 229–30.

Murai, Eiko. "The Enhancement of the Alien's Adjustment through Interpersonal Relationships within the Ethnic Group toward the Socialization into the Host Society: Japanese Women's Case." Ph.D. dissertation, University of Michigan, 1972.

Neumann, A. Lin. "'Hospitality Girls' in the Philippines." *Southeast Asia Chronicle,* 66 (January/February 1979), 18–23.

Okimoto, Daniel I. *American in Disguise.* Tokyo, 1971.

Parise, G. "Strange Sad Story: Sex and Saigon." *Atlas,* 14 (September 1967), 26–31.

Ratliff, Bascom W., et al. "Intercultural Marriage: The Korean-American Experience." *Social Casework,* 59 (1978), 221–26.

"Reagan Signs Bill to Aid Amerasians." *Minneapolis Star and Tribune*, October 23, 1982, 4C

Richardson, Frank D. "Ministries to Asian Wives of Servicemen." *Military Chaplain's Review* (Winter 1976), 1–14.

Risdon, Randall. "A Study of Interracial Marriages Based on Data for Los Angeles County." *SSR*, 39 (1954), 92–95.

Sasaki, Tom. "Social Organization—Towards Larger Community." August 24, 1946. Japanese American Evacuation and Resettlement Study, Bancroft Library, Berkeley, carton 4, no. 49.

Schnepp, G. J., and Agnes Masako Yui. "Cultural and Marital Adjustment of Japanese War Brides." *AJS*, 61 (1955), 48–50.

Scully, Susan B. "Speaking Out: Yurie Horiguchi." *Mainichi Daily News*, July 27, 1977.

"Service Issues Ruling on War Bride 'Visitors.'" *U.S. Immigration and Naturalization Service Monthly Review*, 3 (March 1946), 285.

Sheldon, Walt. *Honorable Conquerors*. New York, 1965.

Smith, J. W., and W. L. Worden. "They're Bringing Home Japanese Wives." *Saturday Evening Post*, January 19, 1952, 26–27.

Strauss, Anselm. "Strain and Harmony in American-Japanese War Bride Marriages." *Marriage and Family*, 16 (1954).

Strong, Nathan Oba. "Patterns of Social Interaction and Psychological Adjustment among Japan's Konketsuji Population." Ph.D. dissertation, University of California, Berkeley, 1978.

Takahisa, Sonnet Carol. "Intercultural Interpersonal Encounters: A Study of Assimilation Patterns of Western-Born Women Married to Japanese Men." A.B. thesis, Harvard University, 1976.

Thompson, Era Bell. "Japan's Rejected." *Ebony*, September 1967, 42–54.

Thompson, Era Bell. "Rest and Recreation." *Ebony*, August 1968, 76–78ff.

Thornton, Michael C. "A Social History of a Multiethnic Identity: The Case of Black Japanese Americans." Ph.D. dissertation, University of Michigan, 1983.

"The Truth about Japanese War Brides." *Ebony*, March 1952, 17–25.

Tsurumi, Kazuko. *Social Change and the Individual: Japan Before and After World War II*. Princeton, 1970.

U.S. Department of the Army. Special Regulations No. 600-24-6, 17 June 1953, "Personnel: Marriages to Non-Nationals within the Far East Command." American University, Foreign Area Studies Division, *US Area Handbook for Japan*, 78–79. Washington, 1964.

U.S. Immigration and Naturalization Service. *Annual Report* (1946), 13–14.

Wagatsuma, Hiroshi. "The Social Perception of Skin Color in Japan." In John Hope Franklin, ed., *Color and Race*, 129–65. Boston, 1968.

Wagatsuma, Hiroshi. "Some Problems of Interracial Marriage for the Japanese." In Irving R. Stuart and Lawrence E. Abt, eds., *Interracial Marriage*. New York, 1967.

Walters, Leon K. "A Study of the Social and Marital Adjustment of Thirty-five American-Japanese Couples." M.A. thesis, Ohio State University, 1953.

"War Brides." *U.S. Immigration and Naturalization Service Monthly Review,* 6 (June 1949), 168.

Watanabe, Yuriyo*, interviewed by the author, July 1972.

Weatherall, William. Article on intermarriages and citizenship. *Japan Times,* June 24, 1978.

Weber, Tom. "The 'Hired Wives' in Thailand—Abandoned, Poor, and Much Older." *San Francisco Chronicle,* April 20, 1976.

Westerfield, Hargis. "Failures in GI Orientation." *Free World,* 2 (1946), 62–63.

Wickersham, Ben. "A Letter from the Far East." *Look,* February 12, 1952, 94–95.

Worden, William L. "Where Are Those Japanese War Brides?" *Saturday Evening Post,* November 20, 1954, 38–39ff.

Yamamoto, George K. "Social Adjustment of Caucasian-Japanese Marriages in Honolulu." M.A. thesis, University of Hawaii, 1949.

Yamamoto, Tamiko T. "Adjustments of War Brides in Hawaii." Romanzo Adams Social Research Library Report 17, University of Hawaii. Honolulu, 1950.

Yoshimura, Evelyn. "G.I.'s and Asian Women." In Amy Tachiki et al., *Roots.* Los Angeles, 1971.

Part III. Jewish Americans

Archival sources

American Jewish Archives (AJA), Cincinnati.

Abbey, Adolph, to the *Hebrew Standard,* July 27 and May 13, 1904.

Bettman, Iphigene Molony, biographical questionnaire, May 9, 1964.

Bettman, Iphigene Molony, interviewed by Stanley Chyet et al., Cincinnati, May 13, 1964. Tape 215.

Bibo Family Papers.

Bureau of Jewish Social Research. "Jewish Population of Los Angeles, California."

Central Conference of American Rabbis. "Resolutions, 1890–1962."

Certificate of Marriage between I. A. Isaacs and Isabelle Hastie, New York, December 6, 1817.

Cook, Michael. "The Debates of the C.C.A.R. on the Problem of Mixed Marriage: 1907–1968."

Deutsch Catalog.

Engel, Irving M. Memoir.

Gilbert, Arthur, to Jacob R. Marcus, Philadelphia, November 26, 1968.

Glasner, Samuel. "Counseling Parents on Problem of Intermarriage." 1962.

Goldberg, David J. "An Historical Community Study of Wilmington Jewry, 1738–1925."

Gould, David Dorman. Autobiographical questionnaire.

Heiss, Jerold S. "Premarital Characteristics of the Religiously Intermarried." In "Sampler of Reform Rabbis' Attitudes."

Ipswich, Massachusetts, Vital Records.

Kerman, Daniel E., to Jacob R. Marcus, Buffalo, N.Y., April 26, 1967.

Kohanski, Dorothy Dellar, to Jacob R. Marcus, Passaic, N.J., January 6, 1976.

Letter from sixteen C.C.A.R. rabbis to their fellow members, April 15, 1973.

Lewis, Ellen Jay. "A Study in Assimilation as Reflected in the Correspondence of the Mordecai Family from the Earliest Days to 1840."

Marcus, Jacob Rader. "A Survey of Intermarriage in Small Mid-Western Towns and Cities."

Moses, Adolph, to William Kriegshaber, Chicago, May 14, 1870.

Report on Orthodox rabbinical conference, New York, May 16, 1916.

"A Sampler of Reform Rabbis' Attitudes toward Mixed Marriage." 1972.

Simons, Leonard M., taped interview, March 24, 1975.

Stern, Malcolm H. "Jewish Marriage and Intermarriage in the Federal Period (1776–1840)."

Stern, Malcolm H., to Jacob R. Marcus, New York, February 1, 1966.

Stern, Malcolm H. "Two Studies in the Assimilation of Early American Jewry." D.H.L. thesis, Hebrew Union College, 1957.

Thompson, Dellight, to Rabbi Stanley F. Chyet, May 4, 1959, Bowling Green, Ohio.

Weiler, Moses Cyrus, to Rabbi Herman E. Schaalman, New York, May 30, 1973.

Weinfeld, Morton. "A Report on Jewish Intermarriage Rates in Canada and the United States." 1975.

YIVO Institute, New York.

Constitution and By-Laws of the First Zborower Sick Benevolent Association. Rev. ed. New York, 1940.

Constitution of the Bombier Benevolent Society, Incorporated. New York, 1916.

Constitution of the Independent First Kudryncer Congregation Sick and Aid Society. New York, 1900.

Constitution of the Kolomear Friends Association. New York, 1904.

Constitution, Plotzker Young Men's Independent Association. New York, 1893.

Konstitushun fun de Yunited Disnere Benevolent Asosieyshon. New York, 1913.

Konstitusion der Progresive Samborer Yong Mens Benevolent Associeyshon. New York, 1896.

Konstitutsion Ershte Zborower Kranken und Vereyn. New York, 1896.

Kremenitzer-Wolyner Benevolent Association. New York, 1915.

Other Sources

Angel, Marc D. "The Sephardim in the United States." *AJYB*, 74 (1973), 77–138.

Asch, Sholem. *East River.* New York, 1946.

Barron, Milton L. "The Incidence of Jewish Intermarriage in Europe and America." *ASR*, 11 (1946), 6–13.

Benedict, George. *Christ Finds a Rabbi.* Philadelphia, 1932.

Berger, Joseph. "Interfaith Marriages: Children's Views." *New York Times*, December 2, 1985, 19.

Berkowitz, Henry. "Should Jews and Non-Jews Intermarry?" *Kansas City Journal*, November 2, 1889.

Berlin, Isabelle. "One Hundred Jewish Working Mothers." Master of Social Service thesis, Graduate School for Jewish Social Work, New York, 1934.

Berman, Louis A. *Jews and Intermarriage: A Study in Personality and Culture.* New York, 1968.

Bigman, Stanley K. *The Jewish Population of Greater Washington in 1956.* Washington, D.C., 1957.

Billings, J. S. "Vital Statistics of the Jews." *North American Review,* 152 (1891), 70–84.

Birner, Louis. "The Interfaith Marriage and Its Effect on the Individual." In Rosenthal, *Jewish Family in a Changing World,* 272–83.

Bressler, Marvin. "Jewish Behavior Patterns as Exemplified in W. I. Thomas' Unfinished Study of the Bintel Brief." Ph.D. dissertation, University of Pennsylvania, 1952.

Brewer, Joseph. *The Jewish Marriage.* New York, 1956.

Cahnman, Werner. "New Intermarriage Studies." *Reconstructionist,* 33 (1967), 7–13.

Cahnman, Werner, ed. *Intermarriage and Jewish Life.* New York, 1963.

Caplowitz, D., and H. Levy. *Interreligious Dating among College Students.* New York, 1965.

Carter, Lewis F. "Racial-Caste Hypogamy: A Sociological Myth?" *Phylon* (1968), 347–50.

Cavan, Ruth Shonle. "Interreligious Marriage: Official Religious Policies and Individual Mate Choice in the United States." *International Journal of Sociology of the Family,* 1 (1971), 83–93.

Central Conference of American Rabbis. *A Sampler of Reform Rabbis' Attitudes toward Mixed Marriage.* Cincinnati, 1972.

Chenkin, Alvin. "Jewish Population in the United States, 1957." *AJYB* (1958), 3–23.

Chenkin, Alvin. "Jewish Population in the United States, 1962." *AJYB* (1963), 57–76.

Chenkin, Alvin. "Jewish Population in the United States, 1964." *AJYB* (1965), 139–54.

Cohen, Bernard. *Sociocultural Changes in American Jewish Life as Reflected in Selected Jewish Literature.* Rutherford, N.J., 1972.

Cohen, Mrs. S. J. *Henry Luria; or, The Little Jewish Convert.* New York, 1860.

Cohen, Steven M., et al., eds. *Perspectives in Jewish Population Research.* Boulder, Colo., 1984.

Coleman, Robert T. "Black and Jewish—And Unaccepted." In Lavender, *Coat of Many Colors,* 229–32.

Collis, Septima M. *A Woman's War Record, 1861–1865.* New York, 1889.

Cowan, Paul, and Rachel Cowan. *Mixed Blessings.* New York, 1987.

Davis, Kingsley. "Intermarriage in Caste Societies." *American Anthropologist,* 43 (1941), 376–95.

Davis, Moshe. "Mixed Marriage in Western Jewry: Historical Background to the Jewish Response." *Jewish Journal of Sociology,* 10 (1968), 177–220.

Dawidowicz, Lucy S., ed. *The Golden Tradition: Jewish Life and Thought in Eastern Europe.* Boston, 1967.

Dean, John P. "Patterns of Association between Jews and Non-Jews." *Jewish Social Studies*, 17 (1953), 247–68.

Della Pergola, S. *Jewish and Mixed Marriages in Milan, 1901–1968*. Jerusalem, 1972.

Digest of Jewish Events. 1932–36.

Doroshkin, M. *Yiddish in America: Social and Cultural Foundations*. Rutherford, N.J., 1969.

Drachsler, Julius. *Intermarriage in New York City*. New York, 1921.

Eichorn, David Max. *Jewish Intermarriages*. Satellite Beach, Fla., 1974.

Eisenstein, Ira. *Intermarriage*. New York, 1964.

Ellman, Israel. "Jewish Intermarriage in the United States." In Schlesinger, *Jewish Family*, 25–61.

Elman, Peter, ed. *Jewish Marriage*. London, 1967.

Engelman, Uriah Zevi. "Intermarriage among Jews in Germany." *SSR*, 20 (1935), 34–39.

Engelman, Uriah Zevi. "Intermarriage among Jews in Germany, U.S.S.R., and Switzerland." *Jewish Social Studies*, 2 (1940), 157–78.

Engelman, Uriah Zevi. "Intermarriage among Jews in Switzerland, 1888–1920." *AJS*, 34 (1928), 516–23.

Epstein, Louis M. *Marriage Laws in the Bible and the Talmud*. Cambridge, "Experiences of a Jew's Wife." *American Magazine*, 78 (1914), 49–52ff.

Federation of Jewish Philanthropies. Commission on Synagogue Relations. *Intermarriage: The Future of the American Jew*. New York, 1964.

Fein, Leonard J. "Some Consequences of Jewish Intermarriage." *Jewish Social Studies*, 33 (1971), 44–58.

Feldman, Ephraim. "Intermarriage Historically Considered." *Central Conference of American Rabbis Journal*, 16 (1908), 271–307.

Feldstein, Stanley. *The Land That I Show You*. Garden City, N.Y., 1979.

Fiedler, Leslie A. *The Jew in the American Novel*. New York, 1959.

Fishberg, Maurice. *The Jews: A Study of Race and Environment*. New York, 1911.

Fisher, Jacob. "Fifty-one Related Family Groups." Master of Social Service thesis, Graduate School for Jewish Social Work, New York, n.d.

Franzblau, Abraham N. "The Dynamics of Mixed Marriage." *Central Conference of American Rabbis Journal* (1954), 284–94.

Friedman, Lester D. *Hollywood's Image of the Jew*. New York, 1982.

Friedman, Peter, et al. *A Population Study of the Jewish Community of Metropolitan Chicago*. Chicago, 1985.

Gallup, G. H. *Gallup Report*, no. 213, June 1983.

Gittelsohn, Roland B. *Consecrated Unto Me: A Jewish View of Love and Marriage*. New York, 1965.

Gittelsohn, Roland B. *Modern Jewish Problems*. Cincinnati, 1943.

Glanz, Rudolf. *The Jewish Woman in America*. New York, 1976.

Glazer, Nathan. *American Judaism*. Chicago, 1972.

Glick, Ira O. "The Hebrew Christians." In Lavender, *Coat of Many Colors*, 415–31.

Goldberg, Nathan. "Intermarriage from a Sociological Perspective." In Federation of Jewish Philanthropies, *Intermarriage*.

Goldman, Benjamin Barcon. "Some Aspects of the Economic Adjustment of Graduates of Cleveland Jewish Orphan Home." Master of Social Service thesis, Graduate School for Jewish Social Work, New York, 1934.

Goldstein, Sidney. *The Greater Providence Jewish Community.* Providence, 1964.

Goldstein, Sidney. *Meaning of Marriage and Foundations of the Family.* New York, 1940.

Goldstein, Sidney, and Calvin Goldscheider. *Jewish Americans.* Englewood Cliffs, N.J., 1968.

Grinstein, Hyman B. *The Rise of the Jewish Community of New York, 1654–1860.* Philadelphia, 1945.

Heller, James G. *Isaac M. Wise.* New York, 1965.

Heller, Max. "Judaism and Intermarriage." *American Israelite,* 50 (1903), 4.

Hellyer, H. L. *From the Rabbis to Christ.* Philadelphia, 1911.

Howe, Irving. *World of Our Fathers.* New York, 1976.

Hurst, Fannie. *God Must Be Sad.* Garden City, N.Y., 1961.

Hutchinson, E. P. *Immigrants and Their Children, 1850–1950.* New York, 1956.

"I Married a Jew." *Atlantic Monthly,* January 1939, 38–46.

"The Issue of Patrilineal Descent—A Symposium." *Judaism,* 34 (1985), 3–135.

Jacobs, Joseph. "Intermarriage." *Jewish Encyclopedia,* 6 (1904), 610–12.

Josephson, Sadie. "Adjustment Histories of Six Jewish Women." Master of Social Service thesis, Graduate School for Jewish Social Work, New York, 1937.

Kagan, Henry Enoch. "Reflections on Intermarriage." In Rosenthal, *Jewish Family in a Changing World,* 284–94.

Kaplan, Benjamin. *The Eternal Stranger: A Study of Jewish Life in the Small Community.* New York, 1957.

Katkov, Norman. *Eagle at My Eyes.* Garden City, N.Y., 1948.

Kaufmann, Myron S. *Remember Me to God.* Philadelphia, 1957.

Kertzer, Morris. *What Is a Jew?* Cleveland, 1953.

Kirshenbaum, David. *Mixed Marriage and the Jewish Future: A Warning and Appeal to the Jewish Community to Counteract the Upsurge of Intermarriage.* New York, 1958.

Kramer, Judith R., and Seymour Levantman. *Children of the Gilded Ghetto.* New Haven, 1961.

Krutza, William J., and Philip P. DiCicco. *Facing the Issues: Three.* Grand Rapids, 1970.

Langer, Marion F. "Story of the Jewish Community of Easton." Master of Social Service thesis, Graduate School for Jewish Social Work, New York, 1935.

Lavender, Abraham D., ed. *A Coat of Many Colors: Jewish Subcommunities in the United States.* Westport, Conn., 1977.

Lazarre, Jacob. *Beating Sea and Changeless Bar.* Philadelphia, 1905.

Lazerwitz, Bernard. "Intermarriage and Conversion." *Jewish Journal of Sociology,* 12 (1971), 41–63.

Lazerwitz, Bernard. "Jewish Christian Marriages and Conversions." *Jewish Social Studies,* 44 (1981), 31–46.

Lehrman, Samuel R. "Psychopathology in Mixed Marriages." *Psychoanalytic Quarterly,* 36 (1967), 67–82.

Lestschinsky, Jacob. "Mixed Marriage." *Universal Jewish Encyclopedia*, 7 (1942), 594–97.

Levin, Bob. "Second-Class Israelis." *Newsweek*, July 13, 1981, 34.

Levine, Jeanne. "Jewish Family Desertion in Cases Carried Cooperatively by the National Desertion Bureau and Other Social Agencies in New York City, 1934." Master of Social Service thesis, Graduate School for Jewish Social Work, New York, 1939.

Levinson, M. H., and D. J. Levinson. "Jews Who Intermarry: Socio-psychological Bases of Ethnic Identity and Change." *YIVO Annual of Jewish Social Science*, 12 (1958), 103–30.

Levitt, Ken. *Kidnapped for My Faith*. Van Nuys, Calif., 1978.

Lewin, Kurt. "Self-Hatred among Jews." In Arnold Rose, ed., *Race, Prejudice, and Discrimination*, 219–33. New York, 1953.

Lewisohn, Ludwig. *The Island Within*. New York, 1940.

Lublin, JoAnn S. "The Crisis in Jewish Identity." *Wall Street Journal*, May 1979.

Luka, Ronald. *When a Christian and a Jew Marry*. New York, 1973.

Made, David R. *Hebrew Marriage*. London, 1953.

Mack, Rebecca E. *You Are a Jew and a Jew You Are!* New York, 1933.

Malamud, Bernard. *The Assistant*. New York, 1957.

Maller, Allen S. "Jewish-Gentile Divorce in California." *Jewish Social Studies*, 37 (1975), 279–90.

Massarik, Fred. *The Jewish Population of San Francisco, Marin County, and the Peninsula, 1959*. San Francisco, 1959.

Massarik, Fred. "Rethinking the Intermarriage Crisis." *Moment*, 3 (June 1978), 29–33.

Massarik, Fred. *Report on the Jewish Population of Los Angeles, 1959*. Los Angeles, 1959.

Massarik, Fred, and Alvin Chenkin. "United States National Jewish Population Study." *AJYB*, 74 (1973), 264–306.

Mayer, Egon. *Love and Tradition: Marriage between Christians and Jews*. New York, 1985.

Mayer, Egon, and Carl Sheingold. *Intermarriage and the Jewish Future: A National Study in Summary*. New York, 1979.

Mayer, John E. *Jewish-Gentile Courtships*. New York, 1961.

Mayer, John E. "Jewish-Gentile Courtships." *New Society*, 10 (1967), 288–90.

Mayer, John E. "Jewish-Gentile Intermarriage Patterns." *SSR*, 45 (1960), 188–95.

Meir, Golda. "The Threat of Mixed Marriage." *American Mercury*, 107 (1971), 51–53.

Mendelsohn, S. Felix. *Intermarriage*. Chicago, 1939.

Merton, Robert K. "Intermarriage and the Social Structure." *Psychiatry*, 4 (1941), 361–74.

Metzker, Isaac, ed. *Bintel Brief*. Garden City, N.Y., 1971.

Mielziner, Moses. *The Jewish Law of Marriage and Divorce*. Cincinnati, 1901.

Mielziner, M. "Upon the Intermarriage Question." *American Israelite*, May 28, 1880, 5.

Mink, Iris Tan. "An Investigation of Intermarriage: A Comparison of Intermarried and Inmarried Jewish Men." Ph.D. dissertation, UCLA, 1971.

Mitchell, William. *Mishpokhe*. New York, 1978.

Mosely, Leonard. *Dulles*. New York, 1978.

Nathan, M. N. *A Defense of Ancient Rabbinical Interpretation of the Prohibitory Law of Deuteronomy XXIII-3*. Kingston, Jamaica, 1861.

Neufeld, E. *Ancient Hebrew Marriage Laws*. London, 1944.

Newman, Louis I. "Intermarriage between Jews and Christians during the Middle Ages." *Jewish Institute Quarterly*, 2 (January 1976), 2–8; (March 1976), 22–28.

Nichols, Anne. *Abie's Irish Rose*. New York, 1927.

Packouz, Kalman. *How to Stop an Intermarriage: A Practical Guide for Parents*. Jerusalem, 1976.

Phillips, Bruce A., and Eleanore P. Judd. *The Denver Jewish Population Study*. Denver, 1982.

Podhoretz, Norman. "My Negro Problem—And Ours." *Commentary*, February 1963, 93–101.

Poll, Solomon. *The Hasidic Community of Williamsburg*. New York, 1962.

Pollett, Sybil H. *Marriage, Intermarriage, and the Jews*. New York, 1966.

Pool, David De Sola. "Intermarriage." *The Hebrew Standard*, February 7, 1919.

Press, Aric. "The Last Nazi Trial?" *Newsweek*, November 26, 1979, 93.

"Reform and Intermarriage." *Liberal Judaism* (1947), 14–17.

"Report of the Committee on Patrilineal Descent." *Reform Judaism* (Spring/Summer 1983), 16.

Resnik, Reuben B. "Some Sociological Aspects of Intermarriage of Jews and Non-Jews." *Social Forces*, 12 (1933), 94–102.

Ringer, Benjamin. *The Edge of Friendliness: A Study of Jewish-Gentile Relations*. New York, 1967.

Rischin, Moses. *The Promised City*. Cambridge, 1962.

Robison, Sophia M., ed. *Jewish Population Studies*. New York, 1943.

Rosenberg, Louis. *Canada's Jews*. Montreal, 1939.

Rosenthal, Erich. "Jewish Intermarriage in Indiana." *AJYB*, 68 (1967), 243–64.

Rosenthal, Erich. "Studies of Jewish Intermarriage in the United States." *AJYB*, 64 (1963), 3–52. Reprinted in Milton L. Barron, ed., *The Blending American*. Chicago, 1972.

Rosenthal, Gilbert S., ed. *The Jewish Family in a Changing World*. New York, 1970.

Rosenthal, Gilbert S. *The Many Faces of Judaism*. New York, 1978.

Roskolenko, Harry. *The Time That Was Then: The Lower East Side, 1900–1914*. New York, 1971.

Roth, Philip. *Goodbye, Columbus*. Boston, 1959.

Roth, Philip. *Portnoy's Complaint*. New York, 1969.

Ruppin, Arthur. *The Jewish Fate and Future*. London, 1940.

Ruppin, Arthur. *The Jews in the Modern World*. London, 1934.

Ruppin, Arthur. *The Jews of To-Day*. London, 1913.

Sanua, Victor D. "Attitudes of Jewish Students toward Intermarriage." In Rosenthal, *Jewish Family in a Changing World*, 204–61.

Sanua, Victor. "Contemporary Studies of Sephardi Jews in the United States." In Lavender, *Coat of Many Colors*, 281–88.

Saperstein, David, and Mark Saperstein. *Who Is a Jew?* New York, 1972.

Sarna, Jonathan D. "The American Jewish Response to Nineteenth-Century Christian Missions." *Journal of American History*, 68 (1981), 35–71.

Sarna, Jonathan. "From Immigrants to Ethnics: Toward a New Theory of 'Ethnicization.'" *Ethnicity*, 5 (1978), 370–78.

Schlesinger, Benjamin, ed. *The Jewish Family*. Toronto, 1971.

Schoenfeld, Eugen. "Intermarriage and the Small Town: The Jewish Case." *JMF*, 31 (1969), 61–64.

Schreiber, Armand. "The Case for Intermarriage." *Harper's Weekly*, 62 (1916), 33–34.

Schulman, Samuel. *Judaism and Intermarriage with Christians*. New York, 1908.

Schwartz, Arnold. "Intermarriage in the United States." *AJYB*, 71 (1970), 101–22.

Seligman, Ben B. "The American Jew: Some Demographic Features." *AJYB*, 51 (1950), 3–52.

Seltzer, Sanford. *Jews and Non-Jews: Falling in Love*. New York, 1976.

Shapiro, Mannheim S. "Intermarriage and the Jewish Community." In Rosenthal, *Jewish Family in a Changing World*, 262–71.

Sharfman, I. Harold. *Jews on the Frontier*. Chicago, 1977.

Shore, Julius. *Intermarriage*. Vancouver, 1935.

Shoulson, Abraham B., ed. *Marriage and Family Life: A Jewish View*. New York, 1959.

Silbert, Celia. "Intermarriage on the East Side." *American Jewish Chronicle*, 1 (1916), 456–57.

Silcox, Claris Edwin, and Galen M. Fisher. *Catholics, Jews, and Protestants*. New York, 1934.

Silver, Samuel M. *Mixed Marriage between Jew and Christian*. New York, 1977.

Singer, David. "Living with Intermarriage." *Commentary*, 68 (July 1979), 48–53.

Singer, Isaac Bashevis. *A Crown of Feathers*. New York, 1973.

Singer, Isaac Bashevis. *The Slave*. New York, 1962.

Sklare, Marshall. "Intermarriage and Jewish Survival." *Commentary*, 49 (1970), 51–58.

Sklare, Marshall. "Intermarriage and the Jewish Future." *Commentary*, 37 (1964), 46–52.

Sklare, Marshall, ed. *The Jews*. Glencoe, Ill., 1958.

Slotkin, J. S. "Adjustment in Jewish-Gentile Intermarriages." *Social Forces*, 21 (1942), 226–30.

Slotkin, J. S. "Jewish-Gentile Intermarriage in Chicago." *ASR*, 7 (1942), 34–39.

Sokolsky, George E. "My Mixed Marriage." *Atlantic Monthly*, August 1933, 137–46.

Sokolsky, George E. *We Jews*. Garden City, N.Y., 1935.

Sonneschein, S. H. "Should a Rabbi Perform the Ceremonies at the Intermarriage between Jew and Gentile?" *American Israelite* (1880), 19–20.

Spickard, Paul R. "Mixed Marriage: Two American Minority Groups and the Limits of Ethnic Identity." Ph. D. dissertation, University of California, Berkeley, 1983.

Stember, Charles Herbers, et al. *Jews in the Mind of America*. New York, 1966.

Stern, Elizabeth Gertrude. *I Am a Woman—and a Jew*. New York, 1926.

Stern, Harry Joshua. *The Problem of Intermarriage*. Montreal, 1944.

Thomas, William I. *The Unadjusted Girl*. Boston, 1923.

Timayenis, Telemanchus Thomas. *The American Jew: An Exposé*, 81–87. New York, 1888. Quoted in Stanley I. Kutler, ed., *Looking for America*, 2:260–63. 2nd ed. New York, 1979.

Tobin, Gary A. *1982 Demographic and Attitudinal Study of the St. Louis Jewish Population*. St. Louis, 1982.

Tobin, Gary A., and Julie A. Lipsman. "A Compendium of Jewish Demographic Studies." In Cohen, *Jewish Population Research*, 137–66.

U.S. Bureau of the Census. *Current Population Reports: Religion Reported by the Civilian Population of the United States, by Color, Sex, and Residence, March 1957*. Series P-20, no. 79. Washington, D.C., 1958.

Weidman, Jerome. *In the Enemy Camp*. New York, 1958.

Weinstein, Jacob. *The Jew and Mixed Marriage*. Cincinnati, 1941.

Weinstock, Harris. "Shall Jew and Christian Intermarry?" In *Jesus the Jew and Other Addresses* (1902), 129–42.

Weisser, Michael R. *A Brotherhood of Memory: Jewish Landsmanshaftn in the New World*. New York, 1985.

Wessel, Bessie Bloom. *An Ethnic Survey of Woonsocket, Rhode Island*. Chicago, 1931.

Wise, Isaac M. "A Clandestine Marriage." *American Israelite* (1880), 4.

Wise, Isaac M. "Intermarriages." *American Israelite* (1883), 25.

Wolfe, George M. D. "A Study of 'Immigrant Attitudes' Based on an Analysis of Four Hundred Letters Printed in the 'Bintel Brief' of the 'Jewish Daily Forward.'" Diploma in Social Work thesis, Training School of Jewish Social Work, New York, 1919.

Wolfe, Thomas. *The Web and the Rock*. New York, 1937.

Yezierska, Anzia. *All I Could Never Be*. New York, 1932.

Yezierska, Anzia. *Bread Givers*. New York, 1975.

Zimmerman, Sheldon, and Barbara Trainin, eds. *The Threat of Mixed Marriage*. New York, 1976.

Zollschan, Ignaz. *Jewish Questions*. New York, 1914.

Part IV. Black Americans

Archival Sources

Howard University Archives, Washington, D.C.
    E. Franklin Frazier Papers (EFF)
        Chicago Documents of Families Coming to the Urban League. Box 81:18.
        "Conflict in My Family." Box 93:9.
        Family Histories—Alabama. Box 5.
        Family Histories—Doris Albert*. Box 85:6.
        Family Histories—Nadine Allen*. Box 85:2.
        Family Histories—Eloise F. Anderson. Box 85:3.

Family Histories—Muriel Avery. Box 85:7.
Family Histories—Otis Bacon*. Box 85:11.
Family Histories—Raymond A. Brownbow. Box 85:23.
Family Histories—John Burke*. Box 85:9.
Family Histories—Wilma Jean Burton. Box 85:24.
Family Histories—Julia Spain Cheevers. Box 86:1.
Family Histories—Analyn Colter*. Box 93:9.
Family Histories—Marcelyn R. Cobbs. Box 86:4.
Family Histories—Dora R. Curtis. Box 86:10.
Family Histories—Harietta Davenport. Box 86:12.
Family Histories—Day Family. Box 86:17.
Family Histories—Martha Hart Green. Box 86:33.
Family Histories—North Carolina. Box 92:7.
Family Histories—Belle Winters*. Box 92:11.
Family Histories of Higher Classes. Box 93:9.
Haskins, Mildred. "The Choice of a Mate." March 1932. Box 82:11.
Hertford County Documents. Box 92:7B.
Hill Family Documents. Box 92:2.
Incidents and Characters in the Chicago Community. Box 82:1.
L. L. "Role of Color in the Development of Personality." Box 108:10.
Louisville Girls Interviewed by Mrs. Thelma L. Colman. Box 109:8.
Miller, Francine*. "History of an Interracial Marriage." Box 36:9.
Mooreland Family Documents. Box 92:3.
Ohio Documents. Box 92:8.
Student Documents on "Choice of Mate." Box 82:11.
Unarranged Family Histories. Box 93:1.
Grimké Family Papers
Archibald H. Grimké Papers
Schlesinger Library, Harvard University.
Vertical File—Black Women
Bowser, Pearl. "The Image of Black Women in the Media."
Wilcox, Ella Wheeler. "An Octoroon." *New York Evening Journal*, no. 7,800, n.d.

Other Sources

Adams, Paul. "Counseling with Interracial Couples and Their Children in the South." In Irving R. Stuart and Lawrence E. Abt, eds., *Interracial Marriage*, 63–79. New York, 1967.
Ai. "On Being ½ Japanese, ⅛ Choctaw, ¼ Black, and ¹⁄₁₆ Irish," *Ms.*, May 1978, 58.
Alba, Richard D., and Reid M. Golden. "Patterns of Ethnic Marriage in the United States." *Social Forces*, 65 (1986), 202–23.
Allen, Bonnie. "It Ain't Easy Being Pinky." *Essence*, July 1982, 67ff.
Allen, Marilyn R. *Alien Minorities and Mongrelization*. Boston, 1949.
"Americans in Ethiopia." *Ebony*, May 1951, 79–80.
"The Anglo-Saxon at Bay." *Crisis*, 30 (1925), 10–11.

"Anti-Intermarriage Bill in Michigan." *Crisis,* 22 (1921), 66.

"Are White Women Stealing Our Men?" *Negro Digest,* April 1951, 52–55.

Armistead, W. E. *The Negro Is a Man.* Tifton, Ga., 1903.

Aryan, Junius [Wilbert Newton]. *The Aryans and Mongrelized America: The Remedy.* Philadelphia, 1912.

Asbury, Herbert. "Who Is a Negro?" *Negro Digest,* October 1946, 3–11.

Askew, C. E. "Yes, I Would Want My Daughter to Marry a Negro." *Negro Digest,* July 1964, 4–8.

Baber, Ray E. "A Study of 325 Mixed Marriages." *ASR,* 2 (1937), 705–16.

"Baha'i Faith." *Ebony,* October 1952, 39–46.

Bailey, Pearl. "This Time It's Love." *Ebony,* May 1953, 122–28.

Baker, Ray Stannard. *Following the Color Line.* New York, 1964; orig. 1908.

Baldwin, James. *Another Country.* New York, 1960.

Baldwin, James. *Blues for Mr. Charlie.* New York, 1964.

Bales, Mary Virginia. "Some Negro Folk-Songs of Texas." *Publications of Texas Folklore Society,* 7 (1928).

Baraka, Imamu Amiri. "Black Woman." *Black World,* 19 (July 1970), 7–11.

Barton, Rebecca Chalmers. *Witnesses for Freedom: Negro Americans in Autobiography.* New York, 1948.

Belafonte, Harry. "Why I Married Julie." *Ebony,* July 1957, 90–95.

Bell, Derick A., Jr. *Race and Racism in American Law.* Boston, 1973.

Berlin, Ira. *Slaves without Masters.* New York, 1974.

Bernard, Jessie. *Marriage and the Family among Negroes.* Englewood Cliffs, N.J., 1966.

Bernard, Jessie. "Note on Educational Homogamy in Negro-White Marriages." *JMF,* 28 (1966), 274–76.

Berry, Bill. "Interracial Marriages in the South." *Ebony,* December 1967, 146–50.

Berzon, Judith R. *Neither Black nor White: The Mulatto Character in American Fiction.* New York, 1978.

Beteille, André. "Race, Caste, and Ethnic Identity." *International Social Science Journal,* 23 (1971), 519–35.

Biegel, Hugo G. "Problems and Motives in Interracial Relationships." *Journal of Sex Research,* 2 (1966), 185–205.

"The Black Sexism Debate." Special Issue of *Black Scholar,* 10 (May/June 1979).

"Blackburn v. Blackburn." *Newsweek,* May 17, 1982, 105.

Blackett, Richard. "Some of the Problems Confronting West Indians in the Black American Struggle." *Black Lines,* 1 (Summer 1971), 47–52.

Blassingame, John W. *Black New Orleans, 1860–1880.* Chicago, 1973.

Bloch, Julius M. *Miscegenation, Melaleukation, and Mr. Lincoln's Dog.* New York, 1958.

Blu, Karen I. *The Lumbee Problem.* New York, 1980.

"Blues Writer in Sweden." *Ebony,* April 1954, 123–25.

Bogle, Donald. *Toms, Coons, Mulattoes, Mammies, and Bucks: An Interpretive History of Blacks in American Films.* New York, 1973.

Bontemps, Alex. "National Poll Reveals Startling New Attitudes on Interracial Marriage." *Ebony,* September 1975, 144–51ff.

Booker, Simeon. "Challenge for the Guy Smiths." *Ebony*, December 1967, 146–50.

Booker, Simeon. "Couple That Rocked the Courts." *Ebony*, September 1967, 78–84.

Borgese, G. A. "A Bedroom Approach to Racism." *Negro Digest*, December 1944, 31–35.

Bowditch, William I. *White Slavery in the United States*. New York, 1855.

Bracey, John H., et al., eds. *Black Nationalism in America*. Indianapolis, 1970.

Britt, May. "Why I Married Sammy Davis, Jr." *Ebony*, January 1961, 96–102.

Brodie, Fawn M. *Thomas Jefferson*. New York, 1974.

Broonzy, Bill. *Big Bill Blues*. London, 1955.

Brotz, Howard, ed. *Negro Social and Political Thought*. New York, 1966.

Brown, Anne. "I Gave Up My Country for Love." *Ebony*, November 1953, 28–38.

Brown, Sterling. "Count Us In." In Moon, *Primer for White Folks*, 364–95.

Brown, Sterling A. "Negro Character as Seen by White Authors." In Emanuel and Gross, *Dark Symphony*, 155–57.

Brown, Sterling A., et al. *The Negro Caravan*. New York, 1969; orig. 1941.

Brownfeld, A. C. "Will the Supreme Court Uphold Mixed Marriages?" *Negro Digest*, March 1965, 72–77.

Brownfeld, Allan C. "Miscegenation and the Law." *New South*, 19 (July–August 1964), 10–15.

Bruce, James D., and Hyman Rodman. "Black-White Marriages in the United States." In Irving R. Stuart and Lawrence E. Abt, eds., *Interracial Marriage*. New York, 1973.

Bryce-LaPorte, Roy Simon. "Black Immigrants." *Journal of Black Studies*, 3 (September 1972), 29–56.

Buckingham, J. S. *The Slave States of America*. London, 1842.

Bullock, Penelope. "The Mulatto in American Fiction." *Phylon*, 6 (1945), 78–82.

Burges, Austin E. *What Price Integration?* Dallas, 1956.

Burke, Ruth. "Protecting a Mixed Marriage." In Larsson, *Marriage across the Color Line*, 40–43.

Burma, John. "Comparison of the Occupational Status of Intramarrying and Intermarrying Couples." *SSR*, 54 (1970), 508–19.

Burma, John. "Interethnic Marriage in Los Angeles, 1948–1959." *Social Forces*, 42 (1963), 156–65.

Buss, David M. "Human Mate Selection." *American Scientist*, 73 (January–February, 1985), 48–51.

Buttery, Thomas J. "Helping Biracial Children Adjust." *Education Digest*, 52 (May 1987), 38–41.

Cable, George Washington. *Madam Delphine*. New York, 1881.

Cahnman, Werner J. "The Interracial Jewish Children." *Reconstructionist*, June 9, 1967, 7–12.

Calhoun, Arthur W. *A Social History of the American Family*. 2 vols. Cleveland, 1917–19.

Calloway, Nathaniel O. "Mixed Marriage Can Succeed." *Negro Digest*, March 1949, 24–27.

Campbell, E. Sims. "Are Black Women Beautiful?" *Negro Digest,* June 1951, 16–20.

Cannon, Poppy. *A Gentle Knight.* New York, 1952.

Cannon, Poppy. "How We Erased Two Color Lines." *Ebony,* July 1952, 47–59.

Cannon, Poppy. "How We Made Our Mixed Marriage Work." *Ebony,* June 1952, 24–40.

Cannon, Poppy. "Love That Never Died." *Ebony,* January 1957, 17–20.

Cannon, Poppy. "Mr. and Mrs. Walter White." In Larsson, *Marriage across the Color Line,* 140–61.

Carey, Archibald J. "Riding the Color Line." *Negro Digest,* August 1951, 7–11.

Carroll, Charles. *The Negro a Beast.* St. Louis, 1900.

Cash, Eugene. "A Study of Negro-White Marriages in the Philadelphia Area." Ph.D. dissertation, Temple University, 1956.

Chase-Ribaud, Barbara. *Sally Hemings.* New York, 1979.

Chesnut, Mary B. *Diary from Dixie.* Boston, 1949.

"Chicago." *Crisis,* 6 (1913), 38–39.

"Children in Interracial Homes." In Larsson, *Marriage across the Color Line,* 67–74.

"Children of the Rainbow." *Newsweek,* November 19, 1984, 120–22.

"Church Wedding for Mixed Couple." *Ebony,* December 1951, 50–52.

Clarke, John Henrik, ed. *Marcus Garvey and the Vision of Africa.* New York, 1974.

Clarke, John Henrik, ed. *William Styron's Nat Turner.* Boston, 1968.

Clay, Cassius M. "Race and the Solid South." *North American Review,* 142 (February 1886), 134–38.

Clayton, E. T. "Famous Negro Sons of White Fathers." *Ebony,* October 1950, 96–100.

Cleaver, Eldridge. *Soul on Ice.* New York, 1968.

"Colored Men and Women Lynched without Trial." *Crisis,* 9 (1915), 145.

"A Coloured Women, However Respectable, Is Lower than the White Prostitute." *The Independent,* 54 (1902), 2221–24. Quoted in Lerner, *Black Women in White America,* 166–67.

Collins, Glenn. "Children of Interracial Marriage," *New York Times,* June 20, 1984.

Comas, Juan. *Racial Myths.* Paris, 1951.

Comer, James P., and Alvin Poussaint. *Black Children.* New York, 1975.

"The Congressmen." *Crisis,* 9 (1914).

Conyers, James E. "Selected Aspects of the Phenomenon of Negro Passing." Ph.D. dissertation, Washington State University, 1962.

Conyers, James E., and T. H. Kennedy. "Negro Passing: To Pass or Not to Pass." *Phylon,* 24 (1963), 215–23.

Cook, Adrian. *The Armies of the Streets.* Lexington, Ky., 1974.

Coombs, Orde. "Black Men and White Women." *Essence,* May 1983, 80–82 ff.

Coombs, Orde. "West Indians in New York." *New York,* July 13, 1970, 28–32.

"Court Takes Woman's White Child after She Has Black Baby." *Minneapolis Tribune,* January 12, 1982.

Cox, Earnest S. *The South's Part in Mongrelizing the Nation.* Richmond, Va., 1926.

Cox, Earnest S. *White America.* Richmond, 1923.

"The Crime of Being Married." *Life,* March 18, 1966, 85–91.

Croly, David G. *Miscegenation.* New York, 1864.

Cronon, E. David. *Black Moses.* Madison, Wis., 1955.

Dance, Daryl C. *Shuckin' and Jivin': Folklore from Contemporary Black Americans.* Bloomington, Ind., 1978.

Daniels, John. *In Freedom's Birthplace.* Boston, 1914.

Davie, Maurice R. *Negroes in American Society.* New York, 1949.

Davis, Allison, and John Dollard. *Children of Bondage: The Personality Development of Negro Youth in the South.* Washington, D.C., 1940.

Davis, Allison, et al. *Deep South.* Chicago, 1965; orig., 1941.

Davis, Sammy, Jr. "Is My Mixed Marriage Mixing Up My Kids?" *Ebony,* October 1966, 124–32.

Degler, Carl. *Neither Black nor White: Slavery and Race Relations in Brazil and the United States.* New York, 1971; rpt. Madison, Wis., 1986.

Dennison, Sam. *Scandalize My Name: Black Imagery in American Popular Music.* New York, 1982.

DePorte, J. V. "Marriages in the State of New York with Special Reference to Nativity." *Human Biology,* 3 (1931).

"Detroit's Most-Discussed Mixed Marriage." *Ebony,* April 1953, 97–103.

De Veaux, Alexis. "Loving the Dark in Me." *Essence,* July 1982, 67 ff.

Dickie-Clarke, H. F. "The Coloured Minority in Durban." In Gist and Dworkin, *Blending of Races,* 25–38.

Dixon, William H. "Colour." In W. H. Dixon, *New America.* London, 1867.

Doherty, Joseph F. *Moral Problems of Interracial Marriage.* Washington, D.C., 1949.

Dollard, John. *Caste and Class in a Southern Town.* 3rd ed. Garden City, N.Y., 1957; rpt. Madison, Wis., 1989.

Dominguez, Virginia R. *White by Definition.* New Brunswick, N.J., 1986.

Douglass, Frederick. *The Life and Times of Frederick Douglass.* London, 1962; orig. 1892.

Dowd, Jerome. *The Negro in American Life.* New York, 1926.

Downs, Joan. "Black/White Dating." In Wilkinson, *Black Male/White Female,* 159–70.

Drachsler, Julius. *Intermarriage in New York City.* New York, 1921.

Drake, St. Clair, and Horace Cayton. *Black Metropolis.* Rev. ed. 2 vols. New York, 1962.

Du Bois, W. E. B. "President Harding and Social Equality." *Crisis,* 23 (1921), 53–56.

Du Bois, W. E. B. "The Social Equality of Whites and Blacks." *Crisis,* 21 (1920), 16–18.

Duncan, Hannibal G. "The Changing Race Relationship in the Border and Northern States." Ph.D. dissertation, University of Pennsylvania, 1922.

Eans, Ernest, Jr. Letter to the editor, *Ebony,* November 1980.

"Eartha Kitt's Search for Love." *Ebony*, November 1956, 83–88.

Edwards, Audrey. "How You're Feeling." *Essence*, December 1982, 73–76.

Egypt, Ophelia Settle, et al. *Unwritten History of Slavery*. Nashville, 1945.

"Emancipation." *Crisis*, 5 (1913), 128–29.

Emanuel, J. A., and Theodore Gross, eds. *Dark Symphony: Negro Literature in America*. New York, 1968.

Erskine, Hazel. "The Polls: Interracial Socializing." *Public Opinion Quarterly*, 37 (1973), 283–94.

Estabrook, Arthur H., and Ivan H. McDougle. *Mongrel Virginians: The Win Tribe*. Baltimore, 1926.

Evans, David W. "My Son Is a Blonde Negro." *Negro Digest*, 7 (March 1949), 43–45.

Evans, Sara. *Personal Politics: The Roots of Women's Liberation in the Civil Rights Movement and the New Left*. New York, 1979.

"Famous Negroes Married to Whites." *Ebony*, 5 (1949), 20–30.

Fanon, Frantz. *Black Skin, White Masks*. New York, 1967.

Farley, Reynolds. *Blacks and Whites: Narrowing the Gap?* Cambridge, 1984.

Fauset, Jessie. *Plum Bun*. New York, 1929.

Feinstein, Herbert. "Lena Horne Speaks Freely on Race, Marriage, Stage." *Ebony*, May 1963, 61–67.

Foerster, Robert F. *The Racial Problems Involved in Immigration from Latin America and the West Indies to the United States*. Washington, D.C., 1925.

Fogel, Robert W., and Stanley L. Engerman. *Time on the Cross*. 2 vols. Boston, 1974.

Foner, Philip S. *The Life and Writings of Frederick Douglass*. New York, 1975.

Fortune, T. Thomas. "Intermarriage and Natural Selection." *Colored American Magazine*, 16 (1909), 379–81.

Fosdick, Franklin. "Is Interracial Marriage Wrecking the NAACP?" *Negro Digest*, July 1950, 52–55.

Franklin, John Hope. *The Free Negro in North Carolina, 1790–1860*. New York, 1971; orig. Chapel Hill, 1943.

Frazier, E. Franklin. *Black Bourgeoisie*. New York, 1957.

Frazier, E. Franklin. *The Free Negro Family*. Nashville, 1932.

Frazier, E. Franklin. *The Negro Family in Chicago*. Chicago, 1932.

Frazier, E. Franklin. *The Negro Family in the United States*. Chicago, 1939.

Frazier, E. Franklin. *Negro Youth at the Crossroads*. Washington, D.C., 1940.

Fredrickson, George M. *The Black Image in the White Mind*. New York, 1971.

Fredrickson, George M. *White Supremacy*. New York, 1981.

Friedman, Lawrence J. *The White Savage: Racial Fantasies in the Postbellum South*. Englewood Cliffs, N.J., 1970.

Gallup, G. H. *The Gallup Poll: Public Opinion, 1972–1977*. Wilmington, Del., 1978.

Gallup, G. H. *The Gallup Poll: Public Opinion, 1978*. Wilmington, Del., 1978.

Gallup, G. H. *The Gallup Poll: Public Opinion, 1983*. Wilmington, Del., 1984.

Gannon, Tim. "Black Freedmen and the Cherokee Nation." *Journal of American Studies*, 11 (1977), 357–64.

Garvey, Amy Jacques. *Philosophy and Opinions of Marcus Garvey.* 2 vols. New York, 1968–69; orig. 1923–25.

Gay, Kathlyn. *The Rainbow Effect: Interracial Families.* New York, 1987.

Genovese, Eugene. *Roll, Jordan, Roll.* New York, 1974.

Gerber, David A. *Black Ohio and the Color Line, 1860–1915.* Urbana, Ill., 1976.

"German Mail Order Bride." *Ebony,* June 1953, 62–64.

Gilligan, Francis James. *The Morality of the Color Line.* Washington, D.C., 1928.

Gilmore, Al-Tony. *Bad Nigger!* Port Washington, N.Y., 1975.

Gilmore, Al-Tony. "Jack Johnson and White Women." *JNH,* 58 (1973), 18–38.

Gist, Noel P. "The Anglo-Indians." In Gist and Dworkin, *Blending of Races,* 39–59.

Gist, Noel P., and Anthony Gary Dworkin, eds. *The Blending of Races.* New York, 1972.

Gitlin, Thyra Edwards, and Murray Gitlin. "Does Interracial Marriage Succeed?" *Negro Digest,* July 1945, 63–64.

Glantz, Oscar. "Native Sons and Immigrants." *Ethnicity,* 5 (1978), 189–202.

Glasser, Alan J. "A Negro Child Reared as White." In Seward, *Clinical Studies in Culture Conflict,* 41–61.

Gloster, Hugh M. *Negro Voices in American Fiction.* Chapel Hill, 1948.

Golden, Joseph. "Characteristics of the Negro-White Intermarried in Philadelphia." *ASR,* 18 (1953), 177–83.

Golden, Joseph. "Facilitating Factors in Negro-White Intermarriage." *Phylon,* 20 (1959), 273–84.

Golden, Joseph. "Patterns of Negro-White Intermarriage." *ASR,* 19 (1954), 144–47.

Golden, Joseph. "Social Control of Negro-White Intermarriage." *Social Forces,* 36 (1958), 267–69.

Grant, Madison. *The Passing of the Great Race.* New York, 1916.

Green, Vera. "Racial versus Ethnic Factos in Afro-American and Afro-Caribbean Migration." In Safa and DuToit, *Migration and Development,* 83–96.

Greenberg, Jack. *Race Relations and American Law.* New York, 1959.

Greene, Lorenzo. *The Negro in Colonial New England.* New York, 1968; orig. 1942.

Griffin, John Howard. *Black Like Me.* New York, 1960.

Grier, William H., and Price M. Cobbs. *Black Rage.* New York, 1968.

Grimké, Francis J. "The Second Marriage of Frederick Douglass." *JNH,* 19 (1934), 324–29.

Grow, Oscar. *The Antagonism of Races.* Waterloo, Iowa, 1912.

Gutman, Herbert G. *The Black Family in Slavery and Freedom.* New York, 1976.

Haley, James T., comp. *Afro-American Encyclopedia.* Nashville, 1895.

Haller, John S., Jr. *Outcasts from Evolution: Scientific Attitudes of Racial Inferiority.* Urbana, Ill., 1971.

Halsell, Grace. *Soul Sister.* New York, 1969.

Halsey, Margaret. *Color Blind.* New York, 1946.

Hansberry, Lorraine. *To Be Young, Gifted, and Black.* New York, 1969.

Hare, Nathan. "Revolution without a Revolution: The Psychosociology of Sex and Race." *Black Scholar,* 9 (April 1978), 2–7.

Harris, Mark. "America's Oldest Interracial Community." *Negro Digest,* July 1948, 21–24.

Harris, Sara. *Father Divine: Holy Husband.* Garden City, N.Y., 1953.

Hedgeman, Rose. "Interracial Marriage." Paper presented at "Crossing the Color Line," Biracial Family Conference, Chicago, June 29, 1985.

Heer, D. M. "Intermarriage and Racial Amalgamation in the United States." *Eugenics Quarterly,* 14 (1967), 112–20.

Heer, D. M. "Negro-White Marriage in the United States." *JMF,* 28 (1966), 264–65.

Heer, D. M. "Prevalence of Black-White Marriage in the United States." *JMF,* 36 (1974), 246–58.

Heim, Oskar. "Why I Want a Negro Wife." *Negro Digest,* July 1951, 64–68.

Hernton, Calvin. *Sex and Racism.* New York, 1965.

"He's Too Light to Be Negro and Too Known to Be White." *Ebony,* March 1950, 22–26.

Hesse, H. H. *Groep sonder Grense.* Bellville, South Africa, 1985.

Hewlett, John. "Four Who Are Passing." *Negro Digest,* April 1957, 41–46.

Higginbotham, A. Leon. *In the Matter of Color.* New York, 1978.

Hill, John Louis. *Negro: National Asset or Liability? The Battle of the Bloods.* New York, 1930.

Hill, Mozell C. "Social Status and Physical Appearance among Negro Adolescents." *Social Forces,* 22 (1944), 443–48.

Hoffman, Frederick L. *Race Traits and Tendencies of the American Negro.* Volume 11 of *Publications of the American Economic Association.* August 1896.

"Hollywood's Most Tragic Marriage." *Ebony,* February 1952, 26–36.

Horne, Lena. "I Just Want to Be Myself." In Watkins and David, *To Be a Black Woman,* 103–12.

Horne, Lena. *Lena.* London, 1966.

Horton, James O., and Lois E. Horton. *Black Bostonians.* New York, 1979.

Huggins, Nathan I. "Marginality in America: Passing is Passé." Colloquium paper, History Department, University of California, Berkeley, November 7, 1979.

Huggins, Nathan I. *Slave and Citizen.* Boston, 1980.

Hughes, Langston. "Mulatto: A Tragedy of the Deep South." In Watkins and Daniel, *To Be a Black Woman,* 23–38.

Huie, William Bradford. "The Shocking Story of Approved Killing in Mississippi." *Look,* January 24, 1956, 46–48.

"I Lived Two Lives for Thirty Years." *Ebony,* December 1958, 156–62.

"Intermarriage." *Crisis,* 5 (1913), 180–81.

"Intermarriage." *Crisis,* 11 (1915), 306.

"Inter-Marriage." *Crisis,* 29 (1925), 251.

"Interracial College Marriages." *Ebony,* July 1954, 89–94.

"Is Mixed Marriage a New Society Fad?" *Ebony,* September 1951, 98–103.

"Jack Johnson." *Crisis* (1913), 121.

Jackson, L. P. "Culture or Color? The Moyetos of San Juan and New York." *Crisis,* 75 (1968), 189–93.

James, Curtia. "A Black-Native American Harvest." *Essence,* November 1983, 87–88.

James, Eddie. Letter to the editor, *Ebony*, October 1970.

Jencks, Albert E. "The Legal Status of Negro-White Amalgamation in the United States." *AJS*, 21 (1916), 666–78.

Jenkins, Lee. *Faulkner and Black-White Relations*. New York, 1981.

Johnson, Charles S. *Growing Up in the Black Belt*. New York, 1941.

Johnson, Charles S. *Patterns of Negro Segregation*. New York, 1943.

Johnson, Guy Benton. "Personality in a White-Indian-Negro Community." *ASR*, 4 (1938), 516–23.

Johnson, Jack. *Jack Johnson—In the Ring and Out*. Chicago, 1927.

Johnson, James Weldon. *Along This Way*. New York, 1933.

Johnson, James Weldon. *The Autobiography of an Ex-Coloured Man*. New York, 1960; orig. 1912.

Johnson, James Weldon. "The Washington Riots." *Crisis*, September 1919.

Johnston, James. "Documentary Evidence of the Relations of Negroes and Indians." *JNH*, 14 (1929), 21–43.

Johnston, James Hugo. *Race Relations in Virginia and Miscegenation in the South, 1776–1860*. Amherst, Mass., 1970.

Jones, Howard O. *White Questions to a Black Christian*. Grand Rapids, 1975.

Jordan, Winthrop D. "American Chiaroscuro: The Status and Definition of Mulattoes in the British Colonies." *William and Mary Quarterly*, 3rd ser., 19 (1962), 183–200.

Jordan, Winthrop D. *White over Black*. Chapel Hill, 1968.

Kaplan, Sidney. "The Miscegenation Issue in the Election of 1864." *JNH*, 34 (1949), 274–343.

Kardiner, Abram, and Lionel Ovesey. *The Mark of Oppression*. Cleveland, 1951.

Kephart, William. "Is the American Negro Becoming Lighter?" *ASR*, 13 (1948), 437–43.

Kiev, Ari. "The Psychiatric Implications of Interracial Marriage." In Irving R. Stuart and Lawrence E. Abt, eds., *Interracial Marriage*, 161–76. New York, 1967.

Killens, James Oliver. *Black Man's Burden*. New York, 1965.

King, C. H., Jr. "I Don't Want to Marry Your Daughter." *Negro Digest*, April 1964, 3–7.

King, Helen Hayes, and Theresa Ojunbiyi. "Should Negro Women Straighten Their Hair?" *Negro Digest*, August 1963, 65–71.

Kitt, Eartha. *Alone with Me*. Chicago, 1976.

Kitt, Eartha. "The Most Exciting Men in My Life," *Ebony*, January 1953, 26–36.

Kronus, Sidney. *The Black Middle Class*. Columbus, Ohio, 1971.

Krutza, William J., and Philip P. DiCicco. *Facing the Issues 3*. Grand Rapids, Mich., 1970.

Kutner, Nanette. "Women Who Pass for White." *Negro Digest*, August 1949, 43–46.

Kuttner, Robert E. "Race Mixing: Suicide or Salvation?" *American Mercury*, Winter 1971, 45–48.

Lacey, Ed. "The Village Is So Quaint." *Opportunity*, 20 (1942), 203–4.

Ladner, Joyce. "Providing a Healthy Environment for Interracial Children." *Interracial Books for Children*, 15, no. 6 (1984), 7–8.

Ladner, Joyce A. *Tomorrow's Tomorrow: The Black Woman*. New York, 1971.

Landay, Eileen. *Black Film Stars*. New York, 1973.

Larsen, Nella. *Passing*. New York, 1969; orig. 1929.

Larsen, Nella. *Quicksand*. New York, 1928.

Larsson, Clotye M., ed. *Marriage across the Color Line*. Chicago, 1965.

Lee, Reba*. *I Passed for White*. New York, 1955.

Leonard, Joseph T. *Theology and Race Relations*. Milwaukee, 1963.

Lester, Julius, ed. *The Seventh Son: The Thought and Writing of W. E. B. Du Bois*. New York, 1971.

"Letters of a Dying Mother to Her Baby." *Ebony*, July 1954, 16–25.

Leven, Nora. "Love in Black and White." *Mpls./St. Paul*, August 1987, 72–74 ff.

Levine, Lawrence. *Black Culture and Black Consciousness*. New York, 1977.

Lewis, Shawn D. "Black Women/White Men: The 'Other' Mixed Marriage." *Ebony*, January 1978, 37–42.

Lieberson, Stanley. "Generational Differences among Blacks in the North." *AJS*, 79 (1973), 550–65.

Lieberson, Stanley, and Mary C. Waters. "Ethnic Mixtures in the United States." *SSR*, 70 (1985), 43–52.

Lieberson, Stanley, and Mary C. Waters. *From Many Strands: Ethnic and Racial Groups in Contemporary America*. New York, 1988.

Lincoln, C. Eric. *The Black Muslims in America*. Boston, 1961.

Littlefield, Daniel F. *Africans and Creeks*. Westport, Conn., 1979.

Littlefield, Daniel F. *Africans and Seminoles*. Westport, Conn., 1977.

Litwack, Leon. *North of Slavery*. Chicago, 1961.

Logan, Rayford, ed. *What the Negro Wants*. Chapel Hill, 1944.

"The Loneliest Brides in America." *Ebony*, January 1953, 17–24.

"A Lynching in Arkansas." *Colored American Magazine*, 9 (1905), 409.

Lynn, Anella. *Interracial Marriages in Washington, D.C.* Washington, D.C., 1953.

Lynn, Anella. "Interracial Marriages in Washington, D.C." *Journal of Negro Education*, 36 (1967).

McCord, Charles H. *The American Negro as a Dependent, Defective, and Delinquent*. Nashville, 1914.

McGee, Mrs. Melvin E. Letter to the editor, *Ebony*, October 1970.

Malcolm X. *Autobiography*. New York, 1965.

Maliver, Bruce L. *Anti-Negro Bias among Negro College Students*. Ann Arbor, 1964.

Mapp, Edward. *Blacks in American Films*. Metuchen, N.J., 1972.

"Marriage of Eartha Kitt." *Ebony*, September 1960, 37–42.

"Marriage to Lenny Hayton Is Open Secret for Three Years." *Ebony*, October 1950, 36.

Massaquoi, H. J. "Would You Want Your Daughter to Marry One?" *Ebony*, August 1965, 82–84.

Matson, T. B. *Segregation and Desegregation: A Christian Approach*. New York, 1959.

Mayo-Smith, Richmond. "Theories of Mixture of Races and Nationalities." *Yale Review*, 3 (1894), 166–86.

Mehlinger, Kermit. "That Black Man–White Woman Thing." *Ebony*, August 1970, 130–33.

Meier, August. *Negro Thought in America, 1880–1915*. Ann Arbor, 1973.

Mencke, John G. "Mulattoes and Race Mixture: American Attitudes and Images, 1865–1918." Ph.D. dissertation, University of North Carolina, 1976.

Meriwether, Louise. "Black Man, Do You Love Me?" *Essence*, 1 (May 1970), 14–15 ff.

Miles, Patrice, and Audrey Edwards. "Black Women and White Men." *Essence*, October 1983, 94–96 ff.

Miller, Herbert Adolphus. "Racial Inter-Marriage." *Crisis* (1931), 337.

Miller, Kelly. *As to the Leopard's Spots*. Washington, D.C., 1905.

Mills, Gary B. *The Forgotten People: Cane River's Creoles of Color*. Baton Rouge, 1977.

Mills, Gary B. "Miscegenation and the Free Negro in Antebellum 'Anglo' Alabama." *Journal of American History*, 68 (1981), 16–34.

"Miss Iowa, the Black Girl from Queens." *New York Times*, June 30, 1970.

"Mississippi: The Place, the Acquittal." *Newsweek*, October 3, 1955, 24–29.

"Mixed Marriage Clubs." In Larsson, *Marriage across the Color Line*, 58–61.

"Mixed Marriage in College." Ibid., 120–39.

"Mixed Marriages and Catholics." *Negro Digest*, March 1945, 85–86.

Monahan, Thomas P. "Are Interracial Marriages Really Less Stable?" *Social Forces*, 48 (1970).

Monahan, Thomas P. "Critique of Heer Article." *JMF*, 36 (1874), 669–72.

Monahan, Thomas P. "Interracial Marriage and Divorce in Kansas." *Journal of Comparative Family Studies*, 2 (1971), 107–20.

Monahan, Thomas P. "Interracial Marriage: Data for Philadelphia and Pennsylvania." *Demography*, 7 (1970), 287–99.

Monahan, Thomas P. "Interracial Marriage in the United States: Some Data from Upstate New York." *International Journal of Sociology of the Family*, 9 (1971), 94–105.

Monahan, Thomas P. "An Overview of Statistics on Interracial Marriage in the United States." *JMF*, 38 (1976).

Moody, Anne. *Coming of Age in Mississippi*. New York, 1968.

Moon, Bucklin, ed. *Primer for White Folks*. Garden City, N.Y., 1945.

Morgan, Edmund. *American Slavery, American Freedom*. New York, 1975.

Morrison, Toni. *The Bluest Eye*. New York, 1970.

Moses, Wilson J. *Black Messiahs and Uncle Toms*. University Park, Pa., 1982.

Murdock, Clotye. "What Happened to the 'Lost Boundaries' Family." *Ebony*, August 1952, 52–66.

Murray, Daniel. "Color Problem in the United States." *Colored American Magazine*, 7 (1904), 719–24.

Murray, Daniel. "Race Integrity—How to Preserve It in the South." *Colored American Magazine*, 11 (1906), 369–77.

Murray, Pauli. *Proud Shoes*. New York, 1957.

"My Daughter Married a Negro." *Harper's*, July 1951, 36–40.

Myrdal, Gunnar. *An American Dilemma*. 2 vols. New York, 1962; orig. 1944.

Myricks, Noel, and Donna L. Ferullo. "Race and Child Custody Disputes." *Family Relations*, 35 (1986), 325–28.

"The NAACP Battlefront." *Crisis*, 35 (1928), 49–50.

Nagan, Winston P. "Conflict of Laws: Group Discrimination and the Freedom to Marry." *Howard Law Journal*, 21 (1978), 1–46.

Neill, Elaine. "Persecution in New York." In Larsson, *Marriage across the Color Line*, 120–39.

Newby, I. A., ed. *The Development of Segregationist Thought*. Homewood, Ill., 1968.

"The Next Step." *Crisis*, 6 (1913), 79.

Norment, Lynn. "A Probing Look at Children of Interracial Families." *Ebony*, September 1985, 158–62.

Ofari, Earl. *"Let Your Motto Be Resistance": The Life and Thought of Henry Highland Garnet*. Boston, 1972.

Oliver, Paul. *Blues Tradition*. New York, 1970.

Orbach, Channing H., and Carl H. Saxe. "Role Confusion in a Negro-Indian Woman." In Georgene Seward, ed., *Clinical Studies in Culture Conflict*, 125–50. New York, 1951.

Oster, Harry. *Living Country Blues*. Detroit, 1969.

Page, Thomas Nelson. "The Great American Question: The Special Plea of a Southerner." *McClure's*, 28 (1907), 565–72.

Page, Thomas Nelson. *In Ole Virginia*. New York, 1887.

Patterson, Haywood, and Earl Conrad. *Scottsboro Boy*. Toronto, 1969; orig. 1950.

Pavela, T. H. "An Exploratory Study of Negro-White Intermarriage in Indiana," *JMF*, 26 (1964), 209–11.

Payne, Buckner H. *The Negro: What Is His Ethnological Status?* Cincinnati, 1867.

Perdue, Charles L., et al., eds. *Weevils in the Wheat: Interviews with Virginia Ex-Slaves*. Charlottesville, Va., 1976.

Perrow, E. C. "Songs and Rhymes from the South." *Journal of American Folklore*, 28 (1915).

"Pinky." *Ebony*, September 1949, 23–25.

Piskacek, Vladimir, and Marlene Golub. "Children of Interracial Marriage." In Irving R. Stuart and Lawrence E. Abt, eds., *Interracial Marriage*, 51–61. New York, 1967.

Pleck, Elizabeth Hafkin. *Black Migration and Poverty: Boston, 1865–1900*. New York, 1979.

"Plastic Surgery: Many Negroes Narrow Noses, Thin Lips through Operations." *Ebony*, May 1949, 19–23.

Podhoretz, Norman. "My Negro Problem—And Ours." *Commentary*, February 1963, 93–101.

Poinsett, Alvin. "A Mississippi Story." In Larsson, *Marriage across the Color Line*, 114–19.

Porter, Frank W. "Strategies for Survival: The Nanticoke Indians in a Hostile World." *Ethnohistory*, 26 (1797), 325–45.

Porter, Kenneth W. *The Negro on the American Frontier*. New York, 1971.

Posey, Darrell A. "Origin, Development, and Maintenance of a Louisiana Mixed-Blood Community." *Ethnohistory*, 26 (1979), 177–92.

Poussaint, Alvin F. "The Stresses of the White Female Worker in the Civil Rights Movement in the South." *American Journal of Psychiatry*, 123 (1966), 401–7.

Powdermaker, Hortense. *After Freedom*. New York, 1967; orig. 1939.

Powers, Charles T. "The Jackson Whites." *Los Angeles Times*, September 29, 1978.

"The Private Life of Lena Horne." *Ebony*, September 1953, 65–70.

"Proposed Negro Legislation." *Crisis*, 22 (1921), 65–66.

Putnam, Carleton. *Race and Reason*. Washington, D.C., 1961.

"Race Intermarriage." *Crisis*, 35 (1928), 118.

"Races: A Marriage of Enlightenment." *Time*, September 29, 1967, 28–31.

Randle, E. H. *Characteristics of the Southern Negro*. New York, 1910.

Raphael, Lennox. "West Indians and Afro-Americans." *Freedomways*, 4 (1964), 438–45.

Reid, Ira DeA. *The Negro Immigrant*. New York, 1969; orig. 1939.

Reuter, Edward Byron. *Race Mixture*. New York, 1969; orig. 1931.

Richards, Leonard. *Gentlemen of Property and Standing*. New York, 1970.

Reiss, I. L. "Premarital Sexual Permissiveness among Negroes and Whites." *ASR*, 29 (1964), 688–98.

Reuter, E. B. *Race Mixture*. New York, 1969; orig. 1931.

Rivierez, Isabelle, and Louis E. Lomax. "Between Two Races." *Negro Digest*, February 1962, 3–8.

Roberts, Robert E. T. "Children of Interracial Marriage." Paper presented to the Biracial Family Conference, Chicago, June 28, 1985.

Roberts Robert E. T. "Self-Identification and Social Status of Biracial Children in Chicago in Comparative Perspective." Paper presented at the International Congress of Anthropological and Ethnological Sciences, Vancouver, August 20, 1983.

Roberts, Robert E. T. "Trends in Marriages between Negroes and Whites in Chicago." In R. E. Holloman and S. A. Arutinov, eds., *Perspectives on Ethnicity*, 173–210. The Hague, 1978.

Rogers, Joel A. *Sex and Race: Negro-Caucasian Mixing in All Ages and All Lands*. 3 vols. New York, 1940–44.

Roosevelt, Eleanor. "Should a Negro Boy Ask a White Girl to Dance?" *Negro Digest*, December 1947, 41–42.

Ross, Michelle. "Is Mixed Marriage Jinxed?" *Ebony*, August 1953, 34–38.

Rothschild, Mary Aickin. *A Case of Black and White: Northern Volunteers and the Southern Freedom Summers, 1964–1965*. Westport, Conn., 1982.

Rubin, Morton. *Plantation County*. Chapel Hill, 1951.

Ruchames, Louis. "Race, Marriage, and Abolition in Massachusetts." *JNH*, 40 (1955), 250–73.

Safa, Helen I., and Brian M. DuToit, eds. *Migration and Development*. The Hague, 1975.

"Sailor to Movie Star." *Ebony*, August 1953, 46–51.

Sams, Conway W. *The Conquest of Virginia*. New York, 1916.

Santini, Rosemary. "Black Man, White Woman." *Essence*, 1 (July 1970), 12–13 ff.

Schell, William Gallio. *Is the Negro a Beast?* Moundsville, W. Va., 1901.

Schulman, Gary I. "Race, Sex, and Violence: A Laboratory Test of the Sexual Threat of the Black Male Hypothesis." *AJS*, 79 (1974), 1260–77.

Schultze, Andrew. *Fire from the Throne: Race Relations in the Church*. St. Louis, 1968.

Schuyler, G. S. *Black and Conservative*. New Rochelle, N.Y., 1966.

Schuyler, George S. *Black No More*. New York, 1931.

Schuyler, George S. *Racial Intermarriage in the United States*. Girard, Kans., 1929.

Schuyler, Mr. and Mrs. George S. "Does Interracial Marriage Succeed?" *Negro Digest*, June 1945, 15–17.

Schuyler, Josephine. "Seventeen Years of Mixed Marriage." *Negro Digest*, July 1946, 61–65.

Schuyler, Lambert. *Close the Bedroom Door!* Winslow, Wash., 1957.

Scott, Anne F. *The Southern Lady*. Chicago, 1970.

Seaman, L. *What Miscegenation Is! And What We Are to Expect Now That Mr. Lincoln Is Re-Elected*. New York, 1864.

Sebring, Deborah L. "Considerations in Counseling Interracial Children." *Journal of Non-White Concerns in Personnel Guidance*, 13 (January 1985), 3–9.

Seidenberg, Robert. "The Sexual Basis of Social Prejudice." *Psychoanalytic Review*, 38 (1952), 90–95.

"Sex Equality." *Crisis*, 19 (1919), 106.

Shackford, Kate. "Interracial Children: Growing Up Healthy in an Unhealthy Society." *Interracial Books for Children Bulletin*, 15, no. 6 (1984), 4–6.

Shadrach, J. Shirley. "Furnace Blasts: The Growth of the Social Evil among All Classes and Races in America." *Colored American Magazine*, 6 (1903), 259–63.

Shannon, A. H. *The Racial Integrity of the American Negro*. Nashville, 1925.

"Should a White Girl Marry a Negro?" *Negro Digest*, December 1948, 13–18.

Sickel, Robert J. *Race, Marriage, and the Law*. Albuquerque, 1972.

Simpkins, Hazel Byrne. "A Negro's British War Bride." In Larsson, *Marriage across the Color Line*, 97–106.

Slater, Jack. "The Real People behind the Jeffersons." *Ebony*, September 1980, 83–93.

Smith, Gerald L. K. *Arkansas: Hungary of America*. Los Angeles, [1950s].

Smith, Gerald L. K. *Congressman John E. Rankin*. Los Angeles, [1950s].

Smith, Gerald L. K. *The Great Issues*. Los Angeles, [1950s].

Smith, Gerald L. K. *Handbook for the Courageous*. Los Angeles, [1950s].

Smith, Gerald L. K. *Matters of Life and Death*. Los Angeles, [1950s].

Smith, Gerald L. K. *The New York Jungle*. Los Angeles, [1950s].

Smith, Gerald L. K. *The Plot to Undermine the Republic*. Los Angeles, [1950s].

Smith, Gerald L. K. *White Man Awaken!* Los Angeles, [1950s].

Smith, Lillian. *Killers of the Dream*. New York, 1945.

Smith, William Gardner. "Black Boy in France." *Ebony*, July 1953, 32–42.

Spaights, Ernest, and Harold E. Dixon. "Socio-Psychological Dynamics in Pathological Black-White Romantic Alliances." *Journal of Instructional Psychology*, 11 (1987), 132–38.

Spivey, Philip. "Growing Up in Interracial Families." *Interracial Books for Children Bulletin*, 15, no. 6 (1984), 11–16.

Spurling, John Jasper. "Social Relationships between American Negroes and West Indian Negroes in a Long Island Community." Ph.D. dissertation, New York University, 1962.

Stampp, Kenneth. *The Peculiar Institution*. New York, 1956.

Staples, Robert. *The Black Woman in America*. Chicago, 1973.

Staples, Robert. "The Myth of Black Macho." *Black Scholar*, 10 (March–April 1979), 24–33.

Staples, Robert. *The World of Black Singles*. Westport, Conn., 1984.

Steinberg, Alfred. "What Is the Law on Mixed Marriages?" *Negro Digest*, May 1949, 47–49.

Stember, Charles Herbert. *Sexual Racism*. New York, 1976.

Stephenson, G. T. *Race Distinctions in American Law*. New York, 1910.

Sterling, Dorothy, ed. *We Are Your Sisters: Black Women in the Nineteenth Century*. New York, 1984.

Stevens, Gladys. "My Father Passed for White." *Ebony*, April 1957, 41–46.

Steward, G. A. "The Black Girl Passes." *Social Forces*, 6 (1927–28), 99–103.

Stewart, Ollie. "How War Brides Fare in America." *Negro Digest*, April 1948, 25–30.

Stewart, Ollie. "What Negro GI's Learned from Women in Europe." *Negro Digest*, September 1947, 24–27.

Still, William Grant. "Does Interracial Marriage Succeed?" *Negro Digest*, April 1945, 50–52.

Stone, A. H. *Studies in the American Race Problem*. New York, 1908.

Stonequist, Everett. *The Marginal Man*. New York, 1965; orig. 1937.

Stuckert, Robert S. "The African Ancestry of the White Population." *Ohio Journal of Science*, 58 (1958), 155–60.

Sutton, Constance R., and Susan R. Makiesky. "Migration and West Indian Racial and Ethnic Consciousness." In Safa and DuToit, *Migration and Development*, 113–44.

Swain, Leo. "How a Negro Minister Passed in Dixie." *Negro Digest*, February 1948, 4–6.

Taeuber, Karl E., and Alma F. Taeuber. "The Negro as an Immigrant Group." *AJS*, 69 (1964), 374–82.

Takaki, Ronald. *Violence in the Black Imagination*. New York, 1972.

Tally, Thomas W. *Negro Folk-Rhymes*. New York, 1922.

"Tate's Night of Passion—Or Sleep? Model Says He Wasn't Alone." *San Francisco Chronicle*, November 2, 1979.

Taylor, Theresa. "Black-Seminole Relations." Student paper, University of California, Berkeley, 1981.

Tilson, Everett. *Segregation and the Bible*. Nashville, 1958.

Toomer, Jean. *Cane*. New York, 1969; orig. 1923.

"Trials of an Interracial Couple." *Ebony*, October 1965, 66–68.

"The Truth about Japanese War Brides." *Ebony*, March 1952, 17–25.

Udry, J. Richard; Karl Bauman; and Charles Chase. "Skin Color, Status, and Mate Selection." *AJS*, 76 (1971), 722–33.

U.S. Bureau of the Census. *Marriage and Divorce, 1867–1906*. 2 vols. Washington, D.C., 1909.

U.S. Bureau of the Census. *Fourteenth Census of the United States, 1920.* Vol. 2: *Population, 1920, General Report and Analytical Tables.* Washington, D.C., 1920.

U.S. Bureau of the Census. *Negro Population, 1790–1915.* New York, 1968; orig. Washington, D.C., 1918.

U.S. Bureau of the Census. *Negroes in the United States, 1920–1932.* Washington, D.C., 1935.

U.S. Bureau of the Census. *1960 Census: Nonwhite Population by Race.* Subject Report PC(2)-1C. Washington, D.C., 1963.

U.S. Bureau of the Census. *1960 Census: Marital Status.* Subject Report PC(2)-4E. Washington, D.C., 1966.

U.S. Bureau of the Census. *1970 Census of Population. General Population Characteristics. U.S. Summary.* Washington, D.C., 1973.

U.S. Bureau of the Census. *1970 Census: Marital Status.* Subject Report PC(2)-4C. Washington, D.C., 1972.

U.S. Bureau of the Census. *1970 Census: National Origin and Language.* Subject Report PC(2)-1A. Washington, D.C., 1973.

U.S. Bureau of the Census. *1970 Census: Negro Population.* Subject Report PC(2)-1B. Washington, D.C., 1973.

U.S. Bureau of the Census. *1980 Census of Population. General Social and Economic Characteristics. U.S. Summary.* PC80-1-C1. Washington, D.C., 1983.

U.S. Bureau of the Census. *1980 Census: Marital Characteristics.* Subject Report PC80-2-4C. Washington, D.C., 1985.

U.S. Bureau of the Census. *Perspectives on American Husbands and Wives.* Current Population Reports, Series P-23, no. 77. Washington, D.C., 1978.

U.S. Congress. House of Representatives. *Intermarriage of Whites and Negroes in the District of Columbia.* Washington, D.C., 1916.

U.S. Department of the Interior. *Population of the United States in 1860.* Washington, D.C., 1864.

van den Berghe, Pierre. "Miscegenation in South Africa." In Pierre van den Berghe, *Race and Ethnicity,* 224–43. New York, 1970.

Van Evrie, John H. *Subgenation.* New York, 1864.

"The Vanishing Mulatto." *Opportunity,* 3 (1925), 291.

Vernier, Chester G. *American Family Laws.* 6 vols. Stanford, 1931.

Walker, David. *Appeal . . . to the Coloured Citizens of the World.* Boston, 1829.

Wallace, Michelle. *Black Macho and the Myth of the Superwoman.* New York, 1980.

"War Babies of Japan." *Ebony,* September 1951.

Wardle, Francis. "Are You Sensitive to Interracial Children's Special Identity Needs?" *Young Children,* 42 (January 1987), 53–59.

Warner, W. Lloyd, et al. *Color and Human Nature: Negro Personality Development in a Northern City.* New York, 1969; orig. 1941.

Washington, Booker T. *The Future of the American Negro.* Boston, 1899.

Washington, Joseph R. *Marriage in Black and White.* Boston, 1970.

Washington, Mary Helen, ed. *Black-Eyed Susans.* Garden City, N.Y., 1975.

Watkins, Mel, and Jay David, eds. *To Be a Black Woman.* New York, 1970.

Weinberg, Meyer, ed. *W. E. B. Du Bois: A Reader.* New York, 1970.

"What Color Will Your Baby Be?" *Ebony*, May 1951, 54–57.

"What Tyne Daly Gains from Her Mixed Marriage." *Globe*, September 4, 1984.

"When Celebrities Intermarry." In Larsson, *Marriage across the Color Line*, 89–96.

"White, but Black." *Century*, 109 (February 1925), 492–99.

"White by Day . . . Negro by Night." *Ebony*, April 1952, 31–36.

White, Newman I. *American Negro Folk Songs*. Hatboro, Mass., 1965; orig. Cambridge, 1928.

"White Queen in Darkest Africa." *Negro Digest*, December 1949, 60–69.

White, Walter. *Flight*. New York, 1926.

White, Walter. *A Man Called White*. New York, 1948.

A White Woman. "I Want to Marry a Negro." *Negro Digest*, August 1948, 9–14.

"Why I Never Want to Pass." *Ebony*, June 1959, 49–54.

Wilkinson, Doris Y., ed. *Black Male/White Female*. Morristown, N.J., 1975.

Williams, Chas. H. "The Negro Problem." *Colored American Magazine*, 6 (1903), 460–63.

Williams, Dennis A. "Roots III: Souls on Ice." *Newsweek*, June 10, 1985, 82–84.

Williamson, Joel. *New People: Miscegenation and Mulattoes in the United States*. New York, 1980.

Williams, Richard L. "He Wouldn't Cross the Line." *Life*, September 3, 1951, 81–94.

Wilson, Barbara Foley. "Marriage's Melting Pot." *American Demographics*, 6 (July 1984), 34–37 ff.

Wilson, William Julius. *The Declining Significance of Race*. 2nd ed. Chicago, 1980.

Wirth, Anna M. "Skin-Deep." *Crisis*, 39 (1932), 126–27.

Wirth, Louis, and Herbert Goldhamer. "The Hybrid and the Problem of Miscegenation." In Otto Klineberg, ed., *Characteristics of the American Negro*. New York, 1944.

Wood, Forrest G. *Black Scare: The Racist Response to Emancipation and Reconstruction*. Berkeley, 1968.

Wood, Peter. *Black Majority*. New York, 1974.

Woods, Sister Frances Jerome. *Marginality and Identity: A Colored Creole Family*. Baton Rouge, 1972.

Woodson, Carter G. "The Beginnings of Miscegenation of Whites and Blacks." *JNH*, 3 (1918), 335–53.

Woodson, Carter G. *Free Negro Heads of Families in the United States in 1830*. Washington, D.C., 1925.

Work, Monroe N., ed. *Negro Year-Book*. 1919–21.

Wright, Richard, *Black Boy*. New York, 1966; orig. 1937.

"Young Women in a 'White World,'" *Ebony*, August 1966, 69–74.

Zabel, William D. "Interracial Marriage and the Law." In Wilkinson, *Black Male/White Female*.

INDEX

523